Visions for Change

Crime and Justice
in the Twenty-First Century

T H I R D   E D I T I O N

ROSLYN MURASKIN

Long Island University—C.W. Post Campus

ALBERT R. ROBERTS

Rutgers, the State University of New Jersey—Livingston College Campus

Prentice Hall

Upper Saddle River, New Jersey 07458

Library of Congress Cataloging-in-Publication Data

Muraskin, Roslyn.
   Visions for change : crime and justice in the twenty-first century / Roslyn Muraskin,
   Albert R. Roberts.-- 3rd ed.
        p. cm.
   Includes bibliographical references and index.
   ISBN 0-13-042030-1
     1. Criminal justice, Administration of--United States--Forecasting. 2. Crime
   forecasting--United States. I. Roberts, Albert R.

HV9950 .M87 2001 *2002*
364.973--dc21   2001036197

Publisher: Jeff Johnston
Executive Assistant & Supervisor: Brenda Rock
Executive Acquisitions Editor: Kim Davies
Assistant Editor: Sarah Holle
Managing Editor: Mary Carnis
Production Management: Naomi Sysak
Production Editor: Naomi Sysak
Interior Design: Naomi Sysak
Production Liaison: Adele M. Kupchik
**Director of Manufacturing
   and Production:** Bruce Johnson
Manufacturing Buyer: Cathleen Petersen

Creative Director: Cheryl Asherman
Cover Design Coordinator: Miguel Ortiz
Formatting: Naomi Sysak
Electronic Art Creation: Mark Ammerman
Marketing Manager: Ramona Sherman
Printer/Binder: R.R. Donnelley, Harrisonburg, VA
Copyeditor: Barbara Zeiders
Proofreader: Tally Morgan
Cover Design: Joseph Sengotta
Cover Illustration: Cici Man, SIS/Images.Com
Cover Printer: Phoenix Color

Pearson Education Ltd.
Pearson Education Australia PTY, Limited
Pearson Education Singapore, Pte. Ltd.
Pearson Education North Asia, Ltd.
Pearson Education Canada, Ltd.
Pearson Educación de Mexico, S.A. de C.V.
Pearson Education—Japan
Pearson Education Malaysia, Pte. Ltd.

10 9 8 7 6 5 4 3 2 1
ISBN: 0-13-042030-1

Dedications

This third edition is dedicated to my husband, Matthew, a constant companion and friend; and to all our children: Tracy and Ted, Seth and Stacy, Craig and Savet, and our two gorgeous granddaughters, Lindsay and Nickia.

—*Roslyn Muraskin*

This third edition is dedicated to my brilliant and loving wife, Beverly, and our son, Herb.

—*Albert R. Roberts*

We jointly dedicate this third edition to all the chapter authors and their families; this is indeed a work of love. Without our diligent team of chapter authors, this book would never have been completed.

Contents

CHAPTER 3
The Situation of Crime Victims in the Early Decades
of the Twenty-First Century
Andrew Karmen

CHAPTER 4
Gangs: Status, Characteristics, Community and Police
Responses, and Policy Implications
Kenneth J. Peak

Contents

CHAPTER 14
Reaffirming Juvenile Justice   265
Peter J. Benekos and *Alida V. Merlo*

CHAPTER 15
A Study of the Criminal Motivations of Sentenced Jail Inmates   287
Robert J. Meadows and *Kimberly L. Anklin*

PART V
TECHNOLOGY IN THE TWENTY-FIRST CENTURY   303

CHAPTER 22
Sentencing into the Twenty-First Century:
Sentence Enhancement and Life without Parole   408
Etta F. Morgan and *Robert T. Sigler*

PART VII
GENDER AND RACE ISSUES IN THE TWENTY-FIRST CENTURY   425

CHAPTER 23
Women and the Law: An Agenda for Change
in the Twenty-First Century   427
Roslyn Muraskin and *Martin L. O'Connor*

Foreword

Sam S. Souryal, Ph.D.
Sam Houston State University

Envisioning change is an awesome task. Originally, it was the domain of the gods. Adam, Abraham, Moses, Buddha, and Mohammed were inspired by them and succeeded to varying degrees. Philosophers including Socrates, Plato, and Aristotle envisioned change through their own power; the first had to give his life for it, and the other two narrowly escaped death. Later, Thomas More and Galileo tried even harder, and were punished severely. Nevertheless, the human race continues to envision change because it is the only way to survive.

Inspiring change—by itself—is hard. O'Toole cites 33 reasons for resisting change. These include fear, ignorance, satisfaction, lack of self-confidence, cynicism, futility, myopia, and self-interest. Envisioning change with some degree of certainty, furthermore, can be risky. If it were not, the Vietnam War would not have been fought, the *Challenger* would still be operating, and the stock market would never have dropped. Yet the human spirit is indefatigable. If only for the survival of the species, human sensibility must be made to prevail. That is why the gods, arguably bored with human insensibilities, created surrogates. In ancient times they were the apostles, and are now the professors. These surrogates, without aid from the gods, must carry the responsibility of preserving today by shaping tomorrow; mixing values with technology, direction with consensus, and risk taking with risk avoidance. In the process they must interpret the courses of events, the contiguity of ideas, and the depth of meanings—all while being sensitive to human suffering, the imperative of goodness, the obligation of justice, and without being foiled by the "cunning" of their reasoning.

In this book human sensibilities are examined in one of their most daring forms—criminal justice. At the end of the criminal justice continuum we are faced with the insensibility of absolute freedom, whereby some people claim the power to promote their own interests by all means possible. The vision here is human liberty. On the other end of the continuum, we are faced with the insensibility of egoism and brutishness, whereby some people are deliberately blind to the needs of others. The vision here is social responsibility. This dialectical dilemma—which will never go away—compels us to consider the truth of who we are, how we are to live together, and the utility of all the laws, courts, police, prisons, and the other criminal justice organs that we have amassed. In this book 31 experienced professors face this very dilemma and offer their solutions by envisioning change and defending their visions intelligently.

Yet the art of envisioning change is not the function of empirical data, evidence, testimony, or even technology, although it should be guided by all of these. A vision is a snapshot of history, a slice of reality, a peek into the unseen, and a prediction of the unusual. Visions also transcend expertise, a quality that no longer is rare in modern societies. Therefore, they can be neither duplicated nor imitated. As such, visions are principally sparks of brilliance that capture the collective mind of a group, a community, a society, or the universe—hence the formidable challenge of the 31 experienced professors in this book. They cover the entire spectrum of criminal justice, from one pole to the other. Their visions address legal, social, and psychological concerns over drugs, gangs, crime victims, pornography, murder, domestic violence, criminal motivations, community policing, the Bill of Rights, gender and race, and of course, capital punishment—the ultimate punishment, traditionally reserved to the gods. These well-thought-out visions are well introduced in the beginning of the book and well summarized at its end.

Whatever the consequence of the bold mixture of visions in this book, the study of criminal justice is never simple or entirely predictable. If that were so, writing more criminal justice books might be unnecessary. Each student (including faculty members and researchers) must have his or her own assessment of the sensibilities or insensibilities of criminal justice based on one's years of interacting with dizzyingly different ideas, changing environments, and transforming personal experiences, expectations, frustrations, and fulfillments. Yet for such assessments to be valuable, they should be based on integrated thinking rather than conformity, reasoning rather than belief, and moderation rather than absolutism. Although these are the characteristics of intellectual humanism, the field of criminal justice is only one of its applications. Consistent with these characteristics, for a visionary assessment of the criminal justice experience in the United States, three questions should be asked: (1) Is it consistent with the highest principles of justice? (2) Is it consistent with the highest level of civility? (3) Is it rational? These three questions sum up the essence of criminal justice today as successive generations of students have grown to know it.

In answer to the first question, we may note that the highest principle of justice is *not* that which is permitted by law, but that which is naturally due by virtue of our humanness. This should not be taken to mean that legal justice is improper; it is only insufficient and therefore inconsistent with our state of social evolution. As citizens of the most open society on earth, we must be able to find innovative ways to prevent "street justice," "basement justice," and "racist justice," among other *injustices*. And as a nation of laws, not of men, it behooves us finally and courageously to proclaim justice in its "original position," one that is pursued under the veil of ignorance, without regard to who might be the criminal or the victim.

In answer to the second question, we may also note that the practice of criminal justice is the nation's foremost test of civility—the way we as Americans handle criminals. In that sense, we have choices to make. Yet the exercise of criminal justice should be applied more by consensus rather than conformity and by education rather than force and humiliation. Furthermore, whatever the choices we make, they must be made not because we can, but because we ought to. In this context, sensationalizing crime and criminals may be as uncivil as parading F. Lee Bailey in leg and waist irons when he was jailed for contempt in a civil court; that pulling cars over by police because of the race or color of their drivers is not the most decent way of enforcing the laws—even if it were shown to be legal; and that putting people behind walls and bars and doing little or nothing to change them is a cheap version of criminal justice.

In answer to the third question, we may also note that criminal justice policies must ultimately pass the rationality test. As such, policies and priorities of crime and corrections must be reviewed regularly and, when necessary, upgraded. In this context, continuing to wage the war on drugs on foreign soils with using military planes and helicopters makes little or no sense because even if it were to succeed in one foreign country, which is unlikely, dozens of other countries will provide the coveted illicit substance as long as the demand for drugs by Americans does not abate. Furthermore, policymakers should consider that women in America are the fastest-growing category of prisoners nationwide, and that more women seek treatment in hospitals for injuries from domestic violence than from all muggings, car accidents, and rapes combined. Even more alarming, policymakers should consider the proposition that women may be being treated more harshly and/or given longer sentences. Allowing such practices to continue is not only irrational but may well illustrate my point regarding the "cunning of reason."

Having said that, the most serious criminal justice challenge facing Americans is largely philosophical: maintaining a *libertarian mind* capable of producing visionary changes. Interestingly enough, such a mind may be a residual product of what Samuel Walker calls the "wildly contradictory attitudes" that Americans have toward crime. As a case in point, it has always been particularly difficult for American scholars to explain to their foreign colleagues why, as a nation endowed with all the ingredients of civility, the United States continues a tradition of crime that stands out among all postindustrial societies. Foreign scholars, on the other hand, have not quite understood the libertarian mind that Americans possess which makes them altogether different from any other society. Through that unique mindset, Americans face up to their failures, admit unjust acts, and strive to restore civic sensibilities. Historically, it was that libertarian mind that rejected the British injustices in the first place, sustained the Union during the Civil War, abolished slavery and attended to its victims, defeated Hitler and rebuilt what he had destroyed, and made human rights a global issue.

Finally, since criminal justice change is bound to continue, it must be made more functional: more conducive to justice, humanity, and rationality. Yet the engine of our ingenuity must always be our libertarian mind, which has served us so well in the past. This book is essential to both university students and criminal justice practitioners. For the former, it can help them learn how to develop sharper visions of change, and for the latter, how to be better prepared to deal with the implications of change.

Sam S. Souryal, Ph.D.
Huntsville, Texas

Preface

It is an accepted fact in the field of criminal justice that courts should dispense justice. Today, advanced technology is transforming the world into a "global village," changing the dimensions of the crime scene as we have known it. This is the third edition of *Visions for Change: Crime and Justice in the Twenty-First Century*. It creates the vision of what is needed today in the twenty-first century as we look back on yesterday.

Most criminal justice books vary distinctly on at least four dimensions in their focus and the kind of detail included in each chapter. In this newest work, we review contemporary issues, the degree to which differing components of the criminal justice process are viewed, the most modern approach to examining the issues of today, and the specific types of crime control and rehabilitative strategies that are necessary.

In this edition we present up-to-date materials bringing us into the new millennium. As an example, there is little doubt that drug users will continue to provide much of the fodder for our rapidly expanding correctional system, well into the new century. During the 1990s our nation easily surpassed Russia and South Africa in incarceration rates, making the United States the leader among industrialized nations in the imprisonment of its citizens. Gangs continue to pose a serious problem in the United States. It should not be assumed that juveniles join gangs solely because of poverty or the pursuit of wealth. Many studies now indicate that large numbers who join gangs are from the middle classes. Deterioration of the family and other social control institutions tend to cause gang activity. We examine the use of obscene and pornographic materials. Here we learn that convicted serial killer Ted Bundy admitted to an addiction to pornography; television, movies, and thus the recording industries are being forced to provide warnings on their products; growing numbers of library books are being censored; while complaints are increasing over the use of young teens and children in advertisements, posing in a suggestive manner.

As we look at elements of community policing, in the first decade of the twenty-first century it has received creditability and has become an acceptable philosophy of policing. We revisit the death penalty by updating all the cases, finding that the sitting justices do not view this penalty as a violation of the Eighth Amendment to the Constitution. It is expected that by 2010 there will be changes in the composition of the Supreme Court, leaving little likelihood that there will be no changes in utilization of the death penalty until perhaps 2050.

In an up-to-date chapter regarding the Bill of Rights, challenges to the amendments are discussed. As an example, the cruel and unusual punishment clause of the Eighth Amendment has been used to attack inequities in sentencing. Embedded in our legal traditions is the notion that there must be proportionality between a crime and its punishment. However, after reviewing all the cases through the last part of the twentieth century, we find that there have been no really substantial changes in the interpretations of the amendments. In fact, in some areas unless there is a dramatic change in the composition of the Supreme Court and/or legislature during the twenty-first century, it is possible that many of the decisions noted in this chapter will stand or get more restrictive interpretations during the first decade of the new century.

In one chapter that talks of victim impact testimony in capital cases, we see the results of research examining the practices of trial courts. A comparative examination of the use of such testimony demonstrates two very different legal, social, and cultural environments. The critical issues that are shaping the twenty-first century are identified through a review of the current policies and issues. Debates continue to flourish with regard to the benefits of incarceration (more people being incarcerated than ever before) versus alternative sentencing.

Gender and race continue to be extralegal factors in determining the outcomes of cases. How concerned is the criminal justice system with questions of gender and race, and what impact does it have on the final adjudication of cases? Racism is very much alive and with us, along with existing concern regarding gender issues. There is a recognized need for a national commitment to end all violence against women.

A discussion of juvenile justice is presented in this newly revised text. The courts have drifted from their original rehabilitative ideal with its focus on prevention toward a much more formal and punitive orientation. The juvenile justice system of the twenty-first century will continue to confront new challenges to its mission of helping young people while preventing delinquency during the ensuing decades.

We look at prison privatization issues. With a dramatic increase in the level of incarceration, correctional administrations at all three levels of government are turning to private, for-profit corporations to manage the burgeoning number of inmates in privately operated correctional facilities. Although private contractors have been introduced into the operation of prisons, it is also noted that during this period, other formerly public service functions have been privatized. Can privatization of elements of the criminal justice system work?

While we review the ramifications of sentencing in this century, we look at community corrections programs which are not identified as treatment programs, which most people have difficulty in identifying as acceptable. There is the thought that if the focus on sentence enhancement and life-without-parole sentences target the number of relatively mild offenders captured by these statutes, the statutes may be revised such that they apply only to those who commit the most serious assault/weapons-linked felonies.

The fastest-growing HIV-infected group being incarcerated are women. Over the past few years tremendous strides have been made in providing treatment for incarcerated populations who are HIV positive, yet there is a glaring deficiency in postrelease treatment. Institutionalized persons are one of society's most ostracized groups. Much like leper colonies of the eighteenth century, today's correctional facilities segregate the disempowered, the poor, drug users, and those who are violent from the rest of society.

Looking at the problems of policing in the twenty-first century, we find that there will be an expansion of private security, higher educational requirements, and antidiscrimination policies applied to women entering the field of policing. Diversity education will be prevalent in the new millennium.

The time has come to reshape the criminal justice system and forgo the rhetoric of the past. The third edition of *Visions for Change* presents the most up-to-date materials for a full discussion of the problems envisioned in this century. The rhetoric alone will not change the system; new policies and plans of action are needed to renew today's visions for tomorrow.

It is vital to blend research with creativity to shape a vision for the future, a vision that moves us well beyond the status quo. In this third edition, much research, time, and thought have gone into this work in order to determine what today's criminal justice system will bring. As always, each chapter examines the most promising and reformed and oriented policies, programs, and technological advances for the new century. New chapters have been added that enhance this work and add to our knowledge of the criminal justice system.

Tremendous thanks to Kim Davies, Prentice Hall editor, a dedicated and very hardworking person who has lent her support, advice, guidance, and patience. Thanks also to Cheryl Adams, an editorial assistant who is always there when needed. Thanks, of course, go to all our contributors for their work in bringing forth the most up-to-date text possible. And to our families, a special thanks for their endurance.

Finally, a special thanks to the reviewers of this book: Dr. Michael Hallett, University of North Florida, Jacksonville, FL; Dr. Ann Geisendorfer, Hudson Valley Community College, Troy, NY; and Michael J. Palmiotto, Wichita State University, Wichita, KS.

Roslyn Muraskin, Ph.D.
C.W. Post Campus—Long Island University

About the Authors and Contributors

ABOUT THE AUTHORS/EDITORS

Roslyn Muraskin, Ph.D., is Professor of Criminal Justice at the C.W. Post Campus of Long Island University. She received her doctorate in criminal justice from the Graduate Center of the City University of New York in 1989. She holds a master's degree in political science from New York University and a bachelor of arts degree from Queens College. She is the Trustee for the northeast region of the Academy of Criminal Justice Sciences (ACJS). Dr. Muraskin was the recipient of the Award for Excellence from the Minorities Section of the ACJS, honored for her work with AIDS education by the Long Island Association for AIDS Care, and was the recipient of the Fellow Award from the Northeastern Association of Criminal Justice Sciences. Her publications include *It's a Crime: Women and Justice* (third edition, Spring 2002), *Morality and the Law*, and is working on a major text in the field of corrections, all published by Prentice Hall. She is also the editor of *The Justice Professional*, a referenced journal published quarterly by Taylor and Francis. She is the author of many major papers and articles, and is often quoted in the media as an expert in women's issues and issues of criminal justice.

Albert R. Roberts, Ph.D., is Professor of Criminal Justice and Social Work at University College, Rutgers University, Piscataway, New Jersey. He is Chairperson of the Administration of Justice Department at Rutgers. He received his doctorate in social work form the University of Maryland, School of Social Work. His M.S. degree is in sociology and criminology from the graduate faculty of Long Island University, and his B.A. is from the C.W. Post Campus of Long Island University. Dr. Roberts is the lead editor on the 130-chapter volume entitled *Social Workers' Desk Reference* (Oxford University Press, 2001) and the *Crisis Intervention Handbook: Assessment, Treatment, and Research*, second edition (Oxford University Press, 2000). He is also the Editor of two different book series with Springer Publishing Company. He is the founding co-editor of the *Journal of Brief Therapy* (with Dr. Gilbert J. Greene).He has numerous publications to his credit, including numerous peer-reviewed journals and book chapters.

ABOUT THE CONTRIBUTORS

Jay S. Albanese, Ph.D., is a Professor in the Department of Criminal Justice at Virginia Commonwealth University. He received his doctorate from the School of Criminal Justice at Rutgers University.

Kimberly L. Anklin has been a graduate student and department assistant in public administration at California Lutheran University. She earned her degree in psychology from California Lutheran University.

William G. Archambeault, Ph.D., is professor in the School of Social Work, Louisiana State University. He earned a Ph.D. in criminology from the Florida State University.

Kimberly R. Jacob Arriola, Ph.D., is a Senior Faculty Associate at Rollins School of Public Health of Emory University. She earned her doctorate from Northeastern University.

David V. Baker, Ph.D., received his doctorate in sociology from the University of California. He is an Associate Professor of Sociology and Chair of the Department of Behavioral Sciences at Riverside Community College.

Peter J. Benekos, Ph.D., is Professor of Criminal Justice and Sociology and the Director of the Center for Justice and Policy Research at Mercyhurst College. He earned his doctorate from the University of Akron.

Ronald J. Braithwaite, Ph.D., is a Professor in the Department of Behavioral Sciences and Health Education at the Rollins School of Public Health of Emory University. He received his doctorate from Michigan State University.

Bruce Bullington, Ph.D., received his Ph.D. in sociology from UCLA. He is Professor of Criminology at Florida State University.

Christopher M. Cevasco, J.D., received his law degree from Emory University where he worked on issues surrounding the death penalty. He is a staff attorney with the Criminal Appeals Bureau of Nassau County Legal Aid Society.

Richard P. Davin, Ph.D., received his doctorate from the University of California, Riverside. He is an Assistant Professor of Sociology and Criminal Justice at Riverside Community College.

Charles B. Fields, Ph.D., is Professor and Chair of the Department of Correctional Services at Eastern Kentucky University. He received his doctorate in criminal justice from Sam Houston State University.

Rosemary L. Gido, Ph.D., is Assistant Professor of Criminology at the Indiana University of Pennsylvania. She served as the Director of the Office of Program and Policy Analysis for the New York State Commission of Correction.

Joseph J. Grau, Ph.D., is a Professor Emeritus in criminal justice at the C.W. Post Campus of Long Island University. He received his doctorate from the University of Pittsburgh.

Kenneth C. Haas, Ph.D., is a Professor in the Department of Sociology and Criminal Justice of Delaware. He specializes in constitutional law with an emphasis on capital punishment.

Donna C. Hale, Ph.D., is Professor of Criminal Justice at Shippensburg University. Dr. Hale is the Editor of *Women and Criminal Justice*.

Michael Hallett, Ph.D., received his doctorate from the School of Justice Studies at Arizona University. He is Associate Professor of Criminal Justice at the University of North Florida.

Vincent E. Henry, is an Adjunct Professor at Long Island University. He received his doctorate from the Graduate Center of the City University of New York. He is a nineteen-year veteran of the New York Police Department.

Robert A. Jerin, Ph.D., is Associate Professor and Chair of the Law and Justice Department at Endicott College. His doctorate is from Sam Houston State University.

Andrew Karmen, Ph.D., is Professor in the Sociology Department at John Jay College of Criminal Justice. He earned his doctorate from Columbia University.

Mark M. Lanier, Ph.D., is Associate Professor of Criminal Justice and Legal Studies at the University of Central Florida. He holds an interdisciplinary doctorate from Michigan State University.

Elizabeth L. Mayfield, Ph.D., is an Assistant Professor of Social Work at the University of North Carolina. Her doctorate is from Florida State University.

C. Aaron McNeece, Ph.D., is Professor of Social Work and Director of the Institute for Health and Human Services Research at Florida State University. His doctorate is from the University of Michigan.

Robert J. Meadows, Ed.D., Ph.D., CPP, is Associate Professor of Criminal Justice Studies at California Lutheran University.

Alida V. Merlo, Ph.D., is a Professor of Criminology at Indiana State University of Pennsylvania. Her doctorate is from Fordham University.

Etta F. Morgan, Ph.D., is an Assistant Professor of Criminal Justice in the School of Public Affairs at the Pennsylvania State University Capital Campus.

Matthew Muraskin, J.D., received his law degree from New York University School of Law. He is Attorney-in-Chief of the Nassau Legal Aid Society, New York.

Peter Nelligan, Ph.D., is an Associate Professor of Criminal Justice at California State University, where he directs the Master's Program.

Martin L. O'Connor, J.D., is an Associate Professor of Criminal Justice at the C.W. Post Campus of Long Island University. He was the Deputy Police Commissioner in charge of legal affairs for both Nassau and Suffolk County Police Departments.

Michael J. Palmiotto, Ph.D., is a Professor of Criminal Justice in the School of Community Affairs at Wichita State University. His doctorate is from the University of Pittsburgh.

Kenneth J. Peak, Ph.D., is a Professor at the University of Nevada, Reno. He entered municipal policing in 1970.

Harriet Pollack, Ph.D., is Professor Emerita of Constitutional Law at the John Jay College of Criminal Justice.

Donald J. Rebovich, Ph.D., is Director of Research for the American Prosecutors Research Institute, Alexandria, Virginia.

Ronald L. Reisner, Ph.D., J.D., received his doctorate degree from Columbia University and his J.D. from the Rutgers University School of Law. He is an Assistant Professor at Monmouth University.

Stephen C. Ruland, is a retired New York City Police Sergeant, where he worked in the office of the Chief of Department, Domestic Violence Unit.

Robert Sigler, Ph.D., teaches at the University of Alabama.

Alexander B. Smith, Ph.D., J.D., is Professor Emeritus of Social Psychology at John Jay College of Criminal Justice.

Sam S. Souryal, Ph.D., is Professor of Criminal Justice at Sam Houston State University. He received his doctorate from the University of Utah.

David W. Springer, Ph.D., is Assistant Professor at the School of Social Work, the University of Texas at Austin. He received his Ph.D. from Florida State University.

Wayne N. Welsh, Ph.D., is Associate Professor of Criminal Justice at Temple University. He received his doctorate from the University of California, Irvine.

PART I

Overview

chapter 1

Looking to the Future of Criminal Justice

Roslyn Muraskin, Ph.D. and Albert R. Roberts, Ph.D.

We are in the twenty-first century and the future is today. But the headlines continue to *scream out* about the criminal justice system as we have known it, and as it has changed:

> *Crime Is Down*
>
> *A Death Row Mistake—DNA Clears Inmate Who Died on Death Row*
>
> *7 Texas Convicts Escape*
>
> *Teen Drug Use Levels Off*
>
> *Four Teens Arrested in Robbery Spree*
>
> *Dip in Youth Killing, but Not in Youth Drug Use*
>
> *Drug Lord's Reward Set; Suspected Aides Arrested*
>
> *New Charges in Ecstasy Cases Are Filed against Mob Figure*
>
> *Closing Arguments Begin in Trial of Police Officers*

This is the third edition of *Visions for Change: Crime and Justice in the Twenty-First Century*. And what is new? Today is the *future*. This work is about the inner workings of the criminal justice system as it develops in this new millennium. Criminal justice remains an integral concern of all human beings and societies around the world. Quantum leaps in technology, growing out of basic science research, continue to transform societies around the world and consequently, the crime scene, criminals, and the criminal justice system. In this new century, emerging changes are demanding more accountability while offering new challenges. In this century there is to be a shift in philosophy from preference for punishment in the disposition of offenders to a preference for treatment as a disposition for criminal offenders.

3

The argument that emerges is that it is not enough to lock people up—something must be done to reduce the likelihood that they will continue to commit crimes. As a result, public sentiment for treatment continues to develop, producing a new wave of treatment-oriented reform.

Since incarceration involves the practice of warehousing criminals (many of whom are violent) in overcrowded and understaffed institutions, it stands to reason that prisons continue to be among the most dangerous places in society. Institutional violence has remained a problem throughout the history of corrections in the United States and will remain as such today.

As pointed out by Andrew Karmen in his chapter, "[w]hile more affluent victims might be able to compel the system to deliver satisfactory service, the most underprivileged strata at the bottom of the social class hierarchy might be forced to fend for itself."

A major dilemma of criminal justice in a democratic society is how to process suspects and punish law violators in a humane and rational manner. The widespread prevalence of court orders to reform unconstitutional conditions of confinement in U.S. jails and prisons, including unprecedented overcrowding, indicates a significant gap in the court's current ability to do so, leaving an important opportunity to change. In this century we look for a coordinated approach to problem analysis and policy design to deal with the scope of jail overcrowding and court-ordered reform.

According to Smith, Pollack, and M. Muraskin, "[w]hat the future holds depends largely on governmental policy in relation to drug trafficking and gun control, chief elements of our present crime problem. But, just as important, the composition of the Supreme Court itself will play a significant role in determining both the thrust and focus of the first ten amendments to the Constitution, at least for the first few decades of this century."

Today's society has to be different from that of the previous centuries. The age of information has taken hold. We are able, instantaneously, to communicate both visually and orally with people anywhere in the world. This century marks a time of significant challenges, expectations, and advanced preparedness. Criminal justice professionals are encountering enormous challenges while experiencing marked changes. Whether or not the technologically advanced changes in criminal justice investigations and crime control reduce rates of violent crime is a subject to be analyzed in future years. Technological and social developments as well as needed policy changes offer much promise for the future which is *now*. Some of the most promising strategies in this century will include the following:

- Increased use of biosensors, lasers, and thermal neutron analysis equipment should greatly assist investigators in their search for missing persons.
- Increased development and use of nonlethal weapons such as laser guns, rubber bullets, and chemical sprays should save thousands of lives each year.
- The use of bionic eyes and eardrums will provide a major aid to police surveillance activities.

- Electronic tracking devices such as subdural implants, bracelets, and anklets should save states millions of dollars by using home detention and electronic monitoring staff instead of incarceration.

- Day reporting, day fines, intensive probation supervision, and restitution should save states and counties millions of dollars in dealing with nonviolent offenders, provided that each jurisdiction has an adequate accounting and monitoring staff.

- Behavior-altering drugs implanted in a sex offender or alcoholic's back can be activated automatically when the offender approaches an elementary school or tavern. The implanted microprocessor would relay physiological reactions to a central monitoring station, which would trigger the release of a small amount of tranquilizer or fact-acting sleep inducer.

Futurist and criminal justice professor Gene Stephens aptly sums up what the world of today holds for law enforcement:

> From a crime-and-justice standpoint, the twenty-first century [will be] either heaven or hell. Police will have new tools that will allow them to better fight crime—or prevent crime from occurring in the first place. These same tools will have the potential for abuse—particularly in the invasions of privacy…[Nevertheless] in [this century], technology and new crime management methods will be able to significantly reduce street crime—the theft and violence that frightens citizens the most.

In the first quarter of this century, many police departments will be using digital technology for automated fingerprint image capture, storage, retrieval, and transmission. As a result, remote positive identification from any part of the United States will be possible within minutes. Automated fingerprint identification systems (AFISs) and other technologically advanced information systems will provide much faster and more accurate fingerprint card processing than that which is possible using the current methods. On-line and efficient access to criminal history and juvenile records will be made available to all police departments within seconds. At the county and city level, a growing number of jurisdictions will establish countrywide criminal justice information networks that link computers from different computer manufacturers and different county agencies into an integrated regional system. This cost-effective strategy to computer networking will allow each authorized operator to transfer information electronically from one agency to another. This system should save local criminal justice agencies hundreds of thousands of dollars each year in time and effort of investigators and computer operators. As an example, a county probation officer or deputy prosecutor will have only to retrieve the information from the authorized computer operator, rather than starting from scratch with duplicating information already collected and entered into the system by one of the local police departments.

Crime laboratories reap the benefits from technology advancements and innovations. The future successes of law enforcement agencies are to be enhanced but those forensic scientists who utilize deoxyribonucleic acid (DNA) for personal identification, and analysis equipment will greatly aid investigators searching for missing persons or toxic wastes. In the case of missing victims, identification will not be made through plaster cases and sculpturing (i.e., skin depth measurements using clay to make a replica of the victim's face). In this century, forensic scientists should be able to do a computer-assisted anthropological study simply by using computer imaging to define what the missing person looks like.

Computer-based technologies and artificial intelligence systems are in use by many criminal justice agencies today. Data-based management systems (DBMs) have already begun to provide important information to jail and court administrators throughout the United States. During this century, we will see continued use of DBMs. Court DBM systems manage case dockets, maintain files on offenders, and enter official court decisions when rendered. DBMs will also interface with telephone and tele-video computer-based tracking systems (CBTSs), producing closed-circuit televisions systems that make it possible for courts to conduct remote bookings, initial hearings, and preliminary arraignments from hundreds of miles away. In local jails and state prisons, retinal identification as well as palm and fingerprint matching will continue to be used widely to control access to restricted areas of institutions.

The Federal Bureau of Investigation (FBI) uses data-based systems (also referred to as expert systems) to analyze criminal behavior patterns among serial killers, rapists, terrorists, and other violent offenders. For many years the FBI's National Criminal Information Center (NCIC) has provided local police departments with criminal history and record checks of suspects within seconds. The NCIC-2000 system enables law enforcement officers to identify missing persons and fugitives rapidly by placing a subject's finger on the fingerprint reader, which is to be located in patrol cars. The fingerprint reader transmits the image instantly to the NCIC-2000 computer at FBI headquarters, and within a few short minutes the computer relays a reply to police officers. Printers, once considered futuristic, will be installed in patrol cars, permitting officers to obtain copies of a suspect's photograph, signature, or tattoos as well as composite drawings of unknown subjects. The FBI has also shared their crime laboratory resources with local departments that investigate homicides (e.g., psychological profiling of serial killers, DNA typing, microscopic fiber analysis, and computer-enhanced imagining of the facial features of persons dead for some period of time).

There is a belief that in this new century, the justice process will become participatory, utilizing a mediation process where victim and defendant will be able to come to satisfactory agreements. Increased resources will and need to become available for such services. A wealthier, older, and culturally diverse population will cause a steady crime increase in the crime rate, with the diversity of crime increasing so that such resources become imperative.

The time is *now* to reshape the future of the criminal justice system, crime prevention, and to redefine its character and method of operation. The future is *now*. The time is ripe to create effective mechanisms for collaboration in the solving of problems faced by the justice system as well as to provide the framework for channels of communication. In this century there must be a revisit of the facilitation, planning, coordination, and implementation of the systems of the last century. We need to improve legislation and its procedures just as there must be a commitment to additional human and financial resources necessary to strengthen the criminal justice system. National policies are needed for crime prevention as well as criminal justice strategies, to contribute to the preservation and reinforcement of democracy and justice based on the rule of law.

Programs must be put into place that give us the capability to plan, implement, and evaluate crime prevention and criminal justice assistance projects—in order to sustain national developments, enhance justice, and gain further respect for human rights. There must be reviews of the criminal law to protect the environment, as well as plans to assess the drug problem, crime prevention in urban areas, juvenile and violent criminality, gender and race problems, and the entire criminal justice system. Efficiency, fairness, and improvement in the management and the administration of criminal justice and related systems must be the theme for this millennium.

There remains the need to place an understanding of compatible information technology to facilitate the administration of criminal justice while strengthening practical cooperation on crime control throughout this country. Both the private sector and criminal justice professionals have to exchange proposals, information on books, and innovations that enhance the operations of our criminal justice system. This book is a collection of chapters, written by persons whose expertise in the field of criminal justice recommends them as harbingers of what has to come in this century. We look at criminal justice from a historical perspective, review what has occurred during the last century, and then suggest what is to be and must be. This third edition is the most up-to-date text available on a system that is so very much a part of our lives, understanding that *the future is truly now*.

PART II

Linking Crime Challenges in the Twenty-First Century

This third edition of *Visions for Change: Crime and Justice in the Twenty-First Century* presents the most up-to-date materials on problems in the justice system. For example, in the chapter on the drug war, we find that it has become clear that incarceration does not break the cycle of illegal drugs and crime, that offenders who are incarcerated tend to recidivate once released, and that drug treatment programs are effective in reducing both drug abuse and drug-related crimes. Treatment has become the key for this century.

In the work by Andrew Karmen, he suggests several situations that can be pursued in anticipation of the problems facing victims of crime. He projects social trends that appear to be emerging that make it possible to paint plausible scenarios about developments in the next decades of this new century. In his chapter, Karmen also indicates ways to predict unheard-of developments that will evolve out of familiar situations. In a review of what has occurred with regard to victim treatment over the years, it has been made clear and sweeping that profound changes can be expected to occur. He notes that "[t]he current trend towards a high-tech service economy coupled with deindustrialization (the decline of American manufacturing) is bringing about pervasive long-term structural unemployment for those lacking the requisite skills." What implication does this have for victims of crime?

In an updated chapter on gangs, we see that they continue to pose a serious social problem for us in the United States. The chapter reviews gangs and their future, their origins, composition, and characteristics as well as all community responses, and possible future strategies for addressing gang problems. We are continually being made aware of gang problems that are not diminishing.

Jay Albanese, in his new chapter on issues of obscenity and pornography for the twenty-first century, talks of explicit songs, movies, cable television shows, talk radio, and computer services that create public concern over the roles of sex and violence in American life in general. Reviewed in Albanese's chapter are the trends in the pornography industry, effects of pornography on behavior, proper action by private citizens, law enforcement remedies, and the ever-growing role of the computer and use of the Internet. Albanese assesses the change in the focus of obscenity from sex to violence. Why is pornography so popular? Due to the current availability of sexually explicit materials, there needs to be a better understanding of why those persons interested in seeing and hearing them are so resilient.

Do the media continue to be at the core of the problems we face in the criminal justice system? Is the media making the headlines, or the criminals? If the media present erroneous and distorted information about the criminal justice system, then we have big problems. If discrepancies are found between the types of crime reported and the official reports of crime, why do we expect "the cultural products of mass media to reflect the social reality of crime"?

chapter 2

The War on Drugs

Treatment, Research, and Substance Abuse Intervention in the Twenty-First Century

C. Aaron McNeece, Ph.D., Bruce Bullington, Ph.D.,
Elizabeth Mayfield Arnold, Ph.D., and David W. Springer, Ph.D.

ABSTRACT

This chapter provides an overview of justice system interventions with drug users, reviews a number of harm reduction approaches, and suggests a different strategy allowing the medical use of marijuana. It concludes by suggesting that we need a paradigm shift away from the prohibitionist policies associated with the "War on Drugs." Overall, a strong argument is made for the decriminalization of drug use, if not for outright legalization.

INTRODUCTION

Three facts have become increasingly clear from the nation's experience with the "war on drugs": (1) incarceration alone does little to break the cycle of illegal drug use and crime, (2) offenders sentenced to incarceration for substance-related offenses exhibit a high rate of recidivism once they are released [Drug Court Clearinghouse and Technical Assistance Project (DCCTAP), 1996:8], and (3) drug abuse treatment has been shown to be demonstrably effective in reducing both drug abuse and drug-related crime [National Institute on Drug Abuse (NIDA), 1999:18–19].

Treatment for substance abuse addiction is seen as a key component in preventing re-offenses. Recent estimates from the National Household Survey on Drug Abuse (NHSDA) and the Uniform Facility Data Set (UFDS) indicate that approximately

5 million drug users needed immediate treatment in 1998, but only 2.1 million received treatment [Office of National Drug Control Policy (ONDCP), 2000:54]. Substance abuse is a long-standing problem in many cities throughout the nation. In the early 1990s, consumers spent $38 billion on cocaine alone. In the war on drugs, three-fourths of the expenditures went for domestic enforcement of drug laws, and only 7% was used for treatment (RAND, 1994). Since the early 1980s, the criminal justice system has felt the impact of the substance abuse problem as the number of offenders arrested on drug-related charges has increased dramatically and prisons throughout the nation have become inundated with drug offenders. There were more than 700,000 marijuana arrests in the United States in 1997 (Federal Bureau of Investigation, 1998).

In 1995, illegal drug use accounted for an estimated $110 billion in total expenses for law enforcement, incarceration, treatment, and "lost revenue." Health care expenditures associated with drug use cost another $12 billion (NIDA, 1998).

JUSTICE SYSTEM INTERVENTIONS WITH DRUG USERS

There is little doubt that drug users will continue to provide much of the fodder for our rapidly expanding correctional system well into the twenty-first century. During the last few decades there have been record increases in the numbers of persons brought under some form of correctional control in the United States. During the early 1990s the nation easily surpassed Russia and South Africa in our incarceration rates, making the United States the standout leader among industrialized nations in the imprisonment of its citizens. At midyear 1999 there were 1,860,520 persons incarcerated in the nation's prisons and jails. This represents a substantial increase, from 1 of every 218 U.S. residents in 1990 to 1 in every 147 in 1999 (Bureau of Justice Statistics, 2000). The highest rate of incarceration was in Louisiana (1025 per 100,000 residents) with the lowest in Vermont (203 per 100,000) (p. 1).

It is also clear that these increases were fueled largely by the war on drugs, as consequences of lengthier sentences and mandatory sentencing for those caught with these illicit substances. By the mid-1990s for example, more than 52% of federal inmates were drug offenders. Drug violators accounted for nearly 30% of prisoners in state facilities (Irwin and Austin, 1994)!

The results of these changes in incarceration rates were often not what had been anticipated by those who fostered them. For example, in Florida it was discovered that various new penal provisions for drug offenders that were passed in the 1980s resulted in serious criminal offenders actually serving less time than they had before, with many violent offenders being released prematurely to increase the availability of prison beds for nonviolent drug offenders who had been incarcerated under mandatory sentencing provisions (Rasmussen and Benson, 1994). Although these trends were eventually halted in the 1990s, they had a marked effect on prison and nonprison correctional populations at the time and will continue to influence the Florida system for some time to come.

Whenever correctional concerns are mentioned, people often think only in terms of prison, although these total institutions have never handled more than a small proportion of those who are serving a correctional sentence. At the present time about 20% of sentenced persons are actually serving time in prisons or jails; the remaining 80% are involved in some alternative sanction provided for under both federal and state justice systems (Clear, 1995). For those not imprisoned, probation is generally thought of as the only available option. Despite this perception, there exists a wide variety of programs that provide alternatives to institutionalization and probation. Recently, these approaches have been labeled "intermediate sanctions" by scholars and researchers in the field, who see them as located between the two extremes of incarceration and probation.

The forms that intermediate sanctions take include a rich diversity of options. Clear (1995) has identified nine distinct methods of intermediate sanctions methods. One of these is *intensive supervision*, an approach that is coupled with either probation or parole. It involves very frequent contacts between those being observed and their supervision agents. In a second method, *house arrest*, the offender is confined to his or her residence either continually or during nonwork hours. A third strategy, *electronic monitoring*, requires that the offender wear a bracelet that signals a homing device when the person has gone beyond an acceptable range. *Urine screening* is a fourth tactic that is used to detect illicit drug or alcohol use by the offender. The fifth method includes *fines*, which are generally used in conjunction with several other approaches. A sixth program type, *community service*, calls for the offender to work for a specified number of hours in a community service project. *Halfway houses* and *work release centers* comprise the seventh strategy. These provide living facilities for offenders, who are usually required to maintain regular employment during the day. An eighth form of intermediate sanction, *shock probation*, provides a brief period of confinement designed to alert offenders to the seriousness of their behavior, followed by intensive supervision on probation. Finally, *treatment programs* can be prescribed for offenders who are ordered to participate in substance abuse programs and related activities. These can include both inpatient and outpatient methods, depending on the person involved and the nature of their chemical dependency problem.

It should be noted that several different goals may be established for these programs. Most can be classified as being principally concerned with controlling offenders, or with changing them through some therapeutic intervention. Given these distinct goals, the various programs identified above may be utilized in several combinations. Offenders are likely to be concurrently assigned to several of these intermediate sanction conditions simultaneously, based on the judge's perception of the nature of their problem, life circumstances, and amenability to specific types of intervention. It has long been believed that the probability of producing favorable outcomes with these populations may be enhanced by careful selection and matching of conditions to individual needs. Of course, the problem remains how we are to accomplish this, especially given the relatively primitive state of our current knowledge.

Intermediate sanctions are seen by supporters as being much less expensive than incarceration and also as more effective at producing desirable outcomes. If such claims are proven to be accurate, these methods should expand considerably in the years to come. While the pressures brought about by the extreme incarceration rates generated during the1990s are subsiding somewhat, there remains considerable interest in lowering the costs of corrections. If intermediate sanctions can produce positive results and at a cost that is but a small fraction of those associated with institutionalization, it seems likely that these programs will receive a great deal of attention.

CURRENT PRACTICES IN DRUG OFFENDER INTERVENTION

Although substance abuse treatment for offenders varies across programs, facilities, and locations, the National Task Force on Correctional Substance Abuse Strategies (1991) notes that "effective programs" have common characteristics: clearly defined missions, goals, admission criteria, and assessment strategies for those seeking treatment; support and understanding of key agency administrators and staff; consistent intervention strategies supported by links with other agencies as the offender moves through the system; well-trained staff who have opportunities for continuing education; and ongoing evaluation and development based on outcome and process data. One of the main issues of contention among researchers and substance abuse providers has been an operational definition of the term *effective treatment*. The Treatment Outcome Working Group, a meeting of treatment and evaluation experts sponsored by the ONDCP, established some results and outcomes that define effective treatment (ONCDP, 1996):

1. Reduced use of the primary drug
2. Improved functioning of drug users in terms of employment
3. Improved educational status
4. Improved interpersonal relationships
5. Improved medical statues and general improvement in health
6. Improved legal status
7. Improved mental health status
8. Improved noncriminal public safety factors

Although some of these desired outcomes are not pertinent to incarcerated offenders receiving treatment, they are appropriate long-term goals following release. Failure to accomplish these goals is likely to lead to continued involvement in future drug use and criminal activity, and possibly, incarceration.

In addition to these criteria, NIDA (1999) believes that "effective treatment attends to multiple needs of the individual, not just his or her drug use" (p. i). To be effective, treatment must address the user's medical, psychological, social, vocational, and legal problems.

One problem in evaluating drug treatment methods and programs for criminal offenders is that recidivism tends to be defined solely in terms of rearrest rates. Yet a number of offenders who successfully complete treatment may continue to use drugs and not be rearrested. Thus, if recidivism is defined only as rearrest, an unknown percentage of subjects may continue to have substance abuse problems, even though they have been defined as successful. Another problem is that offenders may be rearrested for nondrug offenses, resulting in a type of "false positive" in the recidivism statistics.

Looking at data on rearrests may either lead us to underestimate or overestimate the actual rate of continued substance abuse among offenders. One alternative in gaining a better estimate of continued drug use is to examine the substance use level and productivity after treatment completion (Van Stelle et al., 1994). However, monitoring posttreatment offender behavior is difficult unless they are mandated to have follow-up through probation or parole, and urine drug testing. These methods of monitoring are discussed later in this chapter.

We now turn our attention to a discussion of the most common types of intervention and treatment programs. The programs and models below are included either because they represent a prevalent model or because they have shown unusual promise in assisting substance-abusing offenders.

Self-Help Programs

Alcoholics Anonymous (AA), founded by William ("Bill W.") Wilson and Robert ("Dr. Bob") Holbrook Smith, is an abstinence-based 12-step program which maintains that alcoholism is a disease that can be coped with but not cured. Thus, according to the AA philosophy, there are recovering alcoholics, but not cured or ex-alcoholics. Other self-help 12-step programs, such as Narcotics Anonymous (NA), follow the same conceptual framework as that used in Alcoholics Anonymous. AA and NA meetings are held in both adult and juvenile secured correctional settings. Additional self-help groups include Routine Recovery and Women's Sobriety.

Individual, Family, and Group Counseling

Individual counseling might address areas such as depression, faulty cognitions (often referred to in the field as "stinking thinking"), and "using" behaviors. This modality usually entails "talk therapy" between a client and clinical psychologist, social worker, or substance abuse counselor. The goal is to remedy some underlying personality flaw (low self-esteem, etc.) which is believed to have led to the substance abuse problem.

A truism in substance dependency is that families are critical factors to consider when developing a treatment plan for the client. The most commonly used family treatment approach with substance abuse is structural-strategic family therapy (Springer and Smith, 1998). Developed by Salvador Minuchin and his associates (Minuchin, 1974; Minuchin and Fishman, 1981), this approach incorporates family development and a family systems conceptual framework. Studies addressing the efficacy of structural family therapy with youth have revealed positive results when used with drug-abusing families (Fishman et al., 1982; Szapocznik et al., 1986).

Group counseling can take the form of support groups, psychoeducational groups, and interactional therapeutic groups. It is the latter that is the focus here. These groups may be conducted in outpatient and inpatient settings, including settings within the criminal justice system.

Working with groups in the criminal justice system takes on a different connotation than working with groups in the community because of issues of confidentiality, control, and safety. Nevertheless, the primary objective remains the same. The worker should focus on the strengths of the individual, consider group exercises that will emphasize these strengths, and foster the concept of cohesion within the group (Jackson and Springer, 1997). These principles also apply to support groups that are often made available for parents, spouses, siblings, and other family members.

Psychoeducational Approaches

In many corrections settings, both adult and juvenile offenders are required to complete educational classes as a part of their treatment plan. In the justice system, two major types of educational programs for offenders exist: didactic educational programs and psychoeducational methods.

Didactic educational programs closely resemble a seminar or class. In these programs, offenders are presented with information about substance abuse and its effects. Offenders may learn about topics such as the physical effects of drug and alcohol abuse, or the impact of substance abuse on family members, or they may be provided information about substance abuse treatment. In didactic educational programs, offenders are expected to listen to the information provided, and although there may be some interaction, the presenter is the focus of the program and interaction is generally minimal.

Psychoeducational educational methods combine "the presentation of didactic information to increase knowledge with a variety of other techniques to help clients make desired changes and to provide support" (McNeece and DiNitto, 1994:117). In these programs, the emphasis is not solely on the facilitator, and group interaction is encouraged. Structured exercises such as role plays, group discussion on specific topics, and homework assignments are generally a part of psychoeducational programs.

The major objectives of psychoeducational approaches include development of motivation and commitment to treatment through recognition of the addiction history, stages of recovery, and the impact of drug use on physical health and vocational and social functioning; the enhancement of life skills (e.g., managing a checkbook, time management) and communication skills; AIDS education and prevention activities; relapse prevention skills, including recognition of signs and symptoms of relapse, avoidance of active drug users, identification of high-risk situations, and strategies for managing a lapse or relapse; and development of an aftercare plan that incorporates use of community treatment resources (Peters, 1993:53).

Case Management

Case management activities originated in early twentieth century social work practice that provided services to disadvantaged clients. Most descriptions of case management include at least six primary functions: (1) identification and outreach to people in need of services, (2) assessment of specific needs, (3) planning for services, (4) linkage to services, (5) monitoring and evaluation, and (6) advocacy for the client system (Ridgely, 1996). Workers are increasingly engaging in case management activities in their work with substance-abusing offenders.

The importance of workers providing case management services for substance-abusing clients in the criminal justice setting has been supported by Martin and Inciardi (1993), who state that "[d]rug-involved criminal justice clients often face a wider spectrum of problems than other populations targeted by case management, including the life disruptions associated with police and court processing, the perceived stigma of a criminal record, the possibility of lost freedom through incarceration, and the disruptions caused in work, school, and family activities" (p. 89). Others also support the use of case management services, as they have been shown to encourage substance abusers to remain in treatment and reach their treatment goals (Koeofed et al., 1986).

Treatment Alternatives to Street Crime

In the attempt to combat substance abuse in communities, a number of alternatives other than incarceration have been tried in recent years. One of the most widely known of these alternatives is Treatment Alternatives to Street Crime (TASC), a specially designed form of case management initially funded in 1972 with federal monies. TASC targets offenders who appear to have the potential to benefit from treatment and who do not pose significant safety risks to their communities with supervision (Lipton, 1995). The purpose of TASC is to identify, assess, refer for treatment, and conduct follow-up on drug offenders. Offenders in TASC programs are not incarcerated, but rather, are treated outside the court system in community-based programs. Each offender is assigned a case manager who assists in gaining access to treatment, provides linkages to other needed community services, and reports back to the appropriate court officials about the offender's progress. The monitoring function of the case manager is one of the hallmarks of TASC.

Acupuncture

Acupuncture is a form of ancient Chinese medicine that has been used for the last 20 years to treat addictions. The use of acupuncture involves inserting four or five needles into a person's ear for approximately 45 minutes. It is believed that acupuncture may help to reduce the physical signs of withdrawal, including cravings, body aches, headaches, nausea, sweating, and muscle cramping. (The exact mechanisms through which these improvements are supposed to occur have never been clearly identified.) Supporters of acupuncture also claim that it relieves depression, anxiety, and insomnia (Turnabout ASAP, 1997). The needles are believed to produce a powerful response that helps decrease the desire for drugs and/or alcohol, thus helping the brain regain its chemical balance. Once this crucial balance is restored, the abuser will hopefully become more introspective and receptive to therapy (Edwards, 1993). The first substance abuse facility known to use acupuncture with substance abusers is Lincoln Hospital Substance Abuse Center in South Bronx, New York. Acupuncture has become particularly popular among "drug court" programs in the United States.

Despite anecdotal reports of success, few empirical studies exist that have examined the overall effectiveness of acupuncture in treating addictions. Two studies have examined the use of acupuncture with inner-city, cocaine-dependent methadone clients. Margolin et al. (1995) found that the majority (90%) of participants in an eight-week course of treatment remained abstinent for more than one month. Others (Lipton et al., 1990; Brewington et al., 1994) have found that while acupuncture can produce reductions in self-reports of day-to-day cocaine use among chronic crack users, the urinalysis results of participants did not differ from those of the control group.

Urine Drug Testing

A sophisticated technology has been developed to test drug offenders for substance use. During the 1960s these methods were used for the first time to detect the presence of banned substances in the blood and urine of parolees and probationers. At that time urine testing programs were costly, however, and there were few reliable laboratories that could be counted on to minimize the number of faulty readings (both false positives and false negatives).

Today these different forms of drug testing are much more sophisticated than before. Although these latest methods are not foolproof, they do provide much more reliability than the earlier ones did (Timrots, 1992).

Urine drug testing is used in the criminal justice system with offenders in three main ways: (1) as an adjunct to community supervision, (2) as an assessment tool for offenders entering the system, and (3) as an assessment of drug use during mandated drug treatment. The utilization of drug testing serves several purposes in the criminal justice system: to inform judges of an offender's current drug use as a consideration for bail setting or sentencing; to indicate whether an offender is complying with a mandate to be drug-free, and to identify those offenders who are in need of treatment (Timrots, 1992).

The National Institute of Justice Drug Use Forecasting (DUF) program calculates the percentage of offenders arrested in certain cities throughout the country who have positive urine drug screens at the time of arrest. Recent DUF data shows that the percentage of male inmates testing postive for any drug ranged from 51 to 83% (ONDCP, 1997).

Drug testing appears to serve a useful purpose in monitoring offenders with substance problems. However, drug testing alone is not sufficient to keep offenders from using drugs and reoffending. The best approach may be to combine random drug testing with forms of rehabilitative drug treatment to treat the addiction (Graboski, 1986).

We are now urine testing far more people than ever before, including those who are merely workers in an organization who have no official record of drug abuse, as well as parolees and probationers who do. These procedures raise many troubling questions about how far we wish to go as a society to detect illicit use. The technology already exists to test everyone, and fairly inexpensively. If we decide to do this, however, we must decide what to do with this information. When someone is detected using drugs on the job, can we assume that something must be done about it? Are these employees to be fired, forced into some treatment program, warned, or what? Additionally, the question must be resolved of whether testing will occur only during the initial employment interview, periodically throughout one's employment, or only for "cause," such as a supervisor's suspicion that one is using.

It is undeniably true that the existence of this technology considerably enhances the power of the state over citizens. We are now able to tap into their very body chemistry to determine whether they have consumed any illegal substance. Whether the benefits of extending this level of social control over a group of people is really desirable in a democractic society, however, needs to be resolved. Critics have repeatedly argued that a whole wave of new control techniques have been developed since the 1960s, when *diversion* became the catchword for the latest innovation in American corrections, and that these have often not had the intended results. Instead of playing a supporting role as alternatives to incarceration, many of these strategies have simply allowed for and encouraged a "net-widening" effect (Blomberg et al., 1993; Blomberg and Lucken, 1993). Populations that had never before been reached by criminal justice correctional services are now fair game, and many of those sanctioned under these diversion programs appear to be persons who previously would not have been dealt with officially at all. For example, many juvenile courts have implemented juvenile delinquency diversion programs with perfectly good intentions. Many find that rather than diverting the traditional juvenile offender from official court processing, they are "recruiting" new groups of clients from populations of nonoffenders. A teacher hears of a "great diversion program" and refers a "troubled" student who has never been in any legal difficulty. Once that juvenile is into the diversion program, he or she is more likely to be identified and labeled as an "offender."

A close inspection of anyone's life may lead to the observation of a violation of one of the diversion rules. Ultimately, the rigid enforcement of these very strict conditions of probation and parole can actually lead to a swelling of prison and jail populations, with cells being filled with those who could not muster the rules of diversionary alternatives and who are sent to a total institution for these technical violations. If this occurs, it certainly has defeated the purposes for which these alternative programs were established in the first place.

Milieu Approaches

Inpatient and Residential Programs

Inpatient treatment has changed drastically over recent years. The era of 28-day treatment programs is almost extinct. The cost of such programs is too high for most people to pay for out of pocket, and third-party payers overwhelmingly no longer reimburse for such services. Inpatient programs typically provide respite for family, drug education, group encounters with peers, and individual treatment, which may include a pharmacological component.

Longer inpatient (residential) programs for offenders, such as therapeutic communities, also exist. Once admitted into such facilities, clients are encouraged to form close emotional ties with other patients. When successful, clients will perceive themselves as part of a group of peers who act as a support network (Obermeier and Henry, 1989).

There is no evidence to suggest that inpatient treatment is any more effective than outpatient treatment with most substance abusers (Gerstein and Harwood, 1990). However, for many families who avail themselves of extended inpatient treatment for their children or spouses, the treatment period acts as a respite. Changes that do occur within an inpatient setting frequently occur within a vacuum; the typical frustrations and challenges that might encourage alcohol and drug use and abuse are absent in an inpatient setting. Thus, improvements seen in the hospital don't necessarily extend to home settings (Joaning et al., 1986).

Intensive Outpatient Programs

Alternatives to the more expensive and restrictive inpatient and residential care described above are intensive outpatient programs (IOPs) and partial hospitalization programs (PHPs), both of which allow clients to return home each night with his or her family rather than "live" at the facility. Otherwise, IOPs and PHPs provide the same services as inpatient or residential treatment at lower costs (Wells, 1994).

Therapeutic Communities

Therapeutic communities (TCs) may be considered to fall under the realm of residential programs or jail treatment programs. A therapeutic community is a residential treatment environment that provides an around-the-clock learning experience in which the drug user's changes in conduct, attitudes, values, and emotions are implemented, monitored, and reinforced on a daily basis (DeLeon, 1986). Typically, a TC is highly structured, lasting anywhere from three to 15 months. However, due to the confrontational nature of the community, it is common for residents to leave within the first three months of the program (Goldapple, 1990).

The treatment philosophy is that substance abuse is a disorder of the whole person, the problem lies in the person and not the drug, and the addiction is but a symptom and not the essence of the disorder (Pan et al., 1993). The primary goal of the TC approach is to lead the client to a responsible, substance-free life. Although individual, family, and group counseling may be components of the TC, the cornerstone of the program is the peer encounter that takes place in the group process. Rules of the community are specific and enforced by the residents themselves. Generally, the TC staff are themselves recovering substance abusers who have successfully completed treatment in a therapeutic community.

Gerstein and Harwood (1990) found that therapeutic community programs, when closely linked to community-based supervision and treatment programs, can significantly reduce rearrest rates. Therapeutic communities have been tried in correctional settings, but for obvious reasons they must be modified substantially (Lipton et al., 1992). The implementation of therapeutic communities in correctional settings has been hindered at times by a reluctance to provide long-term therapeutic services, by philosophical opposition to the use of staff who themselves are former offenders, by coercive treatment strategies, and by the need for specialized staff training and technical assistance (Peters, 1993). A recent evaluation of several TCs in correctional settings produced mixed results (NIJ, 2000).

Boot Camps

Shock incarceration is derived from the "scared straight" model. Under this approach, juvenile (and sometimes adult) offenders are incarcerated for a brief period (Parent, 1989), then released under close supervision. Boot camps based on a military model are an increasingly popular form of shock incarceration. They are usually small in size; they stress discipline, physical conditioning, and strict authoritarian control (McNeece, 1997). It is precisely these characteristics that have made these camps popular with both politicians and the general public.

Some criminal justice researchers argue that boot camps do not make a long-term impact on juveniles because they do not meet the needs of offenders, and that in fact rearrest rates of boot camp graduates are similar to those of inmates (MacKenzie, 1994; cited in DiMascio, 1995). A recent report conducted by the Florida Department of Juvenile Justice indicates that arrest rates at Florida's six boot camps averaged between 63 to 74% for the first 60 boot camp graduates. The results were similar to comparison groups in other programs. Similarly, the Florida Juvenile Justice Advisory Board released a study indicating a 45% rearrest rate for all youth ($n = 317$) who went through the state's six boot camps during a six-month period (Kaczor, 1997).

Drug Court

A promising and innovative alternative used to combat the growing substance abuse problem in this country is the establishment of diversionary programs known as drug courts. The mission of drug courts is to eliminate substance abuse and the resulting criminal behavior. Drug court is a "team effort that focuses on sobriety and accountability as the primary goals" [National Association of Drug Court Professionals (NADCP), 1997:8]. The team of professionals generally includes the state attorney, public defender, pretrial intervention or probation staff, treatment providers, and the judge, who is considered the central figure in the team. Drug court provides a new role based on "a growing realization that active judicial participation and leadership is crucial to the successful organization, design, and implementation of coordinated anti-drug systems" (NADCP and Office of Community Oriented Policing Services, 1997:5).

Drug courts have generally processed offenders in two ways: (1) through the use of deferred prosecution (herein adjudication is deferred, and the defendant enters treatment), or (2) through a postadjudication process by which the case is adjudicated but sentencing is withheld while the defendant is in treatment [U.S. General Accounting Office (GAO), 1995]. Drug courts tend to be a nonadversarial process (Goldkamp, 1998, in press) which focuses on treatment rather than criminal sanctions.

The great expanse of the drug court movement is due, in part, to the federal monies made available by the Attorney General of the United States under Title V of the Violent Control and Law Enforcement Act of 1994. These grants helped establish drug courts nationwide. As a result, the number of drug courts, the scope of services, and the range of addicted populations served increased [Drug Court Clearinghouse and Technicial Assistance Project (DCCTAP), 1997]. Three hundred and twenty-five drug courts now exist in 48 states, the District of Columbia, Guam, and Puerto Rico, and in 13 Native American Tribal Courts (DCCTAP, 1997).

Judicial supervision may have beneficial effects on reducing recidivism among drug court participants. In a recent three-year study in Oklahoma, Huddleston (1997) compared 48 graduates and 62 nongraduates of a drug court with 47 program graduates and 41 nongraduates of an alternative sentencing precursor to drug court. Findings suggests that there were beneficial effects of judicial supervision in decreasing recidivism rates. Judicial supervision in drug courts, combined with cognitive therapy, increased the success rate for defendants (96%) while decreasing failures (2%), compared to 74 and 39%, respectively, for the comparison group (Huddleston, 1997).

Probation

The main method of monitoring offenders who have not been sentenced to prison is probation. Probation, in combination with counseling, support, and surveillance, is the most common type of treatment used as an alternative to incarceration (Lipton, 1995). With regular probation, an offender lives at home and receives periodic monitoring. Many offenders with substance abuse problems are sentenced to intensive supervision probation (ISP), a more restrictive type of probation than traditional probation. ISP is a method of monitoring that can be used as an alternative to incarceration. ISP requires that the offender and probation officer keep in close contact, which generally includes random home visits to ensure compliance with the requirements of the program. In addition, the offender may have to perform community service, maintain employment, adhere to a curfew, and submit to urine drug testing. Compared to basic probation, ISP is generally more expensive and requires that probation officers have smaller caseloads to accommodate the increase in supervision of the offender. ISP may, however, be more cost-effective than basic probation in the long run, when the alternative for offenders is prison or jail (Edna McConnell Clark Foundation, 1995).

TOWARD A PARADIGM SHIFT IN DRUG POLICY

In our view the United States must experience a paradigm shift in our approach to drug use and abuse if we are ever to make any significant improvements in this area of social policy. Such a paradigm shift would include, at a minimum, a switch from the prohibitionist or zero tolerance concept of drug use to one of harm reeducation, as well as a gradual decriminalization of some currently illicit drugs. On that issue, a possible beginning would be the limited use of marijuana for medical purposes.

Prohibitionist Reduction Approaches

During the 87 years that have elapsed since the Harrison Act's (the landmark federal legislation defining illicit drugs) passage in December 1914, U.S. drug policy has clearly defined an approach to the drug problem that is prohibitionist by design and is dominated by criminal justice agencies, methods, and ideologies. Most often, drug users here have been considered criminals first. Severe sanctions have been applied to violators to discourage their further involvement in illegal enterprises and to deter others from following the same path. Despite these aggressive attempts to control the problem, there is little or no evidence that any of these tactics have had their intended deterrent effects. Indeed, several contemporary observers have remarked that given the degree of our commitment, it is incredible that so little has been accomplished (Currie, 1993).

Over time the financial commitments to fighting a series of drug "wars" have escalated considerably. For example, when President Nixon first declared war on drugs in 1969, a budget of $600 million was set aside for the effort. In contrast, by 1997, President Clinton had committed more than $16 billion to the fight (ONDCP, 1997). Of course, these monies are only a portion of the total amount allocated to the war, as state and local governments spend an amount that is at least equal to that committed by the federal government in their efforts to combat drugs. Just during the last 10 years the federal commitment to the drug war has exceeded $100 billion!

Despite ongoing disagreement among experts, many have come to the conclusion that the drug wars have not produced their intended results (Nadelmann, 1988; Duke and Gross, 1993; Bugliosi, 1996; Bullington, 1997). The evidence that supports this position is easily accessible. For example, the United States continues to have the highest drug use rates of any industrialized, advanced nation (Currie, 1993). Although some modest "gains" have been made in terms of reductions in reported use among high school seniors and other vulnerable population groups during the last 15 years or so, the most recent figures show that such use is once again on the rise. It has also been pointed out that the drug wars were not really targeting these groups at all, as they are mostly casual, recreational users. Rather, the drug wars have been fought against a much smaller group of "problematic" drug users, and that group has not been diminished. In fact, it now appears that the rate of such use has actually gone up, despite the extraordinary efforts made to reduce or eliminate it.

Other indicators of the failure of our drug policy efforts are easily observed. Despite huge increases in police confiscations of drugs, these substances are still available in great supply and in purer form than ever before. For example, the heroin that is currently being sold throughout the United States is now said to be as much as 90% pure, compared with the 3 to 5% purity that was typically found during the 1960s (Coomber, 1997)!

In the face of this compelling evidence, it may be difficult to see how anyone can continue to support the present policies. Of course, many persons do and often vigorously defend the status quo approach to the drug problem. One example of this may be found in recent statements made by Robert L. DuPont (1996), the nation's first appointed drug czar under the Nixon administration: "After more than a quarter of a century in the field of addiction medicine, I have found that the policy of prohibition…remains the bedrock of the modern response to the risks posed by brain-rewarding chemicals…Harm reduction, a compromise between drug prohibition and legalization, is a failed policy since it undermines the clear and powerful message of prohibition" (p. 1,942).

Other experts disagree. They believe that the drug policies that have been aggressively pursued in the United States throughout most of the twentieth century have seemingly failed to accomplish their stated goals. The strong prohibitionist law enforcement and criminal justice orientation favored here has simply not worked. Amazingly, there is very little evidence that the drug wars, whether their most recent iteration or those launched much earlier, have had *any* salutary effects.

Enter Harm Reduction

A strikingly different drug policy approach is currently being implemented enthusiastically, and with considerable apparent success, in several western European nations. This strategy is generally labeled *harm reduction* and promotes a public health rather than criminal justice perspective when determining what to do about drug users and drug problems generally. The police role in these countries is largely restricted to attempts to control large-scale trafficking and sales of illegal substances. The Netherlands has been the clear leader in defining this "new" method for attending to drug problems, although similar approaches are now also being tried in Switzerland, Spain, Italy, and Germany, as well as in the Czech Republic and several other emerging democracies in central Europe.

The harm reduction philosophy is based on several underlying assumptions about the nature of drug use and related concerns. The first of these is that drug use is in a sense inevitable, as we know of no societies, either ancient or contemporary, that have not promoted the use of some substances while opposing the use of others. Thus, the historical record alone provides irrefutable proof that drug use will not go away, regardless of what we may choose to do about it. Given this observation, a policy that is based on the notion that a drug-free society can be achieved, such as that which has been doggedly pursued in the United States during this century, is seen as impractical and doomed to failure.

A second defining characteristic of the harm reduction philosophy is that it treats all drug use, whether of "licit" or illicit substances, as potentially problematic. It is thought that the distinctions made between legal and illegal substances are totally artificial and that they have led to a myopic focus solely on the illicit chemicals. Harm reduction advocates suggest that all drugs have the potential to be used either productively or harmfully. Consequently, no distinction is made between these drugs based on their legal classification alone. Rather, differences are identified on the basis of the real damage and harms that these drugs do. Of course, by this standard, the two generally favored social drugs of tobacco products and alcohol must appear at the head of the list of "problem" drugs. Consequently, they also would be included in any drug policy designed by harm reduction proponents.

A third feature of harm reduction notions is that all drug problems must be seen fundamentally as public health rather than criminal justice concerns. In this model various health agencies and professionals are expected to play key leadership roles in assessing and treating the problematic symptoms associated with the use of these substances. In the harm reduction model, law enforcement continues to play a role in societal efforts to control illegal production, importation, and sales of illicit drugs. The key difference here is that the police are denied the opportunity to pursue users, who are defined here as sick people in need of medical assistance.

Finally, given the obvious reluctance of drug users to volunteer for treatment under the old, police-dominated systems, it is thought that new and very different forms of outreach must be developed to gain their confidence and get them involved in therapeutic interventions. Of utmost concern is the establishment of some contact between health authorities and problematic users. Whereas the prohibitionist approach conditions users to hide and resist efforts to get them into treatment, harm reduction is designed to entice them through nonthreatening interventions and aggressive social work.

Practically speaking, the harm reduction methods that are currently being tried in the Netherlands and elsewhere include the following specific strategies for dealing with users:

- Street social workers establish initial contacts with users.
- Friendly users are enlisted in the efforts to contact their fellows and to encourage them to come in to obtain health services.
- Low-threshold programs are established to provide methadone in low doses to street addicts who are not yet willing to come in for help, and this without any contingent conditions such as that they give up all drug use or submit to urine tests—several methadone buses are used to deliver the drug on a daily basis to these users in their neighborhoods.
- Free needles and needle exchange programs are in place to minimize the potential for HIV infections among injecting users.
- Safe disposal receptacles are provided to individual users, and larger receptacles are placed in the apartments of known sellers.

- Clinics are available for high-dose methadone and regular medical care for those users who are willing to participate.

- "Safe houses" have been established to allow addicts to come off the streets to "fix" in a clean, regulated environment rather than on the streets.

- There has been a liberal dose of public advertising of the potential hazards of particular drugs, unsafe sex, needle sharing and the like.

- An extensive variety of treatment programs have been established to appeal to a wide range of users who are ready to undertake their own rehabilitation.

Each of these tactics has been developed to provide a user-friendly environment in order to bring users back into the mainstream of their societies.

The results of harm reduction methods have been quite impressive thus far. The goal of making treatment an attractive option has resulted in approximately 85% of Dutch drug addicts now being in contact with government agencies and helpers. This figure compares favorably with the estimated 10 to 20% of American addicts who are in contact with health officials (Bullington, 1995). Users throughout the Netherlands and other countries that have adopted similar methods are more likely to be receiving basic health care and nutritional advice; are experiencing fewer drug-related health problems, such as abscesses, hepatitis, and AIDS; and are better able to live somewhat "normal" lifestyles, unlike their North American counterparts.

In assessing the outcomes of these harm reduction programs one must keep in mind the goals of such a philosophy. It is taken as a given that drug use will continue regardless of social attitudes about it and that the dominant theme of intervention approaches must be based on reducing the harms that drugs do to those who consume them! By this measure these programs have been very successful, although they have not, and were never intended to, eliminate drug use altogether. None of this is to suggest, however, that the citizens residing in these nations approve of drug use; to the contrary, they often condemn it in the same manner that U.S. citizens do.

Based on our own failures with criminal justice methods and the apparent successes experienced in these other places, there is reason to hope that many of these methods could be adopted here in the near future. The point is that harm reduction can be undertaken anywhere, regardless of the dominant policy orientation (Erickson, 1996). Thus, even with a prohibitionist policy, it would be conceptually possible to consider how harm reduction could be implemented to minimize drug-related harms. In fact, there is already evidence that harm reduction efforts have been initiated in various locales throughout the United States. For example, a number of cities now promote needle exchange programs or at least the provision of information regarding the use of sterile equipment and bleach to clean injection equipment. There has been considerable resistance to such programs, however, as they are said to encourage or signal societal approval for injecting drug use. In several cases, the practices have been initiated in direct violation of the state and/or local law that prohibits them. Methadone maintenance has also been available here for many years, and well over 100,000 addicts are currently being treated with the substitute narcotic.

Although these programs are supposed to reduce the dosage one takes over time and eventually to wean the addict entirely from the drug, most do not attempt or require this.

Of course, harm reduction can also be implemented as a prevention strategy with those who have not yet experimented with drugs. This would require that all drugs, whether legal or illegal, be included in these discussions; there can be no sacred cows. It also necessitates abandoning the "just say no" claims, which are to be replaced by serious discussions of safe and unsafe use practices. To date, North Americans have been very reluctant to accept such educational tactics, believing instead that this objective stance would ultimately lead to increased use (Rosenbaum, 1996). The evaluations of our current primary prevention methods, however, have revealed that these do not have their intended consequences; in other words, they do not prevent youth from experimenting with drugs.

Ultimately, the adoption of large-scale harm reduction methods would require a significant shift in our dominant prohibitionist drug policy and mind set. For these strategies to be adopted successfully, we would first have to jettison our long-held faith and commitment to punitive tactics in fighting wars on drugs against users. A public health strategy calls for an entirely different view of the user as a sick person in need of basic medical assistance rather than as a criminal who is wilfully subverting the law.

Although many skeptics might argue that these changes seem highly unlikely, we need only look as far back as the nineteenth century to find a time when these substances were treated very differently than they are now. Drugs were not then seen as constituting major social problems, and certainly not as posing a serious threat to the very survival of the nation as they are now. These laissez-faire ideas were not a result of there being few drug users then, however, for there is a formidable array of data supporting the conclusion that there may have been as many serious or problematic users as there are today (Courtwright, 1982). Historian David Musto (1991) reminds us that even in the twentieth century our drug war hysteria has ebbed and flowed with succeeding generations. He argues that the lessons learned about the dangers of drugs by one generation are slowly replaced by a collective naiveté in later cohorts. One consequence of these fluctuations has been that our drug policies have cycled from extreme, often hysterical levels of concern to apathy several generations later. The adoption of harm reduction measures could moderate these national mood swings and provide a much more consistent and enduring set of responses from one generation to another.

Medical Marijuana

As the twentieth century drew to a close, the U.S. government and several states were embroiled in a highly visible public debate regarding the usefulness of marijuana as a medicant. There is little question that the issue will not be quickly resolved, for all sides participating in the debate are fiercely committed to maintaining their respective positions, which are irreconcilable. The group opposing marijuana being used as a medicine typically argue that much more scientific research is needed regarding the drug's actual benefits and liabilities before any reasoned, final decision can be made. Those approving its medical use contend that sufficient evidence to settle the matter has been available for some time and that the call for more research is just a delaying tactic by their opponents. Despite the often acrimonious interactions between members of the various interest groups involved, the issue itself is fascinating and is likely to continue being discussed well into the twenty-first century.

As is true of many current debates about aspects of various national policies, the contestants in this struggle are an odd lot indeed. Those appearing in favor of changing the laws to allow for marijuana use in medicine have included the following: a majority of the voting citizens of the populous states of California and Arizona; activists such as members of NORML (the National Organization for the Reform of Marijuana Laws), who promote a change in the legal status of marijuana for everyone; patients who have used the drug illegally to relieve their symptoms; a small but determined group of researchers, academics, and professionals who have already investigated the drug's medical uses; and a group of political libertarians who are committed to the idea that drug use is an individual choice that the government has no business regulating. These supporters often make strange bedfellows, although their coalition has proven to be a potent force, as their opponents can attest.

A few examples of some of the most prominent participants in this movement may be in order. One interest group is NORMAL (the National Organization for the Reform of Marijuana Laws), a small but vocal national organization that has for several decades been calling for the repeal of all laws regulating the drug. A second constituency is made up of a wide variety of medical patients. Many of these patients are enduring the terminal stages of an illness or disease such as AIDS or cancer and have found that marijuana seems to help them cope with the severe nausea that often accompanies chemotherapy treatment and that it increases their appetite. Others have glaucoma, the progressive eye disease that eventually results in blindness. These patients smoke the drug in order to relieve the painful pressure of fluids building up within the eye itself. A third group of patients with multiple sclerosis have found the drug gives them relief from muscle spasticity and other chronic symptoms of their illness. Another distinct group of participants is comprised of the families and friends of these patients and others who similarly believe that marijuana should be used for these compassionate purposes.

Those opposing any changes in the status of marijuana are a formidable group comprised of government leaders, including the President and his drug czars, both past and present; nearly all national, state, and local politicians; law enforcement leaders and personnel; government-supported scientists; public prosecutors; a number of grass-roots citizen groups; and others. These groups claim that the drug is neither safe nor effective for the treatment of any medical problems. One favored strategy of these claimants has been to suggest that the other side, especially those who wish to use it recreationally, is merely using the medical marijuana issue as a subterfuge to "legalize" the drug for all citizens. A review of the lineup supporting this side of the debate clearly indicates that the weight of the existing law and political machinery is behind them, and as a result, it has proven extraordinarily difficult to effect any major changes in the drug laws.

It should be noted that for hundreds of years marijuana had been used as a popular medication all over the world. The first "modern" concerns with it were raised in Great Britain at the end of the nineteenth century, leading to a large-scale investigation and the Indian Hemp Commission Report of 1898. In its findings the commission suggested that the drug had many practical uses in medicine and that many of the stories then being circulated about its dangerousness could not be documented.

A brief review of the modern history of marijuana in this country might prove helpful in understanding the current dispute over its efficacy in medicine. Despite the drug's relatively low toxicity (especially when contrasted with other popular licit and illicit drugs), it has long served as the touchstone for U.S. drug policies. In one early study of the literature, Howard Becker found that there was little public interest in the drug before about the mid-1930s. That was soon to change. American concerns with marijuana were initially focused on its alleged use by members of "dangerous classes," in this instance male Mexican migrants and black jazz musicians.

In 1937, the Marijuana Tax Act was passed as an addendum to the Harrison Act, our first comprehensive federal drug law, enacted in 1914. This law, like its parent, was ostensibly a revenue measure calling for marijuana dealers to obtain a federal license in order to legally dispense the drug and to pay a tax of $100 per ounce on any sales. Of course, no one did this; even if one were to buy the license, state laws at the time forbade marijuana sales and use and criminalized those found doing it. Interestingly, there was absolutely no debate over the new law; medical practitioners and other interested parties were not even invited to testify at the hearings.

Following the approval of the Marijuana Tax Act, the federal, state, and local police soon had a field day with its users. When one reviews the statistics for this early period, it is readily made apparent that marijuana users were the favored targets of law enforcers. For many years, fully two-thirds of all arrests of drug law violators were for marijuana possession and use only. Given the then-common beliefs and claims about the drug's capacity to induce crimes of violence and to debauch its users, this result could have been expected. Marijuana "addicts" were now fair game for the drug police, and since there were many more of them than there were opiate and cocaine users, they made easy prey.

State and local laws also targeted marijuana in the 1960s when many jurisdictions provided for as much as a life sentence for first offense possession of small amounts of the drug. For example, in a 1967 study, the state of Texas had sentenced 19 persons to life sentences for first-offense possession of small amounts of the drug. Things might have continued in this manner for some time had it not been for the massive youthful rebellions that unfolded in the 1960s . Marijuana use served as another form of resistance to authority for young people who openly disobeyed the law and thereby exposed themselves to the severe sanctions that were then in effect. Many white middle-class youth were arrested for these violations and faced heavy penalties in the form of the prescribed prison sentences for these offenses. Their parents were appalled, however, and soon brought intense pressure on government officials to reassess the utility of U.S. marijuana laws.

During the late 1960s, President Richard Nixon appointed a distinguished commission to study the known effects of marijuana in order to advise officials what to do about the crisis that was brewing. In 1972, the commission issued its final report, *Marijuana: Signal of Misunderstanding*, the culmination of two years of extensive investigations. In reading this account it is readily apparent that all of the earlier archetypal claims about the dangers of marijuana use were not valid; the drug did not lead to crime and insanity. In fact, very little in the way of toxic effects were found, leading the commission to suggest that decriminalization of the drug might be the most appropriate policy for the government to pursue. The President was incensed with this suggestion, however, telling the nation and his own drug czar (who agreed with the report) that he would never accept "legalization" of marijuana.

We should note that the nature of the claimed dangers associated with marijuana use shifted perceptibly over the years. The old horror stories were no longer believed by anyone it seemed. Rather, this drug was now said to cause "amotivational syndrome" among the young, leading them to inactive, unproductive lives. Other damaging health effects were also suggested, such as impotence and breast enlargement among males, short-term memory loss, possible birth defects among children born to mothers who were marijuana smokers, and a permanent loss of brain cells. Although the evidence in support of these claims was weak, health concerns became the most pressing rationale for opposing decriminalization efforts, replacing the crime and degeneracy themes of the earlier generation.

During the first Reagan administration another government research monograph was produced by the federal office of Health and Human Services in 1982. The report was titled *Marijuana and Health* and was thought to be a comprehensive assessment of what was then known about the medical effects of the drug. All of the claims about the serious health effects attributed to the drug had been scrutinized by a panel of experts, but this time they came away with a different set of conclusions than those of the Schafer Commission regarding the health risks associated with marijuana. In fact, they suggested that the earlier report had been incorrect; this was not a harmless substance.

Given such conflicting observations, debate regarding the effects of marijuana smoking have continued almost unabated to the present day. The modern arguments commonly used against any change in its legal status have relied heavily on the dogma that the drug does not have any therapeutic value and that it is likely to have deleterious effects. The latter are only partially known now, however, because there has been little scientific research of marijuana's effects. Thus, at the present time, lack of knowledge about all of marijuana's actual effects is being remedied, we are told, as a result of new federal commitments to fund large-scale marijuana research. The results of these studies will not be known for another decade or so; as with any other substance that has not been tested adequately, the drug must be assumed to be potentially hazardous until proven otherwise.

This brief account of the modern history of marijuana in the United States brings us back to the present. One of the lessons to be learned from these events is that this drug has had tremendous symbolic value here throughout much of this century. Early on it was argued that users were dangerous criminals and that their use of the drug predisposed them to violence and insanity. As evidence accrued that these claims were fallacious, new charges were leveled against the substance. These focused on health-related problems and the "amotivational syndrome" that was said to be a common result of regular use. These arguments have sustained and undergirded the position firmly held by government officials and their supporters ever since.

Modern campaigns against marijuana have undoubtedly had some effect on consumption patterns, although exactly what they are remain unknowable. Several national surveys of high school seniors and respondents from other age groups indicate that use has dropped dramatically since about 1979. These trends are beginning to change, however, and the most recent surveys have reflected increases in youthful use of marijuana. Regardless of the exact number of persons who have used the drug, either recreationally or very regularly, we know for sure that marijuana is far and above the most popular illicit substance in the United States. At the present time we believe that 72 million Americans have used the drug at least experimentally, and about 700,000 are daily users (Zimmer and Morgan, 1997).

These facts may go a long way toward explaining why the government has so strongly resisted any change in its official position with regard to this substance, including the medical marijuana controversy. To admit that they may have been wrong all these years would seemingly open the floodgates to total rejection of the antimarijuana message, and the antidrug message generally, for that matter. Thus the idea that marijuana is a "gateway drug" has been fostered by government sources, suggesting that those who use it, regardless of its potential harmfulness, are likely to go on to use far more harmful substances. Given what we know about the users of this drug, however, this result seems unlikely.

Regardless of the adamant resistance of those defending the official position on marijuana, large numbers of medical patients have clamored for legal access to the drug. In the meantime many have been willing to risk arrest to procure the substance in the illicit market and self medicate. A substantial number of patients have claimed dramatic improvements in terms of the alleviation of some of the most bothersome symptoms that they suffer directly from their illness or as a secondary result of the treatment they have been receiving (especially from radiation and chemotherapy). Meantime, the friends, families, and physicians attending these patients have often become converts based on their own observations of these events.

In 1996, California and Arizona both approved through popular referenda the medical use of marijuana. The specific details of these changes differed somewhat, but both states intended to allow physicians either to prescribe or to recommend marijuana to patients whenever they thought it appropriate to do so and without fear of arrest. The opposition, in this case represented by the federal government, responded by threatening physicians with suspension of their federal prescription-writing privileges if they do approve of marijuana for their patients. The matter is currently under review in the courts.

The struggle over the legal status of marijuana continues. The substance is currently listed federally as a class 1 drug, which means that it has no medical utility and a high potential for abuse. Medical marijuana proponents have been attempting to get it reclassified as a class 2 drug, which would mean that it has medical utility and a high potential for abuse. Although the latter claim (that it has high abuse potential) could certainly be contested, especially in light of the known abuse potential and harms associated with the legal alcohol and tobacco products, this has not been a dominant issue raised in the most recent attempts to change marijuana laws.

The lines have been clearly drawn between supporters of medical marijuana and those who oppose any change in the drug's current status. It is readily apparent that many persons are currently illegally self-medicating with the drug, regardless of the potential harms they could suffer in the form of criminal penalties, fines, asset forfeiture of their possessions, and the like. One may assume that they take these risks because they are personally convinced that this substance works to alleviate some of the symptoms of their illness/disease and that similar relief cannot be obtained with other legally available medications. On the other side of the issue are large numbers of medical professionals, politicians, and others who insist that the drug has no demonstrated medical or therapeutic application that cannot be assuaged with legal medicants such as Marinol (a synthetic form of THC, the active ingredient in marijuana). They either argue that much more research must be completed before the drug can be properly judged one way or the other, or that no additional research is needed, as we already know that marijuana is not an effective medication.

This issue is likely to be resolved legally, at least temporarily, during the next decade. For the first time in recent history the federal government has committed large sums of money to support marijuana research, in contrast to the past decades, when they spent nothing on it. The results of these studies may be pivotal in determining what happens next, at least officially. Unofficially, medical marijuana is being used by many patients despite its illegality, and such use seems destined to escalate among our nation's aging population.

As we write this at mid year 2001, the debate rages on. At this point a total of nine states have medical marijuana laws already in place or approved by the voters. In 1998 the residents of Washington, DC also voted to allow medical marijuana, but Congress blocked the law's approval. The situation in California has still not been resolved either, and the U.S. Supreme Court is deciding the case during its 2001 session.

In the end, of course, the issue will not be resolved on the basis of research results and controlled studies. In truth, medical marijuana is more of a political than a scientific issue, and the exigencies of politics are likely to reign over reason in determining the appropriate course of action. We have repeatedly seen that marijuana has been vilified not because it is so dangerous but because it appears to threaten to undermine the logic of all drug laws. Thus, it is viewed as the hole in the proverbial dike, a weak spot in drug law, that could give way to all kinds of problems.

CONCLUSIONS

The funds we currently spend on drug interdiction, law enforcement, the courts, and incarceration would allow us to make substantial progress in improving treatment and in making treatment available to those who need it. Reducing the number of people arrested and incarcerated for drug possession and other minor drug offenses would also allow the police to concentrate their efforts on more serious crimes, thus making our communities safer.

The decline of our inner cities and the consequent deterioration of the quality of life for the poor and minorities are to a large degree responsible for the epidemic of drug abuse. It is foolish to believe, in the face of declining economic opportunities, that either the threat of criminal punishment or the promise of a short-term treatment program will cause our teenagers and young adults to avoid lives of crime and involvement with drugs. In the long run, stable families, safe neighborhoods, and economically healthy cities are the keys to both drug use and crime.

REFERENCES

BLOMBERG, T., and K. LUCKEN (1993). Intermediate punishment and the piling up of sanctions. In G. Cole (ed.), *Criminal Justice: Law and Politics*. Belmont, CA: Wadsworth, pp. 470–481.

BLOMBERG, T., B. BALES, and K. REEK (1993). Intermediate punishment: Redistributing or extending social control? *Crime, Law and Social Change*, 19:187–201.

BREWINGTON, V., M. SMITH, and D. LIPTON (1994). Acupuncture as a detoxification treatment: An analysis of controlled research. *Journal of Substance Abuse Treatment*, 11(4):289–307.

BUGLIOSI, V. (1996). *The Phoenix Solution*. Beverly Hills, CA: Dove Books.

BULLINGTON, B. (1995). War and peace: Drug policy in the United States and the Netherlands. *Crime, Law, and Social Change*, 22:213–238.

BULLINGTON, B. (1997). America's drug war: Fact or fiction? In Ross Coomber (ed.), *The Control of Drug Users: Reason or Reaction*. London: Harwood Publishers.

BUREAU OF JUSTICE STATISTICS (2000). *Prison and Jail Inmates at Midyear, 1999*. NCJ 181643. Washington, DC: U.S. Department of Justice, April.

CLEAR, T. (1995). Correction beyond prison walls. In J. F. Sheley (ed.), *Criminology*. Belmont, CA: Wadsworth, pp. 453–471.

COOMBER, R. (1997). The cutting of heroin in the United States in the 1990s. *Journal of Drug Issues*, Vol. 29(1), Winter 1999, pp. 17–35.

COURTWRIGHT, D. (1982). *Dark Paradise: Opiate Addiction in America before 1940*. Cambridge, MA: Harvard University Press.

CURRIE, E. (1993). *Drugs, the Cities, and the American Future*. New York: Hill & Wang.

DELEON, G. (1986). The therapeutic community for substance abuse: Perspective and approach. In D. DeLeon and J. T. Zeigenfuss (eds.), *Therapeutic Communities for Addictions: Readings in Theory, Research and Practice*. Springfield, IL: Charles C Thomas, pp. 5–18.

DIMASCIO, W. M. (1995). *Seeking Justice: Crime and Punishment in America*. New York: Edna McConnell Clark Foundation.

DRUG COURT CLEARINGHOUSE AND TECHNICAL ASSISTANCE PROJECT (1996). *Fact Sheet*. Technical Report. Washington, DC: American University, May.

DRUG COURT CLEARINGHOUSE AND TECHNICAL ASSISTANCE PROJECT (1997). *Drug Courts: 1997 Overview of Operational Characteristics and Implementation Issues.* Technical Report. Washington, DC: American University, May.

DUKE, S., and A. GROSS (1993). *America's Longest War.* New York: G.P. Putnam's Sons.

DUPONT, R. (1996). Harm reduction and decriminalization in the United States: A personal perspective. *Substance Use and Misuse,* 31(14):1929–1943.

EDNA MCCONNELL CLARK FOUNDATION (1995). *Seeking Justice: Crime and Punishment in America.* New York: The Foundation.

EDWARDS, B. (1993). Drug court's success rate outstanding. *Tampa Tribune,* June 23, pp. 1–2.

ERICKSON, P. (1996). Comments on "Harm reduction and decriminalization in the United States: A personal perspective" by Robert DuPont, *Substance Use and Misuse,* 31(14):1965–1969.

FEDERAL BUREAU OF INVESTIGATION (1998). *Crime in the United States: 1997.* Uniform Crime Reports. Washington, DC: U.S. Government Printing Office.

FISHMAN, H. C., M. D., STANTON, and B. ROSMAN (1982). In M. D. Stanton, T. C. Todd, et al. (eds.), *The Family Therapy of Drug Abuse and Addiction.* New York: Guilford Press.

GERSTEIN, D. R., and H. J. HARWOOD (eds.) (1990). *Treating Drug Problems,* Vol. 1. Washington, DC: National Academy Press.

GOLDAPPLE, G. (1990). Enhancing retention: A skills-training program for drug dependent therapeutic community clients. Ph.D. dissertation, Florida State University, Tallahassee, FL.

GOLDKAMP, J. S. (1998). Challenges for research and innovation: When is a drug court not a drug court? In C. Terry (ed.), *Judicial Change and Drug Treatment Courts: Case Studies in Innovation.* Sage.

GRABOWSKI, J. (1986). *Acquisition Maintenance Cessation and Re-acquisition: Overview and Behavioral Perspective of Relapse and Tobacco Use.* Research Monograph Series. Washington, DC: National Institute on Drug Abuse.

HUDDLESTON, W. (1997). Summary of drug court evaluation: Recidivism study. *Cognitive-Behavioral Treatment Review & CCI News,* 6(1–2):16–17.

IRWIN, J., and J. AUSTIN (1994). *It's about Time: America's Imprisonment Binge.* Belmont, CA: Wadsworth.

JACKSON, M. S., and D. W. SPRINGER (1997). Social work practice with African-American juvenile gangs: Professional challenge. In C. A. McNeece and A. R. Roberts (eds.), *Policy and Practice in the Justice System.* Chicago: Nelson-Hall, pp. 231–248.

JOANING, H., B. GAWINSKI, J. MORRIS, and W. QUINN (1986). Organizing a social exology to treat adolescent drug abuse. *Journal of Strategic and Systemic Therapies,* 5:55–66.

KACZOR, B. (1997). Legislators let down by boot camps. *Tallahassee Democrat,* June 22, p. 3B.

KOEOFED, L., R. TOLSON, R. ATKINSON, R. TOTH, and J. TURNER (1986). Outpatient treatment of patients with substance abuse and coexisting psychiatric disorders. *American Journal of Psychiatry,* 143:867–872.

LIPTON, D. S. (1995). *The Effectiveness of Treatment for Drug Abusers under Criminal Justice Supervision.* National Institute of Justice Research Report. Washington, DC: U.S. Department of Justice.

LIPTON, D., V. BREWINGTON, and M. SMITH (1990). *Acupuncture and Crack Addicts: A Single-Blind Placebo Test of Efficacy.* Presentation at Advances in Cocaine Treatment, NIDA Technical Review Meeting, August.

LIPTON, D. S., G. P. FALKIN, and H. K. WEXLER (1992). Correctional drug abuse treatment in the United States: An overview. In C. Leukefeld and F. Tims (eds.), *Drug Abuse Treatment in Prisons and Jails.* National Institute on Drug Abuse, Research Monograph Series, No. 118. Washington, DC: U.S. Government Printing Office.

MARGOLIN, A., S. K. AVANTS, P. CHANG, and T. R. KOSTEN (1995). Acupuncture for the treatment of cocaine dependence in methadone-maintained patients. *American Journal on the Addictions,* 2(3):194–201.

MARTIN, S. S., and J. A. INCIARDI (1993). Case management approaches for criminal justice clients. In J. A. Inciardi (ed.), *Drug Treatment and Criminal Justice*, Vol. 27. Thousand Oaks, CA: Sage Publications, pp. 81–96.

McNEECE, C. A. (1997). Future directions in justice system policy and practice. In C. A. McNeece and A. R. Roberts (eds.), *Policy and Practice in the Justice System.* Chicago: Nelson-Hall, pp. 263–269.

McNEECE, C. A., and D. M. DiNITTO (1994). *Chemical Dependency: A Systems Approach.* Upper Saddle River, NJ: Prentice Hall.

MINUCHIN, S. (1974). *Families and Family Therapy.* Cambridge, MA: Harvard University Press.

MINUCHIN, S., and H. C. FISHMAN (1981). *Family Therapy Techniques.* Cambridge, MA: Harvard University Press.

MUSTO, D. (1991). Opium, cocaine and marijuana in American history. *Scientific American,* July, pp. 40–47.

NADELMANN, E. (1988). U.S. drug policy: A bad export. *Foreign Policy,* 70:83–108.

NATIONAL ASSOCIATION OF DRUG COURT PROFESSIONALS DRUG COURT STANDARDS COMMITTEE (1997). *Defining Drug Courts: Key Components.* Washington, DC: NADCP, January.

NATIONAL ASSOCIATION OF DRUG COURT PROFESSIONALS and OFFICE OF COMMUNITY ORIENTED POLICING SERVICES (1997). *Community Policing and Drug Courts/Community Courts: Working Together within a Unified Court System.* Alexandria, VA: U.S. Department of Justice.

NATIONAL INSTITUTE OF JUSTICE (2000). Recent research findings. *NIJ Journal,* March.

NATIONAL INSTITUTE ON DRUG ABUSE (1998). *The Economic Costs of Alcohol and Drug Abuse in the United States.* Rockville, MD: U.S. Department of Health and Human Services.

NATIONAL INSTITUTE ON DRUG ABUSE (1999). *Principles of Drug Addition Treatment: A Research-Based Approach.* NIH Publication 99-4180. Washington, DC: U.S. Government Printing Office.

NATIONAL TASK FORCE ON CORRECTIONAL SUBSTANCE ABUSE STRATEGIES (1991). *Intervening with Substance-Abusing Offenders: A Framework for Action.* Washington, DC: U.S. Department of Justice, National Institute of Corrections.

OBERMEIER, G. E., and P. B. HENRY (1989). Adolescent inpatient treatment. *Journal of Chemical Dependency,* 2(1):163–182.

OFFICE OF NATIONAL DRUG CONTROL POLICY (1996). *Treatment Protocol Effectiveness Study.* Washington, DC: U.S. Government Printing Office, March.

OFFICE OF NATIONAL DRUG CONTROL POLICY (1997). *The National Drug Control Strategy: 1997* NCJ Publication 163915. Washington, DC: U.S. Government Printing Office, February.

OFFICE OF NATIONAL DRUG CONTROL POLICY (2000). *National Drug Control Strategy: 2000 Annual Report.* Washington, DC: U.S. Government Printing Office.

PAN, H., F. R. SCARPITTI, J. A. INCIARDI, and D. LOCKWOOD (1993). Some considerations on therapeutic communities in corrections. In J. A. Inciardi (ed.), *Drug Treatment and Criminal Justice*, Vol. 27. Thousand Oaks, CA: Newbury Park, CA: Sage Publications, pp. 30–43.

PARENT, D. (1989). *Shock Incarceration: An Overview of Existing Programs.* Washington, DC: U.S. Department of Justice, National Institute of Justice.

PETERS, R. H. (1993). Drug treatment in jails and detention settings. In J. A. Inciardi (ed.), *Drug Treatment and Criminal Justice*, Vol. 27. Thousand Oaks, CA: Sage Publications, pp. 44–80.

RAND (1994). *Projecting Future Cocaine Use and Evaluating Control Strategies.* RB-6002. Santa Monica, CA: RAND Corporation.

RASMUSSEN, D., and B. BENSON (1994). *The Economic Anatomy of a Drug War*. Lanham, MD: Rowman & Littlefield.

RIDGELY, M. S. (1996). Practical issues in the application of case management to substance abuse treatment. In H. A. Siegal and R. C. Rapp (eds.), *Case Management and Substance Abuse Treatment: Practice and Experience*. New York: Springer, pp. 1–20.

ROSENBAUM, M. (1996). *Kids, Drugs, and Drug Education: A Harm Reduction Approach*. National Council of Crime and Delinquency. San Francisco: Lindesmith Center.

SPRINGER, D. W., and T. E. SMITH (1998). Treating chemically dependent children and adolescents. In C. A. McNeece and D. M. DiNitto (eds.), *Chemical Dependency: A Systems Approach*, 2nd ed. Upper Saddle River, NJ: Prentice Hall.

SZAPOCZNIK, J., W. M. KURTINES, F. H. FOOTE, A. PEREZ-VIDAL, and O. HERVIS (1986). Conjoint versus one-person family therapy: Further evidence for the effectiveness of conducting family therapy through one person with drug-abusing adolescents. *Journal of Consulting and Clinical Psychology*, 54:395–397.

TIMROTS, A. (1992). *Fact Sheet: Drug Testing in the Criminal Justice System*. Rockville, MD: Drugs and Crime Data Center and Clearinghouse.

TURNABOUT ASAP. (1997). *Acupuncture Treatment for Substance Abuse*. Santa Monica, CA: Turnabout.

U.S. GENERAL ACCOUNTING OFFICE (1995). *Drug Courts: Information on a New Approach to Address Drug-Related Crime*. GAO/GGD Publication 95-159BR. Washington, DC: U.S. Government Printing Office, May.

VAN STELLE, K. R., E. MAUSER, and D. P. MOBERG (1994). Recidivism to the criminal justice system of substance-abusing offenders diverted into treatment. *Crime and Delinquency*, 40(2):175–196.

WELLS, R. A. (1994). *Planned Short-Term Treatment*. New York: Free Press.

ZIMMER, L., and J. MORGAN (1997). *Marijuana Myths: Marijuana Facts*. New York: Lindesmith Center.

chapter 3

The Situation of Crime Victims in the Early Decades of the Twenty-First Century

Andrew Karmen, Ph.D.

ABSTRACT

In the late twentieth century, the basic needs and interests of crime victims were rediscovered after decades of severe neglect. In the early twenty-first century, a number of existing trends will expand the choices and options that victims face. Professional advocates will be assigned routinely to help victims to exercise their formal rights within the criminal justice process. Commercial interests will develop and market a much greater selection of anti-theft and personal security devices. Private prosecution will become possible if victims grow dissatisfied with the services of public prosecutors. Victim-offender reconciliation programs will proliferate and handle a wider variety of cases. Also, differential justice will become recognized as a problem, as the gap widens between the way privileged victims as opposed to second-class complainants are handled by criminal justice agencies.

FORECASTING FUTURE DEVELOPMENTS

Several different strategies can be pursued to try to anticipate what the situation facing crime victims will be like in the first few decades of the twenty-first century. Futurologists can generate informed guesses about social and political arrangements in the years ahead by looking back over the developments of the past several decades in order to see how much can change during this amount of time. A second basis for speculations about what lies just beyond the horizon requires identification of the driving forces for change. By projecting emerging social trends it becomes possible to paint plausible scenarios about likely developments over the next several decades. Such linear extrapolations basically predict "more of the same" but at higher (or lower) levels or to greater (or lesser) degrees. However, this "extrapolation" approach can yield gross inaccuracies if what are really short-run phenomena are mistaken for long-term trends and are extended too far into the future. Furthermore, countervailing pressures could arise that might put up enough resistance to hold the driving forces in check.

Still a third way to make predictions is to speculate that completely new and currently unheard-of developments will evolve out of familiar situations. Although exercising the imagination is the foundation for good science fiction, it generates questionable social science.

Of course, when reviewing the past, describing the present, or imagining what the future holds, "what is" must always be distinguished from "what ought to be." Social scientists have to strive for objectivity and be vigilant that subjective interpretations and personal biases don't find their way into the analysis. Applying this principle of impartiality to forecasting means making a distinction between "what is likely to happen" versus "what would be desirable." Wishful thinking about a better future should not be substituted for a realistic assessment of what is probable.

THE SITUATION VICTIMS FACED IN THE LATE TWENTIETH CENTURY

When the situation of crime victims in the recent past is reviewed, it becomes clear that sweeping and profound changes can occur in a short time span of several decades. As recently as 1970, victims were still largely written off as an undifferentiated mass of faceless, pitiful "losers" who were the unfortunate "casualties" of a growing and intractable street crime problem. A number of commentators characterized them as the forgotten people within the criminal justice process, virtually "invisible" (Rieff, 1979), systematically overlooked, totally excluded from meaningful participation, and beset by pressing needs that were routinely ignored (see Carrington, 1975; Barkas, 1978). The plight of crime victims had not yet been rediscovered by the news media, law enforcement officials, political movements, or academic researchers.

Slowly, public consciousness heightened when the women's liberation movement started to expose and criticize the way the men at the helm of the justice system callously disregarded the best interests of sexually assaulted girls and women (see Griffin, 1971). But there were no rape crisis centers until feminist activists in the San Francisco Bay area challenged police and hospital practices in 1972 (Largen, 1981). In university libraries, students searched in vain for analyses of rape that presented the violated female's point of view (Schwendinger and Schwendinger, 1983:10). Similarly, magazine articles rarely addressed the predicament of battered women trapped in romantic relationships that had turned violent. The *Reader's Guide to Periodical Literature* first introduced the subject heading "wife beating" in 1974 (Loseke, 1989). There were no shelters for battered women to flee to until activists set up a hotline and a refuge in an old house in St. Paul, Minnesota in 1974 (Martin, 1977).

Prosecutors routinely overlooked the needs of their ostensible clients in criminal court proceedings back in 1970. Many victims never found out if anyone was arrested or convicted in their cases, if their stolen property was ever recovered, or if they were entitled to modest witness fees for missing work when called to testify (Lynch, 1976). Half of the decade would pass before the Law Enforcement Assistance Administration began to channel federal funding to county district attorneys to experiment with victim/witness assistance programs to provide support services to people who are needed to testify on behalf of the state (see Schneider and Schneider, 1981; Roberts, 1990). In 1970, the potential of civil lawsuits as a means of recovering financial losses was not yet recognized. It would take a few more years before some legal activists realized that besides suing offenders directly, victims could launch lawsuits against third parties such as businesses, colleges, and psychiatric hospitals whose gross negligence about security matters made it easier for criminals to harm them (Carrington, 1977).

Inspired by the dramatic power struggles of the 1960s involving African-Americans, students, women, gays, soldiers, and even prisoners, victim activists organized self-help and support groups and advocacy organizations during the 1970s. The loose coalition that constituted the victims' rights movement started the process of redressing grievances by publishing newsletters, demonstrating for reforms, monitoring trials, petitioning criminal justice officials, and lobbying lawmakers (see Friedman, 1985). But the earliest proponents of victims' rights (see Hook, 1972) envisioned these new statutes mostly as weapons to counter or even "trump" the expanding rights of "criminals" (suspects, defendants, and prisoners) granted by landmark decisions handed down by the Warren Court. Activists did not yet conceive of victims' rights as a means of empowerment for people who deserved input into how "their" cases were resolved by indifferent officials and remote criminal justice bureaucracies.

Back in 1970, there was no talk about amending the U.S. Constitution to guarantee victims legal standing in criminal justice proceedings. That course of action was not taken seriously until the President's Task Force on Victims of Crime (1982) suggested rewording the Sixth Amendment to include a pledge that "[t]he victim, in every criminal prosecution shall have the right to be present and to be heard at all critical stages of judicial proceedings." It took until the mid-1980s before victim advocacy groups realized that they could be much more successful in their drive to secure new rights by organizing campaigns to amend state constitutions, one at a time [National Organization for Victim Assistance (NOVA), 1986]. Activists made considerable progress: by the close of the twentieth century, 49 states had passed a "Victims' Bill of Rights" and 22 states had enacted amendments to their constitutions that required the provision of certain benefits and options (Tomz and McGillis, 1997). On the federal level, the Clinton administration in 1996 endorsed the campaign to amend the Constitution to guarantee that victims can state their views at court proceedings involving bail, sentencing, and parole, and can receive information, restitution, and reasonable protection from further harm.

Only one area of legal reform was already well under way by 1970: compensating innocent, physically injured victims for their out-of-pocket monetary losses. A few states set up their own funds during the 1960s, while members of Congress were debating whether it was an appropriate area of responsibility and jurisdiction for federal aid. (Before 1970, diehard believers in rugged individualism denounced the thought of spreading a government-sponsored safety net under wounded victims facing financial ruin as "creeping socialism"; see Meiners, 1978). Congress was unable to muster the majority of members needed to authorize the partial funding of state compensation programs until 1984, when the Victims of Crime Act was passed. But these early, faltering steps toward helping certain unfortunate victims pay off some of their devastating medical bills were largely symbolic political gestures that were grossly underfunded, fiscally inadequate, and personally demeaning (Elias, 1983). It took until the 1990s for federal funding to reach modest levels for the Office for Victims of Crime within the Justice Department and for the Crime Victims Fund.

Also on the economic front, few judicial systems (except some juvenile courts) had demonstrated a sustained commitment to revive the ancient practice of restitution by offenders to the parties they harmed (Galaway and Hudson, 1975). It was not until 1975 that a religious group in Canada set up an experimental program to enable offenders to repay their victims as part of an effort to resolve their antagonisms and achieve mutual reconciliation (McKnight, 1981). It took more than a decade for these programs seeking victim–offender reconciliation to evolve into a community-based restorative justice movement.

Victimology—the scientific study of crime victims—had not yet emerged by 1970 as an area of specialization within criminology. Victimologists from around the world did not hold their first professional conference until 1973 in Jerusalem (Drapkin and Viano, 1974). No journal was devoted to publishing studies about crime victims until 1976 (Viano, 1976). Only one scholarly work that could serve as a textbook (Schafer, 1968) was available for college courses, but it was filled with either historical material about a "Golden Age" in the distant past or conjecture about what the future might hold because there were very few actual research findings about the plight of victims for the author to cite.

ANTICIPATING THE SITUATION OF VICTIMS IN THE EARLY TWENTY-FIRST CENTURY BY PROJECTING EXISTING TRENDS

To anticipate what the future holds, the way to proceed is to identify the most important contemporary trends and then to project how they might shape the situation of crime victims in the next few decades. Five significant tendencies currently are at work: the trend toward gaining formal rights, the trend toward commercialization, the trend toward privatization, the trend toward out-of-court dispute resolution, and the trend toward differential case handling.

How the Trend Toward Granting Victims Greater Formal Rights within the Criminal Justice Process Might Lead to the Emergence of Victim Advocates

One likely development over the next few decades will be the emergence of a new kind of criminal justice professional: the victim advocate (see Karmen, 1995). The provision of an advocate by the government, at no cost, probably will become institutionalized in one jurisdiction after another. Upon filing a report with the police, a complainant will be offered the services of an advisor familiar with the increasingly complicated rights, opportunities, options, and obligations victims face. Advocates will look after their best interests in their dealings with detectives, defendants, defense attorneys, prosecutors, judges, probation officers, corrections officials, parole boards, compensation boards, and journalists.

In many jurisdictions, victims are now entitled to know about developments in their cases; to timely notification about optional and required appearances at bail and evidentiary hearings, trials, sentencing hearings, and parole board meetings; to pursue a number of strategies for reimbursement of their out-of-pocket expenses (restitution, compensation, civil lawsuits, insurance coverage); and about how to protect their personal privacy (especially from media exposure in sexual assault cases). In some localities, police chiefs, district attorneys, and judges have granted victims additional privileges above and beyond what procedural law requires as the minimum standard for fair treatment. Special solutions have been devised to address the particular problems burdening abused children, survivors of childhood incest, abused elders, battered women, rape victims, and targets of bias-motivated hate crimes.

To date, only some dedicated volunteers and some overworked and underpaid paraprofessionals are available to assist victims, both outside the criminal justice system (at shelters for battered women and at rape crisis centers, for example) and inside it (such as court appointed special advocates who attend to the needs of abused children in family courts, and counselors working at prosecutors' victim–witness assistance units). But no permanent paid staff of experts is yet at work on a daily basis, looking after the best interests of burglary, robbery, assault, and auto-theft victims, among others, from start to finish in the justice process. Just like attorneys are made available to indigent defendants, advocates could be furnished by a government agency (comparable to the public defender's office) or supplied by an independent nonprofit organization funded by charitable donations (similar to New York's Legal Aid Society). Other advocates will be independent professionals and have their own private practices, such as defense attorneys in law firms, and will be retained for a fee by those who can afford their services.

How the Trend toward Commercialization Will Lead to More Victimization Prevention Devices and Services

Crime prevention programs tackle the "social roots" or social conditions that breed lawlessness. Victimization prevention strategies have much more modest goals: to reduce the risks of violence and theft faced by specific individuals, small groups, and neighborhoods. Commercial interests have demonstrated over and over again their readiness to sell goods and services to ostensibly address all human needs and wants. In the next few decades, there will be a rapid expansion of the market for high-tech victimization prevention gadgetry and professional security services that will be purchased by victims who don't want to be harmed again, by persons who fear victimization, and by organizations that want to protect their employees and customers.

Antitheft devices already abound and will become even more commonplace. Alarm systems will be sold as standard equipment on cars, boats, and new homes. New high-tech gadgets will protect motorists from car thieves and carjackers. Satellite tracking and recovery systems that now help to retrieve stolen vehicles will be used to locate and repossess all sorts of valuable goods. Electronic monitoring systems, surveillance cameras, and emergency transmitters will protect especially vulnerable groups, such as battered women, with orders of protection against their estranged mates, and latch-key children. Security consultants, personal bodyguards, and armed chauffeurs will augment the ranks of night watchmen, store detectives, hotel detectives, doormen, and others who already work in the rapidly growing field of industrial security and loss prevention.

One strong current during the latter part of the twentieth century has been the quest for personal safety in an otherwise unpredictably dangerous world. The rising popularity of gated communities epitomizes how commercial interests can package and sell a sense of security for economic gain. Affluent residents are willing to pay a high price, economically and spiritually, for a predictable, controlled, low-risk environment with no unpleasant surprises. There is a growing demand for such living arrangements by people who feel the need to withdraw from the seemingly chaotic existence of urban dwellers into exclusive and isolated enclaves where the threats posed by burglars, robbers, rapists, and auto thieves can be minimized. Guarded entrances, checkpoints, passes, surveillance cameras, sophisticated alarm systems, high fences, and patrolled perimeters keep intruders at bay (Blakely and Snyder, 1997; Wilson-Duenges, 2000). By 1994, about 30,000 gated communities across the country housed an estimated 4 million residents, as personal security became one of the highest priorities of home buyers (Anon., 1994). The "siege mentality" of "defensible space" against "outsiders who don't belong" will pass for a "sense of community" and "peace of mind" in the early decades of the twenty-first century.

When members of these privileged strata venture out from their fortified sanctuaries to shop or pursue leisure activities, squads of private security forces and surveillance cameras will watch over them. Business improvement districts (BIDs) have been set up nationwide by real estate interests, merchants' associations, and community organizations to attract and reassure apprehensive customers that they will be safe and secure while in the presence of uniformed guards in these reclaimed sections of town. From the early 1970s to the early 1990s, more than 1000 BIDs were established in cities across the country (Lueck, 1994); by the end of the century, that number had risen to 1200, with 40 in New York City alone (Liedtke, 2000).

How the Trend toward Privatizing Criminal Justice Functions Might Lead to Private Prosecution

The trend by government to divest itself of certain responsibilities and tasks within the criminal justice process and to hand them over to nonprofit organizations and profit-oriented enterprises is likely to accelerate in the next few decades. One impact on victims will be to open up the possibility of private prosecution.

All through history, the inherently public and governmental nature of justice and punishment has been symbolized by the badge of the police officer, the robe of the judge, and the uniform of the corrections guard. However, a number of contemporary developments are undermining the government's monopoly over criminal justice functions. Privatization began by nibbling away at the front and back stages of the criminal justice process. At the front end, privatization took the form of furnishing added protection, above and beyond the minimal degree provided by the state from tax revenues (security firms offering guards for hire) and individually financed tailormade investigations (carried out for a fee by "private eyes"). At the tail end, privatization took the form of independently operated nonprofit therapeutic communities and profit-oriented residential and outpatient alcohol and drug treatment programs. During the 1960s and early 1970s, a prisoner's rights movement called for a moratorium on new prison construction and for decarceration and deinstitutionalization—symbolically, a call to "tear down the walls." But the ensuing crackdown on crime demanded by the law and order movement instead generated soaring inmate populations, skyrocketing probation and parole caseloads, and escalating expenditures. During the 1980s, proponents of privatization began to "sell the walls," giving companies a chance to profit from incarcerating the government's growing number of prisoners in detention centers, jails, and prisons (Steinberg, 1984; DiIulio, 1988).

Now the middle stage of adjudication is undergoing privatization, and a dual court system is emerging: criminal courts handling most cases, and neighborhood justice centers practicing dispute resolution on selected cases diverted from the government's system (see the following section for further implications of this development).

What remains to be privatized is the function of prosecution itself. It is likely that activists and advocacy groups within the victims movement soon will launch campaigns demanding the right to private prosecution (see Cole, 1992:718). When they take up this cause, they will encounter another example of how politics creates strange bedfellows. Self-styled militia and "constitutionalist" groups that portray themselves as the backbone of a "patriot" movement already have begun to agitate around the issue of reviving private prosecution (as part of their larger attack on what they perceive to be a corrupt judicial system and an intrusive federal government) (see Roland, 1996).

A branch of the victims' movement might call for private prosecution if frustrations mount with the way that assistant district attorneys handle cases. Victims and the lawyers assigned by the government to "dispose of" their cases can disagree over the goals of the process. A victim might want to press charges, but the prosecutor's office might want to drop some or all charges (or vice versa). A victim might want the offender to admit guilt and to be held responsible for everything in the indictment, by going to trial if necessary, while the prosecutor's office usually will be satisfied with a conviction on a lesser charge, preferably through a timesaving and cost-effective negotiated plea. A victim might want court-ordered restitution from the offender, but the government might not consider reimbursement to be an important priority. Similarly, a victim might want the legal system to compel the offender (perhaps a violence-prone husband or a drug-abusing neighbor) to undergo treatment, but the government might be more intent on securing some other disposition, ranging from a suspended sentence to imprisonment.

The seeds of dissension between victims and "their" lawyers are sown by contradictions within each party's roles. One contradiction revolves around the duality of the victim's role: On one hand, victims are "on the side of the government" in the adversarial system; specifically they are allied with the police and the prosecution in the quest for conviction. On the other hand, victims are independent actors who might want to pursue what they perceive to be their own best interests. Similarly, prosecutors confront a contradiction in their own role whenever they try to bridge a gap by representing both the interests of the government that hires them and the clients they are assigned to help (see Karmen, 1992). The role strain faced by assistant district attorneys was minimal until victims began to exercise their recently granted rights and started to conceive of their personal interests as being separate from those of the bureaucracy that furnished them with a lawyer at no cost to them. Of course, when forced to choose, assistant district attorneys will act in accord with the interests of the agency that employs them rather than in behalf of the injured parties that rely on them.

The underlying philosophy of jurisprudence (which victims are questioning) is that all criminal acts, including interpersonal violence and theft, should be conceptualized as offenses against the state requiring an official response, and are not simply wrongs inflicted on innocent parties that could be righted by individually arranged settlements. Because the government gets drawn in, to safeguard the public interest, victims are relegated to the role of mere complainants who set the machinery of justice into motion by reporting incidents to the police. If their cases are solved (most are not; clearance rates are low) and an arrest is made, victims bear the obligation of testifying for the prosecution; but even as star witnesses, they just provide dramatic evidence of criminal conduct on the part of the accused, and otherwise, lack legal standing.

A new philosophy is emerging from the ranks of the victims movement that challenges the government's monopoly on the exercise of prosecutorial discretion. It proceeds from the assumption that person-against-person crimes such as rape, robbery, assault, and burglary do more than just violate an abstraction known as the criminal law, or threaten the social order, or harm a vague collectivity such as "the People of the State of...," as indictments read. The real flesh-and-blood persons who have suffered emotional damage, physical injuries, and financial losses have a rightful claim to exercise some input into the way the system handles "their" cases, especially given the great latitude concerning the range of penalties written into the law and the considerable discretion exercised by prosecutors and judges. If victims are viewed as "consumers" of prosecutorial "services" made available by the government's "public law firm," shouldn't those attorneys be accountable to their "customers"? If their handling of cases cannot be influenced by their clients, shouldn't these disgruntled complainants be allowed to go elsewhere and choose an attorney of their own to prosecute, perhaps for a fee?

In anger and frustration, people holding this personalized outlook about justice have sought to gain some leverage over prosecutorial decision making, in addition to the long-standing negative, self-defeating strategy of discontinuing cooperation with the authorities. In most jurisdictions, victims are now informed about the terms of a negotiated plea but cannot exercise the privilege of "veto power" over unacceptable deals. Prosecutors have rejected proposals to permit victims to participate directly in negotiations. Through the vehicles of victim impact statements and allocution (personal appearances), victims have attempted to influence sentencing decisions, but their recommendations are just one of many sources of input influencing judges.

Clearly, the attraction of private prosecution is that it would enable a lawyer hired by the victim to pursue what the victim defines as his or her best interests: some mix of retribution, restitution, rehabilitation (of the offender), and/or reconciliation of the two estranged parties. Victims who did not like the way the government attorney was planning to "dispose of" the case could select their own lawyer to press charges, negotiate a plea, or present the case before a jury.

As recently as 1955, this "do-it-yourself" option was permitted in at least 28 states. But by the 1970s, only a few jurisdictions allowed private lawyers hired by complainants to join forces with government attorneys (Sigler, 1979). Over the years, the Supreme Court has handed down a number of rulings (in 1967, 1973, 1977, 1981, and 1983) establishing that victims cannot compel prosecutors to take action and that judges cannot intervene in behalf of victims in their disagreements with prosecutors. Attorneys general and district attorneys retain sole discretion over whether or not to charge defendants with crimes and over which charges to press or drop (Stark and Goldstein, 1985).

Private prosecution is possible in routine criminal matters in most European countries. If European practices are adopted, what must be worked out is whether the victim will be permitted to go forward only if the government prosecutor fails to press charges and whether private prosecution will be allowed only for certain minor interpersonal offenses such as assault and trespass (see Newman, 1986; Sebba, 1992).

It is likely that federal, state, and county prosecutors will consider private prosecution a threat to their job security and professional stature and will oppose this trend toward privatization in ways that will retard its acceptance and implementation.

How the Trend toward Developing More Alternatives to Both Adjudication and Incarceration Might Bring About a Greater Reliance on Victim–Offender Reconciliation Programs

At the close of the twentieth century, punitiveness was the major current within the victims' movement. Given the heavy emphasis on making offenders pay for their crimes, it is not inconceivable that revenge fantasies will come true: perhaps in the near future victims will be invited to a symbolic "lock in" of convicts at brief official ceremonies heralding the start of prisoners' sentences; and that surviving family members of homicide victims someday might be entitled to "pull the switch" at electrocutions of murderers.

But the fixation on "getting even" overlooks a countercurrent that is gaining strength as the century ends: the efforts under way to invent and explore nonpunitive approaches that can peacefully resolve the underlying conflicts that fuel interpersonal violence. One trend likely to accelerate is the practice of diverting cases out of the formal adversarial system of court adjudication into the informal case-processing track of alternative dispute resolution (ADR). Another trend that is sure to persist is the search for effective alternatives to incarceration. The convergence of these two trends will bring about greater reliance on the use of mediation techniques to arrive at out-of-court settlements in which offenders avoid serving time behind bars by making restitution to their victims as a precondition for mutual reconciliation.

For decades, police officers, prosecutors, judges, and court administrators have been weeding out what they consider to be the "garbage" from the case flow. What they deem to be "junk" cases that don't merit much public attention involve people who had prior relationships (as lovers, family members, co-workers, neighbors, etc.) before they became embroiled in minor disputes in which both parties share responsibility for the outbreak of hostilities (Silberman, 1978). After years of neglect, the federal government in the early 1970s provided the seed money to set up several neighborhood justice centers to mediate some of these conflicts diverted from the court system. In 1980, Congress passed the Dispute Resolution Act to further the spread of "storefront justice." By the late 1980s, nearly 300 nonadversarial programs were employing mediators and arbitrators to settle cases in which the labels "totally innocent victim" and "completely guilty perpetrator" did not fit the facts.

At the same time that these alternatives to adjudication were developing, a growing chorus of voices was calling for the development of alternatives to incarceration. Jails and prisons have long been indicted for being overcrowded, disease-ridden, explosively violent, and strikingly counterproductive "schools for crime" that churn out hardened convicts prone to recidivate. By the end of the twentieth century, interest was growing in constructive, cost-effective ways of handling nondangerous offenders without removing them from society.

The first victim–offender reconciliation program (VORP) was established in Indiana in 1978. The initiators were inspired by biblical teachings: that crime symbolized a rupture or wound that afflicted an entire community and had to be healed through reparation rather than retribution. To heal their emotional wounds, both the victim and the offender need to be empowered (authorized to resolve their conflict by themselves). Just as prisons were invented by the Quakers early in the nineteenth century and were then copied by government, the reconciliation model originated by the Mennonites was replicated by nonprofit groups and local agencies throughout the 1980s. The range of cases handled by centers for mediation/restitution/reconciliation quickly expanded. Originally, only quarrels entangling people who knew each other previously or that involved property damage or loss (generally, vandalism, burglary, and other forms of thievery) were considered suitable. But within a few years, cases surrounding assaults committed by strangers were being referred for restitution and reconciliation as well (Umbreit, 1990). By the late 1990s, the National Institute of Justice was encouraging the spread of restorative justice experiments that promised to involve victims and community activists in the process of repairing the harm caused by lawbreakers (Anon., 1997). The number of reconciliation programs grew from about 100 at the start of the 1990s to nearly 300 across the United States (and Canada) by the end of that decade (VORP Information and Resource Center, 2000).

In theory, this particular alternative to incarceration offers advantages to victims, offenders, and crime-plagued neighborhoods. For victims, these evolving programs provide a safe, secure setting to confront their offenders in the presence of trained and skilled intermediaries. When they meet in person, victims get an opportunity to vent pent-up feelings and ask troubling questions. Besides the potential for emotional catharsis, victims ought to be able to leave the negotiations with a satisfactory restitution agreement in hand. For offenders, the encounter offers an occasion to accept responsibility for wrongdoing, express remorse, and ask for the victim's forgiveness. Most perpetrators get the chance to substitute restitution obligations (through work at regular jobs) for hard prison time. For the community, the pragmatic benefit is that negotiated settlements relieve court backlogs as well as jail and prison overcrowding and eliminate the need to build more cells to confine greater numbers of convicts at the public's expense. A less tangible but significant spiritual dividend is that restorative justice nurtures an atmosphere of forgiveness, redemption, acceptance, tolerance, and harmony within the community (Hudson and Galaway, 1975; Umbreit, 1990; Viano, 1990; Wright, 1991).

How the Trend toward Differential Justice Might Increase the Gap in the Way Victims are Handled

It is likely that in the near future, obvious "double standards" in the way that victims are handled by agencies and officials will become a contentious issue. Whereas in the recent past, just about all victims suffered from neglect, now the potential is developing for some victims to receive first-class, VIP treatment, whereas others continue to be relegated to the status of second-class citizens.

One obvious and troubling trend within American society does not have an appropriate, evocative, widely accepted name. It is best referred to as *differential access* but is also called *class privilege* and *dual systems*. The term *differential* is preferable because it is more accurate; *dual* implies only two distinct systems when actually there usually are several: a top track, a bottom track, and one or more gradations in between (with people in the middle classes enjoying some privileges but not others). The phrase *class privilege* accentuates the importance of wealth and power, but it overlooks stratification based on gender, race, and age as well. Differential or dual systems and class privilege in other areas of American society have been studied extensively (e.g., schooling, health care, transportation, recreation, housing). The persistent pattern in each of these areas is that the affluent benefit from the best goods and services that modern technology can deliver and money can buy, while the underclass is grudgingly provided with the minimal, lowest-quality services the system can get away with, without fully exposing its false promises of "equality."

Differential access to justice has been the subject of a great deal of interest, research, and debate. Some argue that in the United States "justice is blind," that the country is run "by laws, not men [sic]," and that there is "equal protection" for all. But others work to expose and put an end to the thinly disguised continuation of the historic trend of differential access to justice, which leads to double standards, in which a perpetrator's and a victim's characteristics are unfairly taken into account in the handling of cases by the system.

As predicted above, the opportunities, rights, and privileges available to victims will proliferate (specifically: providing victim advocates; purchasing anticrime goods and services; permitting private prosecution; allowing mediation/restitution/reconciliation). Differential access to justice will become more blatant, in the sense that the way that cases will be resolved will depend even more on the victim's status and the offender's place in the social order. The victimization of some people will continue to be taken much more seriously than the harming of others. When "important" members of society turn to the legal system for redress, they will receive a more satisfactory and supportive response than they do now. When the meager possessions of "marginal" members of society are stolen, or when they are beaten, robbed, or raped, the same old uncaring, assembly-line disposal of their cases will take place.

Pushing these projections still further, a more blatantly unjust situation than exists at present could develop in the early decades of the twenty-first century. While more affluent victims might be able to compel the system to deliver satisfactory service, the most underprivileged strata at the bottom of the social class hierarchy might be forced to fend for itself.

The current trend toward a high-tech service economy coupled with deindustrial-ization (the decline of American manufacturing) is bringing about pervasive long-term structural unemployment for those lacking the requisite skills. That will further polarize the population into a prospering upper class, struggling middle classes, and a growing "surplus population" (what some call the *underclass* or *outclass* of marginalized, excluded, demoralized, crushed, defeated, self-destructive, and ineffectively rebellious jobless, homeless, and hungry people). Contained within run-down inner-city neighborhoods and scattered pockets of poverty in outlying districts, these victims of economic dislocations will be viciously preyed upon by more desperate people who live among them. Their lives will be written off as unimportant, and their life-and-death struggles will be deemed "private matters" not worthy of governmental intervention. If the authorities turn their backs on these victims of poor-on-poor crimes, the profoundly alienated residents in these areas will be forced to defend their lives and possessions as best they can. They will be driven routinely to impose their own brands of on-the-spot "street justice," vigilante style.

The stark contrast between the sheltered lives of the privileged classes in gated communities (buttressed by a responsive criminal justice system that tends to their needs and wishes should they become victimized), and the misery endured by the inhabitants of out-of-control "free-fire zones" and "no-man's lands" will serve as an indictment of the gross inequities imposed by the problem of differential access to justice—if this nightmare scenario actually materializes.

THE PERILS OF CRYSTAL-BALL GAZING

Will the situation of victims in the first few decades of the twenty-first century be marked by more favorable treatment by criminal justice officials, by technological breakthroughs that enhance personal safety and protect valued possessions, and by universal access to professional advocates, private prosecutors, and mediation/restitution/reconciliation programs? Or will countervailing forces arise to keep today's tendencies in check? When gazing in a crystal ball, it is necessary to recognize the possibility that each action can provoke a reaction, and each trend some resistance and opposition. Will criminal justice officials rally to stop the emergence of dedicated advocates who will force them to live up to their rhetoric about handling victims with dignity and compassion and guaranteeing them notification and participatory rights? Will government attorneys lobby to preserve their virtual monopoly over the exercise of prosecutorial discretion and thereby thwart the revival of private prosecution? Will the punishment-oriented approach stifle the spread of alternatives to adjudication and incarceration that lead to restorative justice? Will egalitarian-oriented organizations fight against any widening of the gap in the way that poor victims are treated in comparison to affluent ones?

Only time will tell.

REFERENCES

ANON. (1994). Circling the wagons: More communities adopt gated-enclave approach. *Law Enforcement News*, November 15, p. 6.

ANON. (1997). Events: restorative justice regional symposiums. *NIJ Journal*, 233, September, p. 26.

BARKAS, J. (1978). *Victims*. New York: Scribners.

BLAKELY, E., and M. SNYDER (1997). *Fortress America: Gated Communities in the United States*. Washington, DC: Brookings Institution Press.

CARRINGTON, F. (1975). *The Victims*. New Rochelle, NY: Arlington House.

CARRINGTON, F. (1977). Victims' rights litigation: A wave of the future? *University of Richmond Law Review*, 11(3), Spring, pp. 447–470.

COLE, G. (1992). *The American System of Criminal Justice*, 6th ed. Pacific Grove, CA: Brooks/Cole.

DIIULIO, J. JR. (1988). What's wrong with private prisons. *The Public Interest*, 92, Summer, pp. 66–83.

DRAPKIN, I., and E. VIANO (1974). *Victimology: A New Focus*, Vols. 1–5. Lexington, MA: D.C. Heath.

ELIAS, R. (1983). *Victims of the System: Crime Victims and Compensation in American Politics and Criminal Justice*. New Brunswick, NJ: Transaction Books.

FRIEDMAN, L. (1985). The crime victim movement at its first decade. *Public Administration Review*, 45, November, pp. 790–794.

GRIFFIN, S. (1971). Rape: The all American crime. *Ramparts*, September, pp. 25–30.

HOOK, S. (1972). The rights of the victims: Thoughts on crime and compassion. *Encounter*, April, pp. 29–35.

HUDSON, J., and B. GALAWAY (1975). *Considering the Victim: Readings in Restitution and Victim Compensation*. Springfield, IL: Charles C Thomas.

HUDSON, J., and B. GALAWAY (1990). *Criminal Justice: Restitution and Reconciliation.* Monsey, NY: Criminal Justice Press.

KARMEN, A. (1995). Towards the institutionalization of a new kind of criminal justice professional: The victim advocate. *Justice Professional*, 9(1):1–16.

KARMEN, A. (1992). Who's against victim's rights? *St. John's Journal of Legal Commentary*, 8(1):157–176.

LARGEN, M. (1981). Grassroots centers and national task forces: A herstory of the anti-rape movement. *Aegis*, 32, Autumn, pp. 46–52.

LIEDTKE, C. (2000). Merchants support cities with business improvement districts. *Nation's Cities Weekly*, 23(6), February 14, p. 7.

LOSEKE, D. (1989). "Violence" is "Violence"…or is it? The social construction of "wife abuse" and public policy. In J. Best (ed.), *Images of Issues: Typifying Contemporary Social Problems*. New York: Aldine de Gruyter, pp. 191–206.

LUECK, T. (1994). Business districts grow at price of accountability. *New York Times*, November 20, pp. 1, 46.

LYNCH, R. (1976). Improving the treatment of victims: Some guides for action. In W. MacDonald (ed.), *Criminal Justice and the Victim*. Thousand Oaks, CA: Sage Publications, pp. 165–176.

MARTIN, D. (1977). *Battered Wives*. New York: Pocket Books.

MCKNIGHT, D. (1981). The Victim–Offender Reconciliation Project. In B. Galaway and J. Hudson (eds.), *Perspectives on Crime Victims*. St. Louis, MO: Mosby, pp. 292–298.

MEINERS, R. (1978). *Victim Compensation: Economic, Political, and Legal Aspects*. Lexington, MA: D.C. Heath.

NATIONAL ORGANIZATION FOR VICTIM ASSISTANCE (1986). NOVA sponsors forum on constitutional amendment. *NOVA Newsletter*, March, pp. 1–2, 7.

NEWMAN, D. (1986). *Introduction to Criminal Justice*, 3rd ed. New York: Random House.

PRESIDENT'S TASK FORCE ON VICTIMS OF CRIME (1982). *Final Report*. Washington, DC: U.S. Government Printing Office.

RIEFF, R. (1979). *The Invisible Victim: The Criminal Justice System's Forgotten Responsibility*. New York: Basic Books.

ROBERTS, A. (1990). *Helping Crime Victims: Research, Policy, and Practice*. Thousand Oaks, CA: Sage Publications.

ROLAND, J. (1996). Private prosecutions. *Modern Militiaman*, 2, July–August, pp. 3–5. (Internet newsletter).

SCHAFER, S. (1968). *The Victim and His Criminal*. New York: Random House.

SCHNEIDER, A., and P. SCHNEIDER (1981). Victim assistance programs: An overview. In B. Galaway and J. Hudson (eds.), *Perspectives on Crime Victims*. St. Louis, MO: Mosby, pp. 364–373.

SCHWENDINGER, J., and H. SCHWENDINGER (1983). *Rape and Inequality*. Thousand Oaks, CA: Sage Publications.

SEBBA, L. (1992). The victim's role in the penal process: A theoretical orientation. In E. Fattah (ed.), *Toward a Critical Victimology*. New York: St. Martin's Press, pp. 195–221.

SIGLER, J. (1979). The prosecutor: A comparative functional analysis. In W. McDonald (ed.), *The Prosecutor*. Thousand Oaks, CA: Sage Publications, pp. 53–74.

SILBERMAN, C. (1978). *Criminal Violence, Criminal Justice*. New York: Random House.

STARK, J., and H. GOLDSTEIN (1985). *The Rights of Crime Victims*. Chicago: Southern Illinois University Press.

STEINBERG, A. (1984). From private prosecution to plea bargaining: Criminal prosecution, the district attorney, and American legal history. *Crime and Delinquency*, 30(4), October, pp. 568–592.

Tomz, J., and D. McGillis (1997). *Serving Crime Victims and Witnesses*, 2nd ed. Washington, DC: Office of Justice Programs.

Umbreit, M. (1990). Victim–offender mediation with violent offenders: Implications for modifications of the VORP model. In E. Viano (ed.), *The Victimology Handbook: Research Findings, Treatment, and Public Policy.* New York: Garland Publishing, pp. 337–352.

Viano, E. (1976). The study of the victim. *Victimology*, 1:1–7.

Viano, E. (1990). The recognition and implementation of victim's rights in the United States: Developments and achievements." In E. Viano (ed.), *The Victimology Handbook: Research Findings, Treatment, and Public Policy.* New York: Garland Publishing, pp. 319–336.

Victim–Offender Reconciliation Programs (VORP) Information and Resource Center. Current news. www.vorp.com.

Wilson–Duenges, G. (2000). An exploration of sense of community and fear of crime in gated communities. *Environment and Behavior*, 32(5), September, pp. 597–612.

Wright, M. (1991). *Justice for Victims and Offenders.* Philadelphia: Open University Press.

chapter 4

Gangs

Status, Characteristics, Community and Police Responses, and Policy Implications

Kenneth J. Peak, Ph.D.

ABSTRACT

In this chapter several aspects of gangs are discussed: their origins, composition, and characteristics; financial aspects; community responses (programs and enforcement strategies); a typology of gang intervention strategies; how the problem is being addressed by community policing and problem solving; and policy implications.

INTRODUCTION

Gangs continue to pose a serious social problem in the United States. In American communities large and small, the fear wrought by teen gangs has spread rapidly. With gang victimizations reported daily, many people have become virtual prisoners in their own homes. In this chapter we examine gangs and what the future holds for them. The following areas are examined: gang origins, composition, and characteristics (including girl gangs, graffiti, and financial aspects of gangs); community responses, possible future strategies for addressing the gang problem, and policy implications.

GANG ORIGINS, COMPOSITION, AND CHARACTERISTICS

Early Formation and Research

Sanders (1994:20) defined a *gang* as "any transpersonal group of youths that shows a willingness to use deadly violence to claim and defend territory, and attack rival gangs, extort or rob money, or engage in other criminal behavior as an activity associated with its group, and is recognized by itself and its immediate community as a distinct dangerous entity. The basic structure of gangs is one of age and gender differentiation, and leadership is informal and multiple."

Although gangs seem to be a recent problem, they have existed for many years. They were present in many American cities in the nineteenth century (Hyman, 1984); it has been estimated that in 1855, New York City alone had over 30,000 gang members (Asbury, 1971). It has also been estimated that some of the Hispanic gang members in Los Angeles are fourth-generation gang members (Donovan, 1988) and that some of the Los Angeles gangs' names date back 60 years (Pitchess, 1979). Hispanic youth gang activity was first recognized early in the twentieth century in the southern California area. Thrasher's seminal study of 1313 gangs in 1927 found that most gangs were small (6 to 20 members) and formed spontaneously in poor and socially disorganized neighborhoods, by

> disintegration of family life, inefficiency of schools, formalism and externality of religion, corruption and indifference in local politics, low wages and monotony in occupational activities, unemployment, and lack of opportunity for wholesome recreation. Such underlying conditions...must be considered together as a situation complex which forms the matrix of gang development. *Among the groups within which the boy delinquent finds expression, the gang is one of the most vital to the development of his personality.* [emphasis in the original] (Thrasher, 1927:33, 339, 346)

Thrasher also observed that the gang functions with reference to these conditions in two ways: "It offers a substitute for what society fails to give; and it provides a relief from suppression and distasteful behavior. It fills a gap and affords an escape" (Thrasher, 1927:33).

Cloward and Ohlin (1960) later asserted that gangs emerged from "blocked opportunities" for legitimate success, resulting in one of three outcomes: juveniles becoming organized or career criminals, wanton violence in search of status, or a retreat into drug use and dropping out. This typology of gangs has been substantially confirmed by a number of subsequent studies in several different cities (see, e.g., Yablonsky, 1962; Huff, 1989; Fagan, 1990; Taylor, 1990).

After this flurry of interest in gangs during the 1950s and 1960s, gang studies and investigations virtually ended. There is little evidence of serious concern about gangs from police or scholars from the mid-1960s to the mid-1970s. In fact, the National Advisory Commission on Criminal Justice Standards and Goals (1976:33) reported that "youth gang violence is not a major problem in the United States." Concern with gangs has experienced a rebirth since then, and it continues today at a high level. Immigration patterns, economic conditions, and increased violence have been identified as factors contributing to the reemergence of gangs (Albanese, 1993).

Gangs and gang membership are a product of socioeconomic conditions, and they tend to develop and expand during periods of rapid social change and instability. However, it should not be assumed that juveniles join gangs solely because of poverty or for the pursuit of wealth. There have been a number of studies indicating that large numbers of gang members come from the middle- and lower-middle classes (Spergal,

1990). Deterioration of the family and other social-control institutions also tend to cause an increase in gang activity. When social conditions deteriorate, the gang tends to serve as an extended family for many juveniles.

Members usually join the gang either by committing a crime or undergoing an initiation procedure. Gang members use automatic weapons and sawed-off shotguns in violent driveby shootings, while becoming more sophisticated in their criminal activities and more wealthy. Crack cocaine and other illegal enterprises have provided gang members with a level of wealth and a lifestyle that they would probably otherwise not have attained. Basically, gangs participate in three types of violence: random violence, intergang violence, and intragang violence. *Random violence* occurs when gang members or "wannabes" attack nongang civilians as a part of a criminal act or to impress their superiors with their savagery (Klein and Maxson, 1989). *Intergang violence* refers to the violence between gangs as they compete for territory, to (1) retaliate for past aggression or acts, (2) protect or compete for territory, or (3) recruit new members, especially in another gang's territory. *Intragang violence* is integral to the gang, and it occurs during group functions such as initiation—it actually serves to strengthen the bonds among members. Other reasons for intragang violence include leadership conflict, disputes over drugs, money, and territory; and one's trying to leave the gang.

Contemporary Status and Types of Gangs

Gangs continue to be a substantial problem in the United States and their members are becoming younger. Most research on youth gangs in the United States has concluded that the most typical age range of gang members has been approximately 14 to 24; researchers are aware of gang members as young as 10 years of age, however, and in some areas (such as southern California, where some Latino gangs originated more than 100 years ago), one can find several generations in the same family who are gang members with active members in their 30s. Youngsters generally begin hanging out with gangs at 12 or 13 years of age, join the gang at 13 or 14, and are first arrested at 14 (Huff, 1998).

The challenge of responding to today's gang problem is indeed great. According to the U.S. Justice Department estimates (see Curry et al., 1996), there are more than 16,000 gangs and over half a million gang members in the United States (Decker and Curry, 2000). Nearly half of all gang members (47.8%) were found to be African-American youth; Hispanic youngsters accounted for 42.7% and Asians totaled 5.2%.

Gangs comprise of three types of members: *hardcore* (those who commit violent acts and defend the reputation of the gang), *associates* (members who frequently affiliate with known gang members for status and recognition but who move in and out on the basis of interest in gang functions), and *peripherals* (who are not gang members but associate or identify with gang members for protection—usually with the dominant gang in their neighborhood). Most females fall into the peripheral category (Witkin, 1991).

Two predominant African-American gangs, the Crips and the Bloods, began in southern California over a quarter century ago and now have affiliations in 32 states and more than 100 cities. Crips address each other with the nickname "Cuzz." Crip graffiti can be identified by the symbol "B/K," which stands for "Blood Killers." Bloods reportedly formed as a means of protection against the Crips, in and near Compton, California. Bloods identify with the color red and address each other as "Blood." Gang graffiti frequently uses the terms "BS" for "Bloodstone" or "C/K" for "Crip Killers." Both Crips and Bloods refer to fellow gang members as "homeboys" or "homeys" (Peak, 2000).

Asian gangs include Chinese and Filipino youths. Chinese gangs can be traced back to the latter part of the nineteenth century with the influx of Chinese immigrants. In 1965 the first Chinese gang was formed in southern California; it is believed that they have continued to flourish because of the exploitation of migrant workers, which led to a breakdown in traditional family ties and crime. Throughout the 1980s, gang leaders found that ethnic Chinese from Vietnam were most suited for criminal activities. Today, the most powerful Chinese gang (especially in California) appears to be Suey Sing, which has taken over the extortion and protection of several gambling houses and in 1990 began brutally executing influential members of rival gangs such as the Wah Ching (Toy, 1992). Filipino gangs began in the Philippines during World War II by many hardcore criminals released from prison. Filipino gang members may be identified by their distinctive tattoos. They also display their gang name in graffiti. Filipino gang members are usually older, often in their 30s.

Hispanic gangs invariably name their gangs after a geographical area or "turf" which they feel is worth defending. Hispanic gang activity often becomes a family affair, with young males (10 to 13) being the "peewees," the 14- to 22-year-old being the hard-core members, and those living beyond age 22 becoming a "vetrano," or veteran. Headgear (knit cap or monickered bandanna), shirts, pants (highly starched khaki or blue jeans), tattoos (of gang identification) and vehicles (prefer older-model Chevrolets, lowered and with extra chrome and fur) are standard fare.

White gangs are also expanding, as growing numbers of young neo-Nazi skinheads are linking up with old-line hate groups in the United States. This unity has bolstered the morale and criminal activity of the Ku Klux Klan and other white supremacist organizations. Numerous skinhead groups have aligned with the White Aryan Resistance, which tends to encourage violence for "self-defense." Skinheads have shaved heads and may sport Nazi and/or Satanic insignia or tattoos. They preach violence against African Americans, Hispanics, Asians, and homosexuals. They range in age from 13 to 25 and associate with "white power" music. Their preferred mode of dress is militarylike in nature, with khaki pants, black leather or tuffy-type jackets, and lace-up black boots (Peak, 2000).

Graffiti and Hand Signals

All social groups and cultures have self-styled communicative methods; teen gangs are no exception. Nonverbal forms of communication allow gang members to have dialogue with each other and with rival gangs. Graffiti also serves to mark the gang's turf: if a gang's graffiti is untouched or unchallenged for a period of time, the gang's control in that area is reaffirmed.

Within the Chicano gang, there is a nonverbal communicative method that has existed for approximately 50 years. This method, called a *placa*, is one that allows the Chicano gang member to express himself, his gang, other gangs, and direct challenges to others. These gangs, having existed since the turn of the century, have developed many standard symbols. Hand signals, or *throwing signs*, are made by forming letters or numbers with the hands and fingers, depicting the gang symbol or initials. This allows the gang member to show which gang he belongs to and issues challenges to other gangs in the vicinity (Peak, 2000).

To have any success at all in investigating gang activities, police agencies must develop expertise in gang movements, activities, nonverbal communication, graffiti, tattoos, and dress codes. As we discuss below, the police have also developed intelligence files on known or suspected gang members.

Girls in Gangs

There is comparatively little recent research that pertains to girls who belong to gangs. Indeed, researchers have been unable to determine with any precision the proportion of gang members in the United States who are female, ranging from around 3 or 4% (Curry et al., 1994) to 8% (Moore and Cook, 1999) and even 10% (Miller, 1992). One survey of eighth graders in 11 cities found that 38% of the students who said they were gang members were females (Esbensen and Osgood, 1997).

Irrespective of the actual proportion of female gang members, recent surveys have suggested an increase in independent female gangs (Curry et al., 1996; National Drug Intelligence Center, 1996). Whether or not female gang members are becoming involved in more serious and violent offending is also unknown, because national trend date are unavailable. Chicago data on gang-related offenses from 1965 to 1994 show, however, that females represented only 5% of victims and 1% of offenders. Female gang violence was more likely to involve simple battery or assault rather than homicide, and female nonviolent crimes consisted mainly of liquor law violations (Block et al., 1996).

A major study of female gangs in 1988, involving a Chicago African-American female gang, found the Vice Queens to be loosely knit and ranging in age from 13 to 19. Unlike their male counterparts, the Vice Kings, the gang did not have a rigid structure; their main interest lay in the achievements of the Kings, but they also had achievements of their own, including criminal activities. Fishman (1988:26–27) placed African-American girl gangs in a larger context:

> There has been little improvement in the economic situation of the black community since 1965. The situation for teenage black girls today is even bleaker…as black girls are increasingly exposed to the worsening conditions within their low income neighborhood where legitimate opportunities become increasingly restricted, then they will increasingly turn to black female auxiliary gangs which provide these girls with the opportunity to learn the skills to make the adaptations to poverty, violence, and racism.

Campbell (1984) concurred, asserting that young African American girls shoulder the burdens of their triple handicaps: race, class, and gender. The lack of recreational opportunities, the long days unfilled by work or school, and the absence of money mean that hours and days are whiled away on street corners and in collective activities.

Revenues and Expenditures

An ethnographic study of street gangs conducted for the National Institute of Justice was very revealing concerning the financial aspects of gangs. Analysis of one large, now defunct gang which consisted of several hundred gang members was particular instructive. The gang included a leadership class (typically, a leader and three officers), a "foot soldier" class (ranging from 25 to 100 members aged 16 to 25 years), and rank-and-file members (usually, 200 persons younger than high school age). More than 70% of the gang's total annual revenue of approximately $280,000 was generated from the sale of crack cocaine. Dues provided some additional gang revenue (about 25%), and extortion directed at local businesses and entrepreneurs represented about 5%. The gang operated in a neighborhood of roughly four city blocks (Venkatesh, 1999).

When a gang member was killed, the gang paid funeral expenses (about $5000 per funeral) and typically provided compensation to the slain member's family. Leaders retained about $4200 per month from the gang's revenues, for an annual wage of about $50,000. The longer a member was in a leadership position, however, the higher was his "salary," which could go as high as $130,000. Officers (runners, enforcers, or treasurer) earned about $1000 per month, and foot soldiers were paid about $200 per month for working about 20 hours per week (but foot soldiers were also allowed to sell drugs outside the gang structure) (Venkatesh, 1999).

The annual death rate among the gang's foot soldiers was 4.2%, more than 40 times the national average for African-American males in the 16- to 25-year-old age group. Most alarmingly, gang members who were active for a four-year period had roughly a 25% chance of dying; members also averaged more than two nonfatal injuries (mostly from gunshots) and nearly six arrests over a four-year period (Venkatesh, 1999).

Although the gang brought in new recruits who were sustained by the powerful belief that they would achieve substantial earnings, such a preconceived accumulation of wealth was not forthcoming. Because most gang members never realize significant material gain, an economic-based explanation for gang membership is not sufficient in itself. Clearly, gang members choose to participate in such activities because of the "family" atmosphere and other reasons described above.

RESPONSES TO GANGS

Programs or Police Crackdowns: Which Method Is Best?

Determining the best course of action for dealing with street gangs is not easy. A number of questions about the origin, activities, and future of gangs are still unanswered. Most experts describe programs in communities with gangs that would include some combination of the following:

- *Fundamental changes in the way that schools operate.* Schools should broaden their scope of services and act as community centers involved in teaching, providing services, and serving as locations for activities before and after the school day.

- *Job skills development for youths and young adults accompanied by improvements in the labor market.* Many youths have dropped out of school and do not have the skills to find employment. Attention needs to be focused on ways to expand the labor market, including the development of indigenous businesses in these communities, and to provide job skills for those in and out of school.

- *Assistance to families.* A range of family services, including parent training, child care, health care, and crisis intervention, must be made available in communities with gangs.

- *Changes in the way the criminal justice system—particularly policing—responds generally to problems in these communities and specifically to gang problems.* Many people feel that police agencies need to increase their commitment to understanding the communities they serve and to solving problems. This shift is currently being addressed through the proactive, community-oriented policing and problem-solving (COPPS) approach (which is described, with examples provided, below).

- *Intervention and control of known gang members.* Illegal gang activity must be controlled by diverting peripheral members from gang involvement and criminal activity. Achieving control may mean making a clear statement—by arresting and incapacitating hard-core gang members—that communities will not tolerate intimidating, violent, and/or criminal gang activity (Conly et al., 1993:65–66).

Support for such a strategy has by no means been unanimous. Observers such as Walter Miller (1990), who has studied gangs for decades, maintain that gang programs have not worked when based on the notion that the solution lies with changing the characteristics of lower-class life (e.g., community conditions). The major assumption that gangs arise out of lower-class life is confounded by the fact that there are lower-class communities with no gangs. Miller advocated programs narrowly focused on gang members and those at immediate risk of membership, organized at the community level, which would provide educational and employment support.

Others believe that the most responsible approach is to invest in prevention and community-wide coordination to address the broad range of social ills in those communities. David Fattah (1994:105–106), cofounder of the House of Umoja in Philadelphia, which provides residential and nonresidential services to juvenile gang members, also argued that much can be done at the community level:

1. Gangs need to attach themselves to positive aspects of their communities; jobs are an important of this positive attachment process.

2. Given the national nature of gang networks, a national task force on gangs should be established, designed, and managed by neighborhood-based organizations working to reduce gang drug dealing and violence.

3. Police, neighborhood-based organizations, and other concerned parties should be trained in how to recognize and respond to the presence of gangs.

4. Immediate efforts should be taken to contain the spread of drug dealing and violence, by preventing drug use and abuse and preventing gang recruitment by targeting preteens.

5. Implementation of a grievance procedure directed toward violence avoidance through counseling, mediation, and conflict resolution training, which has already proven effective with warring gang members.

Something more is needed than police work alone to break the cycle of gang delinquency. A continuing roadblock to prevention has been the lack of community interest and support of gang reduction initiatives. In too many communities, gang violence is tolerated as long as gang members victimize each other and do not bother the rest of society (Horowitz, 1987). Without community support, the contemporary cycle of youth gang activities will continue; even gang members who are imprisoned join branches of their gang behind bars while replacements are found to take their place on the street (Moore, et al., 1978; Jacobs, 1983).

As one observer commented, "if families, schools, and churches don't socialize children to act responsibly, and if the national and local economies don't provide adequate legal opportunity structures, we as a society are in deep trouble" (Huff, 1990:316). Another researcher offered that "community and political institutions, beginning with the family itself, must be better organized and more committed to ameliorating the conditions conducive to gang delinquency" (Albanese, 1993:178).

The recent emergence of gangs in medium-sized and smaller cities is tied up with demographic trends, deindustrialization, the continuing problem of race in our cities, as well as other variables. Hagedorn (1988:167–169) offered three practical lessons from our experiences in trying to "do something" about gangs:

1. Gang members must participate in meaningful programs. Gang programs need to train and hire former local gang members as staff, utilize older gang members as consultants in developing new programs, and make sure that input from gang "clients" takes place.

2. Emphasis needs to be put on creating jobs and improving education, not rationalizing the criminal justice system. While "diversion" or other kinds of community-based programs would be welcome, the emphasis needs to be elsewhere. Although harsh sanctions should be meted out for serious and violent behavior, and any criminal act should merit punishment, a gang member should not be punished merely for who he or she is.

3. Research on gangs is necessary if we are to go beyond the law enforcement paradigm in understanding or policymaking. Why have gangs formed in some cities and not in others? How do we measure the influence of minority institutions and whether that influence is declining? What are the causes for the extreme variation in rates of homicide among gangs? What role is prison playing in gang development in cities where gangs have emerged within the last 10 years?

A Typology

As Petersen (2000:139) observed: "Prevention programs need to be based on realistic measures and goals rather than idealistic ones. It is easy to preach 'just say no,' 'stay out of gangs,' or 'get out of your gang.' These approaches are often impossible to implement or achieve. Many policymakers do not understand the context of offenders' everyday lives."

What appears to be lacking in policy responses to gangs is the focus on combatting crime and delinquency before it occurs. To eliminate or reduce the prevalence of gangs proactively, prevention is key. An effective response to gangs will involve both proximate and fundamental interventions. The only way to address both levels is through institutional and community actions, which affect the values that are the foundation of the gang.

Based on responses from 254 police and social-service agencies nationwide that were part of the National Youth Gang Suppression and Intervention Program, Spergel and Curry developed a typology of five gang intervention strategies (Decker and Curry, 2000):

1. *Suppression* (used as the primary strategy by 44% of reporting agencies): law enforcement and criminal justice interventions such as arrest, imprisonment, and surveillance. These tactics respond to the proximate causes of gangs. To be effective, however, suppression must be part of a broader set of responses to the illegal actions of gang members. By itself, suppression is not likely to have an effect on the growth of gangs or the crimes committed by gang members. Specialized police units may even contribute, in unintended ways, to the growth of gangs by overidentifying a larger gang pattern than actually exists by expanding the pool of gang members through increased labeling. (Suppression efforts by the police are discussed further below.)

2. *Social intervention* (used by 32% of the agencies): includes crisis intervention, treatment for youths and their families, and social service referrals. Such strategies are proximate, designed to address the needs of an immediate nature. Crisis intervention is especially promising. Crisis responses should be available at emergency rooms and be mobilized by police, health care, or community groups. The goals should be the separation of gang members from persons at risk and the provision of mentoring and other social services that extend beyond emergency rooms. Families are an important target of social intervention strategies. Many youths attempt to deceive their parents about their membership in gangs. In addition, most gang members have siblings or cousins whose well-being may be adversely affected by the gang member, which magnifies the impact of family interventions.

3. *Organizational change* (used by 11%): development of task forces for addressing the gang problem. This strategy requires the creation of a broad consensus about gang problems, is targeted at the proximate causes of gangs, and by itself cannot solve gang problems. Organizational change will either lead to an awareness of gang problems in the community and

mobilize efforts to address them, or will produce a new set of relations among agencies and groups responding to such problems. This strategy typically occurs early in the cycle of responses to gangs.

4. *Community mobilization* (9%): focuses on cooperation across agencies, to produce better coordination of existing services. This strategy is designed to address the fundamental causes of gangs and gang membership and to meet needs of gang members. To be effective, this strategy must include both the criminal and juvenile justice systems and immediate social institutions such as the family, schools, community agencies and groups, churches, and public health agencies.

5. *Social opportunities* (5%): stresses education and job-related interventions. More than any other strategy, this confronts the fundamental causes of gang formation and membership. It addresses factors responsible for the creation of an urban underclass and the resultant dislocation of large groups of urban residents; therefore, it may hold the greatest prospects for success. These efforts incorporate job creation and residential placements designed to reshape values, seeking to integrate gang members into legitimate social institutions. These interventions address a primary need of adolescents: to affiliate themselves with a set of peers in age-graded activities.

Spergel and Curry reported that cities with chronic gang problems least often employed social opportunities and community mobilization. Despite this, these were the strategies assessed as being most effective. The Spergel–Curry model has become the basis for major contemporary federal and local responses to gangs (Decker and Curry, 2000).

Related Suppression and Intervention Techniques

Today, about two-thirds of all large cities in the United States with a population of 200,000 or more have a specialized gang unit; about half of all other cities have such a unit (Weisel and Painter, 1997).

A five-year study of gangs in five cities—San Diego, Chicago, Kansas City, Austin, and the metropolitan county of Dade, Florida—determined that all of these agencies, like many others across the country, typically responded to their gang problems by forming some type of special unit—often, suppression oriented—as an initial response to major episodes of gang violence (Weisel and Painter, 1997). Over time, these units integrated investigations, intelligence gathering, and prevention and enforcement activities. Across the country local police are attempting to contain gang problems by assembling gang intelligence units (GIUs) to identify the core members of the gangs and target them for enforcement. Intelligence is collected by questioning suspected gang members who are arrested, talking with rival gang members, and talking with residents in gang neighborhoods. At the same time, officers collect information on gang activities, monitor graffiti, collect information on assaults and homicides of gang members by rival gangs, and observe disputes involving drug sales.

Furthermore, each city typically engaged in some limited form of community outreach—prevention—making presentations to community groups concerning how to recognize if a youth had joined a gang, and so on. The agencies' responses to local gang problems were similar yet unique; rather than implement a "one size fits all" cookie-cutter approach to gang problems, the agencies refined their approaches over time.

One noteworthy trend that was discovered among the five cities in this study was that, over time, most of the agencies studied shifted from an emphasis on suppression to one with more emphasis on education and a much stronger reliance on information gathering by line personnel, rather than relying solely on a gang unit. From these efforts, two major trends have been identified in police responses to gangs: better data collection, management, and dissemination; and enhanced collaboration with agencies external to the police agency (schools, local code enforcement agencies, probation agencies, community groups, etc.) (Weisel and Painter, 1997).

Another increasingly well known police response to gangs is the Gang Resistance Education and Training (GREAT) program, which originated in 1991 in Phoenix, Arizona. GREAT emphasizes the acquisition of information and skills needed by students to resist peer pressure and gang influences; the curriculum contains nine-hour lessons offered to middle-school students, mostly seventh graders.

Few studies have evaluated the GREAT program, and the available evidence has been mixed. For example, Palumbo and Ferguson (1995) found that the GREAT program had a small but positive impact on students' attitudes and resistance skills but not much on whether or not they joined gangs. Overall, they found that the impact of the program was small in relation to huge expenditures of resources. In their national evaluation of 11 GREAT sites, Esbensen and Osgood (1999) found that students completing the program had more prosocial attitudes and lower rates of some types of delinquent behavior than students who did not participate in the program.

One significant reason for the skepticism surrounding the GREAT program is that it tries to do too much with too little. Going into student classrooms for nine hours is hardly enough time to break the cycle of gangs, especially where some children are born into the gang lifestyle. Another reason why such programs fall short is that many do not target teenagers rather than young children. This is, as Petersen (2000:141) noted, "too late in the game." As noted earlier, antisocial and delinquent behaviors, and gang membership, can emerge as early as age 10.

Federal law enforcement initiatives are also working to suppress gang activities. The Immigration and Naturalization Service's Violent Gang Task Force engages in proactive, interagency, multijurisdictional operations against criminal alien gangs. The Bureau of Alcohol, Tobacco, and Firearms (ATF) has also expanded its focus to include criminal gangs, particularly violent gang groups. ATF developed an information database in the mid-1980s; today, ATF maintains five additional data-bases, dedicated to tracking outlaw motorcycle organizations, Bloods and Crips, prison gangs, and Asian gangs (Higgins, 1993).

As noted above, however, enforcement alone provides little relief or solution to the underlying problems, which are vested in social, political, and economic factors. A fundamental question to ask is this: How do we as a society replace the gang's social importance and financial benefits (with children "earning" literally hundreds of dollars a day in drug-related activities) with education or work programs that pay minimum wage? This is a complex issue, with no simple answers.

Applying Community-Oriented Policing and Problem Solving

Community-oriented policing and problem solving (COPPS) brings the community and police together in a partnership to work toward reducing neighborhood disorder and fear of crime (see Goldstein, 1990; Trojanowicz and Bucqueroux, 1990; Peak and Glensor, 1996). Case studies about successes with the COPPS approach to gangs are becoming very commonplace. Following are two examples of gang problems and COPPS activities that were undertaken to quell problems.

Boston, Massachusetts

Boston was suffering from a youth homicide problem, with 155 young people having been either shot or stabbed in a four-year period in three neighborhoods; 60% of the homicides were gang related. An interagency working group was composed, consisting of local, state, and federal law enforcement officers, researchers, probation officers, and gang-intervention street workers. Their responses to the problem focused on both the supply of and demand for guns among gangs.

The guns used in youth homicides were typically manufactured less than two years prior to the crime. This suggested a strategy to the group: identifying and arresting gun traffickers who were supplying guns to gangs. On the demand side of the problem (why young people carried guns and shot one another), the group identified 61 Boston gangs, with about 1300 members, representing only about 3% of the youth in the affected neighborhoods. Youth homicides, it was determined, were committed by a few gang members who committed many crimes. Enhanced penalties ranging from strict curfew checks by probation officers to federal prosecutions for street crimes were created against gang members for violent behavior; extraordinary crimes brought extraordinary punishment. The threat of these penalties was communicated to members firsthand. Homicides of young people dropped 67% from the mean of the previous seven years (Sampson and Scott, 2000).

San Mateo, California

When gang violence spread in San Mateo, primarily because of seven-year warfare between two opposing gangs—involving shootings, stabbings, car bombings, and murder—a street detective requested and received a transfer to the police deparment's community policing unit. After receiving training in problem solving, he first asked a local volunteer mediation agency to assist, and then he enlisted the probation department's help, due to its court-ordered guardianship over many of the more seasoned gang members. He also requested that a juvenile court judge waive the nonassociation clause that was a term of most of the gang members' probation, so that they could meet without fear of court-ordered sanctions (Sampson and Scott, 2000).

The mediation service arranged for separate meetings with the two rival gangs, to be held in a neutral place. Three mediators, two probation officers, and one police officer (the detective) also attended. The groups talked about respect, community racism, the police, and the need to try something new. The idea of a truce was raised, but the two gangs' leaders laughed at the idea. The mediators met individually with each gang four more times; each gang remained curious about the other's commitment, and both seemed tired of the ongoing violence. The gangs finally agreed to meet. Each gang selected five members as spokesmen, who brought a list of items to be addressed; respect was at the top of both lists (Sampson and Scott, 2000).

Finally, an agreement for peace was reached, and handshakes were exchanged; all agreed to a follow-up meeting, where 41 gang members agreed to a truce and that there would be no more violence. They agreed to respect each other, and if a confrontation arose, said they would try to talk through it as opposed to using weapons (Sampson and Scott, 2000). In the four years since this problem-solving effort began, there have been no reports of violence between the two gangs.

These examples demonstrate what can be accomplished when the police collaborate with other citizens and agencies in proactive, problem-solving efforts.

POLICY IMPLICATIONS FOR THE FUTURE

Some authors have maintained that gangs are not inherently evil or totally devoid of any positive attributes; for example, Fattah (1994:106) stated that "gangs offer their members love, companionship, friendship, loyalty, and trust. They also help members and their families with living expenses, such as rent and utility payments, clothing and medicine purchases, and transportation." For most Americans, however, gang activities such as drug abuse, prostitution, and other street crimes are deeply offensive and frightening.

Today, as Thrasher (1927:356) observed long ago, there are "really only two alternatives" in successful reformation of a youth who has come under the influence of a gang: Either remove the person from the gang and the social world it represents, or reform the gang. Both are very difficult to accomplish. Thrasher (1927:356) also asserted that the problem of redirecting a gang turns out to be one of giving life meaning for the youth: "It is a matter of 'definition of the situation,' but this has too often come to mean the process of setting up taboos and prohibitions. We need to make the boy understand what he may not do, but it is more important to lead him to see the meaning of what society wants him to do and its relation to some rational scheme of life."

There are several policy implications for the future. First, as indicated above, youths who join gangs tend to do so at an early age, with an arrest record by age 14. This underscores the urgent need for effective gang-resistance education programs and other primary and secondary prevention and intervention initiatives directed at preteens, especially those who are prone to delinquent and violent behavior (see, e.g., Goldstein and Huff, 1993; Klein, 1995).

Research indicates that although many youths believe that they will be beaten physically if they refuse an offer to join a gang, they can refuse to do so without substantial risk of physical harm. Moreover, they are far better off to resist joining gangs than to expose themselves to the beating they are likely to take upon being initiated (the most common initiation ritual involves gang members assaulting the new recruit to prove that he is "tough," "can take it," and "has heart"), and the increased chances of arrest, incarceration, injury, and death that are associated with gang membership (Huff, 1998).

Because prevention programs will not deter all youths from joining gangs, it is also important to address the brief window of opportunity for intervention that occurs in the year between the "wannabe" stage and the age at first arrest. It is vital that intervention programs that target gang members and divert them from the gang successfully be funded, developed, evaluated, improved, and sustained (Huff, 1998).

A second opportunity to intervene occurs between the time that gang members are first arrested for property crimes and their subsequent involvement in more serious offenses. This period, which lasts about 1.5 to 2 years, affords a chance to divert young offenders from the gang subculture before they further endanger their own lives and victimize other citizens. Gang members are more likely than their nongang peers to sell higher-profit drugs, underscoring the need for prevention and early intervention programs, before they become hooked on illegal earnings (Huff, 1998).

Data suggest that gang members commit a wide variety of personal and property crimes. A sudden increase in those crimes may serve as a "distant early warning signal" that the community needs to consider local gangs in the context of its overall crime problem. Crimes that are especially worth monitoring closely include auto theft, bringing weapons to school, and driveby shootings. Gang members are also likely to possess powerful and highly lethal weapons, although many gang members are not old enough to drive a car legally. Efforts to reduce the number of illegal weapons possessed by youths should be emphasized to reduce gun-related crimes (for successful efforts to reduce gun violence in Kansas City and Boston, see Sherman et al., 1995; Kennedy et al., 1996).

Furthermore, while support must be unflagging for police antigang activities, the community policing and problem-solving strategy holds promise for addressing this problem. Intervention strategies to reduce violence must be built on a foundation of current information about the types of street gangs and street gang activities in each neighborhood where gangs flourish. Initiatives for reducing gang violence must also recognize the difference between turf protection and drug trafficking. A strategy to reduce gang involvement in drugs in a community in which gang members are most concerned with defense of turf will have little chance of success (Block and Block, 1993).

Finally, street gang membership, violence, and other illegal gang activity must be understood in light of both long-term and chronic social patterns. Attempts must also be made to understand rapidly changing street-gang problems stemming from existing economic conditions, weapon availability, drug markets, and the spatial arrangement of street gang territories across a city. The ultimate solution rests on a coordinated criminal justice response, changes in educational opportunities, racial and ethnic attitudes, and job structure.

SUMMARY

In this chapter we have discussed the state of America's gangs, specifically their origins, composition, and characteristics; community responses (programs and enforcement strategies); a typology of gang intervention strategies; how the problem is being addressed by community policing and problem solving, and policy implications.

Gangs are not going to dissipate soon, if ever; where poverty and hopelessness are at their worst, and people live in violent surroundings and seek protection in numbers, gangs will thrive as they have for nearly 100 years. There is cause for hope, however. If the advice of experts is heeded and communities will take the initiative toward developing policy, initiating programs, and providing necessary resources, we may be able to stem the growing tide of illegal gang activities.

We can ill afford to "hurtle into the future with our eyes fixed firmly on the rearview mirror" (Postman, 1991:19). The future will probably not witness the diminution of gang activities unless communities resolve to seek solutions and take action.

REFERENCES

ALBANESE, J. S. (1993). *Dealing with Delinquency: The Future of Juvenile Justice*, 2d ed. Chicago: Nelson-Hall.

ASBURY, H. (1971). *Gangs of New York: An Informal History of the Underworld* (originally published in 1927). New York: Putnam.

BLOCK, CAROLYN R., and R. BLOCK (1993). *Street Gang Crime in Chicago*. Research in Brief. Washington, DC: National Institute of Justice.

BLOCK, C. R., A. CHRISTAKOS, A. A. JACOB, and R. PRZYBYLSKI (1996). *Street Gangs and Crime: Patterns and Trends in Chicago*. Chicago: Illinois Criminal Justice Information Authority.

CAMPBELL, A. (1984). *The Girls in the Gang*. Oxford: Basil Blackwell.

CLOWARD, R. A., and L. E. OHLIN (1960). *Delinquency and Opportunity: A Theory of Delinquent Gangs*. New York: Free Press.

CONLY, C. H., P. KELLY, P. MAHANNA, and L. WARNER (1993). *Street Gangs: Current Knowledge and Strategies*. Washington, DC: U.S. Department of Justice, National Institute of Justice.

CURRY, G. D., R. A. BALL, and R. J. FOX (1994). *Gang Crime and Law Enforcement Recordkeeping*. Research in Brief. Washington, DC: National Institute of Justice.

CURRY, G. D., R. A. BALL, and S. H. DECKER (1996). *Estimating the National Scope of Gang Crime From Law Enforcement Data*. Research in Brief. Washington, DC: National Institute of Justice.

DECKER, S. H., and G. D. CURRY (2000). Responding to gangs: Comparing gang member, police, and task force perspectives. *Journal of Criminal Justice*, 28:129–137.

DONOVAN, J. (1988). An introduction to street gangs. Paper prepared for Senator J. Garamendi's office, Sacramento, CA.

ESBENSEN, F., and D. W. OSGOOD (1997). *National Evaluation of G.R.E.A.T.* Research in Brief. Washington, DC: National Institute of Justice.

FAGAN, J. A. (1990). Treatment and reintegration of violent juvenile offenders: Experimental results. *Justice Quarterly*, 7, June, pp. 233–263.

FATTAH, D. (1994). Drugs and violence in gangs. In A. T. Sulton (ed.), *African-American Perspectives on Crime Causation, Criminal Justice Administration, and Crime Prevention*. Englewood, CO: Sulton Books, pp. 101–107.

FISHMAN, L. T. (1988). The vice queens: An ethnographic study of black female gang behavior. Paper presented at the annual meeting of the American Society of Criminology.

GOLDSTEIN, H. (1990). *Problem-Oriented Policing*. New York: McGraw-Hill.

GOLDSTEIN, A. P., and R. C. HUFF (eds.) (1993). *The Gang Intervention Handbook*. Champaign, IL: Research Press.

HAGEDORN, J. M. (1988). *People and Folks: Gangs, Crime and the Underclass in a Rustbelt Society*. Chicago: Lake View Press.

HIGGINS, S. (1993). Interjurisdictional coordination of major gang investigations. *Police Chief*, June, pp. 46–47.

HOROWITZ, R. (1987). Community tolerance of gang violence. *Social Problems*, 34, December, pp. 437–450.

HUFF, C. R. (1990). Denial, overreaction, and misidentification: A postscript on public policy. In C. R. Huff (ed.), *Gangs in America*. Thousand Oaks, CA: Sage Publications, pp. 310–317.

HUFF, C. R. (1989). Youth gangs and public policy. *Crime and Delinquency*, 35:525–537.

HUFF, C. R, (1998). *Comparing the Criminal Behavior of Youth Gangs and At-Risk Youths*. Research in Brief. Washington, DC: National Institute of Justice.

HYMAN, I. A. (1984). Testimony before the subcommittee on elementary, secondary, and vocational education of the committee on education and labor, U.S. House of Representatives.

JACOBS, J. B. (1983). *New Perspectives on Prisons and Imprisonment*. Ithaca, NY: Cornell University Press.

KENNEDY, D. M., A. M. PIEHL, and A. A. BRAGA (1996). Youth violence in Boston: Gun markets, serious youth offenders, and a use-reduction strategy. *Law and Contemporary Problems*, 59:147–196.

KLEIN, M. W. (1995). *The American Street Gang: Its Nature, Prevalence, and Control*. New York: Oxford University Press.

KLEIN, M. W., and C. L. MAXSON (1989). Street gang violence. In N. Weiner and M. Wolfgang (eds.), *Violent Crime, Violent Criminals*. Thousand Oaks, CA: Sage Publications.

MILLER, W. (1990). Why has the U.S. failed to solve its youth gang problem? In C. Ronald Huff (ed.), *Gangs in America*. Newbury Park, CA: Sage Publications, pp. 263–287.

MILLER, W. B. (1992). *Crimes by Youth Gangs and Groups in the United States*. Washington, DC: U.S. Department of Justice, Office of Juvenile Justice and Delinquency Prevention.

MOORE, J. P., and I. L. COOK (1999). *Highlights of the 1998 National Youth Gang Survey*. Washington, DC: U.S. Department of Justice, Office of Juvenile Justice and Delinquency Prevention.

MOORE, J. W., C. GARCIA, L. CERDA, and F. VALENCIA (1978). *Homeboys: Gangs, Drugs, and Prison in the Barrios of Los Angeles*. Philadelphia: Temple University Press.

NATIONAL ADVISORY COMMISSION ON CRIMINAL JUSTICE STANDARDS AND GOALS (1976). *Report of the Task Force on Juvenile Justice and Delinquency Prevention*. Washington, DC: U.S. Government Printing Office.

NATIONAL DRUG INTELLIGENCE CENTER (1996). *National Street Gang Survey Report*. Johnstown, PA: U.S. Department of Justice, National Drug Intelligence Center.

PALUMBO, D. J., and J. L. FERGUSON (1995). Evaluating gang resistance education and training (GREAT). *Evaluation Review*, 19, December, pp. 597–619.

PEAK, K. J. (2000). *Policing America: Methods, Issues, Challenges*, 3d ed. Upper Saddle River, NJ: Prentice Hall.

PEAK, K. J., and R. W. GLENSOR (1996). *Community Policing and Problem Solving: Strategies and Practices*. Upper Saddle River, NJ: Prentice Hall.

PETERSEN, R. D. (2000). Definitions of a gang and impacts on public policy. *Journal of Criminal Justice*, 28(2):139–149.

PITCHESS, P. J. (1979). Street Gangs. Los Angeles: Human Services Bureau, Los Angeles Sheriff's Office.

POSTMAN, N. (1991). Quoted in D. Osborne and T. Gaebler, *Reinventing Government: How the Entrepreneurial Spirit Is Transforming the Public Sector*. Reading, MA: Addison-Wesley.

SAMPSON, R., and M. SCOTT (2000). *Tackling Crime and Other Public-Safety Problems: Case Studies in Problem-Solving*. Washington, DC: U.S. Department of Justice, Office of Community Oriented Policing Services.

SANDERS, W. B. (1994). *Gangbangs and Drivebys: Grounded Culture and Juvenile Gang Violence*. New York: Aldine de Gruyter.

SHERMAN, L.W., J. W. SHAW, and D. P. ROGAN (1995). *The Kansas City Gun Experiment*. Research in Brief. Washington, DC: National Institute of Justice.

SPERGAL, I. A. (1990). Youth gangs: Continuity and change. In M. Tonry and N. Morris (eds.), *Crime and Justice: A Review of Research*, Vol. 12. Chicago: University of Chicago Press, pp. 171–275.

TAYLOR, C. S. (1990). Gang imperialism. In C. R. Huff (ed.), *Gangs in America*. Thousand Oaks, CA: Sage Publications, pp. 103–115.

THRASHER, F. (1927). *The Gang*. Chicago: University of Chicago Press.

TOY, C. (1992). A short history of Asian gangs in San Francisco. *Justice Quarterly*, 9, December, pp. 647–665.

TROJANOWICZ, R., and B. BUCQUEROUX (1990). *Community Policing: A Contemporary Perspective*. Cincinnati, OH: Anderson Publishing.

VENTAKESH, S. (1999). The financial activity of a modern American street gang. In *Looking at Crime from the Street Level: Plenary Papers of the 1999 Conference on Criminal Justice Research and Evaluation—Enhancing Policing and Practice Through Research,* Vol. 1. Washington, DC: U.S. Department of Justice, Office of Justice Programs, National Institute of Justice.

WEISEL, D. L., and E. PAINTER (1997). *The Police Response to Gangs: Case Studies of Five Cities*. Washington, DC: Police Executive Research Forum.

WITKIN, G. (1991). Kids who kill. *Newsweek*, April 8, pp. 26–32.

YABLONSKY, L. (1962). *The Violent Gang*. Baltimore: Penguin Books.

chapter 5

Looking for a New Approach to an Old Problem

The Future of Obscenity and Pornography

Jay S. Albanese, Ph.D.

ABSTRACT

Explicit songs, movies, cable television, talk radio, and computer services are the latest manifestations of public concern over the proper role of sex and violence in the media and in American life in general. Two national commissions have investigated these issues during the last 30 years and have drawn widely different conclusions. A comparison of the method and conclusions of these investigations is used as a backdrop to propose alternative futures in defining and regulating obscenity and pornography. Recent court interpretation of legislative efforts to control pornography is also examined.

Five major issues are reviewed: (1) trends in the pornography industry, (2) the effects of pornography on behavior, (3) appropriate action to be taken by private citizens, (4) legislative and law enforcement remedies, and (5) the role of computers and the Internet in the distribution of pornography. A closer examination of the consumers of pornography, and a change in the focus of obscenity from sex to violence, are assessed.

NEW CONCERN FOR AN OLD PROBLEM

- Convicted serial killer Ted Bundy admitted prior to his execution that he was "addicted" to pornography.

- Following public complaints, the television, movie, and recording industries are forced to provide warnings on their products in order to warn consumers of their sexual and violent content.

- Growing numbers of library books are being challenged each year for censorship on grounds of offensive descriptions of sex and violence.

- Complaints increase over the use of young teenagers and children in advertisements depicting suggestive poses.

- Bumper stickers, radio announcers, and late-night television proliferate in their references to sexual conduct.

These incidents have combined to create a record level of concern regarding obscenity and pornography in American life. One indication of this concern is that the last 30 years have produced two national investigations into obscenity and pornography in the United States. These investigations were paralleled by similar governmental investigations in Canada and England. Interest and concern about the effects of obscene and pornographic material are international in scope, and an examination of the two U.S. commissions, reporting 16 years apart, provide some insight into the changing views of pornography in American life and what the future holds.

All the pornography investigation commissions were formed in response to what was seen as a dramatic increase in the availability of explicit materials. In the 1960s and 1970s, it took the form of books, magazines, television, radio, and films. From the 1980s to the present, concern has focused on new forms of distribution that did not exist earlier: cable television, video rental and purchases, dial-a-porn, and computer networks. In every instance, the commissions attempted to address the proper balance between free speech, individual privacy, and the public interest.

The mandates of the two U.S. commissions were remarkably similar. The U.S. Commission on Obscenity and Pornography, reporting in 1970, was established to accomplish four specific tasks. It was to "analyze laws pertaining to the control of obscenity and pornography," to "explore the nature and volume of traffic in such materials," to study its "relationship to crime and other antisocial behavior," and to recommend "appropriate action" to "regulate effectively the flow of such traffic" (1970:1). This four-pronged approach was mirrored by the mandate of the U.S. Attorney General's Commission on Pornography, reporting in 1986. That commission was directed to "study the dimensions of the problem of pornography," to examine "the means of production and distribution," to review "available empirical and scientific evidence on the relationship between exposure to pornographic materials and antisocial behavior," and to review "national, state, and local efforts…to curb pornography" (1986:1957).

METHODS AND SOURCES

The two commissions differed greatly in both the time and money they were allocated to accomplish similar goals. The 1970 commission was allocated a budget of $2 million and two years to conduct its investigation. The 1986 Meese commission was granted $500,000 and 12 months to complete its work. These large differences in both time and resources had an effect on both the quality of the investigations of the commissions and on the nature of their findings.

The 1970 commission elected not to hold public hearings until late in its investigation because it felt that "public hearings would not be a likely source of accurate data or a wise expenditure of its limited resources" (1970:3). Instead, it chose to conduct basic research due to "the insufficiency of existing factual evidence as a basis for recommendations" (p. 2). The 1986 Meese commission did "especially regret the inability to commission independent research," so it relied on public hearings and executive sessions among commission members to reach its conclusions (p. 218). As critics of the "public hearing" approach to investigations have recognized, new information is rarely generated in such a forum: "This tactic [public hearings] was inexpensive, dramatic and promised a few good photo opportunities. Unfortunately, hearings were totally ineffective for fact-finding purposes. As the 1970 panel noted, views of most witnesses were predictable" (Nobile and Nadler, 1986:27). The use of public hearings as an investigative tool is less useful than empirical research, especially when simple baseline data are lacking.

The Meese commission was criticized as well for its selection of commissioners. Unlike the 1970 commission, which included a number of behavioral scientists, the Meese commission was made up of 11 members, six of whom had "well-established public records" against sexually oriented material. "The Meese Commission lacked the financial resources of its predecessor, but since its conclusions were preordained, it didn't really need them," as one observer put it (Hertzberg, 1986:21).

WHAT IS PORNOGRAPHY?

Every investigation or discussion of pornography necessarily gets bogged down in defining its target. The 1970 commission correctly noted that the term *pornography* has no legal significance. *Obscenity* is material in violation of existing constitutional standards as established by the U.S. Supreme Court in 1973. This material must "taken as a whole, appeal to the prurient interest in sex," portray sexual conduct in a "patently offensive way," and lack "serious literary, artistic, political or scientific value" (*Miller* v. *California*, 1973). The 1970 commission used *erotica, explicit sexual material*, and *sexually oriented material* interchangeably in its report in referring to its subject matter.

The Meese commission, on the other hand, employed no key term, explaining that either *pornography* or *erotica* is often used to connote any "depiction of sex" or "sexually explicit materials" to which the user objects or disapproves (1986:227–231). As a result, the 1986 Meese commission "tried to minimize" the use of either term, despite the commission's title.

It is clear that both commissions, despite vagaries in definition, were referring to explicit depictions of sex in their investigations. Some authors have found the definition of pornography offered by the Williams Committee in England to be the most understandable. It stated that "pornographic representation is one that combines two features: it has a certain function or intention, to arouse its audience sexually, and also a certain content, explicit representations of sexual material" (Committee on Obscenity, 1979:104; Hawkins and Zimring, 1988:27).

THE PORNOGRAPHY INDUSTRY

Both commissions addressed the size, scope, and operation of the pornography industry. The 1970 commission conducted basic survey research and found that there were approximately 14,000 movie theaters in the United States, attended by 20 million people each week. General release films were found to be shown in 90% of all theaters, and sexual "exploitation" films were found to be shown in about 6% of all theaters. The commission noted the rating system implemented by the motion picture industry in 1968 (i.e., G, PG, R, and X) as a step toward industry self-regulation of sexual content, violence, and suitability for children. The PG-13 and NC-17 ratings were added years later in an effort to make further gradations in scaling objectionable contents.

An attempt was made to discover the number of sex films made each year, but it was found to be "primarily a localized business with no national distribution" that was "extremely disorganized" (p. 22). The 1970 commission found that there was also little money to be made in the stag film industry in the way of large profits: "There are no great fortunes to be made in stag film production. It is estimated that there are fewer than half a dozen individuals who net more than $10,000 per year in the business" (p. 22). The 1970 commission also detailed the size and scope of the "adult" book, magazine, bookstore markets. It also found that 85% of men and 70% of women have some exposure to pornographic materials during their lives. It was found that 75% of adult males have some exposure to explicit sexual materials before age 21, although "the experience seems to be more a social than a sexual one" (p. 25). It was found that American patterns of exposure were similar to those in Denmark and Sweden, where pornography has been decriminalized.

The 1986 commission did not conduct similar research into the nature and volume of traffic in explicit sexual materials. Therefore, it was unable to assess trends in exposure and availability of this material during the intervening 16 years in any objective way. The commission drew conclusions anyway, something that subjected it to criticism. The commission found that the "men's" magazines, sometimes referred to as "male sophisticate" magazines, were objectionable. The commission declared that "*all* of the magazines in this category contain at least some material that we would consider 'degrading'" (p. 281). Concern was also expressed about the sexual content of material on cable television.

The 1986 commission concluded that approximately 80% of all U.S.-produced pornographic films and videotapes are made "in and around Los Angeles, California" (p. 285). The source of this information is not noted. Similarly, the commission found that many video retailers sell or rent pornographic films: "Based on the evidence provided to us, it appears as if perhaps as many as half of all the general retailers in the country include within their offerings at least some material that, by itself, would commonly be conceded to be pornographic" (p. 288). The commission also noted that the adult movie theater "is becoming an increasing rarity" (p. 287) and that the growing popularity of videotape also "has hurt the pornographic magazine industry" (p. 289). Unfortunately, no figures were generated to indicate the precise nature of these apparent changes in the pornography industry. In a highly publicized case, Larry

Flynt, publisher of *Hustler* magazine, pleaded no contest to charges in Cincinnati that he violated city laws in selling X-rated videos there. In 2000, however, he opened a new store to sell nude magazines and "sex toys," but no X-rated videos (Cohen, 2000). This case illustrates that the limits of the law in defining obscenity and distributing sexually oriented material are still being tested.

The other aspect of the pornography industry addressed by both commissions was the influence of organized crime in the manufacture and distribution of pornographic materials. The 1970 commission found that "there is insufficient data to warrant any conclusion" about the involvement of organized crime in pornography (p. 23). The commission cited disagreement among both law enforcement officials and researchers in this regard (p. 142).

The Meese commission came to a different conclusion. It concluded: "[W]e believe that such a connection does exist" (p. 291). This conclusion was reached despite the fact that the director of the FBI testified that "about three quarters of those (59 FBI field) offices indicated that they have no verifiable information that organized crime was involved either directly or through extortion in the manufacture of pornography" (p. 292). The commission concluded that there exists an organized crime–pornography connection, therefore, "in the face of a negative conclusion by the 1970 commission, and in the face of the evidence provided by the FBI" (p. 292). Anecdotal evidence was cited to support this position (dealing with alleged organized criminals operating in pornography in certain cities). The commission's equivocal conclusion reflects the quality of evidence it had on this issue: "Although we cannot say that every piece of evidence we have received to this effect is true, the possibility that none of this cumulative evidence is true is so remote that we do not take it seriously" (p. 296). This lack of clarity in the commission's conclusion is matched only by its poor logic in arguing that the lack of reliable evidence reinforces its belief. The first important difference between the two commissions, therefore, is their conclusions about the link between pornography and organized crime.

THE PORNOGRAPHY–HARM LINK

Perhaps the most significant question to be addressed by these commissions involved the possible effects of pornography in causing antisocial or criminal behavior. The 1970 commission conducted a great deal of research on the subject due to a lack of existing data. The 1986 commission conducted no new research of its own but relied instead on the results of prior investigations.

In a national opinion poll, the 1970 commission found that there was no nationwide consensus among the public about the effects of pornography. Empirical studies found that both genders were equally aroused by explicit sexual material and that exposure appeared to have no effect on frequency of masturbation or intercourse. Similarly, four separate research studies indicated "little or no effect" of erotic stimuli on attitudes "regarding either sexuality or sexual morality" (p. 29). Finally, it was found that, similar to adults, both delinquents and nondelinquents have similar experiences with explicit sexual material, and that there is no evidence of a pornography–crime link (p. 286): "In sum, empirical research designed to clarify the question has found no evidence to date that exposure to explicit sexual materials plays a significant role in the causation of delinquent or criminal behavior among youth or adults. The Commission cannot conclude that exposure to erotic materials is a factor in the causation of sex crime or sex delinquency" (1970:32). This conclusion was echoed by subsequent national commissions in both Canada (Special Committee on Pornography and Prostitution in Canada, 1985) and England (Committee on Obscenity and Film Censorship, 1979) (for a summary of this research, see Malamuth and Donnerstein, 1984).

The 1986 Attorney General's commission came to a different conclusion on the subject of harm. It admitted that the testimony it received from various offenders and victims of pornography may be suspect, and the report offered an extended discussion of the nature of harm, the standards of proof involved, and the problems of valid and reliable evidence of harm (pp. 302–320). Nevertheless, the commission separated sexually oriented materials into four categories that it admitted might be arbitrary. The commission noted that "some items within a category might produce no effects, or even the opposite effects from those identified" (p. 321). These four categories were: sexually violent material, nonviolent but degrading material, nonviolent and nondegrading material, and nudity. The commission drew different conclusions for each of these categories.

With regard to sexually violent material the commission recognized that there was no consensus about its effects on behavior in the research literature. This led the commission to make a number of significant assumptions: "Finding a link between aggressive behavior towards women and sexual violence, whether lawful or unlawful, requires assumptions not found exclusively in the experimental evidence. We see no reason, however, not to make these assumptions" (p. 325). By ignoring a great deal of the empirical evidence, the commission took an ideological approach to the question of harm and concluded that "substantial exposure to sexually violent materials as described here bears a causal relationship to antisocial acts of sexual violence and, for some subgroups, possibly to unlawful acts of sexual violence" (p. 326). The commission found a deleterious effect of this form of pornography on attitudes as well.

The commission recognized that the empirical evidence is divided concerning the effect of nonviolent but degrading material. Nevertheless, the commission made "substantially similar" conclusions as those it made for the effects of sexually violent material, "although we make them with somewhat less confidence and our making of them requires more in the way of assumption than was the case with respect to violent material" (p. 332).

The conclusions of the 1986 commission regarding harm were actually based on supposition. "The absence of evidence should by no means be taken to deny the existence of a causal link" (p. 332). In this category, therefore, it was concluded that "substantial exposure to materials of this type bears some causal relationship to the level of sexual violence, sexual coercion, or unwanted sexual aggression in the population so exposed" (pp. 333–334). It was also found that this type of material results in attitudinal changes regarding personal responsibility for actions and attitudes toward victims of sexual aggression. These conclusions have been challenged by several of the researchers relied upon by the commission. They claim that the commissioners made "serious errors" of "omission" and "commission" in their characterization of the research findings regarding the pornography–harm link (Donnerstein et al., 1987).

On the other hand, the Meese commission found that nonviolent and nondegrading sexual material appear to have no effect on antisocial behavior. It was concluded that there "seems to be no evidence in the social science data of a causal relationship with sexual violence, sexual aggression, or sex discrimination" (p. 378). Nonetheless, it was found that "the material in this category in some settings and when used for some purposes can be harmful" (p. 346).

With regard to nudity, the 1986 commission showed little interest. It found that "by and large we do not find nudity that does not fit within any of the previous categories to be much cause for concern" (p. 349). The differences in the commissions' conclusions about the harm caused by pornography is perhaps the most significant difference between them.

SEX EDUCATION AND CITIZEN ACTION

The third area of investigation for both commissions was positive approaches to be taken by citizens to effect changes in their local communities. The commissions addressed sex education and citizen action groups. The 1970 commission found that parents are frequently "embarrassed or uninformed" about sex, only about half of all medical schools had even elective courses in human sexuality, and that opportunities for training professional workers "are still not widely available" (p. 34). The commission also cited a study which found that girls who had a particular sex education course "were less likely to have illegitimate children" than a comparison group. These facts led the commission to recommend sex education in the schools "because the existing alternatives for communicating about sex with young people are felt by so many people, both adults and young people themselves, to be inadequate or undesirable" (pp. 36, 317).

The 1986 Meese commission also believed that "education is the real solution to the problem of pornography," but it did not recommend sex education in the schools (p. 426). Rather, it limited its attention to the desirability of warnings to children about sexual abuse and exploitation from a variety of sources.

The 1970 commission noted that an evaluation of two organized citizen action groups found that "their practical effect on the availability of erotica in their respective communities had been quite minimal" (pp. 38, 343). On the other hand, the 1986 commission recommended "protesting near the premises of establishments offering material that some citizens may find dangerous or offensive or immoral" (pp. 421–422). Boycotts of an establishment were also seen as desirable.[1]

The 1970 commission also identified industry self-regulation as an important positive approach to sexual material. It recognized the comic book industry, radio, television, and motion picture industries for their self-imposed standards. Greater than

90% compliance with these voluntary standards was seen as an indication of their success within these industries. The 1986 commission did not similarly emphasize the role of industry self-regulation as a positive approach to pornography.

LAW AND LAW ENFORCEMENT

The fourth area addressed by both commissions was the need for laws and changes in law enforcement. Interestingly, both commissions specifically recognized the inability of law to control behavior effectively. The 1970 commission found that legal regulation "is not the only, or necessarily the most effective, method of dealing with these materials" (p. 32). Similarly, the Meese commission believed that "to rely entirely or excessively on law is simply a mistake" (p. 428).

The 1970 commission took its statement to heart and noted that while nearly every state had laws that prohibit the distribution of obscene materials, no federal or state statute defined obscenity at that time. The commission did not "believe that a sufficient social justification exists for the retention or enactment of broad legislation prohibiting the consensual distribution of sexual materials to adults" (pp. 47–48). Therefore, it did not offer a definition of obscenity. In fact, the 1970 Commission made only four legislative recommendations.

First, it recommended that "federal, state, and local legislation prohibiting the sale, exhibition, or distribution of sexual materials to consenting adults be repealed" (p. 57). This was based on the commission's finding that exposure to explicit sexual material does not play a "significant role" in causing social or individual harm. Public opinion also supported the availability of sexually explicit materials for consenting adults. Furthermore, investigations in other countries "all concluded that consensual exposure of adults to explicit sexual materials causes no demonstrable damaging individual or social effects" (p. 50).

Second, the 1970 commission recommended prohibition of the "commercial distribution or display for sale of certain sexual materials to young persons" (p. 62). Although there was no evidence that demonstrated harm to young people, the commission felt that public opinion, as well as insufficient research on the particular effects on children, make prohibition desirable. The commission noted problems of definition but recommended that the prohibited materials be limited to pictures, rather than books, and that the prohibited pictures must depict more than mere nudity.

Third, the commission recommended legislation prohibiting public displays of sexually explicit pictorial materials in order to protect children and nonconsenting adults from exposure they find offensive. Fourth, the commission recommended the establishment of authority for prosecutors to obtain declaratory judgments to determine if material was obscene. This would permit prosecutors to move civilly, rather than criminally, against suspected violators. It would also provide fair notice to the alleged offenders in such actions.

It can be seen that the 1970 commission made only four legislative recommendations, one of which was to abolish the law as it applies to sexually explicit materials available to consenting adults. The commission also placed much emphasis on non-legislative alternatives, noted earlier, such as sex education. As the commission declared, "much of the 'problem' regarding materials which depict sexual activity stem from the inability or reluctance of people in our society to be open and direct in dealing with sexual matters" (p. 53).

The 1986 Meese commission took a different approach in its recommendations for change. It made a total of 86 recommendations, most of which involved calls for new laws and better enforcement of existing laws. The commission's conclusion regarding the existence of a pornography–harm link caused it to reject the adult deregulation approach of the 1970 commission. It also found problems with the city "zoning" approach aimed at grouping or dispersing stores or theaters that offer material containing explicit depictions of sex. The courts have found that "zoning" laws, when used as a guise for "prohibition," are unconstitutional, and "grandfather" clauses in most ordinances do not affect existing establishments, but only future businesses. Similarly, the civil rights approach first attempted in Minneapolis (arguing that pornography violates the civil rights of those portrayed) has been found unconstitutional thus far, because the definitions of obscene material have gone beyond the legal standard set by the U.S. Supreme Court in 1973 (see O'Neill, 1985:177–187). Similar to the 1970 commission, the Meese commission found that there should be preliminary judicial review of material *before* a complaint is filed. This is necessary to protect publishers and distributors from perpetual civil suits.

Of the Meese commission's 86 recommendations, many dealt with the use of forfeiture laws in the prosecution of pornographers to allow for seizure of assets as well as criminal penalties. Fifty of the 86 recommendations dealt with child pornography in some manner. This is interesting inasmuch as the commission made no systematic survey of the extent of the problem. In fact, it concluded that "there now appears to be comparatively little domestic commercial production of child pornography…" and that most is produced as a "cottage industry" rather than through mass production (pp. 409–410).

The emphasis of most of the commission's recommendations was on *greater priority* to obscenity investigations. It was found that obscenity investigations among law enforcement agencies are not common and that prosecutors rarely take these cases to court. Therefore, many recommendations included suggestions for better training, coordination, and resources for investigations in suspected obscenity cases.

The commission made a few recommendations for new legislation as well, although the suggestions broke little new ground. Many involved "tightening" of perceived loopholes in existing law. In addition to greater forfeiture provisions, the commission recommended that *possession* of child pornography be a felony and that photo labs should be required to report suspected child pornography. Clearly, the 1986 commission took a regulatory law enforcement approach to the issue of pornography, whereas the 1970 commission took a deregulation approach, at least with regard to adults.

EXPLAINING THE DIFFERENCES IN THE OBSCENITY COMMISSIONS

Table 1 summaries the major findings of the two national commission investigations of obscenity and pornography during the last 30 years. Seven significant issues that the commissions addressed continue to lie at the heart of the pornography debate today. As Table 1 indicates, the only significant issue on which the two commissions agreed was the prohibition of public displays of explicit material in order to protect children and nonconsenting adults.

The large differences in the findings and recommendations of the two commissions are not difficult to explain. The 1970 commission took an empirical approach to the issue. This was understandable given the presence of three sociologists and two psychiatrists on the commission. Absent a finding of a pornography–harm link in its research, legislation to regulate its distribution to consenting adults appeared unnecessary. The 1986 commission's approach was ideological. Recognizing that the empirical research was imperfect and inconclusive, the commission chose the route to which the commissioners were predisposed. That is, they *believed* that there was some kind of link between pornography and harm, so that is what they concluded (see Albanese, 1987). This is evident in that six of the 1986 commission members

TABLE 1 Comparisons of Conclusions of Two National Commission Investigations	
1970 U.S. Commission on Obscenity and Pornography	1986 U.S. Attorney General's Commission on Pornography
No demonstrated link between exposure to pornography and sexual activity or crimes.	A pornography–harm link exists, although there may not yet be conclusive evidence.
Sex education in school for children and professional workers.	Warn children about sexual abuse and exploitation rather than sex education in school.
Practical effect of citizen protests is minimal.	Protests and boycotts of offending establishments useful.
Self-regulation of film, television, and book industry is largely effective.	Greater priority should be given to civil and criminal enforcement.
Sale of sexual materials to consenting adults should be permitted.	Greater emphasis on prosecution of producers and distributors of pornographic materials.
Prohibit distribution or display of sexual materials depicting more than mere nudity to juveniles.	Fifty recommendations regarding child pornography, including criminalizing its possession.
Public displays of explicit pictorial materials should be prohibited.	Public displays of explicit pictorial materials should be prohibited.

had previously established views on the subject, as mentioned earlier. Their efforts to justify their findings based on available research results were weak, and some of the research the commission characterized as supportive of its positions was later challenged by the researchers themselves as misinterpretations of their work (see Donnerstein et al., 1987).

It is ironic, but none of the significant recommendations of either commission has been enacted into law. The same fate met the Williams Committee report in England (Simpson, 1983:57). This is probably due to the fact that there did not exist wide public support in 1970 for decriminalization of sexually explicit materials for consenting adults. Similarly, in 1986, in a more favorable political climate, there did not exist sufficient public interest in the prosecution approach endorsed by the Meese commission. As the Meese commission recognized, there were only 71 individuals convicted for violation of federal obscenity laws nationwide from 1978 to 1986 (1986:367). There were no federal prosecutions from 1984 to 1985 in Manhattan or Los Angeles, the two largest reputed centers of pornography manufacturing and distribution in the United States (1986:504). Finally, from 1977 to 1984, only one person was convicted for production of child pornography under the Protection of Children from Sexual Exploitation Act of 1977 (p. 604). This low level of enforcement actions and/or incidence of obscenity cases continues to the present.

Arrests and convictions obtained by the U.S. Postal Service for mailing pornographic/obscene materials have fluctuated but dropped overall in the period 1987–1999 (see Table 2). As the table indicates, arrests have dropped 33% and convictions by 24% over a period of 13 years. Therefore, there is either a declining priority given to these investigations, or else fewer instances of distribution of sexual materials are occurring by mail. Fear of the latter possibility of new methods of distribution via the Internet led to new federal legislation beginning in 1996.

TABLE 2   Trends in Arrests and Convictions for Pornogaphy and Obscene Materials Sent or Received by U.S. Mail

Year	Arrests	Convictions
1987	242	194
1990	241	235
1992	245	206
1994	145	150
1996	187	184
1999	163	147
13-year trend	−33%	−24%

Source: Data from U.S. Postal Service, Postal Inspection Service, *Annual Reports* (Washington, DC: U.S. Postal Inspection Service)

THE RISE OF THE INTERNET

The role of the Internet in distributing pornographic text and images led to passage by Congress of Title V of the Telecommunications Act of 1996. Titled the Communications Decency Act, Title V contains two provisions that prohibit "the knowing transmission of obscene or indecent messages to any person under 18 years of age," or sending or displaying "patently offensive messages in a manner available to a person under 18 years of age" (47 U.S.C.A. § 223). The intent of the law was to protect minors from pornographic images and messages on the Internet. The law was challenged in court immediately after it was passed.

In a 1997 ruling, the U.S. Supreme Court held that the terms *indecent transmission* and *patently offensive display* violate the First Amendment's protection of freedom of speech. The Court ruled that the terminology used in the Communications Decency Act was too vague, imprecise, and would "provoke uncertainty among speakers" regarding its applicability. The act was held to be unconstitutional (*Reno* v. *American Civil Liberties Union*, 1997; Johnson, 1999). This is the same argument the Court used in evaluating dial-a-porn operators who offer sexually suggestive telephone messages for a fee. The Court held there, as it did in the Internet case, that obscene messages are illegal, but "indecent" ones are not (*Sable Communications* v. *FCC*, 1989). Unlike radio and television, where one can be "taken by surprise by an indecent message," both dial-a-porn and the Internet "require the listener to take affirmative steps to receive the communication" (at 2836-7). As a result, both indecent and obscene messages are prohibited on television and radio broadcasts, but only obscene messages are prohibited on the Internet or in dial-a-porn (*FCC* v. *Pacifica Foundation*, 1978). The Court concluded that "it is true that we have repeatedly recognized the governmental interest in protecting children from harmful materials. But that interest does not justify an unnecessarily broad suppression of speech addressed to adults" (*Reno* v. *American Civil Liberties Union* at 2346). Quoting itself from an earlier case, the Court remarked, "the level of discourse reaching a mailbox simply cannot be limited to that which would be suitable for a sandbox" (*Bolger* v. *Drug Products Corp*, 1983).

Congress responded to this Supreme Court ruling in 2000 by passing another law, the Child Online Protection Act (47 U.S.C.A. § 231). The intent of the law was to prohibit transmission of objectionable material to minors via the Internet. The U.S. Court of Appeals granted a preliminary injunction on enforcement of this law because of constitutional questions regarding violation of the First Amendment's guarantee of free speech. Attempting to restrict the worldwide access of Internet users, knowing that current technology does not permit a Web publisher to restrict content based on the geographic location of the user, makes it impossible, according to the court, to judge whether material is "harmful to minors" according to "contemporary community standards" as the law mandates (*American Civil Liberties Union* v. *Reno*, 2000; Kim and Paddon, 1999; Miller, 1999). The Court admitted that existing technological limitations may make it impossible to constitutionally restrict harmful material on the Internet, but given rapid technological advances, "what may now be impossible to regulate constitutionally may, in the not-too-distant future, become feasible" (at 164).

In the future, Congress and the various state legislatures are free to write new laws that define objectionable speech and images that employ the accepted legal definition of obscenity set forth in *Miller* v. *California*, and many are doing so (Oder, 2000). It is likely that these legislative efforts will continue, as Internet access grows, abuses by the private sector come to light, and controversial court decisions exacerbate the issue. In 2000, for example, the Federal Trade Commission released a report which indicated that entertainment companies "routinely target children under 17 as the audience for movies, music, and games that their own rating system or labeling system say are inappropriate for children." Industry marketing plans for an R-rated film stated that the "goal was to find the elusive teen target audience and make sure everyone between the ages of 12–18 was exposed to the film." Similarly, of 118 electronic games with a "Mature" rating for violence, 70% were targeted to children under 17 years of age according to the industry's own advertising plans. Twenty-seven percent of music recordings with labels for "explicit content" specially identified teenagers as part of the target audience (Federal Trade Commission, 2000). At the same time, the U.S. Supreme Court held in the 2000 case *United States* v. *Playboy Entertainment Group* that free speech rights make it unconstitutional to prohibit sexually explicit cable television channels from airing their programs only in the late evening and that their signals need not be completely scrambled (allowing for "signal bleed"). The court held that other options exist to protect minors and unconsenting adults from such material, such as having the cable company fully block certain channels. Regulating the distribution and access to objectionable material in our electronic age poses the largest problem for the future.

This continuing concern about objectionable material must account for two issues that have received far too little attention to date. Without such consideration, laws will persist in following behind the latest technology that exploits the large existing consumer market for obscenity and pornography (see Cavazos and Morin, 1994; Hixson, 1996; Lane, 2000).

ISSUES FOR THE FUTURE

Where does this leave the citizen or policymaker who perceives an apparent rise in crime and violence in his or her community that appears to correspond with a rise in explicit sex and violence in books, television, movies, and the Internet? Two significant issues have been either omitted or addressed peripherally in every inquiry into obscenity and pornography: (1) moving from sex to violence in defining obscenity, and (2) identifying causes of the entrenched popularity of pornographic material. These two issues, perhaps more than any other, will chart the course for the future.

Obscenity: From Sex to Violence

Definitions and prosecutions for obscene materials always have been directed at depictions of sexual conduct. A case can be made, however, that there is nothing inherently obscene about *explicit* depictions of sexual conduct. In fact, explicit depictions of sex have long played a role in psychological counseling, physiological education, sex therapy, and art. The terms *patently offensive* and *prurient interest* invariably result in a subjective line drawing in attempting to distinguish gratuitous depictions of sex from those that have "literary, artistic, political, or scientific value." Simply stated, the *value* of sex is an elusive concept, difficult to determine in an objective way. When sexual conduct is carried out in a tasteless manner, there is little social interest involved. This makes it difficult to regulate or prohibit, due to its unclear impact on public health, safety, or welfare.

More objectionable than gratuitous sex are depictions of gratuitous *violence*. A significant social concern arises when sex is depicted in a way that involves *force* against an unwilling victim, against children, or even when unjustified *violence without sex* is depicted. Perhaps the future will witness a move from sex to violence in defining obscenity. Obscenity law might prohibit the depiction of gratuitous *violence* rather than sex alone. Depictions of violent assaultive behavior exhibited without legal justification could be held objectionable and punishable under law. The legal justifications for the use of force (e.g., self-defense, defense of others) are well defined in existing law, as are the definitions of assault. Such a new definition of obscenity might include photographs or broadcasts depicting assaultive behavior committed by persons without legal justification. The inclusion of sex in these depictions of violence could be a sufficient, but not necessary, element of obscenity. The only exception might be factual accounts of real events that have informational or educational value.

Unlike the inconclusive link between depictions of sex and sex offenses, there is a growing body of literature that reports on the effects of depictions of violence on aggressive behavior (National Institute of Mental Health, 1982; Donnerstein et al., 1987:108–136; Federal Trade Commission, 2000:Appendix A). An unusual joint statement to Congress in 2000 by the American Academy of Pediatrics, American Psychological Association, American Medical Association, and American Academy of Child and Adolescent Psychiatry concluded that the average American child spends as much as 28 hours per week watching television and an average of one hour per day playing video games or surfing the Internet. The joint statement declared: "The conclusion of the public health community, based on over 30 years of research, is that viewing entertainment violence can lead to increases in aggressive attitudes, values and behavior, particularly in children" (2000:2). Therefore, it might be argued that descriptions of wanton violence should be declared obscene due to their possible effects on behavior. It could also be claimed that violence without justification is something our society sees as more objectionable than sex without social "value."

Before a proposal like this could be considered, changing the focus of obscenity from sex to violence, better answers to at least two important questions are needed:

- How does the effect of depictions of violence on aggressive behavior compare with other possible influences on aggressive attitudes and behavior (such as family and peer groups)?
- If gratuitous violence was determined to be obscene, what deleterious impact would this have on the creative arts, where books, films, and songs portray fictional violence without legal justification?

Why Is Pornography So Popular?

The 1970 commission conducted studies of the consumers of pornography and found that the vast majority of pornography is directed at the male heterosexual audience. Studies conducted by the commission in a number of different cities found that men also account for 90% of the consumers of sexually explicit materials (1970:10ff.; 1971–1972, 4:16ff.).

Other studies carried out for the commission found that "symbolic materials have a noticeably less arousing and erotic effect on women than they do on men." It was found that in both the United States and Sweden (where depictions of sex are more widely available) there is greater "acceptance of pornography" by men than women and that most pornography is produced by men rather than by women (1971–1972, 9:220; Kinsey et al., 1953). The "traditionally more conservative and restrictive attitudes that women have about virtually all sexual matters" reported by the 1970 commission might be changing, however. A Gallup Poll reported by the Meese commission found that the proportion of young women (18 to 24 years old) who had rented an X-rated videocassette was two-thirds of the male figure (U.S. Attorney General, 1986:920). This apparent trend was ignored by the Meese commission, as was the issue of consumers of pornography in its entirety.

If the availability of sexually explicit materials is identified as a social problem in terms of explicit radio, television, books, films, computer services, and dial-a-porn, it is essential that a better understanding emerge of why those interested in seeing and hearing it are so resilient (see Kipnis, 1996). The questions for which better answers are needed are at least two:

- Why are consumers of pornography predominately male, and are females increasingly consumers of sexually explicit materials?

- Does sex education promote healthier (i.e., less prurient) attitudes toward sex, which, in turn, reduces interest in pornography?

These questions underlie the current debate about the effects of pornography on attitudes toward sex and toward women (Kendrick, 1987; Assiter, 1989; Downs, 1989; Maschke, 1997). The answer to these questions through research and experimentation will make future decisions about obscenity and pornography less a matter of taste and more a matter of fact.

ENDNOTE

1. It should be noted that early in 1986 the executive director of the Meese commission, Alan Sears, notified several corporations that they had been identified as pornography distributors and that unless they proved otherwise within 30 days, they would be described in this way in the commission's final report. This resulted in several chainstores dropping such magazines as *Playboy* and *Penthouse*. Following a suit by Playboy, Penthouse, and the American Booksellers Association, a federal court ordered the commission to retract its letter, six days before it issued its final report.

REFERENCES

ALBANESE, J. S. (1987). Review essay: The accusers, the accused, and the victims in the debate over pornography. *American Journal of Criminal Justice*, 11(1).

AMERICAN ACADEMY OF PEDIATRICS, AMERICAN PSYCHOLOGICAL ASSOCIATION, AMERICAN MEDICAL ASSOCIATION, and AMERICAN ACADEMY OF CHILD AND ADOLESCENT PSYCHIATRY (2000). *Joint Statement on the Impact of Entertainment Violence on Children*. Washington, DC: Congressional Public Health Summit. www.aap.org/advocacy/releases/jstmtevc.htm.

ASSITER, A. (1989). *Pornography, Feminism, and the Individual*. Winchester, MA: Pluto Press.

CAVAZOS, E. A., and G. MORIN, G. (1994). *Cyberspace and the Law*. Cambridge, MA: MIT Press.

Child Online Protection Act (2000). 47 U.S.C.A. § 231.

COHEN, W. (2000). The Flynts' latest hustle in Cincinnati. *U.S. News & World Report*, May 1, p. 26.

COMMITTEE ON OBSCENITY AND FILM CENSORSHIP (1979). *Report*. London: Her Majesty's Stationery Office.

Communications Decency Act (1996). 47 U.S.C.A. § 223.

DONNERSTEIN, E. I., D. G. LINZ, and S. PENROD (1987). *The Question of Pornography*. New York: Free Press.

DOWNS, D. A. (1989). *The New Politics of Pornography*. Chicago: University of Chicago Press.

FEDERAL TRADE COMMISSION (2000). *Marketing Violent Entertainment to Children: A Review of Self-Regulation and Industry Practices in the Motion Picture, Music Recording and Electronic Game Industries*. Washington, DC: FTC.

HAWKINS, G., and F. E. ZIMRING (1988). *Pornography in a Free Society*. Cambridge: Cambridge University Press.

HERTZBERG, H. (1986). Big boobs. *New Republic*, July 14 and 21, pp. 21–24.

HIXSON, R. F. (1996). *Pornography and the Justices*. Carbondale, IL: Southern Illinois University Press.

JOHNSON, L. (1999). The first amendment balance of child's morality and adult's naughty Net play. *Rutgers Computer and Technology Law Journal*, 25:157.

KENDRICK, W. (1987). *The Secret Museum: Pornography in Modern Culture*. New York: Viking.

KIM, G. H., and A. R. PADDON (1999). Cybercommunity versus geographical community standing on online pornography. *Rutgers Computer and Technology Law Journal*, 26, Fall, p. 65.

KINSEY, A. C., W, B. POMEROY, C. E. MARTIN, and P. H. GEBHARD (1953). *Sexual Behavior in the Human Female*. Philadelphia: Saunders.

KIPNIS, L. (1996). *Bound and Gagged: Pornography and the Politics of Fantasy in America*. New York: Grove Press.

LANE, F. S. (2000). *Obscene Profits: The Entrepreneurs of Pornography in the Cyber Age*. London: Routledge.

MALAMUTH, N. M., and E. DONNERSTEIN (eds.) (1984). *Pornography and Sexual Aggression*. San Diego, CA: Academic Press.

MASCHKE, K. J. (ed.) (1997). *Pornography, Sex Work, and Hate Speech*. New York: Garland Publishing.

MILLER, H. L. (1999). Strike two: An analysis of the Child Online Protection Act's constitutional failures. *Federal Communications Law Journal*, 52, December, p. 155.

NATIONAL INSTITUTE OF MENTAL HEALTH (1982). *Television and Behavior: Ten Years of Scientific Progress and Implications for the Eighties*. Washington, DC: U.S. Government Printing Office.

NOBILE, P., and E. NADLER (1986). *United States of America v. Sex*. New York: Minotaur Press.

ODER, N. (2000). Indecency bills in UT, IN, WV, SC. *Library Journal*, 125, March 1, p. 12.

O'NEILL, T. (1985). *Censorship: Opposing Viewpoints*. St. Paul, MN: Greenhaven Press.

SIMPSON, A. W. B. (1983). *Pornography and Politics: A Look Back to the Williams Committee*. London: Waterloo.

SPECIAL COMMITTEE ON PORNOGRAPHY AND PROSTITUTION IN CANADA (1985). *Pornography and Prostitution in Canada*. Ottawa, Ontario, Canada: Minister of Supply and Services.

U.S. ATTORNEY GENERAL'S COMMISSION ON PORNOGRAPHY (1986). *Final Report*. Washington, DC: U.S. Government Printing Office.

U.S. COMMISSION ON OBSCENITY AND PORNOGRAPHY (1970). *Report*. Washington, DC: U.S. Government Printing Office.

U.S. COMMISSION ON OBSCENITY AND PORNOGRAPHY (1971–1972). *Technical Reports*, Vols. 1–9. Washington, DC: U.S. Government Printing Office.

CASES

American Civil Liberties Union v. *Reno*, 217 F.3d 163 (3rd Cir. 2000).

Bolger v. *Drug Products Corp.*, 103 S. Ct. 2875 (1983).

FCC v. *Pacifica Foundation*, 98 S. Ct. 3026 (1978).

Miller v. *California*, 93 S. Ct. 2607 (1973).

Reno v. *American Civil Liberties Union*, 117 S. Ct. 2329 (1997).

Sable Communications v. *FCC*, 109 S. Ct. 2829 (1989).

United States v. *Playboy Entertainment Group*, 120 S. Ct. 1878 (2000).

chapter 6

Murder and Mayhem in the Media

Public Perceptions (and Misperceptions) of Crime and Criminality

Charles B. Fields, Ph.D. and Robert A. Jerin, Ph.D.

ABSTRACT

There are two widely held assumptions concerning the effects of the media on the public's perception of crime and criminality. The first assumes that the mass media (especially television) are the primary sources of our understanding in these areas. The second assumption is that the media present erroneous and distorted information about crime. Are our views distorted by what we read in the newspaper and what we see on television? In this chapter we address the various ways in which crime and related issues are reported, their relationship to the actual crime problem, and influences on public perceptions by the media. Both quantitative and qualitative assessments are employed. Future trends in these areas are also addressed.

INTRODUCTION

Although the public's reaction to crime is influenced by various sources, the media seem to have the greatest effect on the perception of crime and criminality. In one of the first and most important studies examining crime and crime news coverage, Davis (1952) presented evidence that there is no relationship between official crime statistics and crime as reported in the print media. In fact, this study indicated that the public perception of crime depends almost entirely on what is read in the newspapers. However, this study was conducted before widespread television viewing.

There are several competing schools of thought in this area that provide interesting study. Ericson (1991) feels that most previous research on mass media and crime has been deficient because it focused too much on the effect of the mass media on our perceptions of crime and criminals. He addresses this "effects" tradition by critiquing several widely held assumptions, two of which deserve further attention.

The first approach assumes that the mass media (especially television) are the primary sources of our understanding in these areas. It should be noted that some research (Graber, 1979, 1980), however, points out that our knowledge comes from a variety of sources, the media being but one among several. Nevertheless, most research recognizes the growing influence of the media on public opinion and society's understanding of criminal justice issues (Page et al., 1987; Newman, 1990; Hans and Dee, 1991; Schlesinger et al., 1991).

The second assumption is that the media present erroneous and distorted information about crime. The distortion of the extent of crime and its coverage in the news media is well documented. Studies have focused on the extent of crime as reported in local print media (Cohen, 1975, Meyer, 1975, 1976; Antunes and Hurley, 1977; Graber, 1979; Humphries, 1981; Windhouser et al., 1990; Marsh, 1991), the amount on television news reports (Graber, 1979; Surette, 1992), and on comparisons with newspaper coverage of crime in other countries (Marsh, 1991). In assessing the literature in the area, Marsh (1991:67–68) found that "there is an overrepresentation of violent crimes...and the percentage of violent crimes does not match official crime statistics." Additionally, the "emphasis on relatively infrequent violent crimes may contribute to a heightened concern and fear." While Ericson (1991:220) admits that discrepancies can be found between the types and amount of crime reported in the media and official reports of crime, why should we expect the "cultural products of mass media to reflect the social reality of crime"?

These are all important areas of inquiry. Here we address the various ways in which crime and related issues are reported, their relationship to the actual crime problem, the influences on public perceptions by the media, and speculation as to what the future may have in store. Both quantitative and qualitative assessments are employed. We also summarize data that examine the amount and type of crime news as reported in the only national newspaper, *USA Today*, and attempt to discover if there are differences in the amount, type, or seriousness of the coverage of statewide news in the national daily compared to official crime statistics (Uniform Crime Reports), and if state population and crime rates are in any way a determining factor.

CRIME REPORTING AND PUBLIC PERCEPTIONS

Previous research examining the effect of the media's treatment of crime addresses several areas: the study of criminal justice themes in popular culture media (Newman, 1990), the use of public information programming (Sacco and Trotman, 1990), the use of advertising (Eder, 1990), the national print media (Jerin and Fields, 1994), television

(Schelsinger et al., 1991), and combinations of media sources (Sheley and Ashkins, 1981). These studies have all surmised that the true pictures of crime, criminals, and dangerousness are out of proportion to actual crime statistics.

The accuracy of media reports on crime and criminality can have a direct impact on the public's perception of the extent of the crime problem as well as on the operation of the criminal justice system itself. Hans and Dee (1991) correctly recognize that the public's knowledge and views of the law and legal system are largely dependent on what they read in the newspaper and what they see on television; there is little direct experience by the vast majority of citizens with the entire criminal justice system. Victimization data (Macguire et al., 1993) establish that over a person's life the likelihood of victimization is very high; however, fewer than half of these cases are even reported to authorities and from the known crimes, only a very small percentage is pursued to a conclusion in the justice system.

While the amount of coverage given to crime reporting is significant, it may not be greater than that given to other topics (Graber, 1980); it seems, however, that the crimes covered are largely sensational or extraordinary (Surette, 1984; Roberts and Doob, 1990; Marsh, 1992; Jerin and Fields, 1994) and do not reflect the reality of the type or amount of victimization that is occurring.

This information does not seem to reach the general public. As an example, in a USA Today/CNN/Gallup Poll (1993), 69% of the 1000 adults polled (plus an over-sample of 235 blacks) felt that local television news accurately reflects the amount of crime. It should be noted that only 58% of blacks in the sample agreed. The poll additionally found that only 25% of those responding believed that TV news exaggerated the amount of crime and nine out of ten believed that crime was worse than it had been a year earlier. These beliefs do not correspond to official data; the actual amount of crime reported to the police actually fell by 5% over the previous year (Macguire et al., 1993). The link between the public's misconception concerning the amount of crime and the operation of the criminal justice system and whether this trend will continue in the future is an important area for study.

One of the first inquiries into the public's conception of a crime problem and the media's misrepresentation was an examination of how the press fabricated a "crime wave" in 1919 (Schlesinger et al., 1991). Through the use of increased coverage and a call for governmental action, the public was erroneously led to believe that the crime problem was becoming much worse even though actual change was only minimal.

While misrepresentation of crime information is of serious concern, an additional area is the accuracy in how the media portrays the operations of the criminal justice system. False depictions of "crime waves" and other crime-related information (e.g., amount of violent crime) reflect poorly on the police, courts, and corrections. The USA Today/CNN/Gallup Poll (1993) also found that 86% of those surveyed believed that the courts were not harsh enough in dealing with criminals. Given the public's lack of personal contact with what the courts do, this perception of the quality of justice being dispensed is being driven by other sources.

Research has found that "the content of network television news is shown to account for a high proportion of...U.S. citizens' policy references" (Page et al., 1987:23). Extending this information to the criminal justice field, the influence of media sources on the public's view of crime and the criminal justice system is apparent. Since most information reported by the various types of media covers similar kinds of stories, inaccuracies in the information presented can lead to inaccuracies in the public's perception of crime and the job that criminal justice is doing.

In a recent study by the authors of this chapter, a content analysis was conducted on articles reported in *USA Today's* "Across the USA: News from Every State" (Jerin and Fields, 1994). *USA Today* claims to be the foremost daily newspaper in the United States and is the only source that reports news from every state every day. Using Graber's (1979) differentiation of news topics to establish four general headings, the analysis established the central theme of each news *byte* in an effort to reduce duplication of recordings. The topics used in the study were (1) crime and justice, (2) government and politics, (3) economics and social issues, and (4) human interest and family.

In the initial analysis of the news, the different types of news and categories were first examined according to Graber's model. In "News from Every State," the crime and justice section received the least amount of coverage. The percentage of stories that fell into the crime category was 16% ($n = 4236$). The percentage of additional news categories was government/politics, 24.4% ($n = 6412$); human interest/family issues, 26.7% ($n = 7015$); and economic/social issues, 32.8% ($n = 8638$). A relatively small number of summaries ($n = 260$) that were difficult or impossible to categorize were excluded from the analysis. This balance of issues is unique compared to Graber's (1979) earlier study in Chicago (see Table 1). However, further analysis in the crime and justice section confirms previous research.

TABLE 1   Frequency of News Topics (*n*) in *USA Today* (1990) and *Chicago Tribune, Sun-Times*, and *Daily News* (1979)[a] (Percent)

Topic	USA Today ($n = 26,301$)	Tribune ($n = 33,200$)	Sun-Times ($n = 581$)	Daily News ($n = 506$)
Crime and justice	16.1	21.8	28.0	26.7
Government and politics	24.4	41.4	41.5	43.9
Human interest and family	32.8	10.6	5.5	7.9
Economic and social issues	26.7	26.0	23.5	21.5

[a]With the exception of the *USA Today* figures, which were collected by the present authors, the primary data included in the table come from a year-long content analysis of the *Chicago Tribune*. The other two Chicago daily newspapers were analyzed on a more limited basis. For a more detailed discussion of the methodology, see Graber (1979).

It is perhaps unusual that crime- and justice-related news summaries make up the smallest category of "News from Every State" in *USA Today*, while human interest and family summaries constitute the largest. The three papers examined by Graber (1979) all report more news in the areas of government and politics, while crime and justice, or economic and social issues rank second. Human interest and family news ranks last.

The manner in which crime and justice news is reported in the state section of *USA Today* is similar to what was found in earlier research (e.g., Marsh, 1991). The amount of violent index crimes reported is almost 42%, with murder at 28%. Property crimes make up 6% of the crime reported, with white collar/corporate crimes totaling about 10%. The level of drug crimes is the third-highest recorded category, with over 8%. The "other" crime category constitutes 29% of the recordings.

Because of the brevity of the material reported (i.e., two stories per day) the type of crime story that made the news is unique. The material in *USA Today* followed a pattern found in Roshier's work. Roshier (1973) identified four sets of factors which seemed to establish why some crimes are selected in preference to others (pp. 34–35):

1. The seriousness of the offense

2. "Whimsical" circumstances (i.e., humorous, ironic, unusual)

3. Sentimental or dramatic circumstances

4. The involvement of a famous or high-status person in any capacity

Examples of these factors can be found throughout *USA Today's* reporting of state events. In many cases a combination of these factors can be observed in the crimes reported.

The differences between the states are somewhat difficult to analyze because of the subjective descriptions of crimes reported in each state. Typically, in a brief sentence or two, routine crime-related summaries list the location of the offense and describe the offense itself (perhaps naming the offender and victim) but little else. It is a little easier, however, to determine a subjective category in which to list the offense.

The total number of crime-related stories by state ranged from 38 in Alaska to 152 in New York. Many crime categories had no reporting in some states; these include drugs, rape, and robbery. The population of the state in many cases seems to establish the frequency of the crime reporting more than anything else. An additional concern is the high percentage of crimes fitting into the other category. There was a need to redefine this category because of the number of crimes and the important social issues that some address (e.g., hate crimes).

CRIME REPORTING AND OFFICIAL CRIME STATISTICS

Many earlier studies have dealt with the relationship between the extent of crime reporting and actual crime rates (see, e.g., Antunes and Hurley, 1977; Phillips, 1977; 1979; Fedler and Jordan, 1982). In an attempt to assess further the differences between crime rates and crime reporting, statistics for selected offenses from the Uniform Crime Reports (UCR) were compared with the same offenses reported in *USA Today*. Using a ranking system, comparisons between states and the UCR offer some interesting information. States were ranked by population, the UCR index crime rate, and the number and percent of news summaries relating to crime and justice reported in *USA Today*. In addition, four offense categories (murder, rape, drug violations, and corporate crime) were examined and ranked according to the reporting rate for each state.

The five most populated states—California, New York, Texas, Florida, and Pennsylvania—are among the states with the highest number of reported crimes (Macquire et al., 1993), but they are not ranked highest in crime- and justice-related reporting. The inference is that the number of crime and justice summaries is somewhat related to state population.

A comparison of the five areas with the highest UCR index crime rates—Washington, DC, Florida, Arizona, Texas, and Georgia—and the reporting of more serious crimes offers additional insight into crime reporting behavior. None of the states with the five highest crime rates are included in the top five rankings of murder and rape. This difference in reporting may be due primarily to the commonality of major crimes in these states, so that the newsworthiness of serious crimes in these same states may be minimized, and other factors (see Roshier, 1973) may play a larger role.

This comparison is in direct contrast to the five states—West Virginia, South Dakota, North Dakota, Kentucky, and Pennsylvania—with the lowest index crime rates. Three of these states (West Virginia, South Dakota, and Kentucky) are ranked in the top five in rape and rape-related news summaries. This discrepancy may be due to the perception in the media that certain sensational crimes are more "newsworthy" in states with low crime rates.

Even the states with the highest rankings in terms of *USA Today's* crime-related reporting—Arkansas, New Jersey, Wisconsin, Tennessee, and Missouri—are not states with relatively high crime rates. Only New Jersey is in the top half of the UCR index offenses (ranked twenty-second). The fact that Arkansas is ranked number one in terms of total crime- and justice-related reporting, number one in murder reporting, and number two in drug reporting questions the objective reporting of crime-related stories in *USA Today*. Further analysis of this phenomenon reveals that certain sensational crimes may be responsible for the extensive coverage of serious crime in Arkansas.

Although statistical comparisons between official crime rates and the extent of crime-related reporting in *USA Today* may be problematic, there are at least some preliminary indications of a relationship between the reporting of certain crimes and crime rates (see Table 2). When correlations between rape as reported in *USA Today* and the UCR index are examined, it seems that those states with high crime rates were less apt to have rape-related summaries during the year. There is, however, a strong positive correlation between drug-related reporting and official crime rates. No relationship was found between reporting of corporate/white collar offenses, murder, and all offenses combined and official crime statistics. Furthermore, *USA Today* had more drug-related news summaries and total crime-related summaries for small states (in terms of population) than for larger states.

TABLE 2   **Simple Correlations between Uniform Crime Reports (1990) and Crime and Justice Reporting in *USA Today* (Selected Offenses)[a]**

	Crime and Justice Reporting				
	All Offenses	Murder	Rape	Drugs	Corporate
UCR					
Index	0.0193	-0.0032	-0.2346*	0.3663**	0.1742
Violent	0.2313	0.1731	-0.1166	0.3884**	0.1830
Murder	0.0743	0.0259	-0.2215	0.3699**	0.1071
Population	-0.6598***	-0.1141	-0.2557*	-0.4250**	-0.0935

[a]*, $p < 0.05$; **, $p < 0.01$; ***, $p < 0.001$.

In the future, the media's representation of crime and criminality will probably follow the same course. With the evolution of some 500 television channels and the competition that will be generated by these networks, the use of sensationalism and hyperbole seems unavoidable. The print media could also fall victim to perceived market forces that try to increase the public's interest while providing the smallest amount of objective information; the use of sensationalized incidents will continue to distort the true picture of crime.

Notwithstanding the possibility of continued misinformation, the increase in news coverage may also tend to educate the public. The use of cameras in the courtroom, which is occurring in over 45 states (Verhovek, 1991), along with the development of the Courtroom Television Network, will provide the public with coverage of actual court proceedings. Although it is likely that initial coverage by these types of media may be limited to "sensational" crimes and criminals, watching the actual trial without a media filter will provide the public with a more accurate picture of the criminal justice system.

Although sensational crimes have received extensive coverage over the years (e.g., the 1925 Scopes "monkey" trial and the 1935 Lindbergh kidnapping trial), recent sensational cases have provided the public with a greater interest in watching an actual trial unfold. The William Kennedy Smith and Mike Tyson rape trials captured the attention of the public and every media source (Lacayo, 1991; Corliss, 1992), as did the O. J. Simpson murder trial. Although coverage of these trials has been characterized as a media "free-for-all" (Pollitt, 1991; Nack, 1992), the ability of the public to watch the actual trials from start to finish allows for an accurate depiction of part of the criminal justice process that most people never experience.

This type of coverage is not limited to the courts. Law enforcement is also currently the center of attention with television shows such as *COPS* and *Rescue 911*. *COPS* follows actual police officers and allows the officers to narrate the action that the audience is watching. *Rescue 911* reenacts police dramas with the cooperation of the original participants. While what is being covered will focus on appealing law enforcement situations, a more accurate picture of crime and criminals should appear.

The use of these and similar programs is certain to increase due to their low costs of production and the continued prurient interest of the public. The accurate portrayal of the crime problem and the criminal justice system will depend on the media's actions coupled with the public's desire for more information regarding crime and criminality. If the public is only allowed to view a "cut-and-paste" version of these events or has access only to sensational cases, a distortion of both the crime problem and operation of the system will continue.

CONCLUSIONS

The reporting of news events across the United States follows previous patterns found in regional newspapers and other media sources. The print media sensationalize certain crimes and ignore many others. Often, lesser crimes are reported not because of the event, but because of the notoriety of the people involved or the humor that was evoked. However, the breakdown of crime news compared to other areas of interest does not seem out of proportion.

It is suggested that the reporting of major crimes is not based on official crime statistics or state populations. Furthermore, the media reporting of a few sensational crimes in low-crime-rate states can distort the true amount of crime in those states. This study has also found that major factors in a crime being reported by the media is not the crime itself but the circumstances surrounding the crime, the public nature of the offender or victim, and the humorous nature of the incident. This is especially true with minor offenses. It seems that the accuracy of the reporting of criminal acts will always be compromised by the newsworthiness of the incident.

The future may hold more promise for accuracy given the possibility of competing news sources and greater variety that may be available to the general public. Live-action reporting, gavel-to-gavel coverage of court proceedings, and innovations in information technologies should provide the public with increased and more accurate information.

The conscious decision by the public to use these sources instead of continued reliance on the more traditional "news bits" for information can go a long way in assuring the elimination of the public's misperception of crime and criminality.

REFERENCES AND BIBLIOGRAPHY

ANTUNES, G. E., and P. A. HURLEY (1977). The representation of criminal events in Houston's two daily newspapers. *Journalism Quarterly*, 54:756–760.

BACON, J. (1992). Personal communication, February 15.

COHEN, S. (1975). A comparison of crime coverage in Detroit and Atlanta newspapers. *Journalism Quarterly*, 52:726–730.

CORLISS, R. (1992). The bad and the beautiful. *Time*, 139(8):25(2).

DAVIS, F. J. (1952). Crime news in Colorado newspapers. *American Journal of Sociology*, 57, June, pp. 325–330.

DEADEN, J. , and J. DUFFY (1983). Bias in the newspaper reporting of crime news. *British Journal of Criminology*, 23:159–165.

EDER, P. F. (1990). *Futurist*, May–June, pp. 38–41.

ERICSON, R. V. (1991). Mass media, crime, law, and justice. *British Journal of Criminology*, 31(3):219–249.

FEDLER, F., and D. JORDAN (1982). How emphasis on people affects coverage of crime. *Journalism Quarterly*, 59:474–478.

GRABER, D. A. (1979). Is crime news excessive? *Journal of Communication*, 29:81–92.

GRABER, D. A. (1980). *Crime News and the Public*. Westport, CT: Praeger.

HANS, V. P., and J. L. DEE (1991). Media coverage of law: Its impact on juries and the public. *American Behavioral Scientist*, 35(2):136–149.

HEATH, L. (1984). Impact of newspaper crime reports on fear of crime: Multimethodological investigation. *Journal of Personality and Social Psychology*, 47(2):263–276.

HUMPHRIES, D. (1981). Serious crime, news coverage, and ideology: A content analysis of crime coverage in a metropolitan paper. *Crime and Delinquency*, 27:191–205.

JAEHNIG, W. B., D. H. WEAVER, and F. FICO (1981). Reporting crime and fearing crime in three communities. *Journal of Communication*, Winter, pp. 88–96.

JERIN, R., and C. FIELDS (1994). Murder and mayhem in the *USA Today:* A quantitative analysis the reporting of states' news. In G. Barak (ed.), *Media, Process, and the Social Construction of Crime: Studies in Newsmaking Criminology*. New York: Garland Publishing.

JORDAN, D. L. (1993). Newspaper effects on policy preferences. *Public Opinion Quarterly*, 57:191–204.

LACAYO, R. (1991). Trial by television. *Time*, 138(24):30(2).

MACGUIRE, K., et al. (eds.) (1993). *Sourcebook of Criminal Justice Statistics, 1992*. Washington, DC: U.S. Government Printing Office.

MARSH, H. L. (1991). A comparative analysis of crime coverage in newspapers in the United States and other countries from 1960–1989: A review of the literature. *Journal of Criminal Justice*, 19:67–79.

MEYER, J. C., JR. (1975). Newspaper reporting of crime and justice: An analysis of an assumed difference. *Journalism Quarterly*, 52:731–734.

MEYER, J. C., JR. (1976). Reporting crime and justice in the press: A comparative inquiry. *Criminology*, 14:277–278.

NACK, W. (1992). A gruesome account. *Sports Illustrated*, 76(5):24–28.

NEWMAN, G. R. (1990). Popular culture and criminal justice: A preliminary analysis. *Journal of Criminal Justice*, 18:261–274.

PAGE, B. I., R. Y. SHAPIRO, and G. R. DEMPSEY (1987). What moves public opinion? *American Political Science Review*, 81(1):23–43.

PHILLIPS, D. P. (1977). Motor vehicle fatalities increase just after publicized suicide rates. *Science*, 196:1464–1465.

PHILLIPS, D. P. (1979). Suicide, motor vehicle fatalities and the mass media: Evidence toward a theory of suggestion. *American Journal of Sociology*, 84:1150–1174.

POLLITT, K. (1991). Media goes wilding in Palm Beach. *Nation*, 252(24):833 (5).

ROBERTS, J. V., and A. N. DOOB (1990). News media influences on public views of sentencing. *Law and Human Behavior*, 14:451–458.

ROBINSON, M. J., and A. KOHUT (1988). Believability and the press. *Public Opinion Quarterly*, 52:174–189.

ROSHIER, B. (1973). The selection of crime news by the press. In S. Cohen and J. Young (eds.), *The Manufacture of News*. Thousand Oaks, CA: Sage Publications, pp. 29–39.

SACCO, V. F., and M. TROTMAN (1990). Public information programming and family violence: Lessons from the mass media crime prevention experience. *Canadian Journal of Criminology* 32(1):91–105.

SCHLESINGER, P., H. TUMBER, and G. MURDOCK (1991). The media politics of crime and criminal justice. *British Journal of Sociology* 42(3):397–420.

SHELEY, J. F., and C. D. ASHKINS (1981). Crime, crime news, and crime views. *Public Opinion Quarterly*, 45:492–506.

SHOEMAKER, P. J., and S. D. REESE (1990). Exposure to what? Integrating media content and effects studies. *Journalism Quarterly*, 67:649–652.

SURETTE, R. (1992). *Media, Crime and Criminal Justice: Images and Realities*. Pacific Grove, CA: Brooks/Cole.

USA TODAY/CNN/GALLUP POLL (1993). Crime in America. October 28

VERHOVEK, S. H. (1991). News cameras in courts? New York's law disputed. *New York Times*, May 28, pp. B1, B6.

WINDHAUSER, J. W., J. SEITER, and L. T. WINFREE (1990). Crime news in the Louisiana press, 1980 vs. 1985. *Journalism Quarterly*, 67:72–78.

PART III

Policing Now and in the Twenty-First Century

Gazing into the crystal ball of the future may be nebulous, as indicated by Michael Palmiotto, but what we do know is that the role of the police in today's society continues to be the most controversial, yet least understood component of the criminal justice process. Police forces are growing and continue to be made available 24 hours a day. They continue to have the potential in the twenty-first century of maintaining order and improving community unity *(Gemeinschaft)* while lessening family violence incidents. Albert Roberts predicts that by the year 2010, police domestic violence teams will be bolstered by much needed technology.

Domestic violence poses many questions and conflicts for law enforcement personnel. Conflicts over whether to arrest or not to arrest an offender under a mandatory arrest policy are often faced in the field. The diversity of relationships creates conflicts if one is to enforce a must arrest domestic violence policy. The proper response to domestic violence is covered in the chapter by Albert R. Roberts, Stephen L. Ruland, and Vincent E. Henry.

Community policing in the first decade of the twenty-first century has received creditability and has become an acceptable philosophy of policing according to Michael J. Palmiotto. Due to the realization during the last part of the twentieth century that the traditional reactive approach to crime control was not working, there was developed a renewed police strategy, community policing. Community policing is not a new concept: in fact, it was redeveloped during the 1960s and 1970s, but in this first new decade of the twenty-first century, we are once again turning to it as an alternative to traditional policing. There is in most communities the desire to maintain the quality of life in neighborhoods for citizens who live in these neighborhoods.

In this new century, policing is becoming a more demanding process. Both the police and members of the community will share in the crime control function. A trend is developing that will require a better educated police officer as she or he looks to the crime prevention process and functions that are associated with community service. More and more pressure will be placed on the police officer to be proactive while reacting to crime. Through integrated community policies, there will be developed a utilitarian enforcement philosophy that may require curbing legal escapes for factually guilty offenders.

chapter 7

Police Response to Domestic Violence Complaints

Bridging the Present to the Future

Albert R. Roberts, Ph.D., Stephen L. Ruland, and Vincent E. Henry, Ph.D.

ABSTRACT

This chapter focuses on police response to domestic violence—past, present, and future. First, we present a case scenario typical of the year 2010, when technology will have greatly increased the efficiency and speed of police and judicial responsiveness to injured battered women. Also reviewed is the literature on police responses to domestic violence, with particular emphasis on the Minneapolis Domestic Violence Experiment and recent replications in Milwaukee and Omaha. A large data set of domestic violence complaint and arrest rates from a highly populous, ethnically diverse city in the northeastern United States is examined. The study covers six large police precincts during the five-year period 1987–1991 and the four-year period 1992–1995.

INTRODUCTION

It was 1400 hours on September 6, 2010. Two police officers were dispatched by headquarters on a report of a domestic violence complaint. Upon arrival at the scene, the officers spoke to the victim, Wilma R. She stated that her boyfriend Louis had been drinking the night before and became involved in an argument with her that ended with his punching her in the face and choking her. The officers observed that Wilma had a cut on her upper lip and swelling in the area between her nose and mouth.

When the police officers questioned Louis, he said he never touched Wilma. He insisted that the bruises on her face resulted from her being clumsy and falling down the steps while carrying the laundry. He said she was making up the story of being beaten because she was angry at him for staying out late with buddies the previous night.

To determine whether or not Louis had choked his girlfriend, the police officer went to the car and brought in the compact portable laser unit. By aiming the laser at Wilma's neck, the officer immediately obtained laser fingerprints which he compared to Louis'. The results showed an identical match. While the first officer was matching the fingerprints, the second officer went to the car and turned on the MDT computer to run a computerized criminal history on Louis. In less than 30 seconds, Louis's history appeared on the screen: two prior convictions for simple assault against a former girlfriend and resisting arrest. The incidents had occurred three years earlier in another state. In addition, Louis's record showed two arrests for driving while intoxicated during the past three years.

The officers' next step was to obtain a temporary restraining order (TRO) to prevent Louis from having any further contact with Wilma. The TRO was obtained by entering a summary of the police officers' findings at the scene on their portable computer and using the cellular phone to call the judge to inform her that the report was being faxed to her courtroom from their car.

At the courthouse, the court clerk received the report from the fax machine and brought it to Judge Catherine Sloan for her signature. The court clerk then faxed the TRO back to the police car. The entire approval process took only 15 minutes.

Next, the police transported Louis to the county jail, where the nurse practitioner implanted a subdural electronic sensor on Louis's wrist. The police gave a sensing receiver to Wilma to wear externally, on a chain around her neck. The computer at police headquarters monitored these sensors as it had done with the 300 other domestic abuse cases reported to the police department during the past 12 months. The officers informed Louis that if he came within a distance of 500 meters from Wilma, the sensing device would immediately alert the police officers that he had violated the TRO, and Louis would be sent to prison (Roberts, 1996).

POLICE RESPONSE TO DOMESTIC VIOLENCE IN THE MID-1990s

During the past few years, domestic violence has increasingly been defined by a growing number of state criminal codes and family court statutes as a serious crime (i.e., a felony rather than a misdemeanor). In fact, due to the prevalence and life-threatening nature of woman battering, all 50 states have passed civil and/or criminal statutes to protect battered women (Roberts, 1994). As many as 75% of all police calls in some areas involve domestic conflict and/or violence. In the past, police were often reluctant to respond to family violence calls. When they did respond, they were frequently accused of taking the side of the male batterers and subscribing to the view that "a man's home is his castle." In addition, court staff tended to minimize the dangers that battered women encountered and discouraged the women from filing criminal or civil complaints.

Society-at-large has finally recognized that the beating of women (wives, cohabitants, or companions) is a crime and a major social problem. Societal recognition of woman abuse as a major social problem grew out of four note-worthy activities:

1. The women's movement
2. Two national prevalence studies on the extent of domestic violence in the United States (Straus et al., 1980; Straus and Gelles, 1990)
3. Books and news articles on battered women (Fleming, 1979; Walker, 1979; Roy, 1982; Roberts, 1984, 1988; Walker, 1984)
4. Recent litigation and legal reforms (Roberts, 1984, 1998)

Moreover, many police departments now have a pro-arrest or presumptive arrest policy. The road toward implementing effective mandatory or pro-arrest policies for batterers has, however, been bumpy and uneven. Furthermore, research studies on the short-term deterrent effects of arresting batterers is inconclusive.

Nevertheless, Americans have come a long way from the time when the use of violence by men to control their partners was condoned. Mandatory and warrantless arrest laws are just one part of an improved police response to victims of women bat-tering. In addition, police in highly populated cities and counties throughout the nation now provide immediate protection to battered women.

The complex constellation of social, legal, and political issues surrounding the police response to domestic violence is among the most enduring and contentious problems in the recent history of criminal justice theory and practice. The current salience of domestic violence as an issue of national concern for criminal justice theoreticians and practitioners is well illustrated by the degree of attention this subject has recently received in so many diverse spheres, and by the body of research it has generated. Particularly within the past decade, efforts to define and to institutionalize appropriate roles and responsibilities for police in responding to domestic violence have engendered considerable academic research, generated a significant body of statutory and case law, and been the subject of an uncommon degree of public and political discourse.

Social and political pressures for change, in conjunction with the passage of civil and criminal statutes to protect battered women in all 50 states, have considerably altered the way that police officers and agencies currently respond to domestic violence. Police executives and public policymakers, as well as individual police officers, have become more sensitive to the issues involved as they have faced the burden of making appropriate and effective choices from among a range of competing alternative strategies. Because defining and practicing an appropriate police response to domestic violence necessarily entails consideration of a broad array of practical, legal, political and social variables, supervisors, trainers, and street officers confront a difficult task. Despite a host of opinions, policies, agendas, and programs aimed at redressing the social problem and providing relief to victims, there currently appears to be little consensus as to precisely what comprises the most desirable and effective response to domestic violence. It may be that since no single response has proven successful, a multilevel approach should be implemented only after more effective policy research is completed.

Historical Overview

Although the recognition of domestic violence as a pervasive social problem is fairly recent, its cultural bases are deeply embedded in Western history and culture. Even a cursory review of that history reveals the extent to which law and society have traditionally served to implicitly support and perpetuate the subordination of women to their husbands. In South America and Asia, especially in the upper classes, killing a wife for an indiscretion is usually acceptable. The same privilege is not usually extended to women against their husbands. Various cultures and societies have permitted or tacitly encouraged some degree of family violence as a means to maintain that subordination. Demographic analyses of domestic violence offenses reported to the police confirm the observation that domestic violence is most frequently perpetrated by males against their female partners. Males comprise only a small fraction of the total victims in domestic violence cases reported to the police.

As Richard Gelles and Murray Straus (1988) have so aptly noted, domestic violence is intrinsically linked to the maintenance of power and dominance within the family unit. Family violence and spousal assaults are facilitated when a paucity of effective formal and informal social control mechanisms allows the rewards of maintaining power through violence to outweigh the costs of such violence. From this observation we can infer that cultures which define violence within the family unit as unacceptable behavior and which emphatically communicate an attitude of disapproval by applying potent social sanctions (e.g., ostracizing or publicly humiliating the perpetrator) will exhibit lower rates of domestic violence than societies which ignore the issue or which tacitly approve of intrafamily violence will. Similarly, the availability of formal mechanisms of social control (i.e., the legal processes of arrest and punishment) also affects the incidence of domestic violence. Gelles and Straus (1988:17–36) conclude that people use violence against members of their families "because they can."

History reveals that until fairly recently, men were legally empowered to employ relatively unrestrained physical force against their wives and children in order to maintain family discipline. During the 1960s, several discrete trends evolved in policing, in law, and in politics which ultimately converged in the 1970s and 1980s to set the stage for our current concerns and the attention paid to domestic violence issues. The confluence of these trends and pressures created a unique and powerful synergy, forcing American police agencies and lawmakers to reexamine their policies and practices, and to adopt the type of strategies that prevail today.

The Impact of Feminism

First, the feminist movement's focus on the economic, social, and legal disparities between men and women in our patriarchal society raised women's issues in general, and domestic violence in particular, to an unprecedented level of public discourse and debate. Because abuse of women is perpetuated overwhelmingly by males against their female partners, and because it serves to degrade women and maintain (through force) their subordinate role within marital or cohabiting relationships, domestic violence quite properly achieved some prominence in the feminist agenda. As the ranks of feminists swelled, and as they achieved increasing political power, they effected legislative changes and influenced public policy. A central premise of the feminist argument for the arrest of batterers was that such arrests have a potent symbolic content in illustrating the equality of women, and that they demonstrate society's refusal to treat women differently than men on the basis of their sex or social condition. Assaulted women, they argued, should expect and should receive the same criminal justice response whether they were assaulted by a stranger or by a spouse, in the home or outside it.

At about the same time, rising national rates of crime focused public attention on the rights and needs of crime victims, and public policies began to address these needs. Here again, feminist groups took the lead in establishing social service programs for victimized women, and in creating public policies aimed at relieving the traumas experienced by female victims of crime. Prominent among these programs were battered women's shelters (Roberts, 1981). Without the presence of injuries that would raise assault to a felony, police officers frequently remained reluctant to use their discretionary powers of arrest to intrude on the privacy of the domestic relationship in misdemeanor cases of assault. Partly because of this reluctance, police officers rarely invoked their powers of arrest in domestic violence cases when the offense was a less serious misdemeanor assault. Several other trends and forces also militated against arrest in most misdemeanor domestic assaults.

The Impact of Research

Morton Bard (1970, 1973) was the first researcher to develop training for police officers in family crisis intervention and mediation techniques. Specialized training led to increased officer safety and reduced reported levels of domestic violence. By adopting mediation-based policies, the police and other criminal justice agencies believed they could reduce domestic violence and respond to external pressures for change, at the same time avoiding the expensive and time-consuming process of arresting and prosecuting domestic misdemeanor assaults. Bard's research enjoyed great credibility, and consistent with that era's emphasis on enhanced training and police professionalism, many agencies developed mediation-based policies toward policing domestic violence. Since a wealth of federal funds for police training became available through the Law Enforcement Assistance Administration during the late 1960s and early 1970s, many agencies utilized these funds to train officers in family crisis intervention. Sherman and Berk (1984:262), for example, noted that by 1977 over 70% of U.S. police departments employing 100 or more officers had a family crisis intervention training program in place.

In agencies where such mediation-oriented policies existed, the protocol generally called for officers to respond by separating the disputants, interviewing each one to discover the underlying causes for the dispute, and counseling them informally on the spot. In practice, these policies may have helped some families to resolve minor disputes without violence, but in general they rarely proved to be effective deterrents to future disputes or future violence. While the basic theory behind the policies—that mediation and counseling could bring the parties together to work out their difficulties through dialogue rather than through violence—may have had some merit, police were often not trained well enough to deliver effective counseling. Nor did they have the requisite interpersonal skills to identify and deal with the issues leading up to the dispute. Because policing was (and remains) a male-dominated occupation, it might also be argued that despite training, male officers were not sensitive enough to the plight of female victims. They may have wittingly or unwittingly been too sympathetic to the male disputant's point of view. In addition, many officers were simply not disposed to practice what they perceived as time-consuming "social work." Officers who saw themselves as "crime fighters," especially those assigned to busy precincts or beats, may simply have been more interested in completing the assignment quickly and getting back to "real" police work.

To understand the failure of mediation-oriented policies to prevent further violence, it is useful to examine the archetypal family dispute from the responding officers' perspective. Indeed, when experienced officers repeatedly encounter similar or apparently identical patterns of family dysfunction and when a cluster of problems or elements appears to contribute to each of these disputes, officers often tend to conceive of family disputes in generic terms. In time, such common features as alcohol abuse, financial problems or accusations of adultery and extramarital affairs blur the distinctions between disputes. Consequently, officers may lose sight of the unique differences between family disputes. It must also be noted that despite these common features, police officers concurrently view the vast majority of individual family disputes as highly ambiguous and potentially dangerous situations in which the facts and circumstances are not at all clear-cut. The problems and frustrations that give rise to violent disputes are often long-standing and complex, and the disputants themselves may not be fully aware of the causes underlying their present dispute. Instead, the attributed causes they relate to the police may be merely symptomatic of some deep-seated family dysfunction which legitimately lies well beyond the capacity of the police to resolve. Because family crisis intervention is, both by definition and by necessity, short-term counseling, even skilled officers who have been trained in counseling techniques may be unable to discover or to address the larger and more complex issues involved. Officers are still overhead to opine that the solutions to most ongoing family disputes lie either in divorce court or in long-term intensive psychotherapy. Moreover, these situations are potentially dangerous since the disputants may turn on the officers with violence.

The ever-present demands for expedient resolution of these disputes also affected the officers' potential for delivering effective counseling during that era. Particularly in busy or high-crime districts, where time and resources spent in counseling families means less time and fewer resources available to devote to high-priority "real crime" incidents, pressures exist for officers to resolve the disputes as expeditiously as possible so that they are able to return to patrol. Within a context of ambiguity, and in light of the other pressures and constraints placed on the police officers, it should not be difficult to understand that even the most conscientious officers may quickly become cynical and lose faith in their own ability to resolve complex family problems through short-term counseling. Police cynicism is undoubtedly compounded and reinforced by the ultimate failure of mediation to reduce future assaults or disputes, and by the perception that they have been repeatedly called to the same location to deal with the same people and the same problems. Most officers working in a district have intimate knowledge of the family problems they can expect to encounter on a particular chronic call location.

As a consequence of their cynicism, and notwithstanding their training, many frustrated officers have exercised the great discretion afforded them under the mediation model to restore peace temporarily merely by separating the combatants for a period of time. Despite its dubious legality, one strategy frequently employed by police was to order a male aggressor to leave the house for a specified period, threatening arrest if he returned. If the aggressor returned and the dispute continued, the problem would hopefully be passed along to another team of officers.

Several additional factors have possibly contributed to the demise of the mediation model. First, the fact that drug or alcohol abuse, financial difficulties, and other formidable social problems are often correlates of family violence may have impeded the police from dealing with the root causes or the triggers of domestic abuse. The police of that era were (and still remain) largely unable to deal effectively with such profound and deeply embedded problems, which require ongoing therapy and a social support system. In a related vein, and in keeping with the dominant "zeitgeist" of the police professionalism era, the mediation model placed the primary responsibility for crisis intervention and counseling in violent family disputes squarely on the police, who were often considered the first social workers or psychologists on the scene.

The rhetoric and dogma of the police professionalism movement argued adamantly that well-trained police officers were capable of performing an entire range of functions and providing an entire range of services. As a consequence, the police officers and agencies subscribing to this rhetoric were not disposed to cede their authority to external agencies, and were reluctant to utilize services outside the criminal justice sphere. It could well be argued that police reluctance to refer dysfunctional families to community mental health services for ongoing family counseling, as well as an actual paucity of such services within the community, prevented families from accessing the type of long-term counseling which might have reduced further violence. All too often, the police response under the mediation-oriented policies degenerated into a short-term palliative—a "band-aid" approach aimed only at quickly restoring some semblance of order and relieving the critical problem of the moment. Seldom did the police affect the true sources of family dysfunction.

Whatever the reasons, these policies were eventually proven to be ineffective at reducing further incidents of domestic violence: One study determined that in 85% of spousal homicides, the police had been called at least once in the previous two years, and in over half the cases they had been called five or more times. In time, the practical utility and the underlying philosophical premises of this approach were called into question, and the police began to seek other strategies. Police agencies, though, had at least initiated attempts to address domestic violence issues through policy reform, and had begun to use academic research as a basis for domestic violence policymaking.

Research on Deterrent Effects of Arrest

Several studies have been completed on the effect that pro-arrest or mandatory arrest policies have had in reducing calls for domestic violence. The first known study, known as the Minneapolis Experiment, found that arrest was more effective than no arrest or mediation in deterring future battering.

The Minneapolis Domestic Violence Experiment (1981–1982) (Sherman and Berk 1984) was the first research study to test the short-term deterrent effect of arrest in domestic violence cases with both heterosexual married and cohabitating couples, and same-sex couples. In selected police precincts, domestic violence incidents were randomly assigned to one of three police methods of responding:

1. Providing advice and informal mediation

2. Separating the couple by ordering the offender to leave the premises for eight hours to cool off

3. Arresting the alleged offender and detaining him overnight in the local jail

Three hundred and thirty eligible cases were tracked for six months. Repeat incidents of domestic violence were measured through official police department record checks to determine if there were additional domestic violence calls to the same address, as well as follow-up interviews with the victim every two weeks. The findings indicated that arrest was more effective than the two other types of police response in deterring subsequent incidents of domestic violence. Repeat violence occurred in only 13% of the arrest cases, compared with a 19% failure rate among the cases assigned to informal mediation and a 24% failure rate for the cases assigned to "cool off" for eight hours. There were several methodological problems associated with the study: the small sample size, the disproportionate number of cases to which the same officer responded, and inadequate standardization and controls over the treatments actually delivered by the officers. Despite the methodological flaws, the Minneapolis Experiment received widespread national recognition and had a significant impact on arrest policies nationwide. Between 1984 and 1987, police chiefs in thousands of police departments read the laudatory reports in newspaper articles and the National Institute of Justice (NIJ) report which lauded the study and stated that arrest was the best deterrent for abuse against women.

Between 1984 and 1985, in the aftermath of the Minneapolis study, the percentage of large city police departments with preferred- or pro-arrest policies increased from 10% to 46% (Walker, 1992:121). By 1989, thirteen states had enhanced mandatory arrest policies for domestic violence perpetrators. In some of these states arrest is mandatory in misdemeanor and felony-level domestic violence charges, as well as for violating a restraining order. However, in two states (Delaware and North Carolina), arrest is mandatory only when the abuser violates a restraining order (Buzawa and Buzawa, 1990:96). To determine the validity of the Minneapolis Experiment, the National Institute of Justice funded six replications in Atlanta, Georgia; Omaha, Nebraska; Charlotte, North Carolina; Colorado Springs, Colorado; Dade County,

Florida; and Milwaukee, Wisconsin. Similar to the Minneapolis Experiment, the six later studies examined whether arrest is the most effective police response in preventing batterers from committing future acts of abuse.

In sharp contrast to the Minneapolis Experiment, however, none of the six replications found arrest to be a more effective deterrent than other methods of police response. There are three major reasons why arrest was not found to deter future domestic violence at these sites. First, the majority of the batterers in these studies had prior criminal records (50% in Milwaukee; 65% in Omaha; and 69% in Charlotte). Therefore, *arrest in itself does not have the same meaning it would have for first offenders, since it is neither innovative nor unexpected by the lawbreaker.* Second, violence is a common and chronic problem among the sample rather than a first-time occurrence. Therefore, it is unrealistic to expect a short detention to have much of an impact on changing a long-term, chronically violent behavior pattern. Third, there was wide variation in the amount of time that arrested batterers were in custody: "short arrests" averaged 2.8 hours; full arrest 11.1 hours. In Charlotte, the average time in custody was 15.75 hours (Dunford, et al., 1990; Sherman, et al., 1991). In contrast, for the Minneapolis study, the time in custody ranged from approximately 24 hours to one week (168 hours). Finally, arrest alone does not constitute a strong enough societal stigma among persons with previous arrest histories. In many groups, it is a rite of passage.

Lawrence Sherman and associates recently found that arrest did not exert a deterrent effect among a particular subgroup of abusers in Milwaukee. The most promising finding of the above-cited studies indicates that arrest may well lead to an escalation of violence among unemployed persons, and deterrence of subsequent violence by abusers who are employed, married, and white (Sherman et al., 1992). Because of the large sample size (1200 cases were eligible for randomization), the researchers were able to conduct many subclassification and matched-pair comparisons. The other replications were not able to dichotomize and subclassify for as many variables as was done in the Milwaukee study.

Pro-arrest Policies

Since 1984 the trend has been for a growing number of police departments in cities with over 100,000 population to adopt a policy of pro-arrest or probable cause arrests of batterers. Efforts to redefine battering as a crime were boosted significantly by the following four activities and studies:

1. The National Coalition Against Domestic Violence as well as statewide coalitions and advocacy groups work to protect battered women.

2. The Minneapolis Domestic Violence Experiment on the deterrent effects of arrest (Sherman and Berk, 1984).

3. The final report of the U.S. Attorney General's Task Force on Family Violence (1984) citing the Minneapolis Experiment, documenting the

prevalence and intense dangers of battering episodes, and concluding that domestic violence is a major crime problem and that criminal justice agencies should treat it as such.

4. Television network and newspaper accounts of the court decisions that held police liable for failing to protect battered women from severe injuries (e.g., *Thurman* v. *City of Torrington*, 1984).

A highly publicized Supreme Court case in the mid-1980s led to pro-arrest laws and mandated police training on prevention of domestic violence incidents. Tracey Thurman of Torrington, Connecticut, who had been beaten repeatedly by her husband, sued the Torrington Police Department. The basis for Thurman's lawsuit was the failure of the police department and its officers to protect Ms. Thurman despite the fact that she had continually and repeatedly requested police protection over an eight-month period. Even though Ms. Thurman had obtained a court order barring her violent spouse from assaulting her again, it took the police 25 minutes to arrive on the scene of the final and most violent battering. After arrival at Ms. Thurman's residence, the arresting officer delayed arresting Mr. Thurman several minutes, giving the husband, who held a bloody knife in his hand, plenty of time to kick his wife in the head, face, and neck while she lay helpless on the ground. Ms. Thurman suffered life-threatening injuries as the result of this attack, including multiple stab wounds to the chest, neck, and face; fractured cervical vertebrae and damage to her spinal cord; partial paralysis below the neck; lacerations to the cheek and mouth; loss of blood; shock; scarring; severe pain; and mental anguish. Tracey Thurman's award was unprecedented ($2.3 million in compensatory damages against 24 police officers). The jury found that the Torrington, Connecticut police had deprived Ms. Thurman of her constitutional right to equal protection under the law (Fourteenth Amendment of the U.S. Constitution). The jury further concluded that the Torrington police officers were guilty of gross negligence in failing to protect Tracey Thurman and her son, Charles Jr., from the violent acts of Charles Thurman, Sr.

In the wake of the court decision in the *Thurman* case, police departments throughout the nation began immediately implementing pro-arrest policies and increased police training on domestic violence. As a result, during the last half of the 1980s and the first half of the decade of the 1990s, there was a proliferation of police training courses developed on how best to handle domestic violence calls.

By 1988, ten states had passed laws expanding police arrest powers in the cases of domestic assault. Specifically, these new statutes required arrest when there was a positive determination of probable cause (i.e., the existence of visible injury and/or the passage of only a short time between the commission of the act and the arrival of the police on the scene). Police departments are now also legally required to arrest batterers who have violated protective or restraining orders granted to battered women by the courts. As of 1992, protective orders are available to abused women in all 50 states and the District of Columbia. In more and more jurisdictions, women in abusive relationships have been able to obtain protective orders against their abusers from local courts to prevent the abuser from coming to their residence. Police are called upon to enforce protective orders and to arrest the abuser if he violates any of the stipulations set forth in the court order.

Several issues limit the effectiveness of pro-arrest policies. First, in many jurisdictions unmarried couples are not included in the policies' definitions of eligibility. This omission certainly limits the effectiveness of the police response, since it is generally recognized that the police receive proportionally more domestic violence calls from cohabitating women than from legally married women. Second, several studies have indicated that 40 to 60% of batterers flee from the residence before the police arrive on the scene. Therefore, the batterer might not be arrested unless the battered victim signed a criminal complaint. The final issue relates to the fact that experienced police officers are accustomed to making their own discretionary decisions regarding whether or not to arrest the abusive person, and they may resent mandated intrusions upon their traditional discretionary authority. As a result, widespread police compliance with a presumptive or pro-arrest domestic violence policy is going to be a gradual process, taking several years.

Despite all the inherent limitations of a pro-arrest policy, considerable progress has been made within the past decade. While arrest of all suspects in domestic violence calls is mandated by statute in only a small number of states, thousands of police departments nationwide have implemented their own pro-arrest policies and are now requiring arrests when an officer observes signs of bodily injury on a battered woman.

A MODEL DOMESTIC VIOLENCE INTERVENTION PROGRAM

As we have seen in previous sections, domestic violence poses many questions and conflicts for the law enforcement professional. Questions over legal definitions may cause certain types of relationships to be overlooked. Conflicts over whether to arrest or not to arrest an offender under a mandatory arrest policy are often faced in the field. Some even question the effectiveness of mandatory arrest policies for victims of domestic violence. In this section we examine the domestic violence policy of a large eastern city police department. We also look at this department's efforts to redefine its policy, and approach, to this complex problem.

When addressing family violence, the law is specific as to the term *family*. When utilizing a must arrest policy in domestic violence cases some family-type relationships may be excluded. In the state that is relevant to this case, the Family Court Act defines family as "Persons who are legally married to one another; were formerly legally married to one another; are related by marriage; are related by blood; have a child in common, regardless of whether such persons have been married or have lived together at any time."

In today's society there are many different types of family relationships. This diversity of relationships creates a conflict if one is to enforce a must-arrest domestic violence policy. To resolve this conflict, the police department involved expanded its definition to become more inclusive of its population. The department added to its policy the following expanded definition: "Persons who are defined as family in the state Family Court Act *AND* persons who are not legally married but are currently living together in a family-type relationship; are not legally married but formerly lived in a family-type relationship."

The definition now includes common law marriages, same-sex couples, and registered domestic partners, as well as different generations of the same family, siblings, and in-laws. The expanded definition now allows this department to incorporate its city's diverse population into its domestic violence policy. Now when faced with a must-arrest situation, any confusion as to what constitutes a family relationship is greatly reduced. More important, the department has taken the step to recognize and include the various family relationships that exist. It provides inclusive protection under its domestic violence policy and demonstrates a strong commitment to addressing domestic violence in the community. This position will send a strong message to both victims and offenders, by attacking an *atmosphere of tolerance*. Imagine responding to a domestic violence case involving a common law couple. The couple, not legally married, has been living together for several years. By utilizing the narrow family court definition of family, the options available to this couple may not be protected by the department's domestic policy. It may also prohibit the police from taking certain actions allowed under its domestic violence policy. The inability to act will affect the public's perception of this department's domestic violence policy. The message sent to the victim may be interpreted as being that the police do not care and will do nothing to help. The offender may interpret this lack of action as a reinforcement of his or her behavior. Use of the expanded definition allows this department to offer more protection to more diverse family situations. It also improves the public's and victim's perception of the department's domestic violence policy. At the same time, it attempts to prevent any reinforcement of an offender's behavior.

Understanding the definition of family is important, as we will now examine this department's must-arrest domestic violence policy. The department requires that its police officers and/or detectives must arrest an offender in a domestic violence case when certain conditions are met. The first condition is that the relationship between the parties involved fit the expanded definition of family. The next condition is that the incident involves probable cause that an offense was committed between members of the family. *An offense is conduct for which a sentence to a term of imprisonment or to a fine is provided.* They include felony, misdemeanor, and violation. A *felony* is a crime that could result in the imprisonment of a person for a year or more. A *misdemeanor* is a crime that could result in the imprisonment of a person for up to one year. A *violation* is not a crime but an offense, and could result in a fine, imprisonment, or both. Understanding the differences among these offenses is important, as the actions of law enforcement personnel depend on the offense committed.

There is one more item that must be explained before we can go further. An *order of protection* is an order issued by a city criminal court, state family court, or a state supreme court, requiring compliance with specific conditions of behavior, hours of visitation and any other condition deemed appropriate by the court of issuance.

Such orders are usually given to a domestic violence victim by a court and prohibit an offender from contacting a victim and/or engaging in violent, threatening, or disruptive behavior. The provisions of each order of protection will vary—what is important to know is that an order has been issued. Possession of an order by a family member in a domestic violence case is viewed as serious by law enforcement. We examine next the must-arrest policy of this police department. The department's domestic violence must-arrest policy requires that "if an offender is present or the search for an offender was successful and there is probable cause that any *felony* has been committed or an *order of protection* violated, the officer/detective will arrest the offender, even if the victim requests that the offender not be arrested."

This policy makes a strong point on domestic violence. First, it removes all of the discretion not only from the police but also from the victims of domestic violence. As a deterrent, this procedure sends a clear message to an offender: Commit a felony or violate an order of protection and you will be arrested. This policy also removes from the police the ability to mediate. The most important point of this policy is that it provides that an arrest be effected even if the victim does not want the offender arrested. What we see on this last point is that even if an offender, for whatever reason, could convince a victim not to have him or her arrested, an arrest is effected to deter this behavior. What is also seen is a shift by this department from that of deterrence to that of intervention. Safety of the victim is paramount in any police action. A must-arrest policy removes any possibility that an unarrested offender could commit any future violence once the police leave the scene. This ability to intervene is more clearly exhibited in this department's must-arrest policy concerning misdemeanors and violations. This department's domestic violence policy states that "when there is probable cause that any *misdemeanor* has been committed, in or out of the officer's presence, or a *violation* has been committed in the officer's presence, the offender is arrested. An officer must arrest the offender unless the victim specifically states, on his or her own initiative, that he or she does not want the offender arrested. The officer retains the discretion to make an arrest in a misdemeanor case despite the victim's decision not to seek arrest. While the discretion not to make an arrest is removed, this procedure gives the police greater discretion in effecting an arrest.

The primary considerations when a victim does not want an arrest to be made are the prevention of further violence and the safety of all household members. Factors to be taken into consideration include, but are not limited to:

- The past history of the offender and victim
- The officer's observations of the scene and the victim
- Statements of witnesses
- Statements made by the offender
- Threatened use of weapons, the presence of or access to weapons by the offender
- The mental and physical state of the offender
- The presence of other household members who may be at risk

If an officer has any doubts about the continued safety of any household member, *an arrest should be effected*. The misdemeanor arrest procedure is best described by the following example.

The police respond to a domestic violence call. Upon their arrival a 23-year-old woman meets the police. She is suffering from a swollen face, the result of being punched several times by her husband. The woman informs the officers that she had returned home late from visiting her sister. Her husband accused her of cheating on him. During the argument he punched her several times in the face. The woman tells the officers that her husband is a very jealous man and sometimes gets carried away. The victim states that she did not call the police and that everything is fine. Her husband usually calms down after a few hours. She refuses medical treatment and asks the officers to please not arrest her husband. The officers then interview the husband. The husband is still angry. He tells the police that he knows that his wife is fooling around and he has to set her straight. He then yells to his wife, " I'm not done with you yet!" The police then determine that a neighbor had been the one who called the police. One of the officers interviews the neighbor. The neighbor tells the officer that the couple fights all the time. He also informs the officer that the cops sometimes come to the house two or three times on the same day. He also states that last time the cops were here, the victim was removed by an ambulance, unconscious. After reviewing the information, the police arrest the offender for misdemeanor assault, against the victim's wishes.

In reviewing this scenario, several factors are taken into consideration in making the arrest. First, the woman's statement that her husband sometimes gets carried away shows that violence had occurred in the past. Second, the husband is still angry and threatened the wife. Third, the neighbor tells the police that the cops are there several times in one day. These points demonstrate that if the police complied with the victim's wishes not to make an arrest, violence would probably occur after the police left. The police have the authority under this procedure to intervene by making an arrest. Looking at this procedure more closely, you can see that it is no longer a simple question of making or not making an arrest. An officer now is required to conduct an investigation, and if the victim wishes not to press charges, the officer may intervene and make an arrest.

This procedure is a big step: it allows the police to step in and arrest someone to prevent future violence. This procedure also mandates that the police investigate the past history of the household, interview witnesses, and look at other members of the household. This information is critical in determining if and how much the police should intervene. The focus is not on just arrest for a crime committed but is also on the prevention of future violence in the household. But before we examine how this department addresses the intervention and prevention aspect of domestic violence, we must first look at some conflicts over the must-arrest policy.

In responding to domestic violence calls, sometimes a must-arrest policy could work against a victim. For example, if a misdemeanor assault victim wishes the police to arrest his or her attacker, the answer is simple—make an arrest. But what if the offender claims that he or she was also a victim? Now, under the mandatory-arrest policy, the police must arrest both the victim and the offender. This conflict can cause a serious problem for prevention of future domestic violence. How likely is it that a victim, having been arrested once, will call the police again? Does this empower the offender even more in the future? It is presumed that a victim would not risk arrest by calling the police. It is also presumed that an offender would be empowered by this loophole. "Call the police and I will have *you* arrested" is often heard from the offender. It must be understood that often an offender will use a *retaliatory arrest* to maintain control over his or her victim. We see that a savvy offender can use the police must-arrest policy to his or her advantage; it becomes a weapon to use against the victim. This loophole can severely undercut law enforcement's attempts at intervention and prevention. Cross-complaint situations can become difficult to mediate for police personnel. To assist law enforcement, this state enacted a law that requires police to attempt to determine the *primary physical aggressor* in misdemeanor cases. This department incorporated this law into its policy as follows:

In cross-complaint situations, where there is probable cause to believe that more than one family or household member has committed a family offense misdemeanor, in or out of the officer's presence in a single domestic incident, the officer is to attempt to identify the primary physical aggressor after considering the following criteria:

- The extent of any injuries inflicted by and between the parties
- Whether any of the parties are threatening or have threatened future harm against another party or another family or household member
- Whether any of the parties has a prior history of domestic violence that the officer can ascertain
- Whether any such person acted defensively to protect himself or herself from injury

Then, after conferral with a supervisor, the officer may arrest the person identified as the primary physical aggressor and not the victim. This exception does not apply to felonies or violation of orders of protection. This provision does not prohibit the arrest of both parties if the police feel that it is warranted, or an arrest against the victim's wishes. What this provision does allow is an exception to the must-arrest policy. If the police can identify defensive wounds on a person, obtain the household's history, or obtain witness statements showing self-defense, an arrest may not be necessary for both parties.

Look at the following example to see how this procedure may work in the field. A 38-year-old male enters the detective unit wishing to file a complaint against his wife. The male tells a detective that three days ago his wife threatened to kill him with a knife and attacked him, causing scratches to his face. The male further states that the police came and arrested only him, not his wife. He wants his wife arrested, because it's not right that he has to be the one who goes to jail; he was just protecting himself. The six-foot-tall 200-pound male is suffering from scratches on his left cheek but refuses medical aid. The detective then begins an investigation. The detective determines that three days ago the police responded to the male's residence. The male's wife, who is five feet two inches tall and weighs 110 pounds, had been severely assaulted. The woman was beaten with a belt buckle, causing lacerations to her head and arms. She also suffered a broken arm from being pushed to the ground. This is the fourth incident at the household in two years, and resulted in an injury to the wife and the arrest of the husband. The wife was arrested in three of the incidents for threatening the husband with a weapon. All of the cases were dismissed because the victims refused to prosecute. The detective responded to the wife's home to conduct an interview. The wife informs the detective that the other day her husband was beating her with a belt. He was hurting her badly and when she tried to grab the belt from him, she scratched his face. Her husband then threw her to the floor, breaking her arm. He then began to hit her with the belt buckle; bleeding, she managed to run to the kitchen. She then pulled a large kitchen knife out and told her husband to stay away. The police arrived and arrested her husband and she went to the hospital. The woman then told the detective that every time her husband is arrested, he goes to the police and tells them that she threatened to kill him. The police then come and arrest her, because they say they have to. She wants to press charges, but her husband won't drop the charges filed against her unless she drops the charges against him. She tells the detective that since she doesn't want any trouble with the law, she drops the charges. After reviewing the information the detective closes the misdemeanor complaint filed by the husband by not making an arrest. The detective determines that the husband was the primary physical aggressor in the original case. The injuries and threats (misdemeanors) he received were a result of the original victim (the wife) protecting herself. The wife's injuries are consistent with her statements and are defensive in nature (i.e., lacerations and bruising to the head, back, and forearms).

This is important in removing control of the offender over the victim. It also prevents the victim from being victimized twice, once by the offender and then by the system. Again the focus here is the safety of all household members, but it can also assist in the prevention of future violence. This is a step by this department to recognize and address the problems facing victims of domestic violence.

In examining the must-arrest policy of this department, we can gain some understanding of its purpose and its problems. We also see how an approach to such a complex issue as domestic violence requires law enforcement to modify its mission and procedure continually. There is one more issue regarding the must-arrest policy that should be discussed. There is always a strong possibility that after being arrested, an offender may subject the victim to more violence when released. It could be perceived that an arrest may do more harm than good. A victim may only want reconciliation as a remedy. Fear of a home being broken up or of being alone may prevent him or her from seeking police intervention. In reducing domestic violence, protecting victims from future violence, and providing the necessary intervention, law enforcement must become innovative. Next we examine a model police program to demonstrate innovative programs designed to better serve victims of domestic violence.

The police department we have been examining realized that the complex issues created by domestic violence could not be addressed by a must-arrest policy alone. The department set out to improve its ability to police domestic crimes and determined that this could be accomplished by improvements in education, collaboration, enforcement, and prevention. The department also restructured the roles of precinct personnel in its response to domestic violence. Traditionally, each precinct in this department had one to four officers assigned as domestic violence officers. These officers' duties were to review domestic cases as they arrived. They were to enter all information from a domestic incident report into a precinct database. Through review of these records they were to identify and monitor high-risk households. The officers also received specialized training in domestic violence and had established contacts with other social service agencies. One task of the domestic violence prevention officer was to conduct home visits. During the home visit the officer would interview the domestic violence victim. The officer would then assist the victim in several ways. The officer could arrest a wanted offender, develop a safety plan for the victim, or offer the assistance of various social service agencies. The goal was to work with the victim to prevent future violence. We see that arrest of the offender is not the only avenue to reaching this goal. The use of different avenues to prevent domestic violence was expanded on in two pilot precincts. These precincts completely redefined its domestic violence approach and incorporated several innovative programs to better serve domestic violence victims.

These precincts each expanded their domestic violence prevention personnel. Each precinct allocated one supervisor, eight police officers, and two civilian personnel. The precincts chosen for the project were high-volume domestic crime precincts. The civilian personnel assumed the extensive clerical duties formerly performed by the domestic violence officer. The eight officers were to focus on reviewing cases, identifying high-risk locations, and responding in the field. The supervisor reviewed all reports and cases to ensure accuracy and that an appropriate follow-up plan had been established and conducted. Also assigned to the unit were four social workers from a social service agency. They were to work hand in hand with the police, by reviewing cases and providing immediate social service when requested. The social workers also reviewed their records and developed a high-risk locations list for follow-up. The detective unit was also involved directly in the operations of the domestic violence unit. The supervisors as well the personnel of the two units were to work jointly on domestic cases. The detective also maintained a most-wanted domestic offender list for follow-up. The program developed a chain of command up to the headquarters level. This direct line of supervision ensured operational efficiency. These units were also supplied with the resources needed to perform its functions effectively, including an office, computer equipment, phone/fax lines, and an automobile assigned for the unit's exclusive use. All of the personnel involved in the program received extensive training on domestic violence. Topics such as what domestic violence is, evidence collection, department procedure and policy, and legal instruction, as well as how to conduct home visits and develop safety plans, were covered.

Understanding the basic structure of these new units, we can now examine how the department intends to improve its response to domestic violence.

Education

The impact that this program will have on education is seen by the expansion of domestic violence personnel. The goal is to educate victims as well as communities about domestic violence. Each officer is required to attend community meetings, gatherings, and events to educate and distribute information on domestic violence and the resources available. The officers are also encouraged to attend seminars and conferences on domestic violence issues to increase their knowledge in this field. The unit supervisor is required to instruct precinct patrol personnel on domestic violence policy. He or she is to instruct on accurate report taking, procedure, law, and any areas deemed necessary to improve patrols' response to domestic violence in the field. The idea is to educate as many people as possible in recognizing and gaining some understanding of domestic violence. Having informed victims, communities and police will help them to recognize domestic violence and to take the steps necessary to prevent future violence.

Collaboration

Working together is a simple idea but is often difficult in a large agency. Different units or sections often operate by their own rules and procedures. The goal here is to restructure procedures to allow for a collaborative approach to domestic violence. The first step was in the creation of the precinct case management team. This team consisted of the precinct's domestic violence unit, detectives, and social service members. Members of these units would meet regularly to discuss the precinct's domestic violence strategy. Each unit's high-risk household list would be reviewed and discussed. Then together, responses would be developed, and old responses updated and reviewed for effectiveness. Units could request assistance in current cases and work together for a quick response. The focus here is on cooperation and communication to develop a combined approach in addressing domestic violence.

The department then developed a collaborative effort with the district attorney's office. Many domestic violence cases were dismissed due to lack of evidence, uncooperative victims, or lack of additional information. A direct line of communication was established between these program precincts and the district attorney's office, which now had the direct assistance needed for any case. The unit's officers could provide follow-up for evidence, information, and victim contact. The precincts now have direct contact for cases pending or status of offenders. Again, the focus is on cooperation and communication in the prosecution of domestic violence cases.

The department also developed a collaborative effort with probation and parole. It was found that victims of domestic violence were often contacting probation and parole personnel. The offenders were on probation or parole and the victims utilized these agencies for help. Generally, the police were not notified of these incidents and no follow-up contact was made. It was also found that often, domestic offenders on probation and parole were arrested. This was often unknown to probation or parole and no follow-up was conducted. A system of cross-reporting was developed between the police and these agencies. Now any person arrested for domestic violence found to be on probation or parole triggered a direct notification of the appropriate agency. Also, when probation or parole received a report of domestic violence concerning a resident of the project precinct that precinct was notified for the purpose of follow-up action. Here the focus is on cooperation and communication in the monitoring of domestic violence.

Through collaboration, swift intervention and prevention could be achieved. Several new avenues also become available to each of these agencies in their efforts in preventing domestic violence.

Enforcement

Collaboration and a coordinated approach are expected to lead to more appropriate and timely enforcement of domestic violence laws. Increased communication helps identify at-risk locations and allows for swift action by law enforcement personnel. A case may not be enough to hold an offender in jail, but it may be enough to violate his or her probation or parole. Violation of an offender's probation or parole may be the best way to prevent future violence and allow time for intervention. An offender may be more frightened of having his or her probation or parole violated than anything else. It is viewed that this fear will help prevent domestic incidents in the home. An increase in home visits by the precinct domestic violence unit would also increase the timeliness of enforcement. Home visits were made mandatory within 24 hours on an open complaint. The increase in postincident response led to quicker arrests. This quick response also led to better prevention opportunities. The goal is that an offender would be affected by swift and cooperative enforcement.

Prevention

It is hoped that home visits will prevent and reduce recurrent domestic crime. The program aids the precincts by increasing personnel efforts in the field. Units were now required to conduct home visits on all crime complaints received, open or closed. Also, cases would receive a home visit if deemed high risk or requested by another agency. The domestic violence officers would conduct a complete background check on every domestic case received. Every prior incident would be reviewed, and offenders' arrest records, warrants, and probation and parole status would be obtained. This information would then help determine when and how often a home visit would be needed. The goals of the home visit are several. First, there is an increased opportunity for arresting offenders. Second, it allows the police to establish contact with the victim and develop the assistance best needed for him or her. This contact will allow for a discussion of alternatives to police intervention and the establishment of rapport with the victim. The message is that the police are not there just to arrest people, but that they can offer help also. Third, it allows for follow-up contact as a deterrent. The police can visit victims to inquire about their safety and offer assistance. This increased contact or police presence is used to provide victims with reassurance and possible offenders with a deterrent. The home visit demonstrates that the police are there to help and to enforce the law. The role of law enforcement no longer ends by making an arrest in domestic cases. Law enforcement must work directly with victims to tailor the best plan for the victim. The police and the victim could develop a safety plan for the victim. This plan is a course of action that the victim could follow when he or she suspects that an incident of violence may occur. Simply, it would allow the victim to be prepared if an incident of violence may be imminent. Some steps the victim could take are:

- Placing money, keys, and important papers (passport, birth certificate, orders of protection, etc.) in a safe and secure place. Often, an offender will hold a victim's personal effects in an attempt to keep him or her from leaving.

- Finding a safe location to go to: a relative or friend that the victim could stay with if needed. Clothes and personal items are left at this location, as are children's clothes and effects. If a victim needs to leave the location quickly, having items and a place to go ahead of time makes exiting quicker. An offender seeing a victim packing to leave may only become more violent.

- Creating a code word or signal with a relative, friend, or neighbor to call the police. A victim may be able to reach another person to give this prearranged signal. The police may then be able to respond to the location before violence occurs.

- Coordinating a response for the police, future home visits, or phone calls. A victim may feel comfortable with a police presence at times. If violence tends to happen on certain days of the week or month, the victim may want the police to stop by. Also, a stalking victim may benefit from this type of help. For example, a victim may find the abuser standing on the corner of his or her bus stop as he or she comes home from work. This behavior clearly upsets the victim and places him or her in fear. Directed patrol at the bus stop by the police may be enough to intervene and cause the offender to leave.

- Providing a victim with resources and options other than police intervention. Ending a relationship with criminal prosecution may not be the outcome a victim is looking for. A domestic violence prevention officer could refer the family to a variety of counseling services and programs.

The use of home visits is important in the prevention of future violence. By informing the victim and presenting options, victims themselves could prevent future violence.

As law enforcement moves into the twenty-first century it must reevaluate its approach to domestic violence. This complex issue requires much more than a must-arrest policy if it hopes to reduce this type of crime. In examining the policy of this police department, we see the move from mandatory arrests, as a deterrent, to a complete intervention and prevention program. The dedication of resources and the collaborative efforts of this department show its commitment to addressing the problem of domestic violence. We have discussed a very involved program. To demonstrate the process of this program the following scenario is given as an example.

The police on a midnight tour respond to a domestic violence call. At the scene a woman informs the officers that her husband had threatened to kill her with a knife. The husband had fled the scene, and an area search by the police was negative. The officers prepared a report of the domestic incident and a crime report open to the detectives. Response by domestic violence personnel was not done because no unit personnel were working. At 7 A.M. the domestic violence unit received the reports. An officer reviewed the case and a history check was conducted. The domestic history check revealed five prior incidents involving threats with a weapon in the last four months. No other complaints were found. The offender's arrest history revealed two arrests for felony assault and one drug case. No active warrant or order of protection had been issued against the offender. The offender is on parole for an assault case.

The domestic violence officer then retrieves the past reports for review. Review showed that all prior complaints were closed because the victim requested that no charges be pursued. Several home visits were attempted in the past but none were successful. A phone call had been made and the victim stated that everything was all right. The offender's arrests were then followed up and it was determined that two years earlier the offender had stabbed his ex-common law wife over a dispute involving their child. The offender served six months for the crime and is currently on parole. The offender's parole officer is contacted and the information regarding the domestic incidents is given. Parole informs the officer that the offender is to report on the 23rd of each month and has been reporting as scheduled. Based on this information, an immediate home visit was conducted.

At the home visit the domestic violence officers are met by the victim, who relays the following account. The victim states that she has been married to the offender for the last five years. Although they have had problems, he has never been physically abusive. She knew he had had problems with his ex-wife, but she had never met her. He had gone to jail, but he told her that his ex-wife had lied to the police and that's why he had to go to jail. About four months ago the offender started using cocaine. This is when his whole personality changed. The victim tried to leave him because the drugs were taking over his life. He started stealing from her and he stopped working. When she tried to leave, the threats started. The victim states that she is afraid of him. The officers contact social service at the precinct, and referrals and shelter placement are made. The victim then states that she can't leave with the offender still out there. The only reason she let the police in was that her husband was staying with a relative. She feared that if she left, her husband would find her and hurt her. The victim agrees to cooperate but only if her husband was in jail long enough for her to find a safe place to stay. She asks the police not to contact her until her husband is in jail. She then gives the officers her husband's address.

At the station the domestic violence officers, detectives, and social services personnel meet to discuss the case. The case has a high risk of violence and the detectives respond to the offender's new address in an attempt to apprehend him. The domestic violence officer notifies parole of the offender's change of address and the alleged drug use. The officers also prepare an information bulletin to be read to outgoing patrol units. Social service locates shelter placement for the victim when needed. The detectives are unsuccessful in finding the offender. Several days then pass without incident.

The domestic violence officers then receive a call from parole. The offender has reported for his monthly parole visit. The detectives respond and arrest the offender. Parole conducts a drug test at the visit.

At the precinct the district attorney's office is notified and asked to have the offender remanded, due to his past history. The district attorneys office calls back several hours later and states that the victim is reluctant to prosecute the case. The domestic violence officers respond with social service to the victim's home. At the victim's home, a safety plan is developed and a course of action is discussed. The victim agrees to follow up on charges since the offender is still in jail. She feels that this is the only way that he will seek help for his drug habit. The offender was remanded to jail and his parole violated. The victim was relocated, and contact by the domestic violence unit was maintained to provide future assistance.

This scenario should demonstrate how some domestic violence incidents could become complicated for law enforcement to address. The following questions are to help discuss this complex issue and law enforcements efforts to address it.

- What else could have the first officers on the scene done to assist the victim?

- Had a domestic violence prevention officer not reviewed this case, what do you think the outcome would have been?

- What information led the officers to deem this case high risk?

- Why do you think the victim is reluctant to cooperate with law enforcement? What outcome is she is hoping for?

- Was the cooperation between parole, police, and the district attorney helpful or hurtful?

- What if the victim refused any help at all? How far should the police go in their intervention effort? At what point does help become an intrusion on a person's privacy?

- What would you have done differently if you were the officer assigned to this case?

SUMMARY AND CONCLUSIONS

Based on this data analysis, several important general conclusions can be drawn concerning the effect of race and ethnicity on domestic violence report and arrest rates. Again, it must be emphasized that the complaint or report data are representative of the total number of family offenses alleged to have been committed between members of the city's households; because the police may have been summoned more than once to these households, the data do not reflect the number of households affected by domestic violence. In contrast, the arrest data for aggravated (felony) assaults are a highly accurate depiction of the number of assaults in which police had probable cause to believe that a felony was actually committed; because officers have discretion to arrest in simple (misdemeanor) assault cases where the complaining witness refuses to press charges, those data provide a less accurate depiction of the actual rate of bona fide assaults.

The data reveal that the rate of family offenses coming to police attention generally tended to remain fairly constant within precincts between 1987 and 1991, and 1992 and 1995, without regard to race or ethnicity. Annual variances in these intraprecinct rates tended to follow the annual citywide variance.

Nevertheless, dramatic differences in complaint rates are evident for each racial or ethnic group in the subject precincts. The magnitude of these differences in per capita family offense complaint rates suggests strongly that domestic violence offenses come to the attention of the police more frequently within predominantly African-American and Hispanic neighborhoods than in predominantly white neighborhoods. The data set did not permit the authors to discover if this finding was the result of differential police response (an unlikely possibility, given the department's strict regulations) or is attributable to extraneous variables such as differences in employment levels, alcohol or drug abuse, or the failure of arrests to deter further assaults in these communities.

Both the number and rate of arrests for family offenses also tended to remain fairly constant within the precincts selected, and the tremendous differences in complaint rates between ethnically and racially predominant precincts were not reflected in the arrest rates. On the contrary, while these arrest rate data varied, they remained within a fairly consistent and narrow range.

During the four-year period between 1992 and 1995, the overall number and rate of domestic violence complaints remained relatively constant. Although there were years of abnormal growth or decline in domestic violence complaints coming to the attention of police in certain precincts over the four years, these were often isolated occurrences. In fact, of the six precincts analyzed, only one ever experienced a change in the rate of complaint greater than 20% of its four-year average. Other than these isolated fluctuations, each precinct followed the citywide model for total complaints. This trend, which took place between 1992 and 1995, was represented by an initially low complaint rate in 1992 (about 8% off the average), a steady rise over the years 1993 and 1994 represented by an approximate 12% increase over the average, and a more drastic decrease in 1995 to a point just slightly above the initial rate represented by the data of 1992.

This city's pro-arrest policy in domestic violence cases is inferred to be a more effective deterrent in white communities than in minority communities. This assessment is based on the fact that the complaint rate reflects the total number of complaints received by the police rather than the number of people against whom complaints have been made. Because this department's pro-arrest policy is so strictly enforced throughout the agency's jurisdiction, no basis exists to suppose that officers might be enforcing their mandate to arrest more stringently in one neighborhood than in another. Indeed, the compatibility of arrest rates across ethnic and racial lines adds credence to this assertion.

Given the limitations of the data set, an alternative but currently untested explanation for this disparity in complaint rates is that the African-American and Hispanic communities selected for this study are confronted by social problems and conditions which are not as prevalent or as extreme in white communities, and that these problems are contributing factors in the incidence of domestic violence found there. These minority communities may lack many of the resources and continuing social services necessary to achieve a permanent solution to family violence. It is quite possible that batterers in predominantly white communities have the financial resources to access effective counseling programs or that the social stigma attached to arrest within those communities effectively discourages future family violence.

The aggravated assault arrest rate in predominantly white precincts exceeded the simple assault arrest by a substantial margin. In African-American and Hispanic precincts, however, the simple assault arrest rate exceeded the aggravated assault rate. These data suggest that although considerably fewer complaints are received by the police in white communities, the assaults alleged to have occurred there are more severe and result in a greater number of arrests. Two explanations may be posited to account for this finding.

First, police officers in predominantly white neighborhoods may exercise their discretion not to arrest in misdemeanor assaults more frequently than in minority communities. The data did not permit this hypothesis to be tested, and the authors have no empirical reason to assume or question its validity. Another, more intuitive explanation may be that assault victims in white neighborhoods are more reluctant to suffer the embarrassment and stigma of calling the police to intervene in family disputes involving less severe injuries. If this hypothesis is valid, it would imply that these victims are more willing to suffer repeated but less severe assaults, until the increasing violence reaches an intolerable threshold. A corollary to this hypothesis is that the actual rate of domestic assaults against white victims is much higher than the complaint data would suggest. Given the acknowledged frailty of the complaint rate data presented here, that possibility should not be ignored.

REFERENCES AND BIBLIOGRAPHY

BARD, M. (1970). *Training in Crisis Intervention: From Concept to Implementation.* Washington, DC: U.S. Department of Justice.

BARD, M. (1973). *Family Crisis Intervention.* Washington, DC: U.S. Government Printing Office.

BROWNE, A. (1984). Assault and homicide at home: When battered women kill. Presentation at the second National Conference for Family Violence Researchers, Durham, NH.

BROWNE, A. (1987). *When Battered Women Kill.* New York: Free Press.

BUZAWA, E. S., and C. G. BUZAWA (1990). *Domestic Violence: The Criminal Justice Response.* Thousand Oaks, CA: Sage.

DUNFORD, F. W. (1990). System initiated warrants for suspects of misdemeanor domestic violence: A pilot study. *Justice Quarterly*, 7:631–653.

DUNFORD, F. W. et al. (1990). The role of arrest in domestic assault. *Criminology*, 28:183–206.

FLEMING, J. B. (1979). *Stopping Wife Abuse.* Garden City, NY: Anchor Press/Doubleday.

GELLES, R. J., and M. A. STRAUSS (1988). *Intimate Violence.* New York: Simon & Schuster.

GONDOLF, E. W., and E. B. FISHER (1988). *Battered Women as Survivors: An Alternative to Treating Learned Helplessness.* Lexington, MA: Lexington Books.

GONDOLF, E. G., and E. B. FISHER (1991). Wife beating. In R. T. Ammerman and M. Hersen (eds.), *Case in Family Violence.* New York: Plenum Press, pp. 273–292.

HART, B. (1992). State criminal and civil codes on domestic violence. *Juvenile and Family Court Journal*, pp. 3–68.

HASSELT, V. N., R. L. MORRISON, A. S. BELLACK, and M. HERSEN (eds.) (1988). *Handbook of Family Violence.* New York: Plenum Press.

HIRSCHEL, J. D., et al. (1992). Review essay on the law enforcement response to spouse abuse: Past, present and future. *Justice Quarterly*, 9(2):247–283.

PENCE, E. (1983). The Duluth domestic abuse intervention project. *Hamline Law Review*, 6:247–275.

PLECK, E. (1987). *Domestic Tyranny: The Making of American Social Policy against Family Violence from Colonial Times to the Present*. New York: Oxford University Press.

ROBERTS, A. R. (1981). *Sheltering Battered Women: A National Survey and Service Guide*. New York: Springer.

ROBERTS, A. R. (ed.) (1984). *Battered Women and their Families: Intervention Strategies and Treatment Programs*. New York: Springer; 2nd edition, 1998.

ROBERTS, A. R. (1988). Substance abuse and battering: The deadly mix. *Journal of Substance Abuse Treatment*, 12(1):83–87.

ROBERTS, A. R. (1994). Court responses to battered women and reform legislation. In A. R. Roberts (ed.), *Critical Issues in Crime and Justice*. Thousand Oaks, CA: Sage Publications, pp. 240–248.

ROBERTS, A. R. (1996). Police responses to battered women: Past, present, and future. In A. R. Roberts (ed.), *Helping Battered Women: New Perspectives and Remedies*. New York: Oxford University Press, pp. 85–95.

ROBERTS, A. R., and B. J. ROBERTS (1990). A model for crisis intervention with battered women and their children. In A. R. Roberts (eds.), *Crisis Intervention Handbook: Assessment, Treatment and Research*. Belmont, CA: Wadsworth, pp. 105–123.

ROY, M. (ed.) (1982) *The Abusive Partner: An Analysis of Domestic Battering*. New York: Van Nostrand Reinhold.

SHERMAN, L. W. (1991). From initial deterrence to longterm escalation: Short custody arrest for poverty ghetto domestic violence. *Criminology*, 29:821–850.

SHERMAN, L. W., AND R. A. BERK (1984). The specific deterrent effects of arrest for domestic assault. *American Sociological Review*, 49:267–272.

SHERMAN, L. W., et al. (1992). The variable effects of arrest on criminal careers: The Milwaukee domestic violence experiment. *Journal of Criminal Law and Criminology*, 83.

STRAUS, M., and R. GELLES (1990). *Physical Violence in American Families*. New Brunswick, NJ: Transaction Publishers.

STRAUS, M., R. GELLES, and S. STEINMETZ (1980). *Behind Closed Doors: Violence in the American Family*. Garden City, NY: Anchor Press/Doubleday.

SUGG, N. K., and T. INUI (1992). Primary care physicians' response to domestic violence: Opening Pandora's box. *Journal of the American Medical Association*, 267(23):3157–3160.

TRAFFORD, A. (1991). Why battered women kill: Self defense, not revenge is often the motive. *Washington Post*, February 26.

U.S. ATTORNEY GENERAL'S TASK FORCE ON FAMILY VIOLENCE (1984). *Final Report*, Washington, DC: U.S. Department of Justice, September.

WALKER, L. E. (1979). *The Battered Women*. New York: Harper & Row.

WALKER, L. E. (1984). *The Battered Women Syndrome*. New York: Springer.

WALKER, L. E. (1987). *Terrifying Love*. New York: Harper & Row.

WALKER, L. E. (1993). Battered women as defendants. In N. Z. Hilton (ed.), *Legal Responses to Wife Assault*. Thousand Oaks, CA: Sage Publications, pp. 233–257.

CASE

Thurman v. City of Torrington. 595 F. Supp. 1521 (D. Conn.) (1984).

chapter 8

The Influence of Community in Community Policing in the Twenty-First Century

Michael J. Palmiotto, Ph.D.

ABSTRACT

What influence will the community have in community policing in the twenty-first century? The difficulty of projecting the influence of the community on community policing lies with the fact that there exist limited concrete data that community policing is successful. Although community policing is in its infancy it has evolved in the first decade of the twenty-first century. It is anticipated that community policing will continue evolving well into the twenty-first century. Although gazing into the crystal ball of the future is nebulous, certain facets of the community policing concept will survive and have an impact on policing and crime control. The impact and influence of the community on policing should grow and be greater than it was in the last decades of the twentieth century. The influence of the community on policing in the twenty-first century is reviewed in this chapter.

INTRODUCTION

Community policing in the first decade of the twenty-first century has received creditability and has become an acceptable philosophy of policing. In the last quarter of the twentieth century, police practitioners came to the realization that the traditional reactive approach to crimes already committed was not working and that development of a new police strategy was imperative. This new policing concept became known as community policing. The philosophy of community-oriented policing grew out of police strategies known as team policing and *ministations*, which were established in many of our cities during the 1960s and 1970s. In the first decade of the new century, most police practictictioners and an informed public have accepted community policing as a workable alternative to traditional policing.

A driving force behind community policing was the desire to maintain the quality of neighborhoods on the part of citizens who lived in these neighborhoods and the police who had the legal authority to maintain social order in the neighborhoods. Former California Governor Pat Brown had this to say: "As I see it, the single greatest problem over the next twenty years will be keeping the quality of life in the state from deteriorating any further than it already has" (Brown, 1990:8). Citizens' concern about the quality of life has influenced the police to examine the service orientation philosophy of community policing at the expense of the traditional law enforcement model. The average citizen has indicated his or her concern about incivilities that can often devastate a neighborhood.

Herman Goldstein, a noted police scholar of the late twentieth century, developed the concept of *problem-oriented policing*, which compelled police officers to solve nuisance or crime problems. The problem-oriented philosophy became the foundation for the community-oriented approach to policing. Under the community-oriented policing concept, the police are recognizing that they need the support of the community in order to solve crime. With crime on the rise in the latter part of the twentieth century, especially crimes of violence, the fear of crime had also increased. The big hope that community-oriented policing offered was that crime could be prevented and reduced. If the police were successful in these areas, the fear of crime would decline. The major question that has not been answered is whether community-oriented policing will be successful in keeping crime under control. Initially, there existed a wide approach to community-oriented policing, but eventually, evaluation of community-oriented programs made it possible to select its most successful aspects. Both police administrators and line officers came to realize that community-oriented policing had to work if they were to obtain community support and cooperation. The police of the twentieth century became aware that they were successful in solving crimes only when the public cooperated by providing information that could lead to the arrest and conviction of law violators.

During the 1970s, research on policing increased substantially. These findings indicated that the police must make a serious effort to work with people whom they were to serve and protect. The police could not deal with the crime problem alone. The citizen also had a role in preventing and controlling crime. The research of the latter twentieth century was an eye-opener for the police. The major research findings came to the following conclusions (Manning, 1988:41–44):

1. Increasing the numbers of police does not necessarily reduce crime rates or raise the proportion of crime solved; social conditions such as income, unemployment, population, and social heterogeneity are far more important predictors of variation in crime and clearance rates.

2. Randomized motorized patrolling neither reduces crime nor improves the chances of catching criminals.

3. The use of two-person cars neither reduces crime nor helps to catch criminals more effectively than does the use of one-person cars, and police are no more likely to be injured in one-person cars.

4. Although saturation patrolling does reduce crime, it does so at the cost of displacing it to other areas.

5. The legendary "good collar" is a rare event; even more rarely does a police patrol confront a crime in progress.

6. Response time doesn't matter.

7. Criminal investigations are not very effective in solving crime.

THE CRIME PROBLEM

From the mid-1960s to 1993 there was a substantial increase in the crime rate in the United States. During these decades of the century, violent crimes—which include murder, rape, robbery, and aggravated assault—reached 2 million. The clearance rate for violent crimes hovered around 45%. At one point in the early 1990s the number of murders reached over 24,000, compared to 8000 murders during the 1960s (a two-thirds increase in murders in a very short time span). With the increase in the number of murders, the police were less successful in solving them. The solvability rate was over 90% when there were 8000 murders in our country. The solvability rate dropped to less than 70% when the number of murders were over 24,000. During this period the concept of serial murders evolved. A serial murderer is a person who kills a number of people over a period of time. An accurate count of serial murderers on the loose in U.S. society was unknown. This era also saw the evolution of the mass murderer, a person who kills a number of people at the same time, going into fast-food restaurants, shopping malls, and workplaces and killing whoever was in the area. The early 1990s observed the initiation of the recreational murderer as a person who kills simply for pleasure. Most of these murders were senseless, done for the sake of cruelty and without any feeling for the victim as a human being. Many such murderers were juveniles who appeared to have no sense of the value of a human life.

However, beginning in 1994 and continuing into the first decade of the twenty-first century crime took a dramatic twist. It began to decline. For example, the Crime Index from 1994 to 1998 decreased 14% and the Violent Crime Index during this same period decreased 20.6% (*Crime in the United States 1998*, 1999:7, 12). A major factor for the decrease in the national crime rate is that crime in the largest U.S. cities have decreased substantially. For example, New York City in 1994 recorded just over 600 murders compared to 2267 murders in 1990. In 1994, New York City had less murder than it had in 1964. The trend has not abated. For instance, the 1999 crime data revealed that violent crimes fell by 10.4% from the previous year. This crime rate declined for most offenses except rape and sexual assault. Also, property crimes such as burglary, motor vehicle theft, and other types of thefts declined by 9% (Dorning, 2000:1A).

Although the second half of the 1990s saw a decrease in the crime rate, there are several negatives to the nation's crime rate that need to be addressed. There has been an increase in domestic violence, a growing acceptance of marijuana among young people, and drug use is still a serious problem for our nation. Minorities continue to be victimized and arrested at a rate disproportionate to their numbers. Teenagers have a greater chance of being victims of violence than do adults (Hansen, 1998: 81–82).

There is a variety of reasons given for the reduction in crime for the last several years. Ronald Goldstock, chair of the American Bar Association's Criminal Justice Section, says: "The crime reductions we see in the report (ABA report on crime) appear to be due more to the innovative ways in which law enforcement officials now approach their jobs than to changes in demographics and other social conditions" (Hansen, 1998: 81). James Alan Fox, a criminal justice professor at Northeastern University in Boston, attributes the continuing decline in crime rates to "successes in many areas including better police tactics, increase in crime prevention programs, longer prison terms for convicted criminals, the shift in the drug market away from concaine and the aging of the Baby Boom generation" (Dorning, 2000:1A, 8A). However, the author of this article concurs with Alfred Blumstein, professor of criminology at Carnegie Mellon University in Pittsburgh, who believes that the trends of crime declining "can't continue forever, We've seen an indication that at least the leading edge is starting to flatten out" (Dorning, 2000:8A).

COMMUNITY-ORIENTED POLICING

Whatever the cause of the violence, it has been accepted that the United States is a violent country. Crime scholars recognize that the police can only attempt to prevent crime or solve a crime after it occurs. Cooperation from informed citizens who are actively involved in crime prevention is required if the police hope to curb the rising crime rate. Using traditional police strategies, the police have been unable to control crime. The police would not have initiated community-oriented policing if the professional model of policing had been successful in curbing the crime rate. Not only was the violent crime rate high, property crime rates were also high, reaching 13 million crimes in early 1990s, the last decade of the twentieth century. Property offenses include burglary, theft, and arson. With the increase in crime, the public's fear of crime, and the news media's onslaught of crime news, the police had their backs to the wall. Therefore, they adopted a policing philosophy with the argument that it offered a better strategy for preventing crime and reducing the public's fear of crime than did the professional police model.

Community Defined

What does the term *community* mean? The term is used loosely and often has a variety of meanings and perceptions. Peter Wilmot (1987:2) expounds that we may want to distinguish between "*territorial community*, defined by geography and meaning the people living in a specific area; the *interest community*, a set of people with something in common other than just territory (the black community, the Jewish community, the gay community); and the *attachment community*, where there is a kind of attachment to people or place that gives rise to a 'sense of community.'" Wilmot believes that the three types of community can overlap. For example, interest communities can be geographically dispersed. Also, an attachment and sense of community can join people into territorial or interest communities.

The community has functioned as a means of social control, and its importance to the community-oriented policing concept seems evident. The term *community* is often used interchangeably with *neighborhood*. The majority of Americans live in urban and suburban neighborhoods rather than in rural communities. In an industrialized civilization, communities or neighborhoods are drawn along socioeconomic lines, described as underclass or lower class, working class, middle class, and upper class. One's status in this socioeconomical structure is based on wealth, material possession, and the importance of one's position in society's structure.

The lower socioeconomic classes commit many of the predatory crimes that the rest of society considers intolerable. The police have always functioned in controlling the lower socioeconomic classes with the political and economic support of the middle and upper classes. With traditional policing strategies not succeeding in controlling predatory crimes, another strategy was needed. Community-oriented policing became the panacea for preventing and controlling crime. It was also offered as a means to diffuse the fear of crime.

Community-Oriented Policing Philosophy

Mollie Weatheritt (1987:7) writes that "community policing is a conveniently elastic term which is often used loosely to accommodate virtually any policing activity of which its proponents approve." Weatheritt claims that there exists no agreed definition of community policing, nor should there be one. Contrary to Weatheritt, Robert Trojanowicz and Bonnie Bucqueroux (1990:5) have a basic definition for community policing:

> Community policing is a new philosophy of policing, based on the concept that police officers and private citizens working together in creative ways can help solve contemporary community problems related to crime, fear of crime, social and physical disorder, and neighborhood decay. The philosophy is predicated on the belief that achieving these goals requires that police departments develop a new relationship with the law-abiding people in the community, allowing them a greater voice in setting local police priorities and involving them in efforts to improve the overall quality of life in their neighborhoods. It shifts the focus of police work from handling random calls to solving community problems.

Community-oriented policing means a shift away from centralization and control of the line officer. The philosophy of community-oriented policing allows the line officer to be a decision maker and problem solver. The structure of police departments requires them to be more flexible and democratic. Under the concept of community-oriented policing, police work is not incident-driven any longer but instead, emphasizes community problem solving. The goal will be to solve the problem in order to eliminate incidents of disturbances or annoyances to the community or neighborhood. Brown (1988) distinguishes community policing from traditional policing:

1. Community policing is oriented to problem solving and focuses on results. It encourages techniques such as problem identification, problem analysis, and problem resolution.

2. Community policing demands that police departments organize to incorporate citizen input in matters that affect the safety and quality of neighborhood life. Police citizen partnerships and power sharing in crime control efforts are encouraged. Police are expected to be accountable to the community for their actions and results.

3. Decentralization is encouraged. Beats are drawn to coincide with natural neighborhood boundaries to encourage responsibilities for shared "turf." Beat officers are given permanent beat assignments and are encouraged to become actively involved in the affairs of the community and to initiate creative solutions to neighborhood problems. The patrol officer becomes the "manager" of their assigned beat.

4. Performance evaluations are based on problem-solving ability and success in involving citizens in crime-fighting efforts. The criterion for success becomes an absence of incidents such as criminal offenses, traffic accidents, and repeat calls for service.

Herman Goldstein (1993:4–6) claims that if policing is to be improved, the public's expectation of the police must change. Goldstein advocates realistic expectations of what the police can accomplish. By taking a realistic approach, the impossible job the police are asked to perform becomes possible. The police should concentrate on analyzing and responding to specific citizen problems that are brought to their attention. For community policing to be successful, the relationship between the community and the police has to improve. A partnership must develop.

POLICING IN THE EARLY TWENTY-FIRST CENTURY

American society exists in a changing world. The society in which we will live in the early twenty-first century will be different from what it has been in the late twentieth century. The age of information will have taken hold. We will be able to communicate visually and orally with anyone in the world instantaneously. Information about scientific, business, and political issues will be obtained in seconds. Sites for making steel and automobiles will be replaced by communities concerned about pollution products produced by automation. The U.S. economy will become a part of a global economy that became feasible with the fall of communism in eastern Europe in 1989 and the consolidation of western Europe's economy in 1992. Educational institutions will be a key component to the success of individuals and business. The workforce will be trained in high-tech equipment and people will be retrained continuously to keep up to date in new technological developments. More people will be working from their homes than in an office or factory. A substantial portion of the population will be over 65 years of age. The baby boomers of post–World War II will have reached senior status. White males will be a minority in the workforce, being replaced by females and minority groups. The Hispanic population should be approaching 30%, while the Asian and black population will each have about 12% of the population. The United States will have become a more culturally diverse society.

Futurist Gene Stephens (1992:22) believes that the justice process will be participatory, a mediation process where victim and defendant come to a satisfactory agreement. Stephens claims that police will possess tools that could invade individual privacy. A California study found six trends that can affect policing in California cities going into the twenty-first century (Schwab, 1992:16–19):

1. There will be decreased resources.
2. The population will be wealthier, older, and more culturally diverse.
3. There will be a steady increase in the crime rate, and the diversity of crime will increase.
4. The perception of crime by the community will remain stable.
5. Community support should increase.
6. The public's demand for extra service will increase at no extra cost.

Community Influence

In the first decade of the twenty-first century a large number of police departments claim that they have adoped the community-oriented policing philosophy. However, it is extremely difficult to determine if departments are actually committed to the community policing concept or are just attempting to be politically correct. It does appear that many police departments are being influenced by the community policing strategy and that the community policing concept has had an influence on policing in the first decade of the twenty-first century. Community-oriented policing emphasizes listening rather than just talking to people. It takes seriously the concerns and input of citizens who live and work in the community or neighborhood. The police listen because they realize that (Wycott, 1988:105–106):

1. Citizens may legitimately have ideas about what they want and need from the police that may be different from what police believe they need.
2. Citizens have the information about the problems and people in their areas that police need to operate effectively.
3. Police and citizens each hold stereotypes about the other that, unless broken down by nonthreatening contacts, prevent either group from making effective use of the other.

With the police listening to citizens, it will become a common practice for the police in the twenty-first century to conduct periodic *customer surveys*. The police need regular feedback on how they are doing. This feedback can only be obtained from citizen-clients whom the police serve. The police will survey victims, witnesses, and complainants on how the police are performing their job. Customer surveys will ask citizens to rate the police on such areas as concern, helpfulness, knowledge, quality of service, solving the problem, putting the citizen at ease, and professional conduct (Couper and Lobitz, 1991:74). Based on customer service feedback, the police will make adjustments and improvements in their actions.

Citizen Police Academies

In the initial decade of the twenty-first century, the police recognized that they need the assistance of citizen volunteers if they are to keep crime under control. There has been an increase in direct citizen participation to keep crime and neighborhood disturbances under control. One commonly used avenue will be *citizen police academies*, which advance police interaction with citizens and can extend police accountability to the community. These training academies, which are usually offered once a week and taught by police officers, can provide citizens with realistic expectations of what the police can achieve in controlling and preventing crime. Citizens can learn how to prevent crime and how to control the fear of crime and disorders, and they can bring this information back to their communities, where they can put it to practical use. This concept may allow citizens in a neighborhood to police themselves.

Community Advisory Councils

A common practice in the initial decades in the twenty-first century will be the development of *community advisory councils*. These councils will meet on a regular basis and work with operational commanders and police department policymakers to decrease the crime rate, disorder, and the fear of crime. A partnership between the community advisory council and the police will focus on improving the quality of life for community citizens. The council will identify and prioritize problems within the community that a majority of residents want rectified. Once problems are identified, strategies will be devised to solve the problems. There will be an evaluation by the council to determine if the problems identified have been corrected or at least kept under control.

The council will have a variety of activities at its disposal. Under its bailiwick is the *neighborhood information network*, which provides information about crime in the area. The information network will be a direct source of crime information, providing accurate information in place of rumors, gossip, and accounts from the news media. The council would print a newsletter to inform residents of recent crime trends and provide crime prevention techniques to help citizens avoid becoming victims. The council will also have the responsibility to organize citizen patrols and to oversee the selection for this activity with the approval of the police department. Following the lead of the "broken windows" concept, which advocates that graffiti and rundown neighborhoods leave an impression of lack of concern and a crime-infested community, the council working with the police will have graffiti and abandoned cars removed and will strive to clear the neighborhood of any appearance of disorganization. The goal is to establish a sense of community. The council will function as an advisory board to the police and work to provide solutions to community problems.

Civilian Oversight

In the last half of the twentieth century there existed an on-again off-again movement to have civilian review boards or, as it became known in the 1980s and 1990s, *civilian oversight* of police behavior. In the late twentieth century, as a result of police violence and police corruption, community residents demanded the opportunity to review police conduct. In the 1990s it became apparent that police were sometimes unable to clean their own houses. The Mollen Commission in New York City discovered that police officers were robbing drug dealers of their money and drugs and going into business for themselves. Police officers would not only sell drugs but would use illicit drugs such as cocaine while on duty. Officers intentionally abused citizens without any reason other than that someone had annoyed an officer. High-ranking administrators and supervisors looked the other way: They did not want a scandal or negative publicity. Police violence and corruption were not unique to New York; they existed in urban, suburban, and rural communities. In Detroit, two police officers beat a suspect to death. Atlanta police officers were arrested for burglarizing adult entertainment clubs. Savannah, Georgia, had a drug ring operated by a police officer. A New Orleans police officer murdered her partner during a restaurant robbery. Because of police scandals in the last decade of the twentieth century, community leaders have been given the authority to oversee police conduct, directed by the community-oriented police concept, which can operate successfully only if a partnership exists between the community and the police. Under a closed system a partnership does not exist. When police organizations opened their operations to the public, a legitimate partnership came into existence. No longer did a wall of silence exist among police officers. Police administrators and supervisors came to realize that it was in the best interest of the police department to open up their organization to the community. If they did not allow or cooperate with the community in civilian oversight of police behavior, the philosophy of community policing that they advocated would be a fraud.

Civilian oversight would consist only of civilians, who would have the power to investigate and review allegations of police misconduct by members of the police department. The civilian oversight committee would review any police activity involving unnecessary or excessive use of force, discourtesy, abuse of authority, and conduct or behavior. All accusations would be investigated promptly and thoroughly, and upon completion of the investigation, the civilian oversight committee would turn over its findings to a prosecutor for criminal prosecution or to the department for appropriate actions, or if the allegation is unfounded or uncorroborated, the officer, the department, and the accuser would be notified.

The civilian oversight committee would also have input on police promotions, hirings, and reassignments. This committee would provide insight on department policies directly affecting police interaction with citizens. The committee will have the authority to recommend specific training that may be lacking in a police department. For example, some officers may need sensitivity training if they are abrasive and rude when dealing with the community. The committee would be a partner with the police and not function as an adversary. Members of the committee would be recommended by the police department, community organizations such as the chamber of commerce, and elected political officials.

If the police are to be recognized as professionals, their activities have to be an open book. Their conduct and behavior should be above approach. For community-oriented policing to be successful, the community and its citizens must trust and respect the police. How can the community be coproducers in crime prevention, eliminating neighborhood disorganization and controlling the fear of crime, if their only intention is to manipulate the community? There must be a sincere police–community partnership if community-oriented policing is to be successful. This means that in the twenty-first century the community will have a voice in policing.

Privatizing the Police

Because of slow economic growth in the early 1990s, some communities have looked at alternative means for public safety. As a result of financial cutbacks and stagnant budgets, the police have forced the affluent, businesses, and those elements of the community who were concerned about their personal safety to play a larger role. The community-oriented philosophy of policing has been forced to include private security organizations. The conclusions drawn by the Hallcrest Report provide justification for the partnership of private policing agencies with public policing agencies. The Hallcrest report states: "Law enforcement resources have stagnated and in some cases are declining. This mandates greater cooperation with the private sector and its private security resources to jointly forge a partnership on an equal basis for crime prevention and reduction. Law enforcement can ill afford to continue isolation and, in some cases, ignore these important resources" (Cunningham and Taylor, 1985:275).

Private police agencies can be involved in a variety of ways. They can function as alarm monitors and respond to intrusions when burglary and robbery alarms go off. The private police will respond in lieu of the public police. There can be a volunteer police organization under the supervision of the county sheriff or local police chief. The volunteer police organization can operate under a nonprofit, tax-exempt private organization under state law. The organization would have a board of directors with limited police powers. The volunteer police organization can free the police to perform proactive police work. They can check vacant homes while residents are on vacation, or direct traffic.

Privatizing of the police includes establishing guard forces for public housing, directing traffic, and providing security and crowd control for civil centers and publicly owned buildings. The guard force will be used for the management of parking enforcement. Regional shopping centers can use guard forces for public safety. Private police can perform patrol service. For example, San Francisco has had licensed private persons provide patrol services to neighborhoods that wanted additional police protection. They go to the city's police academy to qualify as peace officers; they are armed, uniformed, and are given full police powers. The private patrol officers are expected to respond to calls in their neighborhood just as public police officers do. The key difference is that the private police officers are entrepreneurs.

More private police will serve as switchboard operators in the twenty-first century than in the twentieth century. Public police will contract for this service as well as for records and property management, data processing, and so on. It will be more cost-effective to contract with private police than for the public police to perform these functions.

The list of activities performed by private police involving the privatization of public policing services will be substantial during the twenty-first century. In the twenty-first century, U.S. citizens will decide that private policing agencies have an important role to play in crime prevention and control. The private police and the public police will be partners. The community-oriented policing philosophy will be extended to private police. Since the private police are citizens from the community, their role in private policing will increase the influence of the community in community policing.

CONCLUSIONS

In the last quarter of the twentieth century, police practitioners have come to the realization that the traditional reactive approach to crimes already committed has not worked and that the development of a new police strategy is imperative. This new philosophy has become known as community policing. A driving force behind community policing has been the desire to maintain the quality of life in neighborhoods for citizens who live in these neighborhoods.

The philosophy of community-oriented policing allows the line officer to be a decision maker and problem solver. The structure of the police department requires it to be more flexible and democratic. Under the concept of community-oriented policing, police work is not incident-driven any longer but instead, emphasizes community problem solving.

American society exists in a changing world. The society of the early twenty-first century is different from that of the late twentieth century. The age of information has taken hold. We are able to communicate visually and orally with anyone in the world instantaneously. The U.S. economy is strong and the leader of a global economy. This economy was made feasible with the fall of communism in eastern Europe in 1989 and the consolidation of western Europe's economy in 1992. A substantial portion of the population will eventually be over 65 years of age. Expectations are that white males will become a minority of the workforce, replaced by women and minorities.

In the twenty-first century the community-oriented policing concept will become embedded in the strategies of policing. It will be a common practice for the police to conduct periodic customer surveys. The police will survey victims, witnesses, and complaints on how the police are performing their job. Citizen police academies will become common, with citizens being involved directly in crime prevention and control strategies.

A common practice in the twenty-first century will be the formation of community advisory councils. These councils will meet on a regular basis and work with operational commanders and police policymakers to decrease the crime rate, disorder, and the fear of crime. The council will have a variety of activities at its disposal. Because of police scandals in the last decade of twentieth century, community leaders have been given authority to oversee police conduct. They have been directed by the community-oriented policing concept, which can operate successfully only if a partnership exists between the community and the police.

Because of the anemic economy in the early 1990s and slow economic growth in this decade, some communities have looked at alternative means for public safety. Because of financial cutbacks and stagnant budgets, the police have forced the affluent, businesses, and those elements who were concerned about their personal safety to play a larger role. The community-oriented philosophy of policing has been forced to include private security organizations. Private police have functioned as alarm monitors, volunteer police, guard force, and switchboard operators. Even with an excellent economy in the late 1990s going into the first decade of the twenty-first century, the role of private security has not decreased. With a booming economy, Americans have more material possessions to protect.

REFERENCES

BROWN, L. (1988). *Community Policing: A Practical Guide for Police Officials*. Perspectives on Policing, No. 12. Washington, DC: U.S. Department of Justice, National Institute of Justice.

BROWN, E. G.(1990). To preserve the quality of life. *California Journal*, January.

COUPER, D. C., and S. H. LOBITZ (1991). *Quality Policing: The Madison Experience*, Washington, DC: Police Executive Research Forum.

CUNNINGHAM, W. C., and T. H. TAYLOR (1985). *Private Security and Police in America: The Hallcrest Report*. Portland, OR: Chancellor Press.

DORNING, M. (2000). Crime rates continue to fall. *Wichita Eagle*, August 28.

FEDERAL BUREAU OF INVESTIGATION (1999). *Crime in the United States, 1998*. Uniform Crime Reports. Washington, DC: U.S. Government Printing Office.

GOLDSTEIN, H. (1993). The new policing: Confronting complexity. Paper presented at the Conference on Community Policing, National Institute of Justice, U.S. Department of Justice, Washington, DC, August.

HANSEN, M. (1998). Taking a look at crime. *ABA Journal*, 84, February.

MANNING, P K. (1988). Community policing as a drama of control. In J. R. Greene and S. D. Mastrofski (eds.), *Community Policing: Rhetoric or Reality*. Westport, CT: Praeger, p. 279.

SCHWAB, S. (1992). *Restructuring Small Police Agencies: A Transition toward Customer Service*. Sacramento, CA: Peace Officer Standards and Training, February.

STEPHENS, G. (1992). Drugs and crime in the twenty-first century. *Futurist*, May–June.

TROJANOWICZ, R., and B. BUCQUEROUX (1990). *Community Policing: A Contemporary Perspective*. Cincinnati, OH: Anderson Publishing.

WEATHERITT, M. (1987). Community policing now. In P. Wilmot (ed.), *Policing and the Community*. London: Policy Studies Institute, pp. 7–20.

WILMOT, P. (ed.) (1987). *Policing and the Community*. London: Policy Studies Institute.

WYCOTT, M. A. (1988). The benefits of community policing: Evidence and conjecture. In J. R. Greene and S. D. Mastrofski (eds.), *Community Policing: Rhetoric or Reality*. Westport, CT: Praeger, pp. 103–120.

chapter 9

Legal Issues in Policing

Robert J. Meadows, Ph.D.

ABSTRACT

Policing in the twenty-first century will be a more demanding and delicate process. The police and community will share in the crime control function. Private security services will continue to assist the police in meeting community protection needs. The police will be given more legal freedom mandates, but will continually be held accountable for mistakes. These trends signal a need for the police to be better trained in the total crime prevention process and functions associated with community service.

INTRODUCTION

The modern police officer is confronted with delicate situations, requiring immediate but appropriate responses. The police are an important link between citizens and their government. However, the police must not only be responsive but also accountable to those they are sworn to serve. The police operate under the democratic rule of law process, which means a government of laws, not men. However, it is recognized that the police exercise a great deal of discretion, and at times, this discretion may get out of control. The behavior of the police in the celebrated Rodney King incident demonstrates how the police lost control in a delicate situation. The misuse of discretion in this incident set into motion a series of events where police tactics, policy, and leadership practices were questioned by a number of scholars, public officials, and citizens. The police officers of the future must be responsive to the community and accountable for their performance. In this chapter we explore the police role in addressing crime and violence in the home and the streets. For the police to be more responsive, there is a need for greater involvement from the community. Trends in domestic violence legislation suggest that the police will be required to assume a more aggressive posture. Court decisions in search and seizure cases have permitted the police to "bend the rules." Yet, to assure accountability, legal controls on police behavior and practices will continue to exist.

THE POLICE AND THE COMMUNITY

Given the variety and frequency of police tasks, it is difficult for the police to be totally responsive to the community. A community-wide response is needed to address the crime problem. The concept of community policing is based on a working partnership between the police and the community in addressing crime problems (Wilson and Kelling, 1982; Kelling et al., 1988; Trojanowicz and Bucqueroux, 1990). Generally, the theory of community policing holds that if businesses, community organizations, and residents work together, crime will decrease. In other words, an integrated community effort and a proactive police presence must accompany programs designed to reduce criminal opportunity. In short, the police would go into the community and become not only crime fighters, but community facilitators, working with a law-abiding community. The reactive posture the police have assumed in the past is not enough to address community crime problems. The community must assist in policing itself, and the police must assist in mobilizing the community to accomplish this task. There are three major approaches in meeting future community policing needs. Some of these approaches have already begun.

The first approach is the trend of justice agencies working together in attacking crime problems and targeting serious repeat offenders. In recent years, a number of departments have begun to use proactive, police-initiated procedures in patrolling the community. These programs are referred to as *repeat offender programs* (ROPs). The emphasis on these programs is based on research findings suggesting that a small number of chronic or repeat offenders commit a disproportionately large number of violent crimes (Blumstein et al., 1983). The juvenile delinquency problem in some communities has forged a working alliance between criminal justice agencies.

A program designed to track serious habitual juvenile offenders, referred to as SHO/DI, has been launched in several cities nationwide (Kline, 1993:32–37). The purpose of the program is to develop trust and cooperation between agencies serving juveniles, and to build an interagency information process to identify and track serious habitual juvenile offenders. The ultimate goal is to incapacitate the repeat offender, whether through detention, incarceration, probation, or other measures. It is a process to stop criminal behavior temporarily, and institute efforts to modify the behavior. It is a form of crime prevention whereby the police proactively monitor the serious repeat juvenile offender. The SHO/DI program makes rosters of all juveniles meeting the criteria of serious offenders. The police, district attorney's office, and the probation department work together in tracking these offenders.

Similar programs are targeting gangs and other at-risk youth. Many of these police-sponsored programs not only target the problem offender but conduct a variety of outreach programs, including athletic competition and recreational activities for youth (Weston, 1993:80–84). These approaches are forms of problem-oriented policing (POP) strategies practiced by many departments.

As we move further into the twenty-first century, we find community policing is in full swing. Yet there are concerns as to the required funding to hire more police. Under the proposed 1993 federal crimes control bill, President Clinton's proposal to hire 100,000 more police nationwide was admirable but ridiculously low. The nation's capital and crime capital alone could benefit by 100,000 additional officers, not to mention Miami, New York, and Los Angeles, where gang violence has gripped these cities. As of this writing (2001), we still have not achieved the goal of 100,000 additional officers. If community policing is to be effective, there is a need to hire police at a greater pace than current funding allows. Those recruited into the police ranks must view the community as a force of change, not an adversary. Community policing requires that the police reorganize their response capabilities. The police must assign beat officers, detectives, and other specialists to certain geographical areas of the city. In other words, the police need to decentralize operations to better serve the community (Donahue, 1993:12–22). This approach includes placing the police in a position where they are more visible to the community. Footbeats and storefronts are two examples where the police are accessible to the public. The use of bicycle patrols has proven successful in a number of cities (Ent and Hendricks, 1991).

As pointed out by Goldstein (1990:34–35), "the emphasis on community has two implications. It means looking to the community to define the problems that should be of concern to the police, rather than succumbing to the tendency of the police on their own to define the problems of concern to the community. And it means gaining an understanding of all dimensions of a problem in the total community."

There is a number of examples of community-based policing programs. The Los Angeles police have organized citizens to paint out graffiti and have prompted city agencies to tow away abandoned vehicles. This idea is a form of preventive maintenance, or the philosophy that if one window is broken and not repaired, soon all windows will be broken. In other words, when community disorder and decay are not challenged, the disorder escalates and the decay spreads (Wilson and Kelling, 1989:23).

It is suggested that the community must share in crime control efforts. In 1992, the California Department of Justice published a comprehensive book on community-oriented problem-solving police (COPS). According to a Department of Justice publication (1992:4–5), "the community must recognize the conditions that generate crime, and must accept the challenge and responsibility to assume ownership of their community's safety and well being."

There are a number of COPS programs in effect throughout the country. These programs address gangs, drugs, loitering problems, the homeless, residential and business crime prevention, and other proactive attempts to avert crime. However, there are not enough sworn officers available to carry out these programs. Increased budgetary problems confronting many cities are prohibiting the hiring of additional police. If more police are hired, enforcement focus is often directed toward crime repression and other calls for service. In Los Angeles, for example, which has been victimized by riots, there are only 2.3 officers for every 10,000 residents. This is the lowest officer/citizen ratio of the 10 largest U.S. cities (Anon., 1993b).

In response to the need for increased protection, residents and merchants with the money to spend are hiring private police and security officers to assist in crime control efforts. It is becoming increasingly clear that the police cannot provide the needed protection for everyone; thus the second approach to community policing is through the enlistment of the private security industry. Since the private protection industry outnumbers law enforcement 3 to 1, there is a trend to hire more security to patrol housing tracts, malls, schools, and a variety of other business establishments. Private security is a $64 billion industry, with more than 10,000 firms nationwide. In many respects, real community policing is being done by private security forces and alarm companies (Anon., 1993b).

The benefit of private security has been demonstrated in some communities. In Oceanside, California, the downtown area has been plagued with prostitution and drug activity. The police department has lost 30 officers in three years to budget cuts. In 1992, the city hired a private patrol company on a three-month trial program. The funding was provided by redevelopment funds. The program was so successful that when the funds ran out, downtown merchants each contributed $50 a month to keep the security force. The police, as a result, are able to devote more time and respond more quickly to serious calls.

The increased use of private guards in shopping malls is another trend. Shopping malls are becoming new cities, with some of the same problems as outdoor areas. Increased problems in loitering, gang activity, thefts, and other crimes are finding their way indoors, including the parking lots. Local governments are passing ordinances allowing security officers to write parking citations and enforce reckless driving citations. Security officers provide valuable public relations for tenants and patrons (Anon., 1993d).

In 1993, a bill came under review before the Texas legislature requiring shopping centers to employ security officers. In Minnesota, a Senate bill that authorizes private security officers to request identification of persons who are on the premises. These legislative trends signal an increased recognition of the value of security. In Philadelphia, the police have embraced the support of the private security sector to assist in crime control efforts. The program, entitled *security watch*, utilizes security officers in the downtown area to perform building checks and patrol areas frequented by shoppers, theatergoers, and residents. Security officers are trained by police and their respective agencies. A true partnership has been formed between the police and the private security sector. There has been tangible gain from this partnership, in both the reduction of crime and in the police ability to respond to calls for service (Zappile, 1991:22–23).

Private security officers have replaced police officers in one jurisdiction. In Sussex, New Jersey, a four-member police department was replaced by a private security company. The security company was given a six-month contract to provide police services to the small town. The use of security saved the town over $93,000.

More important, the security officers did a good job and were well received by the citizens (Anon., 1993a). However, a court order forced the town to discontinue the security services because of potential liability in the training of the officers, a problem that could be resolved by legislation.

There is a number of other positive examples of working relationships between public policing and private security. The University of New Haven and Yale University security staffs have developed relationships with the local police. The agencies have carried out a community-based policing philosophy. The police and security staffs meet monthly to discuss mutual crime problems and are involved in joint patrols. The Connecticut Police Chiefs Association has formed a private security committee. The committee is composed of security managers from a number of companies, including Fortune 500 companies (Cain et al., 1993:25). The call for increased use of private security to assist the police has come from scholarly sources as well. The police and community would benefit from the assistance of security and thereby allow the police more control over the security industry. In other words, instead of harassing and resisting the security industry, the police need to coordinate efforts to meet the community crime challenges (Sherman, 1983).

The growth of private protection is attributed to the rising incidents of workplace crime, funding problems in the public sector, fear of lawsuits for inadequate protection, and the growing realization by the public of the availability of protection measures. In five states, the leading cause of death is murder in the workplace. The tragic slayings by disgruntled employees and others in post offices and other public buildings suggest a need to increase security measures. At particularly high risk are people working with valuable money in the retail setting (Anon., 1993c).

For community policing to be effective, there must be increased use of private security; however, it is recognized that private security officers are not trained as well as the police. There is a fear that many security officers are simply thugs in uniform. This perception has some validity. There are trends to upgrade security professionalism, specifically in the training domain. In New York, the legislature in 1992 passed a bill that would establish new mandatory training, licensing, and registration requirements for private security officers employed as contract or proprietary officers. In the same year, there was a bill before the Virginia legislature providing campus security officers the same powers as the police. It passed.

Although a number of states mandate security training, the protection industry lacks serious regulation. There are federal legislative efforts to improve the security industry. These efforts were referred to as the Gore–Martinez training proposals. The bills would not only standardize the training of security officers in every state but also mandate examination, certification, classroom instruction, and on-the-job training for security officers. The 1992 Martinez bill, referred to as House Bill 5931, was more specific than the 1991 Gore bill, in that it provided for specialized training in such areas as law and patrol procedures.

The third approach to meeting the community policing need is the utilization of police reserves and cadet programs stressing higher education. Many law enforcement agencies utilize the services of citizen-reserve officers. In Los Angeles, for example, candidates for the reserve corps must undergo the same preservice training as regular police officers. Reserves are required to volunteer their services every month, without pay. Communities need to recruit qualified citizens to serve as reserves. As in the teaching and nursing professions, funds must be set aside to pay citizens on a per diem basis to assist the police in meeting the community crime challenges.

Reserve programs provide a high-quality pool of officers. There is a need to pass legislation where these officers are paid for their part-time services. In many cities, high school youths begin their police careers in cadet or explorer programs. However, New York City allows youths as young as 16 to take the written exam for a police officer. Those students who pass the exam and stay out of trouble are guaranteed a job when they reach the appropriate age (Osborn, 1992:23).

There is a movement to recruit qualified candidates by offering grants for educational expenses. The New York City Cadet Corps program pays $3000 toward a cadet's last two years of college. After graduation, the student must serve two years with the police department in order to pay the loan in full. There is a need to hire more college-educated officers. Although there is no conclusive evidence that college-educated officers make better officers, there is some evidence that they are more efficient and are less likely to use force than are non-college-educated officers (Carter, 1984). The success of community policing depends on the use of citizens, security officers, and quasi-professionals to perform certain law enforcement tasks, freeing the police for more serious problems.

DOMESTIC VIOLENCE AND THE POLICE

Domestic violence accounts for a significant proportion of calls for police service. It is a problem that pervades every community. Domestic violence includes injuries to married, separated, divorced, and cohabiting couples. Although males can be victims of domestic violence, this aggression is usually directed against females. Verbal threats are also considered abusive but are less likely to result in police intervention (Hirschel et al., 1992:250). There has been an inconsistent response by law enforcement to domestic violence complaints. Reasons for this ambivalence are grounded in policing attitudes about the seriousness of these cases and the reluctance of the police to intervene in private matters. Thus there is a form of unofficial approval of violence (Gelles and Straus, 1988:25).

However, since the 1970s, increased attention to domestic violence cases has surfaced. The police are undergoing training in crisis intervention and other types of violence reduction programs. These training programs are necessary given that between 25 and 30% of all couples will experience a violent incident in their lifetime. Although domestic violence incidents cut across all socioeconomic classes, the poor and undereducated are most often represented in these cases (Hamberger and Hastings, 1988). It is clear that one of the major problems in domestic violence matters is under-reporting. Fearing social disapproval or embarrassment, the middle and upper classes are less likely to report these offenses than are nonwhite and lower-income women (Schulman, 1979).

In the past, domestic violence calls received low police priority (U.S. Commission on Civil Rights, 1982). Police usually viewed these calls as a nuisance and typically left after advising the parties to keep the peace. In recent years, the police have undergone training in crisis intervention and mediation, but there is little evidence that such training has reduced the police handling of these complaints (Oppenlander, 1981).

A further problem concerns the attitudes of the police. Generally, the police did not welcome these changes, often viewing domestic violence training as social work. A number of women's groups filed suits demanding that the police take a more responsive and proactive role in enforcing domestic violence laws. These suits filed on behalf of women victims were based on the denial of due process and equal protection of the law. In other words, in some situations, the police have a duty to the victim to respond in a timely manner to domestic violence complaints. This duty is based on a special relationship to the victim when there is evidence that violence is directed at another, and the police have been notified but fail to respond (*Thurman* v. *City of Torrington*, 1984; *Balistereri* v. *Pacifica Police Department*, 1990).

The current law enforcement movement in addressing domestic violence is termed preferred arrest. In other words, a number of state statutes have been revised, providing the police with broader arrest powers. In 1983, 27 states expanded police arrest powers in domestic violence cases. (Lerman et al., 1983:44). In 1986, six states passed laws requiring arrest with probable cause and the presence of the offender (Ferraro, 1989:61). However, the victim must have signs of physical injury. The police are also asked to arrest abusers who have violated protection orders. Currently, 48 states have such orders (Finn and Colson, 1990). In 10 states, violation of these orders must result in an arrest. Thus, statutory law is limiting police discretion in domestic abuse matters.

The police arrest policy as a means of addressing domestic violence gained support from the Minneapolis domestic violence study (Sherman and Berk, 1984). The study conducted in 1981–1982, was the first to test the deterrent effect of arrest in spousal abuse cases. In this experiment, police arriving at the scene of a domestic violence complaint were assigned one of three responses: (1) advising the couple, (2) separating the couple by ordering the offender to leave the scene for a few hours, and (3) arresting the offender. After a six-month follow-up, it was revealed that arresting the offender resulted in fewer repeat offenses than the other responses.

The study concluded that arrest was more effective in deterring repeat violence. Although there were problems with the study methodology, the finding received national attention and is credited with the movement toward police arrests as the preferred response in domestic violence cases. The validity of arrest as a preferred response was further tested by additional research funded by the National Institute of Justice. The studies conducted in six cities (Omaha; Atlanta; Colorado Springs; Dade County, Florida; Milwaukee; and Charlotte) tested the arrest hypothesis.

Although there was a difference in research designs, the results generally indicated that arrest was not found to be a deterrent to domestic violence. There were a number of reasons for these conclusions, including the fact that some offenders had criminal histories and that arrests are not a new or unusual experience (Dunford et al., 1990:194; Hirschel et al., 1991:37; Sherman et al., 1991:827). More research in Dade County, Florida, however, suggests that mandatory arrest practice does have a deterrent effect on employed suspects. Thus those offenders who are employed or part of the workforce have more to lose than do their unemployed counterparts and are less likely to repeat their abusive patterns (Pate and Hamilton, 1992:691–697).

The future of police responses to domestic violence is not limited to stricter laws and more arrests. As in the community policing concept, a coordinated community response approach to the problem is needed. Like a number of other violent offenders, spousal abusers suffer from social and/or psychological disorders which rehabilitation or prison confinement is unable to cure. Unless legislation is passed requiring mandatory long-term sentencing for abusers, many abusers will leave jail and repeat their crimes. As part of the tough crime control legislation efforts, there was a bill before Congress requiring mandatory life sentencing for those convicted of three violent crimes; however, there are doubts that this bill will pass (Carter, 1993:3200).

Congress considered other punitive approaches. The House Judiciary Committee proposed several crime bills in 1993. The committee approved a measure to establish new legislation aimed at reducing domestic violence. Under the proposed 1993 bill, referred to as HR 1133, the measure would require the police to arrest in cases of domestic violence. The bill was to create a new federal crime for stalkers and provide education programs for judges dealing with domestic violence cases.

As with many other offenses, the punitive response of arrest and imprisonment is often the preferred approach. For many offenders, these approaches are necessary. If for no other reason, these social outcasts will be temporarily out of "the business of abusing." The trends in most states suggest that arrest be the preferred police response, regardless of research findings questioning the value of this approach. However, arrest is only one part of the justice response. Community efforts after the arrest may dictate the success of programs designed to deter domestic violence. An example of a community response program is the Duluth, Minnesota, Domestic Abuse Intervention Project. This project coordinated the efforts of nine law enforcement, criminal justice, and human service agencies. In other words, after an arrest, other agencies were to intervene, providing victim-offender counseling, and so on (Pence, 1983:258–259).

In California, legislation requires the police to arrest anyone inflicting injury to a spouse or to persons of the opposite sex who are cohabiting. The infliction of injury is a felony punishable by up to four years in prison. However, there must be visible injury, not verbal injury (Penal Code Section 273.5). Upon conviction, where probation is granted, the law in California requires the abuser to participate in a batterer's treatment program. This treatment is designed to address the abuser's propensity for violence: in other words, to address the cause of violence rather than treat the symptoms. The role of counseling is introduced to both the victim and the abuser.

The legislative intent in California, as in a number of other states, is to identify domestic violence as a community problem. Spousal abusers are recognized as a "clear and present danger to the citizens." The legislature further finds that the concept of vertical prosecution in which a trained deputy district attorney or prosecution unit is assigned to a case from its filing to its completion is an effective way to assure that abusers are convicted and sentenced (California Penal Code: 273.8). There is a welcome trend to protect the victims. It is a misdemeanor in California to disclose the location of domestic violence shelters or safe houses without the authorization of that shelter (California Penal Code: 273.7). The protection of the victim after an arrest is a high priority.

Another legal approach to enhance the law enforcement role is restraining orders. Most states allow victims to obtain these protection orders if there is evidence of harassment, threats, and so on. Violation of a protection order is a misdemeanor; however, if the victim suffers injury, the law requires that the abuser serve 48 hours in jail whether or not a fine, jail term, or other punishment is imposed [California Penal Code: 273.6(b)]. The problem and treatment of domestic violence are clearly becoming an integrated justice problem-solving approach. In 1994, California had several new laws addressing domestic violence. State marriage fees were increased from $9 to $23 to help finance domestic violence prevention programs. Another new law prohibited any person from owning a firearm for 10 years, upon conviction of spousal abuse or violating a court protection order. In addition, husbands who raped their wives are subject to the same prison penalties as other rapists, and conviction can result in imprisonment for a period of three, six, or eight years (California Penal Code Section 264).

The role of technology is entering the domestic violence arena. In Delaware, there was an experiment with seven county police departments where women who are potential victims of physical abuse installed silent alarms in their homes. The alarms are installed by a security alarm company and are activated by pressing a button in the home or are triggered by pressing a button on a necklace. As evident from the discussion, the police are becoming more proactive in terms of training and arrest practices. The responsibility of the police is to respond quickly to spousal abuse incidents. Upon arrival, the police are accountable for controlling the situation.

However, the response doesn't stop with arrest. Legislation has been enacted in some states to assure that both the offender and victim receive the appropriate assistance. Although it can be criticized that arrest practices are not effective in deterring domestic violence, arrests are valuable in bringing to attention the problem of violence. In other words, arrest is just the first step in the justice process. The arrest is not always viewed as a punitive response but could serve as the catalyst for offender-victim treatment. In any event, the laws in some states are getting tougher on those who physically abuse their spouses.

CONTROLLING THE POLICE

While there are increasing trends to promote and expand community policing and to address problems such as domestic violence, the police will continually be scrutinized by the community and the courts. It is understandable that the police will make mistakes, but they may not always be at fault for their actions. If the public expects more proactive community-oriented policing, there is a risk of the police abusing their authority in carrying out their crime control mandates. Most police departments have some form of administrative control of their officers. Some agencies have civilian review boards that review allegations of police misconduct and other policy matters. However, only about 17% of the 132 largest cities have a citizen board (Walker and Bumpus, 1991). Most departments have internal review boards consisting of officers who investigate misconduct of other officers. Regardless of the method of review, the police can expect increased public scrutiny, especially when the police are accused of corruption or serious misconduct.

The Rodney King incident in Los Angeles resulted in the formation of the 1991 Christopher Commission investigation, which recommended a number of policy changes within the department. This type of investigation illustrates how civilians can influence the policymaking of a police agency. Following on the heels of the Christopher report was the Kolt's report (1992) of the LA County Sheriff's Department. Like the Christopher report, this report was critical of the sheriff's office on matters concerning use of force, hiring, and supervision and other procedural concerns. Other than internal administrative controls and civilian reviews, two legal methods of controlling police conduct are civil litigation and the exclusionary rule. These methods are expected to continue in the future, but with varying results. Unless the police are totally irresponsible, or act without just cause or good faith, their actions, however inappropriate to some, are usually defensible. The courts generally favor police practices, as long as the police do not "break the rules."

CIVIL LIABILITY IN POLICING

The police are confronted with enormous pressures daily. The impact of the Rodney King incident left many citizens wondering if the behavior of the four LA police officers was a planned response, or a demonstration of atypical police behavior. The police can be held liable for inappropriate or wrongful behavior, regardless of their intention. Lawsuits brought against the police can be filed in either state or federal courts.

One of the most common approaches of suing the police for misconduct is under federal law. There are several statutes that allow citizens to file actions against the police. However, the most common is referred to as Title 42 of the U.S. Code, Section 1983. This law has its roots in the early civil rights act of 1871, which is also referred to as the Ku Klux Klan Act. The law was written to protect citizens against the violence of the Klan. The law has been expanded to allow citizens to bring suit against law enforcement officers, police agencies, and municipalities. Title 42 of the U.S. Code, Section 1983, reads:

> Every person who, under color of any statute, ordinance, regulation, custom, or usage, of any State or Territory, subjects, or causes to be subjected, any citizen of the United States or other person within the jurisdiction thereof to the deprivation of any rights, privileges, or immunities secured by the Constitution and laws, shall be liable to the party injured in an action at law, suited in equity, or other proper proceeding for redress.

The application of Section 1983 became entrenched in *Monroe* v. *Pape* (1961). The *Monroe* case held that a Section 1983 case can be brought against the police any time a constitutional right is violated, whether or not the officer was acting within authorized limits. The *Monroe* case opened the door to a flurry of lawsuits against the police and is currently a popular remedy for a number of reasons. It is expected that this type of action will be used extensively in the future. The popularity of this type of suit, as opposed to state actions, is based on the following reasons. First, civil lawsuits are filed in federal court, where discovery is often more liberal than in state courts. This process makes it easier for the plaintiff, or the injured party, to obtain the necessary records and documents from the defendant. Second, suits filed in federal courts do not have to exhaust state remedies, thus reducing delays in the justice process. Another reason for filing in federal court is that the prevailing plaintiff may recover attorney's fees under the Attorney's Fee Act of 1976. In other words, if the case has merit, attorneys are more inclined to accept cases where their fees can be paid by the defendant police officer or agency.

Civil rights lawsuits are used by plaintiffs even though there are also criminal sanctions available. In other words, 1983 suits can be filed whether or not a criminal action is initiated. Civil lawsuits normally follow criminal actions. However, prosecutors may be reluctant to file cases against police officers, or grand juries may not be inclined to indict officers, unless there has been some gross or blatant conduct. Therefore, 1983 actions are filed since only a preponderance of evidence is required to prove wrongdoing rather than beyond a reasonableness as in criminal cases.

There are two basic requirements for a Section 1983 lawsuit. First, the defendant must be acting under color of the law; second, there must be a constitutional violation or violation of some federally protected right. The first requirement requires that the defendant officer be performing an act of public authority. This means that the on-duty officer is performing an act lawfully or unlawfully. Police officers who arrest without probable cause, or administer excessive force, are misusing their authority under the color of law. Committing unlawful acts (e.g., sexual assaults) while on duty can fall under this principle. The second requirement refers to violations of protected rights. Some examples are Fourth and Fifth Amendment violations or police actions violating a person's due process rights. Thus an officer who maliciously beats a prisoner or denies an arrestee needed medical treatment would fall under this principle.

Civil liability under state law is divided into intentional tort and negligent tort. An *intentional tort* is a commission of an act of which an officer intended. An officer who falsely detains another, or uses unreasonable force resulting in injury, is committing an intentional tort. Intentional tort results from a wanton disregard for a person's rights. In contrast, *negligence* is the failure to act or to do something that ought to be done. Negligence generally occurs when an officer fails to protect the public from harm or injury, such as in the case of failure to respond to 911 calls. For negligence under state law to prevail, four elements must be met:

1. There must be a duty on the part of the defendant police officer.
2. There was a failure to perform the duty.

3. There is a proximate cause or relationship between the duty and failure to perform.

4. There is actual damage or injury to the person.

There is a number of court cases that illustrate negligence. In *Sorichetti* v. *City of New York* (1985), for example, a judgment for $2 million against the New York Police Department was upheld for failing to protect a child who was under an order of protection issued by the court. In this case, the police, knowing that the father was in custody of his child in violation of a court order, failed to intervene at the request of the mother. The child was later attacked by the father and severely injured.

In *Irwin* v. *Town of Ware* (1984), the court found that the police had a duty to arrest a drunk driver as required by state statute. The police stopped a drunk driver but failed to make an arrest, resulting in the driver subsequently injuring the plaintiff. In both of these cases, negligence was established because of a special relationship between the police and the plaintiff. The special relationship was established by statute.

In general, the police are not legally obligated to protect a person from harm. The public duty doctrine holds that the police owe a duty to the public, and not to specific individuals. This doctrine was established by the U.S. Supreme Court in *South* v. *Maryland*, (1986). The public duty doctrine prevails in most states but is not without controversy. In *Simack* v. *Risely* (1986), a seventh-circuit decision ruled that the police were not liable for failing to assist a woman who was robbed during an undercover police surveillance. The police owed no duty to protect the woman since there was no special relationship established, or expectation by her for police assistance. The police waited until the attack occurred before they intervened. The Court reasoned that being in a position to observe did not make the police liable for the attack.

If a plaintiff feels that there is a constitutional right to protect, a 1983 action can be filed in federal court. However, it is difficult to establish liability under federal law. The landmark case in this regard is *DeShaney* v. *Winnebago County Department of Social Services* (1989). In this case a 4-year-old was beaten and seriously injured by his father, who had custody of the child after a divorce. Despite a number of complaints by the boy's mother that the child was being abused, the social service agency took various steps to protect the boy but did not remove him from the father's custody. The agency knew that the boy was being abused. The father was later convicted of the crime. A lawsuit was filed alleging that the boy's due process right was violated under the Constitution. The Supreme Court ruled that the due process clause does not impose a duty to protect a person not in state custody. The boy was in the custody of his father.

The use of force is one of the most common suits brought against the police. The police are entitled to use nondeadly or deadly force if the situation allows it. The use of force must be reasonable and appropriate. Otherwise, as seen in the Rodney King incident, the police can be tried criminally under state or federal law. After being acquitted for state charges, two Los Angeles police officers were later convicted in federal court.

The landmark case on police use of deadly force is *Tennessee* v. *Garner* (1985). The case limited the broad shooting discretion used by the police in some jurisdictions. In other words, police officers may not shoot any fleeing felon. The use of deadly force may only be used when a fleeing felon poses a serious physical threat or risk to others. Despite this limitation, the courts recognize the need for the police to use force in split-second decisions (*Graham* v. *Conner*, 1989).

In *Smith* v. *Freland* (1992), the courts balanced the behavior of the police with the need of the situation. In this case, the police shot and killed a suspect in a high-speed chase. The police were sued for excessive force, but prevailed. The court opined that the police must make instantaneous decisions under very threatening circumstances.

The number of lawsuits filed against the police continues to grow. A survey of police chiefs from the 20 largest cities with populations over 100,000 revealed that most officers and supervisors have been sued in the past and expect to be defendants in the future (McCoy, 1987). The survey revealed that the litigations most often brought against the police are:

1. Use of force
2. Auto pursuits
3. Arrests/searches
4. Employee drug tests
5. Hiring and promotion
6. Discrimination based on race, sex, or age
7. Record keeping and privacy
8. Jail management

In Houston, Texas, the number of complaints filed against the police increased by 245% from 1980 to 1985 (Anon., 1986). However, while the number of the lawsuits filed against the police continues to increase, the number of cases imposing liability against the police is low (de Carmen, 1991:3). The number of complaints filed against the police is rising. This increase is due in part to public awareness of their rights, and the stress of policing, where officers may employ force unnecessarily. A survey of police officers indicates that there is fear of being sued by the public. Some officers experience stress when another officer is sued (Scogin and Brodsky, 1991).

Recent research has indicated that the number of cases brought against the police for civil rights (1983) actions is continuing. In a study by Kappeler et al. (1993), there were 1359 section 1983 actions brought against the police between 1978 and 1990. That number is rising in the twenty-first century. Most claims have been for false arrest, excessive force, and search and seizure violations. While the police prevail in over 50% of the cases, there are expenses in defending these cases, as well as negative publicity and morale problems. In response to the threat of civil liability, police departments are making changes in policies and practices. These changes reflect current movements to increase professionalism and accountability. The crime picture for the future looks bleak. The police will be expected to be more proactive and aggressive.

As discussed, some laws are being revised requiring the police to arrest in some situations (e.g., domestic violence). The movement toward community policing may also create more civil liability problems. In other words, as the police assume a more proactive role in community crime control, there may be situations where the police exceed their role. Mandatory arrest policies, for example, may increase the likelihood of violence or abuse initiated against or by the police. In response to these threats, the police tend to recruit persons representative of the community and to prepare these officers to respond to community problems. Police managers must plan now for future recruitment and training. It is expected that there will be rapid changes in the demographics of our population. According to Carter (1991), "by the year 2010, more than one third of all American children will be black, Hispanic, or Asian." Thus Caucasians will become a minority within United States in less than 100 years. There is a need to recruit more women into the police ranks. During the next 10 years it is anticipated that women will dominate the workforce. The need to hire additional women may reduce the problem of civil litigation. One study suggests that women are less likely to use force, are less likely to injure a citizen seriously, are no more likely to suffer injuries, and are more emotionally stable (Grennan, 1988).

In the future, recruitment will focus on multilevel assessments for recruiting police officers. In other words, the emphasis will be on screening out undesirable candidates through a variety of measurements. The assessment center approach utilizes intelligence tests, paper-pencil tests, and role-playing exercises to evaluate a person's capabilities and decision-making abilities. The assessment center approach provides evaluators with an understanding of how a candidate will react under stressful situations. Persons completing the assessment phase successfully will be eligible for employment. Reports on the effectiveness of the assessment approach in selecting police officers have been documented (Pynes and Bernardin, 1992). The assessment approach focuses on measuring a candidate's perception, decision-making decisiveness, ability to direct others, adaptability to policing, oral communications, interpersonal skills, and written communications. This recruitment approach is becoming more popular and is expected to gain in popularity in the future.

In addition to comprehensive recruitment programs, high-quality police training is necessary to assure the effectiveness and performance of police officers. Not only must the police receive training in traditional topics such as firearms and patrol procedures, but training must focus on communication skills, cultural relations, and an understanding of ethnic diversity. Police departments are undergoing training in verbal judo, which is training on the proper use of language as opposed to forcing a physical confrontation. Many police agencies are requiring officers to undergo this training.

The New York and Los Angeles police departments have instituted training on gay and lesbian issues. The Los Angeles Police Department requires officers to complete training in conversational Spanish. In some cities recruit officers are assigned to work in prosecutors' offices, public defenders' offices, and placed with judges to learn about the complexities of sentencing (McCampbell, 1986). Police training in the future will become more holistic and humanistic, incorporating decision-making exercises, not just rudimentary "how to" training that stresses only tactics and procedures.

THE EXCLUSIONARY RULE AND POLICING

The U.S. Constitution prohibits unreasonable searches and seizures of people, houses, and personal property. The Fourth Amendment provides:

> The right of the people to be secure in their persons, houses, papers, and effects, against unreasonable searches and seizures, shall not be violated, and no warrant shall issue, but upon probable cause, supported by oath or affirmation, and particularly describing the place to be searched, and the persons or things to be seized.

Although violation of the rule is not a major problem in policing, it comes into play when a court determines that a search or seizure was unreasonable. Under the rule, which was created to encourage proper police conduct, evidence that results from an illegal (unreasonable) search or seizure is excluded at trial. It is suppressed (inadmissible), and cannot be brought to the jury's attention.

A major case involving the exclusionary rule is *Mapp* v. *Ohio* (1961). The *Mapp* case specifically required the states to exclude from trials evidence that had been seized illegally by the police. In other words, the police need a warrant based on probable cause to search a premises, vehicle, or individual. However, it is not always possible to get a warrant every time the police encounter a situation in which there may be contraband. Consequently, there are judicially interpreted exceptions to the warrant requirement. These exceptions or attacks on the exclusionary rule began about 1970. Since that time there have been a number of cases limiting the scope of the exclusionary rule. There is a number of cases that have limited the intent of the exclusionary rule; however, only a few significant cases are discussed.

Following the "rights for the offenders trend" of the 1960s, the Supreme Court has gradually been chipping away at an offender's Fourth Amendment. The consecutive Burger and Rehnquist Courts have granted the police additional search and seizure exceptions to the warrant requirement. In 1961, the Court in *Mapp* v. *Ohio* allowed the police to "pat down suspicious persons." In this case, the Court ruled that if the police have cause to believe that a person may be armed, and for officer safety, the police can perform a limited search for weapons. In the 1966 case of *Schmerber* v. *California*, the Court allowed the police to use blood samples taken from a drunk driver who was involved in an accident, despite the fact that the driver did not give consent.

The 1970s introduced further erosion to the exclusionary rule. In *Cupp* v. *Murphy* (1973), the Court allowed evidence to be used against a defendant arrested for strangling his wife. Despite his refusal, the police scraped the defendant's fingernails for blood residue before being placed under arrest. One of the exceptions of the search warrant requirement is consent of the citizen. In other words, unless the police have other causes for conducting a search, a citizen has a right to refuse a police search.

In *Schneckloth* v. *Bustamonte* (1973), the police stopped a car for a traffic violation. After the stop, the police asked the occupants if they could search the vehicle. The occupants consented, and the officers recovered evidence of a theft. The occupants were convicted but appealed their conviction on the grounds that the police did not tell them that they had a right to refuse. The Supreme Court upheld the conviction.

Once a person is arrested and placed into police custody, the police may perform a full-scale search of his person. Any evidence discovered by the police, even though unrelated to the initial crime, may be used against the defendant. This was the decision in *United States* v. *Robinson* (1973). In *Rakas* v. *Illinois* (1978), the Supreme Court permitted evidence against an occupant of a car. In this case, the passenger Rakas was arrested for robbery. Even though the police conducted an illegal search resulting in the conviction of Rakas, he had no standing to object to the search because he was only a passenger.

In the 1980s, the assault on the exclusionary rule continued. In *Illinois* v. *Gates* (1983), the Supreme Court ruled that the search and subsequent conviction of two drug dealers based entirely on an anonymous letter sent to the police (accompanied with police surveillance) was permissible. The Court departed from earlier precedent that required corroboration from informants to justify the issuance of a search warrant.

One of the most serious assaults on the *Mapp* case and the exclusionary rule is *United States* v. *Leon* (1984). In *Leon*, the Supreme Court established the so-called "good faith" exception to the exclusionary rule. In other words, if the police conduct a search with a defective warrant, the evidence obtained is still admissible if the police honestly believed that the warrant was valid.

The Court has ruled that there is no privacy protection in open fields. In *Oliver* v. *United States* (1984), narcotics agents relying on a tip, and without a warrant, observed marijuana growing in an open field. The county ruled that there was no expectation to privacy even though a no trespassing sign was posted on the property. In *California* v. *Greenwood* (1988), a warrantless police search of garbage placed on the curb for collection was admissible, despite defendant objections that the garbage was subject to privacy protection.

The conservative trend of the Supreme Court will continue its march into the twenty-first century. As noted in *Illinois* v. *Rodriguez* (1990), the police entered a home without a warrant. The police were granted entry by a person who was victimized by the defendant (the victim did not reside at the home). Upon entry, the police observed drugs that led to the arrest of the defendant. The trial court excluded the evidence based on the warrantless entry; however, the Court ruled that the police had a good basis for entering because the woman said she lived there. In other words, the police were acting under good faith.

In *Maryland* v. *Buie* (1990), the Court extended the right of the police to conduct protective sweep searches of closets and other rooms near the area where a defendant is arrested. This ruling extends the right of the police to protect themselves from harm while making an arrest in a home. Within these protective sweeps, any evidence observed can be used against the defendant.

The problem of drunk driving has created a serious safety problem to the public. In response, the police have instituted checkpoints to detect drunk drivers. Drivers stopped and detained at these checkpoints have raised Fourth Amendment claims. In *Michigan Department of State Police* v. *Sitz* (1990), the Court ruled that the Fourth Amendment does not apply to drivers stopped and detained at these checkpoints.

In another decision, the Supreme Court again tackled the issue of pedestrian searches. In *Minnesota* v. *Dickenson* (1993), the Court ruled that the police pat-down of a suspect revealed drugs were admissible. In this case, the police patted down a suspect for weapons. During the pat-down, the officer felt a soft object in the suspect's pocket. The officer seized the item, which turned out to be illegal narcotics. The Court agreed that the officer's "sense of touch" justified seizing the contraband, even though there was no other reason to suspect that the suspect had narcotics. In short, the case further expanded the Terry decision, allowing the police to retrieve items suspected of being weapons or contraband.

The courts do have limits on how far they will go in allowing the police to search. In *Winston* v. *Lee* (1985), the Supreme Court ruled that the police seizure of a bullet taken from a robbery suspect violated the defendant's Fourth Amendment rights. In this case, a robbery suspect was shot by the victim, arrested by the police, and taken to a hospital, where the bullet was extracted to be used as evidence against the accused. The Court ruled that the surgery violated the defendant's right to privacy.

The famed *Miranda* warning is another area that has seen some erosion. As in search and seizure cases, the courts have allowed the police to exceed certain limits as long as their tactics were reasonable and/or in good faith. Under the *Miranda* rule, the police must advise a suspect of his or her rights before asking incriminating questions or seeking confessions. Suspects must make reasonable waivers before discussing their involvement in a crime. Yet the courts have allowed the police to use trickery and deceit to obtain incriminating evidence. In *Holland* v. *McGinnis* (1992), the police told a suspect that his vehicle was seen at the scene of a crime (a lie). The suspect confessed and the Court ruled that the confession was admissible. In a related case, a suspect was told that his fingerprints were found at a crime scene (another lie), tricking the suspect into confessing. The Court ruled in this case that the police tactic was permissible (*State* v. *Haywood*, 1989).

In *Ahmad A*. v. *Supreme Court* (1989), a juvenile suspect in police custody for murder asked to have a private visit with his mother in the police interrogation room. The youth confessed to his mother his involvement in a killing. The conversation was recorded and the statements used against the youth. The Court ruled that there is no expectation to privacy in police custody, and the statements are admissible. In other words, the Court adopted the concept that the "walls have ears" and that there is no expectation to privacy in police custody. There are limits as to how far the Court will go in permitting police to obtain a confession. When the police threaten a suspect with physical violence, a subsequent confession will not be admitted (*Cooper* v. *Scroggy* 1985). However, threatening a suspect to add additional charges unless the defendant confesses is not always inadmissible. Thus a little threat is permissible as long as it is not physical (*Lindsey* v. *Smith*, 1987).

There are also trends by legislatures, and proposals by governors in several states, to weaken exclusionary rule laws (Glick, 1993:436). In California, for example, the voters passed Proposition 8 in 1982 that allows the use of evidence even though it violated the California constitution (but not the federal Constitution). It is unlikely that the exclusionary rule or *Miranda* warnings will be abolished. However, there will continue to be cases where defendants will find it difficult to challenge police practices as long as the police continue to act reasonably. As long as violent crime continues and society continues to be threatened by ill-intentioned persons, the courts will follow the path of law and order, allowing the justice system greater leeway in using evidence to convict criminals.

CONCLUSIONS

There are indeed challenges for the police in the years ahead. As society experiences more violence from within the household or from the streets, more pressure will be placed on the police to respond. Generally, there is a cry for more punitive approaches to counter violence. These approaches may not solve the underlying social ills resulting from rampant drug use, gangs, unemployment, and so on, but punitive legislation, aggressive policing, and an integrated community-justice response can reduce the threat of victimization. The police will need help from the community to meet the crime problem. There is a welcome trend from the courts and legislatures to warn criminals that enough is enough and violence will not be tolerated in the community. The rights of citizens must take precedence over the rights of the criminals, even if the police need to bend the rules. In other words, a utilitarian enforcement philosophy is needed which may require curbing legal escapes for factually guilty offenders.

REFERENCES AND BIBLIOGRAPHY

ANON. (1986). Policing. *Houston Chronicle*, August 8, p. 3.

ANON. (1993a). *Crime Control Digest*, 27:1, 32.

ANON. (1993b). Laws 1994. *Los Angeles Times*, December 31.

ANON. (1993c). Murder leads workplace deaths in five states. *Los Angeles Times*, November 29.

ANON. (1993d). *USA Today*, December 3, p. 1.

BLUMSTEIN, A., J. COHEN, S. E. MARTIN, and M. H. TONRY (eds.) (1983). *Research on Sentencing: The Search for Reform*, Vol. 1. Washington, DC: National Academy Press.

CAIN, C. M., et al. (1993). No agency is an island. *Security Management*, December, pp. 25–28.

CARTER, D. L. (1984). Theoretical dimensions in the abuse of authority by police officers. *Police Studies*. Washington, DC: Police Executive Research Forum.

CARTER, D. L. (1991). *Your Education and Minority Recruitment: The Impact of a College Requirement*. Washington, DC: Police Executive Research Forum.

CARTER, D. L. (1993). Tough minded Senate adopts crime crackdown package. *Congressional Quarterly*, November 20.

CORWIN, M. (1993). Guns for hire. *Los Angeles Times Magazine*, November 28.

DEL CARMEN, R. V. (1991). *Civil Liabilities in American Policing*. Upper Saddle River, NJ: Prentice Hall.

DEPARTMENT OF JUSTICE (1992). California report on community policing. Sacramento, CA: Department of Justice.

DONAHUE, M. E. (1993). A comprehensive program to combat violent crime: The Savannah experience. *Police Chief*, September, p. 9.

DUNFORD, F. W. (1990). System initiated warrants for suspects of misdemeanor domestic violence: A pilot study. *Justice Quarterly*, 7:631–653.

ENT, C., and J. E. HENDRICKS (1991). Bicycle patrol: A community policing alternative. *Police Chief*, November, pp. 58–60.

FERRARO, K. J. (1989). Policing women battering. *Social Problems*, 36:61–74.

FINN, P., and S. COLSON (1990). *Civil Protection Orders: Legislation Current Court Practice, and Enforcement*. Washington, DC: U.S. Department of Justice.

GELLES, R. J., and M. A. STRAUS (1988). *Intimate Violence*. New York: Simon & Schuster.

GLICK, H. R. (1993). *Courts, Politics and Justice*. New York: McGraw-Hill.

GOLDSTEIN, H. (1990). *Problem Oriented Policing*. New York: McGraw-Hill.

GOULDS (1993). *California Penal Code Handbook*. Longwood, FL: Gould Publishing.

GRENNAN, S. (1988). Findings on the role of officer gender in violent encounters with citizens. *Journal of Police Science and Administration*, 15:78–85.

HAMBERGER, L. K., and J. HASTINGS (1988). Characteristics of male spouse abusers consistent with personality disorder. *Hospital and Community Psychiatry*, 39:763–770.

HIRSCHEL, D. J., I. W. HUTCHISON, C. W. DEAN, J. J. KELLEY, and C. E. PESACKIS (1991). *Charlotte Spouse Assault Replication Project: Final Report*. Washington, DC: U.S. Department of Justice, National Institute of Justice.

HIRSCHEL, D., et al. (1992). Review essay on the law enforcement response to spousal abuse: Past, present, and future. *Justice Quarterly*, 9:2.

KAPPELER, V. E., S. F. KAPPELER, and R. V. DEL CARMEN (1993). Police civil liberty cases: Decisions of the federal district courts, 1978-1990. *Journal of Criminal Justice*, 21:4.

KELLING, G. L., et al. (1988). *Perspectives on Policing: Police Accountability and Community Policing*. Washington, DC: U.S. Department of Justice, National Institute of Justice.

KLINE, E. M. (1993). Colorado springs SHO/DI: Working smarter with juvenile offenders. *Police Chief*, April.

KOLTS, J. G., and staff (1992). *A Report on the Los Angeles County Sheriff's Department*. Los Angeles: Kolts and staff.

LERMAN, L. G., L. LANDIS, and S. GOLDWEIG (1983). State legislation on domestic violence. In J. J. Costa (ed.), *Abuse of Women: Legislation, Reporting, and Prevention*. Lexington, MA: D.C. Heath.

McCAMPBELL, M. S. (1986). *Field Training for Police Officers: State of the Art*. Washington, DC: U.S. Department of Justice, National Institute of Justice.

McCOY, C. (1987). Police legal liability is not a crisis. *Crime Control Digest*, January, p. 1.

OPPENLANDER, N. (1981). The evaluation of law and wife abuse. *Law and Police Quarterly*, 3:382–405.

OSBORN, R. (1992). Police recruitments: Today's standard—tomorrow's challenge. *FBI Law Enforcement Bulletin*, June, p. 21.

PATE, A. M., and E. E. HAMILTON (1992). Formal and informal deterrence to domestic violence: The Dade County spouse assault experiment. *American Sociological Review*, 57:5.

PENCE, E. (1983). The Duluth domestic abuse investigation project. *Hamline Law Review*, 6:247–275.

PYNES, J., and H. J. BERNARDIN (1992). Entry level police selection: The assessment center as an alternative. *Journal of Criminal Justice*, 20:1.

SCHULMAN, M. (1979). *A Survey of Spousal Violence against Women in Kentucky*. Washington, DC: U.S. Department of Justice.

SCOGIN, F., and S. L. BRODSKY (1994). Fear of litigation among law enforcement officers. *American Journal of Police*, 10:41–45.

SHERMAN, L. W. (1983). Patrol strategies for the police. In J. Q. Wilson (ed.), *Crime Control and Public Policy*. San Francisco: ICS Press.

SHERMAN, L. W., and R. A. BERK (1984). *The Minneapolis Domestic Violence Experiment*. Washington, DC: Police Foundation.

SHERMAN, L. W., et al. (1991). From initial deterrence to long term escalation: Short custody arrest for poverty ghetto domestic violence. *Criminology*, 29:821–850.

TROJANOWICZ, R., and B. BUCQUEROUX (1990). *Community Policing: A Contemporary Perspective*. Cincinnati, OH: Anderson Publishing.

U.S. COMMISSION ON CIVIL RIGHTS (1982). *Under the Rule of Thumb: Battered Women and the Administration of Justice*. Washington, DC: U.S. Government Printing Office.

WALKER, S., and V. W. BUMPUS (1991). *Civilian Review of the Police: A National Survey of the 50 Largest Cities*. Omaha, NB: University of Nebraska Press.

WESTON, J. (1993). Community policing: An approach to youth gangs in a medium-sized city. *Police Chief*, August, p. 8.

WILSON, J. Q., and G. KELLING (1982). Broken windows....*Atlantic Magazine*, 249, March, pp. 29–38.

ZAPPILE, R. A. (1991). Philadelphia implements security watch. *Police Chief*, August.

CASES

Ahmad A. v. *Superior Court*, 263 Cal. Rptr. 747 (1989).

Balistereri v. *Pacifica Police Department*, 901 F.2d 696, 9th Cir. (1990).

California v. *Greenwood*, 486 U.S. 35 (1988).

Cooper v. *Scroggy*, 848 F.2d 1385 (1985).

Cupp v. *Murphy*, 412 U.S. 291 (1973).

Deshaney v. *Winnebago County Department of Social Services*, 489 U.S. 189 (1989).

Graham v. *Conner*, 490 U.S. 386 (1989).

Holland v. *McGinnis*, 763 F.2d 1044 (1992).

Illinois v. *Gates*, 462 U.S. 213 (1983).

Illinois v. *Rodriguez*, 110 S. Ct. 2793 (1990).

Irwin v. *Town of Ware*, 467 N.E.2d 1292 (Ma. 1984).

Lindsey v. *Smith*, 820 F.2d 1137 (1987).

Maryland v. *Buie*, 110 S. Ct. 1093 (1990).

Mapp v. *Ohio*, 367 U.S. 643 (1961).

Michigan Department of State Police v. *Sitz*, 110 S. Ct. 2481 (1990).

Minnesota v. *Dickenson*, 113 S. Ct. 2130 (1993).

Monroe v. *Pape*, 365 U.S. 167 (1961).

Oliver v. *United States*, 466 U.S. 170 (1984).

Rakas v. *Illinois*, 439 U.S. 128 (1978).

Schmerber v. *California*, 384 U.S. 757 (1966).

Schneckloth v. *Bustamonte*, 412 U.S. 218 (1973).

Simack v. *Risely*, 804 F.2d 143 (7th Cir. 1986).

Smith v. *Freland*, 984 F.2d 343 (1992).

Sorichetti v. *City of New York*, 484 N.E.2d 70 (1985).

South v. *Maryland*, 59 U.S. (18 How.) 396 (1986).

State v. *Haywood*, 439 N.W.2d 511 (1989).

Tennessee v. *Garner*, 471 U.S. 1 (1985).

Thurman v. *City of Torrington*, 595 F.Supp. 1521 (D. Conn. 1984).
United States v. *Leon*, 82 U.S. 667 (1984).
United States v. *Robinson*, 414 U.S. 218 (1973).
Winston v. *Lee*, 470 U.S. 105 (1985).

PART IV

The Courts and Future Interpretation of Law

In the years following the *Gregg* v. *Georgia* (1976), the U.S. Supreme Court has proceeded with caution. Since 1983, however, the Court has taken a much more aggressive and activist approach toward death penalty cases. This has been demonstrated by the Court in rejecting every major constitutional challenge to the fairness of death penalty laws and sanctioning the execution of 16-year-old offenders, mentally retarded defendants, and those who neither killed nor intended to kill. With the presidency of George W. Bush, it is very likely that executions will continue. The vision presented, however, is that with more executions there will continue to be erroneous executions, more evidence of racial bias and arbitrariness in capital sentencing, more questions about the morality of executing children, the mentally retarded, nonmurderers, or anyone else in a world where human error, caprice, and prejudice are inevitable. Ken Haas predicts that by the middle of the twenty-first century, the American people will repudiate capital punishment and the Supreme Court will declare such a sentence to be cruel and unusual punishment.

The United States remains the only Western democracy to retain the death penalty. The United States is isolated in world that is growing more abolitionist by the day. In so doing, it has executed increasing numbers of foreign nationals, in violation of their rights under the Vienna Convention on Consular Relations. At the same time, numbers of people languished on death row for decades before their death sentences were actually carried out. This has sparked a need for the United States to reexamine the effectiveness of capital punishment as a whole, while examining the flagrant disregard shown for its obligations to the international community. According to Christopher Cevasco in his chapter, the United States must be brought into compliance with international norms.

During the last four decades of the twentieth century, the U.S. Supreme Court has interpreted the Bill of Rights in terms of rights of the defendant as well as the limitations placed on them. In this new century, much depends on the development of governmental policies as they relate to areas such as drug trafficking and gun control, both significant elements of our crime problems. Equally important will be the composition of the Supreme Court and its interpretation of these first 10 amendments. The compromises struck by the Founding Fathers in relation to representation of large states versus small states left many unhappy citizens. However, the biggest complaint revolved around the fact that the Constitution as proposed provided insufficient protection for individual rights. The fear was that we would have in this country a situation similar to that of the old British monarchy. The Bill of Rights guards personal integrity, giving us the right to be left *alone*. It would appear that the function of the Bill of Rights in this century will be to protect minorities, even minorities of one, against majorities. This is the theme discussed in the updated chapter on the Bill of Rights by Smith, Pollack, and M. Muraskin.

In their chapter, Reisner and Nelligan discuss how the past three decades of the twentieth century has brought profound changes in the U.S. criminal justice system. The collapse of the rehabilitative ideal in the mid-1970s, together with a conservative swing in public opinion about crime and criminals, has led to an incarceration rate unprecedented in the nation's history. They argue that a more conservative U.S. Supreme Court has chipped away at many of the expansions of defendants' criminal rights. Their focus is on recent practices in states with the death penalty of allowing family members of capital murder victims to testify at the penalty phase of trials. Their research raises the question of allowing even the most limited elements of emotionality in the jury's penalty deliberation.

Turning to the law and juvenile justice policies, Benekos and Merlo describe the transformation of the last 100 years (last century) of the process of juvenile justice. This is a transformation apparent in waiver legislation and adultification reforms. What is to be the model of juvenile justice during the twenty-first century? Three models are suggested: *prevention and education*, which symbolizes the philosophical orientation of the original juvenile court with increasing reliance on prevention and early intervention programs to deter youth from offending; the *balanced and restorative justice* model, which will emphasize accountability, public safety, and competency for juveniles. Holding youth accountable, compensating victims, and providing treatment are part of this proposed model; and, finally, *retribution, adultification, and punishment* rejects the earlier perspectives on youth and adolescence while supporting a tough, punitive approach to dealing with youthful offenders. This is the result of the *get tough* era of the 1980s. Regardless, the juvenile justice system of this century will continue with its mission of reducing delinquency in this country.

Meadows and Anklin also talk about the increasing number of inmates incarcerated. Their study conducted a few years ago talks about the criminal justice system from the vantage point of those incarcerated. Programs are needed that help the incarcerated focus on transitioning back into the community (i.e., improving their employment and social skills while maintaining some self-esteem). Unlike the twentieth century's focus, there is no need to lock up all offenders who use drugs. Treatment must and does continue to be the preference for such persons, rather than having them pass time through idleness and nonproductive activities.

chapter 10

The Rise and Fall of the U.S. Death Penalty in the Twenty-First Century

Kenneth C. Haas, Ph.D.

ABSTRACT

In this chapter the U.S. Supreme Court's past, present, and future role in monitoring the U.S. system of capital punishment is analyzed. In *Gregg* v. *Georgia* (1976), the Court upheld the constitutionality of death penalty laws that permit a judge or a jury to impose a death sentence only after weighing all the relevant "aggravating" and "mitigating" factors concerning the defendant's crime and character. In the years following *Gregg*, the Court proceeded cautiously, setting strict limits on the applicability of the death penalty by refusing to allow the executions of those who did not actually take another human life and by insisting that judges and juries give due consideration to all mitigating factors in the defendant's conduct and background. Since 1983, however, the Court has taken a much more aggressive and activist approach toward death penalty cases, rejecting every major constitutional challenge to the fairness of death penalty laws and sanctioning the execution of 16-year-old offenders, mentally retarded defendants, and those who neither killed nor intended to kill. These kinds of decisions and George W. Bush's victory in the 2000 presidential election make it very likely that by the year 2010, the number of executions will have increased. Ironically, however, it is predicted that this increase in executions will ultimately convince the American people that the death penalty simply cannot be administered without error, caprice, and discrimination. Abolitionist movements will gain momentum in an increasing number of states, and the Supreme Court will declare the death penalty to be unconstitutional by the year 2050, if not sooner.

INTRODUCTION

On June 29, 1972, the U.S. Supreme Court, ruling in *Furman* v. *Georgia*, put a halt to all executions, thereby removing some 600 condemned prisoners from the nation's death rows (Marquart and Sorensen, 1989:11–13). *Furman* held only that all *then-existing* state and federal death penalty laws violated the Eighth Amendment's cruel and unusual punishment clause because of the arbitrary and discriminatory way in which these laws were applied (*Furman* at 239–374).[1] The decision was, nevertheless, greeted with great optimism by opponents of capital punishment. Many abolitionists saw *Furman* as a decision that left little room to reconcile any death penalty law with the Constitution, and it was predicted that the Court would soon bring an end to the U.S. practice of capital punishment (Meltsner, 1973:289–305).

Four years later, however, the Supreme Court refused to take the next step, declaring the death penalty in and of itself to be unconstitutional. In *Gregg* v. *Georgia* (1976) and its companion cases,[2] the Court upheld new death penalty laws that require the jury (or in a few states, the judge) to conduct a separate penalty hearing in order to consider "aggravating" and "mitigating" factors concerning the capital offender's crime and character. Under most of these *guided-discretion laws*, the jury is instructed to weigh all the relevant factors and circumstances and to return with either a sentence of death or life imprisonment.

On the same day that *Gregg* was decided, the Court struck down another type of death penalty law that several states had enacted in the aftermath of *Furman*. In *Woodson* v. *North Carolina* (1976) and *Roberts* v. *Louisiana* (1976), a five-to-four majority found *mandatory* death penalty laws to be violative of the Eighth Amendment because such laws would undermine the Court's new requirement that sentencing authorities must consider *all* relevant information concerning the nature of the offense and the character of the defendant as an indispensable part of the process of determining which defendants shall live and which shall die (*Woodson* at 302–304).[3]

Today, some three decades after *Furman*, the turnabout can only be described as stunning. Since the *Gregg* decision, the Supreme Court has rejected every major constitutional challenge to the death penalty. The result is that while every other Western democracy has abolished capital punishment, the United States has a death row population of over 3700 men and women (NAACP, 2000:1).

In this chapter we examine the Supreme Court's past, present, and future role in breathing life back into the death penalty. In particular, the chapter analyzes some of the Court's most important post-*Gregg* decisions on the legal status of capital punishment. It is argued that the predominant trend is typified by decisions that limit capital defendants' rights of appeal while expanding the reach of the death penalty to include children, the mentally retarded, and those who have not taken another human life. These decisions make it very likely that by the year 2010, the number of executions will have increased. It is also predicted that the growth in executions will ultimately convince the American people, and the Supreme Court, that the time has come to abolish the death penalty. An increasing number of states will abolish capital punishment in the second, third, and fourth decades of the twenty-first century. Citing this movement away from capital punishment, the Court will conclude that the American people of the middle decades of the twenty-first century have reached a sufficient consensus against capital punishment to justify a Supreme Court holding that the Constitution prohibits capital punishment altogether.

THE POST-*GREGG* CONFUSION

Gregg and *Woodson* established the framework for evaluating the constitutionality of all American death penalty laws. *Gregg* made it clear that the death penalty per se is not forbidden by the Eighth Amendment. But many important questions concerning the constitutional status of capital punishment remained unanswered. Indeed, the 1976 decisions arguably added to the confusion by articulating two major goals that seemed to be quite contradictory. On the one hand, the sentencing authority is commanded by the *Gregg* majority to apply the death penalty evenhandedly and without arbitrariness, thus suggesting that it is paramount to provide judges and juries with clear and objective standards that can be applied the same way in all cases. On the other hand, both *Woodson* and *Gregg* arguably stand for the proposition that the sentencing authority is obligated to place great emphasis on the individual characteristics of each offender and the particular circumstances surrounding his or her crime. These two goals will strike nearly everyone as incompatible; how can the sentencing authority be expected to give full consideration to the uniqueness of each defendant when its discretion has been sharply limited to promote fairness and consistency?[4]

This question has still not been resolved by the Supreme Court, and as a result, it is particularly difficult to predict the future of capital punishment in the United States. The best way to proceed, however, is to examine how the Court has dealt with other important death penalty issues since 1976. As we will see, the clear trend has been to expand the reach of the death penalty. As of today, there is little reason to believe that the Court will alter its course in the near future. It therefore seems likely that there will be fewer procedural safeguards for capital defendants and a greater number of executions by the year 2010.

THE POST-*GREGG* YEARS: 1976–1983

In his book *The Death Penalty in the Nineties*, Welsh White (1991) suggests a useful framework for studying the post-*Gregg* era. As White sees it, from 1976 to 1983, the Supreme Court attempted to clarify the constitutional boundaries of capital punishment by identifying the specific protections that must be afforded capital defendants (White, 1991:5–8). From 1983 to the present, however, the Court has increasingly sought to promote "expeditious executions" (White, 1991:8–24). White's two-phase analysis strikes me as substantially correct, although I would argue in even stronger terms that the Court has increasingly become an activist, pro-death-penalty tribunal. For the most part, the justices, particularly Chief Justice Rehnquist and Justices O'Connor, Kennedy, Scalia, and Thomas, have made little or no effort to camouflage their intentions. These justices exercise their judicial power zestfully while pursuing an activist jurisprudence that emphasizes great deference to legislative bodies and values states' rights far more than individual rights. As a result, the Eighth Amendment has been pushed far into the woodwork and out of the way of the legislative power, thereby expanding the category of death-eligible offenders and curtailing the appellate rights of death row inmates.

From 1976 to 1983, however, the High Court proceeded carefully. *Gregg* and *Woodson* had invalidated mandatory death penalty laws but had given states the green light to enact capital statutes that provide for a bifurcated trial and clear guidelines—aggravating and mitigating factors—for judges and juries to consider in deciding whether to sentence the offender to death. This suggested that guided-discretion statutes such as the one upheld in *Gregg* were generally constitutionally acceptable. But no two states had identical death penalty laws, and many important questions remained to be addressed.

In the years immediately following *Gregg*, the Court seemed inclined to resolve the aforementioned conflict between consistent sentencing and individualized sentencing in favor of the latter alternative. In 1977, for example, the Court reaffirmed its *Woodson* stance against mandatory death penalty laws. In *Roberts* v. *Louisiana*, a sharply divided Court struck down a Louisiana statute that made death the mandatory punishment for anyone convicted of the first-degree murder of a police officer engaged in the performance of his or her lawful duties. A five-justice majority made it clear that the fact that a murder victim was a police officer could be regarded as an aggravating circumstance (*Roberts* at 636). However, the majority held that the sentencing authority must always be permitted to consider such mitigating facts as the youth of the offender, the absence of any prior convictions, or the influence of extreme emotional disturbance (*Roberts* at 637). Because the Louisiana law did not allow the jury to consider these kinds of mitigating factors when the victim was a law enforcement officer, it violated the Eighth Amendment (*Roberts* at 637–638).

A year later, the Court again indicated that promoting individualized sentencing was its foremost priority. In *Lockett* v. *Ohio*, (1978), with Justices Rehnquist and White as the only dissenters, the Court invalidated the sentence of Sandra Lockett, a young black woman who had been condemned to die on the basis of her participation in a pawnshop robbery in which one of her confederates shot and killed the pawnshop owner while Lockett waited in the getaway car. The trial judge had found two statutory aggravating circumstances to exist but could not consider the full range of possible mitigating factors under Ohio's law. This was because the law stipulated that he *must* impose a death sentence unless he found by a preponderance of the evidence that (1) the victim had induced or facilitated the murder; (2) the offender was under duress, coercion, or strong provocation; or (3) the murder was attributable primarily to the offender's psychosis or mental deficiency. By so sharply limiting the number of mitigating circumstances that could be considered, the Ohio statute deprived Lockett of the opportunity to offer into evidence such mitigating factors as her youth and her relatively minor role in the crime (*Lockett* at 589–594).

Reaffirming its commitment to promoting individualized sentencing in capital cases, the Court held that "in all but the rarest kind of capital case," the sentences must not be precluded from considering any mitigating factors bearing on the defendant's character, prior record, or the circumstances of the offense (*Lockett* at 604). The Constitution may not require individualized sentencing in noncapital cases, wrote Chief Justice Burger, but preventing a judge or a jury from giving "independent mitigating weight" to all aspects of the defendant's character, record, and offense is incompatible with the Eighth Amendment (*Lockett* at 604–605). "The need for treating each defendant in a capital case with that degree of respect due the uniqueness of the individual is far more important in capital cases" (*Lockett* at 605). With these words, the Chief Justice established the primacy of individualized decision making in capital cases. Although *Lockett* did not explicitly renounce the objective of reducing arbitrariness and bias in capital sentencing, it certainly signaled that this objective was now subordinate to the goal of promoting individualized capital sentencing. But as will be explained later, the tension between these two conflicting goals still exists and may yet work to the advantage of those who oppose the death penalty.[5]

In the first few years after *Gregg*, the Court also refused to extend death penalty eligibility to crimes other than murder. Thus in *Coker* v. *Georgia*, decided in 1977, six justices agreed that death is an impermissible punishment for the rape of an adult woman. Writing on behalf of a plurality and joined by Justices Brennan and Marshall, both of whom concurred in the judgment on the basis of their belief that capital punishment is in all circumstances unconstitutional, Justice White took the position that rape, although a reprehensible crime deserving severe punishment, simply does not compare to murder in terms of the harm done to the victim and to society (*Coker* at 597–598): "The murderer kills; the rapist, if no more than that, does not. Life is over for the victim of the murderer; for the rape victim, life may not be nearly so happy as it was, but it is not over and normally is not beyond repair" (*Coker* at 598).

Stressing that the Court must look to objective indicators as to whether contemporary society's "evolving standards of decency" (*Trop* v. *Dulles*, 1958, at 101) are incompatible with executing rapists, Justice White found it particularly significant that only three of the 35 states that had enacted post-*Furman* death penalty laws had authorized the death penalty for the rape of an adult woman (*Coker* at 591–594). Thus, the current judgments of state legislatures, though not unanimous, weigh very heavily against death as an acceptable punishment for rape (*Coker* at 596). Moreover, the sentencing decisions actually made by juries in cases in which the prosecutor seeks the death penalty for rape also pointed to a growing consensus that death is a disproportionate punishment for rape (*Coker* at 596–597). In Georgia, for example, juries had sentenced to death only six of 63 convicted rapists since 1973 (*Coker* at 596–597). The jury's rejection of capital punishment for rape in the vast majority of cases, like the legislative response to *Furman*, provided significant and reliable evidence that the American people were now in agreement with the Court's "own judgment, which is that death is indeed a disproportionate penalty for the crime of raping an adult woman" (*Coker* at 597).

Five years later, in *Enmund* v. *Florida* (1982), the Court stood by the principle arguably established by *Coker*—that the death penalty is unique in its severity and irrevocability and therefore must be reserved for those who take another human life or at least intend or attempt to take another human life. Indeed, Earl Enmund, the getaway driver for two robbers who shot and killed an elderly farm couple who resisted their holdup attempt, was parked approximately 200 yards from the scene of the murders (*Enmund* at 784). He did not shoot the victims and there was no evidence that he had planned or even anticipated that lethal force would or might be used in the course of the robbery (*Enmund* at 788). A Florida judge nevertheless sentenced him to die, a decision upheld by the Florida Supreme Court (*Enmund* at 784–787).

With Justice White again writing on behalf of the majority, the Court, by the narrowest of margins, struck down Enmund's death sentence. Justice White began by stressing that "to the maximum possible extent," the Court's decisions as to whether a particular punishment is grossly disproportionate to a particular crime must be informed by objective criteria (*Enmund* at 788–789). Accordingly, he turned first to an analysis of legislative judgments on the appropriateness of executing a nontriggerman such as Earl Enmund (*Enmund* at 788–793). Pointing out that only eight of the 36 states with capital punishment statutes allowed the death penalty to be imposed solely because the defendant somehow participated in a robbery in the course of which an accomplice committed a murder, Justice White found that the legislative consensus "weighs on the side of rejecting capital punishment for the crime at issue" (*Enmund* at 792–793). The sentencing behavior of juries provided even stronger evidence that contemporary American society rejects the death penalty for accomplice liability in felony murders (*Enmund* at 794). Of the 362 executions that had been carried out since 1954, only six were for merely participating in a felony in which a confederate had committed a murder (*Enmund* at 794–795). Moreover, only three of the 739 people who were under sentence of death as of late 1981 had been condemned to die without a finding that they did more than merely participate in an underlying felony that had led to an unplanned murder (*Enmund* at 795).

The final decision, however, must always be made by the Court, and the majority of the justices were in agreement with the judgments of legislators and jurors (*Enmund* at 797). The executions of offenders such as Earl Enmund would serve neither the goal of deterrence (since the threat of death is unlikely to deter when murder is not premeditated) nor the purpose of retribution (since retribution requires penalties that are tailored to fit the offender's *personal* responsibility and moral guilt) (*Enmund* at 798–801). Such executions therefore accomplish "nothing more than the purposeless and needless imposition of pain and suffering" and thus are prohibited by the Eighth Amendment (*Enmund* at 798). Accordingly, death is an impermissible punishment for "one who neither took life, attempted to take life, nor intended to take life" (*Enmund* at 787).

Decisions such as *Lockett, Coker,* and *Enmund* typify the Court's cautious approach to death penalty issues in the 1976–1983 period. With very few exceptions,[6] the Court insisted that the states follow strict procedural guidelines and make reasonable efforts to ensure fairness, reliability, and individualized consideration in the capital-sentencing process. Thus, the Court repeatedly reaffirmed the *Lockett* holding that the sentencer must consider all relevant mitigating circumstances proffered by the defense (*Bell* v. *Ohio*, 1978; *Green* v. *Georgia*, 1979; *Eddings* v. *Oklahoma*, 1982). Similarly, in *Gardner* v. *Florida* (1977), the justices held that capital defendants must always be permitted to confront and cross-examine witnesses who present aggravating-circumstances evidence at the penalty phase. *Godfrey* v. *Georgia* (1980) established that the aggravating circumstances considered by capital juries must be defined clearly enough to avoid the arbitrary imposition of the death penalty. Also in 1980, the Court invalidated an Alabama law that prohibited the trial judge from instructing the jury as to its option to find a capital defendant guilty of a lesser included noncapital offense (*Beck* v. *Alabama*). In 1981, the Court held that a jury's initial vote for life over death was an implied acquittal of death penalty eligibility, thus precluding reimposition of the death penalty after the defendant's reconviction for the same crime (*Bullington* v. *Missouri*). In these and in other cases that invalidated death sentences, the High Court seemed to be acutely aware that "death is a different kind of punishment from any other" (*Beck* at 637) and must always be accompanied by stringent safeguards designed to ensure fairness and consistency in capital sentencing.

THE POST-*GREGG* YEARS (1983–PRESENT)

Toward the end of the 1982–1983 term, the Court began to retreat from its cautious "go-slow" approach to capital punishment. The insistence on strict procedural safeguards was replaced by an attitude that it was time to "get on with it" and stop interfering with the will of the people as reflected by the laws passed by state legislatures.[7] Such deference to the political branches of government would broaden the class of death-eligible defendants and weaken the special safeguards against unfairness and caprice. But as the majority commented in a 1983 case, the states had a legitimate interest in finding a speedier way of handling death penalty appeals, and "not every imperfection in the deliberative process is sufficient...to set aside a state court judgment (*Zant* v. *Stephens*, 1983:884–885).

Space limitations preclude a discussion of all or even most of the dozens of death penalty decisions handed down by the Supreme Court since 1983. But we will look at some of the decisions that most accurately reflect the Court's evolving view of capital punishment, with special emphasis on the holdings that demonstrate the Court's headlong retreat from the positions it had taken in the 1976–1983 period. Although the Court has not reversed its earlier holdings, it has narrowed most of them in ways that are highly disadvantageous for capital defendants and their attorneys.

A good example of this trend is evident in cases raising the issue of whether state death penalty procedures give the defendant a full opportunity to make juries aware of all relevant mitigating evidence. The Court has not repudiated its position that the sentencing judge or jury must be permitted to consider any relevant mitigating circumstances when deciding whether or not to sentence a defendant to death (*Skipper* v. *South Carolina*, 1986; *Hitchcock* v. *Dugger*, 1987). However, the reach of these decisions has been circumscribed by decisions such as *Johnson* v. *Texas* (1993). In *Johnson*, the Court held that the judge's failure to instruct the jury explicitly to consider mitigating evidence about the defendant's age did not *prevent* the jury from considering the mitigating effect of the defendant's youth.

Similarly, in *Buchanan* v. *Angelone* (1998), the attorney for a capital defendant in Virginia requested instructions on the meaning of the concept of mitigation generally and on four statutorily defined mitigating factors that had been placed into evidence—the accused's (1) youth, (2) lack of prior criminal activity, (3) extreme mental or emotional disturbance at the time of the offense, and (4) impaired ability to appreciate the criminality of his conduct or to conform his conduct to the requirements of law. The judge refused to include these instructions but told the jury to base its decision on "all the evidence." Writing for the majority, Chief Justice Rehnquist upheld the trial judge's refusal to instruct the jury on the concept of mitigation generally and on the four specific mitigating factors. The jury instructions, according to the chief justice, were constitutional because by directing the jury to examine "all the evidence," the trial judge had done enough to ensure that jurors would consider mitigating evidence and would not think that they were precluded from considering mitigating evidence (*Buchanan* at 762).

Joined by Justices Stevens and Ginsburg, Justice Breyer issued a strongly worded disserting opinion that accused the majority of ignoring the likelihood that "so serious a misinstruction" had the effect of misleading the jurors and preventing them from considering relevant mitigating evidence (*Buchanan* at 766). Justice Breyer added that by upholding the trial judge's inadequate instructions, the Supreme Court "breaks the promise…that the imposition of the punishment of death will 'reflect a reasoned moral response to the defendant's background, character, and crime'" (*Buchanan* at 766, quoting *California* v. *Brown* at 545).

The Supreme Court also has begun to back away from its *Woodson–Roberts* stance against laws that mandate the death penalty for particular offenses or categories of offenders, but the Court is not yet in full retreat. Most notably, in *Sumner* v. *Shuman* (1987), the Court struck down a Nevada law that required the jury to impose the death penalty in all cases in which a prisoner is convicted of murder while serving a life sentence without the possibility of parole. Interestingly, Justice Blackmun, who had voted to uphold the mandatory death penalty laws at issue in *Woodson* and *Roberts*, wrote the majority opinion in *Shuman*. He reasoned that even when an inmate serving a life-without-parole sentence commits a murder, there might be mitigating factors such as the defendant's age or mental condition, which weigh against a death sentence (*Shuman* at 81–82). To the argument that a mandatory death sentence is necessary in order to deter and provide retribution against life-termers, the majority responded that under a nonmandatory guided-discretion sentencing law, those who deserve to die are likely to receive the death penalty in most cases and those not condemned to die can still be punished in other ways, "such as through a transfer to a more restrictive…correctional facility or deprivation of privileges" (*Shuman* at 83–84). Since the state's legitimate interests in deterrence and retribution can be satisfied through the use of a guided-discretion statute, the Court would not depart from the position that mandatory death penalty laws violate the Eighth Amendment (*Shuman* at 85).

Although *Shuman* remains in effect, the Court in 1990 embraced an element of mandatoriness in capital sentencing. In *Blystone* v. *Pennsylvania*, a five-justice majority held that the existence of a mandatory component in a guided-discretion death penalty statute does not always violate constitutional strictures. Specifically, the *Blystone* Court upheld the constitutionality of a Pennsylvania law that requires the jury to impose the death penalty if it finds that the aggravating circumstances in the case outweigh any mitigating circumstances. Writing for the majority, Chief Justice Rehnquist distinguished *Woodson*, stressing that under the Pennsylvania statute: "Death is not automatically imposed upon conviction for certain types of murder. It is imposed only after a determination that the aggravating circumstances outweigh the mitigating circumstances present in the particular crime committed by the particular defendant, or that there are no such mitigating circumstances" (*BlystoneA at 305*).[8]

In *Blystone*, the Supreme Court merely "chipped away" at past precedents requiring strict scrutiny of death penalty laws. For opponents of the death penalty, this was ominous enough in itself. But in other important cases, the Court has gone much further, jettisoning prior holdings and retreating from the pursuit of fairness and consistency in death penalty cases. To be sure, the Court has continued to invalidate egregiously unconstitutional capital-sentencing provisions.[9] However, the predominant trend has clearly been in the direction of expanding the reach of the death penalty and promoting expeditious executions.

Several 1983 decisions marked the High Court's movement away from the strict regulation of capital-sentencing procedures. For example, in *California* v. *Ramos*, the Court found nothing constitutionally deficient in a law that seemingly gives the jury the mistaken impression that the *only* way to keep the defendant off the street is to execute him. The law in question required judges to instruct the jury that the governor had the authority to reduce a life-without-parole sentence to a sentence that includes the possibility of parole. But it did not require the judge to call the jury's attention to the governor's power to commute a death sentence (*Ramos* at 994–998).

In two 1983 cases (*Barclay* v. *Florida*; *Zant* v. *Stephens*), the Court refused to invalidate death sentences even though the sentencer had considered an illegitimate aggravating circumstance along with two or more legitimate aggravating circumstances. The majority's determination that a sentence of death could rest upon both valid and invalid aggravating circumstances provoked a strong dissent from Justice Blackmun, who wrote, "[t]he end does not justify the means even in what may be deemed to be a 'deserving capital punishment situation'" (*Barclay* at 991).

In a particularly controversial 1983 case dealing with Texas's death penalty statute, the Court upheld the admissibility of testimony by state-hired psychiatrists who routinely predicted that capital defendants would commit future crimes. Writing for the majority in *Barefoot* v. *Estelle*, Justice White acknowledged research studies showing that "expert" predictions about future dangerousness turn out to be incorrect 66% of the time (*Barefoot* at 898–903). He dismissed the importance of such studies, however, noting that psychiatrists are not wrong all of the time, only "most of the time" (*Barefoot* at 901). Since the defense will have the opportunity to cross-examine the state's witnesses and can always call its own witnesses, the jurors will hear both sides of the debate over the defendant's dangerousness and can sort out the differences themselves (*Barefoot* at 898–899). Thus, the scientifically dubious expert testimony does not in and of itself render the sentencing hearing so unfair as to violate the Constitution (*Barefoot* at 905–906). The *Barefoot* majority also bestowed its approval on "expedited review procedures" to be followed by federal courts in order to speed death penalty appeals toward a final resolution (*Barefoot* at 887–896). Ironically, as several legal commentators have pointed out, the procedures approved in *Barefoot* give capital defendants *less time* to prepare their appeals than prisoners who do not face the death penalty (Amsterdam, 1987:889–890; Mello, 1988:547–548).

In 1984, the Court signaled unmistakably that it would no longer uphold all of the strict procedural safeguards that the *Gregg* Court thought would protect capital defendants from the arbitrary, aberrant, or excessive infliction of the death penalty. Both the plurality and concurring opinions in *Gregg* had emphasized the importance of the Georgia statutory provision requiring the state supreme court to "compare each death sentence with the sentences imposed on similarly situated defendants to ensure that the sentence of death in a particular case is not disproportionate" (*Gregg* at 198, 211–212). Indeed, a fair reading of *Gregg* would indicate that the Court viewed such a comparative-proportionality review as an *indispensable* aspect of any constitutionally sound capital-sentencing system. Justice Stewart, after all, had written that "[i]n particular the proportionality review substantially eliminates the possibility that a person will be sentenced to die by the action of an aberrant jury" (*Gregg* at 206). Justice White had added that he was confident that the Georgia Supreme Court would see to it that "death sentences imposed for discriminatory reasons or wantonly or freakishly for any given category of crime will be set aside" (*Gregg* at 224).

In 1984, however, Justice White, writing for a six-justice majority, repudiated the argument that the outcome of *Gregg* had hinged on mandatory proportionality review. In *Pulley* v. *Harris*, the Court considered the case of Robert Harris, a convicted murderer who was sentenced to death under a California law that provided for an automatic appeal of the factual validity of each death sentence but did not require the state's highest court to conduct a comparative proportionality review in all cases. Although Justice White conceded that Gregg had "made much of the statutorily required comparative proportionality review," neither he nor the other justices who constituted the *Gregg* majority meant to declare that such a review "was so critical that without it the Georgia statute would not have passed constitutional muster" (*Pulley* at 45). What the *Gregg* justices really meant to say, according to Justice White, was that whether such a proportionality review would be constitutionally mandated in any given state would depend on what other checks against arbitrariness were included in that state's statutory death-sentencing scheme (*Pulley* at 51–53).

Since the California statute requires the jury to find that at least one aggravating circumstance exists before imposing the death penalty, the statute operates to limit the death sentence to a small subclass of cases, thus minimizing the risk of capricious and standardless sentencing (*Pulley* at 53). The occasional "aberrational outcomes," reasoned Justice White, "are a far cry from the major systematic defects identified in *Furman*" (*Pulley* at 54). Such inconsistencies, he concluded, are inevitable, since there can be no "perfect" procedure for deciding when to extinguish life (*Pulley* at 54). The California procedures provided Robert Harris with enough protection against the evils identified in *Furman* to satisfy constitutional requirements (*Pulley* at 54).

Justice Brennan, joined by Justice Marshall, rebuked the majority for departing from the promises seemingly made in *Furman* and *Gregg* (*Pulley* at 61–64). Arguing that *Gregg* stands for the principle that the irrational imposition of the death penalty can *never* be constitutionally defended (*Pulley* at 63–64), Justice Brennan described comparative proportionality review as an imperfect but necessary method for eliminating some of the racial discrimination and arbitrariness that all too often surround the imposition of death sentences (*Pulley* at 71). A growing body of scholarly evidence, he contended, demonstrated that racial discrimination and other irrationalities continued to infect the post-*Gregg* imposition of the death penalty (*Pulley* at 64–67). He predicted that the majority's refusal to mandate comparative proportionality review would only increase the arbitrariness and racial bias already inherent under the various state capital-sentencing schemes (*Pulley* at 70–73).

With only a few exceptions, the High Court continued to demonstrate its new attitude toward capital punishment in the 1984–1985 and 1985–1986 terms. For example, in *Wainwright* v. *Witt* (1985), the Court by a seven-to-two vote relaxed the long-standing standard that required judges to remove a prospective juror from both phases of a capital trial only when the juror made it "unmistakably clear" that he or she could never vote to impose death in the penalty phase of the trial. This standard, derived from a 1968 decision, *Witherspoon* v. *Illinois*, helped to make capital juries at least somewhat representative of the community at large, a community that typically includes some people who are potentially receptive to the defense attorney's arguments for life as well as the prosecutor's arguments for death. But the *Witt* holding replaced *Witherspoon* with a rule holding that a prospective juror could be eliminated merely on the ground that the judge believed that the juror's doubts about capital punishment would "substantially impair" his or her ability to impose a death sentence (*Witt* at 424–425).

One year later, Justice Rehnquist, the author of the *Witt* majority opinion, again wrote for the Court in *Lockhart* v. *McCree* (1986). Here the holding was that *death qualification,* the practice of removing from capital juries those who were reluctant to impose death in the penalty phase, does not violate the defendant's Sixth Amendment right to a fair trial in the guilt phase of the trial. The *McCree* decision contradicted the findings of numerous social-science studies showing that death-qualified juries were significantly more likely to impose the death penalty than were juries in noncapital cases (Ellsworth, 1988). To opponents of capital punishment, the *Witt* and *McCree* holdings were seen as heralding a new era in which the scales of justice would be weighted against life and in favor of death.

In 1987, many of the worst fears of death penalty abolitionists were realized. In a trilogy of five-to-four decisions, the Court rejected two important challenges to death penalty laws and extended death penalty eligibility to an entire new group of defendants, those who did not actually take another human life. First, in *California* v. *Brown*, Justice Rehnquist authored a majority opinion upholding a death sentence imposed by a jury that had been instructed by the trial judge that it "must not be swayed by mere sentiment, conjecture, sympathy, passion, prejudice, public opinion or public feeling" (*Brown* at 540). The California Supreme Court had found that an instruction to disregard any sympathy factors raised by the defense violated the *Lockett* mandate that juries must be permitted to consider all relevant mitigating evidence before reaching a decision (*Brown* at 539–540). Justice Rehnquist, however, asserted that a reasonable juror would read the instruction as a whole rather than focus only on the admonition against being swayed by sympathy (*Brown* at 542–543). Therefore, he reasoned, the instruction did nothing more than advise jurors to ignore emotional responses that are not rooted in the aggravating and mitigating evidence, thereby minimizing the risk of arbitrary and capricious decisions (*Brown* at 543).

In dissent, Justice Brennan contended that the state supreme court was right in the first place: the antisympathy instruction would almost certainly lead jurors to believe that they could not consider the very kind of mitigating factors that the *Lockett* majority "[had] decreed must be considered by the sentencer" (Brown at 555). The result will be that juries will be confronted with confusing and contradictory instructions, a state of affairs that should not be tolerated when life itself is at stake (*Brown* at 560–561).

Several months after *Brown*, the Court rejected a major systemic challenge to the constitutionality of capital punishment. In *McCleskey* v. *Kemp* (1987), the Court was confronted with strong statistical evidence that post-*Gregg* capital-sentencing procedures were still saturated with arbitrariness and racial discrimination and thus violated both the Eighth Amendment and the Fourteenth Amendment guarantee of equal protection under the law. A comprehensive study (known as the Baldus study)[10] of 2000 murder cases that occurred in Georgia during the 1970s revealed that defendants charged with killing white victims were 4.3 times as likely to receive a death sentence as those whose victims were black (*McCleskey* at 287). Moreover, the death penalty had been imposed in 22% of the cases involving black defendants and white victims, 8% of the cases involving white defendants and white victims, 3% of the cases involving white defendants and black victims, and 1% of the cases involving black defendants and black victims (*McCleskey* at 286).

Did such overwhelming evidence of racial discrimination in capital sentencing establish a constitutional violation? Writing for the majority, Justice Powell answered this question in the negative. The majority assumed that the Baldus study was reliable, but held that to prevail under the equal protection clause, a capital defendant would have to meet the difficult burden of proving "that the decision makers in *his* case acted with discriminatory purpose" (*McCleskey* at 292). To the argument that the statistical evidence demonstrated that the death penalty in Georgia was arbitrarily applied in violation of the Eighth Amendment, Justice Powell responded:

> At most, the Baldus study indicates a discrepancy that appears to correlate with race. Apparent disparities in sentencing are an inevitable part of our criminal justice system…Where the discretion that is fundamental to our criminal process is involved, we decline to assume that what is unexplained is invidious. In light of the safeguards [Georgia has] designed to minimize racial bias in the process…we hold that the Baldus study does not demonstrate a constitutionally significant risk of racial bias affecting the Georgia capital sentencing process (*McCleskey* at 312–313)

In a dissenting opinion, Justice Brennan, joined by Justices Marshall, Stevens, and Blackmun, accused the majority of ignoring "precisely the type of risk of irrationality in sentencing that we have consistently condemned in our Eighth Amendment jurisprudence" (*McCleskey* at 320–321). He vehemently objected to Justice Powell's assertion that the risk of racial bias in Georgia's capital-sentencing system were not "constitutionally significant" (*McCleskey* at 325–328). Pointing out that the Baldus study showed that "blacks who kill whites are sentenced to death at nearly *22 times* the rate of blacks who kill blacks and more than *7 times* the rate of whites who kill blacks," Justice Brennan contended that "we should not be willing to take a person's life if the chance that his death sentence was irrationally imposed is *more* likely than not" (*McCleskey* at 327–328).[11]

The *McCleskey* decision dealt a major blow to opponents of the death penalty, but many abolitionists were even more dismayed by the Court's 1987 holding in *Tison* v. *Arizona*. The *Tison* decision significantly modified the Court's aforementioned 1982 ruling in *Enmund* v. *Florida*, forbidding the execution of those who participate in a felony that leads to murder but who do not actually kill or intend to kill the victim. In *Tison*, the justices considered the fate of Ricky and Raymond Tison, two young brothers who helped their father, Gary Tison, and his cellmate, Randy Greenawalt, escape from the Arizona State Prison in 1978. Several days later, the escape car lost a tire on a desert road, and the group decided to flag down a passing motorist and steal his car. After a Mazda occupied by John Lyons, his wife, his 2-year-old son, and his 15-year-old niece pulled over to offer help, Gary Tison and Randy Greenawalt took the family back to the escape car, held them there at gunpoint, and told the brothers to go back to the Mazda to get some water. When they did so, their father and his friend brutally shotgunned their four captives to death. Although Ricky and Raymond subsequently testified that they were surprised by the shooting, they nonetheless stayed with their father until they were captured several days later after a shootout with the police in which Randy Greenawalt was also captured and their father was killed (*Tison* at 139–141).

The Tison brothers and Randy Greenawalt were all convicted for the murder of the Lyons family and sentenced to death. Randy Greenawalt, one of the actual murderers, certainly was eligible for the death penalty. But could the Tison brothers be executed for murders that the state could not prove that they committed or even intended to commit? The *Enmund* holding would seem to answer this question in the negative, but the Supreme Court disagreed. Writing for the majority, Justice O'Connor reasoned that there was nothing cruel and unusual about executing defendants who neither committed nor intended to commit murder (1) if they participated in a "major" way in the underlying felony that led to murder, and (2) if they demonstrated a "reckless indifference to human life" while doing so (*Tison* at 158). As Justice O'Connor explained it, the defendant's role in the armed robbery and murders in *Enmund* was "minor"; the Tison brothers, on the other hand, participated fully in the escape, kidnapping, and robbery "and watched the killing after which [they] chose to aid those whom [they] had placed in the position to kill rather than their victims" (*Tison* at 152). Focusing only on the question of whether or not the defendant intended to kill, she continued, did not take into account that "reckless disregard for human life may be every bit as shocking to the moral sense as an 'intent to kill'" (*Tison* at 157). She added that "in these midrange felony murder cases...the majority of American jurisdictions clearly authorize capital punishment" (*Tison* at 155).

In a lengthy dissenting opinion joined by Justices Marshall, Stevens, and Blackmun, Justice Brennan challenged both Justice O'Connor's mathematics and her logic (*Tison* at 159–185). Pointing out that Justice O'Connor had excluded from her survey the 14 states that do not authorize capital punishment, Justice Brennan declared that when these states are included along with those that require proof of intent to kill in order to impose a death sentence, "one discovers that approximately three-fifths of American jurisdictions do not authorize the death penalty for a nontriggerman absent a finding that he intended to kill" (*Tison* at 175). He accused the majority of creating "a new category of culpability" and blithely discarding a fundamental principle found in virtually all European and Commonwealth countries: that the death penalty—if it is ever to be used—must be reserved for those who either killed or intended to kill another human being (*Tison* at 170–171). The Court's holding, he concluded, was inconsistent with *Enmund*, violated basic standards of fairness and proportionality, and went well beyond the retributive principle of "an eye for an eye..." (*Tison* at 174–185).[12]

To those who oppose capital punishment, the *Tison* ruling was a chilling indication that the Supreme Court's future decisions would continue to expand the category of death-eligible defendants. This is what the Court in fact has done and is likely to continue to do. Two important 1989 decisions, both announced on June 26 of that year, illustrate the current trend in the Court's death penalty jurisprudence. First, in *Penry* v. *Lynaugh*, the Court held that executing a person who is mentally retarded does not constitute cruel and unusual punishment. Johnny Paul Penry, who was 22 at the time he committed murder, was diagnosed as "moderately" mentally retarded, with an IQ ranging between 50 and 63. This meant that he had the mental capacity of an average 6½ year-old child (*Penry* at 308). But according to Justice O'Connor's majority opinion, this was outweighed in importance by the fact that the state of Texas had found Penry to be competent to stand trial and to have "a reasonable degree of rational understanding...as well as factual understanding of the case against him" (*Penry* at 333). Justice O'Connor suggested that it might be cruel and unusual to execute "profoundly" or "severely" retarded people, but that the mental limitations of someone who was merely "moderately" retarded did not automatically preclude imposition of the death penalty (*Penry* at 333–340). Four dissenting justices failed to convince the majority that "[t]he impairment of a mentally retarded offender's reasoning abilities [and] control over impulsive behavior limit his or her culpability so that, whatever other punishment might be appropriate, the ultimate penalty of death is always...disproportionate to his or her blameworthiness and hence is unconstitutional" (*Penry* at 346).[13]

On the same day the holding in *Penry* was decided, the Court announced its decision in a case that raised the issue of whether the prohibition against cruel and unusual punishment precluded the execution of defendants who were under the age of 18 at the time of their offense. One year earlier, a closely divided Court had held that

15-year-old offenders could not be executed unless and until more states enacted laws authorizing such executions (*Thompson* v. *Oklahoma*, 1988). But in *Stanford* v. *Kentucky* (1989), the Court found that it was already sufficiently clear that there was no national consensus against imposing capital punishment on 16- and 17-year-old offenders. Writing for the majority, Justice Scalia noted that of the states that permit capital punishment, 15 declined to impose it on 16-year-olds and 12 declined to impose it on 17-year-olds (*Stanford* at 372). These numbers, according to Justice Scalia, did not establish enough of a national consensus to show that executing such young offenders was contrary to America's evolving standards of decency and thus violative of the Eighth Amendment (*Stanford* at 372–373). As Justice Brennan pointed out in dissent, the majority's holding would ensure that the United States would remain in the embarrassing company of Rwanda, Barbados, Pakistan, and Bangladesh as the only nations in the world that still execute children (*Stanford* at 389).[14]

Justice Scalia, however, rejected such international comparisons as irrelevant, emphasizing that only *American* conceptions of decency are dispositive (*Stanford* at 369 n. 1). He also repudiated another of Justice Brennan's arguments: that executing those who are too young, immature, and impulsive to take full responsibility for their actions fails to serve the only two penological goals the Court has recognized as legitimate in capital cases—retribution and deterrence (*Stanford* at 377).[15] Indeed, it is this part of Justice Scalia's opinion that is most troubling for those who do not want the United States to become the world leader in executions.

Writing for a plurality (since Justice O'Connor did not join this part of the Court's opinion), Justice Scalia asserted that arguments grounded in the claim that juveniles are less mature, more impulsive, and less likely to possess fully developed cognitive skills than adults must fail because they rest on social science studies rather than the judgment of the American people (*Stanford* at 377–378). Social science studies, according to Justice Scalia, are irrelevant because the Court has no business evaluating such studies in order to determine whether a particular punishment violates the Eighth Amendment (*Stanford* at 378). It is the citizenry of the United States, not judges, who must be persuaded that children are less blameworthy and are therefore ineligible for the death penalty (*Stanford* at 378). Accordingly, the Court in future death penalty cases would ignore "ethioscientific" evidence and consider only "objective indicia," the most important of which are the laws passed by Congress and the state legislatures (*Stanford* at 377–378). In the future, Justice Scalia warned, the Eighth Amendment would be taken literally. A challenged punishment would have to be *both* cruel *and* unusual, as determined by objective factors, to fail the Court's Eighth Amendment tests (*Stanford* at 369). In other words, a cruel punishment will withstand constitutional scrutiny if enough states still authorize it. Just how many states are enough will be determined by the Court on a case-by-case basis.[16]

In the years since *Stanford*, Justice Scalia's brand of jurisprudence—extraordinary deference to laws and procedures that broaden the application of the death penalty—has clearly been in the ascendancy. In the majority of the most important death penalty cases, the conservative majority, led by Chief Justice Rehnquist and Justice Scalia, has prevailed. For example, in *Payne* v. *Tennessee*, Chief Justice Rehnquist ended the

1990–1991 term by authoring a majority opinion that reversed the Court's previous holdings (*Booth* v. *Maryland*, 1987; *South Carolina* v. *Gathers*, 1989) prohibiting the use of "victim-impact" statements in the penalty phase of capital trials. In *Payne*, a six-justice majority rejected Justice Stevens's dissenting argument that permitting juries to base death penalty decisions on such idiosyncratic factors as the victim's reputation and the persuasiveness of the victim's family in describing their loss would distract jurors from examining the character of the defendant and the nature of the crime. This, in turn, would pose a "constitutionally unacceptable risk" that juries would impose the death penalty in an arbitrary and discriminatory manner (*Payne* at 2628–2631).[17]

One other area of the Supreme Court's recent death penalty jurisprudence deserves to be mentioned before we turn to the risky enterprise of predicting the Court's future role in capital punishment. In a series of cases beginning in the 1988–1989 term, the Court has erected exceptionally strict substantive and procedural roadblocks to the use of the federal habeas corpus statute by state death row inmates who wish to appeal their state criminal convictions.[18] Indeed, the Court has managed to eviscerate many of its prior holdings in this area, thereby crippling the power of federal courts to overturn even the most questionable state-court convictions and/or sentences of capital defendants.

Federal habeas corpus law is extraordinarily complex, and space limitations preclude an examination of most of the Supreme Court's recent rulings. However, one decision deserves attention because it not only exemplifies the Court's jurisprudence in this area, but it may yet prove to be a particularly potent symbol and rallying point for opponents of capital punishment. In *Herrera* v. *Collins* (1993), the Court considered the case of Leonel Torres Herrera, a Texas death row inmate who sought federal habeas corpus relief on the ground that he was factually innocent of the murder for which he had been sentenced to die. Most habeas petitions focus on constitutional questions pertaining to the fairness of the defendant's arrest, pretrial proceedings, and trial. Herrera's petition, however, alleged no such deficiencies—no search-and-seizure problems, no *Miranda* problems, no incorrect evidentiary rulings, and no constitutional or other major procedural errors during the trial. Instead, Herrera's claim was that even though he had had a "fair trial," he was nevertheless "actually innocent." He and his attorneys supported this claim with affidavits containing recently discovered evidence indicating that Herrera's now-dead brother was the actual perpetrator of the crime.

Most legal analysts would agree that Herrera's new evidence was not strongly persuasive, but his petition raised two very important questions: (1) Can a death-sentenced prisoner obtain federal habeas corpus relief solely on the ground of newly discovered evidence of factual innocence when he has no accompanying claim of a violation of his constitutional rights in the state criminal proceedings against him? (2) Would the execution of a factually innocent person violate the Eighth Amendment's prohibition of cruel and unusual punishments, the due process clause of the Fourteenth Amendment, or any other provision of the U.S. Constitution? To the dismay of death penalty opponents, the majority opinion, authored by Chief Justice Rehnquist, answered both questions in the negative. With respect to the first question,

Rehnquist stressed that federal habeas corpus review traditionally has been limited to questions of alleged constitutional violations. Accordingly, claims of factual innocence based on newly discovered evidence do not state a ground for relief when they are not accompanied by an underlying constitutional claim (*Herrera* at 860). This rule, Rehnquist added, "is grounded in the principle that federal habeas courts sit to ensure that individuals are not imprisoned in violation of the Constitution—not to correct errors of fact." (*Herrera* at 360).

In response to Herrera's assertion that the Eighth and Fourteenth Amendments prohibit the execution of a factually innocent person, Rehnquist conceded that such an argument "has an elemental appeal" (*Herrera* at 859). But this argument, according to the chief justice, was irrelevant in the context of Herrera's case. The proper judicial proceeding to determine "guilt" or "innocence" is the defendant's trial, and "once a defendant has been afforded a fair trial and convicted of the offense for which he was charged, the presumption of innocence disappears" (*Herrera* at 860). Since the state met its burden of proof at trial, Herrera comes before the Supreme Court not as one who is "innocent" but as one who has been convicted of murder (*Herrera* at 860). "The question before us, then, is not whether due process prohibits the execution of an innocent person, but rather whether it entitles petitioner to a review of his 'actual innocence' claim" (*Herrera* at 864). The answer to this question, Rehnquist reiterated was "no," since "a claim of 'actual innocence' is not itself a constitutional claim, but instead a gateway through which a habeas petitioner must pass to have his otherwise barred constitutional claim considered on the merits" (*Herrera* at 862). Thus, Rehnquist's majority opinion did not answer squarely the question of whether the Constitution prohibits the execution of an innocent person. Moreover, the *Herrera* opinion established a formidable "catch-22" for any death row inmates who might want to raise the question in the future.

Joined by Justices Souter and Breyer, Justice Blackmun issued a dissenting opinion that disagreed with virtually every aspect of the majority opinion. First, Blackmun declared, it is "crystal clear" that execution of the innocent violates both the Eighth and Fourteenth Amendments (*Herrera* at 876–890). Second, he asserted that the majority should realize that even a prisoner who appears to have had "a constitutionally perfect" trial retains a strong and legitimate interest in overturning a wrongful conviction, particularly when he faces the death penalty (*Herrera* at 880). Justice Blackmun argued that claims of actual innocence, even when unaccompanied by a claim of constitutional error, should be reviewed by federal habeas courts in all cases where the petitioner can make a threshold showing that he is "probably innocent" (*Herrera* at 882). In a part of the dissenting opinion in which he spoke only for himself, Justice Blackmun castigated the majority for its "obvious eagerness to do away with any restriction on the States' power to execute whomever and however they please." Permitting an innocent person to be executed, he added, "comes perilously close to simple murder" (*Herrera* at 884).

Five years later, another "catch-22" became apparent in cases in which a condemned prisoner attempts to show that he is factually innocent. Chief Justice Rehnquist's majority opinion in *Herrera* had extolled the virtues of executive clemency as "the historical remedy for preventing miscarriages of justice where judicial process has been exhausted" (*Herrera* at 866). A death-sentenced inmate would not be permitted to bring a freestanding claim of actual innocence to the federal courts in a habeas petition. But, according to Rehnquist, this was appropriate and fair:

> Executive clemency has provided the "fail safe" in our criminal justice system....It is an unalterable fact that our judicial system, like the human beings who administer it, is fallible. But history is replete with examples of wrongfully convicted persons who have been pardoned in the wake of after-discovered evidence establishing their innocence. (*Herrera* at 868)

In dissent, Justice Blackmun countered that although clemency proceedings had saved the lives of some wrongfully convicted people, executive clemency, at best, was an ad hoc exercise of authority by elected officials that was highly fallible in itself and, in fact, had failed to save the lives of a number of factually innocent people (*Herrera* at 876).

The stage was thus set for an important 1998 ruling on the question of whether death-sentenced prisoners were entitled to due process protection during clemency hearings. In *Ohio Adult Parole Authority* v. *Woodard*, Eugene Woodard complained of the lack of procedural protection offered by the Ohio Adult Parole Authority, the state board that votes on clemency petitions and sends its recommendation to the governor. As the ultimate decision maker, the governor has the authority to take a broad range of actions, including commuting a death sentence to a sentence of life imprisonment. Woodard contended that the authority's procedures fell woefully short of fair standards. He complained, in particular, that he was given only 10 days' notice of the date of his clemency hearing, that he was given only three days' notice of his option of requesting an interview with a member of the parole authority, that his attorney was not permitted to be present for any such interview, that his attorney would be permitted to attend the clemency hearing only at the discretion of the parole authority, and that Woodard himself was not allowed to testify or to present documentary evidence at the clemency hearing.

Having praised clemency hearings as the "fail safe" of the criminal justice process, Chief Justice Rehnquist might have been expected to find these procedures to be inadequate, especially in that they gave the condemned man so little time to prepare his case, sabotaged his right to the assistance of counsel, and did not even permit him to testify or present new evidence during the clemency hearing. In *Woodard*, however, Chief Justice Rehnquist, joined by Justices Scalia, Thomas, and Kennedy, took an extraordinarily narrow view, asserting that clemency proceedings simply do not implicate due process (*Woodard* at 275–285). According to Rehnquist, clemency is not an integral part of Ohio's system of adjudicating guilt or innocence and it therefore follows that forcing clemency boards or governors to follow any due process standards "would be inconsistent with the heart of executive clemency, which is to grant clemency as a matter of grace..." (*Woodard* at 280–281). Rehnquist concluded:

> Clemency proceedings are not part of the trial—or even of the adjudicatory process. They do not determine the guilt or innocence of the defendant, and are not primarily intended to enhance the reliability of the trial process. They are conducted by the

> Executive Branch, independent of direct appeal and collateral relief proceedings….While traditionally available to capital defendants as a final and alternative avenue of relief, clemency has not traditionally been the business of courts. (*Woodard* at 284)

The majority of the justices were unwilling to hold that no due process whatsoever is required in capital clemency proceedings. Justice O'Connor, in an opinion joined by Justices Souter, Ginsburg, and Breyer, contended that in capital cases, when life itself is at stake, clemency proceedings implicate due process (*Woodard* at 288–290). These four justices, however, declared that only *minimal* procedural safeguards apply to clemency hearings (*Woodard* at 289). As examples of procedures that might be found to violate due process, O'Connor cited two hypothetical cases—a case where a state denied a death-sentenced prisoner any access at all to its clemency process and a scheme in which a state official flips a coin to decide whether to grant clemency (*Woodard* at 289). Thus, eight justices found that Ohio's clemency procedures were constitutional and that Woodard's due process rights had not been violated. Only Justice Stevens, who pointed out that the Rehnquist opinion would permit clemency procedures to be infected by "the deliberate fabrication of false evidence" (*Woodard* at 290–291) and that the O'Connor opinion provided only "minimal, perhaps even barely discernible" procedural safeguards for condemned people (*Woodard* at 290), was willing to cast a dissenting vote. He would have remanded the case to the lower Ohio courts for an assessment of what particular procedural safeguards are required in capital clemency proceedings (*Woodard* at 294).

Taken together, the *Herrera* and *Woodard* rulings amount to a classic "good news—bad news" answer to the appeals of death-sentenced prisoners by the Supreme Court. The good news is that although we will not permit a federal habeas court to hear your claim of factual innocence unless you can also prove the existence of a major constitutional error by the trial court, you can still take advantage of the executive clemency process. The bad news, however, is that clemency proceedings are not the Court's business, and you are not necessarily constitutionally entitled to testify or offer exculpatory evidence to the clemency board.

Since *Woodard*, the Supreme Court has announced other decisions that raise questions of fairness with respect to the administration of the death penalty. For example, in *Strickler* v. *Greene* (1999), the Court upheld a Virginia man's death sentence despite the prosecution's suppression of important exculpatory evidence that the defense might have used to discredit the state's key eyewitness. That witness had changed her story several times before her testimony at Tommy Strickler's trial for allegedly abducting a woman from a shopping mall and killing her. However, state prosecutors, contrary to state and federal law, never disclosed this to Strickler's defense attorneys. The Court acknowledged that discrediting the testimony "might have changed the outcome of the trial" and that there was a "reasonable possibility" that Strickler would have been spared (*Strickler* at 290). A "reasonable possibility," however, was not good enough. Strickler, the Court concluded, needed to show a "reasonable *probability*" that his conviction or sentence would have been different had the prosecution not suppressed the evidence in question (*Strickler* at 291). Thus, although the question was "close," Strickler's death sentence was affirmed (*Strickler* at 296).

In 2000, the Court announced another decision that exemplifies its increasing willingness to overlook unfair procedures in death penalty cases. In *Weeks* v. *Angelone* (2000), the Court held that a judge presiding over a capital case was not obligated to clear up the jury's confusion over a crucial sentencing instruction. Writing for a five-justice majority, Chief Justice Rehnquist reasoned that the Constitution was not violated when the judge refused to explain, in response to the jury's query, that a death sentence was not mandatory if the jurors found that the state had proved one of two aggravating factors. Rehnquist conceded that there was a "slight possibility" that the jury mistakenly believed a death sentence to be mandatory when the judge responded to the jurors' question simply by telling them to reread his original instructions (*Weeks* at 734). The chief justice, nonetheless, said that "a jury is presumed to understand a judge's answer to its question…and to presume otherwise would require a reversal every time a jury inquires about a matter of constitutional significance, regardless of the judge's answer" (*Weeks* at 733).

Writing for the four dissenting justices, Justice Stevens noted that the jurors spent several hours debating the meaning of the instruction that continued to confuse them and that when the jurors were polled, most of them were "in tears" (*Weeks* at 746). Stevens added that the judge's failure to answer the jury's question in a clearcut way was constitutionally deficient and that it was a "virtual certainty" that the jury was confused (*Weeks* at 740–746).

Will decisions such as *Herrera, Woodard, Strickler,* and *Weeks* eventually convince Americans that even the best minds on the highest court in the land simply cannot figure out a way to administer capital punishment without error, arbitrariness, and inconsistency? In the next section, we will see that this conclusion was reached by former Justice Harry Blackmun. In 1994, Blackmun, shortly before his retirement later that year, cited the growing likelihood of erroneous convictions and unfair death sentences and renounced his former position in support of the constitutionality of capital punishment. Ironically, this indicates that the best hope for the abolitionist dream of eliminating capital punishment may lie in the very trends we have so far discussed. It is possible that the contemporary Supreme Court's growing willingness to expand the death penalty's reach and tolerate arbitrariness and discrimination in its application will eventually lead a future Court to outlaw capital punishment as a cruel and unusual punishment forbidden by the Eighth Amendment.

THE SUPREME COURT AND THE PROSPECTS FOR ABOLISHING CAPITAL PUNISHMENT

Until quite recently, actual execution had been the *least* common cause of death for those condemned to die under post-*Furman* capital punishment statutes. Death row inmates more commonly died from old age, suicide, or murder at the hands of their fellow prisoners (Streib, 1984:443). Indeed, from 1976 to 1983, only 11 death row inmates were executed. In 1984, 21 inmates were executed, followed by 18 in 1985, 18 in 1986, 25 in 1987, 11 in 1988, 16 in 1989, 23 in 1990, 14 in 1991, 31 in 1992, 38 in 1993, and 31 in 1994 (NAACP, 2000:6).

But while executions were carried out from 1984 to 1994 an average of fewer than 23 times per year, the number of defendants sentenced to death each year averaged approximately 250. This sharp numerical discrepancy arguably reflects deep ambivalence toward the death penalty on the part of the American people. In other words, peoples' willingness to endorse capital punishment in the abstract is not necessarily an accurate measure of their willingness to put it into practice. Indeed, recent research shows that even though approximately two out of every three Americans continue to support capital punishment, most of these death penalty supporters acknowledge that they would favor abolishing capital punishment if offenders were given a sentence of life imprisonment without parole combined with a restitution requirement (Bowers, 1993). The result of this ambivalence toward the penalty of death has been obvious—a burgeoning death row population that reached 3703 on October 1, 2000 (NAACP, 2000:1).

To some extent, the gap between the death row population and the number of people executed can be attributed to the length of the appeals process. It generally takes anywhere from 7 to 15 years, and sometimes longer, for condemned inmates to exhaust all of their appeals and postconviction remedies. In June 2000, Columbia University issued a study of 4578 death sentence appeals that had been decided by federal and state appellate courts between 1973 and 1995. In 68 percent of these cases, a federal or state court reversed the conviction or death sentence. Misconduct by prosecutors who suppressed exculpatory or mitigating evidence accounted for 16 percent of the reversals. In 37 percent of the reversals, appeals courts ruled that defendants' attorneys were so incompetent that their performance substantially altered the trial outcome. Overall, 82 percent of the reversed convictions and sentences resulted in defendants receiving lesser sentences, and 7 percent of the defendants were found not guilty in retrials. The report concluded that the U.S. capital punishment system "is collapsing under the weight of its own mistakes." The lead author, Columbia University law professor James Leibman, commented that "[i]t's not just one case, it's not just one state. Error was found at epic levels across the country" (Davies, 2000).

The Columbia University study is one of several noteworthy developments in 2000 that will lead death penalty opponents to believe that change is imminent. For example, in May, the New Hampshire legislature became the first in the nation to vote to abolish capital punishment in the post-*Gregg* era. However, the bill was promptly vetoed by Governor Jeanne Shaheen, a Democrat who was seeking—and won—reelection in November. The legislature could not come close to mustering the two-thirds majority required to override the veto. New Hampshire thus retains its capital punishment law, but arguably nothing has changed; the state has not executed anyone since 1939 (Ferdinand, 2000).

What *is* significant is that among the 38 states with death penalty laws, no other state legislature has even come close to repealing capital punishment since *Gregg*. However, on January 31, 2000, Illinois became the first death penalty state in the modern era to impose a moratorium on executions. Governor George Ryan, a Republican who supports capital punishment, imposed the moratorium because of concerns that the Illinois system of capital punishment was plagued by error and caprice. Since the state reinstated capital punishment in 1977, he pointed out, 12 prisoners had been put to death, but 13 death row inmates had been cleared of murder charges, often only because journalists and students and professors at Northwestern University unearthed pivotal exculpatory evidence that state officials had either missed or ignored (Johnson, 2000).

Governor Ryan also cited a recent series by the *Chicago Tribune* that examined nearly 300 Illinois cases in which a death sentence had been imposed. Of the cases that were appealed, over half were reversed for a new trial or sentencing hearing. In 30 cases death row inmates were found to have been represented by lawyers who were disbarred or suspended from practice. In many other cases, false testimony by witnesses, misconduct by prosecutors, and improper rulings by judges resulted in convictions that had to be reversed. In announcing the moratorium, Governor Ryan stated: "Until I can be sure that everyone sentenced to death in Illinois is truly guilty, until I can be sure with moral certainty that no innocent man or woman is facing lethal injection, no one will meet that fate" (Johnson, 2000).

The 13 exonerated men in Illinois are among 92 death-sentenced inmates who have been freed from death row since 1973 because newly discovered evidence indicated that they had not committed the crimes for which they had been sentenced to die (Rimer, 2001). An important book published in 2000, *Actual Innocence*, by Barry Scheck, Peter Neufeld, and Jim Dwyer, examines many of these cases and finds that the same problems found in Illinois can be found throughout the country. Scheck and Neufeld, the founders of the Innocence Project, a project based at Cardozo Law School, have used DNA testing to clear 37 wrongfully convicted prisoners. The cases recounted in *Actual Innocence* are intended to make Americans aware that poor police work, lying jailhouse snitches, overzealous prosecutors, and mistaken eyewitnesses are all-too-common flaws in our criminal justice system.

But will the American people repudiate the death penalty by 2010? At first glimpse, there would appear to be reason for optimism. Grass-roots moratorium efforts are under way in a growing number of states. Editorials in many of the nation's leading newspapers, including the *New York Times* and *Washington Post*, have praised Governor Ryan and urged other governors to consider a moratorium. More conservative thinkers, such as columnist George Will and Pat Robertson, have voiced criticisms of the capital-sentencing system. And more than ever, leaders in the Western world have chastised the United States for being the only Western democracy to retain capital punishment. Many Europeans expressed dismay that George W. Bush, a man they call the "executioner extraordinaire," was selected to be our next President. The European Union, Pope John Paul II, and United Nations' Secretary General Kofi Annan have joined many other world leaders in calling for a moratorium on executions in the United States (Reid, 2000).

Such events have led many abolitionists to believe that change is imminent. For example, an editorial in *The Nation*, a leading journal of liberal opinion, proclaimed: "The year 2001 could be the one in which America calls a halt to its long love affair with capital punishment. But the people must make it loudly clear to politicians that the death trip is over" (*Nation* editorial, 2001:4). It is typical of the political left to overestimate the humanitarian instincts of "the people"—the American capital punishment system will *not* grind to a halt in 2001 or even by 2010.

Despite the past years' revelations of mistakes, shoddy procedures, inconsistency, and discrimination in the capital sentencing process, the latest Gallup poll shows that public support for the death penalty, though down somewhat, is still strong—66 percent (Reid, 2000). Moreover, the decline in public support is largely attributable to the unusual publicity in the past few years about wrongfully convicted death row inmates, many of whom were exonerated by DNA tests. But as Gregg Easterbook (2000) has pointed out, DNA usually is available only in the aftermath of intimate violent crimes, crimes in which the attacker struggles with the victim and leaves behind blood, semen, saliva, or something else that can be tested. Most murders are committed by people who use guns and do not have intimate contact with the victim. New laws that compel DNA testing for death-sentenced inmates will free a few innocent people from death row, but DNA technology will not help most people convicted falsely. Yet because the public seems to hold DNA testing in such high regard, it will have the effect of making the American people "much more confident that those receiving their last meals really are guilty of a mortal sin" (Easterbrook, 2000). Until the public becomes aware of the limits of DNA technology, popular support for capital punishment can be expected to remain high and perhaps even increase somewhat.

Another change heralded by abolitionists, but one that will actually work to their disadvantage, is the movement toward lethal injection as the sole method of execution in the United States. After a series of botched and bloody electrocutions, Florida in January 2000 switched its primary method of execution to lethal injection, leaving Alabama and Nebraska as the only states that still use the electric chair as their sole method of execution (Rimer, 2000). All other states now use lethal injection or give inmates a choice between lethal injection or another method of execution. But like the availability of DNA testing, this will make people more, not less, supportive of capital punishment. By "sanitizing" the execution process, the use of lethal injection will persuade many Americans that capital punishment is being carried out in a humane, civilized, and relatively painless manner. It will take a while before the evidence accumulates that lethal injection also results in botched and tortuous executions. In fact, on June 8, 2000, Bennie Demps became the first Florida prisoner to die by lethal injection, and, as eyewitnesses reported, nearly everything went wrong.

> Bennie Demps lay on the gurney while technicians struggled for thirty-three minutes to get the needle into four veins in three places. Demps shouted into the microphone dangling over his head: "They butchered me back there. I was in a lot of pain. They cut me in the groin, they cut me in the leg. I was bleeding profusely." The warden of the penitentiary claimed that Demps was just "griping." (Sherrill, 2001:14)

It will take more spectacles like this—and much more understanding about the imperfections of the capital punishment process—before the public will begin to seriously reconsider the death penalty. As for the pressures from abroad, Americans have always been skeptical about the criminal justice policies of other nations, resentful of European criticisms of American penal practices, and extraordinarily reluctant to submit to the rule of international law. For example, as this chapter goes to print, it is clear that the U.S. Senate will not ratify the 1998 Treaty of Rome, which created the world's first permanent international war crimes tribunal (Knutson, 2001).

The most telling indicator of the immediate future of the American death penalty is the selection of George W. Bush as the next President of the United States. As Governor of Texas, Bush has presided over more executions than any governor in American history. He presided over 40 of the 85 executions carried out in the United States in 2000, and he has presided over 152 since his election in 1994 (Yardley, 2000). During his campaign for the presidency, Bush often spoke of his strong support for the death penalty, and when the issue arose during the third presidential candidates' debate, Bush's opponent, Vice-President Al Gore quickly responded "I also support the death penalty." Indeed, in the 2000 elections, no Republican or Democratic candidate for national office campaigned on a platform of opposition to the death penalty. As President, Bush will probably have the opportunity to appoint at least two and perhaps three justices to the Supreme Court in his first term. Chief Justice Rehnquist and Justice O'Connor are widely rumored to be considering retirement and Justice Stevens, who has been on the Court since 1975 and is now 80 years old, may be considering it as well. To say the least, it is highly unlikely that Bush will appoint any justices who do not subscribe to a judicial philosophy that encompasses strong support for the constitutionality of the present system of capital punishment.

Moreover, as we have seen, over the past 17 years, the contemporary Supreme Court has expanded the category of death-eligible defendants, weakened safeguards against unfair death sentences, and streamlined the death penalty appeals process. Will this, in fact, result in the execution of more people in the years to come?

The answer is "yes." Indeed, the trend toward a greater number of executions has already begun. In 1995, there were 56 executions followed by 45 in 1996, 74 in 1997, 68 in 1998, 98 in 1999, and 85 in 2000 (NAACP, 2000:6). The decrease to 85 executions in 2000 from 98 in 1999, like the drops from 1995 to 1996 and from 1997 to 1998, reflect the cyclical nature of execution numbers, which depend on the time frame of appeals that are exhausted in any given year. The overall trend is clearly upward, and in fact it is noteworthy that 300 new death sentences were imposed in 1998 and 272 in 1999, thus adding to a growing death row backlog (Masters, 2000). On October 1, 2000, the American death row population reached a new high of 3703 inmates (NAACP, 2000:1). As the final appeals are exhausted for those now on death row, the annual execution total can be expected to rise.

Equally important, over the next 10 to 15 years, we will undoubtedly see an expansion of the geographical reach of the death penalty. As of December 31, 2000, 603 of the 683 post-*Gregg* executions (88.3%) had been carried out by 17 southern states: Texas (239), Virginia (81), Florida (50), Missouri (46), Oklahoma (30), Louisiana (26), South Carolina (25), Georgia (23), Alabama (23), Arkansas (23), North Carolina (16), Delaware (11), Mississippi (4), Maryland (3), Kentucky (2), and Tennessee (1). Thus, capital punishment remains largely a southern phenomenon; only 80 (11.7%) post-*Gregg* executions had been carried out in nonsouthern states: Arizona (22), Illinois (12), Nevada (8), California (8), Indiana (7), Utah (6), Nebraska (3), Washington (3), Pennsylvania (3), Oregon (2), Montana (2), Ohio (1), Wyoming, (1) Colorado (1), and Idaho (1). But this represents a noteworthy increase; as of March 22, 1988, only six persons had been put to death in nonsouthern states: Nevada (2), Indiana (2), and Utah (2) (Haas and Inciardi, 1988:12). Among the states that have only recently begun to execute offenders are Delaware (11 since March 1992), California (8 since April 1992), Washington (3 since January 1993), Idaho (1 in January 1994), Maryland (3 since May 1994), Pennsylvania (3 since May 1995), Kentucky (2 since July 1997), Colorado (1 in October 1997), and Tennessee (1 in April 2000)(NAACP, 2000).

Even so, seven of the 38 states that currently have capital punishment statutes have not yet executed anyone in the post-*Gregg* era: Connecticut, New Hampshire, New Jersey, New Mexico, New York, Ohio, and South Dakota. However, Ohio, with a growing death row population of 202, is moving toward a resumption of executions (NAACP, 2000:22). Even in New Jersey, with a relatively small death row population of 17, the state's highest court began to uphold death sentences in 1991, ending a nine-year period in which the court had consistently reversed such sentences (Bienen et al., 1990:713–714).

Abolitionists also cannot ignore the possibility that one or more of the 12 states without a capital punishment law may resurrect the death penalty. New York became the thirty-eighth state with a death penalty law on September 1, 1995, and as of December 31, 2000, six people had been sentenced to death under the new law (NAACP, 2000:22). Massachusetts recently came within one vote of becoming the thirty-ninth death penalty state. A capital punishment bill had already been approved by the state senate, and Governor A. Paul Cellucci had promised to sign it. But on November 6, 1997, a state representative, citing his concern that a jury had erred in the celebrated case of an English au pair convicted of murdering a baby under her care, switched his vote. He thereby turned an 81–79 House vote to reinstate capital punishment into an 80–80 tie and blocked Massachusetts from joining the 38 states that have capital punishment laws in place (Dodds, 1997).

It is a virtual certainty that the U.S. government will soon resume executions. There currently are 28 people under a federal sentence of death, seven under U.S. military jurisdiction and 21 under the jurisdiction of the U.S. government (Castaneda, 2001). Moreover, two new laws, the Federal Death Penalty Act of 1994 and the Antiterrorism and Effective Death Penalty Act of 1996, have expanded the number of crimes punishable by death and placed new limits on appeals brought by death-sentenced inmates (Robbins, 2000).

In September 2000, the U.S. Justice Department issued the first comprehensive review of the federal death penalty since it was reinstated in 1988. The Justice Department report disclosed that of the 682 cases in which U.S. Attorneys considered seeking a death sentence, 80 percent of the defendants were black, Hispanic, or members of another minority group. The majority of federal death penalty cases were filed by federal attorneys from Texas, Virginia, and other states with large state death row populations. After review by federal attorneys and by Attorney General Janet

Reno, death penalty prosecutions were authorized in 159 cases, 74 percent of which involved minority defendants. Of the 20 people under a federal death sentence as of December 1, 2000, 14 were black, one was Hispanic, one was Asian, and four were white. Virginia accounted for four federal death row inmates (all black) and Texas for six (five blacks and one Hispanic) (Eggen, 2000).

The report's findings prompted calls by civil rights organizations for a moratorium on federal executions, and President Clinton had the opportunity to impose such a moratorium in late 2000. The execution of Juan Raul Garza, sentenced to die for three drug-related killings in Texas, was scheduled for December 12, 2000 and would have been the first federal execution since 1963. The President rejected the calls for a moratorium, but he did postpone Garza's execution for six months, thus leaving Garza's fate to President-elect Bush (Walsh, 2000).

The racial disparities found on the federal death row differ little from the racial disparities found on Texas's death row during Bush's years as governor. Bush never expressed concerns about the racial composition of death row inmates in Texas, and while presiding over 152 executions, he never granted a reprieve or a pardon on racial discrimination grounds. It is highly unlikely that Bush will impose a moratorium on federal executions or even postpone any executions because of concerns about racial or geographic disparities in the federal death-sentencing process.

Moreover, on December 27, 2000, Timothy McVeigh, convicted of the 1995 Oklahoma City bombing that killed 168 people, requested an end to all appeals of his death sentence, and the trial judge quickly granted his request (Thomas, 2000). McVeigh could change his mind, but if he does not, he will probably be executed in 2001. McVeigh appears to understand the consequences of his decision, and when a condemned person appears to be competent enough to understand the consequences of dropping all appeals, the courts generally will not permit any so-called "next-friend" petitions on his behalf. In all likelihood, McVeigh will be the first federal prisoner to be executed since 1963. He will not, however, be the last.[19]

All things considered, it seems quite likely that by the year 2010 we will see an increase in executions and in the number of jurisdictions that actually execute offenders. In addition to a growing number of federal executions, more nonsouthern states will join the ranks of executing states. Southern states, however, will continue to execute significantly more offenders than will nonsouthern states. In this regard, it is noteworthy that Texas by itself has been responsible for 239 of the 683 executions (35 percent) carried out since the *Gregg* decision.

But how high will the national total of executions go? From January 1, 1990 to December 31, 2000, there were 563 executions, an average of 56 per year for the 1990s. The annual average for the 1990s is, therefore, close to the annual average for the 1950s—68 (Bowers, 1984:50). Will the numbers rise to levels approaching the average of 152 per year (Bowers, 1984:50) who were executed in the 1930s? To the annual average of 118 in the 1940s?

My prediction is that the United States will not return to the levels of the 1930s but that it will return to levels comparable to the 1940s. It is not unreasonable to expect that the average annual number of executions in the first decade of the twenty-first century will be somewhere between 100 and 140. The reason I do not expect it to go higher is that, as explained earlier, support for the death penalty is not nearly as deep as it is broad. The public's ambivalence toward capital punishment may very well turn to discontentment once the number of executed offenders reaches higher levels. Since *Gregg*, American juries, showing that their "bark is worse than their bite," have returned death penalty verdicts in less than 25% of first-degree murder cases (Haas and Inciardi, 1988:11).

Moreover, a growing number of public officials in such death penalty states as Texas and Florida have complained about the crushing financial costs of the death penalty. In Florida, for example, it costs six times more to execute a person than to incarcerate a prisoner for life with no parole. As a result of the heightened due process required in the pretrial, trial, and posttrial stages of capital cases, Florida by 1988 had spent $57.2 million to execute 18 people. Yet a midyear budget cut of $45 million for the Florida Department of Corrections forced the early release of 3000 inmates (Death Penalty Information Center, 1992:4). As the number of executions rises, a growing number of Americans may become increasingly reluctant to allow the death penalty to siphon off scarce resources that could be used to strengthen the police, courts, and correctional agencies.

The best hope for an abolitionist future almost certainly lies in greater public knowledge concerning the death penalty. In *Furman* v. *Georgia* (1972), Justice Marshall asserted that if the American people were given accurate information about capital punishment—its failure to deter crime any more effectively than life imprisonment,[20] its high costs relative to life imprisonment, and the many cases of wrongfully executed defendants—they would renounce the death penalty and replace it with lengthy prison sentences (*Furman* at 360–363). Studies lend support to what has become known as the *Marshall hypothesis*. Interview and questionnaire studies have shown that support for the death penalty is indeed founded on misinformation about the effects of capital punishment and how it is used in our society (Ellsworth and Ross, 1983). Moreover, when representative samples of the American adult population are presented with pamphlets that provide factual, unbiased material on the realities of capital punishment, enough people change their minds to turn what had been minority opposition to the death penalty into a majority (Sarat and Vidmar, 1976).

If anything will turn the current minority position on capital punishment into a majority position, it is the cumulative impact of the Supreme Court death penalty decisions discussed earlier in this chapter. For example, how will Americans react when the evidence mounts that *McCleskey* v. *Kemp* (1987) was wrongly decided? If the evidence becomes irrefutable—and well-known—that human beings simply are incapable of administering the death penalty without racial discrimination, the pendulum of public opinion may very well begin to swing back toward the prevailing attitude in 1966 when a Harris survey found 47% of the public opposed to capital punishment, 38% in favor of it, and 15% unsure (Haas and Inciardi, 1988:11).

A similar shift in public opinion might become evident when the long-term effects of the Supreme Court's 1989 decisions in *Stanford* v. *Kentucky* and *Penry* v. *Lynaugh* become clear. Public support for the death penalty may very well erode noticeably as children increasingly are selected to receive the ultimate penalty. So far, 17 of the 683 post-*Gregg* execution victims have been juvenile offenders (NAACP, 2000), but this figure can be expected to rise. The impact of *Penry* could also contribute to public doubts about the morality of capital punishment. The Court held that Johnny Paul Penry was eligible for the death penalty even though he had a mental age of 6½.[21] One can only wonder where—if anywhere—the court will draw the line here. The *Penry* Court suggested but did not clearly hold that the execution of "severely" or "profoundly" retarded offenders would constitute cruel and unusual punishment (*Penry* at 333). Will the Court countenance the execution of those with a mental age of 2, 3, or 4? And if it does, will the majority of Americans defend such executions as having deterrent or retributive value? What will happen, as seems inevitable, when a greater number of women are executed? Although there are now 53 women on death rows around the country, only five of the 683 post-*Gregg* executions was of a female offender (NAACP, 2000). This suggests a certain squeamishness on the part of the public when it comes to executing women—a chord that may not evoke approval if, as is now possible under current Supreme Court rulings, a 16-year-old girl with a mental age of 6½ were to be put to death.

Tison v. Arizona (1987) also could eventually lead people to rethink their assumptions about the fairness of capital punishment. It is not at all certain that the killing of those who themselves never killed, intended to kill, or attempted to kill will ultimately square with basic American notions of fairness and justice.[22] Are Americans so fearful and angry about crime that they will reject the long-standing principle of "an eye for an eye" and replace it with a principle calling for "an eye for an eye and then some"? (Haas, 1994). This may be a hotly debated issue by the year 2010. And possibly by the year 2020, if not sooner, the answer may turn out to be "no."

There is still another eventuality—made all the more likely by the Supreme Court's recent decisions curtailing habeas corpus appeals by death row inmates—that may prove pivotal in convincing the public that the death penalty can no longer be tolerated. Indeed, it was the chilling impact of this particular eventuality that helped lead to the abolition of capital punishment in England—the execution of defendants who are later discovered to be innocent (Christoph, 1962). Legal scholars have already convincingly demonstrated that the erroneous conviction of people charged with capital crimes has long been, and continues to be, a major problem in the United States. In the most thorough study to date, Michael Radelet, Hugo Bedau, and Constance Putnam (1992) carefully documented the cases of 416 innocent Americans convicted of capital crimes between 1900 and 1991. Although some two dozen of these people were executed, and although the problem of wrongful capital convictions appears to be growing, the magnitude of the problem has so far eluded the American public.

But as a result of inherent human fallibility, the process of determining guilt in capital cases will always be plagued by such problems as mistaken eyewitness identification, perjured testimony, coerced confessions, laboratory errors, overzealous officials who conceal exculpatory evidence, and inattentive or confused jurors. And these kinds of errors can only become more difficult to discover and correct than they have been in the past. The Supreme Court's recent efforts to expedite the capital appeals process may help to reduce somewhat the crushing financial costs of the death penalty, but they will also deprive those who have been wrongfully convicted of a full and fair opportunity to prove their innocence. As more such cases occur and become highly publicized in the print and broadcast media, it stands to reason that a growing number of Americans will have second thoughts about the wisdom of imposing an irreversible punishment on criminal defendants.

My prediction, therefore, is that the Supreme Court's recent death penalty decisions will increase both the number of executions and the geographical reach of executions by the year 2010. I predict that the number of executions will reach levels comparable to those of the 1940s—100 to 140 per year—but will go no higher. I do not expect more than a few states to statutorily abolish capital punishment by 2010, but I do expect to see a growing pattern of reluctance to perform executions in some states.

Although I do not foresee a "deluge" or "avalanche" of executions, there will be enough executions to force Americans to rethink the death penalty in the first decade of the twenty-first century. As a result of the Supreme Court's expansion of the categories of death-eligible defendants, there will be more executions of juvenile offenders and mentally retarded offenders, and it will be more clear than ever that racial bias is the key factor in determining who dies. There will also be more cases in which the death penalty is imposed on nonmurderers and, most disturbingly, on defendants who will be conclusively—but too late—shown to be innocent. As a result, perhaps as early as 2020, a majority of Americans will begin to turn against capital punishment. Abolitionist movements will gain momentum in an increasing number of state capitols and in the U.S. Congress, and a growing number of jurisdictions will abolish capital punishment. Sometime in the mid-twenty-first century, with no more than eight states retaining death penalty statutes, the U.S. Supreme Court, citing the dwindling number of death penalty laws and executions as convincing evidence of a new societal consensus against the death penalty, will declare capital punishment in all cases to be a violation of the cruel and unusual punishment clause of the Eighth Amendment.

If this scenario proves correct, the American public will have gone through the same transition as Justice Harry Blackmun. Justice Blackmun had joined not only in the *Gregg* majority but had supported the *mandatory* death penalty laws under review in *Woodson* v. *North Carolina* (1976) and *Roberts* v. *Louisiana* (1977). But on February 23, 1994, after 24 years on the Supreme Court, Justice Blackmun repudiated capital punishment. In *Callins* v. *Collins*, he pointed to the central dilemma underlying all of the Supreme Court's post-*Gregg* jurisprudence. How can an appropriate balance be struck between the promise of consistency and equality in capital sentencing and the seemingly contradictory requirement of individualized sentencing in capital cases? Justice Blackmun's answer was that these two goals simply cannot be reconciled. "It seems that the decision whether a human being should live or die is so inherently subjective—rife with all of life's understandings, experiences, prejudices and passions—that it inevitably defies the rationality and consistency required by the Constitution" (*Callins* at 1134–1135). A quarter of a century of handling the hundreds of death penalty cases that came to the nation's highest court, he wrote, had convinced him that human beings are not capable of devising procedural or substantive rules that can prevent the inevitable intrusion of arbitrariness and racial discrimination into the capital-sentencing process (*Callins* at 1135–1136).

Justice Blackmun also made it clear that his decision to renounce capital punishment was heavily influenced by what he called the Court's "obvious eagerness to do away with any restrictions on the States' power to execute whomever and however they please" (*Callins* at 1137). He singled out the Court's 1993 decision in *Herrera* v. *Collins* for especially strong criticism (*Callins* at 1137–1138). The *Herrera* majority, he asserted, had not only refused to afford Leonel Torres Herrera an evidentiary hearing "despite his colorable showing of actual innocence," but it had erected "nearly insurmountable barriers" to any capital defendant's ability to get a federal habeas corpus hearing on a claim of actual innocence (*Callinsa* at 1138). The result of *Herrera*, he predicted, will be an increasing number of innocent people who will never have a full and fair opportunity to challenge their conviction and death sentence (Callins at 1138). Under these circumstances, he declared, he would no longer "tinker with the machinery of death" (*Callins* at 1130). He was optimistic, however, that "this Court will eventually conclude that…the death penalty must be abandoned altogether" (*Callins* at 1138).

To be sure, Justice Blackmun's hope will not become a reality in the near future. As noted earlier, President-elect George W. Bush is all but certain to appoint Supreme Court justices whose judicial philosophy includes enthusiastic support for the constitutionality of capital punishment and a strong tendency to value notions of finality and states' rights over concerns about erroneous convictions and unfair procedures. It is noteworthy that Bush's nominee for Attorney General, former Missouri Governor John Ashcroft, like Bush himself, is widely known as an aggressive advocate of capital punishment (Edsall, 2000). If Ashcroft's nomination is approved by the Senate, he will be the most influential member of the Bush administration not only when there are vacancies to be filled on the Supreme Court, but when it comes to the appointment of what will surely be several hundred federal trial and appellate court judges. Moreover, the 95 U.S. Attorneys that Bush will appoint in the next year undoubtedly will be more strongly inclined to seek the death penalty in federal cases than were their Clinton-appointed predecessors.

But there will undoubtedly be some changes in the composition of the Supreme Court by the year 2010 and, of course, *many* more by the year 2050. If, by then, the American people, like Justice Blackmun, become convinced by the weight of the evidence that the death penalty is useless, dangerous, and self-defeating, the Supreme Court will surely reach the same conclusion.

CONCLUSIONS

In a thought-provoking book, *Capital Punishment and the American Agenda*, Franklin Zimring and Gordon Hawkins (1986:148) argued that "America has outgrown the death penalty but is reluctant to acknowledge [it]." I agree. But what will it take to convince the American people to "acknowledge it"? Ironically, the answer may lie in the U.S. Supreme Court's recent death penalty jurisprudence. Since 1983, the Court has weakened the procedural protections available to convicted defendants, created formidable procedural obstacles to federal appellate review of capital appeals, ensured the continuing pervasiveness of racial discrimination in capital sentencing, and extended the reach of the death penalty to juvenile offenders, mentally retarded offenders, and those who never killed or intended to kill. By the year 2010, the short-term effects of these decisions will be evident—more executions in more states. But with more executions will come more erroneous executions, more evidence of racial bias and arbitrariness in capital sentencing, and more questions about the morality of executing children, the mentally retarded, nonmurderers, or anyone else in a world where human error, caprice, and prejudice are inevitable. By the middle part of the twenty-first century, the American people will repudiate capital punishment and the Supreme Court will declare it in all cases to be a cruel and unusual punishment forbidden by the Eighth Amendment.

NOTES

1. For detailed discussions of *Furman*, see Polsby (1973) and McFadden (1972).
2. See *Proffitt* v. *Florida* (1976) and *Jurek* v. *Texas* (1976).
3. Among the many good analyses of *Gregg*, *Woodson*, and the other 1976 death penalty cases are Barry (1979) and Rhoads (1977).
4. This issue is discussed at length by Sundby (1991).
5. This possibility and other implications of the *Lockett* decision are examined by Radin (1980).
6. See, for example, *Dobbert* v. *Florida* (1977) (holding that changes in Florida's capital punishment law between the time of the murder and the defendant's sentencing did not amount to an ex post facto violation) and *Estelle* v. *Smith* (1981) (excluding psychiatric testimony on *Miranda* grounds, but pointedly noting that psychiatric evidence as to a defendant's "future dangerousness" is generally admissible).
7. Arguably, the Court's emerging new attitude first became apparent in Justice Rehnquist's dissent from a denial of certiorari in *Coleman* v. *Balkcom* (1981). Urging his colleagues to take all necessary steps to expedite the administration of the death penalty, Justice Rehnquist referred to the slow pace of executions as a "mockery of our criminal justice system" (*Balkcom* at 958). Pointing to the lengthy appeals process in capital cases, Justice Rehnquist lamented that "[g]iven so many bites at the apple, the odds favor petitioner finding some court willing to vacate his death sentence because in its view his trial or sentence was not free from constitutional error" (*Balkcom* at 957).
8. See also *Boyde* v. *California* (1990) (applying the reasoning of *Blystone* and thus upholding a sentencing scheme that requires the imposition of a death sentence when aggravating circumstances outweigh mitigating circumstances).
9. See, for example, *Ake* v. *Oklahoma* (1985) (overturning a death sentence on the ground that an indigent capital defendant was denied access to a psychiatric examination that was necessary to prepare an effective defense based on his mental condition), *Francis* v. *Franklin* (1985) (invalidating a conviction and death sentence on the ground that the instructions to the jury violated the Fourteenth Amendment requirement that the state must prove every element of a criminal offense beyond a reasonable doubt), *Caldwell* v. *Mississippi* (1985) (vacating a death sentence because the prosecutor, citing the inevitability of appellate review, urged the jury not to view itself as actually determining whether the defendant dies), *Maynard* v. *Cartwright* (1988) (reversing a death sentence because one of the statutory aggravating circumstances was unconstitutionally vague), *Mills* v. *Maryland* (1988) (vacating a death sentence imposed under a state law that led jurors to believe that they could not consider all relevant mitigating factors), *Lankford* v. *Idaho* (1991) (invalidating a death sentence in a case in which the prosecution

announced that it would not seek the death penalty and the trial judge failed to provide adequate notice that death could still be imposed as the punishment), *Dawson* v. *Delaware* (1992) (reversing a death sentence imposed by a jury that had been told to consider the defendant's racist political views as an aggravating circumstance), and *Morgan* v. *Illinois* (1992) (invalidating a death sentence because the defense was not permitted to challenge the eligibility of jurors who would *automatically* impose the death penalty after a conviction).

10. For a detailed analysis of the study, its implications, and its treatment by the courts, see Baldus et al. (1990).

11. See Kennedy (1988) for a good critique of *McCleskey* v. *Kemp*.

12. The *Tison* holding is critically analyzed by Bass (1988).

13. The *Penry* decision has been greeted with an outpouring of criticism. See especially Dick-Hurwitz (1990), Cohen (1991), and Reed (1993). It will strike many as paradoxical that in *Ford* v. *Wainwright* (1986), the Court held that the Eighth Amendment prohibits the execution of insane death row inmates. The *Ford* case and its implications are examined by Miller and Radelet (1993).

14. For a penetrating critique of *Stanford* and *Penry*, see Miller (1990). The most comprehensive overview of the historical and contemporary practice of subjecting minors to capital punishment is by Streib (1987).

15. In *Gregg* v. *Georgia* (1976:184–187), the Court cited retribution and deterrence as two legitimate penological rationales for the death penalty. Surprisingly, the Court has never officially recognized a third justification—incapacitation. Many avowed opponents of capital punishment will acknowledge that this rationale is not totally without merit. Studies consistently show that convicted murderers are less likely to commit murders in prison or after release than are inmates convicted of such lesser crimes as robbery, burglary, and aggravated assault (Sellin, 1980:103–120). Nevertheless, there are some death row inmates who appear to be incorrigible, willing to kill guards or fellow inmates, and capable of escape. It thus can be argued that the death penalty is the only way to be 100% certain that a sociopath or a serial killer will never kill again. On the other hand, the noted attorney and abolitionist Anthony Amsterdam has responded to this argument by declaring that "[y]ou cannot tell me…that a society which is capable of putting a man on the moon is incapable of putting a man in prison, keeping him there, and keeping him from killing while he is there" (Amsterdam, 1982:354).

16. See Gey (1992) for an insightful analysis of Justice Scalia's death penalty jurisprudence.

17. The *Payne* decision continues to provoke highly critical commentaries in law reviews. See, for example, Oberlander (1992), Casimir (1993), and Levy (1993).

18. See especially *Teague* v. *Lane* (1989) (determining that new constitutional rulings benefiting defendants cannot be applied retroactively in habeas corpus proceedings), *Murray* v. *Giarratano* (1989) (holding that indigent death row inmates have no right to counsel in habeas corpus petitions), *Butler* v. *McKellar* (1990) (holding that the Teague retroactivity doctrine bars state death row inmates from invoking a new rule, one that was "susceptible to debate among reasonable minds" and was not clearly dictated by precedent, in a federal habeas corpus proceeding), *McCleskey* v. *Zant* (1991) (finding that a death row inmate's failure to raise a Sixth Amendment claim, a claim based on facts that he and his attorney did not become aware of until later, in his first habeas corpus petition constituted "an abuse of the writ" that precluded a second habeas corpus hearing), *Coleman* v. *Thompson* (1991) (deciding that an attorney's error in filing a notice of appeal from the denial of state postconviction relief one day late did not constitute a "cause" for death row inmate's procedural default and that the inmate thus was procedurally barred from seeking federal habeas corpus relief), *Keeney* v. *Tamayo-Reyes* (1992) (holding that the "cause-and-prejudice standard" governs question of whether a death row inmate forfeited his right to federal habeas corpus review by failing to fully develop his claim

in state court proceedings), *Gomez* v. *District Court* (1992) (ruling that the claim that execution by cyanide gas violates the Eighth Amendment was waived when not presented in an earlier federal habeas corpus petition), *Sawyer* v. *Whitley* (1992) (requiring a federal habeas petitioner bringing a successive claim to prove by clear and convincing evidence that but for a constitutional error, no reasonable juror would have found him eligible for the death penalty), and *Calderon* v. *Coleman* (1998) (holding that even when state judges give capital juries improper instructions that contain inaccurate information and divert the jury's attention from mitigating evidence, federal courts should not grant habeas relief unless it is clear that the improper instructions had a "substantial and injurious" influence on the jury's decision to impose a death sentence. These and other noteworthy decisions are discussed by Robbins (2000).

19. Timothy McVeigh was executed on June 11, 2001, after a one-month delay due to the failure of the FBI to turn over 300 pages of evidence.

20. After over 50 years of research and dozens of published studies, the evidence is overwhelming that the death penalty is no more effective than life imprisonment in deterring murder. Moreover, a growing body of research indicates that executions may have a "brutalizing effect" that causes a small but discernible short-term *increase* in the murder rate. See generally Bowers (1988) and Cochran et al (1994).

21. Although the 1989 *Penry* decision upheld the constitutionality of executing Penry, the Court nevertheless vacated his death sentence because the original trial jury had not been properly instructed to take Penry's mental retardation into account as a mitigating circumstance. Penry was subsequently resentenced to death. But in November 2000, with Penry's execution only days away, the Supreme Court stayed his execution and agreed to review the question of whether his second sentencing jury, like the first, did not receive proper instructions as to how to weigh Penry's mental retardation as a mitigating factor (see Bonner, 2000).

22. In fact, recent studies indicate that the majority of Americans soundly support the principle of proportional justice and reject the death penalty as a fair punishment for felony-murder accessories. See Finkel and Duff (1991) and Finkel and Smith (1993).

REFERENCES

AMSTERDAM, A. G. (1982). Capital punishment. In H. A. Bedau (ed.), *The Death Penalty in America*, 3rd ed. New York: Oxford University Press, pp. 346–358.

AMSTERDAM, A. (1987). In favorem mortis. *Human Rights*, 14:889–890.

BALDUS, D. C., G. WOODWORTH., and C. A. PULASKI, JR. (1990). *Equal Justice and the Death Penalty: A Legal and Empirical Analysis*. Boston: Northeastern University Press.

BARRY, R. V. (1979). *Furman* to *Gregg*: The judicial and legislative history. *Howard Law Journal*, 22:53–117.

BASS, W. K. (1988). *Tison* v. *Arizona*: A general intent for imposing capital punishment upon an accomplice felony murderer. *University of Toledo Law Review*, 20:255–292.

BIENEN, L. B., N. A. WEINER, P. D. ALLISON, and D. L. MILLS (1990). The reimposition of capital punishment in New Jersey: Felony murder cases. *Albany Law Review*, 54:709–817.

BONNER, R. (2000). Killer deemed retarded wins review of his death sentence. *New York Times*, November 28, p. A14.

BOWERS, W. J. (1984). *Legal Homicide: Death as Punishment in America, 1864–1982*. Boston: Northeastern University Press.

BOWERS, W. J. (1988). The effect of executions is brutalization, not deterrence. In K. C. Haas and J. A. Inciardi (eds.), *Challenging Capital Punishment: Legal and Social Science Approaches*. Thousand Oaks, CA: Sage Publications, pp. 49–89.

BOWERS, W. J. (1993). Capital punishment and contemporary values: People's misgivings and the court's misperceptions. *Law and Society Review*, 27:157–175.

CASIMIR, G. (1993). *Payne* v. *Tennessee*: Overlooking capital sentencing jurisprudence and stare decisis. *New England Journal on Criminal and Civil Confinement*, 19:427–458.

CASTANEDA, R. (2001). Man condemned in Beltsville slayings. *Washington Post*, January 4, p. B1.

CHRISTOPH, J. B. (1962). *Capital Punishment and British Politics: The British Movement to Abolish the Death Penalty, 1945–57*. Chicago: University of Chicago Press.

COCHRAN, J. K., M. B. CHAMLIN, and M. SETH (1994). Deterrence or brutalization? An impact assessment of Oklahoma's return to capital punishment. *Criminology*, 32:107–134.

COHEN, V. S. (1991). Exempting the mentally retarded from the death penalty: A comment on Florida's proposed legislation. *Florida State University Law Review*, 19:457–474.

DAVIES, F. (2000). Death-row cases often filled with error, study says. *Philadelphia Inquirer*, June 12, p. A2.

DEATH PENALTY INFORMATION CENTER (1992). *Millions Misspent: What Politicians Don't Say about the High Costs of the Death Penalty*. Washington, DC: The Center.

DICK-HURWITZ, R. (1990). *Penry* v. *Lynaugh*: The Supreme Court deals a fatal blow to mentally retarded capital defendants. *University of Pittsburgh Law Review*, 51:699–725.

DODDS, P. (1997). Au pair case helps bar death penalty in Massachusetts. *Philadelphia Inquirer*, November 8, p. A2.

EASTERBROOK, G. (2000). DNA and the end of innocence: The myth of fingerprints. *New Republic*, July 31, pp. 20–21.

EDSALL, T. B. (2000). Ashcroft will face a grilling in Senate. *Washington Post*, December 25, p. A1.

EGGEN, D. (2000). Executioners in Indiana await the President's order. *Washington Post*, December 5, p. A3.

ELLSWORTH, P. C. (1988). Unpleasant facts: The Supreme Court's response to empirical research on capital punishment. In K. C. Haas and J. A. Inciardi (eds.), *Challenging Capital Punishment: Legal and Social Science Approaches*. Thousand Oaks, CA: Sage Publications, pp. 177–211.

ELLSWORTH, P. C., and L. ROSS (1983). Public opinion and capital punishment: A close examination of the views of abolitionists and retentionists. *Crime and Delinquency*, 29:116–169.

FERDINAND, P. (2000). A death penalty bellwether? *Washington Post*, May 18, p. A3.

FINKEL, N. J., and K. B. DUFF (1991). Felony-murder and community sentiment: Testing the Supreme Court's assertions. *Law and Human Behavior*, 15:405–429.

FINKEL, N. J., and S. F. SMITH (1993). Principals and accessories in capital felony-murder: The proportionality principle reigns supreme. *Law and Society Review*, 27:129–156.

GEY, S. G. (1992). Justice Scalia's death penalty. *Florida State University Law Review*, 20:67–132.

HAAS, K. C. (1994). The triumph of vengeance over retribution: The United States Supreme Court and the death penalty. *Crime, Law and Social Change*, 21:127–154.

HAAS, K. C., and J. INCIARDI (1988). Lingering doubts about a popular punishment. In K. C. Haas and J. A. Inciardi (eds.), *Challenging Capital Punishment: Legal and Social Science Approaches*. Thousand Oaks, CA: Sage Publications, pp. 11–28.

JOHNSON, D. (2000). Illinois, citing verdict errors, bars executions. *New York Times*, February 1, p. A1.

KENNEDY, R. L. (1988). *McClesky* v. *Kemp*: Race, capital punishment and the Supreme Court. *Harvard Law Review*, 101:1388–1443.

KNUTSON, L. L. (2001). Clinton authorizes U.S. role in permanent war-crimes court. *Philadelphia Inquirer*, January 1, p. A3.

LEVY, J. H. (1993). Limiting victim impact evidence and argument after *Payne* v. *Tennessee*. *Stanford Law Review*, 45:1027–1060.

MARQUART, J. W., and J. R. SORENSEN (1989). A national study of the *Furman*-commuted inmates: Assessing the threat to society from capital offenders. *Loyola of Los Angeles Law Review*, 23:5–28.

MASTERS, B. A. (2000). Legal scrutiny slows pace of executions in Virginia. *Washington Post*, December 26, p. B1.

MCFADDEN, G. T. (1972). Capital sentencing: Effect of *McGautha* and *Furman*. *Temple Law Quarterly*, 45:619–648.

MELLO, M. (1988). Facing death alone: The post-conviction attorney crisis on death row. *American University Law Review*, 37:513–607.

MELTSNER, M. (1973). *Cruel and Unusual: The Supreme Court and Capital Punishment*. New York: Random House.

MILLER, E. (1990). Executing minors and the mentally retarded: The retribution and deterrence rationales. *Rutgers Law Review*, 43:15–52.

MILLER, K. S., and M. L. RADELET (1993). *Executing the Mentally Ill: The Criminal Justice System and the Case of Alvin*. Thousand Oaks, CA: Sage Publications.

NAACP LEGAL AND EDUCATIONAL DEFENSE FUND (2000). *Death Row U.S.A. Reporter*. New York: NAACP, Fall.

Nation editorial (2001). Executioner's swan song. *The Nation*, January 8, pp. 3–4.

OBERLANDER, M. I. (1992). The *Payne* of allowing victim impact statements at capital sentencing hearings. *Vanderbilt Law Review*, 45:1621–1662.

POLSBY, D. D. (1973). The death of capital punishment? *Furman* v. *Georgia*. In P. Kurland (ed.), *The Supreme Court Review: 1972*. Chicago: University of Chicago Press, pp. 1–40.

RADELET, M. L., H. A. BEDAU, and C. E. PUTNAM (1992). *In Spite of Innocence: Erroneous Convictions in Capital Cases*. Boston: Northeastern University Press.

RADIN, M. J. (1980). Cruel punishment and respect for persons: Super due process for death. *Southern California Law Review*, 53:1143–1185.

REED, E. F. (1993). *The Penry Penalty: Capital Punishment and Offenders with Mental Retardation*. Lanham, MD: University Press of America.

REID, T. R. (2000). Europeans see Bush as executioner extraordinaire. *Washington Post*, December 17, p. A36.

RHOADS, M. D. (1977). Resurrection of capital punishment: The 1976 death penalty cases. *Dickinson Law Review*, 81:543–573.

RIMER, S. (2000). Florida passes bill to quicken execution pace. *New York Times*, January 8, p. A1.

RIMER, S. (2001). Two death-row inmates exonerated in Louisiana. *New York Times*, January 6, p. A7.

ROBBINS, I. P. (2000). *Habeas Corpus Checklists: 2000 Edition*. St. Paul, MN: West Group.

SARAT, A., and N. VIDMAR (1976). Public opinion, the death penalty, and the eighth amendment: Testing the Marshall hypothesis. *Wisconsin Law Review*, 1976:171–206.

SCHECK, B., P. NEUFELD, and J. DWYER (2000). *Actual Innocence*. New York: Doubleday.

SELLIN, T. (1980). *The Penalty of Death*. Thousand Oaks, CA: Sage Publications.

SHERRILL, R. (2001). Death trip: The American way of execution. *The Nation*, January 8, pp. 13–34.

STREIB, V. L. (1984). Executions under the post-*Furman* capital punishment statutes: The halting progression from "let's do it" to "hey, there ain't no point in pulling so tight." *Rutgers Law Journal*, 15:443–487.

STREIB, V. L. (1987). *Death Penalty for Juveniles*. Bloomington, IN: Indiana University Press.

SUNDBY, S. E. (1991). The *Lockett* paradox: Reconciling guided discretion and unguided mitigation in capital sentencing. *UCLA Law Review*, 38:1147–1208.

THOMAS, J. (2000). Judge grants McVeigh's request to stop appeals; execution date can be set. *New York Times*, December 29, p. A14.

WALSH, E. (2000). Clinton stays killer's execution. *Washington Post*, December 8, p. A12.

WHITE, W. S. (1991). *The Death Penalty in the Nineties: An Examination of the Modern System of Capital Punishment*. Ann Arbor, MI: University of Michigan Press.

YARDLEY, J. (2000). Texas' busy death chamber helps define Bush's tenure. *New York Times*, January 7, p. A1.

ZIMRING, F. E., and G. HAWKINS. (1986). *Capital Punishment and the American Agenda*. Cambridge: Cambridge University Press.

CASES

Ake v. *Oklahoma*, 470 U.S. 68 (1985).

Barclay v. *Florida*, 463 U.S. 939 (1983).

Barefoot v. *Estelle*, 463 U.S. 880 (1983).

Beck v. *Alabama*, 477 U.S. 625 (1980).

Bell v. *Ohio*, 438 U.S. 637 (1978).

Blystone v. *Pennsylvania*, 110 S. Ct. 1078 (1990).

Booth v. *Maryland*, 482 U.S. 496 (1987).

Boyde v. *California*, 494 U.S. 370 (1990).

Buchanan v. *Angelone*, 118 S. Ct. 757 (1998).

Bullington v. *Missouri*, 451 U.S. 430 (1981).

Butler v. *McKellar*, 494 U.S. 407 (1990).

Calderon v. *Coleman*, 528 U.S. 141 (1998).

Caldwell v. *Mississippi*, 472 U.S. 320 (1985).

California v. *Brown*, 479 U.S. 538 (1987).

California v. *Ramos*, 463 U.S. 992 (1983).

Callins v. *Collins*, 114 S. Ct. 1127 (1994).

Coker v. *Georgia*, 433 U.S. 584 (1977).

Coleman v. *Balkcom*, 451 U.S. 949 (1981).

Coleman v. *Thompson*, 111 S. Ct. 2546 (1991).

Dawson v. *Delaware*, 112 S. Ct. 1093 (1992).

Dobbert v. *Florida*, 432 U.S. 325 (1977).

Eddings v. *Oklahoma*, 455 U.S. 104 (1982).

Enmund v. *Florida*, 458 U.S. 782 (1982).

Estelle v. *Smith*, 451 U.S. 454 (1981).

Ford v. *Wainwright*, 477 U.S. 399 (1986).

Francis v. *Franklin*, 471 U.S. 307 (1985).

Furman v. *Georgia*, 408 U.S. 238 (1972).

Gardner v. *Florida*, 430 U.S. 349 (1977).

Godfrey v. *Georgia*, 446 U.S. 420 (1980).

Gomez v. *District Court*, 112 S. Ct. 1652 (1992).
Green v. *Georgia*, 442 U.S. 95 (1979).
Gregg v. *Georgia*, 428 U.S. 153 (1976).
Herrera v. *Collins*, 113 S. Ct. 853 (1993).
Hitchcock v. *Dugger*, 481 U.S. 393 (1987).
Johnson v. *Texas*, 509 U.S. 350 (1993).
Jurek v. *Texas*, U.S. 262 (1976).
Keeney v. *Tamayo-Reyes*, 111 S. Ct. 1715 (1992).
Lankford v. *Idaho*, 111 S. Ct. 1723 (1991).
Lockett v. *Ohio*, 438 U.S. 586 (1978).
Lockhart v. *McCree*, 476 U.S. 162 (1986).
Maynard v. *Cartwright*, 486 U.S. 356 (1988).
McCleskey v. *Kemp*, 481 U.S. 279 (1987).
McCleskey v. *Zant*, 111 S. Ct. 1454 (1991).
Mills v. *Maryland*, 486 U.S. 367 (1988).
Morgan v. *Illinois*, 112 S. Ct. 2222 (1992).
Murray v. *Giarratano*, 492 U.S. 1 (1989).
Ohio Adult Parole Authority v. *Woodard*, 523 U.S. 272 (1998).
Payne v. *Tennessee*, 111 S. Ct. 2597 (1991).
Penry v. *Lynaugh*, 492 U.S. 302 (1989).
Proffitt v. *Florida*, 428 U.S. 242 (1976).
Pulley v. *Harris*, 465 U.S. 37 (1984).
Roberts v. *Louisiana*, 428 U.S. 325 (1976).
Roberts v. *Louisiana*, 431 U.S. 633 (1977).
Sawyer v. *Whitley*, 112 S. Ct. 2514 (1992).
Skipper v. *South Carolina*, 476 U.S. 1 (1986).
South Carolina v. *Gathers*, 490 U.S. 805 (1989).
Stanford v. *Kentucky*, 492 U.S. 361 (1989).
Strickler v. *Greene*, 527 U.S. 263 (1999).
Sumner v. *Shuman*, 483 U.S. 66 (1987).
Teague v. *Lane*, 489 U.S. 288 (1989).
Thompson v. *Oklahoma*, 487 U.S. 815 (1988).
Tison v. *Arizona*, 481 U.S. 137 (1987).
Trop v. *Dulles*, 356 U.S. 86 (1958).
Wainwright v. *Witt*, 469 U.S. 412 (1985).
Weeks v. *Angelone*, 120 S. Ct. 727 (2000).
Witherspoon v. *Illinois*, 391 U.S. 510 (1968).
Woodson v. *North Carolina*, 428 U.S. 280 (1976).
Zant v. *Stephens*, 462 U.S. 862 (1983).

chapter 11

The Future Impact of International Law on the U.S. Death Penalty

Christopher M. Cevasco, J.D.

At the dawn of a new millennium, the United States remains the only Western democracy to retain the death penalty. Indeed, holdings such as that of the Supreme Court in *Stanford v. Kentucky* (1989) have rendered the United States increasingly isolated in a world that is growing more abolitionist by the day. Rather than acknowledge this widespread condemnation of capital punishment as indicative of customary international law, however, the United States has actually increased its rate of executing criminals over the past decade, and in so doing, has executed increasing numbers of foreign nationals in violation of their rights under the Vienna Convention on Consular Relations and a startling number of juvenile offenders in violation of a wide array of international instruments. Many of these individuals languished on death row for decades before their death sentences were actually carried out, raising questions about the psychological impact of such delays. Just as the sheer numbers of recent execution have sparked a need for the United States to reexamine both the fairness and the effectiveness of capital punishment as a whole, flagrant disregard for its obligations to the international community has created a situation in which the United States must soon come to terms with those obligations or risk alienating friend and foe alike. International pressure will become an increasingly important factor in bringing the United States into long-overdue compliance with customary international norms and several international treaties, all of which abhor the death penalty.

INTRODUCTION

International law and U.S. law are distinct but often complementary systems. Increasingly, the two have been merged with regard to the enforcement of human rights. Nevertheless, it remains difficult to pin down the enforceability of international law within the United States. Some countries have adopted a "dualist" approach in which international law is not judicially enforceable unless there has been some form of implementing legislation (e.g., the United Kingdom). Other countries have adopted a "monist" approach in which international law is deemed a part of and generally of equal or greater priority to national law (e.g., Austria, Belgium, the Netherlands). The United States exhibits elements of both systems.

Article VI, Clause 2 of the U.S. Constitution provides: "This Constitution, and the Laws of the United States which shall be made in Pursuance thereof; and *all Treaties made, or which shall be made*, under the authority of the United States, shall be the supreme Law of the Land; and the Judges in every State shall be bound thereby, any Thing in the Constitution or Laws of any State to the Contrary notwithstanding" [emphasis added].

Generally, a treaty provision will supersede an earlier federal statute in conflict with it or any inconsistent state legislation only if it is self-executing.[1] Toward the end of the nineteenth century, however, the U.S. Supreme Court held that the enforcement of international treaties is a matter for negotiations and reclamations between countries and the courts neither have anything to do with this process nor are in a position to give redress.[2] Indeed, courts continue to remain reluctant to enforce U.S. international obligations, although they have done so on a number of occasions. Generally, however, Justice Scalia's opinion expressed in *Stanford* v. *Kentucky* that only *American* conceptions of decency are relevant has been the prevailing view of the nation's high court. Presumably Justice Scalia's view disregards conceptions of decency set forth in various international instruments even where the United States has become a party thereto. Nevertheless, a court's refusal to enforce such obligations does not, in theory, diminish those obligations. To the contrary, the United States continues to remain bound by such treaties and may be subject to appropriate international sanctions.

INTERNATIONAL OBLIGATIONS OF THE UNITED STATES

When U.S. federal and state courts and administrative agencies have applied international law, they have done so pursuant to three strategies. First, if the right for which one is seeking advancement is guaranteed by a self-executing treaty clause,[3] courts or agencies may apply the clause directly. Second, if the right is protected by an international customary norm, judges and administrative officials may enforce it. Third, courts and agencies may, at their own discretion, find certain clauses of international instruments "persuasive" in construing open-ended provisions of national law. While direct incorporation pursuant to either of the first two strategies binds courts effectively, various rules of interpretation and application create certain obstacles.[4] Additionally, direct incorporation is much more likely to result in a decision that will be reversed on appeal. Any of these three strategies stands a much better chance of success if there has been an incorporation of or reference to the given international standard in a federal or state statute. As such, legislative initiatives are often just as important as judicial ones.

Customary International Law

Customary international law (or customary norms) is also applied by U.S. courts as indicated above, subject to restrictions created by statute and precedent. A practice is considered part of customary international law when it reflects widespread (although not necessarily unanimous)[5] acquiescence among governments. At the close of 2000, a total of 75 countries' legal systems did not provide for the death penalty for any crime whatsoever, regardless of the defendant's age.[6] Most recently, on March 21 and July 23, 2000, respectively, Malta and Côte d'Ivoire became the first and second countries to abolish the death penalty for all crimes in the new millennium. In addition, another 13 countries provide for the possibility of the death penalty only for exceptional crimes (e.g., crimes under military law) or crimes committed under exceptional circumstances (e.g., wartime).[7] For example, in 2000, Albania ratified Protocol No. 6 to the European Convention on Human Rights, abolishing the death penalty for all peacetime offenses. Furthermore, another 20 countries retain the death penalty for ordinary crimes (e.g., murder) but either have not executed any criminal during the past 10 years or more or have made an international commitment to impose a moratorium on executions.[8] Thus, a total of 108 countries are abolitionist in law or practice, while the remaining 87 countries, including the United States, retain the use of the death penalty for ordinary crimes.[9] With more than half the countries in the world opposing the death penalty, and given the number of recent converts to this point of view, an evolving sense of humanity becomes apparent. Indeed, of the 108 abolitionist countries, 22 stopped executing criminals during the 1980s and another 38 stopped during the 1990s.[10] Nevertheless, as recently as 1998, the United States ranked third worldwide behind China and Congo in sheer numbers of executions, with countries such as Rwanda, Yemen, Pakistan, and Lebanon ranking far below us.

Arguably, the fact that well more than half the nations on earth oppose the death penalty, with over 60 of those nations having done away with the death penalty over the past two decades alone, a customary international norm against the death penalty has been firmly established. Such a norm is binding on all governments, including those that have not recognized it, as long as those governments have not expressly and persistently objected to its development.[11] When a court is faced with an argument that it should apply a customary norm, it must first decide whether the asserted principle has indeed developed into a norm. In determining this, U.S. courts have looked to the sources enumerated by the Supreme Court in *United States* v. *Smith* (1820). According to the *Smith* Court, "The law of nations...may be ascertained by consulting the works of jurists, writing professedly on public law; or by the general usage and practice of nations; or by judicial decisions recognizing and enforcing that law" (*Smith* at 160–161). It is a standing principle of U.S. law that "courts must interpret international law as it has evolved and exists among the nations of the world today."[12] In other words, new norms must be applied as they emerge. As such, a ruling that a particular principle has not developed into a norm would not prohibit relitigation of the issue at a future time. If it is determined that a rule has developed into a norm, a separate inquiry must be made into whether that particular norm is judicially enforceable. In the United States, however, when a court has found an asserted customary norm to be in conflict with an existing federal statute or executive act, the statute or act has generally been given precedence.

During the past 15 years, a number of attempts have been made to use international norms relating to the death penalty in arguing against the legality of execution practices within the United States.[13] Although there have been a number of notable successes in this arena, the overall results have been inconsistent and ambiguous at best. In reaching its plurality decision in *Thompson* v. *Oklahoma* in 1988, for example, the Supreme Court relied in part upon international practice and instruments in holding that the execution of those below the age of 16 violates the Eighth Amendment. Just a year later, a different Supreme Court plurality in *Stanford* v. *Kentucky* upheld the constitutionality of capital punishment for those aged 16 or 17 at the time of the crime, despite international norms and practices to the contrary. Justice Scalia rejected such international comparisons as irrelevant, emphasizing that only American conceptions of decency are dispositive (*Stanford* at 369 n. 1). He also repudiated another of Justice Brennan's arguments: that executing those who are too young, immature, and impulsive to take full responsibility for their actions fails to serve the only two penologic goals the Court has recognized as legitimate in capital cases: retribution and deterrence (*Stanford* at 377).[14] Indeed, it is this part of Justice Scalia's opinion that is most troubling for those who do not want the United States to become the world leader in executions.

Joan Fitzpatrick, professor of law at the University of Washington, suggests three possible explanations for why U.S. courts assessing the legality of capital punishment have been largely impervious to the international aspect of the questions confronting them: (1) our theories of customary law in the death penalty area have been flawed and therefore deservedly unconvincing; (2) our theories have been valid but our advocacy has been deficient; or (3) our theories have been valid and our advocacy has been appropriate, but the courts have rejected or ignored both because of the peculiar political sensitivity of capital punishment (Fitzpatrick, 1996:167). The analytical efforts to which many judges and justices have gone to avoid finding the existence of applicable international norms regarding capital punishment suggest that the third explanation is the most reflective of reality. Furthermore, in light of the recent efforts of federal courts to progressively deregulate state death penalty systems by constricting the scope of the Eighth Amendment and precluding federal habeas corpus review (e.g., the Antiterrorism and Effective Death Penalty Act of 1996), it has been unlikely that courts would place the U.S. death penalty system under the control of international law. In Fitzpatrick's words, "the death penalty in the United States has little to do with penology and little to do with law. It is politics, and symbolic politics at that" (Fitzpatrick, 1996:180).

Fitzpatrick maintains that there are two basic options for challenging the legality of execution practices in the United States, each with its own advantages and detriments. These options are: (1) proof of a customary norm of international law that invalidates contrary U.S. state law under the Supremacy Clause of the U.S. Constitution; or (2) reliance on an international norm as a standard of decency to interpret the "cruel and unusual" punishment clause of the Eighth Amendment of the U.S. Constitution.

The first approach has the benefit of both simplicity and historical recognition of customary law as enforceable in U.S. courts. The strengths of this approach are undermined, however, by three factors. First, success under this approach is contingent upon satisfying a number of theoretical objections to the existence of customary norms (see Fitzpatrick, 1996:168–177). Second, while the hierarchy of customary international law over state statutes is clear under the Supremacy Clause, there is little direct precedent to support it. Finally, courts that are skeptical of the legal nature of customary law are unlikely to be inclined to give it force in the face of contrary law adopted by state political actors, even if precedent for such judicial action exists.

As for the Eighth Amendment interpretive approach, the lack of a need to satisfy the technical requirements for proving a customary norm is a distinct advantage. In addition, international treaties serve as strong indicators of contemporary international standards of decency absent any need to prove their binding effect on the United States. Traditionally, however, international practice and treaty norms have been given little importance in U.S. courts. Indeed, in the case of a clear conflict between a U.S. constitutional provision and an existing customary or treaty norm, precedent suggests that the Constitution would control.[15] Where constitutional norms are vague, however (as in the context of the Eighth Amendment), Fitzpatrick maintains that there are strong reasons for judges to interpret unclear provisions so as to be consistent with international norms where possible. First, such an interpretation helps to ensure and advertise the international law-abiding character of the United States. Furthermore, it helps to avoid a clash between two important legal-interpretation principles—that state and federal statutes should be construed, where possible, as both consistent with the Constitution[16] and consistent with international law.[17]

International Treaties

A number of international instruments, particularly those promulgated by the United Nations (UN) and the Organization of American States, contain provisions relevant to capital sentencing. The United States is bound by these instruments, however, only to the extent that it has ratified or adopted them or that the provisions contained therein are indicative of customary international law. Otherwise, it is not required to respect the terms of these instruments whatsoever.

The Universal Declaration of Human Rights, for example, was adopted and proclaimed by the UN General Assembly in Resolution 217 (III) of December 1948 and represents customary international law which is binding on the United States—at least in theory. As most of the protections which this document affords criminal defendants are encompassed in one form or another by the U.S. Constitution, however, it has never been necessary to place exclusive reliance on it in a U.S. court. Similarly, the UN's Safeguards Guaranteeing Protection of the Rights of Those Facing the Death Penalty (UN Safeguards), adopted and proclaimed by the General Assembly in Resolution 44/128 of December 15, 1989, include a number of provisions that have been variously identified as customary norms. But the Safeguards have only a "norm creating" function, inasmuch as they are intended to create a consciousness and open up a debate on the subject of the rights of those facing the death penalty. The principles in this resolution, which provide *inter alia* that countries which have not abolished the death penalty may only impose capital punishment for the most serious crimes, only upon persons 18 years of age or older, and only in a manner that will inflict the minimum possible suffering, have acquired substantial support from the international community. The Safeguards themselves, however, are promotional rather than protective and have no real binding force.

On the other hand, the United States did sign the international Convention against Torture and Other Cruel, Inhuman or Degrading Treatment or Punishment (Convention against Torture) on April 18, 1988, and proceeded to ratify it on October 21, 1994. This convention provides a definition of torture which includes "any act by which severe pain or suffering, whether physical or mental, is intentionally inflicted on a person" for purposes which include "punishing him for an act he or a third person has committed or is suspected of having committed" (Convention Against Torture, Article 1, § 1). Article 16(1) of this convention further provides that "each State Party shall undertake to prevent in any territory under its jurisdiction other acts of cruel, inhuman or degrading treatment or punishment which do not amount to torture as defined in article I, when such acts are committed by or at the instigation of or with the consent or acquiescence of a public official or other person acting in an official capacity." The United States, through its reservations to this convention, has limited itself to be bound by Article 16 only insofar as the term *cruel, inhuman, or degrading treatment or punishment* has the same meaning as the cruel, unusual, and inhumane treatment or punishment prohibited by the Fifth, Eighth, and Fourteenth Amendments to the U.S. Constitution. Most significantly, the United States, in its ratification of this convention, has specifically expressed the understanding that the convention does not restrict or prohibit the United States from applying the death penalty consistent with the Fifth, Eighth and Fourteenth Amendments, including any constitutional period of confinement prior to the imposition of the death penalty. Further, the United States has specifically declared itself not to be bound by Article 30(1), which provides for arbitration and, in irreconcilable cases, referral to the International Court of Justice in instances where two or more state parties are in dispute over the interpretation or application of this convention.

The United States also signed the International Covenant on Civil and Political Rights (ICCPR), on October 5, 1977, and proceeded to ratify it on June 8, 1992. Again, this ratification came with five express reservations, four interpretative declarations, and another five "understandings." And as recently as 2000, the Supreme Court denied certiorari to a death row inmate, Michael Domingues, who argued that his execution would violate the ICCPR because he was only 16 years old at the time of his crime [Death Penalty Information Center, 2000(b)]. The treaty does prohibit the execution of juvenile offenders, but one of the U.S. attached reservations allows for the execution of those who committed crimes while under the age of 18. Even given these limitations, however, the United States is bound by certain commitments under the ICCPR. First the United States has made no reservations to ICCPR Article 6 on capital punishment other than to Article 6(2), which relegates the death penalty exclusively to the most serious crimes, and to Article 6(5), which prohibits the death penalty for crimes committed by minors below the age of 18.[18] As such, the United States has accepted Article 6(1)'s provisions that every human being has an inherent right to life (and has committed itself to protect this right through law) and that no one shall be deprived of his or her life *arbitrarily*. The United States has also recognized and accepted the provision of Article 7 of the ICCPR that no one shall be subjected to torture or to cruel, inhuman, or degrading treatment or punishment. However, it has qualified its acceptance by indicating that it considers itself bound by this article only to the extent that the meaning of "cruel, inhuman, or degrading treatment or punishment" is consistent with the Fifth, Eighth, and Fourteenth Amendments to the U.S. Constitution.[19] Similarly, the United States has recognized and accepted the provisions of Article 14 of the ICCPR mandating that all persons are equal before courts and tribunals and that in the determination of any criminal charge against an individual, all persons are entitled to a fair and public hearing by a competent, independent, and impartial tribunal established by law. It has also accepted under this article that in the determination of any criminal charge all persons are entitled to defend themselves in person or through legal assistance of *their choosing* and to have legal assistance assigned to them where the interest of justice so requires and without payment if they lack sufficient means to cover the costs of that assistance. The United States has limited these rights, however, inasmuch as it has expressed its understanding that Article 14 does *not* require the provision of a criminal defendant's counsel of choice when either (1) the defendant is provided with court-appointed counsel due to indigence, (2) the defendant is financially able to retain alternative counsel, or (3) imprisonment is not imposed.

A Second Optional Protocol to the ICCPR was adopted and proclaimed by the UN General Assembly in Resolution 44/128 of December 15, 1989 and entered into force on September 2, 1990. The first article of this instrument provides that no one within the jurisdiction of a state party to the protocol shall be executed and that each state party shall take all necessary measures to abolish the death penalty within its jurisdiction. Unsurprisingly, the United States has neither signed nor ratified this protocol and is thus not bound by it in any way.

Two additional UN instruments, the International Convention on the Elimination of all Forms of Racial Discrimination (ICERD) and the Convention on the Rights of the Child (CRC), bear indirectly on the manner in which the death penalty may be carried out. The United States signed the ICERD in September 1966 and proceeded to ratify it in October 1994. Again, however, this ratification came with three reservations, one declaration, and one "understanding." Nevertheless, even given these limitations, the United States has undertaken, consistent with Article 2(1) of the ICERD, to adopt effective measures to review governmental, national, and local policies, and to amend, rescind, or nullify any law or regulation that has the effect of creating or perpetuating racial discrimination wherever it may exist. Consistent with Article 5(a) and in compliance with the obligations set forth in Article 2, the United States is also bound to prohibit and eliminate all forms of racial discrimination and to guarantee the right of everyone to equality before the law without distinction as to race, color, or national or ethnic origin. Notably, this equality includes enjoyment of the right to equal treatment before tribunals and all other organs administering justice. As the racial disparity of capital punishment has been called increasingly into question of late, the ICERD has the potential to significantly affect the future of the death penalty in the United States.

In addition to its obligations as a member of the UN, the United States has certain obligations as a member of the Organization of American States (OAS), and there are a number of procedures within the Inter-American system that permit people to lodge complaints against governments alleging that they have been victims of violations of those rights guaranteed by various OAS instruments. For example, a complaint may be made against any OAS member state to the Inter-American Commission of Human Rights that the member state has violated the rights guaranteed in the American Declaration of the Rights and Duties of Man. The commission exercises its jurisdiction over states by virtue of their membership in the OAS, and no explicit acceptance of the procedure is required. When a state becomes a party to the Convention, it thereby accepts the commission's competence to entertain complaints against it lodged by individuals or nongovernmental organizations (article 44). However, a state may also recognize the competence of the Inter-American Court to consider cases brought against it (article 62). The Inter-American Court of Human Rights has both advisory and continuous jurisdiction, and since its creation has delivered a number of important judgments in the field of human rights. Article 45 of the Convention also provides that a state may accept the competence of the commission to receive complaints made against it by another state party to the convention.

There is a handful of OAS instruments of particular relevance to the implementation of the death penalty within member states, but as with the UN instruments, the United States is bound only to the extent that it has ratified or adopted them or that the provisions contained therein are indicative of customary international law. Most important among these, the American Declaration of the Rights and Duties of Man (1948) is binding in its entirety inasmuch as it has been deemed representative of customary international law. This document provides, among other things, that every person has the right to life, liberty, and the security of his or her person, that every person deprived of his liberty in accordance with law shall enjoy the right to humane treatment during the time that he or she is in custody, and the right not to receive cruel, infamous, or unusual punishment.

The American Convention on Human Rights (ACHR) was approved in 1969 and came into effect on July 18, 1978, through the required eleventh deposit of an instrument of ratification. The United States signed this convention on June 1, 1977 but has yet to ratify it. Article 18 of the Vienna Convention on Treaties (1980) requires a government in this situation "to refrain from acts which would defeat the object and purpose of [the] treaty...until it shall have made its intention clear not to become a party." But U.S. courts have not applied Article 18 to treaties the United States has signed but not ratified. Rather, to the extent that they have relied on such instruments, they have looked to them as evidence of customary law or as aids in interpreting provisions of U.S. law. Article 4 of the ACHR provides, among other things, that (1) no one shall be arbitrarily deprived of his life; (2) in countries that have not abolished the death penalty, it may be imposed only for the most serious crimes;

(3) the death penalty shall not be reestablished in states that have abolished it; (4) in no case shall capital punishment be inflicted for political offenses or related common crimes; and (5) capital punishment shall not be imposed upon persons who at the time a crime was committed, were under 18 years of age or over 70 years of age; nor shall it be applied to pregnant women. Article 5 provides that "every person has the right to have his physical, mental, and moral integrity respected, no one shall be subjected to torture or to cruel, inhuman, or degrading punishment or treatment, [and] all persons deprived of their liberty shall be treated with respect for the inherent dignity of the human person."

Finally, the Protocol to the American Convention on Human Rights to Abolish the Death Penalty, adopted on June 8, 1990, prohibits the imposition of the death penalty within states party to this instrument. The United States has neither signed nor ratified this protocol, however, and is therefore not bound by its terms.

THE DEATH ROW PHENOMENON

Increasingly, considerable worldwide attention has been paid to what is known as the *death row phenomenon* or the *death row syndrome*. These labels describe a fairly common and dehumanizing situation in which death row inmates face prolonged delays between the date of sentencing and the proposed date of execution, delays that are exacerbated by harsh and degrading conditions of confinement. A number of foreign courts have begun to accept this phenomenon as a mitigating reason for overturning capital sentences.[20]

More important for the United States, foreign and international courts are considering the death row phenomenon when reviewing requests for the extradition of alleged criminals to the United States when those criminals could face the death penalty. In the 1989 decision, *Soering* v. *United Kingdom*, the European Court of Human Rights decided for the first time that such extradition would be a breach of Article 3 of the European Convention for the Protection of Human Rights and Fundamental Freedoms. This article provides that "[n]o one shall be subjected to torture or to inhuman or degrading treatment of punishment." Soering himself was a German national who was wanted for murder in the state of Virginia. He had fled to Europe and was arrested in England on unrelated charges. The United States requested his extradition, as did the then Federal Republic of Germany, which had abolished the death penalty and also had jurisdiction to try him for the alleged murders. Soering was found to be extraditable to the United States by the British courts, but Soering had filed a complaint with the European Commission of Human Rights in the meantime. As such, the extradition was delayed pending an investigation by the commission. The commission decided against Soering but referred the case to the European Court of Human Rights.

The court unanimously found a real risk that a Virginia court would sentence Soering to death and that, if surrendered for trial, his rights would be violated under Article 3. This determination was based on the court's assessment of the appallingly harsh conditions on death row at the Mecklenburg Correctional Center, where Soering would have been housed. Particular attention was also paid to the fact that the average time between trial and execution in Virginia was six to eight years, due primarily to a strategy by convicted prisoners to prolong the appeal process as much as possible. The court noted that:

> just as some lapse of time between sentence and execution is inevitable if appeal safeguards are to be provided to the condemned person, so it is equally part of human nature that the person will cling to life by exploiting those safeguards to the full. However well-intentioned and even potentially beneficial is the provision of the complex of post-sentence procedures in Virginia, the consequence is that the condemned prisoner has to endure for many years the conditions on death row and the anguish and mounting tension of living in the ever-present shadow of death. (Soering at 106).

It has been suggested that the court would not have invalidated Soering's extradition but for the unusual factors of Soering's age (18 years), alleged mental disorders, and the request by the Federal Republic of Germany for his extradition. However, these factors were not as determinative as the court's rejection of the argument that the Virginia appeal process was designed to protect the death row inmate, and that the inmate could always opt to accelerate the process by waiving his appeal rights.

In 1991, however, the Supreme Court of Canada considered a similar case, *Re Kindler* v. *Minister of Justice*, and refused to block extradition of a fugitive appellant to the United States. By a majority of four to three, the court held that "the psychological stress inherent in the death-row phenomenon...ultimately pales in comparison to the death penalty. Besides, the fact remains that a defendant is never forced to undergo the full appeal procedure...It would be ironic if delay caused by the [appellant]...should be viewed as a violation of fundamental justice" (*Kindler* at 838). The minority, however, expressed strong disagreement with the holding of the court, and went so far as to suggest that the death penalty is per se cruel and unusual punishment.

In the United States, the Supreme Court has never directly addressed the death row phenomenon in carrying out death sentences. As recently as 1999, the Court declined to hear an appeal from two death row inmates (*Knight* v. *Florida* and *Moore* v. *Nebraska*) concerning the cruelty of the amount of time they had spent on death row. Nevertheless, Justice Breyer, dissenting from the court's decision, wrote that "[b]oth of these cases involve astonishingly long delays flowing in significant part from constitutionally defective death penalty procedures. Where a delay, measured in decades, reflects the State's own failure to comply with the Constitution's demands, the claim that time has rendered the execution inhuman is a particularly strong one" (*Knight* at 461). The language in several other U.S. cases also evinces at least a tacit recognition of the unusually severe consequences of such conditions. As early as 1890, Justice Miller noted in *Ex parte Medley* (at 172) that "when a prisoner sentenced by a Court to death is confined in the penitentiary awaiting the execution of the sentence, one of the most horrible feelings to which he can be subjected during that time is the uncertainty during the whole of it—as to the precise time when his execution shall take place." Similarly, in 1972's *Furman* v. *Georgia* decision, Justice Brennan provided the following as one of his reasons for concluding that capital punishment is per se unconstitutional: "[M]ental pain is an inseparable part of our practice of punishing criminals by death, for the prospect of pending execution exacts a frightful toll during the inevitable long wait between the imposition of a sentence and the actual infliction of death" (*Furman* at 288). As the wait increases, so too does the mental suffering; indeed, the Supreme Court recognized in *In re Kemmler* (1890) that "Punishments are cruel when they involve…a lingering death…something more than the mere extinguishment of life" (*Kemmler* at 447). Prolonged delay between sentencing and execution could certainly be classified as this type of cruel and lingering death. If so held, the death row phenomenon would be a clear violation of the Eighth Amendment of the U.S. Constitution, which prohibits the infliction of cruel and unusual punishment. As indicated above, however, the U.S. Supreme Court has yet to address this issue.

There have, however, been some fledgling attempts at shining a flashlight at the death row phenomenon in lower U.S. courts. In California, for example, Caryl Chessman argued that years spent on death row had caused him great mental suffering and was "cruel and unusual punishment." Although he had been on death row for close to 12 years by the time his case reached the appellate level, the Court of Appeals for the Ninth Circuit denied a stay of execution and held as follows:

> It may show a basic weakness in our government system that a case like this takes so long, but I do not see how we can offer life (under a sentence of death) as a prize for one who can stall the process for a given number of years, especially when in the end it appears the prisoner never really had any good points. If we did offer such a prize, what year would we use as a cutoff date? I would think that the number of years would have to be objective and arbitrary.
>
> But counsel for petitioner suggests that we take a subjective approach on this man's case. We are told of his agonies on death row. True, it would be hell for most people. But here is no ordinary man. In his appearances in Court one sees an arrogant, truculent man, …spewing vitriol on one person after another.
>
> We see an exhibitionist who never before had such opportunities for exhibition. (All this I get from the record.) And, I think he has heckled his keepers long enough. *Chessman* v. *Dickson* (1960 at 607–608).

Not only does this opinion evince an inappropriate attempt to punish the petitioner for his mannerisms, it fails to establish why his personality would in any way reduce the degree of his mental suffering below that required for an application of the constitutional "cruel and unusual punishment" standard. More recently, in *Potts* v. *State* (1989), the Supreme Court of Georgia rejected a plea that a period of over 13 years on death row justified the setting aside of a death sentence. The narrow reasoning of this 1989 opinion placed significant emphasis on the suggestion that suffering on death row was no worse than suffering endured by patients with terminal illness. No further attempts to analyze the issue were made.

Nevertheless, some U.S. courts have rendered more progressive opinions. In 1972, the Supreme Court of California held in *State* v. *Anderson* (1972) that the death penalty violated Article 6 of the state's constitutional prohibition against cruel and unusual punishment. In articulating this holding, the court stressed the torturous nature of delays involved in carrying out death sentences, specifically referring to "the dehumanizing effects of the lengthy imprisonment prior to execution during which the judicial and administrative procedures essential to due process of law are carried out.…An appellant's insistence on receiving the benefits of appellate review…does not render the lengthy period of impending execution any less torturous or exempt such cruelty from constitutional proscription" (*Anderson* at 894–895). Similarly, the Supreme Judicial Court of Massachusetts held in *District Attorney for Suffolk District* v. *Watson* (1980) that the death penalty violates the Massachusetts Constitution, which also prohibits cruel punishment. Again, the delay factor involved in capital punishment was a major part of the court's rationale. The California State Constitution was later amended so as to exempt the death penalty from the prohibition against cruel or unusual punishment. Although this effectively overruled the California Supreme Court's 1972 decision, the reasoning of both this court and the Massachusetts Supreme Court still evinces an understanding and acceptance of the harsh realities of the death row phenomenon.

THE EXECUTION OF JUVENILE OFFENDERS

Arguably, an international customary norm exists which prohibits the execution of children, but as seen above, U.S. courts have had a difficult time defining children in terms of age. Among other international instruments, the UN Safeguards prohibit the execution of those under the age of 18, and the CRC defines a child as someone below the age of 18. The United States signed the latter on February 16, 1995 and is currently considering its ratification. In the meantime, although 191 other nations are parties to the CRC, the United States and Somalia remain the only two nations on earth not to have ratified this convention (Amnesty International, 2000b).

Perhaps unsurprisingly, then, the United States leads the world in executing juveniles–persons under 18 at the time of the commission of their crime. Since 1990, only six other countries—Iran, Pakistan, Saudi Arabia, Nigeria, Yemen, and the Democratic Republic of Congo—have done so, but none of these countries has executed as many juveniles as the United States (Amnesty International, 2000b). Over the past decade, 14 executions of child offenders have been carried out in the United States (half of these took place in Texas alone), as compared to six in Iran, two in Yemen, and one each in Congo, Nigeria, Pakistan, and Saudi Arabia during that same 11-year period (Amnesty International, 2000b). Since the beginning of 1994, however, Yemen and Pakistan, along with Barbados, Zimbabwe, and China, have changed their laws to eliminate the use of the death penalty against child offenders, and Saudi Arabia has ratified the CRC (Amnesty International, 2000b). As of October 2000, 16 U.S. states were holding a total of 83 child offenders on death rows, so these numbers can only be expected to increase in the foreseeable future. Although the United States has not yet ratified the CRC, however, the mere fact that it has signed this convention obligates it under international law to do nothing to defeat the underlying objectives of said convention. Every time the United States executes a juvenile offender, however, it does just that.

THE EXECUTION OF FOREIGN NATIONALS

One final area in which the world beyond America's shores may begin to have an increasingly great impact on the death penalty within the United States bears mentioning. It involves the execution of foreign nationals by the United States. An increasing number of countries are objecting strenuously to America's failure to comply with the guarantee under the Vienna Convention on Consular Relations (officially ratified by the United States in 1969) that foreign inmates be advised of their rights to contact their own government through their embassies in the United States. This failure is particularly offensive in light of the fact that the United States "aggressively demands that this right be accorded to American citizens detained abroad" (Anon., 2000). Nonetheless, the Supreme Court has remained reluctant to intervene in such cases. For example, in its 1998–1999 term, the Supreme Court denied an application by the German government to file a complaint and a motion for injunction against the United States and the governor of Arizona to stop the execution of German citizens, Walter and Karl LaGrand, and the previous year, the Court denied a similar petition for certiorari by Paraguay on behalf of Paraguayan national Angel Francisco Breard, each asserting a violation of the Vienna Convention given that none of these defendants had been informed of his right to contact his country's consulate (Death Penalty Information Center, 2000b). Breard was executed by the state of Virginia on April 14, 1998, and Karl and Walter LeGrand were executed on February 24 and March 3, 1999, respectively. Even more recently, Joseph Stanley Faulder, whose rights under the Vienna Convention were similarly violated, was the first Canadian to be executed in the United States since 1952, after the Supreme Court rejected his arguments. His execution took place in Texas on June 17, 1999, 22 years after he had been sentenced to death (Death Penalty Information Center, 2000a).

But these cases hardly amount to isolated incidents. At the end of 2000, there is a total of 90 foreign nationals reported to be on death row in the United States (Death Penalty Information Center, 2000a). Nearly half of these inmates are Mexican.[21] Again, unsurprisingly, Texas leads the nation with 26 foreign nationals on that state's death row, followed closely by California (23), and more distantly by Florida (9), Arizona (6), Ohio (4), Illinois (4), Oklahoma (3), Washington (2), Pennsylvania (2), Arkansas (1), Montana (1), Louisiana (1), Virginia (1), Oregon (1), and Delaware (1). Additionally, there are currently three foreign nationals who have been sentenced to death by the federal government (Death Penalty Information Center, 2000a). Georgia, South Carolina, and New Jersey presently house no foreign nationals on their respective death rows, but there is as yet no reliable data on the subject from several U.S. states with significant death row populations, such as Pennsylvania, Mississippi, Tennessee, Kentucky and Missouri (Death Penalty Information Center, 2000a). As such, it is quite conceivable that the actual number of foreign nationals serving death sentences in the United States approaches 100— nearly 3% of the nation's overall death row population of 3703 inmates as of this writing.

Since the Supreme Court revived the death penalty with *Gregg* v. *Georgia* in 1976, 15 foreign nationals have already been put to death—all since 1993 and five in 1999 alone, marking a significantly increasing trend (Death Penalty Information Center, 2000). Not one of these fifteen men were advised of their consular rights under the Vienna Convention (Death Penalty Information Center, 2000a). Most recently, Mexico sent a formal protest to the U.S. State Department in late 2000 in an effort to halt the execution of a Mexican citizen, Miguel Angel Flores. Indicative of nearly all such cases, Flores was never advised of his right to contact the Mexican embassy, and Mexican officials did not even become aware of the 1989 Texas rape and murder charges against Flores until nearly a full year after he had been *sentenced.* According to the Mexican government, had it been notified in a more timely fashion, it would have provided Flores with a lawyer and ensured that Spanish-speaking members of Flores' family would have been available to testify on his behalf. Significantly, while Flores himself was 20 years old at the time of the crime and had no history of criminal behavior or violence, his court-appointed lawyer (who did not speak Spanish), failed to call a single character witness or present any mitigating evidence whatsoever (Anon, 2000). Notwithstanding both Mexico's request for the State Department to intercede so as to help in having Flores' sentence commuted to life in prison as well as a last-minute appeal filed with the Supreme Court, Flores was executed on November 9, 2000. Presumably, Texas officials were unpersuaded by the State Department's statement that it "took seriously" the failure of states to advise defendants of their consular rights, and Texas failed to respond in any meaningful way to the State Department's request for an explanation regarding Texas' failure to so advise Flores (Anon., 2000).

The inability and apparent unwillingness of either the Supreme Court or the State Department to intervene effectively in such cases leaves the battleground for reform at the grass-roots level, where several recent reforms may be indicative of a first response to the pressure being exerted by foreign governments. In 1999, for example, California became the first state to pass legislation requiring law enforcement agencies to incorporate language based on the Vienna Convention into policy, procedure, and training manuals and requiring every peace officer to advise foreign nationals of their consular rights upon arrest and booking or detention (Death Penalty Information Center, 2000a). Similar provisions have also been implemented at the local level, notably in Colorado's Pueblo County, Illinois' Cook County, and New Jersey's Hudson County (Death Penalty Information Center, 2000a). In October 2000, in response to specific complaints by the Mexican and Polish governments regarding violations of the rights of their respective citizens, the Chicago Police Department began posting signs in Spanish and Polish in each of that department's detention facilities notifying arrested foreigners of their consular rights (Death Penalty Information Center, 2000a).

Although these are all steps in the right direction, many countries have nevertheless been driven to sue the United States in the International Court of Justice (also called the World Court) at The Hague, seeking reparations for executions where there was a failure to implement this type of compliance. Dissatisfied with a mere admission by the State Department that Arizona officials failed to notify Walter and Karl LaGrand of their Vienna Convention rights, for example, Germany brought suit seeking an official finding of guilt against the United States and assurances from the United States that future German arrestees will be notified of said rights. Oral arguments in *Germany* v. *United States* were heard at the ICJ over the week of November 13, 2000, but whether this and other such suits will ultimately prove successful (or the resulting judgments enforceable) remains to be seen. Should the World Court actually rule in Germany's favor, a flurry of similar suits will probably follow. One thing is certain, however; if the United States continues to execute increasing numbers of foreign nationals in violation of their rights under the Vienna Convention, international pressure in one form or another from a variety of nations—many of whom are strong allies of the United States—will only increase.[22]

CONCLUSIONS

Admittedly, the United States has never been known to buckle under international pressure; if it did, the American death penalty would long since have been a thing of the past. As seen in Chapter 10 by Kenneth Haas, however, with regard to the death penalty there are already major, albeit fledgling, strides being made toward abolition within the United States. Ironically, this movement seems to have been sparked by the dramatic increase in sheer numbers of executions over the past 15 years. Similarly, as the public learns of increasing numbers of juvenile executions and as our international neighbors publicly condemn or sue the United States over repeated failures to extend foreign defendants their consular rights, some form of backlash will become increasingly likely. When such factors are added to the already volatile mix of questions surrounding the fairness of capital punishment in the United States, it seems all the more likely that by the mid-twenty-first century, the American people will join the rest of the international community in repudiating the death penalty, and the Supreme Court will declare it a cruel and unusual punishment that is both forbidden by the Eighth Amendment and violative of global perspectives on human rights.

ENDNOTES

1. See *Foster* v. *Neilson* (1829).
2. See *Head Money Cases* (1884).
3. The Supreme Court first articulated the self-executing requirement in *Foster* v. *Neilson* (1829), in which it held that a clause is self-executing and thus "equivalent to an act of the legislature, whenever it operates by itself without the aid of any legislative provision." Subsequent cases and Restatements of Law have focused on the express or implied intent of the parties. A test that has been deemed particularly relevant to multilateral human rights treaties is a three-step inquiry proposed by Riesenfeld (1970) in his article, "The Doctrine of Self-Executing Treaties and Gatt: A Notable German Judgment." This test deems a treaty self-executing if it "(a) involves the rights and duties of individuals; (b) does not cover a subject for which legislative action is required by the Constitution; and (c) does not leave discretion to the parties in the application of the particular provision."
4. For a discussion of such obstacles as political questions, sovereign immunity, standing, failure to state a claim, national policies in contradiction of customary norms, acts of state, foreign sovereign immunity, statutes of limitations, damages, and choice of law, see Newman and Weissbrodt (1990):621–654, and pp. 137–139 in 1994 Supp.).
5. See, e.g., *Forti* v. *Suarez-Mason (Forti II)* (1988).
6. Andorra, Angola, Australia, Austria, Azerbaijan, Belgium, Bulgaria, Cambodia, Canada, Cape Verde, Colombia, Costa Rica, Côte d'Ivoire, Croatia, Czech Republic, Denmark, Djibouti, Dominican Republic, East Timor, Ecuador, Estonia, Finland, France, Georgia, Germany, Greece, Guinea-Bissau, Haiti, Honduras, Hungary, Iceland, Ireland, Italy, Kiribati, Liechtenstein, Lithuania, Luxembourg, Macedonia (former Yugoslav Republic), Malta, Marshall Islands, Mauritius, Micronesia (Federated States), Moldova, Monaco, Mozambique, Namibia, Nepal, Netherlands, New Zealand, Nicaragua, Norway, Palau, Panama, Paraguay, Poland, Portugal, Romania, San Marino, Sao Tomé and Principe, Seychelles, Slovak Republic, Slovenia, Solomon Islands, South Africa, Spain, Sweden, Switzerland, Turkmenistan, Tuvalu, Ukraine, United Kingdom, Uruguay, Vanuatu, Vatican City State, and Venezuela.

7. Albania, Argentina, Bolivia, Bosnia-Herzegovina, Brazil, Cook Islands, Cyprus, El Salvador, Fiji, Israel, Latvia, Mexico, and Peru.

8. Bhutan, Brunei Darussalam, Burkina Faso, Central African Republic, Congo (Republic), Gambia, Grenada, Madagascar, Maldives, Mali, Nauru, Niger, Papua New Guinea, Samoa, Senegal, Sri Lanka, Suriname, Togo, Tonga, and Turkey.

9. Afghanistan, Algeria, Antigua and Barbuda, Armenia, Bahamas, Bahrain, Bangladesh, Barbados, Belarus, Belize, Benin, Botswana, Burundi, Cameroon, Chad, Chile, China, Comoros, Congo (Democratic Republic), Cuba, Dominica, Egypt, Equatorial Guinea, Eritrea, Ethiopia, Gabon, Ghana, Guatemala, Guinea, Guyana, India, Indonesia, Iran, Iraq, Jamaica, Japan, Jordan, Kazakstan, Kenya, Kuwait, Kyrgyzstan, Laos, Lebanon, Lesotho, Liberia, Libya, Malawi, Malaysia, Mauritania, Mongolia, Morocco, Myanmar, Nigeria, North Korea, Oman, Pakistan, Palestinian Authority, Philippines, Qatar, Russian Federation, Rwanda, Saint Christopher and Nevis, Saint Lucia, Saint Vincent and Grenadines, Saudi Arabia, Sierra Leone, Singapore, Somalia, South Korea, Sudan, Swaziland, Syria, Taiwan, Tajikistan, Tanzania, Thailand, Trinidad and Tobago, Tunisia, Uganda, United Arab Emirates, United States of America, Uzbekistan, Vietnam, Yemen, Yugoslavia (Federal Republic), Zambia, and Zimbabwe. The Chilean senate recently voted to end the death penalty and increase the number of years that must be served under a life sentence. Before it becomes law, however, the bill must be submitted to the constitutional committee for review (Death Penalty Information Center, 2000).

10. Based upon data compiled from Amnesty International's "The Death Penalty: List of Abolitionist and Retentionist Countries" (1999) and Amnesty International's "Abolitionist and Retentionist Countries" (2000b).

11. See Restatement (Third) of the Foreign Relations Law of the United States, § 102, comment d (1987).

12. See *Filartiga* v. *Peña-Irala* (1980 at 881).

13. For a detailed analysis of this subject, see Fitzpatrick (1996).

14. In *Gregg* v. *Georgia* (1976:184–187), the Court cited retribution and deterrence as two legitimate penologic rationales for the death penalty. Surprisingly, the Court has never officially recognized a third justification—incapacitation. Many avowed opponents of capital punishment will acknowledge that this rationale is not totally without merit. Studies consistently show that convicted murderers are less likely to commit murders in prison or after release than are inmates convicted of such lesser crimes as robbery, burglary, and aggravated assault (Sellin, 1980:103–120). Nevertheless, there are some death row inmates who appear to be incorrigible, willing to kill guards or fellow inmates, and capable of escape. It thus can be argued that the death penalty is the only way to be 100% certain that a sociopath or a serial killer will never kill again. On the other hand, the noted attorney and abolitionist Anthony Amsterdam has responded to this argument by declaring that "[y]ou cannot tell me…that a society which is capable of putting a man on the moon is incapable of putting a man in prison, keeping him there, and keeping him from killing while he is there" (Amsterdam, 1982:354).

15. See Restatement (Third) Foreign Relation Law of the United States § 115(3) (1987); *Reid* v. *Covert* (1957) (Black, J., plurality opinion).

16. See, e.g., *NLRB* v. *Catholic Bishop of Chicago* (1979) at 499–501.

17. See, e.g., *Murray* v. *Schooner Charming Betsy* (1804); *Chew Heong* v. *United States* (1884). The "Charming Betsy" principle, as it has come to be called, is premised upon the attribution of an internationally law-abiding character to legislators' unclear enactments.

18. Both of these Article 6 reservations have been deemed "incompatible with the object and purpose of the Covenant" by the U.N. Human Rights Committee. Additionally, 11 State Parties to the Covenant have made similar objections to the reservation to Article 6(5).

19. Again, the U.N. Human Rights Committee has expressed the opinion that such an "understanding" is not permissible under international law. By adopting this definition, the United States has insulated itself from allegations that prolonged judicial proceedings in capital cases (the "death row syndrome") could constitute cruel, inhuman or degrading treatment under Article 7. It has also insulated itself from allegations under this article that corporal punishment or solitary confinement might constitute cruel, inhuman, or degrading treatment.

20. See, e.g., *Catholic Comm'n for Justice and Peace in Zimbabwe* v. *Attorney-General, Zimbabwe* (1993) (decision of the Zimbabwe Supreme Court recognizing prolonged delay and harsh conditions as sufficient to require vacating the death sentences imposed upon four prisoners); *Vatheeswaran* v. *State of Tamil Nadu* (1983) (decision of the Supreme Court of India setting aside the appellants' death sentences and substituting life imprisonment where there had been an illegal imposition of eight years of solitary confinement following sentencing); *Javed Ahmed* v. *State of Maharashtra* (1985) (decision of the Supreme Court of India substituting life imprisonment for the death penalty following a delay of two years and nine months); *Triveniben* v. *State of Gujarat* (1989) (decision of the Supreme Court of India holding that no fixed period could be held to make a sentence of death inexecutable, overruling a prior decision that had arbitrarily established a two-year period); *Madhu Mehta* v. *Union of India* (1989) (decision of the Supreme Court of India substituting life imprisonment for the death penalty following a delay of over eight years in awaiting a decision on a mercy petition to the President of India). A number of other courts in the West Indies have also considered appeals based on delay but have declined to overturn sentences of death—*Riley* v. *Attorney General of Jamaica* (1982) and *Abbott* v. *Attorney General of Trinidad and Tobago* (1979), for example.

21. Specifically, of the 90 foreign nationals currently on death row in the United States, Mexico has 44 of its citizens so situated. The remainder of the foreign death row inmate population breaks down as follows: Cuba (5), Germany (3), Jamaica (3), Colombia (3), Estonia (2), Canada (2), El Salvador (2), Honduras (2), United Kingdom (2), and 1 each from Yugoslavia, Lebanon, Peru, Iraq, Iran, France, Poland, Spain, Trinidad, Belize, Guyana, Argentina, Phillippines, Cambodia, Laos, Thailand, Hong Kong, Bangladesh, Vietnam, Nicaragua, and Haiti (Death Penalty Information Center, 2000a).

22. For in-depth analysis of the issues surrounding the execution of foreign nationals by the United States, see O'Driscoll (2000), Quigly (1998), and Kadish (1997).

REFERENCES

Amnesty International (1999). The death penalty: List of abolitionist and retentionist countries (last modified Dec. 18). www.amnesty.org/ailib/intcam/dp/abrelist.htm.

Amnesty International (2000a). Abolitionist and retentionist countries (last modified Nov. 23). www.web.amnesty.org/rmp/dplibrary.nsf/http://www.web.amnesty.org/rmp/dplibrary.nsf/ba4 275cdead20d858025677e0059735b/daa2b602299dded0802568810050f6b1.

Amnesty International (2000b). Children and the death penalty (last updated Dec. 14). web.amnesty.org/ai.nsf/Index/ACT500102000.

Amsterdam, A. G. (1982). Capital punishment. In H. A. Bedau (ed.), *The Death Penalty in America*, 3rd ed. New York: Oxford University Press, pp. 346–358.

Anon. (2000). U.S. bid to execute Mexican draws fire. *New York Times*, October 30. www.nytimes.com/2000/10/30/national/30DEAT.html.

Death Penalty Information Center (2000a). Foreign nationals and the death penalty in the United States (last updated December 16). www.deathpenaltyinfo.org/foreignnatl.html.

Death Penalty Information Center (2000b). News from the U.S. Supreme Court (last modified Nov. 27). www.deathpenaltyinfo.org/supremecourt.html.

FITZPATRICK, J. (1996). The relevance of customary international norms to the death penalty in the United States. *Georgia Journal of International and Comparative Law*, 25:165.

KADISH, M. J. (1997). Article 36 of the Vienna Convention on Consular Relations: A search for the right to consul. *Michigan Journal of International Law*. 18:565.

NEWMAN, F., and D. WEISSBRODT (1990). *International Human Rights: Law, Policy, and Process*. Cincinnati, OH: Anderson Publishing (and 1994 supplement).

O'DRISCOLL, C. S. (2000). The execution of foreign nationals in Arizona: Violations of the Vienna Convention on Consular Relations. *Arizona State Law Journal*, 32:323.

QUIGLY, J. (1998). Execution of foreign nationals in the United States: Pressure from foreign governments against the death penalty. *ILSA Journal of International and Comparative Law*, 4:589.

RIESENFELD, S. A. (1970). The doctrine of self-executing treaties and Gatt: A notable German judgment, 65 Am. J. Int'l L. 548, 550.

SELLIN, T. (1980). *The Penalty of Death*. Thousand Oaks, CA: Sage Publications.

AMERICAN CASES

Chew Heong v. *United States*, 112 U.S. 536 (1884).

Chessman v. *Dickson*, 275 F.2d 604 (9th Cir. 1960).

District Attorney for Suffolk District v. *Watson*, 411 N.E.2d 1274 (Mass. 1980).

Ex parte Medley, 134 U.S. 160, 172 (1890).

Filartiga v. *Peña-Irala*, 630 F.2d 876 (2d Cir. 1980).

Forti v. *Suarez-Mason* (Forti II), 694 F. Supp. 707 (N.D. Cal. 1988).

Foster v. *Neilson*, 27 U.S. (2 Pet.) 253 (1829).

Furman v. *Georgia*, 408 U.S. 238 (1972).

Gregg v. *Georgia*, 428 U.S. 153 (1976).

Head Money Cases, 112 U.S. 580 (1884).

In re Kemmler, 136 U.S. 436 (1890).

Knight v. *Florida*, 120 S. Ct. 459 (1999).

Moore v. *Nebraska*, 120 S. Ct. 459 (1999).

Murray v. *Schooner Charming Betsy*, 6 U.S. (2 Cranch) 64 (1804).

NLRB v. *Catholic Bishop of Chicago*, 440 U.S. 490 (1979).

Potts v. *State*, 376 S.E.2d 851 (Ga. 1989).

Reid v. *Covert*, 345 U.S. 1 (1957).

Stanford v. *Kentucky*, 492 U.S. 361 (1989).

State v. *Anderson*, 493 P.2d 880 (Cal. 1972).

Thompson v. *Oklahoma*, 487 U.S. 815 (1988).

United States v. *Smith*, 18 U.S. (5 Wheat.) 153 (1820).

FOREIGN CASES

Abbott v. *Attorney-General of Trinidad and Tobago*, 1 W.L.R. 1342 (PC) (1979).

Catholic Comm'n for Justice and Peace in Zimbabwe v. *Attorney-General, Zimbabwe* (1993) (4) S.A. 239 (Zimbabwe Supreme Ct).

Germany v. *United States*, 1999 I.C.J. 9 (1999) (International Court of Justice).

Javed Ahmed v. *State of Maharashtra*, A.I.R. 1985 S.C. 231 (1985) (Supreme Ct. of India).

Madhu Mehta v. *Union of India*, 3 S.C.R. 775 (1989) (Supreme Ct. of India).

Riley v. *Attorney-General of Jamaica*, 3 All E.R. 469 (PC) (1982).

Re Kindler v. *Minister of Justice*, 2 S.C.R. 779 (Supreme Ct. of Canada 1991).

Soering v. *United Kingdom*, App. No. 14038/88, 11 Eur. H.R. Rep. 439 (European Ct. of Human Rights 1989).

Triveniben v. *State of Gujarat*, 1 S.C.J. 383 (1989) (Supreme Ct. of India).

Vatheeswaran v. *State of Tamil Nadu*, A.I.R. 1983 S.C. 361 (1983) (Supreme Ct. of India).

INTERNATIONAL TREATIES AND OTHER INSTRUMENTS

American Convention on Human Rights, O.A.S. Treaty Series 36, 1144 U.N.T.S. 123 entered into force July 18, 1978, reprinted in *Basic Documents Pertaining to Human Rights in the Inter-American System*, OEA/Ser.L.V/II.82 doc.6 rev.1 at 25 (1992).

American Declaration of the Rights and Duties of Man, O.A.S. Res. XXX, adopted by the 9th International Conference of American States (1948), reprinted in *Basic Documents Pertaining to Human Rights in the Inter-American System*, OEA/Ser.L.V/II.82 doc.6 rev.1 at 17 (1992).

Convention Against Torture and Other Cruel, Inhuman or Degrading Treatment or Punishment, G.A. res. 39/46, annex, 39 U.N. GAOR Supp. (No. 51) at 197, U.N. Doc. A/39/51 (1984), entered into force June 26, 1987.

Convention on the Rights of the Child, G.A. res. 44/25, U.N. GAOR Supp (No. 49) at 171 U.N. Doc. A/44/49 (1989), entered into force September 2, 1990.

European Convention for the Protection of Human Rights and Fundamental Freedoms, 213 U.N.T.S. 222, entered into force September 3, 1953 (as amended by Protocols Nos. 3, 5, and 8, entered into force September 21,1970, December 20, 1971, and January 1, 1990 respectively).

International Convention on the Elimination of all Forms of Racial Discrimination, 660 U.N.T.S. 195, entered into force January 4, 1969.

International Covenant on Civil and Political Rights, G.A. res. 2200A (XXI), 21 U.N. GAOR Supp. (No. 16) at 52, U.N. Doc. A/6316 (1966), 999 U.N.T.S. 171, entered into force March 23, 1976.

Protocol to the American Convention on Human Rights to Abolish the Death Penalty, O.A.S. Treaty Series No. 73 (1990), adopted June 8, 1990, reprinted in *Basic Documents Pertaining to Human Rights in the Inter-American System*, OEA/Ser.L.V/II.82 doc.6 rev.1 at 80 (1992).

Safeguards Guaranteeing Protection of the Rights of Those Facing the Death Penalty, E.S.C. res. 1984/50, annex, 1984 U.N. ESCOR Supp. (No. 1) at 33, U.N. Doc. E/1984/84 (1984).

Second Optional Protocol to the International Covenant on Civil and Political Rights, Aimed at the Abolition of the Death Penalty, G.A. res. 44/128, annex, 44 U.N. GAOR Supp. (No. 49) at 207, U.N. Doc. A/44/49 (1989), entered into force July 11, 1991.

Universal Declaration of Human Rights, G.A. res. 217A (III), U.N. Doc. A/810 at 71 (1948).

Vienna Convention on Consular Relations, 596 U.N.T.S. 261, signed April 24, 1963, entered into force March 19, 1967.

Vienna Convention on Treaties, 1155 U.N.T.S. 331, entered into force January 27, 1980.

chapter 12

The Bill of Rights in the Twenty-First Century

Alexander B. Smith, Ph.D., J.D., Harriet Pollack, Ph.D., and Matthew Muraskin, J.D.

ABSTRACT

For the past thirty years, the U.S. Supreme Court has interpreted the Fourth, Fifth, Sixth, and Eighth Amendments of the Bill of Rights in a manner protective of the rights of suspects, defendants, and prisoners. In recent years, the focus of the Court has shifted from restrictions on the police and the conduct of trials, to concerns about sentencing and punishment. What the future holds depends largely on government policy in relation to drug use and trafficking and gun control, the chief elements of our crime problems.

When the text of the Constitution emerged from the Constitutional Convention in 1787 and was presented to the states for ratification, it was not greeted with universal acclaim. The compromises struck by the Founding Fathers in relation to representation of large states versus small, the slave trade, and other controversial issues left many people unhappy. The biggest complaint, however, was that the proposed Constitution provided insufficient protection for individual rights, and indeed, that the new government-to-be might be as tyrannical as the old British monarchy. In many states it was only the promise that a bill of rights protecting individual liberties would be enacted immediately that enabled the Constitution to be ratified.

It is, in fact, true that while the Constitution itself set up the framework for a majoritarian representative government, it is the Bill of Rights, that is, the first 10 amendments to the Constitution, that protects individuals from the unwarranted intrusion of government into their daily lives. It is the Bill of Rights that guards personal integrity, that gives us the right to be left alone.

The government is the only institution in society that has a legitimate right to exert physical force over us. Therefore, the right to be left alone means, above all, the right not to be arrested and punished for what we have said or done except under certain clearly specified conditions. It is not surprising, thus, that five of the first 10 amendments concern how U.S. Supreme Court interpretations of those five amendments—the First, Fourth, Fifth, Sixth, and Eighth—have shaped the substance of the criminal law as well as the rules of criminal procedure, and second, those questions, currently unresolved, which have the potential for further changes in the system.

INTRODUCTION

For the last four decades of the twentieth century, the United States Supreme Court interpreted the Bill of Rights in terms of defendant's rights and limitations upon them. As we moved into this century, however, the focus of the Court has shifted from restrictions on the police and the conduct of trials, to concerns about sentencing and punishment. What the future hold depends largely on governmental policy in relation to drug trafficking and gun control, which are the chief elements of our present crime problem. But, just as important, the composition of the Supreme Court itself will play a significant role in determining both the thrust and focus of the first 10 amendments to the Constitution for at least the first few decades of this century.

When the text of the Constitution emerged from the Constitutional Convention in 1787 and was presented to the states for ratification, it was not greeted with universal acclaim. The compromises struck by the Founding Fathers in relation to representation of large states versus small, the slave trade, and other controversial issues left many people unhappy. The biggest complaint, however, was that the proposed Constitution provided insufficient protection for individual rights, and indeed, that the new government-to-be might be as tyrannical as the old British monarchy. In many states, it was only the promise that a bill of rights protecting individual liberties would be enacted immediately that enabled the Constitution to be ratified.

It is, in fact, true, that although the Constitution itself set up the framework for a majoritarian representative government, it is the Bill of Rights, that is, the first 10 amendments to the Constitution, that protects individuals from the unwarranted intrusion of government into their daily lives. It is the Bill of Rights that guards personal integrity, that gives us the right to be let alone.

The government is the only institution in society that has a legitimate right to exert physical force over us. Therefore, the right to be let alone means, above all, the right not to be arrested and punished for what we have said or done except under certain clearly specified conditions. It is not surprising, thus, that five of the first 10 amendments concern the workings of the criminal justice system. It is our purpose in this chapter to discuss, first, how United States Supreme Court interpretations of those five amendments, the First, Fourth, Fifth, Sixth, and Eighth, have shaped the substance of the criminal law as well as the rules of criminal procedure, and second, those questions, currently unresolved, which have the potential for further changes in the system.

THE STATE OF THE LAW AS OF THE END
OF THE TWENTIETH CENTURY

First Amendment

> Congress shall make no law respecting an establishment of religion, or prohibiting the free exercise thereof; or abridging the freedom of speech, or of the press; or the right of people peaceably to assemble, and to petition the Government for a redress of grievances.

The First Amendment is not usually discussed in terms of its impact on the criminal justice system, yet in the context of the right not to be arrested or punished for speech-related activities, it is very important. Actually, with the exception of the short-lived Alien and Sedition Act of 1798, there was no federal regulation of speech until World War I in the Sedition and Espionage Acts. Although the states may have punished certain types of speech, the federal government did not, and although the road from the post–World War I period to the present traversed serious bumps in the form of Red scares and McCarthyism, at the present time we are living in an era of great freedom for both speech and religion. The United States Supreme Court has held virtually all speech to be constitutionally protected, except for speech that is pornographic or creates a danger of imminently inciting riot or rebellion. Speech, moreover, has been broadly defined as communication, meaning art, music, sculpture, drama, picketing, and street demonstrations. Some of these forms of communication obviously involve action as well as speech and can be restricted more than speech unmixed with action. Nevertheless, the Supreme Court generally has sided with the speaker, going so far as to indicate that in the case of a speaker with a hostile audience, the police, wherever possible, must restrain the audience and protect the speaker.

Although there continues to be discussion that "hate crime" legislation punishes thoughts and thereby runs afoul of the First Amendment, the Supreme Court has had no such problem with laws imposing sanctions because of the bias of the perpetrator toward a targeted group or person. In *Wisconsin* v. *Mitchell* (1993) a black man was convicted of leading a racial assault on a white teenager. Under the state's hate crime law, the sentence was doubled because of the racial motivation of the defendant. The defendant claimed that his First Amendment rights were violated in that his political beliefs enhanced the sentence. Wisconsin argued that it was the additional potential for violence that increased the term, not the perpetrator's political beliefs. The Court ruled that the state's interest in controlling violence outweighed any First Amendment claim.

Religion has been almost entirely free from regulation by the criminal law except for two relatively recent cases, one involving the use of peyote, a hallucinogenic drug, in religious rituals, and the other a form of animal sacrifice. In both cases the United States Supreme Court upheld the state law that outlawed the forbidden practice.

Fourth Amendment

> The right of the people to be secure in their persons, houses, papers and effects, against unreasonable searches and seizures shall not be violated, and no Warrant shall issue but upon probable cause supported by Oath or affirmation, and particularly describing the place to be searched or the person or things to be seized.

The Fourth Amendment is the amendment that quintessentially restrains the police. It tells the police that they must have probable cause to arrest, that they must have a warrant to search, and that the warrant must specify where and what is to be seized. Given the complexity of the interactions between the public and the police, there is an enormous body of law dealing with the details of these restrictions on police action. The Court has said that probable cause is something more than mere suspicion and that the permissible thoroughness of the search must vary with the degree of certainty that the police officer has regarding the guilt of the suspect. *Terry* v. *Ohio*(1968) held that where a police officer merely suspects that someone is about to commit a felony, he may stop and frisk the person in a public place, but he may not conduct a full-scale search or arrest of such a person without additional information.

A police officer may also conduct a search without a warrant if given consent by a person authorized to give such consent (e.g., the owner of the premises the police wish to search). In the case of a valid arrest, the officer may also, without a warrant, search the premises immediately adjacent to the suspect. These procedural rules regarding arrests and searches are, for the most part, not new, but within the last 40 years or so, the Court has greatly expanded its impact on the police by ruling that evidence illegally seized (i.e., in violation of these rules) cannot be used in court to obtain a conviction. Evidence gained through leads obtained by illegal means is, moreover, to be considered fruit of the poisonous tree and cannot be used either.

This exclusionary rule led to a revolutionary change in police training and attitudes. It is generally agreed that, historically, American law enforcement, especially on the local level, was conducted without regard for constitutional niceties, until the decision in *Mapp* v. *Ohio* (1961), which removed most of the incentive and imposed penalties for illegal police activity. Since then, gradually, the police have become both better trained and more professional. The exclusionary rule, of course, was criticized severely by those who felt that the hands of law enforcement officials were being tied and criminals were being coddled. Crime did increase for some years after the *Mapp* decision; it has since decreased. Despite the firm belief of many police officials to the contrary, *Mapp* and the exclusionary rule seem to have had little impact on the rate of crime. Their chief effect has been on police training and culture. The exclusionary rule, moreover, has been modified by the Supreme Court to provide for good faith exceptions where the totality of the circumstances were such that the officer had reason to believe that he or she was acting legally (see *Illinois* v. *Gates*, 1983; *New York* v. *Quarles*, 1984; *Nix* v. *Williams*, 1984; and *United States* v. *Leon*, 1984).

The Court has also dealt with other intrusions on personal privacy, such as wiretapping, and after a long period of denying that wiretapping fell under the aegis of the Fourth Amendment, finally admitted that wiretapping was indeed a search that should be regulated by Fourth Amendment standards, *Berger* v. *New York* (1967). Subsequent to the Berger decision, Congress enacted legislation regulating wiretapping, and although wiretapping still remains the dirty business that Justice Holmes called it, the situation is much better controlled.

In more recent times, the Court has dealt with more esoteric issues, such as the question of whether a person has a right to privacy in the garbage he has discarded. In *California* v. *Greenwood* (1988), a warrantless search of garbage revealed drug paraphernalia which the Court admitted into evidence, holding that Greenwood had no right to privacy in the garbage once it has been placed on the curb. Similarly, in *Oliver* v. *United States* (1984), marijuana growing in a secluded, fenced, open field marked "No Trespassing," was permitted into evidence on the ground that there was no right to privacy in an open field.

The Court also addressed the problem of warrantless arrests. Such arrests are permitted when in hot pursuit of the suspect, but traditionally, had also been permitted when the suspect was thought to be hiding in private premises. The Court held that not only did the police require an arrest warrant to enter such premises, but a search warrant as well, if there was no prior consent to their entry (see *Payton* v. *New York*, 1980; *Steagald* v. *United States*, 1981).

One of the most difficult areas for the Court has been deciding the constitutionality of various types of automobile searches and seizures, particularly in illegal drug cases. The multitudinous decisions in this area are truly bewildering and require a chapter of their own, but the clear tendency has been to allow the police more latitude in making such searches, both of the vehicle itself and of containers within the vehicle.

Fifth Amendment

No person shall be held to answer for a capital, or otherwise infamous crime, unless on a presentment or indictment of a Grand Jury, except in cases arising in the land or naval forces, or in the Militia, when in actual service in time of War or public danger; nor shall any person be subject for the same offense to be twice put in jeopardy of life or limb; nor shall be compelled in any criminal case to be a witness against himself, nor be deprived of life, liberty, without due process of law; nor shall private property be taken for public use, without just compensation.

Of all the guarantees mentioned in the Fifth Amendment, probably the most important in terms of impact on the criminal justice system is the protection against forced self-incrimination. In British law, from which we derive many of our legal traditions, suspects are warned that incriminatory statements that they made could be used against them, and that they had a right to remain silent under police questioning. In the United States, the Fifth Amendment was thought to provide the same protection. However, until *Miranda* v. *Arizona* (1966), there was no specific penalty imposed on the police for ignoring this protection. *Miranda* for the first time required that the police give a specific set of warnings to suspects under arrest, informing them of their right to remain silent and their right to have a lawyer present during questioning by the police. Any statements obtained without regard for these protections would be inadmissible for the purpose of obtaining a conviction at a trial.

Like *Mapp*, *Miranda* was extremely unpopular not only with the police but with the public as well, who felt that voluntary admissions of guilt were being excluded on the basis of technicalities. Despite the furor, *Miranda* has never been overruled, although it has been modified in many respects. *Miranda* applies only to suspects who are in custody at the time of questioning, and custody has been defined very narrowly by the Court. Thus, people brought in by the police for questioning, unless they have been formally arrested, are not covered by *Miranda*, even though they may think that they are under arrest.

Eleven years after the decision, the Court refused to overturn *Miranda* even in a case that presented an excellent opportunity. In *Brewer* v. *Williams* (1977), the suspect, accused of kidnaping, raping, and killing a child, was being transported on Christmas eve from one city to another. In the course of the ride, the sheriff, who had promised the suspect's counsel not to question him, made remarks designed to elicit a confession from Brewer, a known religious zealot. The Court refused to admit Brewer's confession, holding that the sheriff's statement, although not direct questioning, was designed improperly to pressure the suspect to confess. At the start of this century, when given another clear opportunity to overrule *Miranda*, the Supreme Court did not and held that the required warnings of the case were now part of our culture.

Another modification of *Miranda* was the *Quarles* decision where Quarles, while attempting to hold up a supermarket, was captured and handcuffed. While thus confined, the police, without giving him *Miranda* warnings, asked him where he had thrown his gun. Quarles told them, and the gun was admitted into evidence at the trial. The Court held the admission proper, holding that because of the imminent danger to public safety, the police had not had time to give *Miranda* warnings.

Another protection of the Fifth Amendment is the protection against double jeopardy. *Double jeopardy* basically means that a person cannot be tried and punished twice for the same crime. However, since the United States is a federation of states rather than a unitary system, there is dual sovereignty exercised over every person. It is settled law that although a state may not try an accused person twice for the same crime, the federal government may institute a second prosecution for that crime regardless of the outcome of the first prosecution, and vice versa. Thus, when the local sheriff was acquitted of murder charges in the case of three civil rights workers in Mississippi, he was tried and convicted in federal court of violating the civil rights of the three men by murdering them.

Sixth Amendment

> In all criminal prosecutions, the accused shall enjoy the right to a speedy and public trial, by an impartial jury in the State and district wherein the crime shall have been committed, which district shall have been previously ascertained by law, and to be informed of the nature and cause of the accusation; to be confronted with the witnesses against him; to have compulsory process for obtaining witnesses in his favor, and to have the Assistance of Counsel for his defense.

Closely related to the privilege against self-incrimination is the right to counsel at all times after arrest. At the pretrial stage, the purpose of the attorney is to see that the defendant's rights are not violated by torture or improper questioning. The purpose of the attorney at trial is to see that the defendant receives a fair trial with the opportunity to confront and cross-examine witnesses against him, present evidence in his own behalf, and have a judge and jury untainted by pretrial prejudicial publicity. *Escobedo* v. *Illinois* (1964), a forerunner of *Miranda*, involved a defendant who asked for, but was denied, the presence of his lawyer during police questioning. The Court held his confession inadmissible.

Similarly, in *Massiah* v. *United States* (1964), Massiah, an indicted defendant in a drug case, was induced by his indicted codefendant, who had turned informer, into making incriminating statements. The Court refused to admit Massiah's confession on the ground that after indictment, questioning of a defendant may not take place without the presence of his or her lawyer, and that use of an undercover informer constituted improper questioning.

Eighth Amendment

> Excessive bail shall not be required, nor excessive fines imposed, nor cruel and unusual punishment inflicted.

The purpose of bail is to ensure the presence of a defendant at trial. If the crime, however, is egregious enough, there is a strong possibility that the defendant may run away and never come back. Therefore, very large amounts of bail, or indeed, the total denial of bail, have been imposed in certain kinds of cases.

The courts have always been conflicted over whether it is proper to use a money device to ensure the presence of the defendant at trial. On the one hand, the effect of money bail may be to keep poor people who pose little risk to the community in jail because they cannot make bail. On the other hand, releasing a defendant who can make bail may mean releasing a dangerous criminal. The riddle has not yet been resolved.

To alleviate the hardship of money bail on the poor, there have been many pilot projects that enable suspects with roots in the community and stable lifestyles to be released without bail. These projects have had a mixed record of success, depending on how well they have been administered, but well-run programs have managed to allow poor defendants their freedom pending trial and to ensure their return for adjudication.

To address the second part of the bail riddle, some jurisdictions have enacted preventive detention laws that deny bail altogether to suspects thought to be too dangerous to be released. Such laws must be drawn narrowly and contain safeguards against long-term, unreasonable pretrial detention if they are to pass constitutional muster. In short, not much has changed since 1835, when a judge named Krantz was asked to set bail for a suspect who had attempted to assassinate President Jackson. He set bail at $1500 but complained that "if the ability of the prisoner alone were to be considered, $1500 is too much, but if the atrocity of the offense alone were to be considered, it was too small."

The cruel and unusual punishment clause of the Eighth Amendment was probably meant to prevent the infliction of barbarous methods of punishment, such as boiling in oil or drawing and quartering. However, in more recent years, the cruel and unusual punishment clause has been used to challenge the conditions under which prisoners have been incarcerated. In the earlier cases, the conditions brought to light were truly horrifying, as in *Holt* v. *Sarver* (1972), which dealt with the Arkansas prison system having used inmate trustees to perform the duties of prison guards. Trustees flogged inmates, used electric shock devices attached to their genitals, and applied burning cigarettes to their bodies. Many inmates were murdered and their bodies buried. In more recent cases, however, the abuses charged have been much less flagrant and relate to overcrowding, lack of medical care, poor food, and so on.

There have also been challenges to restrictions of prisoners' First Amendment rights, including the right to receive uncensored mail, to be interviewed by journalists, and the right to practice their religion and observe special holy days. In the last quarter of the twentieth century, as a result of suits brought by inmates under the Eighth Amendment, a large proportion of the state prisons systems of the United States came under federal court orders to improve conditions under which inmates are held. Despite the Supreme Court's subsequent retreat to a more limited role in prison condition cases, as well as the Prison Litigation Reform Act of 1995, the twentieth century ended with the major inmate claims alleging restrictions of First Amendment rights being resolved in the prisoners' favor.

The cruel and unusual punishment clause has also been used to attack inequities in sentencing. Embedded in our legal traditions is the notion that there must be proportionality between a crime and its punishment. As far back as 1910, the U.S. Supreme Court held that a 15-year sentence at hard labor, chained at the ankle and wrist, was a disproportionate sentence for a wrongful entry in a cash book by a government employee (*Weems* v. United States) In more recent times, disproportionality in sentencing has been challenged in relation to mandatory sentencing laws for drug offenders, which have resulted in very harsh sentences for what are frequently low level offenders.

The main challenges in sentencing, however, have come in relation to the death penalty. The death penalty was at first challenged on a per se basis, that is, that execution in and of itself was unconstitutional. The Court, in *Furman* v. *Georgia* (1972), denied that argument. Since then, however, the Court has attempted, by imposing rigorous procedural requirements, to eliminate the randomness of the death penalty, possible racial bias, and to limit the types of offenses for which the death penalty may be imposed. In capital cases, two trials are now required, one for the determination of guilt and one to decide whether the death penalty should be imposed.

From 1967 to 1977 the federal courts declared a moratorium on executions, pending resolution of legal challenges to their constitutionality. Since the moratorium ended, executions have taken place at an increasing pace, although fewer than before the moratorium, and mainly in the southern states. In the 1990s there was a quickening of executions, especially in Texas and Florida, but at the same time there was a slight drop in public support for the death penalty. This attitudinal change may be the result of concern over executing the innocent as the media carried several stories of persons on death row being exonerated. Indeed, as the century ended, Illinois imposed a moratorium on executions because a dozen inmates waiting to be put to death had their convictions overturned.

NEW ISSUES FOR THE TWENTY-FIRST CENTURY
First Amendment

As noted before, the First Amendment is usually not involved in a discussion of constitutional issues relating to criminal justice, especially since the climate for free speech is extraordinarily free at the present time. Controversy, however, over "social" issues such as abortion and minority rights, have given rise to Supreme Court decisions that bear on the peacekeeping activities of the police. The most publicized of these was *Schenck* v. *Pro-Choice Network* (1997), concerning the right of groups opposed to abortion to hinder the operation of clinics where abortions were being performed, and to prevent or dissuade women seeking abortions from entering the clinics. In 1990, three doctors, four abortion clinics, and the Pro-Choice Network of Western New York filed a complaint in Federal Court in the Western District of New York against 50 individuals and three organizations, of which Operation Rescue was one. The defendants were accused of blockading clinics and conspiring to deprive women of abortion services by marching, kneeling, sitting, or lying in driveways, yelling, pushing, and shoving. The demonstrations were so large and violent that the police were overwhelmed. A temporary restraining order obtained from the Court by the plaintiffs was breached by Schenck on the ground that it violated his First Amendment rights. The Court affirmed its order, holding that it merely regulated the time, place, and manner of the demonstration, not the content. It concluded that in view of the defendant's tactics, a 15-foot buffer zone which demonstrators could not infringe was needed to protect persons wishing to enter the clinic. The Circuit Court of Appeals, en banc, affirmed the lower-court ruling. On appeal, the United States Supreme Court held unanimously that although a 15-foot buffer zone around a clinic was permissible, a 15-foot "bubble" around persons seeking to enter the clinic, no matter where they were located, was a burden on Schenck's free speech rights. It is not unreasonable to expect that the first few years of the twenty-first century will see additional cases before the Supreme Court, further fine tuning the rights of antiabortion demonstrators to protest in front of and around abortion sites.

Another free speech case, *Hurley and South Boston Allied War Veterans* v. *Irish-American Gay, Lesbian and Bisexual Group* (1995) involved the refusal of the sponsors of the annual St. Patrick's day parade in Boston to permit Irish homosexuals to march as an identified unit in the parade. The gays claimed that since the parade had received a permit from the city, and used the city streets, it should be open to all Irish persons in whatever unit they chose to march. The United States Supreme Court disagreed, holding that to force a private parade sponsor to include identified units of which they disapproved violated the sponsor's First Amendment right not to say something they didn't wish to say.

Limitations on bias crime legislation continues to come before the Supreme Court, but the discussion is about the Fifth and Sixth Amendments, not the First. In *Apprendi* v. *New Jersey* (2000), the Supreme Court held that enhancement of the defendant's sentence beyond the statutory maximum because his crime was racially motivated was improper because the Fifth Amendment due process clause and the notice and jury trial guarantees of the Sixth Amendment require that any factor other than a prior conviction that enhances the sentence must be submitted to the jury and determined, by them, beyond a reasonable doubt. However, in *People v. Rosen* (2001), the New York Court of Appeals held *Apprendi* did not require a jury trial a sentence was being enhanced because of three prior felony corrections even though the trial court had to make the additional determination that the circumstances warranted the increased sentence.

The First Amendment cases cited above are important and interesting, but as indicated, most of the criminal justice decisions of the United States Supreme Court involve the Fourth, Fifth, Sixth, and Eighth Amendments. Contrary to many people's expectations, since 1990, despite a change in the political climate of the country and of the membership of the Court, there have been no really substantial changes in the interpretations of those amendments. Rather, the Court has modified some of its earlier decisions in a more punitive direction. The *Mapp* and *Miranda* decisions, which imposed the exclusionary rule on illegally obtained evidence and confessions, were, in many ways, the high-water marks of constitutional change in our criminal justice system. They still stand, although in modified form. The tide of protection for defendants has been ebbing, but slowly and not dramatically. The newer interpretations are important not only to the litigants, but as a reflection of changes in our society.

One caveat needs to be addressed, however. Although it is true that the substance of Fourth, Fifth, Sixth, and Eighth Amendment jurisprudence has not changed markedly, the procedural rules for getting such cases to the U.S. Supreme Court have changed considerably, especially in relation to habeas corpus petitions. A habeas corpus petition is a device for bringing the custodian of an accused person or prisoner into court for the purpose of challenging the legality of the confinement. It is used, for example, to challenge the admissibility of evidence that might have been seized illegally, the admissibility of confessions that might have been involuntary, and most important, in death penalty cases, the constitutionality of an impending execution. The most significant use of habeas corpus has been to obtain federal oversight of state criminal procedure, since a writ of habeas corpus obtained in a federal court commands state officials to justify their actions. In legal terms, habeas corpus granted by a federal court for the purpose of examining a state court ruling results, in effect, in federal supervision of state practices. Understandably, state officials resent such suits, and the collateral relief process results in very long, complex, and expensive litigation, which congests both state and federal courts.

The United States Supreme Court has responded to this situation by limiting the granting of habeas corpus in certain kinds of situations. In 1976 in *Stone v. Powell*, the Court ruled that federal courts could not hear Fourth Amendment habeas corpus petitions from state prisoners, arguing that illegally seized evidence should have been excluded from their trials as long as each inmate had received a full and fair chance to make the argument in state court appeals. In addition to Court-imposed restrictions on Fourth Amendment habeas corpus appeals, Congress has enacted several statutes designed to restrict prison inmates from filing multiple habeas corpus appeals. Most of the challenges to these statutes have been rejected. *Felker v. Turpin* (1997) considered the question of whether severe restraints on the right to file habeas corpus petitions might not be construed as a total denial of the constitutional right to habeas corpus. Felker was convicted of murder and sentenced to death. He filed one unsuccessful habeas petition, followed by a second habeas petition. When the second petition was denied by a federal court of appeals, his attempt to appeal to the United States Supreme Court was forbidden by a 1996 congressional statute which denied appellants permission to appeal such a denial to the Supreme Court. The Supreme Court granted certiorari on the question of whether the statute amounted to an unconstitutional total denial of habeas corpus. A unanimous court held that the 1996 statute was constitutional and the Court could refuse to hear an appeal from the circuit court. Felker, however, could apply for habeas corpus in an original petition directly to the United States Supreme Court, thus preserving his constitutional right to habeas corpus.

One of the few decisions relating to habeas corpus favorable to defendants, was *Lindh* v. *Murphy* (1997), which questioned the retroactivity of a 1966 congressional statute designed to make it harder for state prison inmates to file habeas corpus petitions in federal court. Lindh was convicted in Wisconsin of murder and attempted murder. He filed several applications for habeas corpus, but while his appeals were pending, Congress changed the rules regarding habeas corpus, so that Lindh's applications became invalid. He appealed to the United States Supreme Court, which held, in a 5-to-4 decision, that Congress did not intend for the law to be applied retroactively.

Unless there is a dramatic change in the composition of the Supreme Court and/or legislative change vis-á-vis habeas corpus, both of which seem unlikely, the present limitations on habeas corpus will stand and may very well get more restrictive in the next decade.

Fourth Amendment

Aside from habeas corpus restrictions, there have been very few changes in Fourth Amendment jurisprudence. In *Florida* v. *Bostick* (1991), a police officer who had no legal basis for suspecting a particular passenger, boarded a bus and at random asked for and received a passenger's consent to search his luggage after telling the passenger that he could refuse permission to search. The resulting search revealed contraband. The Supreme Court held that as long as the officer's request was not so coercive that the passenger was not free to refuse, the search was a legal consent search, even though the passenger, being on a bus, was not free to leave. Bostick expanded the meaning of "consent" in consensual searches, which are free from the requirements of probable cause or a warrant. However, in *Bond* v. *United States*, in 2000, the Supreme Court held that a traveler's personal luggage is clearly an "effect" protected by the Fourth Amendment, and merely exposing the luggage to the public does not cost a petitioner his or her reasonable expectation that his or her bag will not be physically manipulated.

Two other cases also involve motor vehicles. In *Ohio* v. *Robinette* (1996), a unanimous Supreme Court held that it would be unreasonable to require the police to inform a driver, before making a request to search a car, that he or she is free to refuse the request and go on his or her way. The police need not inform the driver of his or her right to leave. In another case, *Maryland* v. *Wilson* (1997), the police stopped a car for speeding and noticed that the front-seat passenger appeared to be very nervous. The officer ordered him to get out of the car, and when he did, a package of cocaine fell out. In *Pennsylvania* v. *Mimms* (1977), the Court had ruled that a police officer had the right to order the driver of a stopped vehicle out of the car. The question in *Wilson*, however, was whether a passenger could also be so ordered. The Court held 7 to 2 that the passenger could be ordered out on the grounds that the safety of the policeman must prevail over the minimal intrusion on the passenger's privacy.

A more important case, perhaps, is *Richards* v. *Wisconsin* (1997), involving proper implementation of a search warrant. Police officers obtained a search warrant for Richard's hotel room, which specifically forbade them to enter the room without announcing their presence. Because this was a drug case and the police feared that Richards would destroy the evidence before admitting them, they broke down the door before knocking. Cocaine was found and Richard's motion to suppress the evidence as being illegally seized was denied by both the trial and appellate courts. On appeal to the U.S. Supreme Court, the question presented was whether in cases such as drug cases, where the evidence might be destroyed, the police have a right to enter without announcing themselves. A unanimous Court held that although there is no blanket exception to the no-knock rule, where the police had reasonable suspicion that the evidence would be destroyed, the search was not illegal.

Fifth Amendment

The most notable development in Fifth Amendment jurisprudence was the refusal of the Court to extend the habeas corpus restrictions that it had applied to cases relating to illegally seized physical evidence to cases involving allegedly illegally obtained confessions. In *Withrow* v. *Williams* (1993), in a 5-to-4 decision, the Court refused to extend to confessions the limitation on habeas corpus that it had imposed on search and seizure cases in *Stone* v. *Powell* (1976). Withrow involved a defendant who claimed a violation of the *Miranda* rule and challenged the admissibility of his incriminating statements. To the surprise of most Court watchers, who expected the ban on habeas corpus in cases involving searches and seizures to be extended to cases involving incriminating statements, the Court granted his petition. The issue may not be entirely closed, however, because of the closeness of the vote and the fact that in another case, *Brecht* v. *Abrahamson* (1993), another 5-to-4 decision, the Court refused to permit habeas corpus petitions alleging constitutional errors committed by the state at trial unless the defendant could show that the error had a "substantial and injurious effect on the jury's verdict" and that he suffered from "actual prejudice from the error."

Double jeopardy is, however, a problem that continues to plague the courts, both because of our federal system, which gives separate jurisdictions to both the states and the federal government, and because the law recognizes both civil and criminal offenses, which carry separate punishments and which may result in a defendant being punished twice for an infraction relating to the same set of facts. In *United States* v. *Dixon* (1993), the Court upheld a second prosecution for a man who had beaten his wife after he had already been tried for violation of a court order of protection. The decision was 5 to 4, and some recent events have reopened public discussion of the fairness of the dual sovereignty–dual jeopardy rules.

In Los Angeles, California, the acquittal in a state trial of four white policemen shown on television tape severely beating a black man in the course of an arrest aroused such public outrage that the federal government instituted a new trial. Although the acts were the same, the charge in federal court was violation of the victim's civil rights, and some of the previously acquitted defendants were convicted. The original state verdict, however, had led to severe rioting in Los Angeles, in the course of which a white truck driver was badly beaten by black rioters. The beating was filmed by a reporter. At the ensuing trial, only one defendant was convicted of a felony, which carried punishment far less than the original highest count in the indictment. There were some calls for a federal trial of the defendants, on the ground that the jury had been terrorized by the fear of a replay of the riots. There was no retrial of the black defendants, but the two cases provoked much discussion of when and whether a second trial by a different sovereign (i.e., the state or federal government) was appropriate.

In this new century, second trials, usually by the federal government, in cases where the state crime also makes out a federal civil rights violation, although not routine, are becoming more common. Indeed, prosecutors even get together before bringing charges to determine the appropriate jurisdiction within which to bring the case. These, of course, are political decisions since the prosecutors involved have broad discretion in deciding whether to bring charges at all.

Some double jeopardy cases involve, not prosecutions by different sovereigns, but multiple prosecutions by the same governmental unit. In *United States* v. *Usery* (1996), the question presented to the Court was whether civil forfeiture and criminal prosecution for the same illegal drug activity constituted double jeopardy. Usery's house was seized by the federal government in *in rem* proceedings after he had been found guilty of facilitating illegal drug transactions. After he had settled the *in rem* claims, he was indicted for and convicted of manufacturing marijuana, and sentenced to prison. The lower courts found for Usery, but on appeal, the United States Supreme Court ruled that the civil *in rem* proceeding was neither criminal nor punitive in nature and therefore the criminal conviction and punishment did not constitute double jeopardy. In *Hudson* v. *United States*, the United States Supreme Court agreed to review a 1996 decision of the 10th Circuit, which involved the question of whether a defendant was subjected to double jeopardy if he was criminally indicted for a banking violation after he had paid a fine for the same offense. Hudson had misapplied bank funds and had been convicted civilly and fined $46,000 when, in fact, the losses caused by his malfeasance were $900,000. The prosecution argued that since the fine was so small, it was only remedial, not punitive, and therefore a punitive criminal conviction would not constitute double jeopardy.

Even more unsettling was the denial of certiorari by the U.S. Supreme Court to a case involving the retrial for murder of a defendant who had previously been acquitted of the same offense. Harry Aleman was acquitted in a nonjury trial in Illinois of the murder of a union official (*Aleman* v. *Illinois*, 1987). At the time, the prosecutor felt strongly that the case had been fixed by bribing the judge. Subsequently, a federal investigation begun in the 1980s of corruption in the Cook Country court system led to testimony by one Robert Cooley, a lawyer in Cook County, who had volunteered to be an undercover informer for the government, that the trial judge had been bribed. Illinois then retried and convicted Aleman on the original charge, reasoning that if the judge had been bribed, Aleman had never been in jeopardy. Aleman appealed his conviction on double jeopardy grounds ultimately to the U.S. Supreme Court which denied certiorari (*Aleman* v. *Illinois*, 1997). Although denial of certiorari does not set a precedent, it is somewhat startling for the Court to have refused to hear a case that appears to have put in question all previous precedents on double jeopardy by retrial for the same offense after acquittal.

As we entered the twenty-first century, it appeared momentarily that the settled law of *Miranda* v. *Arizona* was about to be overturned. In the wake of the *Miranda* decision in 1966, Congress enacted section 3501 of title 18 of the U.S. Code, which in essence set forth that the admissibility of a statement should turn only on whether it was voluntary. The statute lay dormant until the Fourth Circuit Court of Appeals, making reference to the section cited above, reinstated a confession that had been excluded at the trial level because of a failure to give the accused the appropriate *Miranda* warnings. Writing for a 7-to-2 majority, in *Dickerson* v. *United States* (2000), Chief Justice Rhenquist noted that the warnings of *Miranda* were now part of our culture and that *Miranda*, being a constitutional decision, could not be overturned by an act of Congress. The Court went on to state that *Miranda* and its progeny continue to govern the admissibility of statements made during custodial interrogation in both state and federal courts.

Sixth Amendment

Very few cases in recent years have come to the Court regarding the Sixth Amendment, and Sixth Amendment law seems to be fairly well settled. However, in 1996, the Court decided *Cooper* v. *Oklahoma*, in which Cooper challenged the right of Oklahoma to put the burden of proof on him to prove that he was incompetent to stand trial. Cooper had been accused of felony murder and was found to be incompetent to stand trial. He was committed to a state mental health facility for treatment and was released three months later when the doctors found him to be competent to stand trial. His behavior at the trial, however, was extremely bizarre, and he refused to cooperate with his counsel. Despite defense arguments that he was incompetent, he was convicted because the court held that Cooper had not met the burden of proving his incompetency. In a unanimous decision, the U.S. Supreme Court reversed, holding that to place the burden of proof of incompetency on the defendant offended a principle of justice that was deeply rooted in the traditions and conscience of the American people.

Another fair trial case, accepted for review in 1997, was *United States* v. *Scheffer* (1997), where the Court agreed to consider the question of whether a defendant can be barred from presenting favorable polygraph evidence as part of his right to present his defense under the Sixth Amendment. Rule 707 of the Military Rules of Evidence bars polygraph evidence in court-martial proceedings. Does the rule apply to evidence for the accused as well as evidence against him?

Eighth Amendment

In over 200 years of existence, the United States Supreme Court paid almost no attention to the criminal justice system—until the 1960s. The post–World War II years have been a period when increasingly the Court has been concerned with individual rights rather than property rights, and part of that concern reflected itself in new interpretations of the Fourth, Fifth, Sixth, and Eighth Amendments. The Fourth Amendment dealing with police procedure was the first to receive attention, followed over the years by the Fifth Amendment, dealing with confessions and double jeopardy, and the Sixth Amendment, dealing with the right to counsel and fair trial. At the present time, however, it is the Eighth Amendment, dealing with sentencing that is at the top of the Court's agenda in the area of criminal justice.

The Eighth Amendment speaks of cruel and unusual punishment. The cases coming before the Court divide themselves roughly into three categories: cases dealing with the death penalty, with unsatisfactory prison conditions; and with disproportionate sentencing in nondeath penalty cases. Most of the appeals from the death penalty come via a writ of habeas corpus asking the federal court to review certain procedural questions that the prisoner alleges violated his or her constitutional rights.

In *Herrera* v. *Collins*, (1993), Herrera alleged that newly discovered evidence of his innocence had been discovered that entitled him to a new trial. The evidence consisted in part of affidavits tending to show that his now dead brother had committed the murders, evidence that was not available to him at the time of his original trial. Herrera's claim, however, was made 10 years after his original conviction, while under Texas law a new trial motion based on newly discovered evidence must be made within 30 days of the imposition of sentence. The United States Supreme Court denied Herrera's motion holding that the Texas limitation on the introduction of new evidence, even evidence purporting to show the defendant's innocence, was not a denial of fundamental fairness and did not violate Herrera's due process rights.

In another case, *McCleskey* v. *Zant* (1991), McCleskey claimed in his petition for habeas corpus that the evidence used to convict him had been obtained improperly from a prisoner in an adjoining cell and should have been excluded on the basis of the decision in *Massiah* v. *United States* (1964). In the Massiah case, the police had wired Massiah's codefendant, who had agreed to turn informer, and had him elicit damaging admissions after Massiah had been indicted and was without the presence of his attorney. McCleskey's problem, however, was that although he might have prevailed on the merits of his *Massiah* claim, he had previously made several petitions for habeas corpus at both the state and federal levels, some of which did not include the *Massiah* claim, although 18 other claims had been made. The United States Supreme Court rejected his application for habeas corpus on the ground that he had abused the writ by filing multiple claims, some of which did not raise the *Massiah* issue. In both *Herrera* and *McCleskey*, three justices dissented, holding that in the case of the death sentence and its ultimate finality, technical procedural rules should not bar meritorious claims.

More recently, the attitude of the Court concerning technical procedural rules has, on the whole, become increasingly punitive. In *Lambrix* v. *Singletary* (1997), when Lambrix was convicted of first-degree murder in Florida, the jury was erroneously instructed on one of many aggravating factors. He was sentenced to death and appealed his sentence. While the appeal was pending, the Supreme Court decided *Espinosa* v. *Florida* (1992), which held that neither the judge nor the jury can consider invalid aggravating circumstances. Lambrix claimed that *Espinosa* should be applied retroactively to his sentence. In a 5-to-4 decision written by Justice Scalia, the Court held that *Espinosa* could not be applied retroactively because the *Espinosa* decision was a new rule, and the Court has a general policy against new rules being applied retroactively.

Another application of the "new rule" principal was *O'Dell* v. *Netherland* (1997). O'Dell was convicted of rape and murder in 1988, and sentenced to die. The jury was never informed that had it rejected the death sentence, O'Dell could have been sentenced to life imprisonment without the possibility of parole. Six years later, in 1994, in *Simmons* v. *South Carolina* (1994), the U.S. Supreme Court ruled that a capital defendant who is described as a future threat to society (as was O'Dell) has a due process right to have the jury know that he or she will never get out of prison if the jury spares his or her life. In 1997, O'Dell had not yet been executed. The question before the Court, thus, was whether the *Simmons* precedent should apply, invalidating O'Dell's death sentence. In a 5-to-4 decision, written by Justice Thomas, the Court held that new rules of constitutional law should not be available to state prison inmates who are seeking federal court review through petitions of habeas corpus. The *Simmons* holding was a new rule and therefore did not apply to O'Dell. The dissenters, Justices Stevens, Breyer, Souter, and Ginsberg, held that Simmons was not a new rule but a bedrock principle of a full and fair hearing.

Another death penalty case not involving the propriety of a request for a writ of habeas corpus was *Payne* v. *Tennessee* (1991). Payne was convicted of first-degree murder of a mother and her 2-year-old daughter and assault on her 3-year-old son. At the penalty phase of Payne's trial, the state called as a witness the victim's mother, who described the devastating effect on the family, and especially on the remaining child, of the crime. The constitutional question presented was whether a capital sentencing jury could, under the Eighth Amendment, consider victim impact evidence. Two previous precedents, *Booth* v. *Maryland* (1987) and *South Carolina* v. *Gathers* (1989), barred the admission of victim impact statements during the penalty phase of a capital trial, on the ground that the jury should consider only evidence relevant to the character of the offense and the character of the defendant. Impact statements that tend to differentiate victims on the basis of their different roles or value to society served no purpose but to inflame the jury. In *Payne* the Court overruled the two previous precedents and held that the impact might properly be considered as an aggravating circumstance, related to the crime itself.

Another group of cases decided recently by the United States Supreme Court deals with prison conditions. In *Wilson* v. *Seiter* (1991), Wilson claimed that the overall prison conditions under which she was confined constituted cruel and unusual punishment. The Court rejected her claim, holding that it is incumbent on the petitioner to specify both the particulars of the allegedly unconstitutional conditions of confinement and to relate them to a policy of deliberate indifference on the part of prison officials.

On the other hand, in *Hudson* v. *McMillian* (1992), Hudson alleged that his Eighth Amendment rights were violated by the beating he received by state correctional officers. He was beaten while handcuffed and shackled following an argument with Officer McMillian, one of the prison guards. Hudson received minor bruises, facial swelling, loosened teeth, and a cracked dental plate. The supervisor on duty watched the beating and simply told the guards "not to have too much fun." At the federal court of appeals level, Hudson's claim was disallowed on the ground that inmates alleging excessive force in violation of the Eighth Amendment must prove significant injury, and since Hudson required no medical attention, his claim was dismissed. In a 7-to-2 decision, the United States Supreme Court disagreed, holding that unnecessary and wanton infliction of pain violated the Constitution regardless of the extent of the injury.

In 1993, in *Helling* v. *McKinney*, McKinney brought suit against Nevada prison officials, claiming that his health was jeopardized by his cellmate, who was a heavy smoker, forcing him to breathe secondhand smoke whenever he was in his cell. The United States Supreme Court agreed that it was not necessary for McKinney to show that his confinement represented deliberate indifference on the part of the prison administration to his health needs, but that he was not entitled to a directed verdict, only to a hearing in which he could prove that the cigarette smoke was injurious to his health.

The remainder of the Eighth Amendment cases relate to disproportionate sentences—determining whether, as Gilbert and Sullivan said, "the punishment fits the crime." Many of these cases were triggered by the relatively recent implementation of federal sentencing guidelines, which punish drug possession very harshly and also allow for forfeiture of property thought to have been obtained through illegal drug activities. RICO (racketeer-influenced corrupt organizations), a federal law that provides for property seizure before conviction, is also giving rise to increasing litigation in this area.

In *Harmelin* v. *Michigan* (1991), the Court permitted imposition, under Michigan law, of a mandatory sentence of life imprisonment without parole for a nonviolent first offense: possession of more than 650 grams of cocaine. Harmelin contended that the mandatory nature of the sentence did not permit consideration of mitigating factors in his case. In a 5-to-4 decision the Court held that although such a severe penalty might be unconstitutional for some crimes, Harmelin's sentence under Michigan law for having 2 pounds of cocaine in his possession was constitutional, even though under federal law he would have been sentenced to about 10 years. Two justices, Scalia and Rehnquist, went so far as to say that short of the death sentence, proportionality in sentencing was irrelevant in terms of the Eighth Amendment—that any prison sentence was constitutional. Justices Kennedy, O'Connor, and Souter, however, said that although Harmelin's sentence was acceptable, the Eighth Amendment could invalidate grossly disproportionate sentences. White, Blackmun, Stevens, and Marshall dissented, holding that the sentence was disproportionate and unconstitutional. White noted that only one other state, Alabama, imposed a mandatory life sentence without parole for a first-time drug offender. Under Michigan law, Harmelin would have received a five-year sentence.

The Court revisited the excessive punishment question in *Kansas* v. *Hendricks* (1997). In 1994, Kansas enacted the Sexually Violent Predator Law, which allowed for the civil commitment of persons who, due to a mental abnormality or personalty defect, are likely to engage in predatory acts of sexual violence. The act was invoked for the first time to commit Leroy Hendricks, an inmate who had a long history of sexually molesting children, and who had scheduled for release from prison shortly after the act became law. Hendricks, who had been sentenced to 10 years in prison, challenged the law as violating the federal constitution due process, ex post facto, and double jeopardy clauses. The question before the Court was whether Hendricks could be confined in a state hospital for the mentally ill after he had completed his prison term even though he did not meet the standards for civil commitment under state law. Once again, Justice Thomas held in a 5-to-4 decision that Hendricks' continued confinement was not punishment but was a method the state had chosen to protect communities from violent sexual predators. The same dissenters as in O'Dell disagreed, holding that Hendricks' confinement was basically punitive because he was simply being restrained, not treated for his mental problems. The law could be constitutional if it were applied prospectively and if it provided treatment and not simply incarceration.

In Hendricks, Kansas sought to imprison an offender for longer than his original sentence. *Lynce* v. *Mathis* (1997), however, originated in Florida's attempt to shorten sentences as a means of clearing out overcrowded prisons. In 1983, because of overcrowding in its prisons, Florida enacted a law giving early release credit to inmates when the population of the prisons exceeded certain limits. In 1992, frightened by the number of violent criminals who were being released, Florida passed another law canceling credits for certain types of offenders. Lynce had been sentenced to 22 years in 1986 for attempted murder and was released in 1992 before enactment of the new law on the basis of the credit accumulated under the 1983 law. When the 1992 law went into effect, he was rearrested because his release credits had been canceled. He then went to federal court asking for a writ of habeas corpus on the ground that the application of the 1992 law was ex post facto and therefore, unconstitutional. On appeal, the U.S. Supreme Court held 7 to 2 for Lynce.

Several 1993 cases related to seizure of property from criminals and suspects, particularly in drug cases. In *United States* v. *a Parcel of Land* (1993), the Court, by a 6-to-3 vote, interpreted a federal drug forfeiture law to provide an exception for innocent owners. A woman was permitted to defend her house against forfeiture on the ground that she did not know that the money used to buy the house came from her boyfriend's drug dealing. In a second case, *Austin* v. *United States* (1993), the Court unanimously left to the lower courts the decision as to when a forfeiture violated the

Eighth Amendment. Austin was the owner of a small body shop in South Dakota and lost his business and his mobile home, worth a total of $38,000, in addition to $4000 in cash, when he sold 2 grams of cocaine to an undercover agent.

In a third case, *Alexander* v. *United States* (1993), the owner of a chain of adult bookstores and movie houses forfeited his businesses and almost $9 million in profits after he was convicted of racketeering by selling obscene material. Alexander had raised both an Eighth Amendment claim against excessive fines and a First Amendment claim relating to the destruction of books and other materials that were not obscene. His Eighth Amendment claim was unanimously upheld, but his First Amendment claim was narrowly rejected by a 5-to-4 vote. A remaining issue that the Court has undertaken to decide is the right to advance notice and hearing in forfeiture cases.

CRIMINAL JUSTICE ISSUES NOT RELATED TO THE BILL OF RIGHTS

An old issue that has surfaced for the Court in a new form is the question of how much control the federal government has over state and local enforcement of a federal law. Gun control brought the issue to a head. In 1968, Congress passed the Gun Control Act, which prohibited firearms dealers from selling handguns to certain categories of persons, such as minors or convicted felons. In 1993, Congress amended the act by enacting the Brady Bill, which required gun dealers to have prospective purchasers fill out certain forms to show that they are not in the prohibited classes. These forms were to be submitted to the chief law enforcement officer of the district, who was to ascertain whether the purchaser had a right to buy a gun. The sheriffs of two counties in Montana and Arizona challenged the constitutionality of the act, claiming that the federal government could not impose such duties on them. In *Printz* v. *United States* (1997), Justice Scalia, writing for the majority of the Court, agreed, holding that the federal government may not compel the states to enact or administer a federal regulatory program. In dissent, Justice Stevens wrote that the commerce power provided sufficient ground to support the regulations, besides which, the intent of the Founding Fathers, as expressed in the *Federalist Papers*, was to enhance the power of the new government to act directly upon local officials.

CONCLUSIONS

The function of the Bill of Rights in the twenty-first century, even as in the eighteenth century, will be to protect minorities, even minorities of one, against majorities. Criminal defendants are minorities, and the last 30 years, on the whole, have seen a generous interpretation of the Bill of Rights in their favor, a generosity which at the time of this writing appears to be waning somewhat. But the body of the Constitution exists to create and maintain a government for the benefit of the majority. The question then becomes: Whose rights shall prevail?

The post–World War II era has been a time of concern for minority rights, probably in reaction to the horrors resulting from the wholesale overriding of those rights in such countries as Germany and the Soviet Union. At the present time there seems to be no likelihood that there will be a sweeping denial of basic human rights in the foreseeable future in the United States, but increasing crime and violence are straining the social fabric. The degree of success in dealing with those strains will determine the shape of the criminal justice system in the twenty-first century.

CASES

Aleman v. *Illinois*, 136 L.Ed.2d 868 (1997).

Alexander v. *United States*, 113 S. Ct. 2766 (1993).

Apprendi v. *New Jersey*, 540 U.S. 466 (2000).

Austin v. *United States*, 113 S. Ct. 2801 (1993).

Berger v. *New York*, 388 U.S. 41 (1967).

Bond v. *United States*, 529 U.S. 334 (2000).

Booth v. *Maryland*, 482 U.S. 496 (1987).

Brecht v. *Abrahamson*, 113 S. Ct. 1710 (1993).

Brewer v. *Williams*, 430 U.S. 387 (1977).

California v. *Greenwood*, 486 U.S. 35 (1988).

Cooper v. *Oklahoma*, 517 U.S. 348 (1996).

Dickerson v. *United States*, 147 L.Ed.2d 405 (2000).

Escobedo v. *Illinois*, 378 U.S. 478 (1964).

Espinosa v. *Florida*, 505 U.S. 1079 (1992).

Felker v. *Turpin*, 518 U.S. 1051 (1997).

Florida v. *Bostick*, 111 S. Ct. 2382 (1991).

Furman v. *Georgia*, 408 U.S. 238 (1972).

Harmelin v. *Michigan*, 111 S. Ct. 2680 (1991).

Helling v. *McKinney*, 113 S. Ct. 2475 (1993).

Herrera v. *Collins*, 113 S. Ct. 853 (1993).

Holt v. *Sarver*, 309 Fed. Supp. 881 (1972); affirmed 501 F.2d 1291 (5th Cir. 1974).

Hudson v. *McMillian*, 503 U.S. 995 (1992).

Hudson v. *United States*, 92 F.3d 1026 (10th Cir. 1996), accepted for review by U.S. Supreme Court, April 14, 1997.

Hurley and South Boston Allied War Veterans v. *Irish-American Gay, Lesbian and Bisexual Group*, 132 L.Ed.2d 487; 515 U.S. (1995).

Illinois v. *Gates*, 462 U.S. 2113 (1983).

Kansas v. *Hendricks*, 138 L.Ed.2d 501; 521 U.S. (1997).

Lambrix v. *Singletary*, 520 U.S. 518 (1997).

Lindh v. *Murphy*, 138 L.Ed.2d 481 (1997).

Lynce v. *Mathis*, 137 L. Ed.2d 63; 519 U.S. 443 (1997).

Mapp v. *Ohio*, 367 U.S. 642 (1961).

Maryland v. *Wilson*, 519 U.S. 408 (1997).

Massiah v. *United States*, 377 U.S. 201 (1964).

McClesky v. *Zant*, 111 S.Ct. 2841 (1991).

Minnesota v. *Dickerson*, 113 S. Ct. 2130 (1993).

Miranda v. *Arizona*, 384 U.S. 436 (1966).

New York v. *Quarles*, 467 U.S. 649 (1984).
Nix v. *Williams*, 467 U.S. 431 (1984).
O'Dell v. *Netherland*, 138 L.Ed.2d 351 (1997).
Ohio v. *Robinette*, 519 U.S. 33 (1996).
Oliver v. *United States*, 466 U.S. 170 (1984).
Payne v. *Tennessee*, 111 S. Ct. 2597 (1991).
Payton v. *New York*, 445 U.S. 573 (1980).
Pennsylvania v. *Mimms*, 434 U.S. 573 (1977).
People v. *Rosen*, _____ N.Y.2d _____ (2001).
Printz v. *United States*, 521 U.S. 98 (1997).
Richards v. *Wisconsin*, 520 U.S. 385 (1997).
Schenck v. *Pro-Choice Network*, 519 U.S. 357 (1997).
Simmons v. *South Carolina*, 512 U.S. 154 (1994).
South Carolina v. *Gathers*, 109 S. Ct. 2207 (1989).
Steagald v. *United States*, 451 U.S. 204 (1981).
Stone v. *Powell*, 428 U.S. 465 (1976).
Terry v. *Ohio*, 392 U.S. 1 (1968).
United States v. *a Parcel of Land*, 61 U.S.L.W. 4189 (1993).
United States v. *Dixon*, 113 S. Ct. 2849 (1993).
United States v. *Leon*, 468 U.S. 897 (1984).
United States v. *Scheffer*, 117 S. Ct. 1817 (1997).
United States v. *Ursery*, 518 U.S. 267 (1996).
Weems v. *United States*, 217 U.S. 349 (1910).
Wilson v. *Seiter*, 111 S. Ct. 2321 (1991).
Wisconsin v. *Mitchell*, 113 S. Ct. 2194 (1993).
Withrow v. *Williams*, 113 S. Ct. 1745 (1993).

chapter 13

A Comparative Analysis of Victim Impact Testimony in Capital Cases in New Jersey and Texas

Ronald L. Reisner, Ph.D., J.D. and Peter J. Nelligan, Ph.D.

ABSTRACT

The past three decades have brought profound changes to the U.S. criminal justice system. The collapse of the rehabilitative ideal in the mid-1970s and a conservative swing in public opinion about crime and criminals has led to an incarceration rate unprecedented in the nation's history. In a related development, a more conservative U.S. Supreme Court has chipped away at many of the expansions of criminal defendants' rights developed during the era of the Warren Court. Finally, with the rediscovery of crime victims by U.S. society and the criminal justice system, a broad-based effort is being made to reintegrate them into the criminal justice process (see Friedman, 1993:305–309). All three of these trends converge in the recent practice in states with the death penalty of allowing the family members of capital murder victims to testify at the penalty phase of trials.

INTRODUCTION

In this chapter we report the results of research examining the practices of trial courts in presenting victim impact testimony to juries in two jurisdictions, the entire state of New Jersey and Smith County, Texas, during the 1990s. Although both New Jersey and Texas provide for the death penalty in their homicide statutes, and both states permit victim impact testimony at the sentencing phase of capital murder trials, they could hardly be more different in the way this evidence is presented. The two jurisdictions may be viewed as ends of a continuum in the latitude given prosecutors to present victim impact testimony and provide a unique insight into actual courtroom practices in these high-stakes cases.

We begin the discussion with a brief overview of the historical role of victims in legal systems as well as the rise of the victims' rights movement in the United States. We then turn to the relevant statutory and case law context in both states. Finally, we present a quantitative and qualitative analysis of victim impact testimony in 28 capital murder trials, 14 from New Jersey and 14 from Texas.

THE CHANGING LEGAL ROLE OF VICTIMS

The history of the changing legal role of victims has been well researched and often recounted (see Ziegenhagen, 1977; Tobolowsky, 1999). Prior to the establishment of centralized political authority associated with the rise of the nation-state, wrongs were typically private matters between victim and offender in the context of their kinship groups. Justice was achieved when the victim was satisfied. Ziegenhagen (1977) notes that as social differentiation increased concomitant with the rise of the nation sate, victims were marginalized and victim satisfaction declined as the focus of justice processes.

Even though the expropriation of the victim's right to act against and punish wrongdoers proceeded slowly, and was from time to time resisted, its advance was inexorable (Ziegenhagen, 1977:61–69). The rise of social contract theory as the major philosophical justification for the state and criminal law effectively undercut any rationale for victims to have any more recognized interest in the outcome of his or her case than any other citizen. Beccaria's (1953) late eighteenth century, influential essay on *Crimes and Punishments* asserted that the proper role of the criminal justice system was the suppression of crime. Punishments were to be as certain as possible, as prompt as possible, and only severe enough to balance the wrong done to the whole of the society and to deter offenders. Punishment was solely the right and duty of the sovereign acting on behalf of the collectivity. Although Beccaria took harm into account in establishing penalties, it was harm to the community. He abhorred anything that inserted irrationality, discretion, or emotion into judicial proceedings, so the idiosyncratic preferences of victims, as well as the particularities of individual offenders, had no place in his system. By implication, given Beccaria's emphasis on rational deterrence, wrongdoers would only be punished for the foreseeable consequences of their offenses.

Looking more generally at legal evolution, Galanter (1966) proposed a number of characteristics of modern legal systems that differentiate them from less complex systems. Generally, modern legal systems consist of stable, impersonal, uniform, rational rules applied to objective facts and administered in a bureaucratic system by a highly differentiated cadre of professionals. Acts, not statuses, are supposedly relevant to legal outcomes. The subjective, the personal, the idiosyncratic, and the emotional are not ideal features of modern legal systems. Insofar as these features are associated with crime victims, it is understandable why they have been of decreasing importance as legal systems have modernized.

In sum, anthropologists, historians, and sociologists have found that the rise of social complexity, social differentiation, the power of the state, and the rationalization of law have been accompanied by a decline in the role of the victim in addressing wrongdoing. There has been a progressive deinstitutionalization of the role of the victim and reduction of the victim to a mere witness in criminal proceedings. Now we find a reassertion of the claims of victims and a drive to reinstitutionalize the victims in the criminal justice process. Yet our legal culture is uneasy with this development and it remains to be seen just how this can be done without conflicting with established values and practices of the U.S. criminal justice system (Nelligan, 1998).

THE VICTIMS' RIGHTS MOVEMENT

The rediscovery of crime victims in the late 1960s was an outgrowth of the nascent feminist movement (see Griffin, 1971). The maltreatment of rape and domestic violence victims by the criminal justice system was a central theme of early feminist consciousness-raising groups, and rape law reform during the 1970s was a major focus of feminism. Rape victim advocates contended that rape victims have a legitimate personal interest not only to decent treatment by the criminal justice system, but to a satisfying outcome. They also suggested that participation in the criminal justice process is, with the proper outcome, healing and therapeutic. This aspect of the rape law reform movement quickly generalized to similar consideration of the wishes and interests of all crime victims.

The crime victims' rights movement has had remarkable success at a number of levels. One of the earliest reforms was the establishment by all states and the District of Columbia of victim compensation programs to alleviate the financial consequences of violent crime (Kelly and Erez, 1997). Most states, as well as the federal government, have provided crime victims at least the right to be informed about critical decisions. The most significant success for crime victims' rights came in 1982 with the establishment by President Reagan of the President's Task Force on Victims of Crime, which researched and documented the mistreatment of crime victims in the nation and developed a long list of recommendations for reform of all phases of the criminal justice system. The Office for Victims of Crime was established within the Justice Department to implement the task force's recommendations. Within four years many states had passed into law task force recommendations (see U.S. Department of Justice, 1986:4). Most notably, the task force recommended a constitutional amendment to augment the rights of crime victims. Such an amendment has been introduced in Congress and was supported by President Clinton. At present, all states have statutory provisions ensuring victims' rights, and 32 states incorporate victims' rights in their constitutions (Kilpatrick et al., 1998).

Many of the victims' rights provisions are not controversial. Few oppose compensation for and decent treatment of crime victims or even the right to be notified of events in case processing. However, provisions that make crime victims decision makers in the criminal justice process are much more controversial. Some worry that expansion of crime victims' rights into this area compromises civil liberties and legal impartiality (see Elias, 1983, 1993; Orvis, 1998).

VICTIM IMPACT STATEMENTS

One mechanism that provides for crime victim influence on case outcomes is the victim impact statement. This mechanism permits consideration as part of sentencing of written or oral statements by the crime victim or family members (in the case of homicide victims). Every state and the federal government permit victim impact statements (Kelly and Erez, 1997). Numerous benefits have been suggested in the literature for the use of impact statements (see Erez and Tontodonato, 1990). However, the principal rationales involve (1) that full information on specific harm to victims increases the accuracy of sentencing, and (2) allowing the victim or victims' family to participate will increase satisfaction and have a therapeutic effect (Kilpatrick and Otto, 1987; Young, 1997).

The use of victim impact statement in the courts has not been without criticism, particularly in capital murder trials, where the issues become much more focused and intense. It may be that increased victim participation in the criminal justice process will be aggravating rather than therapeutic for victims (Rubel, 1986). Phillips (1997) contends that inclusion of victim impact statements in capital murder trials has costs that outweigh benefits. She argues that the use of victim impact statements simply exaggerates the existing tendency of juries in homicide cases to consider victim characteristics to the detriment of due consideration of case characteristics and the defendant's moral culpability.

The U.S. Supreme Court also has had difficulty conceptualizing victim participation in sentencing decisions in capital cases. In *Booth* v. *Maryland* (1987), the first case to put to the test written victim impact evidence in a capital case, the court found that consideration at sentencing of the crime's physical and psychological impact on the victim's family, as well as the family members' characterizations of the brutality of the crime, violated the Eighth Amendment. The court worried that introduction of victim harm would make use of the death penalty arbitrary and that victim characterizations of the crime would serve no purpose other than to inflame the jury. The court followed similar reasoning in *South Carolina* v. *Gathers* (1989) when it disallowed statements made by the prosecutor at the sentencing hearing which discussed the victim's religiosity and good citizenship.

In an abrupt about-face, the court ruled in *Payne* v. *Tennessee* (1991) that the controlling principle on which the *Booth* and *Gathers* cases had been decided was erroneous. Evidence relating to the specific harm to a victim and the victim's family is relevant in capital sentencing, and the Eighth Amendment does not prohibit states from permitting it at trial. Justices Marshall, Blackmun, and Stevens dissented in *Payne*, the latter rejecting the interjection of the victim's character in the trial as irrelevant and the former two contending that victim impact evidence draws the jury's attention from the defendant and the crime to "such illicit considerations as the eloquence with which family members express their grief and the status of the victim in the community" (p. 846).

Empirical studies of victim impact statements are starting to appear in the literature and focus on the issues of sentence impact and victim satisfaction. With regard to the effects of victim statements on sentences, the results are mixed. The research generally shows that particulars of the crime and the offender are more important than an impact statement (Erez and Tontodonato, 1990; Davis and Smith, 1994), but in one study, impact statements did affect the relative likelihood of prison or probation, although they did not affect the length of the prison sentence (Erez and Tontodonato, 1990). Erez and Laster's (1999) recent survey of the victim impact literature concludes that the studies show that "...the inclusion of victims in the process has had little effect on processing or sentencing in criminal cases" (p. 531). They blame a resistant practitioner (judges, prosecutors, defense attorneys) culture which objectifies and thereby minimizes the subjective experiences of crime victims.

On the second issue, the effects of making impact statements on the victim, the results are also mixed. Early studies revealed little victim interest in participating in the criminal justice process and little effect on victim satisfaction (Davis and Smith, 1994b). Erez and Tontodonato's (1990) study of a large sample of Ohio felony cases showed only a very small increase in satisfaction among victims who had filed impact statements over those who had not. Whatever the effects of victim impact statements on sentences arising out of routine felony cases, it is doubtful that such findings may be generalized to capital cases. In these cases the family member of the victim usually sits face to face with the jury and testifies about the victim and the harm and loss caused by the offender's actions. The conditions would seem to be maximized for effective victim impact testimony.

Some research specific to participation of the family members of homicide victims is also beginning to appear. A preliminary analysis by Day and Weddington (1996) of interview data from family members of homicide victims suggests that the criminal justice process does affect the grief and anger of the family members of homicide victims. Their findings suggest that the effects relate more to satisfactory interactions with criminal justice officials, especially prosecutors, than to case outcomes.

VICTIMS' RIGHTS IN TEXAS

Texas has followed the general pattern in the development of victim services and rights. In 1979 the legislature passed the Crime Victims' Compensation Act, which established the Crime Victims' Compensation Fund. As of 1998, more than $300,000,000 has been paid out of the fund (Morales, 1998). In 1985 the legislature made a statutory delineation of crime victims' rights and has refined the law in each biennial legislative session (*Texas Code of Criminal Procedure*, Art. 56.02). The original enactment, which has been revised several times, provides for victim impact statements to be provided to and considered by the courts prior to the imposition of a sentence (Art. 56.03). In 1989, the legislature passed, and the voters overwhelmingly ratified, a constitutional amendment incorporating basic victims' rights in the Texas Constitution In addition to statutory changes affecting court operations, agencies such as the governor's office, the Texas Department of Criminal Justice, and local prosecutors' offices have developed services focusing on crime victims. However, neither statutory law nor the Texas Constitution specifically authorizes the introduction of victim impact testimony at the sentencing phase of capital murder trials.

CAPITAL MURDER AND CAPITAL PUNISHMENT IN TEXAS

Capital murder trials are a regular feature of Texas courthouses, and by any measure Texas is the state whose citizens are most committed to the use of capital punishment. Between 1976 and June 14, 2000, Texas has executed 220 persons, constituting more than one-third of all persons executed in the United States during that period. As of April 1, 2000, Texas had 460 death row inmates, exceeded only by the 568 in California. However, in 1999, California executed only two persons, whereas Texas executed 35 (Death Penalty Information Center, 2000). A 1999 poll that asked Texans their opinion about the death penalty found that 80% support it as punishment for murder. A significant number would extend it to other crimes; 46% approve of it for rape, 36% for treason, 31% for kidnapping, and 17% for arson or armed robbery (Longmire and Hignite, 1999).

Capital murder trials in Texas in which the state seeks the death penalty are bifurcated. If the jury finds the defendant guilty of capital murder, the sentencing phase ensues. The jury is not asked directly whether the defendant should be executed, but rather is asked to answer three special issues, regarding (1) if the defendant constitutes a future danger to society, and (2) "whether the defendant actually caused the death of the deceased or did not actually cause the death of the deceased but intended to kill the deceased or another or anticipated that a human life would be taken" [*Texas Code of Criminal Procedure*, Art. 37.071, §. 2(b)]. If the jury answers both questions in the affirmative, it then shall answer (3): "Whether, taking into consideration all of the evidence, including the circumstances of the offense, the defendant's character and background, and the personal moral culpability of the defendant, there is sufficient mitigating circumstance or circumstances to warrant that a sentence of life imprisonment rather than a death sentence be imposed" [*Texas Code of Criminal Procedure*, Art. 37.071, § 2(e)]. This provision of the capital murder sentence was added by the legislature after the state lost *Penry* v. *Lynaugh* due to the fact that the sentencing issues in the existing statute had no provision for juries to consider mitigating factors. Ironically, it was the mitigation provision that opened the door for victim impact testimony at the sentencing phase of capital murder trials.

Since Texas prosecutors began using victim impact testimony soon after the *Payne* decision, and since all Texas death penalty verdicts are automatically appealed to Texas's criminal court of last resort, the Texas Court of Criminal Appeals soon began to consider the propriety of such testimony. It had no easier time than the U.S. Supreme Court. In *Ford* v. *State* (1996), arising out of a 1993 trial, the defendant argued that victim impact testimony should not have been permitted since it was not relevant to any of the three special issues the jury was required to answer. He also argued that the prejudicial effect of the testimony of the victims outweighed its probative value. The court upheld admissibility citing *Payne* and provisions of the *Texas Code of Criminal Procedure* [Art. 37.071, § 2(a)] permitting admission of evidence at sentencing proceedings of "as to any matter the court deems relevant to sentence." It also cited the *Texas Rules of Criminal Evidence* (402) that generally provides for the admissibility of all relevant evidence. Regarding the second issue, the court ruled that the trial court did not abuse its discretion in deciding that the victim impact testimony had more probative value than prejudicial effect.

In *Smith* v. *State* (1996), decided on the same day as *Ford*, the issue was whether the trial court erred in permitting testimony regarding the victim's good character. The court ruled that such evidence was inadmissible unless introduced to rebut a defense attack on the victim's character. However, the court did not reverse the death sentence, finding the trial court's error harmless.

The character issue continued to be troubling. In *Mosley* v. *State* (1998) the court admitted that "Our jurisprudence in this area has been somewhat inconsistent and confusing" (p. 262). It decided "to announce a consistent, if not always clear-cut rule to be followed in future cases." It opined as follows: "Both victim impact and victim character evidence are admissible, in the context of the mitigation special issue, to show the uniqueness of the victim, the harm caused by the defendant, and as rebuttal to the defendant's mitigating evidence" (p. 262).

The court cautioned, however, that the evidence must focus on humanizing the victim and showing the harm done rather than suggesting the comparative worth of the victim in relation to other members of society. The court called on trial judges to exercise "sound discretion in permitting some evidence about the victim's character and the impact on others' lives while limiting the amount and scope of such testimony" (p. 262). Subsequent objections to victim impact and character testimony have been rejected citing the *Mosley* case (*Griffith* v. *State*, 1998; *Jackson* v. *State*, 1999; *Ladd* v. *State*, 1999; *Prytash* v. *State*, 1999).

VICTIMS' RIGHTS IN NEW JERSEY

New Jersey was not immune to the national political forces that developed in the 1960s and gathered momentum in succeeding decades. It took significant steps to advance the rights of victims and their survivors in the judicial process. (For a complete analysis of the development of victims' rights policy in New Jersey, see Reisner, 1998.) Recognizing as early as 1971 the importance of victims in the criminal justice equation, New Jersey established the Violent Crimes Compensation Board (N.J.S.A. 52:4B-3), an administrative body that was granted authority to compensate victims for personal injury or death resulting from violent crimes.

In 1985, New Jersey adopted the Crime Victims' Bill of Rights (N.J.S.A. 52:4B-46). A statutory enactment, it simply clarified the rights to victims to be notified of various critical stages of the judicial process as it related to the defendant. It allowed for a victim's role in the preparation of a statement to be included in the presentence report prepared for the judge. In 1986, the legislature adopted a statute allowing family members of murder victims to include a written statement in the presentence report (N.J.S.A. 2C:44-6). In 1991, the legislature adopted a statute allowing the county prosecutor to file a written statement about the impact of the crime on the family to be made prior to the filing of formal charges. It also permitted victims to make personal statements in noncapital cases [N.J.S.A. 52:4B-36(m)(n)].

The 1991 Victims' Rights Amendment to the New Jersey Constitution (N.J. Constitution, Art. I, para. 22) was the penultimate action, setting the stage for the 1995 adoption of the Victim Impact Statute [N.J.S.A. 2C:11-3c(6)]. The constitutional amendment was approved by 85% of the voters on November 5, 1991 (New Jersey Legislator, 1992:903). It is as important for what it does say as for what it does not say. It provides that crime victims be treated with dignity and respect. They are provided a constitutional right to attend judicial proceedings unless excluded as witnesses. Victims were further "entitled to those rights and remedies as may be provided by the Legislature" (N.J. Constitution, Art. I, para. 22). This was a fairly broadly worded enabling clause that the legislature would use four years later as authority for adoption of the victim impact statute (for a fuller discussion, see Reisner, 1998).

CAPITAL MURDER AND CAPITAL PUNISHMENT IN NEW JERSEY

New Jersey presents an interesting contrast with Texas with regard to the public's views regarding the death penalty. Although a majority of New Jerseyans favor the death penalty, there is slightly less support than in the nation as a whole. In a recent poll, 63% of statewide respondents say they favor the death penalty for persons convicted of murder. Twenty-three percent oppose it and 15% reported that it would depend on the situation or had no clear opinion. Opinions appear to vary with the factual circumstances presented. When offered the alternative of "life in prison with absolutely no possibility of parole," an option not available under New Jersey law, support for the death penalty drops to 44%, with 37% preferring life in prison. Nineteen percent expressed difficulty in choosing (Eagleton Institute, 1999).

Further, by a margin of 57 to 37%, New Jerseyans believe that a poor person is more likely than someone else to get the death penalty for the same crime. Forty-two percent agree that a black person is more likely than a white person to receive the death sentence for the same crime (Eagleton Institute, 1999).

Compared to the 460 death row inmates in Texas, New Jersey's death row is sparsely populated. As of April 1, 2000, there were 16 death row inmates (Death Penalty Information Center, 2000). There have been no executions in the state since 1963, despite the fact that the death penalty was reenacted in 1982. The low number of death row inmates is the result of judicial reversals of death sentences and delays due to appeals by the current inmates.

As in Texas, capital murder trials in New Jersey are bifurcated. If a jury finds a defendant guilty of murder, the trial proceeds to the penalty phase during which aggravating and mitigating factors are admitted and evaluated by the jury (N.J.S.A. 2C:11-3C). The New Jersey Legislature had been attentive to both the national political winds as well as the changing federal constitutional law on the subject of victim impact testimony. After the reversal by the U.S. Supreme Court in *Payne*, states had wide latitude to set guidelines for the introduction of such testimony. The removal of the federal constitutional prohibition thus allowed New Jersey to move further along a path it had already begun to follow several years earlier.

The final piece of legislative action, setting the stage for the New Jersey Supreme Court's landmark decision in *State of New Jersey* v. *Rasheed Muhammad* (1996), came in 1995 with the adoption of the Victim Impact Statute [N.J.S.A. 2C:11-3c(6)]. After a lengthy legislative debate in which the issues were forcefully argued by all affected parties (see Reisner, 1998, for a full discussion of the legislative history), the legislature opted for a moderate, compromised approach in which victim impact testimony would be admitted only if the defendant introduced mitigating evidence of his or her own character or record. In other words, victim impact testimony would not be independently admissible as an aggravating factor, that is, as a factor that the jury may consider in reaching a death penalty decision.

The statute provides as follows:

> When a defendant at a sentencing proceeding presents evidence of the defendant's character or record pursuant to subparagraph (h) of paragraph (5) of this subsection, the State may present evidence of the murder victim's character and background and of the impact of the murder on the victim's survivors. If the jury finds that the State has proven at least one aggravating factor beyond a reasonable doubt and the jury finds the existence of a mitigating factor pursuant to subparagraph (h) of paragraph (5) of this subsection, the jury may consider the victim and survivor evidence presented by the State pursuant to this paragraph in determining the appropriate weight to give mitigating evidence presented pursuant to subparagraph (h) of paragraph (5) of this subsection. [N.J.S.A. 2C:11-3c(6)].

What is noteworthy is the limited circumstance under which victim impact testimony may be introduced. The legislature took a cautious, moderate path, allowing such testimony only when necessary to rebut mitigating evidence introduced by the defendant with respect to his or her character and record. It would be left to the New Jersey Supreme Court, in *Muhammad*, to determine if this limitation was sufficient to protect the defendant's constitutional right to a fair trial, free of undue prejudice.

The New Jersey Supreme Court was thus asked to determine whether the New Jersey Constitution, and more specifically the Victims' Rights Amendment, provided sufficient authority for the Victim Impact Statute, and if so, whether such statute meets state and federal constitutional requirements of due process. A deeply divided New Jersey Supreme Court fashioned its own compromise. Departing from its prior decisional framework, it looked to the broadly worded Victims' Rights Amendment and found adequate basis to justify legislative authority for the adoption of the statute. The overwhelming passage of the amendment, by 85% of the electorate, was a fact not lost on the court.

The court had, in the past, expressed grave reservations about the death penalty generally and had refused to allow executions for more than a decade since it was reinstituted. More important, it had a long decisional history opposing the introduction of victim impact testimony. It thus proceeded, in *Muhammad*, to creatively fashion a set of limitations that it deemed necessary to protect the essential due process interests of capital defendants. Although this artful balancing of interests did not, in theory, revise the statute substantively, it imposed limits not necessarily envisioned by the framers of the statute.

Under *Muhammad*, victim impact testimony would be carefully reviewed, in advance, by the trial court. Absent extraordinary circumstances, it could only be delivered by one adult survivor who would read from a previously approved written script. Such a statement would be devoid of emotional outburst and could not address issues of the defendant's character or the sentence that the survivor thinks may be appropriate. Comments would be limited solely to the character of the victim and the impact of his or her loss. No reference to the comparative worth of the defendant and victim—to society—would be tolerated. Were these procedural revisions only? Or is there a substantive element to these limitations? Probably, a little of both, reflecting the precarious road the court traveled in fashioning its decision.

The court thus ratified the policy adopted by the legislature but modified it as well, revealing a sensitivity to political realities and a capacity for creative judicial policymaking while protecting the critical elements of due process demanded by the state and federal constitutions. The success of the court's formulation will be tested in its implementation.

With this background, we now turn to a consideration of the actual practices of the trial courts in New Jersey and Texas.

METHODOLOGY

To determine how victim impact testimony is being presented in capital murder trials in Texas and New Jersey, we compiled transcripts of testimony from both states. The Texas data are from Smith County in the northeast corner of the state along the Interstate 20 corridor, about equidistant from Shreveport and Dallas. Smith County's population is 170,000. The county seat and largest city is Tyler, with a population of about 85,000. From 1990 through 1999 there have been 16 capital murder trials of persons indicted during this time period in which the prosecution presented victim impact testimony at the sentencing phase. One defendant was tried twice, due to an appellate reversal of the original conviction (*State of Texas* v. *Rickey Lynn Lewis*, 1-91-32). Transcripts were obtained from 14 of the trials. One transcript could not be located, and the transcript from a recent trial has not yet been completed.

The New Jersey data also consist of 14 transcripts derived from 13 trials (in one trial where the defendant was convicted of killing two unrelated persons, members of both families presented victim impact testimony) which represent the entire population of sentencing phase victim impact testimony for the whole state from 1997 to the present.

Since no prior research has been discovered which reports a systematic analysis of victim impact testimony in capital murder cases, the authors had no definite expectation of what elements would appear. We decided to empirically derive a coding scheme from a close reading of all the transcripts and then to go back through them to code each one. This methodology enables us to present quantitative data and a two-state comparison of the frequency with which certain testimonial elements appear. On a qualitative level a close comparison of the two sets of transcripts enables us to discuss the broader similarities and differences in the testimony in the two settings.

RESULTS

The style of presentation of victim impact testimony in New Jersey and Texas could hardly be more different. The trial transcripts reveal that New Jersey trial judges have been very concerned about following the letter and the spirit of the strictures laid down in the *Muhammad* decision. The transcripts reveal several important practices. First, in all 14 cases the victim impact testimony was written out in advance. It was reviewed by the prosecution, defense, and judge, and often edited prior to presentation to the jury. Second, for each murder victim only one family member was permitted to present impact testimony on behalf of the entire family. Third, in most of the 14 cases the witness was first placed on the witness stand, with the jury not present, for the judge to satisfy himself or herself that the witness could deliver the testimony without any display of emotion. The witnesses are cautioned that if they cannot meet this requirement, they will not be permitted to testify. Fourth, once the witness takes the stand, he or she reads the testimony without deviation. Finally, neither the prosecution nor the defense are permitted to ask the witness any questions. Although it can hardly be stated that victim impact testimony in New Jersey is unemotional, it is relatively brief, highly scripted, and controlled. In particular, emotional breakdowns on the witness stand are not permitted.

The Texas courts do not face the *Muhammad* restrictions. Rather, the trial judges in Smith County merely need to avoid abusing their discretion in admitting testimony that is not relevant to the question of the defendant's moral culpability and in which the prejudicial effect exceeds the probative value. From the time of the *Ford* decision in 1996 to the *Mosley* decision in 1998, there was uncertainty whether testimony about the character of the victim could be admitted. After Mosley, it was clearly acceptable. In any case, the trial judges could take comfort from the fact that even if they admitted victim impact testimony improperly, the Texas Court of Criminal Appeals was likely to hold it "harmless error."

The use of victim impact testimony in Smith County differs in major respects from the New Jersey practice. First, there is no requirement that the testimony be written in advance and reviewed by prosecution, defense, and court. It does not appear from the transcripts that any witnesses read statements, and in most cases it is clear that they did not. In several cases (e.g., *State of Texas* v. *Donal Loren Aldrich*, 1-93-1105, Transcript Vol. 36, p. 30) the prosecutor asks the witness if he or she (the prosecutor) has discussed the testimony with the witness and the witness denies it. Second, impact testimony is not limited to one member of the family. Of the 14 cases, five had one witness, five had two witnesses, and four had three witnesses. Third, it is clear that in all 14 cases the witness did not present testimony out of the presence of the jury before presenting it to the jury. Fourth, while in several cases (e.g., *State of Texas* v. *Donal Loren Aldrich*, 1-93-1105, Transcript Vol. 36, pp. 30–37; *State of Texas* v. *Napolean Beazley*, 4-94-226, Transcript Vol. 59, pp. 447–462) the witness is able to give mostly narrative testimony, the common pattern is for the testimony to be elicited by the prosecutor by a sequence of questions. Although the defense frequently objected to the relevance of the testimony, the defense did not cross-examine the witnesses concerning the truthfulness or details of their statements. Finally, displays of emotion were not discouraged by the Smith County courts. In several of the 14 transcripts there is allusion to breakdown or sobbing by the witness. In one case, when the prosecutor himself broke down and could not continue questioning the witness, he had to pass the witness to a colleague. His further emotional display in the court caused the defense to move for a mistrial based on possible effect on the jury, but the motion was denied (*State of Texas* v. *Christopher Andre Wells*, 7-95-260). The Texas transcripts do not show that any witness was cautioned not to show emotion during his or her testimony.

As might be expected, the content of victim impact testimony is most importantly influenced by the particular facts and circumstances of the case, as well as the nature of the relationship between the witness and the murder victim. For example, the mother of an 11-year-old female murder victim (*State of Texas* v. *Tony Nesha Chambers*, 4-91-57) presents impact testimony that is much different from that of the 80-year-old wife of a man to whom she had been married for nearly 60 years (*State of Texas* v. *Christopher Andre Wells*, 7-95-260). The matter is complicated by the fact that witnesses frequently testify not only about the impact of the murder on themselves but on other family members. This is especially true in New Jersey, where only one family member may speak for the whole family. Nevertheless, we found similar elements in the testimony across cases within each state and between the states.

In the Texas cases the prosecutor usually followed a sequence of questions that sought to establish several points. First, the prosecutor would ask the witness to characterize the closeness of his or her relationship with the victim, including frequency of contact, if they did not live together. Second, when permitted by the court, the prosecutor tried to elicit information about what kind of person the victim was. Third, questions would be asked about how the witness or others were affected (psychologically or physically) upon discovering or being informed of the murder and in its short-term aftermath. Finally, the prosecutor would ask about long-term effects.

The difference in the form of the New Jersey testimony, being written out in advance, results in differences in its content. Instead of the witness being led through a series of questions, to which he or she responds extemporaneously, the New Jersey statements are more planned, organized, and rich in description. These differences are revealed by the relative frequency with which victim characterizations and specific impacts are mentioned in the two states.

Tables 1 to 4 present the quantitative component of the analysis of the transcripts in the form of simple frequencies with which witnesses mentioned particular relationships, victim characteristics, and short- and long-term impacts. To permit comparability between the Texas data set, where nine of the cases had more than one victim impact witness, and the New Jersey data set, where only one witness was permitted per case, the Texas data were collapsed so that an item was coded as present if any witness in the case mentioned it. The rationale for this procedure is that the jury heard of the impact at least once but that repetitiousness across witnesses does not weight the findings. We also found it a needless complexity to attempt to identify in the testimony precisely who experienced the impact. Sometimes the witness referred to himself or herself, sometimes to specific members of the family, sometimes to the entire family, and sometimes it was not clear who was affected. For this reason we coded an impact if it was mentioned as affecting anyone.

RELATIONSHIPS

First, we were interested in who testified. In Texas there was a total of 27 witnesses in the 14 trials, and in New Jersey, 14 witnesses in 13 trials. Table 1 presents the data for each state on the frequency with which the various types of relatives appeared as victim impact witnesses. In Texas the most frequent relative of the victim was an adult son or daughter of the victim; in New Jersey, it was a parent. In Texas, the "other" category consisted of a fiancé (twice), the fiancé's sister, and an ex-husband. In New Jersey, the "others" were a fiancé, a cousin, and a stepfather.

Obviously, victim impact is dependent on the closeness of the relationship, and the prosecutors in Texas as well as the victims in New Jersey seek to establish this at the outset. In 11 (79%) of the Texas transcripts and nine (64%) of the New Jersey transcripts, the witness characterized the relationship as "close." Some witnesses referred to dependence (e.g., advice giver) and some to the victim as a "best friend" or "buddy." Several examples will illustrate this type of testimony.

TABLE 1   Relationship of Witness to Murder Victim

Relationship	New Jersey	Texas
	Number of Witnesses	
Parent	6	6
Child	0	10
Spouse	1	1
Sibling	3	4
Niece/nephew	1	1
Cousin	0	0
Ex-husband	0	1
Cousin	1	0
Fiancé	1	2
Sister of fiancé	0	1
Stepfather	1	0
In-law	0	1
Total	14	27

State of Texas v. *Napolean Beazley*, 4-94-226, Transcript Vol. 59, p. 449

    Q: Can you tell the jury how close you were to your father?

    A: As I was saying, he was my best friend throughout life. I suppose that—
we were as close as father and son—as even a father and son can be.

State of Texas v. *Justin Chaz Fuller*, 241-80814-97, Transcript Vol. 40, p. 9

    Q: Were you and your son close, Mr. W_____?

    A: Yes, sir.

    Q: Even after your son moved out, Mr. W_____, how often would he call
you and Mrs. W_____?

    A: He called six, seven, eight times a day, four or five times a night.

    Q: All right. And why would he call you and his mother that many times a day?

    A: We just loved each other, loved to talk to each other, loved to be with each
other quite a bit.

State of New Jersey v. *Lupkovich*, Monmouth County, Ind. 96-02-0281

    "Even though his parents were divorced, J_____ was close to both of them."

    "We have a very large family and everybody loved L_____. She was close
to her aunts, uncles, also her great aunts and uncles."

    "L_____ and her mother would spend days in the kitchen cooking and hav-
ing lots of fun together."

State of New Jersey v. *Koskovich*, Sussex County, Ind. 97-07-0150

    "It could be said that the bond of father and son was complete. So, when my
son was killed, my husband not only lost his son, but also a good buddy."

    "From the start, J_____ had a bond with Mommie and Daddy."

State of New Jersey v. *Wright*, Cape May County, Ind. 96-0346

    "E_____ was my daughter, my co-worker, and my best friend."

State of New Jersey v. *Hoyte*, Essex County, Ind. 561-2-96

    "To his youngest brother, Oscar, who is 11 years old, he was the perfect role
model."

State of New Jersey v. *Timmendequas*, Mercer County, Ind. #94-10-1088

    "M_____'s love for her mother was extra special…something special existed."

    "M_____ and her brother Jeremy were 18 months apart. Jeremy lost not
only his little sister, but his best friend as well."

State of New Jersey v. *Rasheed Muhammad*, Essex County, Ind. 2285-6-90

> "K_____ also has siblings, a brother, Isaiah, and two sisters, I_____ and I_____. Her life with them was short, but wonderful. K_____ would read to her twin sisters every day.

CHARACTER TESTIMONY

We found a marked difference between the Texas and New Jersey testimony in reference to the character or characteristics of the victim. This is probably the result of two factors. First, during the period of most of the trials in Texas (until the *Mosely* case in 1998) judges were doubtful as to its admissibility. However, it often did creep in indirectly. Second, the New Jersey written statements seem to lend themselves more to rich characterizations and the extensive use of adjectives than do the Texas' extemporaneous responses to questions. So in the New Jersey transcripts we found many more characterizations of the victims than we did in the Texas cases. Table 2 presents the frequencies of the most frequent characterizations of the victims. Some of the other terms that were used were: "helpful," "kind," "trusting," "peacemaker," "bubbly," "meticulous," "courage," tenacity," "leadership," "reliable," "funny," "creative," and "decent."

Some examples of character testimony follow.

State of Texas v. *Christopher Andre Wells*, 7-95-260, Transcript Vol. 44, pp. 10–11.

> Q: Ms. R_____, tell the jury a little bit about your father and what you remember about your father.

TABLE 2   Most Frequent Characterizations by Victim Impact Witnesses

	New Jersey	Texas
Character	Number of Witnesses	
Employed	8	2
Hardworking/diligent	11	4
Honest/integrity	4	3
Religious	5	1
Generous	10	2
Happy/good natured	10	2
Thoughtful	1	1
Gentle	2	0
Caring/loving	1	2
Outgoing	2	0
Compassionate	2	0

A: My father was an honest, decent, caring, person with integrity, who was respected by everyone who knew him. He devoted his life to being a father and a husband and a provider...I can honestly say that all children loved him. I did, my kids did, and my grandson does, and all the children who knew him. He was a very gentle person. He was a very kind and generous person.

State of New Jersey v. *Kostner*, Essex County, Ind. 95-01-0093

"R_____ was a compassionate child. One year I asked both children if they would like to have lamb for Easter instead of turkey. R_____ told me that he does not eat cute little baby animals, and that he would not eat lamb."

State of New Jersey v. *Simon*, Gloucester County, Ind. 95-08-0380

"My uncle was an extremely dedicated police officer and he exemplified leadership, courage, and devotion to his profession. Those qualities were recognized when he was promoted to Sergeant on September 26, 1989."

"Our family admired my uncle for all he accomplished and for all the awards he has received, but they admired him the most for his tenacity, his passion for his work, and above all his courage. Despite all of the awards, he never lost sight of his duties as a police officer or of his obligations to the citizens he took an oath to protect."

"Whether he was lending out his car, his house, or even his time, he was always willing to help anybody who needed it. I don't think anything was ever too big a favor to ask. He was always there for anything."

State of New Jersey v. *Hoyte*, Essex County, Ind. 561-2-96

"J_____ was a very special person. As a human being, he possessed many qualities and virtues. He came to this country full of dreams and hopes. He came with the thought of helping his G_____, the name he had for his mother."

"M_____ was a deeply religious man."

State of New Jersey v. *Minett*, Union County, Ind. 96-05-550

"The first thing that came to everyone's mind when I asked about H_____ was Tweety Bird. H_____ was truly a child at heart with her love for Tweety Bird. H_____ wore Tweety Bird clothes and had Tweety Bird decorations throughout her home."

State of New Jersey v. *Rasheed Muhammad*, Essex County, Ind. 2285-6-90

"K_____ was a person who loved her music just so she could dance. She also loved doll houses...K_____ dreamed when she got older she would be a nurse."

State of New Jersey v. *Wright*, Cape May County, Ind. 96-0346

"E____ was a very gentle, loving, and compassionate person. She saw only the good in people."

"E____ was a unique individual in that she was exceptional with all people she came in contact with, both personally and professionally, including children, the elderly, and mentally handicapped persons as well."

SHORT-TERM IMPACT

In both Texas and New Jersey cases we found reference to short-term physical and psychological impact. Texas prosecutors specifically asked about how witnesses reacted to the discovery or news of the murder, such as physical symptoms or varieties of emotional reaction. Texas prosecutors probed about the effect of the witness having to make funeral arrangements, attending the funeral, and viewing (or not being able to view) the victim's body. In New Jersey, victims also sometimes mentioned short-term physical or psychological impact. Table 3 presents the frequencies.

Some examples of testimony about short-term impact follow.

TABLE 3   Witness Statements of Short-Term Impact

Short-Term Impact	New Jersey	Texas
	Number of Witnesses	
Appetite loss	1	1
Anger	2	0
Medical problems	1	2
Sleeplessness	2	3
Fear	2	3
Crying/sobbing	7	4
Sedation	0	1
Hospitalization	2	1
Suicide attempt	0	1
Upset: holidays/birthdays	2	4
Upset: funeral and arrangements	0	3
Upset: body viewing	0	2
Guilt	1	1
Depression	1	0
Job loss	1	0
Panic attacks	1	0
Terrible pain	0	0

State of Texas v. *Thomas Wayne Mason*, 4-91-943, Transcript Vol. 43, p. 5510

Q: How did you feel when they told you what had happened?

A: I just went numb. I mean, you know, it's just like they cut part of your body apart is all it is.

State of Texas v. *Allen Bridgers*, 114-81252-97, Transcript Vol. 33, p. 68

Q: How did that first affect you when you found out that your sister was gone?

A: I really didn't want to believe it, but when I got over there and it was her, it just—knocked me, and I really wished I had not ever went into see what I saw. I wished I would never have went in.

State of Texas v. *Justin Chaz Fuller*, 241-80814-97, Transcript Vol. 40, pp. 15–18

Q: Now can you describe to the jury how it was, Mr. W_____, from that Tuesday that you realized that you felt someone had taken your son and— someone had taken your son against his will, tell the jury how that was to feel that your son had been kidnapped or taken against his will, that something had happened to him, and you didn't know where he was, you didn't know whether he was alive or dead or what happened to him? Can you look over here and tell the jury how that was to go through when you first realized that?

A: I couldn't eat, I couldn't sleep, I couldn't do nothing but cry....

Q: How were you able to try to—what was happening to you during that period of time, Mr. W_____, when you didn't know where your son was?

A: What do you mean what's happening?

Q: Well, I mean how was it affecting you, Mr. W_____?

A: I couldn't eat, sleep, couldn't do nothing. I had to be taken to a doctor. He said I was heading for a heart attack or stroke or whatever because my blood pressure was so high from it....

Q: What did you do, Mr. W_____, when the police came out and told you that they had found your son and the body was so decomposed that you couldn't see him?

A: Just started crying and asking why.

Q: Asked the police why?

A: No, asking the Lord, "Why? Why me?"

Q: Asked the Lord why?

A: It's hard to understand.

State of Texas v. *Charles Daniel Tuttle*, 4-95-396, Transcript Vol. 44, p. 394

> Q: Ms. G_____, I think you testified earlier about how you were notified of C_____'s murder and how you came up to Tyler. So let me just move on and ask you if you could express to the jury in your own words the effect or impact—let me first ask you—of the death of C_____ on your parents at their age.

> A: Well, about a week after this happened, Mother and Daddy both ended up in the hospital. Two separate hospitals because Daddy had heart problems and mother was in another hospital. So my husband had to stay with Dad and I stayed with Mother. They stayed there for a week and then took them back home and we all took care of them for about two months. And it's like they just gave up after this happened.

State of New Jersey v. *Simmons*, Cape May County, Ind. 96-10-0575

> "My initial reaction was shock and bewilderment, then anger came into play and draw into a rage and that emotion is the same this very moment. Upon my notifying family members of the incident, they expressed this same bewilderment, sorrow and revulsion."

LONG-TERM IMPACT

Victim impact witnesses in both states mentioned an extensive list of long-term impacts. There do not appear to be marked differences between the states. As one would expect, most of the testimony focuses on the various dimensions of loss. Recurrent thoughts of the victim are commonly reported, especially when prompted by objects or birthday and holidays associated with family gatherings. Some witnesses testified that the entire family was "ruined." There were two mentions in each state of the need to seek counseling. A few witnesses in both states mentioned continuing fear and insecurity. Perhaps surprisingly, financial loss was mentioned only in two cases in New Jersey. Ironically, in four cases in Texas at least one witness mentioned that attending the trial, viewing at trial photos of the body, and hearing autopsy evidence increased their trauma. Table 4 presents the frequencies.

Some examples of testimony about long-term impact follow.

State of Texas v. *Samhurmundre Widemann*, 241-80839-97, Transcript Vol. 70, pp. 14–15

> Q: Can you, in your own words, tell this jury what the effect of this situation has been on you and on the members of your family, Mr. W_____?

> A: It just tore holes in our hearts. Just can't get it filled or nothing, and we just can't be a normal—function like a family, because we feel like a partial family, because they took my son away from me. And my son was always with us and around us. We done things together. We—he just ain't there no more.

TABLE 4 Witness Statements of Long-Term Impact

Long-Term Impact	New Jersey	Texas
	Number of Witnesses	
Family ruined	9	4
Lost best friend/confidant	8	6
Lost meaning/direction	6	5
Reminders: objects	7	5
Reminders: holidays/birthdays	3	7
Children/grandchildren deprived	9	3
Need to relocate	1	1
Psychological counseling	2	2
Recurrent thoughts of victim	6	11
Continuing fear	2	6
Upset by trial testimony/photos	0	4
Anger/rage	2	2
Sleeplessness	0	4
Medication	1	1
Loss of appetite	1	1

State of Texas v. *Allen Bridgers*, 114-81252-97, Transcript Vol. 33, pp. 68–69

> Q: You indicated earlier that you've been having—that your health has declined since M_____'s death. What kind of health problems have you had?

> A: I have had a heart condition, stressed heart, and I was placed in the hospital for that, and so I—my health has just gone down.

State of Texas v. *Robert Charles Ladd*, 114-80305-97, Transcript Vol. 47, pp. 205–206

> Q: T_____, let me just ask you, if you could to tell the jury in your own words, in terms of the impact of your sister's murder, what that's going to mean—that impact and that loss of your sister at the hands of this Defendant, what type impact is that going to have on you from now on, you and your other family members, in terms of the changes that's resulted in?

> A: That was a very important part of our life that's missing now. At the time of her funeral, my father made a statement regarding that our family circle was broken now, and it always will be. This man over here didn't just take one life when he chose to do what he did, he shattered the lives of a bunch of people, those people out there who knew V_____ and who loved V_____.

State of Texas v. *Thomas Wayne Mason*, 4-91-943, Transcript Vol. 43, p. 5509

> Q: Mr. D_____, I'm going to—first of all I'm going to ask you what the effect was on you personally losing your sister, M_____ B_____?
>
> A: Like the end of the world. I mean, you lose over half your family, it just tears you up.

State of Texas v. *Thomas Wayne Mason*, 4-91-943, Transcript Vol. 43, p. 5473

> Q: Mr. B _____, if you will, I don't have many more questions for you, and I know this is difficult on you. Can you tell this jury what the effect has been on you of the loss of your mother and grandmother?
>
> A: My mom was 54 years old, and I think, you know—my grandmother was 80. And I just keep thinking that my mom was stolen from me. I could have had her for 26 more years. I'll never have children that she'll be able to see. Holidays, I won't have to leave town. I hate holidays. I can't be around people that talk about things or moms, and dads, or moms and grandmothers. It's hard to go to church, because I go to church, I go to church and I hear a song and I have to leave.

State of Texas v. *Donal Loren Aldrich*, 1-93-1105, Transcript Vol. 36, pp. 36–37

> Q: If you will, Mr. W_____, can you tell the jury about the effect this had on you and your family?
>
> A: (Witness gives extended narrative description of the family and impact of the murder including the following.) Even today after six or seven or eight months, still one of the hardest things is to go to the cemetery and just be there, because it's so final. When he's not around it's like, you know, he's going to be back in a day or two. He's gone, but when we go to the cemetery, it's always just the hardest time. We've gone through birthdays, and like I said, our birthdays were always a big thing, and Mother's Day and Father's Day. His birthday is next Thursday, and will be his first birthday since he's died. The memories are always there.

State of New Jersey v. *Cevallos-Bermeo*, Hudson County, Ind. 0323-02-96

> "…her mother expresses how she is going to learn how to write her name and in the future she will look back and see all she has accomplished. But little Andrea has been deprived of the opportunity to share with her mother, her school years, her college years, and even her wedding day."

State of New Jersey v. *Simon*, Gloucester County, Ind. 95-08-0380

> "I can tell you that nothing I do, nothing N_____ does, nothing my parents do, nothing my brother does is the same since B_____ and R_____ died. We cry a lot. Holidays are particularly tough for the entire family. We

have not videotaped a Christmas or any other event since B_____ and R_____died."

"I have an extremely hard time watching children as they walk to the school bus in the morning. Because seeing neighborhood children on their way to school is so troubling, I deliberately leave the house later than I should to get to work in the morning. I do this to avoid seeing the children. It has been difficult to make friends in Florida."

"…I am going through the motions of living. I am not really living. There are times when one day at a time is simply too long. I try to get through the next hour, the next minute, the next second." "There exists only empty days, sleepless nights, and dreaded dreams."

State of New Jersey v. *Simon*, Gloucester County, Ind. 95-08-0380

"Everything is a constant reminder. That is something his family will have to live with for the rest of their lives. The pain, the sorrow, the anger, the emptiness are all indescribable."

State of New Jersey v. *Lupkovich*, Monmouth County, Ind. 96-02-0281

"Needless to say, R_____ and D_____ have had a great deal of difficulty coping with this tragedy because of the nature of his death, and also because they cannot grieve privately." "Both are under doctors' care and require antidepressant medication."

"Because of his absence, his family now struggles to find joy in the simple pleasures of daily living."

State of New Jersey v. *Koskovich*, Sussex County, Ind. 97-07-0150

"Since then their marriage has been up and down, kind of like a yo-yo. Anger and outrage pours out of T_____at times."

State of New Jersey v. *Hoyte*, Essex County, Ind. 561-2-96

"Since the murder of their poppy, our children have had a very difficult time in school."

"When my husband M_____ was murdered, more than he was killed. A part of the whole family died with the death of my husband. Our entire family suffered a great and irreparable loss and we are still suffering."

State of New Jersey v. *Timmendequas*, Mercer County, Ind. 94-10-1088

"The moments that will be missed will be the constant interfering in our lives, the fifth place setting at the dinner table, the little head popping up and down in the rearview mirror in the car, the constant love and affection for Abbey, the family dog, the constant updating of community affairs, a true mediator between mom and dad, brother and sister, the bald-headed dolls that were everywhere around the house, the little domestic around the house, the giving and sharing of love we all took for granted."

"It has been necessary for J_____ and J_____ to undergo therapy sessions to deal with the loss of their little sister M_____. J_____ still has nightmares and has been found screaming in his closet in the middle of the night...After M_____'s death , they (J_____ and sister J_____) could not bear to return to the room they shared with her..."

"The only peace that we have as parents are the moments during sleep when we don't have to deal with the harsh reality of our everyday lives. And upon wakening when for the briefest of moments we think it was all a bad dream, only to have reality set in and know that it was not. She was—she is the last thought on our mind when we got to sleep and the first thought on our mind when we wake up."

"It has been almost three years since M_____'s death and time has stood still for our family. It feels as raw as if it had happened yesterday. We want life as it was back and don't know it can ever be again."

State of New Jersey v. *Rasheed Muhammad*, Essex County, Ind. 2285-6-90

"I can't imagine life without her....They [others] don't know what it is like to outlive K_____ knowing how she died."

State of New Jersey v. *Minett*, Union County, Ind. 96-05-550

"Every time we see Tweety Bird, tears come to our eyes. We know that this pain will ease in time, but it will never completely go away. We have an emptiness inside that can never be filled by anyone else. It is a void that will last forever....There is now an emptiness in our hearts that can never be filled again."

State of New Jersey v. *Wright*, Cape May County, Ind. 96-0346

"As her mother, I can say I will never be the same. I get up every morning and it is as if someone winds me up to get through the day....Time is supposed to ease the pain, but the void we feel does not seem to decrease. A voice, a smell, a certain hair color or style, or a song remind us how deeply affected we are by E_____'s untimely death at 24 years of age. "

CONCLUSIONS

This comparative examination of the use of victim impact testimony in two very different legal, social, and cultural environments is instructive in several ways. First, from a purely content-analytical perspective, the data indicate that despite significant differences in style of presentation dictated by vastly different legal and constitutional settings, the impact testimony in both states falls neatly into four categories: the nature of the relationship with the victim, the nature of the victim's character, the short-term impact of the victim's death, and long-term impacts. Within each category there were some noted differences—such as the greater depth of character descriptions included in New Jersey testimony, which is prepared in advance. Despite these differences, however, the overall content of impact testimony is categorically similar.

Second, the manner in which victim impact testimony is prepared and delivered is a direct reflection of the vast differences in political cultures of Texas and New Jersey. Texas is a strong death penalty state, with public opinion clearly supportive of the execution of 220 persons since 1976 and the future execution of the 460 inmates currently on death row. It is not surprising therefore to find that prosecutors are given free rein to elicit testimony containing significant emotional content. New Jersey, on the other hand, although nominally supportive of the death penalty, as evidenced by 63% approval in a recent public opinion poll, is far less demonstrative in that support. No one has been executed since 1963, and only 17 men await their fate on death row, some of whom have been there for nearly two decades. The New Jersey Supreme Court barely approved the constitutionality of victim impact testimony and did so in the most limiting fashion, reflecting its underlying doubts about the efficacy and fairness of such testimony. These limitations—including the requirement of written testimony, prepared in advance, reviewed by defense counsel, approved by the judge, and usually subjected to a dry run to test for emotionality—clearly indicate the reluctance with which New Jersey has incorporated victim impact testimony in the penalty phase of capital trials.

Finally, the research raises questions about the legitimacy of allowing even the most limited elements of emotionality in the jury's penalty deliberations. The public seems strongly supportive of the use of impact testimony. Victims' advocates have criticized the muting, by practitioners—mainly judges and lawyer—of the emotional content of such testimony (Erez and Laster, 1999). On the other hand, one must necessarily question the basic premise of inclusion of such testimony in the determination of capital crime penalties, inasmuch as disparities in impact cannot fairly serve as the basis for disparate sentencing if due process is to be preserved. Texas and New Jersey clearly offer interesting contexts for the examination of contrasting approaches to the use of such testimony.

ACKNOWLEDGMENT

This chapter was originally a paper presented to the annual meeting of the Academy of Criminal Justice Sciences, New Orleans, Louisiana, March 22, 2000.

REFERENCES

BECCARIA, C. (1953). *On Crimes and Punishments*. Stanford, CA: Academic Reprints.

DAVIS, R. C., and B. E. SMITH (1994a). The effects of victim impact statements on sentencing decisions: A test in an urban setting. *Justice Quarterly*, 11:453–469.

DAVIS, R. C., and B. E. SMITH (1994b). Victim impact statements and victim satisfaction with justice: An unfulfilled promise? *Journal of Criminal Justice*, 22:1–12.

DAY, L. E., and M. M. WEDDINGTON (1996). Grief and justice in families of homicide victims: Initial results from a study of the impact of the criminal justice system. Paper presented at the annual meeting of the American society of Criminology.

DEATH PENALTY INFORMATION CENTER (2000). www.deathpenaltyinfo.org.

EAGLETON INSTITUTE OF POLITICS, RUTGERS UNIVERSITY (1999) Jump start the chair: New Jersey favors capital punishment. State has reservations, but wants pace of executions moved up. Press release SL/EP 73-4 (EP123-4), October 10.

ELIAS, R. (1983). *The Politics of Victimization: Victims, Victimology, and Human Rights. New York: Oxford University Press.*

ELIAS, R. (1993). Victims Still: The Political Manipulation of Crime Victims. Thousand Oaks, CA: Sage Publications.

EREZ E., and K. LASTER (1999). Neutralizing victim reform: Legal professionals' perspectives on victims and impact statements. *Crime and Delinquency*, 45(4):530–553.

EREZ, E., and P. TONTODONATO (1990) The effect of victim participation in sentencing outcome. *Criminology*, 28:451–474.

FREIDMAN, L. M. (1993) . *Crime and Punishment in American History*. New York: Basic Books.

GALANTER, M. (1966). The modernization of law. In M. Weiner (ed.), *Modernization*. New York: Basic Books.

GRIFFIN, S. (1971). Rape: The all-American crime. *Ramparts*, 10, September, pp. 26–35.

HOGBIN, I. (1934). *Law and Order in Polynesia*. London: Christophers.

KELLY, D. P., and E. EREZ (1997). Victim participation in the criminal justice system. In R. C. Davis, A. J. Lurigio, and W. G. Skogan, (eds.), *Victims of Crime*, 2nd ed. Thousand Oaks, CA: Sage Publications.

KILPATRICK, D. G., and R. K. OTTO (1987). Constitutionally guaranteed participation in criminal proceedings for victims: Potential effects on psychological functioning. *Wayne Law Review*, 34:7–28.

KILPATRICK, D. G., D. BEATTY, and S. S. HOWLEY (1998). *The Rights of Crime Victims—Does Legal Protection Make a Difference*? Research in Brief. Washington, DC: National Institute of Justice.

LONGMIRE, D. R., and L. HIGNITE (1999). *Texas Crime Poll*. Huntsville, TX: College of Criminal Justice, Sam Houston State University.

MORALES, D. (1998). *Crime Victims' Compensation: Annual Report, 1998*. Austin, TX: Office of the Attorney General of Texas.

NELLIGAN, P. J. (1998). Crime victims' expectations for individual justice: Some unintended consequences of the victims' rights movement. Paper presented at the annual meeting of the Academy of Criminal Justice Sciences, Albuquerque, NM.

NEW JERSEY LEGISLATOR (1992). *Manual*, p. 903.

ORVIS, G. P. (1998). The evolving law of victims' rights: Potential conflicts with criminal defendants' due process rights and the superiority of civil remedies. In L. J. Moriarity and R. A. Jerin (eds.), *Current Issues in Victimology Research*. Durham, NC: Carolina Academic Press.

PHILLIPS, A. K. (1997). Thou shalt not kill any nice people: The problem of victim impact statements in capital sentencing. *American Criminal Law Review*, 35:94–118.

REISNER, R. (1998). Victim impact testimony in New Jersey capital cases: A case study in criminal justice policy development. *Criminal Justice Policy Review*, 19:3–4.

RUBEL, H. C. (1986). Victim participation in sentencing proceedings. *Criminal Law Quarterly*, 28:226–250.

TOBOLOWSKY, P. M. (1999). Victim participation in the criminal justice process: Fifteen years after the president's task force on victims of crime. *New England Journal on Criminal Law and Civil Confinement*, 25:21–105.

TURNER, J. H. (1972). *Patterns of Social Organization: A Survey of Social Institutions*. New York: McGraw-Hill.

U.S. DEPARTMENT OF JUSTICE (1986). President's Task Force on Victims of Crime: Four Years Later. Washington, DC: U.S. Government Printing Office.

YOUNG, M. A. (1997). Victims rights and services: A modern saga. In R. C. Davis, A. J. Lirigio, and W. G. Skogan (eds.), *Victims of Crime*, 2nd ed. Thousand Oaks, CA: Sage Publications.

ZIEGENHAGEN, E. A. (1977). *Victims, Crime, and Social Control*. Westport, CT: Praeger.

CASES

Booth v. *Maryland*, 482 U.S. 496 (1987).

Ford v. *State*, 919 S.W.2d 107 (Tex. Crim. App. 1996).

Griffith v. *State*, 983 S.W.2d 282 (Tex. Crim. App. 1998).

Jackson v. *State*, 992 S.W.2d 469 (Tex. Crim. App. 1999).

Ladd v. *State*, 3 S.W.3d 547 (Tex. Crim. App. 1999).

Mosley v. *State*, 983 S.W.2d 249 (Tex. Crim. App. 1998).

Payne v. *Tennessee*, 501 U.S. 808 (1991).

Penry v. *Lynaugh*, 492 U.S. 302 (1989).

Prytash v. *State*, 3 S.W.3d 522 (Tex. Crim. App. 1999).

Smith v. *State*, 919 S.W. 2d 96 (Tex. Crim. App. 1996).

South Carolina v. *Gathers*, 490 U.S. 805 (1989).

State of New Jersey v. *Cevallos-Bermeo*, Hudson County, Ind. 0323-02-96.

State of New Jersey v. *Hoyte*, Essex County, Ind. 561-2-96.

State of New Jersey v. *Koskovich*, Sussex County, Ind. 97-07-0150.

State of New Jersey v. *Kostner*, Essex County, Ind. 95-01-0093.

State of New Jersey v. *Lupkovich*, Monmouth County, Ind. 96-02-0281.

State of New Jersey v. *Minett*, Union County, Ind. 96-05-550.

State of New Jersey v. *Rasheed Muhammad*, 145 N.J. 23 (1996).

State of New Jersey v. *Simmons*, Cape May County, Ind. 96-10-0575.

State of New Jersey v. *Simon*, Gloucester County, Ind. 95-08-0380.

State of New Jersey v. *Timmendequas*, Mercer County, Ind. 94-10-1088.

State of New Jersey v. *Wright*, Cape May County, Ind. 96-0346.

State of Texas v. *Allen Bridgers*, 114-81252-97 (Smith County). Reporter's Record of Testimony.

State of Texas v. *Charles Daniel Tuttle*, 4-95-396 (Smith County). Reporter's Record of Testimony.

State of Texas v. *Christopher Andre Wells*, 7-95-260 (Smith County). Reporter's Record of Testimony.

State of Texas v. *Donal Loren Aldrich*, 1-93-1105 (Smith County). Reporter's Record of Testimony.

State of Texas v. *Justin Chaz Fuller*, 241-80814-97 (Smith County). Reporter's Record of Testimony.

State of Texas v. *Napolean Beazley*, 4-94-226 (Smith County). Reporter's Record of Testimony.

State of Texas v. *Rickey Lynn Lewis*, 1-91-32 (Smith County). Reporter's Record of Testimony.

State of Texas v. *Robert Charles Ladd*, 114-80305-97 (Smith County). Reporter's Record of Testimony.

State of Texas v. *Samhurmundre Wideman*, 241-80839-97 (Smith County). Reporter's Record of Testimony.

State of Texas v. *Thomas Wayne Mason*, 4-91-943 (Smith County). Reporter's Record of Testimony.

State of Texas v. *Tony Nesha Chambers*, 4-91-57 (Smith County). Reporter's Record of Testimony.

Texas Code of Criminal Procedure.

chapter 14

Reaffirming Juvenile Justice

Peter J. Benekos, Ph.D. and Alida V. Merlo, Ph.D.

ABSTRACT

Juvenile justice has undergone a major transformation in the last 100 years. The court has drifted from its original rehabilitative ideal and its focus on prevention toward a much more formal and punitive orientation. This transformation is most apparent in waiver legislation and adultification reforms that have characterized juvenile justice in recent years. The juvenile justice system will continue to confront new challenges to its mission of helping youth and preventing delinquency in the next decade. Rather than abandoning the original juvenile court ideal, three models of juvenile justice have emerged which will characterize the juvenile court of the future.

INTRODUCTION

As demonstrated in California by support for *The Gang Violence and Juvenile Crime Prevention Initiative* (Proposition 21), citizens continue to favor putting more youthful offenders into adult courts where they would be sentenced to adult prisons (Initiative Info, 2000). Proposition 21 requires (1) more juveniles to be tried in adult court, (2) certain juveniles to be held in local or state correctional facilities, and (3) longer sentences to be imposed on an expanded list of violent and serious offenses (California Secretary of State, 2000). This no doubt reflects a continuing reaction to sensationalized and dramatized cases of youth violence and explains Shepherd's concern that "the future of the juvenile court is in question" (1999:21). As a result of similar juvenile justice "reforms," several states now have legislation that further lowers the age at which youth can be transferred to criminal court and sentenced to adult time (Merlo et al., 1997; Finley and Schindler, 1999). The Justice Department reports that in 1997, 7400 juveniles were convicted as adults and admitted to state prisons; this is a 118% increase from the 3400 juveniles admitted to state prisons in 1985 (Johnson, 2000:A1; Strom, 2000:1).

This "adultification" of juvenile offenders was illustrated in the case of Nathaniel Abraham, who was 11 years old when he was charged with first-degree murder in the October 1997 shooting of an 18-year-old stranger, Ronnie Greene, Jr., in Pontiac, Michigan. In November 1999, Abraham was found guilty of second-degree murder, and in January 2000 he was sentenced to serve seven years in a maximum security juvenile detention center (Bradsher, 2000). In Abraham's case, he was the youngest child in Michigan to be charged, tried, and convicted as an adult for murder. This was possible as the result of a 1996 state law which "allows prosecutors to seek judges' permission to try any juvenile as an adult, no matter how young" (Bradsher, 1999:A21).

The sentencing judge, Eugene Arthur Moore, rejected the prosecutors' request for additional time and publicly criticized the state's juvenile laws as "weighted too heavily toward punishment instead of rehabilitation" (Bradsher, 2000:A1). The statement made by Judge Moore and his "lenient" sentence contrast sharply with the 111-year sentence (without the possibility of parole) imposed on another juvenile murderer, Kip Kinkel, who killed his parents, two students, and wounded several other students at a school shooting near Portland, Oregon (Bradsher, 2000). Both the Kinkel school shooting and the Abraham random shooting are tragic but extreme cases that received intense media attention, which served to further distort public understanding and diminish support for juvenile justice.

As critics and supporters look back to the first 100 years of the juvenile court, both can agree that the founding principles and original intent of a separate court for youth have been severely challenged. Critics would argue that flawed assumptions and failed performance should justify the dismantling of the system. Proponents, however, would see transformations and emerging paradigms as evidence of a system capable of adapting to social and political change and meeting challenges in the twenty-first century. In contributing to this discussion on the future of juvenile justice, this chapter is organized into four sections: (1) the history and lessons from the first 100 years; (2) the rationale for optimism about juvenile justice; (3) evidence of successful strategies; and (4) issues and models that will persist in shaping (and reshaping) the juvenile justice system.

HISTORY OF JUVENILE JUSTICE

Readers are familiar with the orthodox view that at the end of the nineteenth century well-intentioned reformers championed the cause of "wayward" children whom they believed needed benevolent supervision, guidance, and socialization (Albanese, 1993). The founding of a juvenile court in 1899 in Illinois signaled a rejection of the prevailing practice of punishing youth as little adults and instituted an informal process to determine the best interests of youth and to seek therapeutic interventions in reforming youthful miscreants. Guided by the doctrine of *parens patriae*, a kind and benevolent judge would rely on "substantive" rationality to order social welfare agencies to divert youth from negative influences and to correct their delinquent tendencies (Bortner, 1988).

Since this new jurisprudence was concerned with child-saving and not criminal prosecution, youth did not require due process or protections for their rights. Delinquent acts were not viewed as crimes but as symptoms of problems that needed treatment (Albanese, 1993:68). A new lexicon was used to denote the distinction between juvenile and criminal court, and as this separate system was established throughout the country (all but two states had a separate court by 1925), the concept of adolescence as a unique developmental phase gained acceptance (Bilchik, 1999a:1): "A century ago, the focus of the juvenile justice system was on the juvenile offender—rather than the offense…and on the principle that youth are developmentally different from adults and more amenable to intervention."

Transformation

While the intent of this informal, child-centered social welfare approach was recognized, the performance of the system began to raise objections. From 1905 when the Pennsylvania Supreme Court upheld the informal, rehabilitative model of the juvenile courts (*Commonwealth* v. *Fisher*) until the 1967 landmark decision establishing procedural safeguards (*In re Gault*), critics objected to the mistreatment of youth, the abuse of judicial discretion, and failure of rehabilitative programs (Albanese, 1993).

As a result of court decisions in the 1960s and 1970s that required more formal procedure and due process in the juvenile court, the distinction between the separate courts was diminished and the courts began to converge. In addition, as crime became more politicized and as a more conservative, punitive model of criminal justice emerged in the 1970s, the rehabilitative model was challenged and replaced by crime control as the salient jurisprudence of criminal justice. These developments—increasing crime, politicized crime policy, punitive dispositions, and an ideological shift to the right—also influenced the direction of juvenile justice.

In his critique of these developments, Feld (1993) credits (1) the procedural convergence, (2) the jurisprudential shift to crime control and punishment, and (3) the jurisdictional changes of removing status offenders from the juvenile court and waiving serious youthful offenders to criminal court with transforming the juvenile court into a barely separate but equal system that was no longer needed or justified. With the juvenile court under scrutiny, the confluence of four factors raised doubts about a future for juvenile justice: guns, gangs, drugs, and race.

Beginning in the mid-1980s, and aggravated by the (1) "epidemic" of crack cocaine, (2) growing numbers of youth gangs, and (3) proliferation of guns, policies toward youth have become more politicized and punitive. The images of younger and younger offenders using firearms to kill innocent citizens have precipitated more retributive and get-tough policies that—intended or not—have reinforced a link between race and youth crime that resulted in the "targeting" of young black men (Feld, 1999a; Finley and Schindler, 1999). In his assessment of the transformation of the juvenile court, Feld noted the importance of race as an impetus for get-tough sentencing and waiver policies (1999a:361): "The politicization of crime policies and the connection in the public and political minds between race and youth crime provided a powerful political incentive for changes in waiver policies that de-emphasized youths' 'amenability to treatment' and instead focused almost exclusively on 'public safety.'"

Racial Disparity

One salient consequence of this impetus has been *disproportionate minority confinement*. As defined by Snyder and Sickmund, the issue is "whether the proportion of minorities in confinement exceeds their proportion in the population" (1999:192). A related dimension focuses on the "disparity" of outcomes, including the length of detention and the security level of the detention facility. In their review, the authors conclude that "for most jurisdictions across the country, (data) show that minority (especially black) youth are overrepresented within the juvenile justice system, particularly in secure facilities" (p. 193).

Several factors may explain the differences, but offending rates of minorities is not one of them. Based on their data, Snyder and Sickmund found evidence that "suggests that disparity is most pronounced at the beginning stages" of juvenile justice processing (p. 193). While representing 15% of the U.S. population ages 10 to 17 in 1996–1997, black juveniles represented (Snyder and Sickmund, 1999:192):

- 26% of all juvenile arrests
- 44% of juvenile arrests for Violent Crime Index offenses
- 45% of delinquency cases involving detention
- 40% of juveniles in residential placement
- 46% of cases judicially waived to criminal court

As these data suggest, and as Feld (1999a) concluded, get-tough attitudes and politicized policies have created not only a more punitive juvenile justice system but one that disproportionately targets black youth. Similarly, a study of school disciplinary practices also found that black students are disproportionately expelled or suspended under "zero tolerance" policies that have been implemented in the wake of school shootings (Claiborne, 1999). For example, in San Francisco where "blacks constitute 16 percent of the enrollment, they account for 52 percent" of the school disciplinary removals (Claiborne, 1999:1). Focusing on these issues of race and minority overrepresentation is crucial to efforts to promote both juvenile justice and social justice. As Finley and Schindler conclude: "Elected officials must stop using fear and stereotypes to justify an increasingly and unnecessarily punitive juvenile justice system that disproportionately impacts minority youths and communities" (1999:14).

Media reports, especially television news, of open drug dealing, driveby shootings, inner-city gang warfare, and images of young black male gang-bangers created public panics and precipitated a series of legislative reforms that lowered age of exclusion, increased penalties for crimes committed with firearms, and sent large numbers of minority youth to prisons. Even though crime rates, especially for violent crimes, have been dropping for several consecutive years for both adults and juveniles, a lingering suspicion of youth has sustained get-tough attitudes and punitive public policies. And after a series of well-publicized school shootings, the tolerance for youthful offending was further eroded. Reactionary, punitive crime control policies and a demonized portrayal of youth highlighted the close of the twentieth century.

Lessons from the First 100 Years

If a fundamental principle of the juvenile court is that youth are developmentally different and therefore should be separated from adults, this has been obscured by the tyranny of a small number of young violent offenders. Among all youth ages 10 to 17, less than 1% is arrested for committing a violent crime (Snyder and Sickmund, 1999). The slogan "adult crime–adult time" and the accompanying legislation that automatically waives 14- and 15-year-olds into adult courts and institutions reflects reactionary, emotional, and bankrupt responses to youth. This, however, is consistent with Bernard's thesis that juvenile justice cycles between get-tough and do-nothing policies (1992). In contrast to comparatively liberal and lenient policies in the 1960s and 1970s, the juvenile crime problem of the 1980s and 1990s was met with hardened attitudes and tough punishments. By limiting the possibility of leniency, Bernard believes that (1992:155) "justice officials eventually will reach the point when they have only harsh punishments available for responding to delinquents. They then will be forced to choose between applying those harsh punishments and doing nothing at all." He predicts that extreme harsh punishments will function "to reintroduce leniency in the responses to juvenile offenders" (p. 155). If Bernard's analysis about the softening–hardening–softening cycles is accurate, a challenge for juvenile justice is to find "balance" in the response to youth. This is discussed in the next section.

In response to the challenge of defining the juvenile court for the twenty-first century, there are five encouraging developments which suggest optimism in assessing future directions for juvenile justice:

1. Crime is decreasing and the trend is continuing.

2. As a result, issues other than crime are receiving public and political attention.

3. There is increasing evidence of effective prevention programs and intervention strategies.

4. There is public support for prevention and treatment programs.

5. Alternative models of juvenile justice have been developed.

In this section we briefly review these developments and examine some strategies, initiatives, and directions for the future of the juvenile justice system.

EMERGENT THEMES AND TRENDS IN JUVENILE JUSTICE

Good News: Crime Continues to Decline

In 1999, for the eighth consecutive year, overall crime rates continued to decline; homicide rates dropped to the lowest levels last seen before 1969 (Dorning, 2000). The homicide rate was 6.3 per 100,000, a 7% decline between 1997 and 1998 (from 18,210 homicides in 1997 to 16,914 in 1998). Victimization rates for violent crimes also dropped to the lowest level in 25 years: 36 victimizations per 1000 population, down from 51.2 in 1994 (Bureau of Justice Statistics, 1999b). These declines have been attributed to policing tactics, economic prosperity, sentencing policies, stabilization of the crack markets, and efforts to reduce gun violence (Butterfield, 1999:A16).

The good news about juveniles is that the arrest rate for juvenile violent crime decreased 39% from 1993 to 1997: In 1997, "juveniles accounted for 12 percent of all violent crimes cleared by arrest" (Snyder, 1998:1). The violent crime rate for juveniles in 1997 was 31 crimes per 1000 youth, down from 52 per 1000 in 1993 (Forum on Child and Family Statistics, 1999a). In addition, while homicides and violent crimes committed by juveniles have declined, the rate of serious crimes committed against youth has also declined: "youth from ages 12 to 17 were the victims of violent crime at a rate of 27 per 1,000 in 1997, down from 44 per 1,000 in 1993" (Forum on Child and Family Statistics, 1999b:3).

In his critical analysis of juvenile crime trends using both Uniform Crime Reports (UCR) and National Crime Victimization Survey (NCVS) data, Bernard concluded that with the exception of increased juvenile arrests for homicide between 1984 and 1993 ("linked to guns"), essentially there has not been a juvenile crime wave in the United States (1999:353). "In fact, nearly 9 out of every 10 counties nationwide did not have a juvenile murderer and 1 out of every 4 juvenile murderers were located in eight counties" (Forum on Child and Family Statistics, 1999a:1). And in the larger context, less than 1% of youth in the United States is arrested for a violent crime (Snyder and Sickmund, 1999).

These data dispel concerns about a coming generation of "superpredators" and raise questions about reactionary, counterproductive "reforms" that focus on waiver and punishment, and transformation of the juvenile court (Sentencing Project, 1999). However, as juvenile crime continues a downward trend, intense media coverage of school shootings has contributed to misperceptions and new fears about school dangerousness and new reactionary policies against youth. In the aftermath of the April 1999 school shootings and 15 deaths at Columbine High School in Littleton, Colorado, students returning to schools in fall 1999 faced increased zero-tolerance policies and increased security measures. In Montgomery County, Maryland, students were required to display photo identifications (Anon., 1999c); five students in South High School in Cleveland, Ohio, were arrested on charges of "planning" to commemorate and replicate the Columbine shootings (Anon., 1999a; Meredith, 1999); in Littleton, a 17-year-old who threatened to "finish the job" started by Eric Harris and Dylan Klebold was arrested and held in jail on $500,000 bail (Keene-Osborn and Glick, 1999).

Based on these media reports, it is understandable why the public believes that school violence is escalating. The data, however, illustrate that schools have in fact become safer and "school-related violent deaths" have decreased (Powell, 1999; Justice Policy Institute 2000; Repenning et al., 2000).

With crime continuing to decline and with schools now safer and more secure, this presents an opportunity to rationally assess the performance of juvenile justice and to consider prevention and intervention strategies, especially in the context of schools, which are effective in reducing delinquency. In addition, since crime is down, other issues are being recognized as national priorities.

Politics, Public Opinion, and National Issues

In the 2000 presidential campaign, issues other than crime captured public attention and political rhetoric. Based on public surveys, "education" was a leading public concern, overshadowing crime, which had dominated the list of issues for several years. A September 1999 Washington Post/ABC News survey asked adults which issue was "very important" in the 2000 presidential election (Balz, 1999). Results placed "improving education and the schools" at the top of the list, followed by concerns for the economy, crime, and Social Security. While posturing on crime is integral to presidential politics, the prevailing get-tough ideology has essentially eliminated serious debate on crime policy and centered political platforms on punishment (Merlo and Benekos, 2000). Since the priority of crime as an issue has diminished, speeches and debates are beginning to focus on other domestic issues and social problems (Balz, 1999).

However, rather than focusing on punitive reactions to youth crime as in the past, substantive policies addressing these issues have the potential to ameliorate conditions that contribute to crime and delinquency. Essentially, this is about the quality of life (poverty, family, schools) and improving conditions for children, and evidence suggests that these efforts can be effective as delinquency "prevention" strategies (Greenwood, 1998, 1999). With attention on these issues, policy debates are more likely to shift away from punitive, retributive juvenile justice legislation that emphasizes statutory waiver and instead begin to focus on assessing strategies that can reduce risks of delinquency and enhance protective factors.

Prevention and Early Intervention

As discussed above, the receding "crime wave" offers a respite from a "crisis management" mode of reacting to juvenile crime and creates an opportunity to consider strategies that prevent delinquency, especially youth violence. Coincidentally, there is a growing literature that presents empirical evidence of the effectiveness of such strategies (Kracke, 1996; Grossman and Garry, 1997; Sherman et al., 1997; Greenwood, 1998, 1999; Kumpfer and Alvarado, 1998; Ohlin, 1998). Greenwood reports that not only is the tide slowly beginning to turn, but policymakers are "beginning to recognize that wise investments in early prevention are not only effective ways of reducing crime, but reduce the need for future prison cells as well" (1998:137).

As policymakers seek information on promising strategies, reports such as those provided by the National Institute on Drug Abuse (NIDA) have identified several "prevention principles" for drug abuse that generally apply to developing and supporting delinquency prevention programs (1997). The principles include family-focused efforts; media campaigns, community programs, skill development (e.g., peer relationships, assertiveness, communications), age-specific interventions, programs that enhance "protective factors" and reduce known "risk factors," and collaborative, comprehensive partnerships.

Prevention and early intervention strategies that incorporate these principles can lead to some of the following outcomes (Greenwood, 1999): improved parent–child relationships, increased emotional and/or cognitive development for children, improved educational outcomes, and decreased criminal activity. Evidence that these types of strategies and programs can reduce crime and delinquency, and do so with cost savings, provides important support for initiatives to counter or at least contain the "waiver" mania that continues to transform juvenile justice (Feld, 1993, 1999a,b; Schiraldi and Ziedenberg, 1999). With arguable evidence that legislative exclusion and prosecutorial discretion have not been effective strategies in reducing crime, and may have detrimental consequences for youth and society (Schiraldi and Ziedenberg 1999), the next era of juvenile justice may be better served by focusing on more cost-effective, primary prevention strategies.

Public Support for Prevention

Although fear of crime remains a salient public concern, recent surveys indicate that "a clear majority" of citizens still favor "governmental efforts designed to intervene with families and children" (Cullen et al., 1998:197). In their study on public attitudes, Cullen et al. found citizen support for early intervention with youth, and they concluded that "policies that seem harsh toward at-risk children are inconsistent with the public mood" (p. 198). In their research on prosecutorial waiver, Schiraldi and Soler (1998) found that almost twice as many respondents were "strongly opposed" to this practice as "strongly supported" it (29% to 16%). Just as there is evidence that supports the effectiveness of intervention strategies, there is evidence that get-tough strategies are an "overreaction" which are not effective. Butts and Harrell (1998a) suggest that looking to the adult criminal justice system for solutions to juvenile crime is counterproductive: The "one-size-fits-all" approach "simply isn't fair" and leads to abuses. In addition, Schiraldi and Ziedenberg (1999) report on the risks that youth face in adult institutions and the doubtful effectiveness of waiver on reducing recidivism. With evidence of public support, as well as support from policymakers who are receptive to more progressive, cost-effective responses to crime and delinquency, this is a crucial juncture in determining the future of juvenile justice.

Future Models for Juvenile Justice

Based on his critical and provocative analysis of the history of juvenile justice, Feld concluded that it is time to abolish the juvenile court and treat youthful offenders as adults (1993). Essentially, Feld argued that the intent of the juvenile court—to seek the best interests of children through an informal process guided by the doctrine of *parens patriae*—has failed. He identified three reforms that have transformed the juvenile court from an informal, child-centered, welfare-based court into a more formal, rational-legal, and retributive process which parallels the adult criminal justice system. The consequences of these reforms—jurisdictional, jurisprudential, and procedural—are the convergence of juvenile and criminal courts and a juvenile court in which youth receive the "worst of both worlds": incomplete due process protections and ineffective care and treatment.

While dismissing a reaffirmation of the juvenile court, Feld poses two options: maintain the present practice of parallel but separate courts or abolish the juvenile court and provide due process and punishment to all offenders, with a "youth discount" for age-diminished culpability. Butts and Harrell, however, maintain that this is a "simplistic substitution" of "treating youth as miniature adults" (1998a:2). While many states are lowering the age that youth can be tried as adults (Merlo et al., 1997; McLaughlin, 1999), the performance of the criminal justice system also leaves much to be desired and does not instill optimism for this type of legislative reaction (Schiraldi and Soler, 1998).

As noted above, the extreme reactions to youth crime in the 1990s have begun to create "a national backlash against a decade of 'get tough' policies aimed at children who commit crimes" (McLaughlin, 1999:1). For example, Schiraldi and Soler found that the public did not support many of the provisions of Senate Bill 10 such as (1998:592–595): confining teenagers and adults in jails for indefinite periods of time; "housing status offenders in adult jails;" requiring schools "to expel teenagers for up to six months for regular use of tobacco;" and making "juvenile felony arrest records available to colleges."

The confluence of economic prosperity, decreasing crime rates, concern about the quality of schools and education, empirical evidence of effective intervention strategies, and the issues in the 2000 presidential campaign suggest that the "cyclic nature of juvenile justice" (Bernard, 1992, 1999) is on the edge of an emerging era. Some of the effective strategies in this emerging model are reviewed below.

PROMISING STRATEGIES FOR YOUTH INTERVENTION

Specialty Courts

An alternative to the abolitionist perspective favored by Feld (1993) is the vision of preserving the juvenile court with some modifications. One opportunity involves the implementation of a number of *specialty courts* designed to address youthful offending (Butts and Harrell, 1998b). These courts target specific groups of offenders who have unique needs that can best be addressed by agencies and organizations that have staff and treatment programs to serve the identified population.

Teen Courts

Teen courts, also referred to as *youth courts* and *peer courts*, have been in existence since the early 1990s. In 1995, 25 states had established teen courts (Godwin, 1996:1); by 1998, there were more than 450 such court programs operating in 42 states and the

District of Columbia (Gordon, 1998; cited in Minor et al., 1999). Teen court jurisdiction can be adjudicatory or dispositional, depending on the criteria established in each state. For example, Kentucky has teen courts at 10 sites, and their role is strictly prescribed. Judges refer youth for disposition to these courts after a finding of involvement or guilt in the juvenile court. Most teen courts operate similarly; the youth are required to admit to the charges brought against them in order to be eligible for a teen court disposition (Butts et al., 1999:1). The most common case-processing system utilizes an adult judge with youth in the roles of attorneys, jurors, clerks, and other court personnel (Butts et al., 1999:1). In fact, this model exists in 47 percent of the teen courts surveyed in 1998 (Butts et al., 1999:1).

The rapid pace in which teen courts have been established throughout the United States has not necessarily been based on empirical evidence of their effectiveness. Nevertheless, teen courts appear to require more community involvement than traditional dispositions and are perceived favorably by the juvenile court staff and the community.

Drug Courts

Although drug courts are more widely utilized in the adult system, there are approximately 45 such courts for juveniles in the United States. Typically, the courts require offenders to participate in drug treatment while receiving strict monitoring. In their review of the drug court initiatives, Inciardi et al. (1996) contend that these courts offer great promise, not only as a relevant approach for dealing with the drug offender, but also as an incentive to make system improvements that are necessary in order to develop and implement effective drug court programs (p. 88; Merlo and Benekos, 2000:154). In their study of juvenile offenders and eligibility for drug court, Roberts and Benekos found that a large majority of youth arrested for drug- or alcohol-related offenses (77%) were eligible for the intensive supervision, comprehensive treatment, and incentives offered by drug court (1999). They concluded that " juvenile drug courts seem to be an encouraging option for providing treatment while still ensuring accountability" (p. 6). Based on their evaluation of the Orange County (Florida) Juvenile Substance Abuse Treatment Court, Applegate and Santana also concluded that "the drug court model shows promise for youthful drug offenders" (2000:297).

Gun Courts

Drawing on the success of the drug courts, gun courts operate with a similar orientation. Gun courts target first-time nonviolent offenders and require parental education (Office of Juvenile Justice and Delinquency Prevention, 1999b:153). Several jurisdictions that have established diversion programs for youth involved in weapons offenses require a firearms education course and classroom presentations by experts, victims, and/or their survivors who have been affected by firearm violence. Programs also provide social services for youth and their families (Office of Juvenile Justice and Delinquency Prevention, 1999b:153).

The gun court program in Birmingham, Alabama, was established in 1995. It is an intense program with strict supervision guidelines; and it requires parental involvement in a seven-week workshop. Youth who admit their involvement in a gun violation are sent to a boot camp program for short-term incarceration and then placed on maximum supervision probation for 30 days to six months (Office of Juvenile Justice and Delinquency Prevention, 1999b:161). In addition, while on probation, youth are required to complete the Alabama Substance Abuse Program. Data indicate that youth who complete gun court had a lower recidivism rate than pre–gun court youth and were less likely to return to the juvenile court on offenses related to gun charges (Office of Juvenile Justice and Delinquency Prevention, 1999b:162).

Preliminary research suggests that youth who complete the program tend to have somewhat lower rates of new charges compared to youth who do not complete the program. The new charges are more likely to be status offenses or misdemeanors (88%) rather than felonies (12%). By contrast, the majority of youth who did not complete the program tended to be referred for felonies (65%) rather than for misdemeanors (35%) (Office of Juvenile Justice and Delinquency Prevention, 1999b:164).

These specialized courts offer insight into alternative approaches that can be used to work with youth who are involved in property offenses, drug offenses, and weapon violations. By targeting specific offenders and providing intensive treatment and certain sanctions, there is an opportunity to conduct research and determine which strategies are most effective and which strategies need to be reexamined and perhaps discarded. Such efforts are important in preventing future offending and expanding or revising program initiatives.

In addition to specialty courts, there are a number of interventions that target at-risk youth to provide them with a comprehensive array of programs and services. The most promising strategies to prevent youth from engaging in delinquency or to deter youth who have already been involved in some law violating behavior are collaborative efforts that include family, school, and the community. Rather than simply focusing on the youth, these programs involve cooperation among agencies and organizations; and they can begin at various stages in a child's development. Early intervention efforts are especially appealing because they have the potential to prevent youth from engaging in predelinquent or delinquent activities and thus to preclude contact with the juvenile justice system. However, it appears that success can also occur after youth have been involved in some types of delinquent activity.

Collaborative Intensive Community Treatment Program

In their study of community alternatives to juvenile placement, Garase and Sonnenberg found that the increase in the number of juvenile placements in one jurisdiction could be significantly reduced by screening and selecting eligible youth for a comprehensive, community-based treatment strategy (1999). As an alternative to secure residential placement, the Collaborative Intensive Community Treatment Program (CICTP) developed a "managed care" approach to allocating scarce resources for youth programming. The program was based on principles of the "balanced and restorative justice model" and emphasized competency development, community service, and offender accountability (p. 7). In their preliminary evaluation of CICTP, Garase and Sonnenberg found that the program was effective in reducing the number of residential placements as well as the costs of juvenile programming, and was successful in providing a continuum of services and treatment programs while maintaining accountability for juvenile offenders (p. 18). The CICTP is an example of an effective collaboration by treatment providers, school officials, juvenile court personnel, and child and youth caseworkers.

Project CRAFT

Another type of collaborative effort is the vocational training program sponsored by the Home Builders Institute. Project CRAFT (Community Restitution and Apprenticeship Focused Training Program) began in 1994 (Hamilton and McKinney, 1999:1) and has been implemented in North Dakota, Tennessee, Maryland, Florida, and Texas. Utilizing a holistic approach that incorporates career training, community service activities, support services such as social skills training, employability training, and case management, this program demonstrates how private business (the construction industry) can collaborate with the juvenile justice system to assist youth (Hamilton and McKinney, 1999:1).

In addition to job training, Project CRAFT is a comprehensive approach to high-risk youth. In partnership with schools, court staff, drug and alcohol counselors and treatment programs, private organizations, mentors, local governments, and juvenile court judges, Project CRAFT demonstrates the importance of addressing youth difficulties through a cooperative and inclusive strategy. An independent evaluation of Project CRAFT illustrates that over a four-year period, graduates of the program had a very high job placement in the home building industry; the recidivism rate for youth who were involved in the program at three of the sites was 26%, which was significantly lower than the national average; and the program has been success- ful in continuing to work with youthful offenders long after they have been placed in jobs, particularly those youth who were in residential facilities (Hamilton and McKinney, 1999:2).

Identifying Risk Factors

Project CRAFT successfully demonstrates that agencies and organizations can inter- vene collaboratively in the lives of troubled youth. However, to prevent youth from engaging in delinquent conduct, it is helpful to identify risk factors (Catalano et al., 1999:1). The Office of Juvenile Justice and Delinquency Prevention convened 22 researchers for the Study Group on Serious and Violent Juvenile Offenders. They con- cluded that there are a number of interventions that have demonstrated positive effects in reducing risk and enhancing protection against adolescent antisocial behaviors. Family, school, and community interventions are critical in preventing children from becoming violent (Catalano et al., 1999:1).

One of the 10 effective intervention programs that the study group identified is Behavioral Monitoring. This program is designed to provide disruptive, low-achieving seventh-grade students with close supervision and rewards for positive behavior. For two years, intervention staff and teachers met regularly to assess student tardiness, class preparedness, performance, and behavior (Catalano et al., 1999:2). In addition, staff members worked with students in small group sessions and reviewed their school behavior. Staff members continued meeting with teachers and held small review sessions for students every two weeks for one year after the interventions (Catalano et al., 1999:2).

The results indicate that the comprehensive intervention strategy was successful. Students who were monitored had significantly higher grades, better attendance, and engaged in far fewer problem behaviors at school than students in a comparison group which received no interventions (Bry and George, cited in Catalano et al., 1999:2). Even after five years, youth who had received the intervention were far less likely to have a juvenile court record than youth who were not in the program (Bry cited in Catalano et al., 1999:2).

The study group also identified comprehensive community intervention programs. Of particular interest were the collaborative community intervention efforts that were designed to deter youth smoking and alcohol use in Minnesota (Catalano et al., 1999:6). Project Northland, an alcohol prevention program, was initiated when children were in the sixth grade and demonstrates another effective collaborative effort. The project included a special curriculum in the school and community-wide task force activities that involved parents and peer leadership. After three years, children who completed the program had lower scores on a tendency-to-use-alcohol scale and showed considerably lower rates of alcohol use. The participants were also less at risk for drug use (Catalano et al., 1999:6).

Parenting Programs

Parenting programs are also an integral component of a comprehensive prevention strategy. One of the more successful interventions focuses on parenting skills that identifies youth who are at risk, reduces their risk factors, and attempts to prevent them from becoming involved in delinquent activities by augmenting protective factors. Preparing for the Drug Free Years began in 1987 and is designed for adult learners (i.e., parents) who have children in grades four through seven (Haggerty et al., 1999). The goal of the program is "to empower parents of children ages 8 to 14 to reduce the risks that their children will abuse drugs or alcohol or develop other common adolescent problems" (Haggerty et al., 1999:1).

Preparing for the Drug Free Years is delivered through video presentation and requires a minimum of 10 hours. The program is typically offered by two trained workshop leaders from the community, and they are encouraged to increase the number of hours and topic areas as appropriate. Thus far, there have been over 120,000 families in 30 states who have participated in the program (Haggerty et al., 1999:1,6).

Preliminary evaluations indicate that the program is effective in teaching important parenting concepts to a wide audience. Parents appear to adopt the approaches, including family meetings, which are an important part of the curriculum. The utilization of instructors who are community leaders also appears to be effective. In addition, when parents volunteer to participate, they generally attend most of the sessions. Although more evaluation is needed, the Preparing for the Drug Free Years Program is easily disseminated, inclusive, and a successful strategy for parents of children who may be at risk for becoming delinquent (Haggerty et al., 1999:9).

Low-Birth Weight Babies

Recent research suggests the importance of intervention efforts before or shortly after birth. In their longitudinal analysis of low birthweight and its relationship to early-onset offending of minority youth in Philadelphia, Tibbetts and Piquero (1999) found that individuals with low birthweight who were from a low-socioeconomic status group were more likely to have an early onset of offending (p. 865). Low birthweight is often associated with a number of factors, including lack of prenatal care for pregnant women, drugs and/or alcohol use, smoking cigarettes during pregnancy, poor diet, low socioeconomic status, and low educational attainment level (Tibbetts and Piquero, 1999:848). The good news is that low birthweight can be prevented through early intervention programs; and these strategies reduce the complications associated with low birthweight (Tibbetts and Piquero, 1999:868–869). Effective intervention policies which include good-quality prenatal care and nurse home visitation programs can be developed in communities.

Although there are many other successful programs that target youthful offenders, the programs described above provide evidence that successful strategies can be implemented and refined to deliver services to at-risk youth and their families. These programs are more cost-effective and more humane than punishment and long-term incarceration for juvenile offenders. Rather than developing reactive programs, juvenile justice is in an unprecedented position. With sufficient resources, it will be able to expand programs with demonstrable success (Merlo, 2000).

ISSUES FOR THE FUTURE

In the early decades of the twenty-first century, the juvenile justice system will devote increasing attention to at least four issues: gangs, disproportionate minority representation, the death penalty, and juveniles incarcerated in adult institutions. In addition, rather than simply retaining or abolishing the tenets of the original juvenile court, there will be a greater emphasis on balancing and integrating three alternative models for handling juvenile offenders.

Gangs

In the closing decades of the twentieth century, sensationalized media attention to gangs and gang violence helped to exacerbate public concern with youth crime. Esbensen (2000) notes that the "superpredator" model that DiIulio and Fox predicted helped foster the belief that gang members were the forerunners of this coming wave of a new breed of young criminals. Even though their projections regarding violent youth have not been realized, attention has focused on gang crimes as well as female involvement in gangs. Although some evidence suggests that females may comprise more than one-third of gang members (Esbensen and Winfree, 1998; Miller and Brunson, 2000:422), Snyder and Sickmund observe that the number of girls and nonminority males who view themselves as gang members is much greater than the official law enforcement records indicate (1999:78).

Girl gang members are not identical to their male counterparts, and in fact, have a number of differences. In their study of 58 male and female gang members (who ranged in age from 12 to 20) in St. Louis, Missouri, in 1997 and 1998, Miller and Brunson (2000) found that when describing their risk of victimization, young girls and young boys perceived different risks. Whereas males verbalized fear of being "lethally victimized" (i.e., killed) by a rival gang, female gang members perceived that their greatest risk was being "jumped and beaten up" (2000:442). Miller and Brunson contend that it is important to study variations in gangs to fully understand the risks faced by females. Although many of the gangs' activities are mundane, some of them are quite dangerous (2000:443).

Gang composition is dependent on the location and size of the community. For example, the 1998 National Youth Gang Survey found that whites comprise 11% of gang members in larger cities and approximately 30% of gang members in rural counties and small cities (National Youth Gang Survey Center, in press, cited by Esbensen, 2000:3). Although gang migration was thought to be responsible for the increasing presence of gangs in various parts of the United States, there is no evidence to substantiate that claim. To the contrary, most gang members are residents of the urban, suburban, or rural area where their gangs exist (Snyder and Sickmund, 1999:78).

From available research, it appears that delinquent activity, which typically precedes gang involvement, is enhanced through gang membership (Snyder and Sickmund, 1999; Esbensen 2000:6). This suggests that prevention efforts have to target at-risk youth as well as youth who have already joined gangs (Esbensen, 2000:6; Wyrick, 2000:2). In particular, some important steps to discourage gangs and gang membership include (Howell and Decker, 1999:9) (1) early identification of at-risk youth in rural as well as urban areas, (2) implementation of comprehensive community-based programs, (3) programs to reduce truancy and keep youth in school; (4) employment opportunities for youth; (5) increased efforts to remove guns from the street; and (6) community participation in a collaborative strategy designed to deter youth from engaging in delinquent behavior.

Disproportionate Minority Representation

Despite attention on racial profiling, disproportionate minority representation in the juvenile justice system will persist and strategies to reduce the overrepresentation of minorities will need to focus on broader social issues. As discussed earlier, minority youth are overrepresented in the juvenile justice system in every stage of the process.

Snyder and Sickmund contend, however, that there is evidence "that disparity is most pronounced at the beginning stages" of juvenile justice (1999:193). It is arrest, detention, and intake where the greatest disparity in outcomes occurs, and it is these actions that have profound consequences for youth (Bilchik, 1999b:3).

In 1997, minorities comprised 34% of the total juvenile population in the United States and 62% of all juveniles detained (Office of Juvenile Justice and Delinquency Prevention, 1999a:4). Black youth were almost twice as likely to be detained as white youth, even when researchers controlled for offense. Black youth charged with drug offenses were most likely to be detained (p. 9).

Although these findings pertain to confinement in juvenile facilities, Bilchik contends that "disproportionate minority confinement sends a signal that we need to take a closer look at how our society treats minority children, not just those who become offenders" (1999b:1). Even as Feld (1993, 1999b) has advocated for the abolition of the juvenile court, he has recognized the importance of "providing a hopeful future for all young people," which includes "the pursuit of racial and social justice" and "public policies that reduce and reverse the proliferation of guns among the youth population" (1999a: 394). His analysis of the social structural changes that contributed to "the disproportionate overrepresentation of minority youth in the juvenile justice system" underscores the importance of focusing policy on reducing poverty, urban disorder, minority alienation, and violence.

Capital Punishment

Use of the death penalty for juveniles will continue, but this issue will be more strenuously contested. In 1988, in *Thompson* v. *Oklahoma*, the U.S. Supreme Court ruled that the death penalty could not be utilized for juveniles who are under 16 years of age at the time of the offense. In 1989, in *Stanford* v. *Kentucky*, the U.S. Supreme Court determined that the Eighth Amendment does not preclude the utilization of capital punishment for youth who are 16 or 17 at the time of the offense (Snyder and Sickmund, 1999:211). Currently, there are 20 states that authorize capital punishment for juveniles who were 16 when they committed the offense and four states that authorize capital punishment for youth who were 17 when the offense was committed (Bartollas and Miller, 2001:152). From 1973 to 1998, Texas sentenced more offenders to death (42) who were under age 18 than any of the other states (Snyder and Sickmund, 1999:212).

Recently, the controversy regarding the use of the death penalty for both youth and adults has become more public. This is due, in part, to DNA testing, which has resulted in some adult offenders being exonerated and released from death row. Although the death penalty is still supported by the public, increased media attention and debate regarding capital punishment and egregious flaws in the system have lowered support for executions. The current criticisms of the death penalty will probably lead to two changes: more interest in the DNA testing of persons suspected of committing a serious crime and more monitoring to assure that indigent offenders are represented by attorneys who specialize in capital cases.

Adultification

As more juveniles are transferred to adult court, greater demands will be placed on adult correctional institutions and their staff. This will necessitate construction or renovation of jails, construction of new "juvenile prisons" for youthful offenders, and renovation of adult institutions to accommodate the changing demographics of the prison population. In 1997, there were 9100 youth under the age of 18 held on any given day in adult jails (Snyder and Sickmund, 1999:208) and 7400 inmates in state prisons were under age 18 (Johnson, 2000:A1; Strom, 2000:3).

Adolescents in adult institutions pose a formidable challenge for administrators. Not only do they face a greater risk of suicide and violent victimization, but they are also less likely to have the insight and maturity of the adult population (Ziedenberg and Schiraldi, 1997). As a result, they are more likely to be victims of sexual assault and staff abuse. A youthful offender serving a life sentence with no possibility of parole may also be a particularly difficult inmate to manage.

Models of Juvenile Justice

In addition to these specific challenges, responses to youthful offenders will continue to reflect competing ideologies and politicized public policies. Rather than adhering to a strict punishment or treatment model, juvenile justice in the twenty-first century will be characterized by a multifaceted approach that will incorporate three models: Prevention, Education and Treatment (PET), Balance and Restorative Justice (BARJ), and Retribution, Adultification, and Punishment (RAP).

The Prevention, Education, and Treatment (PET) model symbolizes the philosophical orientation of the original juvenile court. In this model, there is increasing reliance on prevention/early intervention programs to deter youth from offending. As evidenced by the recent research by Cullen et al. (1998), the public appears to be supportive of early intervention/prevention programs. Child-centered strategies, which were once the mainstay of juvenile justice, have been expanded to include parenting programs, prenatal care, and preschool programs, along with prevention programs for adolescents. These are comprehensive strategies such as antigang programs for adolescents, special after-school programs for at-risk youth, and counseling programs for youthful offenders.

The Balanced and Restorative Justice (BARJ) model, which emphasizes accountability, public safety, and competency development for juveniles, has been adopted in several jurisdictions (Bazemore and Umbreit, 1995). Rather than focusing solely on youth, this model incorporates community safety and protection along with holding youth accountable, compensating victims, and providing treatment. Programs such as teen courts, drug courts, boot camp programs, and victim restitution/community service programs are emblematic of this perspective. With the inclusion of accountability, punishment, and public safety in the purpose clause of juvenile court statutes, it is clear that this perspective has been endorsed and supported (see Bilchik, 1999a).

The third model, Retribution, Adultification, and Punishment (RAP), rejects earlier perspectives on youth and adolescence and supports a tough, punitive approach to dealing with youthful offenders. This is the legacy of the get-tough era of the 1980s and 1990s and legislative reforms that politicized youth policies. The manifestations are evident in the number of states that lowered the age for transfer to adult court, the number of youth waived to adult court, the increased number of youth incarcerated in adult institutions (some sentenced to life without possibility of parole), and the number of states that enacted blended sentences (statutes that authorize the courts to utilize juvenile and/or adult correctional sanctions) (Bilchik, 1999a:19).

The continuum of these "trifurcated" approaches incorporates the themes of early intervention and prevention, accountability and public safety, and punishment and retribution. This conceptualization more accurately reflects juvenile justice policies that embody both preventive interventions and reactive sanctions. Rather than being limited to one approach, public policies for dealing with delinquent offenders will utilize strategies that reflect these perspectives. Juvenile justice is poised to proceed in this direction. Even though get-tough political rhetoric and adultification legislation have characterized juvenile justice in the last 15 years, the juvenile justice system will continue with its mission to help youthful offenders and reduce delinquency.

REFERENCES

ALBANESE, J. S. (1993). *Dealing with Delinquency: The Future of Juvenile Justice*, 2nd ed. Chicago: Nelson-Hall.

ANON. (1999a). Fifth student pleads innocent to plot. *Erie Times News*, November 6, p. A5.

ANON. (1999b). Expulsions for bringing weapons to school down sharply. *New York Times*, August 10. nytimes.com/yr/mo/day/late/guns.html.

ANON. (1999c). For kids, a badge is no shield. *Washington Post*, October 10, p. B6.

APPLEGATE, B. K., and S. SANTANA (2000). Intervening with youthful substance abusers: A preliminary analysis of a juvenile drug court. *Justice System Journal*, 21(3):281–300.

BALZ, D. (1999). Autumn marks a season for substance. *Washington Post National Weekly Edition*, September 13, p. 11.

BARBOZA, D. (2000). Boy, 6, accused in classmate's killing. *New York Times*, March 1. nytimes.com.

BARTOLLAS, C., and S. J. MILLER (2001). *Juvenile Justice in America*. 3rd ed. Upper Saddle River, NJ: Prentice Hall.

BAZEMORE, G., and M. UMBREIT (1994). *Balanced and Restorative Justice: Program Summary*. Office of Juvenile Justice and Delinquency Prevention. Washington, DC: Office of Justice Programs, October.

BAZEMORE, G., and M. UMBREIT (1995). Rethinking the sanctioning function in juvenile court: Retributive or restorative responses to youth crime. *Crime and Delinquency*, 41(3):293–316.

BENEKOS, P. J., and A. V. MERLO (2000). The future of the juvenile court: Reaffirmation or requiem?" Paper presented at the annual meeting of the Academy of Criminal Justice Sciences, New Orleans, LA, March 21.

BERNARD, T. J. (1992). *The Cycles of Juvenile Justice*. New York: Oxford University Press.

BERNARD, T. J. (1999). Juvenile crime and the transformation of juvenile justice: Is there a juvenile crime wave? *Justice Quarterly*. 16(2):337–356.

BILCHIK, S. (1999a). *Juvenile Justice: A Century of Change*. Office of Juvenile Justice and Delinquency Prevention. Washington, DC: Office of Justice Programs, December.

BILCHIK, S. (1999b). *Minorities in the Juvenile Justice System*. Office of Juvenile Justice and Delinquency Prevention. Washington, DC: Office of Justice Programs, December.

BORTNER, M. A. (1988). *Delinquency and Justice: An Age of Crisis*. New York: McGraw-Hill.

BRADSHER, K. (1999). Murder trial of 13-year-old puts focus on Michigan law. *New York Times*, October 31, p. A21.

BRADSHER, K. (2000). Boy who killed gets 7 years; judge says law is too harsh. *New York Times*, January 14, pp. A1, 21.

BUREAU OF JUSTICE STATISTICS (1999a). Serious violent crime levels continued to decline in 1998. ojp.usdoj.gov/bjs/glance/cv2.htm.

BUREAU OF JUSTICE STATISTICS (1999b). National Crime Victimization Survey, crime trends, 1973–1998. ojp.usdoj.gov/bjs/glance/viotrd.txt.

BUTTERFIELD, F. (1999). FBI study finds gun use in violent crimes declining. *New York Times*, October 18, p. A16.

BUTTS, J. A., and A. V. HARRELL (1998a). *One-Size-Fits-All Justice Simply Isn't Fair*. Washington, DC: Urban Institute, December 1.

BUTTS, J. A., and A. V. HARRELL (1998b). *Crime Policy Report: Delinquents or Criminals: Policy Options for Young Offenders*. Washington, DC: Urban Institute.

BUTTS, J. A., D. HOFFMAN, and J. BUCK (1999). *Teen Courts in the United States: A Profile of Current Programs*. Office of Juvenile Justice and Delinquency Prevention, Office of Justice Programs. Washington DC: U.S. Department of Justice, October.

CALIFORNIA SECRETARY OF STATE (2000). 2000 California primary election ballot measure summary. Vote2000.ss.ca.gov/VoterGuide/summary_21_22.htm.

CATALANO, R. F., R. LOEBER, and K. C. MCKINNEY (1999). School and community interventions to prevent serious and violent offending. *Juvenile Justice Bulletin*, October, pp. 1–12.

CLAIBORNE, W. (1999). *Study: Racial Disparity in School Discipline*. Washington, DC: Center on Juvenile and Criminal Justice, December 17. cjcj.org/jpi/washpost121799.

CLINES, F. X. (1999). Columbine spurs pilot computer program to spot potentially violent students. *New York Times*, October 24, p. A16.

CULLEN, F. T., J. P. WRIGHT, S. BROWN, M. M. MOON, M. B. BLANKENSHIP, and B. K. APPLEGATE (1998). Public support for early intervention programs: Implications for a progressive policy agenda. *Crime and Delinquency*, 44(2):187–204.

DORNING, M. (2000). Dramatic drop in U.S. crime continued in '99. *Chicago Tribune*, August 28. Chicagotribune.com/news/printededition/.

ESBENSEN, F.-A. (2000). Preventing adolescent gang involvement. *Juvenile Justice Bulletin*, September, pp. 1–11.

ESBENSEN, F.-A., and L. T. WINFREE, JR. (1998). Race and gender differences between gang and non-gang youth: Results from a multisite survey. *Justice Quarterly*, 15(3):505–526.

FELD, B. (1993). Juveniles (in) justice and the criminal court alternative. *Crime and Delinquency*, 39:403–424.

FELD, B. (1999a). The transformation of the juvenile court, Part II: Race and the "crack down" on youth crime. *Minnesota Law Review*, 84(2):327–395.

FELD, B. (1999b). *Bad Kids: Race and the Transformation of the Juvenile Court*. New York: Oxford University Press.

FINLEY, M., and M. SCHINDLER (1999). Punitive juvenile justice policies and the impact on minority youth. *Federal Probation*, LXIII (2):11–15.

FORUM ON CHILD AND FAMILY STATISTICS (1999a). Indicators of youth violent crime and victimization show continuing declines, July 8. childstats.gob/ac1999/teenrel.asp.

FORUM ON CHILD AND FAMILY STATISTICS (1999b). Federal agencies report on nation's children, July 8. childstat.gob/ac1999/pressrel.asp.

FRAZIER, C. E., D. M. BISHOP, and L. LANZA-KADUCE (1999). Get-tough juvenile justice reforms: The Florida experience. *Annals of the American Academy of Political and Social Science*, 564, July, p. 167. wysiwyg://bodyframe.16/http://ehostweb11.epnet.com/fulltext.asp.

GAMBLE, T. J., A. CUZZOLA-KERN, S. SONNENBERG, and L. ROBERTS (1999). Assessing the impact of a screening instrument on secure detention utilization in Erie County Pennsylvania. Paper presented at the annual meeting of the American Society of Criminology, Toronto, Ontario, Canada, November.

GARASE, M., and S. L. SONNENBERG (1999). Community alternatives to juvenile placements. Paper presented at the annual meeting of the American Society of Criminology, Toronto, Ontario, Canada, November.

GODWIN, T. M. (1996). *A Guide for Implementing Teen Court Programs*. Office of Juvenile Justice and Delinquency Prevention Fact Sheet 45. Washington, DC: Office of Justice Programs, August, pp. 1–2.

GOLDBERG, C., and M. CONNELLY (1999). Fear and violence have declined among teen-agers, poll shows. *New York Times*, October 20, pp. A1, 20.

GREENWOOD, P. (1998). Investing in prisons or prevention: The state policy makers' dilemma. *Crime and Delinquency*, 44(1):136–142.

GREENWOOD, P. (1999). *Costs and Benefits of Early Childhood Intervention*. Office of Juvenile Justice and Delinquency Prevention Fact Sheet. Washington, DC: Office of Justice Programs, February.

GROSSMAN, J. B., and E. M. GARRY (1997). *Mentoring: A Proven Delinquency Prevention Strategy*. Washington, DC: Office of Juvenile Justice and Delinquency Prevention, Office of Justice Programs, April.

HAGGERTY, K., R. KOSTERMAN, R. F. CATALANO, and J.D. HAWKINS (1999). *Preparing for the Drug Free Years*. Juvenile Justice Bulletin. Washington, DC: Office of Juvenile Justice and Delinquency Prevention, July, pp. 1–11.

HAMILTON, R., and K. McKinney (1999). Job Training for Juveniles: Project CRAFT. Office of Juvenile Justice and Delinquency Prevention Fact Sheet. Office of Juvenile Justice and Delinquency Prevention, Office of Justice Programs, Washington, D.C. (August): pp. 1–2.

HOWELL, J. C., and S. H. DECKER (1999). *The Youth Gangs, Drugs, and Violence Connection*. Office of Juvenile Justice and Delinquency Prevention Fact Sheet. Washington, DC: Office of Justice Programs, January, pp. 1–12.

INCIARDI, J. A., D. C. McBRIDE, and J. E. RIVERS (1996). *Drug Control and the Courts*. Thousand Oaks, CA: Sage Publications.

INITIATIVE INFO (2000). Stop the attack on youth! noprop21.org/Pages/info.html.

JOHNSON, K. (2000) "Youths in adult prisons double." USA Today. (February 28) p. A1.

JUSTICE POLICY INSTITUTE (1999). New report shows no increase in school shooting deaths over six-year period. cjcj.org/jpi/schoolhousepr.html.

JUSTICE POLICY INSTITUTE (2000). *School House Hype: Two Years Later*. Cjcj.org/schoolhousehype/.

KEENE-OSBORN, S., and D. GLICK (1999). Columbine's tragic wake. *Newsweek*, November 1, p. 42.

KRACKE, K. (1996). *Safe Futures: Partnerships to Reduce Youth Violence and Delinquency*. Washington, DC: Office of Juvenile Justice and Delinquency Prevention, Office of Justice Programs, December.

KUMPFER, K. L., and R. ALVARADO (1998). *Effective Family Strengthening Interventions.* Washington, DC: Office of Juvenile Justice and Delinquency Prevention, Office of Justice Programs, November.

LEVRANT, S., F, T. CULLEN, B. FULTON, and J. E. WOZNIAK (1999). Reconsidering restorative justice: The corruption of benevolence revisited? *Crime and Delinquency*, 45:3–27.

MAXSON, C. L. (1998). *Gang Members on the Move.* Washington, DC: Office of Juvenile Justice and Delinquency Prevention, Office of Justice Programs, October, pp. 1–11.

McLAUGHLIN, A. (1999) Easing get-tough approach on juveniles. *Christian Science Monitor*, August 16, p. A1.

MEREDITH, R. (1999). City shaken by reports of school shooting plot. *New York Times*, November 1, p. A10.

MERLO, A. V. (2000). Juvenile justice at the crossroads. Presidential address delivered at the Academy of Criminal Justice Sciences annual meeting, March 23, 2000, New Orleans, LA. *Justice Quarterly*, 17(4):701–723.

MERLO, A. V., and P. J. BENEKOS (2000). *What's Wrong with the Criminal Justice System: Ideology, Politics and the Media.* Cincinnati, OH: Anderson Publishing.

MERLO, A. V., P. J. BENEKOS, and W. J. COOK (1997). "Getting tough" with youth: Legislative waiver as crime control. *Juvenile and Family Court Journal*, 48(3):1–15.

MILLER, J., and R. K. BRUNSON (2000). Gender dynamics in youth gangs: A comparison of males' and females' accounts. *Justice Quarterly*, 17(3):419–448.

MINOR, K. I., J. B. WELLS, I. R. SODERSTROM, R. BINGHAM, and D. WILLIAMSON (1999). Sentence completion and recidivism among juveniles referred to teen courts. *Crime and Delinquency*, 45(4), October, pp. 467–480.

NATIONAL INSTITUTE ON DRUG ABUSE (1997). *Prevention principles for children and adolescents*, April 2. nida.nih.gov/Prevention/PREVPRINC.html.

NAUGHTON, K., and E. THOMAS (2000). Did Kayla have to die? *Newsweek*, March 13, pp. 25–29.

OFFICE OF JUVENILE JUSTICE AND DELINQUENCY PREVENTION (1999a). *1999 National Report Series: Minorities in the Juvenile Justice System.* Washington, DC: U.S. Department of Justice, Office of Justice Programs, December.

OFFICE OF JUVENILE JUSTICE AND DELINQUENCY PREVENTION (1999b). *Promising Strategies to Reduce Gun Violence.* Washington, DC: U.S. Department of Justice, Office of Justice Programs, February.

OHLIN, L. E. (1998). The future of juvenile justice policy and research. *Crime and Delinquency*, 44(1):143–153.

POWELL, H. (1999). School violence: Statistics reveal school violence declining. *The Mentor* (Center for Justice Research and Policy, Mercyhurst College), 1(1):4–6.

REPENNING, K., H. POWELL, A. DOANE, and H. DUNKLE (2000). Demystifying school violence: A national, state, and local perspective on the phenomenon of school violence. Paper presented at the annual meeting of the Academy of Criminal Justice Sciences, New Orleans, LA, March.

ROBERTS, L. M., and P. J. BENEKOS (1999). Assessing the feasibility of drug courts for youthful offenders. Paper presented at the annual meeting of the American Society of Criminology, Toronto, Ontario, Canada. November.

SCHIRALDI, V., and M. SOLER (1998). The will of the people: The public's opinion of the Violent and Repeat Juvenile Offender Act of 1997. *Crime and Delinquency*, 44(4):590–602.

SCHIRALDI, V., and J. ZIEDENBERG (1999). *The Florida Experiment: An Analysis of the Impact of Granting Prosecutors Discretion to Try Juveniles as Adults.* Washington, DC: Justice Policy Institute.

SCHIRALDI, V., and J. ZIEDENBERG (2000). *New Report Finds Public's Worries Grow Even As Schools Become Safer*. Washington, DC: Justice Policy Institute/Children's Law Center, April 12.

SENTENCING PROJECT (1999). *Briefing Paper: Prosecuting Juveniles in Adult Court*. Washington, DC. The Project. sentencingproject.org/brief/juveniles.html.

SHEPHERD, R. E., JR. (1999). The juvenile court at 100 years: A look back. *Juvenile Justice*, 6(2), December, pp. 13–21.

SHERMAN, L. W., D. GOTTFREDSON, D. MACKENZIE, J. ECK, P. REUTER, and S. BUSHWAY (1997). *Preventing Crime: What Works, What Doesn't, What's Promising*. Washington, DC: National Institute of Justice.

SNYDER, H. N. (1998). *Juvenile Arrests 1997*. Washington, DC: Office of Juvenile Justice and Delinquency Prevention, Office of Justice Programs.

SNYDER, H. N., and M. SICKMUND (1999). *Juvenile Offenders and Victims: 1999 National Report*. Washington, DC: National Center for Juvenile Justice. Office of Juvenile Justice and Delinquency Prevention, Office of Justice Programs, September.

STROM, K. J. (2000). *Profile of State Prisoners under Age 18, 1985–97*. Washington, DC: Bureau of Justice Statistics, Office of Justice Programs.

TIBBETTS, S. G, and A. R. PIQUERO (1999). The influence of gender, low birth weight, and disadvantaged environment in predicting early onset of offending: A test of Moffitt's interactional hypothesis. *Criminology*, 37(4), November, pp. 843–877.

WYRICK, P. A. (2000) *Vietnamese Youth Gang Involvement*. Washington, DC: Office of Juvenile Justice and Delinquency Prevention, Office of Justice Programs, February 1–2.

ZIEDENBERG J., and V. Shiraldi (1997). *The Risks Juveniles Face When They Are Incarcerated with Adults*. Washington, DC: Justice Policy Institute.

CASES

Commonwealth v. *Fisher*, 213 Pa. 48, Supreme Court of Pennsylvania (1905).

In re Gault, 387 U.S. 1; 87 S. Ct. 1248 (1967).

Stanford v. *Kentucky*, 492 U.S. 361 (1989).

Thompson v. *Oklahoma*, 102 S. Ct. (1988).

chapter 15

A Study of the Criminal Motivations of Sentenced Jail Inmates

Robert J. Meadows, Ph.D. and Kimberly L. Anklin, B.A.

ABSTRACT

The number of inmates at the federal, state, and local level is rising at an alarming rate. The most recent statistics and public outcries bring not only the demand for more prison and jail space, but more important, for ways to reduce recidivism, especially at the local level. To gain insight we need to obtain clarification about prisoner perceptions regarding criminal motivations and feelings about the effectiveness of confinement. One hundred three sentenced male inmates from the Todd Road Jail, Santa Paula, California, were interviewed. Utilizing this information, persons working in the social science fields may be better able to understand patterns of offenders, leading to improved methods of prediction, treatment, and reducing the problem of recidivism.

INTRODUCTION

There are a number of psychological and sociological theories explaining the causes of crime (Wilson and Herrnstein, 1985; Raine, 1993; Denno,1994). Modern research now supports a variety of physiological factors never before considered (Raine, 1993; Hickey, 1997). From environmental conditions, such as chemical toxins and pollution, to allergies and diet, in-depth studies allow such possibilities to be explored when attempting to understand criminal behavior. At the same time, society's patience and tolerance is decreasing, as has been proven by many recent policy changes. Each of us as private citizens can attest to the calamitous presence of malevolence in our daily lives (Goldberg, 1995). We are outraged when we hear of the ever-increasing crime rate and feel helpless as we are subjected to the 24-hour media coverage. These feelings are only exacerbated when such violent acts as car-jacking and shootings are committed close to home. Punitive legislation and longer prison sentences add pressure to an overburdened justice system. The economics of crime is shocking. Funds spent to sustain existing facilities and to build additional jails and prisons are at an all-time high. The costs of criminal behavior far surpasses the deficit, inflation, or any other economic problem (Rubenstein, 1995). In one year, 1992, the direct costs in cash, cars, and personal property came up to approximately $18 billion. However, this is only a fraction of the total costs, which include the cost to the victims. Mental and physical trauma, including depression and fear, can reduce a person's ability to function. Long periods of absenteeism at work can last a lifetime, and the costs nationally can reach $500 billion in one year.

Excluded from that figure are the funds spent on public safety. State and local governments spend over $80 billion per year on law enforcement, courts, prisons, and parole systems. The U.S. Department of Justice (USDOJ), Bureau of Justice Statistics (BJS) reported that in 1995, 1,585,400 persons were incarcerated in the United States (BJS, 1996). This means that one of every 167 U.S. citizens was incarcerated. Of every 100,000 residents, 600 were being held in a state, federal, or jail facility. Of the total incarcerated population, state and federal prisoners accounted for two-thirds (1,078,357 inmates) and the local jails supervised the remaining third (507,044 inmates). From 12 months prior, the total inmate population increased 7.3%, which is an average increase of 2064 inmates per week. Within the 10-year span 1985–1995, the incarcerated population increased 113%. Of every 100,000 U.S. residents, the total number of inmates increased from 200 to 409. State and federal prisoners averaged a 6.7% increase over a five-year span (1990–1995) and jails experienced a 4.6% increase. It is clear why there is so much pressure to build more prison facilities. Although it is estimated that the total number of incarcerated persons was close to 1.6 million in 1995, that number is only a portion of the more than 5 million people under some form of correctional supervision (BJS, 1996). These figures include state and federal prison, jail, probation, and parole. In 1995 the United States had the highest prisonization rate, four times greater than Canada, five times greater than England, and 14 times greater than Japan (Rubenstein, 1995).

Regarding the local jail population, the BJS (1996) reported that in 1995 the nation's jails supervised over 541,913 offenders. Ninety-four percent (507,044 inmates) were housed in local jails and the remaining 6% (34,869 inmates) were supervised by an alternative program. The BJS defines jails as "locally-operated correctional facilities that confine persons before or after adjudication" (1996:9). The majority of inmates sentenced to jail serve a year or less. At the same time, those incarcerated tend to be within a wide range of categories. They can include persons who are pending arraignment and are held awaiting trial, conviction, or sentencing; readmittance of parole and probation violators; housing inmates for federal or state authorities because of overcrowding; to those held for the military or for contempt of court, and mentally ill persons waiting to be moved to appropriate health facilities. The alternative supervision is used for those who are not housed in a conventional jail but rather, supervised outside a jail facility. Some of the these programs include electronic monitoring, home detention, and community service.

Who are the people occupying the jails? The gender and ethnic makeup for the national jail population, as of midyear 1995, shows that almost 90% are male and 10% are female (BJS, 1996). Sixty percent of jail inmates belonged to racial or ethnic minorities; blacks, 44%; whites, 40%; Hispanics, 15%; and 2%, other than black, Hispanic, or white. The data for the crimes committed are not detailed, but the BJS (1995a) report states that the largest source of growth among jailed inmates was those charged or convicted of drug offenses. In 1983, the total for drug offenders was 20,800. That figure rose to 91,000 in 1989, and by 1993, more than 105,800, five times as many as 1983. In 1983, one of every 10 inmates was in jail for a drug offense, and in 1989 the ratio was 1:4. Between 1983 and 1989 violent offenses decreased from 31% to 23%; property offenses were also reduced by 8%.

It has been suggested that drug use is a primary motivating factor when examining other crimes, especially those violent in nature (BJS, 1988). The BJS gives three reasons for this relationship of drugs and crime. First is the psychopharmacology argument. Drug use relaxes inhibitions and stimulates aggression, which can lead to the reduction of legitimately earning income. Second, in terms of economic compulsivity, those who have developed dependence on an illegal drug must find a way to obtain additional funds, and pay the black market prices, due to laws that control for illegal drug trafficking. The third reason is systemic: Due to the illegal drug trafficking, more serious crimes such as assault, extortion, and homicide are more frequent. Supporting the BJS's reasoning, the University of Nebraska conducted a recent study summarized in the National Institute of Justice's (NIJ, 1996) report and entitled "Adult Patterns of Criminal Behavior." Their results indicated that of the 658 newly convicted inmates, illegal drug use was related to all four measures of offending (any crime, property crime, assault, and drug crime). Their results suggest that by using drugs, the odds of committing a property crime increased by 54%. The probability of assault increased by over 100% and when committing any crime, drug use increased the chances sixfold. In an area known for its illegal drug market, the state of California was ranked third in violent crime per 100,000 residents in 1994 (FBI, 1996). Another related fact is the reduction of age and drug use.

Inciardi and Pottieger (1991) conducted a study of 254 adolescent crack users. Their findings indicated that within a one-year time frame, approximately 223,000 crimes (880 per subject) were attributed to these youths alone. Courts typically fail to consider a youth as a chronic offender until the person has been arrested five to six times, despite the fact that the offenders were arrested for only one of every 555 crimes. Calculating these figures suggests that within a year, each of these youths committed 2775 to 3330 crimes (Duncan et al., 1995). It seems clear that for those who abuse drugs, their drug dependency becomes a major motivator for criminal behavior.

Other variables contribute to reasons why people make choices leading to jail. More important, the continuation of these choices occurs after experiencing life behind bars or being placed on parole. As disturbing as it is to understand how many people go to jail the first time, it is equally disturbing to comprehend the high percentage of repeat offenders. There are some estimates reaching as high as one-half to almost three-fourths of the present prison population as having been previously incarcerated (Allen, 1996). Of those released from prison during any given year, as many as 60 to 70% will return within five years (Allen, 1996).

For some offenders, the pattern of recidivism and the escalation into more serious crimes seems almost predictable. There are personality disorders that show common-alties such as lack of concern for others. What begins as a mistake ends at the state and federal level or even on death row. However, does a crime begin as just a "mistake"? Or are we witnessing the results of a mental disorder, such as attention deficit disorder (ADD) or attention deficit/ hyperactivity disorder (ADHD), manifesting into a personality disorder? All of the criteria for these mental and personality disorders have the tendency of undertaking risky and criminal behaviors (e.g., drug use). Hyperactivity and attention deficits have long been recognized in children who exhibit chronic behavioral problems (Goldstein, 1996). ADD and ADHD are being taken more seriously, especially since there seems to be a strong connection to criminal behavior (Goldstein and Goldstein, 1995; Quinsey and Reid, 1996; Wilson, 1997).

Mental health and criminal justice professionals are recognizing that as children exhibiting these patterns grow into adolescence and adulthood, they are at a higher risk of offending. Some of the characteristics of ADD in adults (Amen, 1997) are as follows:

- Past history of symptoms of ADD as a child, including distractibility, short attention span, impulsivity or restlessness, frequent behavior problems in school, and family problems.
- As an adult, one has a short attention span and can easily be distracted. Examples can be trouble with details and listening to directions.
- Restlessness and constant motion, which may include leg movement and fidgetiness.
- An internal sense of anxiety or extreme nervousness.
- Impulsivity that can be seen by frequent traffic violations, frequent and impulsive job changes, tendency to embarrass others, and/or lying or stealing on impulse.
- Negative internal feelings, including mood swings and a sense of impending doom.
- Problems with interpersonal relationships. May have trouble maintaining relationships and trouble with intimacy, can lack empathy, be verbally abusive, have a short fuse, and experience trouble with authority.
- Frequently searching for high stimulation, including gambling, race car driving, bungee jumping, and the need to be in a high-stress job.
- Cognitive dysfunctions, including frequently getting stuck in a thought or behavior. May show signs of dyslexia or turning words around in a conversation. May have poor writing skills, poor handwriting and coordination difficulties.

The *Diagnostic and Statistical Manual*, fourth edition (DSM-IV) (American Psychiatric Association, 1994:629) defines antisocial personality disorder (ASPD) as "an enduring pattern of inner experience and behavior that deviates markedly from the expectations of the individual's culture, as pervasive and inflexible, has an onset in adolescence or early adulthood, is stable over time, and leads to distress or impairment." One of the criteria is that the person be 18 years old; prior to that age, a similar pattern would be diagnosed as conduct disorder (CD).

Both disorders show a pattern of violation of and disregard for the rights of others. Those with ASPD have little or no empathy for others, are deceitful, and manipulate to obtain personal profit or pleasure. The term *ASPD* has also been interchangeable with *psychopathy* and *sociopathy* (Beck and Freeman, 1990). In fact, most of the empirical research used subjects who were criminals instead of psychiatric patients. Although there is overlapping in all three terms, there is no universal set of defining criteria. The reason for addressing these disorders is that moral maturity and cognitive development are stunted in these people. Simply, their behavior is that of a young child who is unable to think abstractly, or consider the rights of others, with poor impulse control. The only conceptual abilities they rely on are concrete and immediate rewards. Therefore, treatment must be behavior modification and cognitive reconstruction. Prisons and jails must be consistent with their rewards and punishments.

Aside from those with ASPD and/or psychopathy for a moment, how do we reach those who want to live life differently? The best of programs can be offered, but if self-efficacy and self-worth are lacking, the programs will lose their effectiveness. By fear of inability, the offender will surely return. If there is a way to teach self-worth along with social skills, employment, and education, can we reduce the rate of recidivism and the escalation of crime?

The purpose of the present study is to collect local statistics and gain insight into the inmates' thought processes. Information on state and federal inmates is very complete and detailed but not on those serving shorter sentences in local jails. Certainly, reasons for not compiling such data would include cost, but also the data would quickly be obsolete because of the short sentences. However, more information is needed as to what brings a person to jail in the first place and why they return. To aid local law enforcement agencies and officials it would seem beneficial to obtain such information and to customize programs better suited for this population. Developing programs that reduce recidivism rates and teach impulse control need to begin with the basic understanding of why people make the choices that lead them to jail in the first place. Before one can change behavior, one must recognize that he or she has a lifestyle problem and must want to do something about it. What better place to start than with those who have the best chance, people who are going to serve a year or less before they escalate to more serious crimes?

Out of the 25 largest local jail jurisdictions, California ranked first in frequency, with seven of its counties included (BJS, 1996). Florida was second with five counties and Texas third with four counties. The two jurisdictions with the most inmates nationally were Los Angeles County and New York City. Together, they housed more than 36,300 inmates; at the time the two jurisdictions accounted for 7% of the total local jail inmate population. In Ventura County, California, there are three jails: the Ventura County Jail, the Ojai Honor Farm, and the Todd Road Jail. The Todd Road Jail facility opened March 15, 1995 and is located in Santa Paula. Its purpose was to reduce the overcrowding of the Ventura County Jail, and at the same time, operate with less staff than that of similar-sized facilities, thereby reducing costs to taxpayers. This 230,000-square foot complex has 400 cells and accommodates up to 800 inmates with plans to expand over the next 20 years to house 2300 inmates. Those prisoned in the Todd Road Jail are sentenced men. As indicated by the BJS (1995b), the increase in incarcerated individuals has remained mostly male, minority, and young. It was for this reason that we chose our sample from the Todd Road Jail. Contrary to what one might believe, information gained through interviews with inmates is generally reliable (BJS,1995b). Usually, inmates' responses agree with data from official records, and findings do not differ much from information reported by correctional authorities. Information from separate surveys fit coherent and consistent patterns, as the self-reporting data indicate. By surveying inmates at a local jail we will gain an understanding as to how they perceive their crime, their confinement, future plans, and so on. Do they possess the desire not to repeat the past, and has serving time deterred them in any way?

A copy of the questionnaire appears in the appendix to this chapter. It addresses the following issues:

- What was the offender's primary motivating factor?
- Was the crime planned?
- Was the crime committed alone?
- Did the inmate have any fear of being caught?
- What reason would most likely have prevented the person from committing the crime?
- Was the victim someone the offender knew?
- Was any harm inflicted on the victim?
- Did the offender experience any remorse, either at the scene or afterward?
- Was a weapon used?
- Was there any drug and/or alcohol use during the crime?
- Has the offender served any time in a state prison?
- What would keep the person from returning to jail?
- Was the offender on probation or parole at the time of the current offense?
- Is there a history or record of violence as a juvenile?
- With regards to the three-strikes law, how many strikes does the inmate have thus far?

METHOD

Participants

One hundred three sentenced male inmates from the Todd Road Jail participated in the study. However, 22 inmates terminated the interviews or did not want to answer all the questions. As a result, there were 81 responses. The interviews were conducted between October 1996 and March 1997. The participants ranged in age from 18 to 60, with a mean age of 30.45 (SD = 8.90). Of this sample, 59.3% were Hispanic, 28.4% were Caucasian, 3.7% were African-American, and 8.6 % chose not to disclose their ethnicity. Crimes committed by subjects in this study included drug offenses (26%), property offenses (38%), crimes against persons (30%), and parole violations (5%).

Procedure

The survey research method employed followed a structured interview process. The interviewers consisted of students and one faculty member. A 16-item questionnaire was developed to interview the inmates. The questionnaire was derived from several sources, including previous research on victimology and offender motivation (Cromwell, 1996; Erickson and Stenseth, 1996) and suggested questions from the Todd Road Jail staff. The questionnaire was pretested with the general staff and volunteer inmates for clarity. The interviews were conducted by criminal justice and psychology students from California Lutheran University. The participants were reassured that the information reported would be kept confidential and were told that they had the right to terminate the interview at anytime. The percentages were calculated for all the variables. For the percentages of each variable, see Table 1. Percentages may not add up to 100%, due to rounding or missing data.

DISCUSSION

The sample showed that the percentage of Hispanics (59%) was much greater than the national representation of 15%; however, the Hispanic population is greater in southern California and this should not be considered significant. Inmates under the age of 35 years represented 90% of the population. National data for the average age at the jail level were not available. However, the BJS (1995b) reported that 68% of the state prison population were younger than 35 years in 1991. In terms of the type of crimes committed, our sample of parole violators accounted for only 5% of the total. However, 77% were on probation or parole during the time of the current offense. Property and drug offenses accounted for 64% of the crimes committed. Examples of a property crime included stealing cars and breaking into a residence or business, and the purchase and/or sale of illegal drugs were common among drug offenders. As mentioned earlier, the University of Nebraska study found that these two offenses, as well as those who committed crimes including violence, were highly related (NIJ, 1996). As indicated, drug offenders represented most offenders, which is not different from the previous data. Thirty-seven percent reported their reason for committing their crime as a need for money to obtain drugs. Twenty-five percent answered "excitement/thrill" as the primary motive, which may be an indication of ADHD and/or ASPD. In other words, these offenders admitted that they didn't think about the consquences of their actions, suggesting impulsive behavior. For those who chose "other" as their option, some of the responses included "maintaining a certain lifestyle," "under the influence," and "just wasn't thinking." These answers seem to concur with the behavior that using drugs subjects a person to act on impulse,

TABLE 1 Variables Examined for Todd Road Jail Represented in Percent and Frequency (Percents Rounded)

	N	%		N	%
Type of crime			Idea		
Drug	21	26	Own idea	58	72
Property	31	38	Coaxed by another	8	10
Violent	24	30	Mutual decision	3	4
Parole breach	4	5	Valid cases	69	
Valid cases	80		Missing cases	12	
Missing cases	1		Alone		
Race			Alone	56	69
White	23	28	With one other	15	19
Black	3	4	With more than one	10	12
Hispanic	48	59	Valid cases	81	
Valid cases	74		Missing cases	0	
Missing cases	7		Fear		
Age			Yes	24	30
35 yr	54	90	No	52	64
18–24	23	28	Concerned	2	3
25–34	31	38	Valid cases	78	
35–44	19	19	Missing cases	3	
45–54	5	6	Prevention		
55–64	2	1	Security officer	12	15
65+	0	0	Camera equipment	5	6
Valid cases	79		Victim carries gun	7	9
Missing cases	2		Long prison term	9	11
Motive			Alarms	3	4
Money for drugs	30	37	Neighborhood watch (signs indicating such)	1	1
Need cash/property	2	3	On probation	5	6
Excitement/thrill	20	25	Other	39	48
Other	29	36	Valid cases	81	
Valid cases	81		Missing cases	0	
Missing cases	0		Victim knowledge		
Planning			No	55	68
Planned	14	17	Acquaintance	17	21
Unplanned	67	83	Knew personally	0	0
Valid cases	81		Valid cases	72	
Missing cases	0		Missing cases	9	

TABLE 1 *(continued)*

	N	%		N	%
Victim Harm			Avoid returning to jail		
No	60	74	Good job	28	35
Yes	13	16	Family support	25	31
(unintentional)			Relocating	1	1
Yes	1	1	Fear of arrest	9	11
(intentional)			(and returning to jail)		
Valid cases	74		Other	16	20
Missing cases	7		Valid cases	79	
Remorse			Missing cases	2	
No	30	37	Probation/parole during current offense		
Yes	42	52	Yes	62	77
Other	9	11	No	18	22
Valid cases	81		Valid cases	80	
Missing cases	0		Missing cases	1	
Weapon used during crime			Juvenile record for violence		
Gun	5	6	Yes	37	46
Knife	8	10	No	43	53
None	62	77	Valid cases	80	
Other	5	6	Missing cases	1	
Valid cases	80		Three-strikes law		
Missing cases	1		(how many strikes currently)		
Use of drugs/alcohol at time of offense			None	40	49
Yes	24	30	One	10	12
No	57	70	Two	21	26
Valid cases	81		Don't know	1	1
Missing cases	0		Valid cases	72	
State prison time served			Missing cases	9	
Yes	52	64			
No	29	36			
Valid cases	81				
Missing cases	0				

thereby functioning in a certain lifestyle that is often unstable. Also, 83% of the inmates said they did not plan their crime, that it was done on impulse. It would there-fore seem reasonable to believe that 69% committed their crimes alone and 72% came up with idea themselves, which is another indication of impulsive, reckless behavior and disorganized thinking.

The majority were not afraid (64%) of arrest or getting caught, and in fact 77% were on probation or parole at the time of the current offense. Our findings support past research conducted by Neal Shover and David Honaker (1992), as cited in Cromwell (1996), that for the most part, a criminal's decision making does not include the possibility of arrest and confinement. Probation or parole status is not a major factor in prevention. Their study acquired a sample of 60 recidivists who were all property offenders nearing their release date. Sixty-two percent said the thought of arrest did not enter their mind. The remaining 38% admitted fear of arrest, but either quickly and easily dismissed the thought or made a conscious effort to block the thought from their mind and proceeded with the crime.

Cromwell (1996:14) used the following analogy to help explain the true lack of fear existing: "Just as bricklayers do not visualize graphically or deliberate over the bodily carnage that could follow from a collapsed scaffold once there is a job to be done, many thieves apparently do not dwell at length on the likelihood of arrest or on the pains of imprisonment when proceeding to search out or exploit suitable criminal opportunities." From our sample, 30% admitted the fear of arrest. Also, when asked if they felt remorse for their crimes, 52% answered "yes," but only after some time had passed. Unquestionably, this percentage is inflated, as many want to answer in a positive manner. It also suggests that feelings of remorse and fear are used to persuade a person to consider new patterns of thinking and relating.

In terms of inmates' view of measures preventing them from committing the crime in the first place, security measures accounted for 34%. In other words, inmates specifically felt that patrolling security officers, a civilian carrying a gun, closed-circuit cameras, and alarms on or at the property are good deterrents. They expressed no thoughts of detection or apprehension otherwise. Once again, these tactics are concrete and the consequences are immediate. For the morally immature or opportunists, security measures appear to be deterrents for a number of inmates. In a study of armed robbers incarcerated in state prisons, this theory is supported (Erickson and Stenseth, 1996). One of the most important findings was that the presence of an armed security officer was a good robbery deterrent. Stores with poor escape routes and privately owned stores where owners were more likely to possess a gun were reported by inmates to be deterrents.

In contrast, criminal justice measures (e.g., probation, parole, long sentences) do not deter as well, as they are intangible and often inconsistent. If, for instance, a criminal commits a crime, is not caught, or receives a light punishment, it produces an effect opposite to that the justice system intended. Unfortunately, this only serves as reinforcement to increase or intensify existing behavior. In fact, our sample indicates that 52 inmates (64%) had previously served time in a state prison, and 46% (37 inmates) had juvenile records that included violence. Interestingly, the community measure of posting neighborhood watch signs accounted for only 1% prevention. This type of prevention suggests that criminals have the ability to foresee consequences. With this understanding it is generalized that the criminal's only concerns center around immediate gratification and self-preservation.

The majority of our sample (68%) did not know their victim. A victim includes anyone who is harmed physically or financially due to some form of criminal activity. Typically, when one thinks of a victim, one tends to think of a person who has been assaulted. At the same time, someone who has lost property (i.e., burglary) has also suffered a loss due to criminal activity and therefore is also defined as a victim.

Seventy-four percent reported not inflicting any harm on their victim, which may correlate with the high percentage (77%) not using a weapon during the crime. Their intentions may not have included harming another; however, if approached, the offender would not hesitate to inflict injury. Thirty percent of the sample (24 inmates) committed a violent crime in which 17% inflicted harm intentionally and 16% used a weapon to do so. When asked what would prevent them from returning to jail, 35% said having a good-paying job, 31% stated family support, such as an understanding wife, and 11% indicated that the fear of returning to jail was the primary reason. Working at a well-paying job is construed as not having the need to steal. Whether that relates to having more money to buy expensive and illegal drugs or the ability to live in a better environment is unknown and certainly suggests the need for further research. Incidentally, only one inmate said that relocation would deter him from committing a crime after release. Twenty percent answered "other" to this question, such as worrying about their families' financial well-being and feelings of embarrassment and guilt.

The three-strikes law took effect in California on March 7, 1994. Some argue that it is credited with decreasing violent crime in California's most populated areas (Reuters, 1997). From our sample, 31 inmates had one or more strikes and 40 inmates (almost 50%) had no strikes against them. The inmates with strikes admitted to fear of getting another strike and returning to prison. All the inmates who served time in a state prison did not want to return. However, the inmates agreed that serving time in prison was better than serving a sentence in a county jail (prisons provide more opportunities, programs, etc.). Although we addressed some of the perceptions that the male population of jailed inmates have, it is recognized that this is only the beginning of the process. Further probing questions will enhance a follow-up study and lead to more answers, aiding those already in the correctional system. With this information, sociologists, prison officials, and others who work with this population can judge the results and effectiveness of particular policies and programs as well as learn more about factors that contribute to or deter crime.

The information obtained in the present study can be used as a base on which to build further in areas such as the following:

- Identifying patterns of offending for high-risk offenders
- Violent crime events understood in terms of time, place, and persons involved
- Victims' roles: educating the community on how to avoid becoming a victim
- The role of drug and alcohol use in crime and in the criminal histories of offenders

- Programs for parents and teachers that aid in recognizing signs that may predict a possible future pattern of criminal behavior, including the warning signs of ADD and ADHD
- For those already incarcerated, identifying and treating those with ADD and ADHD with medication and/or behavior modification programs
- Programs that train law enforcement officers to recognize ADHD and how to address those with ADHD

In other words, what is needed are programs that help the incarcerated focus on transitioning back into the community, specifically, improving their employment and social skills and their self-esteem and family connections. We must also reconsider the policy of locking up all drug offenders. Not all drug offenders are threats to the population. Treatment for some is preferrable to incaceration in a facility with limited help programs. It is clear that jails are merely holding facilities, with inmates passing time through idle, nonproductive activities.

ACKNOWLEDGMENTS

The authors wish especially to thank the following California Lutheran University criminal justice and psychology student interviewers: Jeff Barry, Amy Fischer, Shoshona Fontaine, Shante Riveria, Stephen Seper, and Sabina Taj.

REFERENCES

ALLEN, A. A. (1996). Criminology. In *Colliers Encyclopedia CD-ROM*, Vol. 7.

AMEN, D. (1997). cs.stanford.edu.

AMERICAN PSYCHIATRIC ASSOCIATION (1994). *Diagnostic and Statistical Manual of Mental Disorders*, 4th ed. Washington, DC: APA.

BECK, A. T., and A. FREEMAN (1990). Antisocial personality disorder. In *Cognitive Therapy of Personality Disorders*. New York: Guilford Press.

BUREAU OF JUSTICE STATISTICS (1988). *Drug Use and Crime*. Washington, DC: U.S. Department of Justice.

BUREAU OF JUSTICE STATISTICS (1995a). *Jails and Jail Inmates, 1993–1994*. Washington, DC: U.S. Department of Justice.

BUREAU OF JUSTICE STATISTICS (1995b). *Survey of State Prison Inmates, 1991*. Washington, DC: U.S. Department of Justice.

BUREAU OF JUSTICE STATISTICS (1996). *Prison and Jail Inmates, 1995*. Washington, DC: U.S. Department of Justice.

CROMWELL, P. (1996). Criminal lifestyles and decision making. In *In Their Own Words*. Los Angeles: Roxbury Publishing.

DENNO, D. W. (1994). Gender, crime, and criminal law defenses. *Journal of Criminal Law and Criminology*, 85.

DUNCAN, R. D., W. A. KENNEDY, and C. J. PATRICK (1995). Four-factor model of recidivism by male juvenile offenders. *Journal of Clinical Child Psychology*, 24:250–270.

ERICKSON, R. J., and A. STENSETH (1996). Crimes of convenience. *Security Management*, October.

FEDERAL BUREAU OF INVESTIGATION (1996). www.census gov/ftp/pub/statab/ranks/pg 13.txt.

GOLDBERG, C. (1995). The daimonic development of the malevolent personality. *Journal of Humanistic Psychology*, 35:7.

GOLDSTEIN, S. (1996). Attention deficit/hyperactivity disorder implications for the criminal justice system. www.fbi.gov/leb/june973.htm.

GOLDSTEIN, S., and M. GOLDSTEIN (1995). Attention deficit disorder in adults. *Directions in Psychiatry*, 14:18

HICKEY, E. W. (1997). *Serial Murderers and Their Victims*, 2nd ed. Belmont, CA: Wadsworth.

INCIARDI, J. A., and A. E. POTTIEGER (1991). Kids, crack and crime. *Journal of Drug Issues*, 21:257–270.

NATIONAL INSTITUTE OF JUSTICE (1996). *Adult Patterns of Criminal Behavior*. Washington, DC: U.S. Department of Justice.

QUINSEY, V. L., and K. S. REID (1996). Mentally disordered offenders' accounts of their crimes. *Criminal Justice and Behavior*, 23:472–488.

RAINE, A. (1993). *The Psychopathy of Crime*. San Diego, CA: Academic Press.

REUTERS (1997). California crime rate drops 12 percent; murders down 18 percent. March 12.

RUBEINSTEIN, R. (1995). The economics of crime. *Vital Speeches*, 62:19–23.

SNOW, K. (1991). Contemporary theories of crime. *Criminal Justice and Behavior*, 4:491–493.

WILSON, J. Q. (1997). *Moral Judgement*. New York: Basic Books.

WILSON, J. Q., and R. J. HERRNSTEIN (1985). *Crime and Human Behavior*. New York: Simon & Schuster.

APPENDIX: INMATE STUDY

Current crime: Interview date:

Your race: Interviewer:

Your age:

1. **Motivation:** Regarding your current sentence, what motivated you *most* to commit the crime? (Select one.)
   a. need for money to buy drugs
   b. just needed cash/property
   c. excitement/thrill
   d. anger/revenge
   e. other

2. **Planning:** Did you plan the crime or was it done on the spur of the moment?
   a. planned (with someone else or a group)
   b. unplanned/spur of the moment

3. **Idea:** Did anyone encourage or convince you to commit the crime?
   a. no, it was my idea
   c. I was talked into it by someone else
   d. it was a mutual decision
   e. other

4. **Alone:** Were you alone when you committed the crime?
   a. I was alone
   b. I was with another person (partner)
   c. I was with a group/gang (more than two persons)

5. **Fear:** Were you fearful of getting arrested?
   a. yes
   b. never thought about it or did not care
   c. was concerned, but felt I would get away with it
   d. other

6. **Prevention:** Which *one* of the following reasons would *most* likely prevent or stop you from committing a crime against someone (such as robbery, burglary, etc.)?
   a. a uniformed security officer patrolling the property
   b. closed circuit TV cameras on property
   c. knowledge that the victim or property owner may be armed with a handgun
   d. strict sentencing laws resulting in a long prison term if caught/convicted
   e. alarms on property (car, home, business)

    f. signs indicating neighborhood watch or patrols

    g. if I was on probation/parole

    h. other reason

7. **Victim knowledge:** Concerning your present crime, did you know the victim(s)?

    a. did not know the victim(s)

    b. knew who victims(s) were, but not personally

    c. knew victim(s) personally

8. **Victim harm:** Did you physically harm or injure the victim(s) during the commission of the crime (if not for present crime, any crime in the past)?

    a. no

    b. yes, but not intentionally/didn't mean to

    c. yes, because they deserved it/I meant to

    d. other

9. **Remorse:** Did you feel sorry or regret committing the crime, or injuring the victim afterward (or any crime in the past)?

    a. no

    b. yes, but only after a while

    c. other

10. **Weapon:** Did you carry a weapon during the crime?

    a. firearm

    b. knife

    c. no weapon

    d. other

11. **Using alcohol/drugs:** Were you under the influence of any drug or alcohol during the crime?

    a. yes (indicate type of drug)

    b. no

    c. other

12. **Prison time:** Have you served time in state prison?

    a. yes

    b. no

13. **Recidivism:** After release, what would be the *most important reason* for staying out of jail/prison or becoming a repeat offender?

    a. having a good-paying job

    b. family support (spouse, children, parents, etc.)

    c. a move to a different area (city, state)

    d. fear of arrest and going back to jail

    e. other

14. **Probation:** Were you on probation/parole when you committed the crime you are presently jailed for?

    a. yes

    b. no

15. **History of violent crime(s) as a juvenile:** Do you have juvenile record for a violent crime (assault, robbery, sex crimes, battery, etc.)?

    a. yes (how many)

    b. no

16. **Three-strikes law:** How many strikes do you have?

    a. none

    b. one

    c. two

    d. don't know

PART V

Technology in the Twenty-First Century

The use of technology in this new century is most important in understanding crime as it exists: how its theories, the very nature of crime, and the role of the criminal justice system will be based on technological innovations. Grau discusses the quantum leaps in technology that have grown out of basic science research and continues to grow in this century, thereby affecting the way crime will be viewed and handled.

A major development during the 1990s was the theme of workforce investment. Complex demographic, economic, and educational conditions have caused emerging problems in the workforce and a shortage of skilled workers necessary for the twenty-first century. To function properly there will exist a model for criminal justice organizational changes that will both proactive and reactive to problems of crime. An improving economy, according to Rosemary Gido, has not resulted in either a public- or private-sector commitment to a long-term solution to the endemic problems of unskilled workers and the skills gap. The Clinton administration sponsored a National Skills Summit on April 11, 2000, focusing on the U.S. workforce skills shortage.

Prosecuting environment crime in this new century will be of major concern to those involved in criminal justice. Groups looking to protect the environment have taken to setting fires and using graffiti to mar new buildings because they believe they we need to protect the land. Rebovich's chapter indicates the direction that we must take in order not simply to protect the environment but to prevent "terroristic types of acts" from occurring. It is suggested that local prosecutors must have a sensitivity to a problem long overlooked. As an example, public pressure to control pollution in the United States has helped lead to the criminalization of offenses against the environment. There needs to be environmental equity in this millennium.

Archambeault looks at the impact that computer-based research will have on criminal justice. He explains the nature and impact of the information society on American criminal justice, while logically linking information dependency to computer dependency. He believes that through evolving technologies, including that of the use of artificial intelligence and virtual reality, we will see a changing criminal justice system. The prediction is that the line between science fiction and scientific fact will not only blur but that it will no longer exist as we have known it in the twentieth century. As indicated, if the past is an indicator of the future, it then becomes logical for us to take current evolving technologies while projecting their future use. The only limitations on the future applications of computers in the criminal justice system will be human imagination, ethics, and law.

chapter 16

Technology and Criminal Justice

Joseph J. Grau, Ph.D.

ABSTRACT

Quantum leaps in technology, growing out of basic science research, are transforming societies around the world, and consequently, the crime scene, criminals, and the criminal justice system. The crime scene is worldwide and crime is being democratized. As technology knits societies together through rapid, easier communication, the world shrinks to a "global village."[1] One's "neighbor" may be on another continent, reached in seconds, and capable of responding immediately.

Although technology is changing the social context within which wrongdoing occurs, it does not cause crime; rather, by adding a new dimension to the social situation, it opens new opportunities for expanded freedom and more effective social control. Human beings can use it for good or evil, for legal or illegal purposes. Personal and corporate assets take new forms, such as plastic and electronic money: Greater availability and expanded use of intangible property (e.g., information) raise intriguing legal questions concerning human rights of freedom and privacy. In technological society, tangible and intangible property can be exchanged legitimately or fraudulently; personal space can be subtly invaded or expanded.

TECHNOLOGICAL SOCIETY

Criminal justice is an integral concern of all human beings and societies around the world. Understanding the crime problem, the nature and role of the criminal, and criminal justice systems requires elaboration of the ways technological innovations have transformed the social context within which crime occurs. Data highways supplement transportation systems. Cyberspace is the new milieu overlaying physical space; it does not replace, but adds a new dimension to, the crime scene. *Time* defines cyberspace and its social consequences:

> Cyberspace is the globe-circling, interconnected telephone network that is the conduit for billions of voice, fax and computer-to-computer communications....Every night on Prodigy, CompuServe, Genie and thousands of smaller computer bulletin boards, people by the hundreds of thousands are logging on to a great computer-mediated gabfest, an interactive debate that allows them to leap over barriers of time, space, sex and social status. Computer networks make it easy to reach and touch strangers who share particular obsessions or concerns.[2]

Within cyberspace, love notes, explicit sexual messages, graphics, coded plans for terrorist attacks, and invasions of personal space may be communicated. In this environment, for example, "two anonymous people (or maybe more) may sit at their computer terminals in different parts of the world, exchanging written descriptions of erotic arts performed with each other in an imaginary boudoir."[3] John Schwartz, a reporter for the *Washington Post*, brings "net sex" or "virtual sex" closer to home with the story of "an eight-year-old girl attempting computer conversations with a group of transvestites. Seemingly safe at home, the child was playing with her favorite $2000 toy, using her computer and modem to make new friends online."[4] Internet can be used to "wire digitized child pornography to those who want it."[5] One can enter a computer discussion group where questions can be raised such as: "Has anyone ever experimented with flogging or caning on the soles of the feet? Is there any reason this should be avoided? If not, is there a preferred way to go about it? Anyone with knowledge, please advise."[6] In the flow of data and information through computer networks, such as Internet, ethical and law enforcement controls are lacking. No one is in charge, not even the government. Legislation and regulations are urgently needed to assure decency, justice, and fairness.

In this chapter we focus on cyberspace and information technologies which have a significant impact on (1) the crime scene; (2) forms, rates, and qualities of crime; and (3) the criminal justice system. Reference is made to technological developments in other fields, such as molecular biology and social science research, but these aspects of the technological revolution are not treated extensively. To begin, we point to a few technological resources available and used in crime control: remotely controlled surveillance, chemical and genetic testing, DNA typing, and a wide array of computer and telecommunications exchange systems; computer models, psychological profiles, composite sketches and maps that facilitate tracking offenders and assessing potential recidivists; electronic events scheduling, task coordination, and monitoring to replace paper-based manual procedures; and computer caseload management for moving criminal cases through the criminal justice system for report–investigation–arrest to judicial proceedings and various correction applications.

Before discussing the relationship between technology and the criminal justice system, the "global village" concept requires further elaboration because it sets the parameters for the discussion that follows. Teleputing—the convergence of television, telephone, and computer—has intensified the cybernetic revolution. Whereas mechanical inventions, one by one, increased our physical powers, electricity has expanded mental functions; electronics created a new dimension— cyberspace. As industrialization gave birth to urban and suburban areas, electrification internationalized and, to some extent, democratized human societies. Now, billions of people around the world can reach out to the minds, hearts, and emotions of each other. In the 1970s during the Vietnam War, we experienced televised military conflict in our living room; more recently we shared in the suffering of people in Somalia, the Middle East, and the former Yugoslavia through televised newscasts, while in the same way experiencing the tragedies, disasters, violence, and crimes of our "local" neighbors. Russian newscasts for the Russian people are received simultaneously by us and many other people around the world through satellite transmission. Wilson P. Dizard, Jr., former consultant on telecommunications and information policy for the U.S. Department of State, said that "for the first time in human history, there is a realistic prospect of communication networks that will link everyone on earth." He was optimistic that the "United Nation's goal of a telephone within an hour's walk of every village" would "be realized in the next century," despite the fact that presently there are some gaps in the "basic connection for most people" and in the "array of computers and other information resources," especially in Third World countries.[7]

Already, telecommunication linkage among the powerful and volatile financial, commercial, and industrial centers of the world, such as New York, London, and Tokyo, is operating around the clock. Simultaneously, each receives the same updated information, such as stock quotes, interest rates, and currency changes. All these markets are sensitive to the slightest change in the financial fortunes, productivity, and political developments in European, Asian, and Pacific Rim countries, to mention only a few. This "new global financial market" was poignantly described by Walter Wriston, former chairman of Citicorp:

> The new global financial market is not a place on the map; it is more than 200 thousand monitors in trading rooms all over the world that are linked together. With this technology no one is really in control. Rather, everyone is in control through a kind of global plebiscite on monetary and fiscal policies of the governments issuing currency...news will march across the tube, traders will make judgments and a value will be placed on a currency that will be known instantly all over the globe.[8]

At the present time, the world socioeconomic fabric is knit together into a global village. For example, by the use of only one computer network, the Internet, an estimated 15 million people in 50 countries are connected; nearly 40% of personal computers have modems facilitating the transmission of messages— often by fax.[9]

Telecommunication is pulsating through the academic community, not only in research endeavors, but also in the social life of students. In a special report on technology, the *Wall Street Journal* described one of the "hottest night spots" on the campus of the University in Michigan, namely, the courtyard at Angel Hall:

> Students flock here to write love notes, send letters to their parents, turn in homework to their professors, post classified ads, catch up on campus news, talk about Rousseau and Locke on a special bulletin board for members of a political science class (more than 25% of all classes have their own discussion boards), and look one another up in an electronic phone directory (complete in some cases, with such personal details as "male, blond, nice guy").[10]

They engage in, what *Newsday* called "riding the information highway." In this electronic social center, which from the outside "looks like a giant funky cafe," it is chic to have a computer address with "the *funny* @ in the middle."[11]

Although this chapter focuses on this global electronic information world, we shall also refer to genetic and chemical research contributions insofar as they significantly affect criminal justice. Through biologically based techniques, human birth and death are engineered: individuals are genetically tested and evaluated. The 15-year, $3 billion federally funded Genome Study, begun in 1988 by the National Research Council of the National Academy of Sciences, is currently identifying and mapping the estimated 100,000 human genes. Further research will demonstrate genetic relationships to specific human physical, behavioral, and psychological conditions. An in-depth treatment of genetic engineering would require detailed discussion well beyond the limits of this chapter. However, biologically based techniques such as DNA fingerprinting and other biometric identification measurements deserve a special note. Genetic research, at this time, does not affect all aspects of the criminal justice system, as does information technology. In the future, molecular biology may have more extensive applications, as suggested by the fact that gene technology research is being applied today for identification of war crimes perpetrators in Yugoslavia, Korea, and Argentina.[12]

THE HIGH-TECH CRIME SCENE

The high-tech crime scene is set on a technosocial stage, being integrally woven into the global social fabric. Advanced electronics provide an easily accessed, user-friendly environment for wrongdoing. In a button-pushing society, young and old, weak and strong, brilliant and the less intelligent, male and female, people of high and low social status have equal opportunities for instantaneously transferring assets or obtaining money and information. It is not unusual for us to draw or transfer money through an automatic teller machine (ATM) or to engage in computerized credit or debit card purchases at local stores, by telephone, or by computer. Modem data bank access to valuable information is so easy that even a grade-school child can do it. The purchase and know-how for using advanced electronic equipment are available everywhere—in magazines, catalogs, and newspapers at local stores, by merchants, and on electronic bulletin boards. For example, *Virtual Reality World*, a magazine devoted to the "hottest" advanced technology, appears regularly on newsstands; academic institutions and entertainment centers such as Disney World offer virtual reality experiences.[13] Note that this electronic world of teleputing, telecommunicating, computing, and, in fact, any electrical device operates rain or shine, day or night, in any place (home, bedroom, office, car, airplane, satellite, or outer space), as well as within and across national and international jurisdictional lines.

In this technological user-friendly easily accessed electronically-wired social setting, the crucial issue is access control. This access raises many questions concerning personal identification. Which person (or persons) has been authorized? For what specific purpose? To use which electronic equipment? These questions surfaced when a highly publicized crime, the case of the Hannover Hacker, occurred in 1980.[14] Young West German hackers, operating from a small cramped room in Hamburg, Germany, logged onto computers without authorization at the University of California's Lawrence Berkeley Laboratory and at NASA headquarters in Washington, DC. They found access to Internet through University College, London, and then to a computer bank of Mitre Corporation modems which saved the last number dialed. When redialing these numbers, they happened to enter a computer at the Anniston Army Depot and Optimis, a U.S. Defense Department computer base, with information about military studies.[15] The unsophisticated computer security of that time allowed the hackers to type "anonymous" as a log-in and "guest" as a password. In another case (1988), Robert T. Morris, a 22-year-old Cornell University graduate student, gained notoriety by placing a flawed computer program, a worm, into a network system. He experienced how quickly and easily it moved through the telecommunications system. After putting final touches on his program around 7:30 P.M., he typed in a few commands, hit the return button, and went out to eat. "In the time it took Robert to put on his jacket after pressing Return, the program began to spread. Within a few minutes it was already fanning out over the network. Computers started infecting one another like toddlers in a day care center."[16] The released worm quickly jammed about 6000 computers linked to Internet because of the speed with which the command was executed.[17] Today, this spread would be considered slow time because electronic impulses are often measured in as little as a nanosecond or billionth of a second.

Not only can hackers disrupt computer systems and enter cybernetic space unauthorized, but thieves easily and quickly tap phone systems, running up exorbitant toll charges on other people's bills. For example, Ron Hanley, an executive at Dataproducts in New England in Wallingford, Connecticut, was notified by ATT that his company had been hacked. Within two days he had a bill confirming that "in one twenty-four-hour period, street corner phone users in New York had made some two thousand calls to the Caribbean on the company's line, ringing up about $50,000 in tolls."[18] Don Delaney, computer consultant and retired New York State Police senior investigator, explains how the complex network allows phone freaks almost impenetrable cover of anonymity:

> Tens of thousands of computers are interconnected nationwide and internationally over telephone lines. These interconnections are networks with such names as Internet, Milnet, Arpanet, Telenet, and Tymnet. Many of these linked computers enable the individual

dialing in to out-dial to another computer. If a criminal initiates the first call using a stolen telco credit card or a PBX on an 800 number, and then loops through several network computers, he or she virtually ensures anonymity.[19]

Note that the convergence of telecommunication systems involves transmission through both fiber optic wires and airwaves. Furthermore, hundreds of thousands of mobile cellular phones, using both types of transmission, have been cloned (i.e., reprogrammed with illegally copied numbers). A user can make roughly a month's worth of free international calls before being caught.[20] Clone phone cheats park their large, expensive cars along city streets where people, migrant aliens and nonaliens who cannot afford telephone service, enter and make calls to their relatives and friends in faraway places in the Middle East and South America.

A group of hackers, Masters of Deception (MOD), led by Mark Abene, alias Phiber Optic, got access to computers that controlled all the regional telephone companies and ATT. They made unbillable calls and freely used other services that cost hundreds of thousands of dollars. They traveled the Tymnet highway frequented by banks and the government. Just before being arrested at his parents' house, Phiber Optic had been using his laptop computer in his bedroom, but he did not know that he was being hacked back by two New York Telephone employees.[21]

The high-tech crime scene, characterized by wire and wireless communication that links commercial and government computers locally, nationally, and internationally, creates opportunities for savvy criminals. Only a few of their many fraudulent scams have been illustrated, and they were basically at the individual and lower level of the financial system. In addition, more costly crimes at the upper institutional level occur, where on an average day trillions of dollars are moved by electronic funds transfer (EFT). National and international money exchange involves wire transfers, automated clearing house (ACH) procedures, cash management, online teller, and computerized check processing, which are vulnerable to high-tech fraudulent manipulations.

To prevent such fraud, personal identification numbers (PINS) and passwords are standard safeguards. Computer security experts have implemented sophisticated protection programs to keep one step ahead of hackers and criminals who also use computers to transfer and launder money, steal commercial inventories, and communicate with each other.[22] In this teleputing environment, the thief's traditional tools—mask, gun, and getaway car—are crude instruments. Theft and misuse of passwords and access codes, manipulation of computer programming, and system glitches present opportunities for wrongdoing that never existed before; furthermore, plastic and electronic money are new forms of assets waiting to be misused. The criminal has adapted quite well to the high-tech crime scene by implementing a variety of effective electronic modi operandi that fit with the electronic world.

High-Tech Crime Scene Infobanks

The high-tech crime scene provides not only opportunities for costly telecommunications disruptions, fraudulent use of services, and financial scams, but also easy button-pushing access to a new type of bank, the *infobank*, which holds computer-generated information.

The introduction of the microchip in the 1970s and the inundation of our homes and offices with personal computers made it possible for anyone with a modem to obtain invaluable personal information from thousands of databases or mainframe infobanks in the United States and around the world. Again, global source access has shrunken this planet so that global villagers can know just about everything about anyone.

The basis for this statement is the fact that for several decades computers have been collecting, filing, and storing private details gathered from personal applications. Few people realize that whenever they apply for a mortgage, license, or even telephone service, their personal life history enters the infobank system. We all know that a driver's license contains much more information than one's driving history. Among the computerized items on that little card are date of birth, place of residence, color of eyes, height, weight, color of hair, and even a photograph of the driver. Because of all this information, it is the most readily accepted and frequently used form of identification. Furthermore, credit bureaus, such as TRW in Orange (Calif.), Equifax in Atlanta, and Trans Union Credit Information in Chicago, collect and store financial status information on about 170 million people on a half million computer files. To this must be added all the financial information held by Internal Revenue Service from income tax returns which reveal more about one's lifestyle than is apparent. In preparing credit profiles, credit bureaus look into a subject's payment history, public records that may contain liens, judgments, or bankruptcies, personal debt load, banking relations or affiliations, employment, credit performance, and verification of social security number.

Although access restrictions apply to credit bureau reports and income tax returns, many other data banks in the public domain are computer accessible without many restrictions. They contain information on property ownership, professional licenses, bankruptcy searches, professional reputation, criminal convictions, address verification, bank affiliations, liens/judgments, civil litigations, motor vehicle ownership, business affiliations, education verification, employment history, secondary residence, and telephone verification. Incidentally, *public domain* refers to information available to everyone. In addition, there is an almost inexhaustible supply of infobanks related to other areas of life, such as health, entertainment, and sports. For our purposes we focus on those most relevant to law enforcement and the high-tech crime scene.

The National Crime Information Center (NCIC), monitored and controlled by the Federal Bureau of Investigation (the FBI), contains computerized files on criminal histories, missing persons, warrants, stolen property and securities, registered property, such as guns and vehicles, and even persons considered dangerous to the President of the United States. NCIC holds criminalistic lab information and Canadian arrest warrants. It is consulted approximately a half million times a day by local authorities.

The Treasury Enforcement Communications System (TECS) was instituted for the U.S. Treasury Department and operated by the U.S. Customs Service in the fight against crime, especially in the areas of money laundering and drug smuggling. Scrambled messages are transmitted through more than 1600 terminals throughout the country. To log on, users must identify themselves to the operation systems and enter the day's secret access code. An agency uses the TECS hardware and generic software but sets up its own database. An agency may shield its information from other agencies on the system. Upon written request, other federal agencies and even Interpol may seek the input data from a TECS subsystem. The Organized Crime Information System (OCIS) is a computerized database, maintained and controlled by the FBI to provide specific information about known and suspected organized crime fighters and their activities.

Some computer systems (e.g. "Big Floyd" and "Scorecard") were designed to access databanks on known and potential criminals for the purpose of "thinking through" their activities. They can identify the contacts and associates of wanted individuals and make suggestions as to where a fugitive might be or which other parties might be able to lead to that person. This type of relational database file retrieves and searches out clues and relationships between clues.

All states have computerized law enforcement networks with subsystems that include criminal history, firearm control, stolen vehicles identification, wanted persons, missing persons, stolen property identification, and many others. Information can be accessed by local, state, and federal law enforcement agencies, even from mobile units in the field.

The Automatic Fingerprint Identification System (AFIS) scans fingerprints submitted by law enforcement agencies, creating a unique pattern and library index of individual prints, even latent prints. The American Standard for Information Exchange allows the matching of fingerprints taken from crime scenes with known prints from other jurisdictions. In addition to traditional finger and palm prints, research in molecular biology provides support for DNA fingerprinting tests that involve comparing the DNA of blood, semen, or hair roots found at the scene with the DNA of a suspect. This technological enhancement is virtually foolproof because no two people, other than identical twins, have the same genetic characteristics.

The National Center for the Analysis of Violent Crime (NCAVC), located in the FBI's National Academy, Quantico, Virginia, is comprised of two units: the Behavioral Science Instruction and Research Unit and the Behavioral Science Investigative Support Unit. The overall Behavioral Science Unit, formerly known as a psychological profiling unit, provides characteristics of offenders based on their behavior before, during, and after committing a crime to requesting law enforcement agencies in the United States and free world.[23] Violent crime is reported to NCAVC for pattern analysis and classification which can reveal multidimensional trends and profiles in the crime data.

The FBI Violent Crime Apprehension Program (VICAP) computer system stores information on unresolved homicides reported to the NCAVC. Crime reports are entered on-line from NCAVC at Quantico using a secure telecommunication network. The VICAP compares over 100 selected categories of each new case with all other cases stored in the database, producing a hardcopy report listing in rank order the top 10 matches in the violent crime data bank (i.e., a template pattern match).

The profiling and consultation program uses a series of crime pattern recognition computer programs to detect and predict the behavior of violent criminals. Applying the same approach, the Arson Information Management System facilitates law enforcement's ability to predict the time, date, and location of future incidents and the most probable residence of the suspect. In general, artificial intelligence procedures are being used to manipulate data and compute the probable hierarchies and interactions of complex organizations to interdict organized crime, terrorist, and gang activity. Computer-assisted linguistic analysis techniques facilitate content evaluation of written and oral communication in extortions, bombings, and terrorist incidents to assess authorship and threat viability.

As we have seen, not only the criminal justice system, but countless other services and agencies collect and record data about people living in the United States and around the world. Thirty or forty years ago this information was paper-recorded and filed in large cabinets; today, a pinhead microchip can electronically classify, store, and retrieve the same data. What was costly, time consuming, and limited by space has become inexpensive, lightning fast, and almost boundless. As a result, public and private institutions collect, maintain, and exchange huge quantities of data, much of it personal. Instantaneously, one's personal life may become an open book, flashed to the mass media and across the city, to a mobile police cruiser or credit office, or even the entire world.

The computer transforms raw data into meaningful, usable information. Infobanks organize, cross-index, and create composite files from which conclusions are drawn and decisions made. Police, license and credit bureaus, housing and welfare agencies, insurance and mortgage companies, educational institutions, and innumerable government agencies routinely exchange this information about people without their knowledge or consent. Exchanges between the Central Intelligence Agency, Internal Revenue Service, and the Federal Bureau of Investigation are sometimes performed without adequate audit trail procedures. As a result, the original source of the data and the circumstances under which it was gathered cannot be traced. Data accumulates in public and private administrative institutions that may limit a person's benefits or preclude employment.

The standards for maintaining confidentiality in information transferral from one agency to another vary not only between the public and private sectors but also among federal, state, and local governments. This sharing can lead to privacy invasion, especially when public officials are not sensitive to privacy concerns. However, even in private business transactions confidentiality may be violated and information divulged, misused, or at least not handled in a way that indicates personal consideration. The following incident reported in *Business Week* illustrates the point.

> Last spring, the long arm of American Express Co. reached out grabbed Ray Parrish. After getting his credit card in January, the twenty-two-year old New Yorker promptly paid bills of $331 and $204.39 in February and March. Then he got a surprising call. His credit privileges were being suspended, an American Express clerk informed him, because his checking account showed too small a balance to pay his April charge of $596. A contrite American Express now says that it should have asked before peeking, and it reinstated Parrish after he paid his bill from his savings and cash on hand. But that was beside the point. "I felt violated," says Parrish who has kept his card because he needs it. "When I gave them my bank account number, I never thought they would use it to routinely look over my shoulder."[24]

That was his introduction to the information age. In the beginning he did not realize that by signing the credit card application, he allowed American Express the right to snoop.

The establishment of data banks at all levels of government, business, and military service and subsequent information exchanges subtly whittle away rights to privacy. *Business Week* succinctly summarized the private protection legislation that has been passed and the many loopholes that in practice make it quite ineffective. For example, the Fair Credit Reporting Act restricts the sharing of information but allows it for "legitimate business needs." The Privacy Act "bars federal agencies from letting out information they collect for one purpose to be used for a different purpose," but "exceptions let agencies share data anyway," and the law applies only to federal agencies. The Right to Financial Privacy Act sets procedural rules when federal agencies go through a customer's bank records but does not cover state and local governments. Furthermore, the FBI and U.S. government agencies are exempt in an increasing number of instances. The Computer Matching and Privacy Protection Act "regulates computer matching of federal data for verifying eligibility for federal benefits programs or for recouping delinquent debts" and gives the individual an opportunity to respond before the federal government takes adverse action, but because of the law's narrow scope, matches for "law enforcement and tax purposes" are now exempt. New privacy protection legislation is forthcoming as we move into the twenty-first century. For example, when the video rentals of Robert Bork, a nominee for the U.S. Supreme Court, were identified through a computer search and published in Washington *City Paper*, lawmakers were outraged. As a result, they passed the (1988) Video Privacy Protection Act.[25]

Not only the large number of infobanks, but their vulnerability to searches creates enormous problems. It is relatively easy, or at lest an exciting challenge, for someone who understands computer technology to search an infobank with or without authorization. Even the computer illiterate through social engineering can gain access to computerized information. Many low-level computer operators, unconcerned about keeping their records private, provide medical and financial data to anyone who gives a good reason for wanting to know. Private investigators are particularly adept at obtaining confidential information.

Difficulties involved in controlling the quality of input data and the person's limited opportunities to expunge or delete errors in a file open a Pandora's box of personal problems and legal questions. Even if a person knows or suspects that certain files are being kept, the specific information and its accuracy often cannot be verified. Information in government or private files may be misleading or blatantly false because it was not checked thoroughly. For example, an insurance company investigator may ask a neighbor a question. The response received is local gossip, hence false, or at least of questionable reliability and validity. If the investigator has no way of knowing this, it may enter the infobank as fact. To delete false or irrelevant information, assuming that the person has had an opportunity to identify it, can be a long, tedious, costly struggle.

High-Tech Crime Surveillance Technology

In addition to computer-driven searches, relatively inexpensive and widely available sophisticated surveillance technology has expanded the power of our five senses, especially the eye and ear. Parabolic listening devices, night vision cameras and scopes, cellular and laser devices, motion detectors, and microwave developments enhance our ability to see and hear. A former New York City detective and presently a corporate business investigator, in summarizing available technological equipment, identifies more than two pages of eavesdropping devices (bugs) used by law enforcement personnel as well as by ordinary citizens. "In today's business climate, the availability of over-the-counter products and inventions have fashioned a growing recourse to industrial espionage, armchair private investigators, do-it-yourselfers, and the professional eavesdroppers."[26] Other electronic equipment described includes the 360 Tracking System, the LoJack system activated through computerized microprocessing and coding, video and infrared surveillance, voice scramblers, digital voice changers, mail screening, x-ray spray, fiber-optic video transmission, wireless alarm systems, teleconferencing, and satellite communications. As noted, technological equipment is neither good nor bad, but rather more effective or efficient. It can be, and in fact, is used by criminals, law enforcement personnel, and the average person. For example, a mother may buy an eavesdropping device (bug) to monitor the crying of her baby in another room, or an estranged husband and wife may find surveillance instruments useful during their breakup.

In addition to the availability of surveillance and teleputing equipment in local stores and through catalogs, extremely deadly, rapid-fire weapons and explosives can also be obtained legally or illegally with little difficulty. Even the material and know-how for constructing and detonating a nuclear bomb are not beyond the reach of some people and nations. As a general safeguard against misuse of telecommunications by criminals, especially in plotting criminal activities, the U.S. government introduced an encrypting device, the Clipper Chip, in 1994.

The Clipper Chip

The Clipper Chip, a tiny computer chip attached to telephones, scrambles sounds and information for privacy protection. As with all technology, it is a double-edged sword, raising a storm of controversy among law enforcement officials, the computer industry, and civil libertarians. "Vice President Al Gore dubbed encryption a 'law and order issue' because criminals use it to bypass wiretaps."[27] The Clinton administration wants it adopted by the United States as the one and only legitimate coding system for protecting telephone and computer communications. Controversy is currently raging over who should hold the decoding or unscrambling key. In response to the computer industry and civil libertarians' fear that it would violate privacy rights, the administration proposed the following measures to protect the public against misuse or abuse by the government:

One of the two components of the key embedded in the chip would be kept with the Treasury Department and the other component with the Commerce Department's National Institute of Standards and Technology. Any law enforcement official wanting to wiretap would need to obtain not only a warrant but the separate components from two agencies. This, plus the super strong code and key system, would make it virtually impossible for anyone, even corrupt government officials, to spy illegally.[28]

Presently, law enforcement engages in eavesdropping (i.e., interception of telecommunication through electronic surveillance) by obtaining court authorization, which includes stringent requirements for execution. In somewhat the same way, the FBI wants universal application and control of the Clipper Chip by the U.S. government so that it will be able to intercept teleputing communications by organized crime. If criminal elements are allowed to have their own coding and decoding system, the agency contends that it would not be able to function effectively. Dorothy E. Denning, chair of computer science at Georgetown University and author of *Cryptography and Data Security*, said that "the Constitution does not give us absolute privacy from court-ordered searches and seizures, and for good reason. Lawlessness would prevail."[29] The computer industry and civil libertarians believe that people should be free to use their own scrambling codes and that the government's exclusive control of the Clipper Chip would be an invasion of privacy.

Such controversies will continue into the twenty-first century because of the basic dilemma involved: namely, freedom versus control. The key issues are crucial to the maintenance of our way of life and security. How can we balance the individual's rights to privacy with the government's need to know? When "technology as a productive force rolls on, while its contribution to social stability grows weaker" it may be worthwhile to consider the following paradoxes cataloged by a French sociologist, Jacques Ellul:[30]

- All technical progress exacts a price; that is, while it adds something on the one hand, it subtracts something on the other.

- All technical progress raises more problems than it solves, tempts us to seek the consequent problems as technical in nature, and prods us to seek technical solutions to them.

- The negative effects of technological innovations are inseparable from the positive. It is naive to say that technology is neutral, that it may be used for good or bad ends; good and bad effects are, in fact, simultaneous and inseparable.

- All technological innovations have unforeseeable effects.

The High-Tech Criminal

Who can be a high-tech criminal? Anyone who participates in, or has access to, an advanced technological society that shapes the crime scene. Teleputing and surveillance equipment is user-friendly and available to anyone at a relatively modest cost. Therefore, assuming a high-tech scene, anyone can be a criminal. Indeed, technology has democratized crime. August Bequai, attorney and author of several books on the technological society, entitled a chapter "Democratizing Crime: The Myth of the Supercriminal." He said that "even the amateur with access to a keyboard can do it." For example:

> Michele Cubbage, twenty-seven, was a housewife in Oxon Hill, Maryland. There was nothing unusual about her; she had no computer training. She learned from watching the television program "60 Minutes" how easy it was to steal by computer. And she did, taking People's Security Bank for more than $36,000.
>
> Until May 1983, Stanley Slyngstad worked for the Washington State Division of Vocational Rehabilitation. An unemployed friend of his needed money to buy a truck, and Stanley decided to help. He took more than $17,000 from his employer by programming the department's computer to issue twenty-five bogus checks to "people who were down on their luck." Stanley had never stolen a nickel before this; neither did he know what "computer crime was all about."
>
> Eryie Ann Edgerly, thirty-seven, and Jennie L. Barger, thirty-eight, were two inconspicuous Maryland housewives. Their neighbors were startled to learn that the two had been implicated in a $500,000 fraud involving a Washington, D.C., pension fund. They did it by filling out phony computer sheets, which listed Eryie as a beneficiary; the computer issued a total of 608 checks to her.
>
> In England a salesman for a chemical company defrauded his employer of more than $100,000 by programming the computer to double his sales commissions. This was his first brush with the law.[31]

Despite the fact that, theoretically, all have an equal chance to engage in telecommunication and computer fraud, persons involved directly with computer functions on a daily basis, such as data-entry operators, computer operators who control and monitor programmers who test and maintain programs, system analysts who design and implement systems, and database administrators who design and program guidelines for use have greater and more frequent opportunities. They are in a position to engage in internal computer crimes, employing covert instructions that alter the computer program (e.g., Trojan Horse, Logic Bomb, Trap Door, or virus infection); they are able to access teleputing systems through phreaking, hacking, misuse of telephones, and use of illegal bulletin boards. They can undertake manipulative fraudulent acts electronically, without manual paper pushing and a paper trail. Law enforcement needs more than a fingerprint on a keyboard to get a conviction. Indeed, computer button-pushing facilitates the creation of fictitious loans, insurance policies, membership lists, or addresses as well as the deletion or change of grades, inventory, or merchandise shipments.

Computers can assist criminals by providing databases to support criminal enterprises, such as drug distribution, prostitution, pornography, and illegal gambling. Finally, theft of high-tech equipment is a lucrative business, especially microchips, which are tiny and much more difficult to trace than paper money, coins, and drugs.

Applying a modus operandi based on advanced technology has given rise to a new vintage of criminals, such as techno-terrorists, software pirates, infobank blackmailers, and extortionists, and even those ingenious murderers by computer. Techno-terrorists' strategic global plans can be implemented through remotely controlled or time-delayed high-explosive detonations. Within our advanced technological age, their methods are beginning to shift from seizing radio and television stations to invading and attacking computer network systems and infobanks to bring about a serious social disruption.[32] Software piracy has become commonplace, and opportunities for blackmail and extortion, personal and international, multiply with the infobank explosions. Computer-monitored lifesaving hospital equipment is vulnerable to deadly reprogramming or deletions.

Hackers can be utilized in spy operations. In the following incident, hacking, but not espionage, was involved. The Belgian newspaper *De Standaard* reported that a man using a personal computer spent three months rummaging through the electronic mail and files on the Belgian Prime Minister and cabinet members. Apprehended, he showed reporters exactly how he broke into and "read the personal files of about ten government ministers" and gained access to the government's agenda.[33] While demonstrating his skills, he met up with and talked to another "burglar" via his computer. Although this crime did not become a serious international or even a national problem, deceptive access and illegal use of government information did become a crucial matter in the Aldrich Ames CIA spy case. Hackers can play a key role in spy operations, as revealed in the Hannover Hacker case when unauthorized computer-accessed information was sold to the former Soviet Union. The hacker may be the only distinctly new type of criminal. Be that as it may, the fact remains that this form of criminal behavior will only increase and play an ever more significant role in the crime scene as the technological developments advance.

TECHNOLOGY AND CRIMINAL JUSTICE MANAGEMENT

Advanced technology has transformed the crime scene, facilitating both crime commission and control. At the same time, criminal justice management has changed from reliance on manual, paper-based procedures to electronics. High-tech teleputing assists by providing a fast, effective way of communicating through the bureaucratic quagmire and coordinating activities so that steps in the justice process occur in a more orderly manner.

Teleputing helps by saving wasted resources and by building public confidence in the administration of justice through more efficient case handling. Engulfed by its sheer number of cases, persons involved, and the complexity of the system, this bureaucracy can employ teleputing to work out solutions to some of its problems. Consider how it could be applied in the following situations:

1. A police officer appears in court on his day off, drawing overtime pay. The hearing is rescheduled, but he or she never received a notice.

2. A laboratory technician works long hours on a piece of evidence, but the case was dismissed and that person does not know about it.

3. A prosecuting attorney informs appropriate personnel that he or she will be out of town at a law seminar, but a case is scheduled for the prosecuting attorney on that day.

4. One municipal courtroom is jammed to capacity, while another down the hall is empty and not used because its caseload was disposed of early due to many no-shows.

5. A justice professional tries to find a case folder, but it is not where it should be, and no one knows where it might be.

6. A probation officer spends an hour investigating a new probationer, only to discover later that all the information he or she gathered had been acquired previously by another agency.

7. A detainee whiles away many hours in a detention center because that unit did not receive notification that bail was paid. Furthermore, the detainee was not even guilty.

Teleputing, by electronically controlling events scheduling, task coordination, and task monitoring, can facilitate the resolution of such situations. In general, each event in the criminal justice system (e.g., an arraignment) has a number of tasks associated with it, such as a formal complaint. The arraignment cannot occur and the case be moved on to the next event until the task of filing the complaint is accomplished. Computerized management makes it easier to complete these functions and their associated tasks. Teleputing has extensive applicability because the criminal justice system is complexified by innumerable other tasks requiring coordination, such as preparing investigation reports, serving subpoenas, and preparing for the hearing. Computerization of bureaucratic operations assists in the smooth running of any system.

Furthermore, telecommunication infobanks, discussed previously, employ computer crime mapping analysis to handle the huge volume of information generated in the investigative process. Electronically, clusters of criminal activity are located and graphically mapped in terms of such variables as time of occurrence, place, and type of crime. Moreover, through computer analysis trends are extrapolated and probable future events predicted. As a result, law enforcement's ability to properly identify and apprehend criminals improves, internal operations become more efficient, and in general, the public benefits.

The following teleputing pilot program, New York City's I-Net (international network) project, illustrates high-tech application of video, voice, and data transmission in criminal justice management at the precinct level. Ross Daly, reporting for the *Newsday* series "Riding the Information Highway," describes an application of teleputing at the police precinct level:

> Officer Tom Buckley sat down in front of the assistant district attorney, calmly reviewing the facts of a domestic assault the night before. The husband, Buckley told Phil O'Hene, had battered his wife with a baseball bat. The attorney and the cop reviewed the facts, O'Hene typed up a criminal complaint, and Buckley signed it.
>
> Their meeting finished, Buckley stood up from the table in the 122nd Precinct station house in Staten Island. O'Hene stood, too—at the Targee Street Criminal Court, a 45-minute drive away. But Buckley didn't have to make that drive because he was using a video link-up between the precinct station house and the court.[34]

The dedicated fiber-optic, coaxial cable lines carry interactive pictures that allow participants to share each other's personal expressions and to make eye contact. As one officer said: "It's just like being there." Forty cities have brought forth suggestions for other applications and the city department of telecommunications and energy will be outlining future uses of the network.

CONCLUSIONS

Technological society introduced the high-tech crime scene and electronic criminal justice management. Teleputing—the convergence of telephone, television, and computer—added a new dimension, cyberspace. Sophisticated surveillance technology surfaced an almost inexhaustible supply of public and private information. Stored like money in the bank, this intangible asset assists law enforcement in identifying, apprehending, processing, convicting, and punishing offenders. At the same time, computers house invaluable information assets that can become targets for criminal activities.

The critical issue in this cybernetic world is how to work out a balance between freedom and social control. Knowledge is a powerful tool in the hands of social controllers. The government as a social control agent needs to know. Therefore, it conducts a census. Payment for services provided requires taxation, which to be equitably applied, necessitates information gathering. The criminal justice system functions to ensure lawful exercise of power. Technology has enhanced the government's capacity to know and, as a result, its power lies at the expense of personal and collective freedoms and privacy. Adjusting to this dilemma is the challenge of the future.

Being a double-edged sword, technology provides the means for our becoming a more fully informed society in which individual members can exercise self-control and informally regulate their behavior in the interest of social harmony, thus offering the possibility of a "computopian" society. On the other hand, advanced electronics also present the potentiality for implementing an Orwellian Big Brother global village. Jacques Ellul suggested a third, most likely, possibility: good and bad effects are inseparable. Hence we may continue to experience both positive and negative effects simultaneously.

In general, the high-tech stage is set: (1) Cyberspace overlays a more powerfully explosive physical environment; (2) teleputing provides abundant opportunities for mental wrongdoings as well as crime control; and (3) remotely controlled operations provide the cover of anonymity for the criminal as well as a means for more effective and efficient criminal justice management.

As actors on the stage we write the script, create social space, and design the beliefs, values, and standards by which we live. Fortunately, in this creative role we have the power to rearrange society to better meet our needs and express our values, always remembering that every action has intended and unintended consequences which may not always occur at the same time.

ENDNOTES

1. Technology: Global villager, *Wall Street Journal Reports*, November 15, 1993, p. R12.
2. Cyberpunk cover story, *Time*, February 8, 1993, p. 60.
3. The love connection, *Newsday*, November 7, 1993, p. 3.
4. Ibid.
5. Technology, *Wall Street Journal Reports*, November 15, 1993, p. R16.
6. Ibid.
7. W. P. Dizard, Jr., *The Coming Information Age*, 3rd ed. New York: Longman, 1989, p. 1.
8. The decline of the central bankers, *New York Times*, Forum, September 20, 1989.
9. Technology, op. cit., p. R4.
10. Ibid.
11. Ibid.; see also Riding the information highway, *Sunday Newsday*, Special Reprint, July 1993.
12. Scientist as detective, *Newsday*, February 21, 1994, p. 14.
13. *Virtual Reality World*. Westport, CT: Mecklermedia.
14. K. Hafner and J. Markoff, *Cyberpunk: Outlaws and Hackers on the Computer Frontier*. New York: Simon & Schuster, 1991, pp. 141–249. See also C. Stoll, *The Cuckoo's Egg*. New York: Pocket Books, 1990.
15. Cyberpunk, op. cit., pp. 186–187.
16. Ibid, pp. 301–302.
17. Computer terrorism, *National Times*, February 1993, p. 58.
18. Hanging up on hackers, *Crain's New York Business*, October 12, 1992, p. 21.
19. D. P. Delaney, Investigating telecommunications fraud, in J. J. Grau (ed.), *Criminal and Civil Investigation Handbook*, 2nd ed. New York: McGraw-Hill, 1994, pp. 35–35.
20. 2 Charged in big "clone" scam, *Newsday*, February 17, 1993.
21. Hacker gets logged into U.S. prison, *Newsday*, November 4, 1993, p. 6
22. J. F. Markey, Money laundering: An investigative perspective, in J. J. Grau (ed.), op. cit.
23. R. M. Pierce, Criminal investigative analysis, in J. J. Grau (ed.), op. cit.
24. Is nothing private? *Business Week*, September 4, 1989, p. 74.
25. Ibid., p. 77.
26. B. Jacobson, Technological advances and investigations, in J. J. Grau (ed.), op. cit.
27. White House faces backlash on policy to protect private telecommunications, *Wall Street Journal*, February 7, 1994, p. B4.
28. D. E. Denning, The clipper chip will block crime, Viewpoints in *Newsday*, February 22, 1994, p. 35.
29. Ibid.
30. J. Ellul, The technological order, *Technology and Culture*, 3, Fall 1962, p. 394, as referenced and quoted by W. P. Dizard, op. cit., p. 13.
31. A. Bequai, *Techno-Crimes*. Lexington, MA: Lexington Books, 1987, pp. 49–50.
32. Dizard, op. cit., p. 209.
33. A byte back at crime, *Newsday*, October 22, 1988, p. 8.
34. R. Daly, Taking a byte out of crime, *Newsday*, Special Reprint, July 1993, p. 16.

chapter 17

The Technoeconomic Revolution

Reengineering Criminal Justice Organizations and Workplaces

Rosemary L. Gido, Ph.D.

ABSTRACT

The American economy is being reshaped by a technoeconomic revolution comparable to the Industrial Revolution in terms of its impact on the definition of work, organization, and worker. Fueled by complex demographic, economic, and educational forces, the emerging workforce problem centers around a shortage of skilled workers and a continuing wage gap for the average U.S. wage earner. Issues for the criminal justice workplace of the future include attracting a high-quality workforce in the face of increased competition, affording opportunities to an increasingly diverse workforce, and embracing new organizational work models. The integration of information technologies will require dynamic organizational structures and employee participation inputs. The traditional reactivity and inertia of criminal justice organizations and workplaces will need to change. Elements of community policing recruitment and implementation are reviewed as a model for criminal justice organization and workplace change.

INTRODUCTION

The reshaping of the U.S. economy has appropriately been labeled a *technoeconomic revolution*, comparable to the Industrial Revolution in terms of its impact on the definition of work, organization, and worker (Snyder, 1996:9). The major forces driving this revolution include (1) rapid technological change, particularly information technology; (2) continued globalization of the U.S. economy; (3) rapid economic growth in populous, export-oriented developing nations, particularly in Asia and Latin

322

America; (4) deregulation and economic liberalization of international trade markets; and (5) the impact of the aging of nearly 83 million U.S. baby boomers (Jury and D'Amico, 1997:11–50).

With the current U.S. economy booming and exhibiting the unusual combination of low inflation and low unemployment (Shea, 1997), economists are reexamining some of the gloom and doom projections of the 1980s, which forecast dramatic skilled worker shortages, worldwide worker surpluses, and the demise of the American Dream (Peterson, 1993).

WORKFORCE ISSUES FOR THE DECADE

Changes in U.S. Workforce Composition

The first labor force analysis to gain national attention was *Workforce 2000*, published in 1987 (Johnston, 1987). *Workforce 2000* focused on the changing composition of the workforce and the demographic, economic, and educational trends that would exacerbate the skills deficit of U.S. workers into the next century.

Recently, the Hudson Institute published a sequel, *Workforce 2020*, which reexamined and refined some of the earlier findings and trend projections (Jury and D'Amico, 1997:4, 118–119, 121):

- The workforce will grow slowly, due to slow population growth and baby boomer retirements.

- Women will make up 50% of the 2020 workforce.

- There will be a gradual growth in the ethnic diversity of the national population and workforce. White non-Hispanics will make up 68% of the workforce in 2020. Hispanic and Asian proportions of the population and workforce will be greatest in western states such as California.

- With no changes in U.S. immigration policy, immigrants will comprise an increasing share of workers early in the century. Without improvements in educational preparation, these immigrants will be the growing pool of Americans who lack a high school education.

- The labor market of 2020 will demand a highly technologically skilled and highly educated workforce. There will be a continual decline in low-skill, low-pay U.S. jobs, which can now be done by workers throughout the world.

- Manufacturing's share of total employment in the United States will decline, fueled by automation and globalization. High productivity and highly skilled manufacturing jobs will remain and demand higher wages than in any other historical period.

In the last two years, U.S. labor force participation rates expanded to almost twice the rate of other years in the 1990s, bringing about 4 million additional workers into a growing economy. Most of the new entrants have come from the ranks of young women, persons nearing retirement, Hispanics, and from eastern states and prospering southern states such as Kentucky. *These new workers are primarily filling in at the lower end of the salary scale as other workers shift to better jobs* (Uchitelle, 1997a). Yet a recent analysis of U.S. economic expansion finds that it is onlly since 1996 that opportunities for workers at the low end of the labor market have improved (Whalen, 2000).

At the same time, a resurgence in blue-collar job growth—a record 32.8 million recorded in the spring of 1997—has suggested that contrary to forecasts, job growth in this sector will continue for the next 10 years (Hershey, 1997). Yet the "composition" of blue-collar work has clearly changed, away from manufacturing and toward communications, transportation, and law enforcement. Supporting the predictions, the fasting-growing new blue-collar jobs are technician types in the service sector (Hershey, 1997:D2).

It is doubtful that these short-term shifts will affect the *wage gap* and the two decades of "stagnant living standards weathered by the bottom three-quarters of Americans....[A]verage wages remain lower, after adjusting for inflation, than their all-time peak in 1973" (Anon., 1997). And as reported in *The State of Working America, 2000–01* (Economic Policy Institute, 2000):

> In spite of the widespread living standard improvements accompanying the strong recovery of the late 1990s, the fundamental economic situation, given the dramatic broad-based wage erosion and rising inequalities of the 1979–95 period, can still not be considered "good." For instance, over the 1989–99 period, productivity, which might be considered the economy's "ability to pay," or its yardstick to measure good growth, rose 20.5%. However, typical workers received virtually none of this increase—the median hourly wage among men was slightly less in 1999 than in 1989, while for women it was up just 4%.
>
> Between 1989 and 1998, the inflation-adjusted incomes of the median, or typical, family grew just 0.4% per year—identical to the disappointing average growth rate of the 1980s and well below the 2.6–2.8% average rate from 1947 to 1973. Even the income gains of the late 1990s—median inflation-adjusted income grew 2.5% a year—fell short of the average rate achieved during the first 30 years of the postwar period....Between 1989 and 1998, the share of total income received by the bottom 20% of households fell 0.4 percentage points, while the share received by the top 5% grew from 17.9% in 1989 to 20.7% in 1998.

Moreover, an improving economy has not resulted in either a public- or private-sector commitment to a long-term solution to the endemic problems of unskilled workers and the skills gap. The Clinton administration sponsored a National Skills Summit on April 11, 2000, focusing on the U.S. workforce skills shortage. It echoed an earlier analysis based on the 1987 Hudson Institute study (Gido, 1996:273):

> The stagnation of earnings among the young and less educated raises more critical long-term issues. High level jobs resulting from technological change are not likely to go to those most disadvantaged by lack of education, discrimination, or language barrier. To what degree will such patterns of uneven economic growth and opportunity and change in the structure of jobs erode communities and increase the risk of crime and violence (Currie, 1987)? Will national policy priorities for the year 2000 emphasize job creation and training/retraining for disadvantaged and displaced workers? Will our nation continue to rely on expansion of the criminal justice system as a response to those displaced from the labor market who turn to crime?

The degree to which there is public commitment to these labor market strategies will directly affect the role of the criminal justice system in the 21st century. At the same time, the criminal justice workplace will face similar dilemmas to that of the private sector: managing an increasingly diverse workforce; affording opportunities to women; retaining and retraining seasoned and new employees; and embracing new organizational models which permit flexibility, employee participation, and proactive human resources strategies.

Information Technology and Workplace Organization

The most dramatic changes in the workplace are unfolding as information technology (IT) reframes the structure and content of work environments. *Distributed workforces* are becoming the norm as electronic technology has made it possible to link workers and functions at various locations (Barner, 1996). Corporate and public employment downsizing has actually increased reliance on such virtual organizations and has resulted in reengineering workplaces that support group decision making, teamwork, and employee empowerment (Gido, 1996:275).

The integration of information technology into work organizations supports a more flexible and dynamic organizational structure. The term *learning organization* refers to a more flexible and adaptable work setting, with the emphasis on continuous improvement and work defined more fluidly as projects managed in teams (Garvin, 1993; Barner, 1996).

The need to produce both technically trained employees and those capable of adaptability, self-direction, motivation, and team communication points to "a mismatch between higher education and economic conditions and trends" (Jury and D'Amico, 1997:139). The U.S. skills gap will not disappear as long as "more degrees in the United States are awarded in home economics than in mathematics" (Jury and D'Amico, 1997:139).

TWENTY-FIRST CENTURY WORKFORCE TRENDS: PERSONNEL DILEMMAS FOR CRIMINAL JUSTICE ORGANIZATIONS AND WORKPLACES

The workforce trends outlined above will present significant personnel-related dilemmas for criminal justice administrators in the future. Specifically (Gido, 1996):

- The creation of higher-paying, higher-skill jobs in the private sector will make it more difficult to attract such talent to the traditional criminal justice work environment. The smaller size of the labor pool will increase competition for such qualified workers, driving up salaries that will be impossible to match by police and corrections agencies.

- The remaining worker pool will be largely semiskilled and unskilled. Even more qualified workers displaced by reengineering may not be available to the criminal justice workplace, as they are likely to be quickly absorbed by the private sector, given the smaller labor pool. As entry level jobs decline and reengineering or a slowing in current economic growth stalls new job creation, will the criminal justice system have to recruit from a less qualified labor pool?

- Women, minorities, and immigrants represent a potential resource for recruitment to the criminal justice workplace. Women are now more likely than men to graduate from high school and complete college (Mishel and Teixeira, 1991). Will criminal justice administrators attract these groups as affirmative action policies are being dismantled?

- The implementation of virtual organizations and learning organizations are advancing in today's workplace. To what degree will such criminal justice innovations as community policing and unit management go forward if more qualified employees cannot be attracted and retained? Similar to the private sector, will reengineering and the introduction of computer-based technologies into the criminal justice workplace enhance productivity with fewer workers (Archambeault, 1996)?

The effects of the technoeconomic revolution on the criminal justice work environment of the future are directly related to present criminal justice management and personnel practices. It is clear that criminal justice agencies need to address both organizational structures and human resource policies that are resistant to internal and external change. These structural and cultural barriers are obstacles to the reengineering of proactive human resource policies, flexible organizational models, and employee decision making—all essential elements to high-quality criminal justice workplaces in the future.

BARRIERS TO CRIMINAL JUSTICE ORGANIZATIONAL CHANGE

Reactivity and Inertia

Foremost among the impediments to change across criminal justice agencies is the reactive nature of the criminal justice business. Unlike private-sector employers, the public sector serves the public, and public-safety dictates often preclude long-term fiscal planning and personnel training. Although the 1990s have brought tremendous increases in state corrections budgets, funding has been directed at building more prisons, with little allocated for employee development. At the federal level, Crime Bill allocations for police have been more likely to be spent on equipment and defensive armaments. High-profile police corruption cases in large cities such as New York and Philadelphia point to continuing deficits in law enforcement screening, recruitment, and training.

Organizational inertia is often cited as the enemy of change and innovation. Despite integration of the concepts and language of "emerging and new organizational paradigms" in publications for police (DeParis, 1997), the extent to which policing has changed in the United States is a subject of debate given the diffusion of community policing. In a review of police patrol practices of the past decade, Mastrofski found that American police are "becoming more susceptible to broader forces of purposive change"

(Mastrofski, 1990:2). Yet research has documented that implementing management strategies based on empowerment and participation alone will not solve resistance to the implementation of community policing (Gaines and Swanson, 1997).

Gender and Racial Barriers

Assessments of the status of women and minorities in police work indicate that most of the blatant discrimination practices of the past have been eliminated (Martin, 1989). There are, however, still obstacles in the formal and informal structures of police work organizations related to gender and race (Martin, 1989:302). Hale and Wyland (1993), for example, find that despite evaluation studies which indicate that women are successful as patrol officers, the organizational culture of policing has resisted women's integration into this role over the last 20 years. They cite three types of organizational resistance to blocking the recruitment and retention of female patrol officers. Technical resistance includes both the failure to adapt police uniforms and equipment adequately for women, as well as the continued emphasis on physical testing and firearms during training. Political and cultural resistance is evidenced in the failure to develop child care programs, flexible and gender-neutral shifts, and maternity–paternity policies (Hale and Wyland, 1993:5).

Zupan (1992) has also documented cultural and structural roadblocks to women correctional officers in all-male prisons. Tokenism, differential treatment, and discrimination by first-line officers in the assignment of women officers and continued opposition to women by male co-workers still exist.

While some researchers have noted the dramatic effects on police agencies of the assimilation of African-Americans and other minorities into the police (Maghan, 1992), the recruitment and promotion of minority officers is still at issue. Continued reliance on written examinations and negative image of policing as an occupation for people of color hinder recruitment efforts. The underrepresentation of minority officers above the patrol level as well as lack of access to informal "white-power networks" within the outside police departments represent obstacles to promotion.

Despite these major obstacles to organizational change and workplace quality, there are some positive models of change that have been developed and implemented in criminal justice agencies of today. These innovations represent the basic change agents that will enable criminal justice organizations to become more flexible, respond to employee needs, and attract and retain qualified personnel.

EMERGING MODELS OF CRIMINAL JUSTICE ORGANIZATION CHANGE

Community Policing

Despite the intransigence of policing resistance to change, problem-oriented and community policing hold the best hope for institutional change. Program complexity, variation in scope, and limitations in research design have been cited as barriers to comprehensive evaluations of community policing efforts (Cordner, 1995:7). Nonetheless, some experts locate the chances of long-term success for strategic policing in (1) the qualitative changes that are taking place in police recruitment and training, and (2) implementation strategies that are aimed at long-term comprehensive organizational change.

Bittner (1990) acknowledges that a college degree is a key factor in police officer candidates who will be successful in proactive policing. As there may be significant competition for college graduates for other occupational fields, the essential element for change must take place within training academies. These graduates are a cadre of young officers who have the potential to change existing departments.

Research on community police officers' job satisfaction and community perceptions and attitudes have found beneficial effects, particularly for those who are volunteers or members of special units (Cordner, 1995:7). Clearly, recruitment efforts must be focused on candidates who match skill and motivation profiles that include problem solving, decision making, critical thinking, and creativity. Support for the empowerment of officers comes from changes in recruitment standards and training, new guidelines for the exercise of discretion, and the inculcation of values to guide decision making (Goldstein, 1993).

Changes in the work environment beyond the development of new management styles are critical to the success of community policing. The major obstacle to achieving full implementation of community policing has been the failure to "engage and elicit a commitment from those having management and supervisory responsibilities" (Goldstein, 1993).

The implementation of organization-wide change to effect community policing, as opposed to a narrower focus on "new" management strategies such as empowerment and participative management, has been proposed (Cordner, 1995). Such a comprehensive change strategy includes (Gaines and Swanson, 1997:5–6):

1. *Goals and strategy.* Drawing on the key building blocks of community partnership and problem solving, administrators must develop new policies at all department levels to ensure diffusion and commitment to the new philosophy and focus.

2. *People.* Complete restructuring of human resource systems to attract appropriate personnel as outlined above is necessary as well as training and policies that are specific to the program and community.

3. *Services.* Replacement of the traditional reactive service model with a citizen "client-based" system is the key. This includes citizen input into problem solving and forming police goals and objectives.

4. *Technology.* Police information systems are utilized to scan the environment as a routine part of proactive problem solving and a basis for developing police tactics to address the problem.

CONCLUSIONS

Workforce investment is a major economic development theme as the U.S. economy moves through a technoeconomic revolution. Critical to this transition is the degree to which income disparity and job displacement can be translated into high-value jobs and "informated" workplaces. The challenge for this society is to allocate the resources to support citizen access to higher education and training, technical competencies, and high-quality workplaces. The alternative is a future where criminal justice agencies and agents continue to function as reactive forces to crime and violence as enacted by those permanently displaced from the labor market.

REFERENCES AND BIBLIOGRAPHY

ANON. (1997). Sharing prosperity. *Business Week*, September 1, pp. 64–70.

ARCHAMBEAULT, W. G. (1996). Impact of computer based technologies on criminal justice: Transition to the 21st century. In R. Muraskin and A. R. Roberts (eds.), *Visions for Change*. Upper Saddle River, NJ: Prentice Hall.

BARNER, R. (1996). Seven changes that will challenge managers—and workers. Futurist, March–April, pp. 14–18.

BAYLEY, D. (1994). *Police for the Future*. New York: Oxford University Press.

BITTNER, E. (1990). Some reflections on staffing problem-oriented policing. *American Journal of Police* 9(3):189–196.

BOLMAN, L. G., and T. E. DEAL (1991). *Reframing Organizations: Artistry, Choice, and Leadership*. San Francisco: Jossey-Bass.

BRIGGS, V. M. (1996). Immigration policy and the U.S. economy: An institutional perspective. *Journal of Economic Issues*, 30(2):371–387.

CORDNER, G. W. (1995). Community policing: Elements and effects. *Police Forum*, 5(3):1–8.

CURRIE, E. (1987). *What Kind of Future? Violence and Public Safety in the Year 2000*. San Francisco: National Council on Crime and Delinquency.

DEPARIS, R. J. (1997). Situational leadership: Problem-solving leadership for problem-solving policing. *Police Chief*, October, pp. 74–86.

ECONOMIC POLICY INSTITUTE (2000). *State of Working America, 2000–01*. www.epinet.org//books/swa2000/swa2000intro.html.

GAINES, L. K., and C. R. SWANSON (1997). Empowering police officers: A tarnished silver bullet? *Police Forum*, 7(4):1–7.

GARVIN, D. A. (1993). Building a learning organization. *Harvard Business Review*, July–August, Reprint 93402, pp. 78–91.

GIDO, R. L. (1996). Organizational change and workforce planning: Dilemmas for criminal justice organizations for the year 2000. In R. Muraskin and A. R. Roberts (eds.), *Visions for Change*. Upper Saddle River, NJ: Prentice Hall.

GOLDSTEIN, H. (1993). *The New Policing: Confronting Complexity*. Research in Brief. Washington, DC: U.S. Department of Justice.

HALE, D. C., and S. M. WYLAND (1993). Dragons and dinosaurs: The plight of patrol women. *Police Forum*, 3(2):1–6.

HERSHEY, R. D. (1997). The rise of the working class: Blue-collar jobs gain, but the work changes in tone. *New York Times*, September 3, pp. D1, D2.

JOHNSON, J., J. R. BALDWIN, and B. DIVERTY (1996). The implications of innovation for human resource strategies. *Futures*, 28(2):103–119.

JOHNSTON, W. (1987). *Workforce 2000*. Prepared for the U.S. Department of Labor. Indianapolis, IN: Hudson Institute.

JURY, R. W., and C. D'AMICO (1997). *Workforce 2020: Work and Workers in the 21st Century* (sequel to *Workforce 2000*). Indianapolis, IN: Hudson Institute.

MAGHAN, J. (1992). Black police officer recruits: Aspects of becoming blue. *Police Forum* 2(1):8–11.

MARTIN, S. (1989). Female officers on the move? A status report on women in policing. In R.G. Dunham and G. P. Alpert (eds.), *Critical Issues in Policing*. Prospect Heights, IL: Waveland Press.

MASTROFSKI, S. D. (1990). The prospects of change in police patrol: A decade in review. *American Journal of Police*, 9(3):1–79.

MISHEL, L., and R. A. TEIXEIRA (1991). *The Myth of the Coming Labor Shortage: Jobs, Skills and Income of America's Workforce 2000*. Washington, DC: Economic Policy Institute.

PETERSON, P. G. (1993). *Facing Up: How to Rescue the Economy from Crushing Debt and Restore the American Dream*. New York: Simon & Schuster.

SCHWARTZ, J. E. (1997). *The American Dream in Question*. New York: W.W. Norton.

SENGE, P. M. (1990). *The Fifth Discipline: The Art and Practice of the Learning Organization*. New York: Doubleday.

SHEA, C. (1997). Low inflation and low unemployment spur economists to debate "natural rate" theory. *Chronicle of Higher Education*, October 24, p. A13.

SNYDER, D. P. (1996). The revolution in the workplace: What's happening to our jobs? *Futurist*, March–April, p. 8–13.

TROJANOWICZ, R. C., and D. L. CARTER (1990). The changing face of America. *FBI Law Enforcement Bulletin*, January, pp. 7–12.

UCHITELLE, L. (1997a). U.S. job machine absorbing fresh workers. *New York Times*, July 10, pp. A1, D5.

UCHITELLE, L. (1997b). That was then and this is the 90s: Today looks a bit like the golden post-war years until you look more closely. *New York Times*, June 18, pp. D1, D6.

WHALEN, C. J. (2000). Economic trends. *Business Week*, August 28, p. 38.

ZUPAN, L. (1992). The progress of women correctional officers in all-male prisons. In I. Moyer (ed.), *The Changing Roles of Women in the Criminal Justice System*. Prospect Heights, IL: Waveland Press.

chapter 18

Prosecuting Environmental Crime in the Twenty-First Century

Donald J. Rebovich, Ph.D.

ABSTRACT

In this chapter we trace environmental crime prosecution from its early days in the 1970s at the federal level, through the 1980s, when state attorneys general proceeded to initiate environmental crime prosecutions at growing levels, to the present, when many of the prosecution responsibilities have shifted into the hands of district attorneys and county prosecutors. Based on these trends and recent empirical research, projections are furnished that characterize environmental prosecutions of the future.

   Part of the discussion on environmental prosecution in the future centers on the building pressure of the public to demand criminal punishment of offenders and protection from the results of their criminal activities and the manner in which prosecutors will probably respond to such pressure. Recent role expansions of local district attorneys are emphasized as the wave of the future for environmental prosecution. The chapter concludes with a discussion of a future research agenda in this area.

INTRODUCTION

The process of criminalization of human behavior judged to be harmful to the public is typically one that builds slowly in common law jurisdictions. Momentum gained through problem identification and pressures exerted by special-interest groups can easily span decades before undesirable actions are classified as "crime" through legislative enactment. A rare exception to this problem is the relatively speedy transformation of acts of pollution into official *crimes against the environment*. National media coverage of toxic tragedies like those occurring at Love Canal, New York, in the late 1970s and at Times Beach, Missouri, in the early 1980s altered forever the American public's perception of the improper disposal of hazardous waste and sparked the quick passing of criminal laws on both federal and state legislative levels prohibiting offenses against the environment.

Entrusted with implementing these new laws is a growing army of prosecutors specializing in environmental crime prosecution that will assume broad responsibilities for the control of environmental crime as we enter the twenty-first century. Once found exclusively within the U.S. Department of Justice, environmental crime prosecutors now populate many state attorney general offices as well as the offices of local district attorneys in urban–metropolitan jurisdictions. In this chapter we examine the problems that these prosecutors face, the future implications of recent environmental studies of local, state, and federal environmental crime prosecutions, and how certain factors can be expected to affect the prosecution of environmental crime in the future. These factors include recent changes in standards for the admissibility of scientific evidence into the courtroom, an enhanced public awareness of the dangers of environmental crime, the growing acceptance of the crime problem as an equity issue, and criminal displacement caused by tougher enforcement. We also project improvements in the effectiveness of environmental crime prosecution brought about by the widened availability of specialized training and greater experimentation with new technology and prosecution strategies. We conclude with an agenda for prospective research that can serve to complement the work of criminal prosecutors in the forefront of this rapidly evolving crime area.

A NEW CRIMINAL ROLE: THE LOCAL ENVIRONMENTAL PROSECUTOR

Gradually, and without abatement, grass-roots movements have helped elevate the issue of environmental protection to a serious matter of community safety that, increasingly, is being seen by local public officials as an important obligation (Bullard, 1991). Community leaders and the public they represent are turning to their elected crime control leaders—local prosecutors—for the type of protection they have come to expect from these officials on more traditional predatory crimes. In response to this groundswell, district attorneys, particularly in densely populated jurisdictions, are preparing their personnel to confront the mammoth task of solving and prosecuting these crimes locally rather than passing them up to federal or state agencies, a common practice in the past (Metz, 1985). Through this direct involvement, local prosecutors are seizing the opportunity to demonstrate their level of concern for constituents' well-being, rather than deferring enforcement responsibilities to other government agencies through claims of lack of ability or expertise (Meehan, 1991).

State and federal agencies traditionally responsible for the enforcement of environmental laws have been characterized by some in the early 1990s as isolated, specialized, and only mildly empathetic to local issues (Murphy, 1991). Lack of involvement of state/federal environmental enforcement agencies in local issues has tended to further their isolation from other public safety functions of local government. As we move toward the twenty-first century, local prosecutors are filling this vacuum by bringing to this area an integration of environmental prosecutions into the routine function of law enforcement at the local level. Counteracting what some have called the federal "boutique" approach to environmental crime enforcement, this response by local prosecutors symbolizes their sensitivity to a crime problem too long overlooked (Jensen, 1991).

As seen by the Environmental Protection Agency (EPA) in its *Enforcement in the 1990s Project Report*, greater district attorney involvement in criminal prosecutions would provide a faster response to environmental crimes, reducing environmental risk or damage. Prosecution by district attorneys is also expected to deter criminal behavior within a class of violators too numerous for EPA and the states to reach. In addition, operations can be tailored to indigenous community conditions to meet community needs, and cooperative relationships can be built among local, state, and federal agents to form task forces necessary to investigate and prosecute environmental crimes efficiently and effectively (Herrod et al., 1991).

BARRIERS TO EFFECTIVE ENVIRONMENTAL PROSECUTION: WHAT IS CURRENTLY KNOWN

Despite recent gains made in the investigation of environmental offenses (Metz, 1985; Hawke, 1987), hurdles to achieving consistency in environmental prosecution success remain. The most frequently expressed prosecution-related problems, as reported through a 1988 prosecutors' survey, dealt with difficulties in juror and judicial interpretation of complex criminal laws and regulations (Rebovich, 1992). Ohio, Pennsylvania, Vermont, and Virginia were states that found this complexity to be particularly troublesome. In these states, juror and judicial uncertainty of interpretation of relevant laws and regulations was thought to jeopardize the attainment of guilty verdicts. Even in cases resulting in convictions, prosecutors in Virginia claimed that time spent on the courtroom clarification of the statutes resulted in substantial processing-time delays. There have been some indications that local prosecutors have avoided the prosecution of clearly criminal environmental violations out of fear of losing the cases because of such cases' highly technical nature.

Since 1992, three separate publications have been produced that furnish valuable new insight into characteristics of environmental crime and its prosecution. A fourth work presents results of a national survey that can help us in taking a peek at what is in store for all with regard to environmental crime/crime control.

Dangerous Ground: The World of Hazardous Waste Crime (Rebovich, 1992) laid out the results of a study of hazardous waste crime in the northeastern United States between 1977 and 1985 and efforts to stem its growth on the state enforcement/prosecution level. While state criminal enforcement/prosecution agencies studied were found to be dedicated and responsible for major inroads into environmental crime, they were also found to be routinely undercut by failures of state regulatory agencies and by a paucity of resources to address adequately all environmental crime reported. The book warns of the potential of amendments to the Resource Conservation and Recovery Act (Pub. L. No. 98-616, 1984, U.S.C., 6901–6987, 1982) in widening the defining parameters of environmental crime and, in turn, widening the population of those subject to criminal prosecution.[1]

In "Environmental Crime and Punishment: Legal/Economic Theory and Empirical Evidence on Enforcement of Federal Environmental Statutes" (1992), Cohen presented empirical information on 703 environmental crime prosecutions on the *federal* level by the Department of Justice's Environmental Crimes Section between 1983 and 1990. Cohen's analysis found that the average firm charged with environmental crime on the federal level is larger than the average firm charged with nonenvironmental federal crimes. Cohen further projects the growth of the proportion of large companies charged with federal environmental crimes based on his assertion of a trend toward criminalizing and prosecuting regulatory noncompliance and street liability offenses on the federal level.

Hammett and Epstein's NIJ-supported "Local Prosecution of Environmental Crime" (1993a) shifts the focus of environmental crime control to the local government level in the presentation of its results of case studies of five local prosecutors' offices. The report portrays some progressive local prosecutors' offices as vigorously taking on the challenge of controlling environmental crime and dispelling the myth that these cases are inherently too complex and expensive for district attorneys to handle. Environmental crime is presented as varying in its makeup from locality to locality, with local prosecutors and police departments representing agencies appropriately attuned to local community needs, but heretofore underused in the fight against environmental crime.

The most recent empirical study of environmental prosecution was a NIJ-supported national assessment of the abilities and needs of environmental prosecutors on the local government level: district attorneys (Rebovich and Nixon, 1994). The study found that over 75% of the 100 urban prosecutors' offices surveyed have prosecutors assigned specifically to environmental crime cases, with half of the offices operating special environmental prosecution units. According to the study, between January 1990 and June 1992 the volume of environmental cases prosecuted by the prosecutors more than doubled (i.e., 667 to 1352). Community pressure to criminally prosecute environmental offenses was perceived by the majority of respondents as far outweighing pressures applied by the business community to withhold prosecutions. The access to and use of technical experts in environmental crime cases were considered to be of extraordinary value to prosecutors' decision making in charging and to their effectiveness at trial.[2] To improve their effectiveness, respondents were almost unanimous in their expression of need for increased technical assistance and specialized training.

Synthesized along with qualitative case study data, the study results illustrate how district attorneys have been compelled to assume greater responsibility for controlling environmental crime. The results also show how district attorneys have gravitated toward specializing professional personnel in environmental crime prosecution and have become more active in developing task forces dedicated to environmental crime control (Rebovich, 1998).

FACTORS AFFECTING ENVIRONMENTAL PROSECUTION IN THE FUTURE

Based on our knowledge of environmental crime, its prosecution, and the needs of environmental prosecutors, it is apparent that the future offers many new challenges for those prosecuting environmental crime. There are several key areas, however, that warrant special attention. They are areas in which patterns of change should have noticeable impact on the manner in which environmental crime is prosecuted in the future and the level of its effectiveness. These areas include changes in public and system sentiment toward environmental crime, particularly with regard to punishment, growing dissent in low-income areas about environmental crime control, and the spillover of environmental crime to suburban and rural districts. Of a more technical nature, changes in evidence admissibility standards, in education for improvement of prose- cutorial skills, and in the testing of new technologies and strategies will probably influence the state of environmental crime prosecution in the twenty-first century. The following is a projection of what we can come to expect in each of these areas.

Wider Acceptance of Strict Penalties for Environmental Offenses

After years of setbacks in their plight to raise environmental violations to the level of "criminal behavior," prosecutors of environmental crime are now on the verge of witnessing a change in the winds of sentiment on this issue. In the 1991 second national environmental opinion study conducted by Environmental Opinion Study Inc., U.S. citizens were found, overwhelmingly, to favor terms of incarceration for corporate or government officials convicted of deliberately violating pollution laws (Environmental Opinion Study, 1991). The U.S. Sentencing Commission's proposal on how to sentence corporations for environmental crimes seemed to further reflect a toughening on acts of environmental crime. Determination of fines under the proposed guidelines requires sentencing judges to calculate factors such as economic gain derived from the criminal act and costs attributed to the pollution (e.g., cleanup costs, actual environmental harm) and to merge their calculations with an ordinal grading of offense severity set out by the commission. Judges are also encouraged, through the proposed guidelines, to put defendants on probation for one to five years. Altogether, the guidelines have drawn much protest from certain business community groups and conservative legal foundations as being "draconian" in nature (DeBenedictis, 1993).

The public's disgust with environmental crime and the government's new proclivity to react was typified by the "Rocky Flats affair," a case that should prove to be a lasting catalyst to intensified criminal prosecution of environmental offenses and sentence impositions for some time to come. In 1992, Rockwell Corp., a nuclear weapons facility in Rocky Flats, Colorado, pled guilty to federal criminal violations involving the illegal disposal and storage of hazardous wastes. Although the plea bargain did result in a $18.5 million penalty for Rockwell, federal prosecutors sought no individual indictments against Rockwell employees. The most noteworthy aspect of the case is that federal grand jury members chose to disregard the prosecutor's decision not to pursue individual indictments and attempted, instead, to indict Rockwell employees on their own.

This incident, plus questions regarding the handling of other environmental pollution cases by federal prosecutors, eventually became the target of a House oversight committee chaired by Rep. John Dingell (D-Mich.). The Dingell panel was assembled to review Justice Department policy on environmental crime and to investigate changes of leniency toward polluting corporations. Although the panel ostensibly represented a feasible avenue for unearthing information on patterns of a "soft" approach under the Bush administration toward violations of federal environmental laws, it also received sharp criticism for what was charged as an assault against the concept of prosecutorial discretion. These allegations became more pronounced when Dingell's staff was allowed by Attorney General Janet Reno to interview career attorneys at the Department of Justice about their cases (LaFranire, 1992; Anon., 1993).

The genesis of environmental offense criminalization has taken us from a point in the past where the average American equated hazardous waste dumping to "throwing out the garbage," to a point where after years of rising numbers of incidents of these offenses—and media attention to them—the public outcry to punish severely has reached a pitch heard plainly by those in political power. Environmental crime control officials have worked diligently to change the normative climate on pollution and are finally seeing some genuine results.

Federal sentencing patterns for environmental crimes analyzed by Cohen highlight a sentencing toughness unparalleled in the past. Federal sentencing guidelines propose to put more teeth into punitive options, and leniency toward corporate polluters is questioned at the highest levels of government. But while environmental prosecutors overall should be satisfied with such results, the possibility exists that their voracity, aimed at tendering more punitive sanctions, may become their own unique conundrum: *How "tough" is "tough" when it comes to environmental crime?* By raising the level of consciousness of the public and government officials on the "criminality" of acts of pollution, prosecutors may have also raised expectations that even they cannot meet. A more aware public will, in the coming years, be more demanding of prosecutors on all government levels to treat polluters harshly. This means an expectation of a reduction in leniency in plea negotiations in cases that will now place prosecutors under a magnifying glass, much like their experiences with more traditional high-profile crime cases. As state and local prosecutors intensify their efforts to prosecute environmental crimes, they will also undergo greater public and media scrutiny, held to a higher standard than they themselves will have created, a standard that may indirectly limit prosecutorial discretion.

Despite evidence that the general public has not wavered in its support of meeting environmental infractions with strong and swift control responses, efforts to roll back stricter enforcement have not been totally absent from the national scene. Eclipsing the less-than-successful political maneuverings by conservative members of Congress to weaken environmental programs has been resisted by some state governments against vigorous enforcement of federal environmental laws. In some instances this resistance has escalated into ideological battles over states' rights. In 1997, the EPA cited

Virginia as a leading example of such resistance coming at a time when states have gained more responsibility in environmental enforcement. The differences between the Virginia Department of Environmental Quality and the EPA came into sharp relief in early 1997, when the EPA filed a $125 million suit against Smithfield Foods for pollution of the Pagan River at the company's meat plants in Smithfield, Virginia, after the Virginia DEQ had sought far lighter penalties than the EPA had wanted. This came in the wake of a report by the Virginia General Assembly's review commission that the Virginia DEQ had demonstrated a steadily declining rate of environmental case referrals for criminal prosecution from 1989 to 1997. The Virginia DEQ's defense of their heavy reliance on the use of consent orders rather than the pursuit of civil or criminal penalties to contain environmental violations is emblematic of efforts by some states to grant generous flexibility in disposal practices to private businesses.[3] In what has the potential for materializing into a setback for environmental prosecutors of the future, states like Virginia have gone as far as enacting legislation protecting waste-generating firms from disclosure and punishment when the firms detect pollution violations in self-inspections and remedy them (Cushman, 1997).

Self-Auditing Privileges

Into the twenty-first century, we can expect that the legislative changes that will have the most significant impact on environmental crime enforcement will be those changes granting self-auditing privileges to waste-generating companies. In the 1990s, private businesses were afforded new incentives to conduct internal environmental audits, incentives such as the protection of the confidentiality of environmental audits and the reduction of penalties for firms reporting audits or self-reporting violations. This was a result of the strong lobbying of Congress and state legislatures, by industry, to offer incentives for performing environmental audits. The argument made by representatives of industry was that the vulnerability of audits to disclosure discourages business managers to conduct audits. The business industry movement to encourage the adoption of self-auditing privileges has resulted in the birth of two types of incentives for the performance of audits. The first type, the audit privilege, protects the confidentiality of the audit only. Self-auditing policies under which regulatory agencies provide lenient treatment to companies that perform audits represent the second type. Through 1997, eighteen states had enacted audit privilege programs intended to provide incentives for the performance of self-audits.[4] Oregon adopted audit privileges that protect the confidentiality of voluntary audits of their compliance programs and management systems rendering environmental audit reports inadmissible as evidence in legal actions (Oregon Revised Statutes 468.963 [1]; McCoy, 1997).

By 1997, environmental auditing privileges had become highly politicized on the national level. Environmentalist organizations as well as the EPA and federal and local prosecutors have vigorously opposed self-auditing privileges. Although it is generally agreed that self-audits have the potential to be important in confirming compliance with environmental regulations and the minimizing of waste in manufacturing, criminal justice officials have expressed deep concern about the latitude of control businesses can enjoy under these privileges and the extent of protection they may receive. Those from the crime control community objecting to self-audit privileges contend that the presence of the incentives will mean the addition of new, formidable obstacles to the effective enforcement of environmental laws. The scenario depicted by these officials is that the new laws would be exploited by polluters to sidestep responsibility for their criminal acts. Criminal prosecutors are particularly worried that the laws would prevent prosecutors from seizing as evidence materials routinely relied upon in investigations of the illegal disposal of hazardous waste (Cushman, 1997; McCoy, 1997; Rebovich, 1998).

The EPA publicly stated its strong disapproval of audit privileges and promised to take a position of ignoring any state legislation granting them. The EPA's repsonse to calls by political conservatives for enhanced environmental audit incentives was its *Project XL*, designed to provide greater flexibility in regulation. The initiative was developed to encourage companies to create their own regulatory game plans for pollution control. After the plans are developed, local government, environmental group, and private citizen "stakeholders" are brought into negotiations to approve the company's plans. As a laboratory for new regulatory approaches, however, the project became the target of harsh criticism from groups like the Silicon Valley Toxics Coalition with regard to the Project XL agreement struck between the EPA and Intel Corporation and the amount of leverage the public was allowed in the process. At present, it is uncertain just how much impact the EPA's Project XL will have on appeasing interests backing the environmental audit incentive movement (McCoy, 1997; Skrzycki, 1997).

Legal experts such as William McCoy (1997) remind us that environmental audit incentives are still relatively new and that laws, regulations, and policies affecting them are unsettled. As we move into the twenty-first century, the issue of audit incentives should continue to be a subject of debate in state and local politics leading to possible rapid changes. The implications of these laws should become less cloudy as private businesses and enforcement/regulatory agencies become more familiar with them. We can only speculate, however, on the effects the laws will have on the behavior of those employed by waste-generating companies and on the effectiveness of criminal prosecution of polluters, *unless* there are controlled, empirical evaluations of the implementation of the laws in the states that have enacted them.

Environmental Equity

As environmental prosecutors enter the twenty-first century, it is likely that they will, more than ever, be required to consider carefully the ramifications of the issue of environmental equity. As defined by the EPA, *environmental equity* refers to the distribution of environmental risks across population groups and policy responses to them. In 1990, EPA's 30-member task force on environmental equity concluded that minority communities experience greater than average exposure to environmental hazards including lead, air pollutants, and toxic wastes (EPA, 1990). Activists representing the lower class lay claims that industry consciously locates its most polluting plants in low-income, minority areas, with the tacit approval of government (Weisskopf, 1992). The close proximity of these plants, landfills, and incineration facilities add up to a disproportionate amount of pollution in these areas, along with the creation of a local culture tolerant of the illegal abandonment of hazardous waste. This has taken its most insidious form in such areas as the Altgeld district of Chicago, where "fly dumping"— hit-and-run waste dumping—has become a common practice (Ervin, 1992).

In *Environmental Equity: Reducing Risk for All Communities* (EPA, 1992), the EPA pledges to address the inequity of low-income population proximity to chemical dangers by making a number of recommendations for improvement. These include the selective review and revision of EPA's permit, grant, monitoring, and enforcement procedures in low-income communities and improvement of the manner in which EPA communicates with racial minorities.

Up to the present, the most graphic demonstration of EPA's new stance on environmental equity occurred in September 1997, when the EPA blocked a request for a chemical plant to be built in a poor, predominately black Louisiana town. In this landmark case, the EPA ruled that emissions from a polyvinyl chloride plant proposed by Shintech Inc. in Convent, Louisiana, would exceed air pollution standards under the Clean Air Act. EPA contended that the building of the Shintech plant, a producer of PVC pipe used in construction, would make the city of Convent unlivable because of the presence of close to a dozen chemical facilities in the surrounding area. In her decision, EPA administrator Carol Browner stated that EPA's action in this case reflected what would be a long-term program by EPA to ensure that minority and low-income communities are not subjected disproportionately to environmental hazards (Hoversten, 1997).

Criminal enforcement, however, has yet to effect a plan to address the environmental crime violations occurring as by-products of the disproportionate presence of plants, landfills, and incinerators in these areas. As pressure grows from activist groups to arrest this problem, the crime control burden will probably fall on the shoulders of state and local prosecutors. It is foreseen that those prosecutors progressive enough to realize the gravity of environmental equity will open avenues of communication with minority-group community leaders to identify environmental patterns in low-income areas and begin to direct their task force resources toward those locations at greatest risk.

Displacement of Environmental Crime

As prosecutors become more proficient at controlling environmental crime in those urban, highly populated areas most likely to be victimized, it is anticipated that rising incidents of environmental crime will "spill over" into adjoining suburban and rural districts. In the study by Rebovich and Nixon (1994) mentioned previously, interviews with local prosecutors warn that this infiltration is occurring now in some areas. Less populated counties with less experienced enforcement units are becoming the unsuspecting recipients of environmental offenders migrating from those areas where environmental enforcement task forces have perfected their crafts and where prosecutors are aggressive in their prosecution. In addition, in many cases, poorer rural counties make some of the best targets for midnight dumpers because of their isolated geography.

One recent examination of district attorneys prosecuting environmental crime in the south noted that prosecutors there were observing an influx of companies and individuals possessing records of environmental offenses. Speculation by the Bureau of National Affairs in 1991 to explain this trend was that environmental offenders from the north were keenly aware of the relatively lower level of sophistication of environmental crime control in the south and were capitalizing on this knowledge. A more recent assessment of charging trends among rural prosecutors by the Bureau of Justice revealed that environmental crime was considered to be one of a select number of emerging areas in rural jurisdictions that posed special complications for those uninitiated to cases of this type.

The solution to this problem may well lie in the wisdom of prosecutors in suburban and rural America to accept the spread of environmental crime into their districts as inevitable and to consider the dire consequences of *not* preparing their work forces with adequate training in environmental investigation and prosecution. If they ignore the problem, they risk becoming an unintentional casualty of the earnest control efforts of their urban neighbors. Absent organized education programs for prosecutor offices in nonurban regions, these regions could conceivably become "legal havens" for the future's environmental criminals.

Standards for the Admissibility of Scientific Evidence: The Daubert Test

A looming problem for prosecutors of environmental crime cases is the degree to which recent Supreme Court decisions affect their capacity to prove physical harm or the extent of physical harm caused by wastes improperly disposed. At the heart of this problem is the change in the standards of admissibility of scientific evidence in the courtroom, evidence that could be pivotal in determining the dimensions of harm posed that can have a significant bearing in penalty severity at conviction.

The traditional standard emerging in *Frye* v. *United States* (1923) was that the validity of scientific evidence considered for admission must be ensured through general acceptance within the relevant scientific community. The standard was developed as a fairly strict test of acceptance through evaluation of those most qualified to determine the worth of the scientific technique in question. This long-standing test has recently been replaced by one born out of a 1993 Supreme Court decision in *Daubert* v. *Merrell Dow Pharmaceutical, Inc.* (1993), in which Merrell Dow was sued by the guardians of infants to recover from birth defects allegedly caused by the mothers' ingestion of an oral drug. The decision dramatically liberalizes the standard for admissibility of scientific evidence in that the trial judge largely becomes the determinate of evidential validity. As described by Busloff in her analysis of the landmark decision's effect on the horizontal gaze nystagmus test for sobriety (Busloff, 1993:221): "The trial judge must determine whether the subject of an expert's testimony is "scientific knowledge" and whether the testimony can be supported by appropriate validation. Moreover, there must be a valid scientific connection between the testimony and the pertinent inquiry. In other words, Daubert asks judges to make decisions on a case by case basis."

The Daubert decision may prove to be a double-edged sword for prosecutors of environmental crime. The relaxing of standards of scientific evidence admissibility may open the door for the use of expert testimony on scientific techniques, demonstrating connections between chemical exposure and physical harm that may have been considered inadmissible under the prior standard, due to the relative newness of the particular methods. Thus prosecutors may find themselves in a better position to rely on such emerging technology to verify resultant harm and buttress arguments for the imposition of tougher penalties. On the other hand, presenting the trier of fact with expanded authority in concluding scientific method validity can also have a damaging impact for environmental prosecutors. The shift in standards conceivably can have the effect of turning the courtroom into a raging battleground, pairing expert witnesses for the prosecution against those for the defense, arguing over the finer points, levels of toxicity and degrees of harm of wastes disposed, with the judge wielding wide discretion in deciding which information meets the test of acceptability at trial. Prosecutors can find themselves at a distinct disadvantage in light of the deep pockets that corporate defendants may have to call upon for persuasive technical testimony. Furthermore, the *Daubert* decision may act unintentionally to elevate the credibility of certain "coincidence" defenses. These defenses allow the proliferation of hazardous chemicals by widening the latitude of acceptability for waste sample analysis results matching disposed wastes to their sources.[5]

Training

The national survey of local environmental prosecutors stressed the growing need for specialized training in environmental prosecution skills. It wasn't until 1981 that any organized training in environmental crime prosecution was generated for state government prosecutors. At that time, the Northeast Hazardous Waste Coordination Committee—a regional consortium of state attorney general offices and state regulatory agencies—began developing and administering specialized training to state prosecutors. Since then the EPA has provided funding for the creation of three similar regional consortiums covering most of the United States. Environmental crime prosecution training on a national level directed exclusively at local prosecutors was established in 1993 by the National Environmental Crime Prosecution Center. Training of federal prosecutors in environmental crime prosecution is ongoing and predates that of state and local prosecutors. It is furnished by the EPA and the FBI.

Although the past has seen a paucity of channels for environmental crime prosecution training, it is clear that we are now embarking on a period in which government is more willing to fund formal education for those responsible for prosecuting offenses against the environment. Some training programs, like that of the National Environmental Crime Prosecution Center, are supported primarily through forfeiture funds contributed by local district attorneys. In the early 1990s a degree of fractionalism arose between the four regional consortiums and the National Center. In some respects local prosecutors became the beneficiaries of this dispute with competition spurring the establishment of more training programs for local prosecutors than were ever before available. However, the hope is that the training providers will collaborate to complement programs to ensure that training *quality* is not sacrificed for training *quantity* in the quest to equip prosecutors with necessary skills. One recent attempt to coordinate such training efforts on local, state, and federal government levels has been the development of EPA's National Environmental Training Institute, the results of which remain to be seen.

For now we can say that environmental prosecutors of the future should at least have greater access to organized education programs. Those who avail themselves of these programs should be better able to lead effective environmental crime investigations taking advantage of knowledge gained from investigative strategies from other crime-specific areas (e.g., drug enforcement) and from veterans of successful environmental crime investigations.[6] In addition, those trained should be better prepared to under-stand the nuances of directing multiagency responses, to make decisions to initiate civil or criminal proceedings, to use technical experts at trial, and to present general and defense strategies common to environmental crime cases.

Experimentation with New Technologies/Strategies

Findings of the American Prosecutors Research Institute's national survey of local prosecutors exposed this group's wish for a marked upgrading of their technical abilities to match those of environmental case defense attorneys. In the courtroom, this desire translates, to a great degree, into a need for the capacity to simplify complicated descriptions of the harmful chemical properties of wastes that are illegally disposed, transported, or stored. Also needed are skills to reduce the complexities entailed in depicting chemical procedures used during investigations to link illegally disposed wastes to their source to verify criminal culpability of the defendant(s).[7]

As prosecutors continue to pursue environmental crime cases and begin to take advantage of the wider array of training opportunities offered by regional/national environmental control education organizations, it is expected that they will display a greater tendency to rely on technological advances in the submission of complex evidence. This presentation can include experimentation in areas such as the use of three-dimensional computer simulations to recreate the commission of environmental crimes, the tracing of disposed wastes to their source, and the events leading up to accidents resulting in hazardous disasters such as oil spills.[8] Experience with refined methods of presenting simple demonstrative evidence in these cases is also anticipated as being enhanced in the future.

With regard to special strategies that environmental crime prosecutors will be more likely to use in the future, the use of Racketeer Influenced and Corrupt Organizations (RICO) laws on local, state, and federal levels holds much promise. Enacted in 1970 on the federal level (RICO, 18 U.S.C. 1961–1965), the law makes it a crime to acquire, receive income from, or operate an enterprise through a pattern of racketeering and permits prosecutors to abandon a reliance on discrete statutes. Instead, RICO allows prosecutors to prosecute *patterns* of criminal acts committed by direct and indirect participants in criminal enterprises. Twenty-nine states have enacted their own versions of this law. So far there have only been a handful of situations where prosecutors have turned to RICO in environmental crime cases.[9]

A 1993 national survey on the use of state RICO statutes by local prosecutors provided information that while RICO statutes were found to be used infrequently by local prosecutors overall, metropolitan prosecutors were showing signs of a greater willingness to employ these statutes in organized/white-collar crime cases. With adequate training and the development of effective screening criteria for its use, local prosecutors claimed a higher likelihood that their confidence in using this progressive prosecutorial tool would be enhanced (Rebovich et al., 1993).[10] In many states, these statutes carry criminal penalties stricter than those associated with more traditional laws typically used in environmental crime cases. They also provide prosecutors with other powers, such as those relating to the forfeiture of assets, that can prove to be potent weapons in the battle against environmental crime.

DISCUSSION AND IMPLICATIONS FOR FUTURE RESEARCH

Since the emergence of environmental pollution offenses as bona fide environmental crime, there has been increasing concern regarding the refinement of prosecution capabilities to catch up to the maturing crime commission patterns of environmental offenders. In terms of sheer numbers of environmental prosecutors, we are light-years ahead of where we were only two decades ago. Tracing the history of environmental prosecution in the United States is analogous to picturing an inverted funnel, with the top represented by the small number of federal environmental prosecutors beginning their campaigns in the 1970s, the middle represented by the somewhat greater number of state attorneys general expanding the prosecution coverage in the 1980s, and the widest area symbolizing the much larger number of local prosecutors' offices prosecuting environmental crime in the 1990s. While we can feel fairly secure that even more will be prosecuting environmental offenders in the future, there is less certainty on how effective environmental prosecutors will be and by what measure they will be judged.

In this chapter we have offered some projections on what environmental prosecution will be like in the future given certain events and patterns forming at the present. The important factors presented can be categorized as those that are sociopolitical in nature (e.g., public/system sentiment on environmental crime, equity in the distribution of environmental risk, the burden of increased environmental crime in suburban/rural regions caused by effective control programs in urban areas) and those that are profession-specific technical issues (e.g., changes in evidentiary standards, progress in training, advances in methods and technologies). Although some of these may not materialize as *leading* change elements, clearly, the role diversification of this profession should be emphasized as the wave of the future for environmental prosecutors.

Undoubtedly, tomorrow's environmental prosecutor will be required to wear several hats: those of law enforcer, protector of public health, environmental technician, and community leader. This diversity will mean that certain inevitable compromises will be forced on the environmental prosecutor to satisfy new community expectations. The increasing public and media pressures to prosecute polluters vigorously and simultaneously, to safeguard the welfare of the general public will prompt prosecutors to weigh carefully issues that, given fallout from the Rocky Flats affair, may not be easy to balance. To guarantee the expedient elimination of health threats emanating from criminal disposals, prosecutors may sometimes be obliged to structure plea negotiation decisions to revolve around promises of defendant remediation of the disposal sites (i.e., environmental cleanup) and grudgingly forsake desired degrees of punitiveness. Prosecutors may also find that they will have to reconcile public insistence on the imposition of tough penalties with some residual judicial hesitancy to mete out such penalties. Consequently, we may see more environmental prosecutors exploring the possibilities of subtly graduated penalties for situational offenders that could include community service and more creative alternatives such as the disqualification of professional certifications and the newspaper publication of criminal act admissions by offenders.

Although some of these predictions may be arguable, it is generally agreed that whatever course the environmental prosecutor of the future takes, changes in role definition will necessitate a new agenda for future research that will supply the environmental prosecutor with information facilitating a proactive position and permitting him/her to meet the challenges of the new role. Past environmental crime studies have afforded some rewarding insights into the metamorphosis of environmental criminality and the strategies developed concerning environmental crime control. Those conducting this research have sometimes disagreed on what characteristics seem to be most representative of environmental criminals (Block and Scarpitti, 1985; Hammitt and Reuter, 1988; Rebovich, 1992). The work of these researchers, however, stimulated additional interest in studying the conditions and circumstances that are determinants of environmental crime and what elements are needed to suppress these violations. Through empirical research, it has been posited that the ideal equation for the reduction of environmental crime is: tightened environmental legislation + toughened enforcement + increases in legitimate disposal alternatives = reduced rates of environmental offenses (Rebovich, 1994, 1996, 1998b). But little research has been done to determine if this theoretical equation is an accurate representation of the dynamics necessary for environmental crime reduction. Over the last two decades there have been sharp pendulum shifts in government sentiment on the issue of environmental crime control, ranging from the stringent 1980s amendments to the Resource Conservation and Recovery Act to congressional attempts in the mid-1990s to slash funding for environmental enforcement programs. It is expected that those conducting environmental crime research in the future will assess what impact fluctuations in elements of the environmental crime reduction equation have on the volume of environmental crime incidents.

Tomorrow's envornmental crime prosecutor should be prepared to adjust to greater demonstrations of crime commission ingenuity, especially the strategic shifting of locations in which illegal disposals are committed. Expect polluters to refine their methods of crime commission in an effort to escape quickly evolving enforcement strategies. Liberal federal definitions of recycling demand research on offenses in which hazardous substances are blended with innocuous substances to create aggregates represented as being legitimate recycling products. Prosecutors should also be on the alert for changes in the makeup of criminal conspiracies as a reaction to advances in environmental crime control programs. Imbalances among states, counties, and municipalities in environmental crime enforcement effectiveness should continue despite the diligent attempts of government and criminal practitioner associations to devise progressive models for environmental enforcement and state legislation. Enforcement method evolution should force offenders to search aggressively for jurisdictional "havens," states and counties with weaker laws and enforcement.

Although not exhaustive, the following list provides a glimpse at some of the possible research endeavors that could help usher the environmental prosecutor into a new era of professional growth.

- *Study of offender behavior.* This would enable appropriate proactive enforcement mechanisms to be identified and targeted for specific crime commission types. Prosecutors could establish the relationships, if any, between the financial status of offenders at the time of the offense and the offense committed. Prosecutors could also isolate characteristics common to offending corporations. This information is vital to EPA ideas of "pollution prevention" to target only "good citizen" corporations for voluntary compliance.

- *Identification of the types of business most likely to commit environmental offenses and their location in rural or urban areas.* Research is needed to predict the kinds of people and companies likely to commit environmental crimes (e.g., profile study of criminal corporations with comparison control group of noncriminal corporations).

- *Significant outsiders to criminal core acts* (e.g., unregulated "treatment brokers," "private labs"). Needed is a comparison of study of prosecutors' offices in states with regulation in these areas and those without such regulation. This study would be an examination of the extent to which significant outside groups and individuals can pave the way for the unencumbered commission of environmental offenses at the local level and the avoidance of meaningful punishment.

- *Decision to charge.* We need a content analysis study of a comparison of environmental crime cases dismissed versus cases charged. What factors are most important in charging or not charging? Are they the best reasons for all? What formal and informal procedures are used by prosecutors to reduce felonies to misdemeanors, to relegate criminal cases to civil proceedings, or to dismiss altogether?

- *Success or failure of environmental crime cases prosecuted.* This research would be based on discriminate analysis of environmental crime conviction rates by characteristics of cases (level of evidence, complexity of cases, source of discovery, degree of harm, type and volume of chemical, proximity to popular areas). The independent variable would be success or failure of the cases. With this study we could establish predictability standards as is done in other crime areas so that planning can be done efficiently. In essence, this type of analysis would be the foundation of a system to predict statistically the chances of conviction for use in helping to decide which environmental cases to criminally prosecute.

- *Study of penalties.* Studies are required on sentencing at a local level: quality and types of penalties by types of offenses. Data could lead to a study of environmental offense recidivism and collection of supplemental data on the impact of sanctions on company profits in later years as well as on attitudes of shareholders.

- *Study of intermediate environmental sanctions and prevention strategies.* This study would deal with equations of "risk" and "harm" with levels of punitive sanctioning (e.g., occupational disqualification of corporate executives, community service, tax-incentive programs for waste reduction).

ENDNOTES

1. A host of heretofore unregulated industry procedures related to hazardous waste generation are now regulated under the 1984 amendments. Most significant is the amendment regarding small waste generators. Section 221 lowers the cutoff volume level of those previously exempt because of low levels of waste generation.

2. More than 75% of those environmental prosecutors responding to the survey believed these utilities of technical experts (e.g., expert witnesses on properties of wastes disposed) to be important. Supplemental qualitative data indicated that defense knowledge of the technical capacity of prosecutors strengthened the environmental prosecutor's position during plea negotiations and during trial, and the use of technical expert testimony strengthened evidence credibility in the eyes of jurors.

3. In this case, actions that the EPA considered continuing violations involving discharges of fecal bacteria, phosphorus, ammonia, cyanide, and oil were within the limits of a consent order that the Virginia DEQ had negotiated with Smithfield Foods. The consent order allowed Smithfield Foods time to connect its meat operations to sewage treatment plants.

4. These states are Arkansas, Colorado, Florida, Idaho, Illinois, Indiana, Kansas, Kentucky, Minnesota, Mississippi, Missouri, New Hampshire, Oregon, South Carolina, Texas, Utah, Virginia, and Wyoming.

5. One of the best-known incidents where this position was used recently involved the Monsanto Co. plant in Sauget, Illinois, the nation's largest producer of PCBs before PCBs were banned in 1979. EPA officials found themselves deadlocked by Monsanto claims that their generation of PCBs and the clusters of PCB dumps along nearby Dead Creek were mere coincidence. Monsanto's position that their proximity to Dead Creek and likelihood of disposal there was irrelevant and that the disposal could have been committed by others was found to present early obstacles to the strategy of matching chemical composition of wastes to their source.

6. An example of this type of investigative strategy training is environmental "reverse sting" operations, presented at the National Environmental Crime Prosecution Center's National Conference on the Prosecution of Environmental Crime in Phoenix, Arizona, in April 1993. A traditional part of the drug investigator's repertoire, it involves the use of undercover agents posing as business officials paying the suspected offenders to dispose of hazardous wastes. Although heretofore used rarely by environmental prosecutors, instances where it has been used have led to fruitful results. One of the most notable was orchestrated by the Suffolk County,

New York, District Attorney's Office in 1992. The "toxic avenger" sting took four months for investigators to set up the transaction with representatives of plating industry/silicon transistor manufacturing companies to transport and dispose of hazardous wastes illegally (American Prosecutors Research Institute, 1992). Information from successful operations such as this is increasingly forming the foundation of new training programs for environmental prosecutors.

7. These methods can include the injection of chemical dyes into the waste stream and the tracing of the journey of the dyed wastes, or the physical tracing of special painted markings, or qualities of drums containing wastes.

8. Such technology has already been employed in criminal trials involving vehicular homicide and in manslaughter cases against police in which bullet trajectory angles are critical to the determination of the physical positions of victims and defendants.

9. On the state government level, one of the best-known RICO prosecutions associated with environmental crime occurred in 1983 in the Pennsylvania State Attorney General's case against *Lavalle & Son Co.* Lavalle, the head of a trucking company that transported hazardous wastes, was charged with illegally disposing hazardous wastes and using more than $580,000 in illegal profits to create a "legitimate" transport business. Through the use of its state RICO law, Pennsylvania was able to prove that an organized and consistent pattern of criminal activities surrounded Lavalle's operations. Lavalle was found guilty of violating the RICO statute on two separate counts: theft by deception and use of stolen funds (Rebovich et al., 1993).

    The most noteworthy federal RICO prosecution in an environmental crime case is *United States* v. *A&A Land Development et al.*, a 1990 case in which three individuals and seven waste disposal and real estate development agencies were convicted of RICO and mail fraud violations. The violations involved the illegal transfer and disposal of hazardous wastes on Staten Island. Penalties resulted in the seizure of the companies and assets for liquidation and recovery and sentences of incarceration for all three individuals.

10. Sixty percent of the respondents reporting the prosecution of organized crime were from jurisdictions representing over 250,000 in population. Prosecutors who used RICO statutes contended that they offered versatile sanctions to a wide variety of offenses and that these sanctions were not available under other laws. Some advantages specified included the obtaining of injunctions to prevent RICO violators from continuing to operate businesses in which criminal activity was focused. RICO laws were also asserted to be valued as prosecution "hammers" during plea negotiations because of the strict penalties that could result from conviction.

REFERENCES AND BIBLIOGRAPHY

ABT ASSOCIATES, INC. (1985). *National Small Quantity Hazardous Waste Generator Survey.* Washington, DC: U.S. Environmental Protection Agency, Office of Solid Waste.

ADLER, F. (1991). Offender specific versus offense specific approaches to the study of environmental crime. Presentation at the American Society of Criminology Annual Conference, San Francisco, November 21.

AMERICAN PROSECUTORS RESEARCH INSTITUTE (1992). *The Local Prosecution of Environmental Crimes: A Literature Review.* Alexandria, VA: APRI, August 14.

ANON. (1993). General Dingell. In *Review and Outlook,* Wall Street Journal, July 8, p. A12.

BENSON, M. L., W. MAAKESTAD, F. CULLEN, and G. GEIS (1988). District attorneys and corporate crime: Surveying the prosecutorial gatekeepers. *Criminology,* 24(3):505–519.

BLOCK, A., and F. SCARPITTI (1985). *Poisoning for Profit: The Mafia and Toxic Waste in America.* New York: William Morrow.

BLUMENTHAL, R. (1983). Illegal dumping of toxins laid to organized crime. *New York Times,* June 5, pp. 1, 44.

BULLARD, D. (1991). Environmental racism in America? *Environmental Protection*, June, p. 25.

BUREAU OF JUSTICE ASSISTANCE (1993). *Violent Crime and Drug Abuse in Rural Areas: Issues, Concerns, and Programs*. Washington, DC: Justice Research and Statistics Association.

BUSLOFF, S. (1993). Can your eyes be used against you? The use of horizontal gaze nystagmus test in the courtroom. *Journal of Criminal Law and Criminology*, 84(1):203–238.

CALIFORNIA BUREAU OF CRIMINAL STATISTICS AND SPECIAL SERVICES (1988). Racial, ethnic and religious crimes project. In *Criminal Justice Analysis in the States: The Role of Measurement in Public Policy Development*. Washington, DC: Criminal Justice Statistics Association.

COHEN, M. (1992). Environmental crime and punishment: Legal/economic theory and empirical evidence on enforcement of federal environmental statutes. *Journal of Criminal Law and Criminology*, 82(4):1055–1107.

CRIMINAL JUSTICE STATISTICS ASSOCIATION (1988). Measuring bias motivated crime. In *Criminal Justice Analysis in the States: The Role of Measurement in Public Policy Development*. Washington, DC: CJSA.

CUSHMAN, J. (1997). Virginia seen as undercutting environmental rules. *New York Times*, January 19, p. 22.

DE BENEDICTIS, D. (1993). Few like pollution guidelines. *ABA Journal*, June, pp. 25–26.

ENVIRONMENTAL OPINION STUDY (1991). *Environmental Issues Ranked*. Washington, DC: EDS, Inc.

ENVIRONMENTAL PROTECTION AGENCY (1990). *Reducing Risk: Setting Priorities and Strategies for Environmental Protection*. Washington, DC: U.S. EPA.

ENVIRONMENTAL PROTECTION AGENCY (1992). *Environmental Equity: Reducing Risk for All Communities*. Washington, DC: U.S. EPA.

EPSTEIN, S., L. BROWN, and C. POPE (1982). *Hazardous Waste in America*. San Francisco: Sierra Club Books.

ERVIN, M. (1992). The toxic doughnut. *Progressive*, January, p. 15.

GOLD, A. (1991). Increasingly, prison term is the price for polluters. *New York Times*, February 15.

HAMMETT, T., and J. EPSTEIN (1993). Local prosecution of environmental crime. *Issues and Practices*. Washington, DC: U.S. Department of Justice, National Institute of Justice.

HAMMETT, T., and J. EPSTEIN (1993). Prosecuting environmental crime: Los Angeles County. *Program Focus*. Washington, DC: U.S. Department of Justice, National Institute of Justice.

HAMMITT, J. K., and P. REUTER (1988). *Measuring and Deterring Illegal Disposal of Hazardous Waste*. Santa Monica, CA: Rand Corporation.

HAWKE, N. (1987). Crimes against the environment. *Anglo-American Law Review*, 16(1):90–96.

HERROD, S., L. PADDOCK, S. PATTI, H. HOLDEN, G. LIE, and J. BAYLSON (1991). Utilizing local government. In *Enforcement in the 1990's: Recommendations of the Analytical Workgroup*. Washington, DC: U.S. Environmental Protection Agency.

HOLLINGER, G., and M. ATKINSON (1988). The process of criminalization: The case of computer crime laws. *Criminology*, 26(1).

HOVERSTEN, P. (1997). EPA puts plant on hold in racism case. *USA Today*, p. A3.

JENSEN, G. (1991). America's new environmental populism. *Prosecutor's Brief*, 2nd Quarter, pp. 4–5.

KRAJICK, K. (1981). When will police discover the toxic time bomb? and Toxic waste is big business for the mob. *Police*, May, pp. 6–20.

LAFRANIERE, S. (1992). Pollution leniency alleged: Dingell panel to review Justice Department policy. *Washington Post*, September 18, p. 1.

MCCOY, W. (1997). The new self-auditing incentives and site assessments. In Touchstone Environmental Incorporated (ed.), *The Complete Guide to Environmental Liability and Enforcement in Pennsylvania*. North Vancouver, British Columbia, Canada: STP Specialty Technical Publishers.

MEEHAN, J. (1992). Policy issues in environmental crimes for America's metropolitan prosecutors. Presented at the NDAA Annual Conference for Metropolitan Prosecutors, Washington, DC.

METZ, B. (1985). *No More Mr. Nice Guy: Hazardous Waste Enforcement Management in the USA*. Groningen, The Netherlands: Ministry of Housing, Physical Planning and Environment, Regional Inspectorate for the Environment.

MUGDAN, W. E., and B. R. ADLER (1985). The 1984 RCRA amendments: Congress as a regulatory agent. *Columbia Journal of Environmental Law*, 10(2):215–254.

MURPHY, W. (1991). Presentation at the National Environmental Enforcement Council, Washington, DC.

MUSTOKOFF, M. (1981). *Hazardous Waste Violations: A Guide to Their Detection, Investigation and Prosecution*. Washington, DC: National Center on White Collar Crime, Department of Justice, Law Enforcement Assistance Administration.

REBOVICH, D. (1987a). Exploring hazardous waste crime characteristics. *Law Enforcement Intelligence Digest*, 2(1).

REBOVICH, D. (1987b). Policing hazardous waste crime: Issues in offense identification and prosecution. *Criminal Justice Quarterly*, 9(3).

REBOVICH, D. (1992). *Dangerous Ground: The World of Hazardous Waste Crime*. New Brunswick, NJ: Transaction Publishers.

REBOVICH, D. (1996). Prosecutorial decision making and the environmental prosecutor: Reaching a crossroads for public protection. In S. Edwards, T. Edwards, and C. Fields (eds.), *Environmental Criminality: Definitions, Explanations, Prosecutions*. New York: Garland Publishing.

REBOVICH, D. (1998a). Evolving toward a specialization of environmental crime prosecution at the county level: Issues and concerns of county prosecutors within local environmental task forces. In M. Clifford (ed.), *Environmental Crime: Enforcement, Policy and Social Responsibility*. Gaithersburg, MD: Aspen Publishers.

REBOVICH, D. (1998b). Environmental crime research: Where we have been, where we can go. In M. Clifford (ed.), *Environmental Crime: Enforcement, Policy and Social Responsibility*. Gaithersburg, MD: Aspen Publishers.

REBOVICH, D., and R. NIXON (1994). *Environmental Crime Prosecution: A Comprehensive Analysis of District Attorneys' Efforts in This Emerging Area of Criminal Enforcement*. Washington, DC: U.S. Department of Justice, National Institute of Justice.

REBOVICH, D., K. COYLE, and J. SCHAAF (1993). *Local Prosecutor of Organized Crime: The Use of State RICO Statutes*. Washington, DC: U.S. Department of Justice, Bureau of Justice Statistics.

REUTER, P. (1983). *Disorganized Crime: The Economics of the Visible Hand*. Cambridge, MA: MIT Press.

SHERMAN, R. (1987). Pillars or polluters: Prosecutors play hardball with corporate managers. *New Jersey Law Journal*, August 6, p. 1.

SKRZYCKI, C. (1997). The regulators: Critics see a playground for polluters in EPA's XL plan. *Washington Post*, January 24, p. D1.

SZACZ, A. (1986). Corporations, organized crime, and the disposal of hazardous waste: An examination of the making of a criminogenic regulatory structure. *Criminology*, 24(1):1–28.

U.S. DEPARTMENT OF JUSTICE (1991). *Environmental Crimes Manual*. Washington, DC: U.S. Government Printing Office, January.

WALD, M. (1992). Jury battled prosecutor on Nike plant. *New York Times*, September 30.
WEISSKOPF, M. (1992). Minorities pollution risk is debated. *Washington Post*, January 16.
WOLF, S. (1983). Hazardous waste trials and tribulations. *Environmental Law*, 13(2).

CASES

Daubert v. *Merrell Dow Pharmaceutical, Inc*, 113 S. Ct. 2786, 53 CRL 2313 (1993).
Frye v. *U.S.*, (293) F1013 [D.C. Cir. 1923].
Lavelle & Son Co. (1983).
United States v. *A&A Land Development et al.* (1990)

chapter 19

The Impact of Computer-Based Technologies on Criminal Justice

Transition to the Twenty-First Century

William G. Archambeault, Ph.D.

ABSTRACT

In this chapter we explain the nature and impact of the information society on American criminal justice, logically linking information dependency to computer dependency. We trace the evolution of computers and computer-based technologies, then discuss the applications of computers in American criminal justice of the 1990s. Computer applications are discussed under the headings of data-based management, organizational communications, computer-assisted diagnosis/education/training, computer-assisted monitoring of offenders, and computer-related crime. Evolving technologies, including artificial intelligence and virtual reality, are discussed in terms of their future applications. The chapter concludes by noting that the future applications of computers in criminal justice will be limited only by human imagination, ethics, and law.

INTRODUCTION

As the twentieth century yields to the twenty-first, computers and computer-based technologies (CBTs) play critically important roles in American criminal justice. As defined today, computers are electronic devices that have at least four basic definable functions: input,[1] storage,[2] processing,[3] and output.[4] There are at least three common groupings of computers: PCs or microcomputers,[5] minicomputers,[6] and mainframe computers. Computer-based technologies (CBTs)[7] comprise a wide range of integrated technologies that employ computers (PC, mini, or mainframe) or computer microchip integrated logic circuitry into their design as critical or essential components.

Computers and CBTs are the heart of organizational information systems. In a recent National Institute of Justice report discussing the importance of computers to law enforcement, Sparrow (1993:1) notes:

> At one time, information technology was thought to be best left to technicians so managers could concentrate on the serious business of management. However, that might have been an effective division of labor only when computers were used solely to automate well-defined administrative functions, such as batch processing of payroll....Now, information systems are the essential circuitry of modern organizations, often determining how problems are defined and how progress is evaluated. They frequently determine how work gets done, often who does it, and sometimes what the work is....Organizational strategy no longer can be separated from informational technology strategy, for the organizational effects of information systems no longer are limited to efficiency gains.

Sparrow's comments are indicative of a fundamental reality in the external environment of all criminal justice organizations, namely, that the United States, like most other industrialized countries of the world, has evolved into a society which is totally dependent on information: its content, its flow, and its speed of delivery.

This dependency manifests itself in two fundamental ways in all criminal justice organizations. *First, information and its flow within organizations are critical to efficient operations, the delivery of services, and the safety of criminal justice workers.* The most obvious example of this need is seen in the dispatching and delivery of police emergency services. Accurate information and its rapid flow can literally have life or death consequences. Similar levels of criticality and information dependency can also be seen in the operation of courts, jails, and correctional facilities.

Second, the criticality of information and its flow in American criminal justice has led to the widespread use of computer-based technologies and recurring cycles of ever-increasing dependency on the technology. Most criminal justice organizations are totally dependent on information and the technology for managing it. Within these organizations there is great pressure to acquire, store, manage, retrieve and analyze raw data and to convert it to usable information.[8] This continuing pressure propels these organizations to apply more powerful computers to handle the information load. The irony of this process is that more powerful computers produce more data and information than the human beings in the organizations can utilize or even comprehend. In turn, this multiplication increases the pressure to obtain ever more powerful computers that lead to even greater dependency and produce even more information. Paradoxically, computer dependency is a relatively recent phenomenon, as the following sketch of history indicates.

RISE OF THE INFORMATION SOCIETY AND COMPUTER DEPENDENCY

For centuries the term *computer* referred to human beings who performed mathematical computations in accounting, budgeting, engineering, astronomy, and navigation-related computations. When President John F. Kennedy announced the goal of landing men on the moon, NASA was still using human computers. However, by July 20, 1969, when American astronauts first walked on the moon, the word *computer* had evolved into its present meaning, but only a few programmers and systems analysts had any contact with computers. A small number of large police departments or government agencies used computers or computer services. The vast majority of criminal justice organizations maintained manual (paper and file folder) records and information storage. The idea of using computers in police cars or courtrooms or officers carrying video-telephone devices were *Dick Tracy–* or *Flash Gordon–*quality comic book fiction.

By 1979, a decade later, much had changed. Most criminal justice organizations were automating or at least experimenting with the use of computers in a desperate effort to keep up with the demand for information. However, it was still science fiction:

1. That human beings could interact verbally with computers
2. That computers could "learn" anything on their own
3. That CBT retinal scans could be used for the identification of persons entering or leaving correctional confinement
4. That CBT crime labs could conduct DNA analysis and identify rapists
5. That police could use computers in routine police cars
6. That CBT CADS could interact with satellites, dispatch emergency vehicles to specific locations, or provide electronic maps of the shortest way to travel to the scene of the emergency
7. That computers could be effectively used in employee training or offender education

By 1989, however, the computer revolution and the information society were realities. Most of what had been "science fiction" in 1969 or even 1979 had become operational realities of criminal justice in the United States. In society, computers were as normal as pencils. Computer literacy became second in importance only to reading literacy. The use of computer-based education and training became common in criminal justice organizations.

COMPUTER-BASED TECHNOLOGIES AND CRIMINAL JUSTICE OF THE 1990s

Ongoing research into computer technology and CBT applications continues to redefine human definition of computers and of their potentials. Changes as radical as the cumulative changes experienced since the 1970s may occur by the year 2000 or shortly thereafter. Anticipation and understanding of these projected changes begin with a comprehension of today's computer. With few exceptions, most contemporary computers and CBT devices exploit defendant fourth-generation computer technologies which are human dependent: human beings enter data and input processing instructions, and instruct computers on how to analyze data and how to output the results. There are, however, some exceptions. These are computers with some attributes of evolving fifth-generation technology.

Emerging fifth-generation computers add a fifth function to the basic definition of a computer: *the capacity to learn without human assistance*. This ability is loosely called *artificial intelligence* (AI). At the present time, true artificial intelligence does not exist. What does exist are incremental technological steps leading to AI and rudimentary forms of artificial intelligence which are often labeled "smart," "expert," "brilliant," or even "genius." These have some, but not all, of the characteristics of AI.

True artificial intelligence has two sets of functional "learning" characteristics. Without human intervention, the computer has the ability to acquire new data or information and to alter its basic programming. In the first context, learning refers to a computer's capability to acquire new data, analyze them, and make decisions based on them without human direction or control. Today's most advanced computers are programmed to acquire new data or information on their own but in a very narrow frame of reference. These computers are labeled "smart," "expert," or "brilliant." These are illustrated by the performance of the computer-directed guidance system of the Patriot Missile during the 1991 Gulf War. Hundreds of times a second the missile was able to receive data on its location and that of its target, analyze the data, and alter its course. These functions are also found in the most sophisticated computers in American criminal justice, such as the computers used by the FBI's National Center for the Analysis of Violent Crime (NCAVC) (Reboussin, 1990), the Automated Fingerprint Identification System (AFIS) in wide use today, in genetic research and DNA matching, in telecommunication, and in emergency dispatching systems.

Current "smart" or "expert" systems are incremental developments that will eventually lead to true artificial intelligence, but are not true AI. Although such machines can "learn" or acquire new data, they can do so only within narrow parameters controlled by the computers' basic programming. For true AI to exist, a computer must be able to "learn" on its own from a wide range of inputs in its environment, just as humans can learn from a wide variety of different life experiences and integrate them into some new conceptual model of reality. More important, the true AI computer must be able to modify its own programming through a process that parallels that of a human child who is developing a sense of personal morality about the world. By way of analogy, a Patriot missile guidance system in flight cannot suddenly decide that it no longer wants to be a missile, conclude that all killing is wrong, and resolve not to destroy what it hits. An "expert" AFIS system cannot suddenly decide that it wants to become a communications system instead. A "brilliant" genetics research computer cannot suddenly reach a dilemma and philosophize about the ethics and morality of genetic engineering. Only true artificial intelligence could do any of these things. In the near future, AI research may totally redefine current ideas of what computers are and what they can do. Before exploring future potentials of AI, it is necessary to understand how computers and CBTs are applied in American criminal justice.

In the operational environment of the 1990s, computers and computer-based technologies are used extensively in at least four areas of American criminal justice: (1) database management, (2) computer-assisted communication, (3) computer-assisted instruction and training, and (4) computer-assisted monitoring of offenders. In addition to being tools of criminal justice, computers are also creating new crime forms. Space limitations permit only a superficial description of each of these areas.

Database Management

Database management (DBM) is the application of computer-based technology to the systematic input, storage, retrieval, and analysis of data (encoded facts) or information (encoded facts with meaning). Computers make it possible to store and access huge volumes of data and information, which could not be done manually with any acceptable degree of efficiency.

Database management, the core of most computer utilization in criminal justice, depends on rapid access to accurate information that may have life and death consequences. Most other application areas interface with DBM systems. Consequently, it is not surprising to find that there are many different kinds of DBM applications in criminal justice. Some involve the simple storage of files or records. Others, called *management information systems* (MISs), are designed to provide managers with information and organizational activities, budgets, personnel actions, and historic and projected future demands for services needed for planning. They may track employee work and vacation schedules; personnel records dealing with payroll, promotions, retirement; vehicle mileage, and replacement and maintenance schedules; and other related information that managers and administrators need to make decisions about the organization.

Other types of DBM systems provide information needed for criminal justice operations. Jails and courts use DBM systems to ensure that offenders are properly charged, booked, and scheduled for hearings or trials, as well as to make sure that the right offender shows up in the right courtroom with the right assigned judge (Weinberg, 1989; Block, 1990; Manchester, 1991). Court DBM systems manage case dockets, maintain files on offenders, and enter official court decisions when rendered. Many courts can directly access current laws and case precedents (Gruner, 1989; Churbuck, 1991) as well as offender records at time of sentencing. DBM systems interface with telephone and tele-video CBTs to produce closed-circuit television systems that make it possible for courts to conduct remote bookings, initial hearings, and preliminary arraignments from miles away. DBM systems make it possible to track offender cases through the maze of legal and judicial steps that comprise the American criminal justice system.

In jails, prisons, and other custody settings, retinal scan identification, as well as hand-palm and fingerprint matching, are used to control access to restrictive areas of institutions. A DBM system contains identification files that contain previously recorded retinal, hand-palm, and fingerprint data. Voice print recognition is also used and information stored in a similar manner.

Still other DBM systems store all known information on characteristics, behavioral patterns, actions, and victims of known serial killers (Larson, 1989; Bardege, 1990; Clede, 1990). The Federal Bureau of Investigation (FBI) employs "expert systems" to analyze criminal behavior stored in the DBM system at the National Center for the

Analysis of Violent Crime (NCAVC) (Reboussin and Rafoya, 1990). Other DBM systems may contain information on known terrorists such as the ones who placed a car bomb in the New York Trade Center parking garage or may contain general information on offenders in a prison system (Jameson and Megerman, 1990; Saylor, 1990). Many DBMs record information and evidence as it is collected and evaluated, while others allow police officers to run a records check in seconds, such as searching the files of the National Criminal Information Center (NCIC) in Washington, DC.

Portable crime lab computers operate in the field at crime scenes to collect data and analyze some evidence. Other collected field data are transmitted to powerful forensic computers in crime labs for detailed analysis. Analysis possibilities include a broad array of evidence, including DNA typing, blood matching, microscopic fiber analysis, computer-enhanced imaging of the facial features of persons long dead, and behavioral profiling of serial killers, among others.

Police and other 911 emergency dispatchers can receive a call for service, verify the caller's address and phone number, prioritize the call, determine which available units are closest to dispatch, and notify these units of the call and the best route to follow in getting to the emergency—all in a matter of seconds. Some systems require human dispatchers to access databases that store addresses, phone numbers, and street maps (Dertouzos, 1991; Sikes, 1991); others perform this function automatically. Some "smart" systems are capable of interfacing with communications satellites that can pinpoint objects and terrain features of only a few inches from thousands of miles out in space, determine the exact location of any vehicle on a computerized street map and dispatch units without human intervention. Computers in police cruisers and computer-aided dispatch (CAD) of emergency services are common in many large metropolitan areas today.

Sheriff's deputies in New York City carry handheld computers that allow satellite interface with mainframe computers that contain hundreds of thousands of unpaid parking tickets and public ordinance fines (Parks, 1990), allowing the City of New York to collect millions of dollars in unpaid fines. Other DBM systems may contain plans to buildings, including banks, high rises, apartment buildings, and others. Crime pattern analysis allows police agencies to deploy limited patrol resources most efficiently in any geographical area by time of day.

Computer-Assisted Organizational Communications

There are three areas of organizational communications that employ CBT extensively: written, electronic, and verbal. *Written communications* refers to operational manuals, memos, letters, or any other form of information communications that requires a reader to see and interpret meaning from printed words or symbols. *Electronic communications* refers to the transmission and reception of written communications via a video screen or CRT, fax machines, or the transmission of voice messages through voice mail. With the advent of in-car computers, electronic communications are rapidly replacing many forms of both verbal and written communications. *Verbal communications* refers to the transmittal of human voice communications through interpersonal exchanges, over the airwaves or through some other medium.

Computer-assisted writing (CAW) is the application of CBTs to the preparation, editing, and dissemination of printed documents in an organization. Word processing and desktop publishing are two of the most common uses of CBTs in any organization. CAW allows writers to assemble their written statements or documents, then edit them for readability and reading comprehension before they are distributed. CAW can also be used to distribute the completed information as well. Many criminal justice organizations have tried, with varying degrees of success, to become "paperless" so far as the distribution of internal documents is concerned. The CAW signals the intended recipient that a message is waiting. The recipient can read the message (document) on the computer screen, then print it out if a hard or paper copy is needed (Dean, 1989). Other CAW systems allow the message to be sent to all intended recipients through a facsimile (fax) system. The document is prepared in the word processor, then sent to the fax system to be distributed to from one of several hundred different locations ranging from a few feet away to thousands of miles. Still other CAW systems make it possible to send documents directly to a central distribution center, where it is printed on paper and sent to intended recipients. Often, these communications are prepared through the use of desktop publishing programs that give a professional print quality to the final publication.

In addition, most justice organizations also depend on CBT radio, microwave, or cellular technologies to send human voice communications as well (Parks, 1990; Dertouzos, 1991; Harman, 1991). However, perhaps the most important of the recent CBT developments is in the area of computer-assisted dispatch systems (CADs). Sparrow (1993:6) notes:

> The development of police technology during the 1980s focused principally on the acquisition by police departments of two major types of systems: CAD (computer-aided dispatch, sometimes called "enhanced") and AFIS (automated fingerprint identification systems). CAD systems have been augmented by the use of mobile display terminals (MDTs) in patrol cars, by automatic vehicle locator systems, and by integrations of geographic information (GIS) capabilities into CAD control systems. AFIS frequently has been tied to existing criminal history data bases.

In many metropolitan areas an emergency call for assistance might be received either by a human dispatcher or by a computerized voice recognizer. Under optimal operating conditions, within 1 to 3 seconds after a call is received, the information is entered into a database, the priority determined, and an order to respond is sent to the closest available unit. The CAD systems can then route the emergency unit to the scene of the emergency by the quickest route. Additional information on the call is transmitted while police cruisers are heading toward their destination. Unfortunately, in many areas the high volume of high-priority calls (e.g., shootings, robbery in progress, major traffic accidents with life-threatening consequences) utilize all available units. Consequently, CADs often do not result in improved response time to less serious emergency calls (e.g., minor traffic accident, home burglary not-in-progress). Also, field computers and portable crime lab computers are used to collect and measure crime scene field data, which are often transferred electronically via CBTS microwave radio technology back to base stations and powerful forensic crime computers for detailed analysis.

Federal agencies such as the FBI and DEA employ video-telephones that allow agents in the field to see and talk to superiors in Washington, DC. They also allow interaction with agency databases as well as giving supervisors data on the location of agents. CBT high-tech monitoring devices make it possible to aim a microwave dish at a building or automobile hundreds of feet away, listen in on conversations, and obtain video images and other information. CBT observation and intelligence-gathering equipment employ technologies that do not fit traditional definitions of "wiretapping," about which right to privacy laws have been written in many states. There are issues of concern and debate.

Computer-Assisted Diagnosis, Instruction, and Training

CBTs are being employed in all forms of diagnosis techniques, from assessing the operation of a modem automobile to medical diagnosis of illnesses to psychological testing of human beings (Waldron et al., 1987:41–58; Cash and Brown, 1989; Anthes, 1991). Computer-assisted diagnosis of personality disorders, or reading and educational deficiencies, are commonplace in many clinics and school settings today. Some probation departments are generating prehearing and presentence evaluations, social history reports, and risk analysis ratings using computers. Although there are many different forms of this technology in use today, most involve sitting a person down in front of a computer that asks the subject to respond to questions. Sometimes the person is aided by another person, who may read the questions to the test subject and record the subject's responses. In all forms, the computer scores and analyzes the test results, producing a report. Some research suggests that computers are much more accurate than human testers in administering psychological tests. The FBI and other law enforcement agencies employ programs that allow the analysis and profiling of criminal personality types. Psychological and psychiatric diagnoses of human pathologies are also possible using current technology.

Computer-assisted diagnosis is also used with two other CBT applications: computer-assisted instruction (CAI) and computer-based training. CAI is a term that is used for a variety of applications which involve using computers to augment or substitute for human classroom teaching. The vast majority of CAI applications involve augmentation rather than substitution. CAI places the learner in direct interaction with a computer and a computer program that presents information to the learner and then tests learning levels. CAI was generally unheard of two decades ago. Today, it is used in hundreds of thousands of classrooms throughout the United States. CAI often combines video and CD-ROM technologies to place the learner in a two-dimensional video learning equipment.

CAI is used in correctional institutions in teaching subjects ranging from GED (general education development) preparation to teaching academic subjects such as math, reading, and history. CAI is also useful in alternative school settings.

Some students who have trouble relating to human authority figures or who find traditional classrooms to be too difficult can find great success in learning through CAI. Consequently, CAI has great utility for various kinds of alternatives to traditional schools.

Computer-based training refers to application of the same technology to the training of people and employees for specific jobs or positions (Booker, 1990; Fritz, 1991; Orlin, 1991). It is used extensively in police training simulations and to a lesser extent in the training of correctional personnel. It is used in the skill training of offenders both inside and outside correctional institutions. Much more sophisticated computer-based training has been borrowed from military simulation trainers. Simulators present pilots and tank drivers with video scenery that interacts with the actions of the trainee. Simulation training has led to the development of *virtual reality* (VR) technologies that allow humans to become part of computer-generated "reality." Through virtual reality, human body movement is part of the computer program allowing a person to move about the three-dimensional surrealistic world of the computer in much the same manner as did the fictional characters in the movie *TRON*.

VR allows architects, as well as aircraft designers, to "see" and "walk" through computer-generated simulations based on the plans. Changes and errors can be detected in construction before the plans are ever built. Current discussions and debates revolve around how VR technology could be used in teaching and training people, as well as how it might be used in the treatment of the mentally ill. VR may also have great potential for the treatment and rehabilitation of offenders in the future.

Computer-Assisted Monitoring of Offenders

Computer-assisted monitoring of offenders (CAMO) is defined (Archambeault and Archambeault, 1989:170–171) as having two unique properties: "First is the notion that a computer, through some form of sensory input and with minimum human intervention, can systematically assimilate, store, analyze and retrieve information about individual offenders. Second is the notion that the computer assisted monitoring system has the ability to directly or indirectly influence or control the behavior of the offender." CAMO is commonly discussed under the heading of *electronic monitoring or home arrest*. CAMO is in its infancy and may become the single most significant sentencing and correctional alternative of the twenty-first century. Currently, there may be as many as 70,000 offenders under some form of CAMO control, and this number may well triple by the year 2000.

However, current legal, ethical, and economic issues, combined with a lack of creative thinking, have retarded the development of CAMO technologies thus far this century. Legal controversies involving CAMO often revolve around issues of privacy—that of the offender and those who live in the same location with him or her. Current "rule of thumb" legal standards generally hold that it is legal to monitor an offender's time-related activities and location. However, unless a substance abuse issue is involved, it may not be legal to monitor offender physiology or biology. It may also not be legal to invade the privacy of other people (e.g., family friends) who may live with the offender. These standards restrict the type of CBT that can be incorporated into legal CAMO devices.

Ethical issues are many and varied. Some revolve around questions such as: How much external state control over an offender's life, outside a prison or jail, is justified? Does the state, through its law enforcement and correctional control social institutions, have the right to monitor every aspect of an offender's life? To what degree must the offender be free to choose whether or not to commit crime again? If the state is allowed to restrict to the maximum degree that CBT allows the rights and movement of offenders in the community, what is to stop it from using the same "big brother" technology to restrict the rights of other classes of citizens?

Economic issues are directly linked to legal and ethical issues. Although manufacturers have the capability of producing significantly more sophisticated CAMO systems, they would be much more expensive than current products. Legal and ethical considerations have influenced manufacturers to concentrate on marketing less controversial and less effective CBT devices.

The problems associated with current market-driven CAMO technologies prompt some critics to argue that electronic monitoring and criminal justice-related CBT systems are merely passing fads (Corbett and Marx, 1991). Others disagree (Lilly, 1992). Moreover, such conclusions often do not reflect an accurate understanding of the range of CBT applications that could be employed in a CAMO context. To aid in the understanding of the real potential of CAMO, this writer developed and presented a seven-category continuum typology (Archambeault and Archambeault, 1989:170–187) and later elaborated on it (Archambeault and Gould, 1990). This continuum typology includes:

1. Computer-assisted diagnosis and instructional systems
2. Computerized offender transaction databases
3. Fixed-location detector devices
4. Mobile-location detectors
5. Mobile-location and biophysical data transmission devices
6. External behavior altering and monitoring systems
7. Intracranial stimulation and subcutaneous control devices

Space limitations will not allow a detailed discussion of each. However, the following seven summary comments are appropriate.

First, moving from CAMO type 1 to 7, the extent of external control or influence over offender behavior and activities increases in addition to the amount of information on subjects which is collected and analyzed by computer.

Second, computer-assisted diagnosis and instructional systems[9] (CAMO type 1) and computerized offender transaction databases (CAMO type 2) are the most common and widely accepted forms of CAMO.

Third, although a wide variety of CBT integrated technologies is used in "offender monitoring" devices today, most are CAMO type 3, which transmit only three basic pieces of information: (1) time, (2) fixed location, and (3) subject identification using early 1980s technology.[10] Currently, there are many problems with CAMO type 3 devices. For example, to track an offender's movement from point A (home) to B (work), fixed monitors must be installed in both locations. There is no continuous monitoring during movement. Perhaps the worst feature of current monitoring practices is the great number of paper reports that must be read by human probation, or parole or community control, officers to detect patterns of violating behavior. Often, stacks of daily reports are placed in files, lost, thrown away, but not read. Reports are sometimes generated on a 24-hour basis, while monitoring agencies themselves are only open 8 to 12 hours a day. When a violation occurs during an agency's "closed hours," it may be 12 to 18 hours before anyone knows it. This is obviously time enough for the offender to disappear or return to his or her assigned location. Consequently, the effectiveness of the "control" aspect is sometimes questioned.

Fourth, the technologies for CAMO type 4, mobile location detectors, and type 5, mobile location and biological data transmitters, currently exist, but few products are currently marketed in the United States. For example, CAMO type 4 devices could be constructed out of the same technologies that create CAD (computer-aided dispatch), AVL (automatic vehicle locator), and other emergency CBT systems. Mobile emergency medical technologies monitoring systems could be added to create CAMO type 5 devices. These systems would allow continuous point-to-point monitoring of offender behavior and actions. However, this technology is much more expensive than type 3 devices. Additionally, legal and ethical issues concerning their use are still unresolved in some jurisdictions.

However, during the 1980s, the emphasis on DWI or DUI enforcement led to the acceptance of the use of some of this technology in detecting substance abuse violations. Consequently, there are several devices that are capable of detecting substance abuse violations and reporting them in the process of offender monitoring. Most of these either use the breath from the subject or measure toxins on the surface of the skin to detect violations. Although the products currently on the market are fairly primitive, much more sophisticated technology already exists in the medical, biomedical, and space research programs. These state-of-the-art biomedical sensors and transponders are able to monitor a wide range of biological and biophysical functions of the human body, in addition to the detection of a wide spectrum of gases and toxin exposures to human skin surface. For example, in Japan a system is being developed that will allow drivers, as well as monitoring authorities, to detect when a driver is too tired to drive safely by reading the buildup of certain chemical compounds on the skin surface. Similar systems already exist in other countries that alert drivers and authorities when too much alcohol has been consumed.

Fifth, external behavior altering and monitoring systems (CAMO type 6) and intercranial stimulation and subcutaneous control devices (CAMO type 7) offer the most potential for correctional control of offenders but are also the most controver-

sial. Currently, these CBT applications are not legal correctional control methods and exist only as theoretical CAMO types. They extend the concept of monitoring from that of simply collecting information on offenders to that of intervening directly in offender behavior and actions. Arguably, crude forms of CAMO type 6 can be seen in the devices that will not permit a driver who has consumed alcoholic beverages to be able to start his vehicle. Slightly more advanced prototype devices contain prom chips and voice synthesizers; when alcohol or drug toxins are detected, the devices can make instant records and generate verbal warnings. In theory, these could warn a probationer or parolee that he or she is around illegal substances and might, as a consequence, have his or her probation or parole revoked. Others might produce minor shocks and be used in combination with a behavioral modification reinforcement regime. Still other devices might allow the release of drug agents onto the surface of the skin that counter the effects of the drug or produce an adverse physical reaction.

However, much more sophisticated mechanisms are currently in use in medical treatment and biotechnical research. Computers are now able to communicate directly with brain cells; future potentials may allow computers to abstract information from human brains that may be lost to the conscious mind. Many forms of medical patches or external devices are used to monitor patient electrochemical balances in the body. These patches might also offer potential application in the control, monitoring, and treatment of selected offenders with biologically or physically based mental problems or with substance abuse addictions.

CAMO type 7 devices extend this technology of control into the human body itself through implants. Although no devices are currently marketed for use in monitoring offenders, much of the technology needed to implant miniaturized computer devices in the body, especially the brain, already exists. For decades there has been continuous medical and physiological research into human brain-body connections. Research, for example, has shown that the artificial stimulation of selected parts of any organism's brain can give that organism the greatest pleasure or pain that the organism is capable of experiencing. Other research has extended the use of miniaturized computers that are surgically implanted in the brain, central nervous system, or other parts of the body. These devices can monitor body motor activities or functions, or stimulate brain or sensory feelings and sensations. Other devices can regulate the body's own chemistry and electrophysiology. When combined, these technologies make it theoretically possible to both monitor and control the organism. The implications of this technology for the future are awesome.

Sixth, the range of CBT biomedical technologies that could potentially be used for the monitoring and control of offenders is developing much more rapidly than the legal and ethical issues which they create can be resolved. More sophisticated CBT human control technologies currently exist than were ever conceptualized by George Orwell in his book *1984.*

Finally, a lack of creative thinking and void of adequate theory also hinder the efficient use of CAMO. The phenomenon of CAMO has not been adequately conceptualized in terms of theory development. Terms such as *electronic monitoring* or *house arrest* obscure the nature of CAMO and hinder understanding. Combined with a lack of creativity in thinking about how current CBTs could be used, CAMO has not advanced much beyond the early 1980s capabilities.

Computer-Related Crime

Computers have also altered the nature and characteristics of crime and criminals. The 1990s continued to experience an increase in computer-related crime, including electronic fraud, viruses, terrorism, and security system violations (McCullock, 1990; Rosenblatt, 1990; Alexander, 1991; Rotenberg, 1991). This technological crime has engendered much debate about privacy issues (Weinberg, 1991) and the potential threats posed by the emerging electronic information highway. It has also increased the demand and utilization of more powerful and "smarter" computer systems for the protection of data systems as well as the detection and investigation of computer-related crimes (Clede, 1990). The nature of computer crime will change, as will the investigative tools of law enforcement as a function of the development of artificial intelligence and virtual reality.

CRIMINAL JUSTICE IN THE TWENTY-FIRST CENTURY: IMPLICATIONS AND CONCLUSIONS

If the past two decades are indicators of the future, the line between science fiction and scientific fact will continue to blur as the twenty-first century approaches. On any given day, computer research may dramatically redefine state-of-the-art technology as it has so many times over the past few years. Computer technology which existed only in "sci-fi" movies and literature of the 1960s and 1970s became operational reality in the 1980s and early 1990s. In part, this progress occurs because computer technology evolves as an end in itself and is propelled by theoretical, futuristic thinking. It is left to others to determine how to apply the technology to different functions.

If the past is an indicator of the future, it is logical to take current evolving technologies and project their use into the future. Three emerging computer technologies have significant implications for criminal justice of the twenty-first century: artificial intelligence, virtual reality, and biomedical research into direct brain-computer linkage.

Research in artificial intelligence may totally revolutionize current concepts of computers. In the near future, for example, it may be possible for users to interact verbally (talk) with computers, inputting data and instructions without having to touch a keyboard. Computers will clarify what they are supposed to do by asking the user questions. Computers will be able to provide users with verbal output information, in addition to printing reports or graphics. Emerging AI technology will also make it possible to develop network linkages among currently incompatible data bases.

These advances will be incorporated into criminal justice communication and crime analysis capabilities. Increasingly, crime scene evidence will be collected and analyzed in the field or at crime scenes. New verbal interactions between officers on the street and centralized computers may change the meaning of *partner*. These advances may result in improved accuracy of evidence. Courts—judges, prosecutors, defense attorneys—may be able to interface directly with legal databases during trials, allowing the introduction of higher court decisions to be applied instantly after they are made. Computers may guide all the court actors as to procedures, leading to fewer errors.

Corrections will use AI to manage its huge offender data systems. However, AI advancements will also lead to more secure correctional facilities and more effective treatment programs. CAMO effectiveness will be strengthened by allowing AI to screen offender monitoring reports and making more efficient use of probation officer or community control officer time.

AI, in combination with virtual reality technology, may have tremendous implications for criminal justice. For example, today, computer-generated graphical arrays and displays are already being used to illustrate events surrounding crime scene investigations and traffic accidents in U.S. courts. Further developments in AI–VR CBT may enable computer simulations to be generated as witnesses testify as to what they observed. Drawing from current research on a direct brain–computer interface (VR–AI) may allow witnesses to recall subconscious or suppressed memories. Conceivably, it may even be possible to question a subject and obtain accurate perceptions of facts and events without consent; such use would have obvious constitutional implications.

The integration of artificial intelligence, virtual reality, and computer-assisted instruction may have great potential for offender therapy and rehabilitation. For example, in the future it may be possible for people to read sensory or action words (e.g., hot, ice, wind, run) and experience the physiological sensations associated with them. In this context it may enhance the learning process and enable students who have difficulty learning through conventional methods to learn better. It may also speed up the process of learning for normal learners, allowing the acquisition of knowledge more rapidly than through conventional methods. Under therapeutic counseling conditions, offenders may be able to relive their crimes and experience the reactions and feelings of their victims. Similar technology may allow the probing of deep psychological, emotional, and social learning problems.

The VR–AI technology may have some negative effects as well. The same technology may also create new forms of addiction that could be more powerful than biology-based drug addiction. It could also be used to "brainwash" or alter human learned value systems. The future applications of computers in criminal justice will be limited only by human imagination, ethics, and law.

ENDNOTES

1. *Input* refers to the fact that the device is capable of receiving electronic coded data or information. Input can come from a *user* or person who operates the computer through keyboard commands, or from already stored data, or from the output of some other program. Input can also come from sensor readings; from data transmitted over wire, radio waves, or microwaves; or from hundreds of other sources.

2. *Storage* refers to the fact that the electronic device is capable of storing or saving the input data or information for future use. Storage can either be for a short period of time or can be permanent or long term. For example, data saved by a computer only until it is turned off are said to be *held in memory*. On the other hand, data are said to be "stored" when they are saved to electronic media, such as disks, tapes, CD-roms, or other devices, and if they are present even after a computer is turned off and on again. The distinction between *memory* and *storage* in many computers is whether the user input data remain are retrievable after the computer is turned off.

3. *Processing* refers to the capability of the device to do something with the input data or information. Normally, processing involves the manipulation, use, or analysis of the stored data or information. It is the reason for the computer in the first place. The user controls the computer either through direct instructions to it, which is another form of input, or through programs. *Programs* are sets of prewritten instructions or applications. A few of the most common application programs today are word processing, spreadsheets or accounting ledgers, statistical analysis, games, and telecommunications processing, to mention only a few. Through all of these, the input data are transformed into a more usable format by the computer for the human user. Word processing or telecommunications facilitate human communications. Statistical analysis and spreadsheets allow the user to summarize and analyze numerical data. Games allow the user to play according to the rules of the program. Processing may also involve the monitoring or controlling of production machines, robots, the flight of aircraft, or thousands of different functions.

4. *Output* refers to the ability to get the processed data or information out of the computer. Frequently, output takes the form of alphanumeric or graphic print formats such as those that are produced through word processing, statistical analysis, or graphics. Other times, the output function is to cause another device to be manipulated or controlled, such as the use of computers to regulate heating and cooling in a building or to regulate the flow of fuel in a modern car's injection system. Other times, the output function of one program may be the input functions of another. Where these functions occur, they are said to be looped or linked together. For example, the output function of a word-processing program may be the simultaneous printing of a document, the saving of the document file, and the creation of a backup of the file. Many other types of output functions are also possible.

5. Personal computers (PCs) are stand-alone systems which include CPU, disk drive(s), CRTs, or monitors and keyboards. These may be connected to peripheral devices including modems, faxes, printers, and tape drivers, among others. PCs are generally intended for one user, although PC networks can interconnect many PCs and users.

6. Minicomputers and mainframe computers are central memories that are accessed through remote terminals. Both mini and mainframe computers are designed by multiple users to run multiple programs. Minicomputers are small mainframe computers which are generally much more powerful than PCs. Minicomputers are sometimes used in PC networks as file servers or central computers. Mainframe computers are the most powerful computers in existence. They are often able to service thousands of users who are running hundreds of different programs.

7. In the environment of the 1990s, there are literally tens of thousands of different CBT applications in use and hundreds more being created daily. These include programmable TVs, radios, VCRs, satellite dishes, coffeepots, alarm clocks, digital wristwatches or video games, microwave ovens, memory typewriters, motion detectors or lights, voice-activated security systems, voice-activated dictation equipment, cellular telephones, printers, modems, fax machines, copying machines, memory telephones, electronic fuel injection, and emissions systems in most newer vehicles. Whole areas of operations depend on integrated computer technologies, including robotics, telephone, cable, microwave and radio-wave communications devices, biomedical treatment and research monitors, laser surgery, CAT scans, and radiation therapy, among others.

8. Data are raw facts or computer-encoded numeric symbols. Information refers to facts that communicate meaning to the human being.
9. For discussions on why these are included in the CAMO typology, refer to citations given above.
10. Refer to Archambeault and Archambeault (1989:172–180) for a discussion of different specific characteristics of different types of equipment used.

REFERENCES AND BIBLIOGRAPHY

ALEXANDER, M. (1989). Hacker stereotypes changing. *Computerworld*, April, p. 101.

ALEXANDER, M. (1991). Justice unit spurred on by cross-border hackers. *Computerworld*, October 21, p. 5.

ALLEMAN, T. (1990). The computerized prison: Automation in a penal setting. In F. Schmalleger (ed.), *Computers in Criminal Justice: Issues and Applications*. Bristol, IN: Wyndham Hall Press.

ANTHES, G. H. (1991). Computers play part in addicts' recovery. *Computerworld*, September, p. 45.

ARCHAMBEAULT, W. G., and B. J. ARCHAMBEAULT (1989). *Computers in Criminal Justice Administration and Management*, 2nd ed. Cincinnati, OH: Anderson Publishing.

ARCHAMBEAULT, W., and L. GOULD (1990). The computer assisted monitoring of offenders (CAMO): An emerging alternative to incarceration. In F. Schmalleger (ed.), *Computers in Criminal Justice: Issues and Applications*. Bristol, IN: Wyndham Hall Press.

BARDEGE, S. (1990). Technology boosts law enforcement. *American City and County*, February, p. 14.

BLOCK, M. H. (1990). Computer-integrated courtroom: Moving the judicial system into the twenty-first century. *Trial, 26*, September, pp. 30–52.

BOOKER, E. (1990). Grading high-tech teaching. *Computerworld*, February 19, p. 114.

BRANSCOMB, A. W. (1991). Common law for the electronic frontier. *Scientific American*, September, pp. 154–158.

BRANWYN, G. (1990). Computers, crimes and the law. *Futurist*, 24(5):48.

CASH, T. F., and T. BROWN (1989). Validity of Million's computerized interpretation system for the MCMI: Comment on Moreland and Onstad. *Journal of Consulting and Clinical Psychology*, 57(2):311–312.

CHURBUCK, D. (1991). The computer as detective. *Forbes*, December, pp. 150–155.

CLEDE, B. (1990). Computer-aided investigation. *Police Chief*, April, p. 45.

CORBETT, R., and G. T. MARX. (1991). Critique: No soul in the new machine: Technofallacies in the electronic monitoring movement. *Justice Quarterly*, 8(3):399–414.

DEAN, J. M. (1989). Computers are like cars…. *Federal Probation*, June, pp. 61–64.

DERTOUZOS, M. L. (1991). Communications, computers, and networks. *Scientific American*, September, pp. 63–69.

DWORETZKY, T. (1991). Mechanimals. *Omni*, March, pp. 50–56.

FRITZ, M. (1991). Future looks a little brighter for CBT. *Computerworld*, April, p. 16.

GEAKE, E. (1991). Transputers speed up medical diagnosis. *New Scientist*, August 24, p. 24.

GRUNER, R. S. (1989). Sentencing advisor: An expert computer system for federal sentencing analysis. *Santa Clara Computer and High Technology Law Journal*, February, pp. 51–73.

HARMAN, A. (1991). Photophone. *Law and Order*, February, pp. 28–30.

HITT, J., and P. TOUGH (1990). Terminal delinquents. *Computerworld*, December, pp. 174–178; 182–183; 211–219.

JAMESON, R., and C. MEGERMAN (1990). Automation in medium-sized jail. *Corrections Today*, July, pp. 180–182.

JOHNSON, W. (1989). Information espionage: An old problem with a new face. *Computerworld*. October, p. 85.

KAPOR, M. (1991). Civil liberties in cyberspace. *Scientific American*, September, pp. 158–164.

LARSON, R. (1989). The new crime stoppers. *Technology Review*, November–December, pp. 28–31.

LILLY, J. R. (1992). Review essay: Selling justice: Electronic monitoring and the security industry. *Justice Quarterly*, 9(3):493–503.

MANCHESTER, R. E. (1991). Office organization in the computer era. *Trial*, 27, January, pp. 29–31.

McCULLOCK, D. J. (1990). Computer based security systems save money, boost safety. *Corrections Today*, July, pp. 86, 88, 90–91.

MEYER, G., and J. THOMAS (1990). The "baudy" world of the byte bandit: A postmodernist interpretation of the computer underground. In F. Schmalleger (ed.), *Computers in Criminal Justice: Issues and Applications*, Bristol, IN: Wyndham Hall Press.

MORELEY, H. (1990). Computer viruses: High technology automated crime. In F. Schmalleger (ed.), *Computers in Criminal Justice: Issues and Applications*. Bristol, IN: Wyndham Hall Press.

NAGELHAUT, M. (1992). Caller ID: Privacy and blocking issues. *Public Utilities Fortnightly*, March, p. 31–33.

ORLIN, J. M. (1991). Alien technology made familiar. *Training and Development*, November, pp. 55–58.

PARKS, C. M. (1990). Handheld police computers: The ticket of the future. *Police Chief*, April, pp. 36–40.

REBOUSSIN, R. (1990). An expert system designed to profile murderers. In F. Schmalleger (ed.), *Computers in Criminal Justice: Issues and Applications*, Bristol, IN: Wyndham Hall Press.

REBOUSSIN, R., and W. RAFOYA (1990). The development of artificial intelligence expert systems in law enforcement. In F. Schmalleger (ed.), *Computers in Criminal Justice: Issues and Applications*, Bristol: IN: Wyndham Hall Press.

ROBERTS, L. (1991). GRAIL seeks out genes buried in DNA sequence. *Research News*, 8, November, p. 805.

ROSENBLATT, K. (1990). Deterring computer crime. *Technology Review*, February–March, pp. 35–40.

ROTENBERG, M. (1991). Let's look before we legislate: Laws are adequate to handle computer crime; "Net Police" not needed. *Computerworld*, October 21, p. 40.

SAYLOR, W. (1990) Federal Bureau of Prison systems tracks inmate populations. *Corrections Today*, July, pp. 24, 26, 28.

SCHMALLEGER, F. (ed.) (1990). *Computers in Criminal Justice: Issues and Applications*, Bristol, IN: Wyndham Hall Press.

SIKES, A. (1991). Brink of revolution. *Newsweek*, January 14, p. 8.

SPARROW, W. (1993). Information systems and the development of policing. *Perspectives on the Police*, Washington, DC: U.S. Department of Justice, March, pp. 1–11.

STEPHENS, G. (1990). Impact of emerging police and corrections technology on constitutional rights. In F. Schmalleger (ed.), *Computers in Criminal Justice: Issues and Applications*, Bristol, IN: Wyndham Hall Press.

WALDRON, J., B. ARCHAMBEAULT, W. ARCHAMBEAULT, L. CARSONE, J. CONSER, and C. SUTTON (1987). *Microcomputers in Criminal Justice*, Cincinnati, OH: Anderson Publishing.

WEINBERG, D. (1989). Computers are talking in America's courts. *Judges' Journal*, 28, Spring, pp. 4–7.

WEINBERG, D. (1990). Prison à la carte. *Economist*, September 8, p. 57.

WEINBERG, D. (1991). Computers and privacy: The eye of the beholder. *Economist*, May 4, pp. 21–23.

WEINBERG, D. (1992). Police computer fuels fears of "European Connection." *New Scientist*, 4, January, p. 14.

PART VI

Correctional Issues
in the Twenty-First Century

The real task in administering all correctional facilities, large and small, is a problem presenting very real challenges for criminologists. The prison is supposed to incapacitate offenders, control and restrict their movements, deter them from committing further crimes while changing offenders' value orientations and teaching them new vocational skills. How realistic are these goals? The chapters in this section examine major problems inherent in today's correctional institutions, while predicting major riots and skyrocketing crime rates (though nationwide crime rates are down), unless our prisons fail to reflect the needs of the twenty-first century.

According to many indexes the American economy was at its strongest ever near the close of the twentieth and at the beginning of the twenty-first century. However, the American incarceration rate was at its highest ever, 682 per 100,000 per Hallett. We saw an increasing rate of incarceration during the last century, reflected still in this new century. With the dramatic increases in the level of incarceration, there is some thought that correctional administrators at all levels of government should turn to private-opened correctional facilities. There are three key areas in which the government is concerned: private financing and construction of prisons; private industry involvement inside prisons; and private management, construction as well as operation of whole prison facilities by independent contractors. We wait to see if this is the wave of the future.

Another major dilemma facing criminal justice is how to process suspects and punish law violators in a humane and rational manner. In an attempt to reform unconstitutional conditions of confinement within American correctional facilities, there is needed, according to Welsh, a coordinated approach to problem analysis. It is Welsh's claim that there exist substantial shortcomings in both policy design and research on jail problems. We have been witness over the last century to how court orders have raised an awareness of jail problems while creating a more receptive climate for sentencing alternatives, public education, and other needed innovations. Overcrowding in correctional facilities is a result of a dynamic confluence of social, political, and legal forces. A *quick fix* is not always available. There needs to be in this new century relevant informed policy research so that the problems of yesteryear are solved today.

In this new century the conclusion is that community corrections programs are being framed in terms of alternative sanctions, yet continue to be developed and expanded. According to Morgan and Sigler, punishment and treatment represent two extremes on a continuum of approaches for the disposition of offenders found guilty. Orientation toward the punishment or treatment of convicted offenders has continually vacillated from treating the offender as if he or she had no rights or reason, to expecting help to treat the offender as a person who retains his or her rights. Contemporary concern with the perceived increase in the amount and severity of violence may moderate the response to modify sentencing provisions. In this new century, it is highly likely that mandatory sentence enhancements will be softened. It will be interesting to note the changes of determinate sentences that are keyed to the crime rather than to the characteristics and needs of the offenders, while still allowing for treatment programs to work.

chapter 20

An Introduction to Prison Privatization

Issues for the Twenty-First Century

Michael Hallett, Ph.D.

ABSTRACT

This chapter presents a summary of the growing number of issues associated with the privatized operation and management of correctional facilities in the United States. By summarizing the history, rationale, current scope, and operational performance data generated by privatized prison facilities over the past 15 years, the chapter presents a synopsis of issues relevant to prison privatization in the twenty-first century.

INTRODUCTION: FORCES DRIVING PRISON PRIVATIZATION

While according to many indexes the U.S. economy was at its "strongest ever" near the close of the twentieth century—with the lowest rates of unemployment and inflation in a generation, with more people living in their own homes than ever before, and a tight labor market pushing wages higher—another, less widely cited, index clouded this picture of robust societal health: the U.S. incarceration rate was at its highest ever, 682 per 100,000 (Bureau of Justice Statistics, 1999:497).[1] As depicted in Figure 1, a rapid increase in the rate of incarceration took place during the latter part of the century. Particularly during the years 1980–2000, the U.S. incarceration rate roughly quadrupled and, as reflected in Table 1, on June 30, 1999, stood at unprecedented levels.

As a result of this dramatic increase in the level of incarceration, correctional administrations at all three levels of government (federal, state, and local) turned to private, for-profit corporations to manage the burgeoning number of inmates in privately operated correctional facilities. In addition to the introduction of private

371

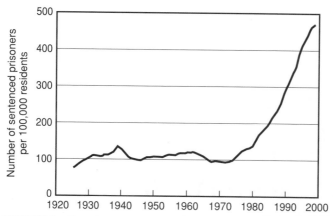

FIGURE 1   Rate (per 100,000 resident population) of sentenced prisoners under jurisdiction of state and federal correctional authorities on December 31, 1925–1999[a]

[a]The rates for the period before 1980 are based on the civilian population. The civilian population represents
the resident population less the armed forces stationed in the United States. Since 1980, the rates are based on
the total resident population provided by the U.S. Bureau of the Census. Data for 1999 are as of June 30.

Source: Bureau of Justice Statistics, 1999.

contractors into the operation of prisons, however, it should also be noted that during
this period many units of government, from local to federal, increasingly sought to
privatize other former public service functions, including waste disposal, education,
mass transit, infrastructure repair and construction, and other criminal justice functions
such as probation and parole and community corrections (e.g., halfway houses,
probation monitoring, house arrest, process servers) (Touche Ross & Co., 1987;
Thomas, 1995; Gilbert, 2000a). As discussed below, however, the privatization of
prisons is a unique phenomenon, imposing unique burdens and responsibilities upon
its constituent parties. In the realm of private operation and management of prisons,
however, privatization has taken place in three key areas:

1. Private financing and construction of prisons, particularly to avoid the need
    for issuing public bonds to finance construction of new facilities
2. Private industry involvement inside prisons, particularly in the provision of
    services to prisoners and in the utilization of prisoners as laborers
3. Private management, construction, and operation of entire prison facilities
    by independent contractors

This chapter addresses issues related to the latter form of privatization, that of
privately owned firms managing, operating, and often owning entire correctional
facilities on a for-profit basis. The chapter outlines several key issues facing the
private prisons industry at the turn of the century, all of which need resolving in
the twenty-first century.

TABLE 1   Number and Rate (per 1000,00 Residents) of Persons in State and Federal
Prisons or in Local Jails, United States, 1985, 1990–1999[a]

	Total Inmates in Custody	Prisoners in Custody		Inmates in Local Jails	Incarceration Rate[b]
		Federal	State		
1985	744,208	35,781	451,812	256,615	313
1990	1,148,702	58,838	684,544	405,320	458
1991	1,219,014	63,930	728,605	426,479	481
1992	1,295,150	72,071	778,495	444,584	505
1993	1,369,185	80,815	828,566	459,804	528
1994	1,476,621	85,500	904,647	486,474	564
1995	1,585,586	89,538	989,004	507,044	600
1996	1,646,020	95,088	1,032,440	518,492	618
1997	1,743,643	101,755	1,074,809	567,079	648
June 30, 1998	1,802,187	107,381	1,102,344	592,462	667
Dec. 31, 1998	NA	110,793	1,111,643	NA	NA
June 30, 1999	1,860,520	117,995	1,136,582	605,943	682
Percent change, 6/30/98 to 6/30/99	3.2	9.9	3.1	2.3	X
Annual average percent increase, 12/31/90 to 6/30/99	5.8	8.5	6.1	4.6	X

[a]Jail counts are for June 30; counts for 1994–1999 exclude persons who were supervised outside a jail facility. State and federal prisoner counts for 1985 and 1990–1997 are for December 31. NA, not available.

[b]Number of prison and jail inmates per 100,000 U.S. residents in each reference year.

Source: Bureau of Justice Statistics, 1999.

Mandatory Sentencing

The dramatic rise in the use of incarceration during the latter part of the twentieth century is widely attributed to policies associated with the "war on crime," undertaken by both conservative and liberal administrations, beginning with Lyndon Johnson in the mid-1960s (Quinney, 1974:60–81). A key strategy in the war on crime was the implementation of a *determinate* or *mandatory minimum* sentencing scheme, which sought both to lengthen the duration of time served by offenders to reduce the level of discretion provided judges and parole boards in enabling reductions of time served by convicted offenders (Clear and Cole, 1994:81). Drug-related crimes became a particular target of mandatory minimum sentencing schemes by the early 1980s, with even nonviolent drug crimes such as possession of marijuana being assigned mandatory minimum prison sentences in numerous states (Donziger, 1996:15, 25). As a result of these drug war policies, the U.S. incarceration rate increased dramatically. It is also important to note that evidence clearly demonstrates that the expanded use of incarceration during this period was not the result of increasing crime rates, but rather, the result of changes in criminal justice policy (Petersilia 1994; Donziger, 1996; Bohm and Haley, 1997:327; Austin and Irwin, 2001). That is, the shift to mandatory minimum sentencing was brought about not by an explosion in the level of crime, but rather, by a *shift in philosophy* regarding how best to respond to crime. In a study of incarceration rates in California, for example, the state with the nation's highest rate of incarceration, Joan Petersilia concluded that public fear of crime, rather than actual increases in the rate of crime, best explained the adoption of mandatory sentencing schemes in that state (1994:165). According to Petersilia, as fear of crime increased, "the nation shifted its focus away from addressing the 'root causes' of crime and the rehabilitation of criminals toward making crime penalties more swift, certain, and severe.…The state passed the Determinate Sentencing Law in 1977, which, among other things, embraced punishment as the purpose of prison, required mandatory prison sentences for many offenses formerly eligible for probation, and dramatically increased the rate at which probation and parole violators were returned to prison. As a result, California's corrections populations skyrocketed" (1994:165).

The trend toward expanded use of privately operated prisons, then, is one driven by several forces operating in unison. First and foremost is the above-illustrated increase in the incarceration rate itself and the corresponding increase in the number of prisoners housed in the country's prisons. Second, the rapidly increasing incarceration rate resulted in two corresponding difficulties, an increase in the level of prison *overcrowding* and an increase in the *costs* to taxpayers of operating expanding prisons. Included in these costs are the costs of new prison construction and the expanded use of diversionary programs such as boot camps and intensive probation supervision while new prisons were being built and monies shifted around in state budgets for expanded incarceration programs (McCarthy, 1987; Duffee and McGarrell, 1990; Petersilia, 1994; RAND, 1997). According to Petersilia, in California, by the early 1990s, spending on prison construction outpaced spending on education (Petersilia, 1994).

Prison Overcrowding and Cost of Incarceration

As a result of the swift increase in the use of incarceration, by the early 1990s prisons became overcrowded and dangerous, with roughly two-thirds of U.S. correctional facilities being placed under federal court order to reduce overcrowding for violations of inmates' Eighth Amendment rights under the Constitution (Bohm, 1997:327). A key consequence of overcrowding is a higher prevalence of violence and injury to inmates and staff, as well as higher use of disciplinary "good time" revocation and higher rates of staff turnover (Silberman, 1995). As overcrowding-related problems increased, the option of trying to relieve overcrowding through the use of private prison facilities became more attractive. Indeed, the world's largest private prison corporation,

Corrections Corporation of America (CCA), based in Nashville, Tennessee, was literally founded during a forced special session of the Tennessee state legislature brought about by an overcrowding crisis (Hallett and Lee, 2000).

Like many states in the late 1970s, Tennessee began its own crusade to lower crime rates through implementation of mandatory minimum sentencing. Predictably, this created tremendous overcrowding, which led to a federal court order placing caps on the prisoner population. By 1985 the situation reached a crisis point, with rioting and several deaths, and the declaration of the state's oldest prison at Nashville as unconstitutional. Tennessee found itself very quickly in need of roughly 7000 additional prison beds and called for spending an additional $380 million to build six new prisons (Tennessee Select Oversight Committee on Corrections, 1995). During that special session, cofounder of CCA Tom Beasley introduced CCA's first proposal to manage a statewide prison system. Said Beasley in 1985: "Our proposal is simple—we will pay the state for the right to manage the system under the state's supervision; we will spend private capital to improve the system and draw our profit out of more efficient use of the state's regular operating budget. That is a $250 million—one quarter billion dollar—turnaround in the state budget without a tax increase! We believe this is absolutely a win–win situation and an unprecedented opportunity to make Tennessee a leader in this most difficult area (Corrections Corporation of America, 1985:2, as cited in Hallett and Lee, 2000:230).

According to a 1998 survey of state and federal correctional administrators conducted by Abt Associates, Inc., reduced overcrowding (not cost savings) is, in fact, the leading reason that jurisdictions opt to utilize private prisons. The report ranks the objectives of prison administrators in regard to privatization in the following order (1998:16):

1. Reducing overcrowding   86%
2. Speed of acquiring additional beds   75%
3. Gaining operational flexibility   61%
4. Construction cost savings   57%
5. Improving caliber of services   43%
6. Reducing legal liability exposure   39%
7. Other   21%

Current Use of Private Prisons

According to the U.S. Department of Justice *Sourcebook of Criminal Justice Statistics* (Bureau of Justice Statistics, 1999), as of December 1999 there were 13 private contractors operating adult correctional facilities in the United States, with a total inmate population of nearly 140,000 (Table 2). The two largest of these, Corrections Corporation of America and Wackenhut Corrections Corporation, together held 80% of the total U.S. prisoners housed in private facilities. It is also worth noting that CCA currently dominates the prison privatization market, holding 52% of the available contracts, while Wackenhut holds roughly 20% (Abt Associates, 1998:18).

TABLE 2   Private Adult Correctional Facility Management Firms by Capacity of
Facilities under Contract, United States, Dec. 31, 1997, 1998, and 1999

Management Firm	Capacity of All Facilities under Contract[a]		
	1997	1998	1999
Total	103,730	127,262	138,726
Alternative Programs, Inc.	340	340	340
Aviation Correctional Services, Inc.[b]	150	350	350
The Bobby Ross Group	2,825	464	464
CiviGenics, Inc.	3,563	3,563	2,791
Cornell Corrections, Inc.	3,882	5,916	7,138
Correctional Services Corporation	2,629	6,891	6,517
Corrections Corporation of America[c]	52,095	69,530	71,250
Correctional Systems, Inc.	170	272	272
The GRW Corporation	362	362	362
Management & Training Corporation	4,259	6,447	9,177
Maranatha Production Company	500	500	500
U.S. Corrections Corporation	5,259	NA	NA
Wackenhut Corrections Corporation[c,d]	27,696	32,627	39,565

[a]Includes correctional facilities, facilities under construction, and planned expansion of existing facilities.
[b]Formerly Aviation Community Services, Inc.
[c]Includes facilities under contract outside the United States.
[d]The Wackenhut Corrections Corporation did not respond to the survey; data were estimated.

Source: Bureau of Justice Statistics, 1999.

By comparison, then, CCA's inmate population is larger than that of most states (71,250). In the late 1990s, for example, the state of Tennessee had an inmate population of roughly 17,000. In effect, CCA runs the sixth-largest correctional system in the United States, behind states like California, New York, and Texas. Wackenhut's total inmate population for 1999 was 39, 595 (Bureau of Justice Statistics, 1999:82). In total, over 150 private correctional facilities were operational in the United States in 1999 and housed roughly 5% of the total inmate population in the country (Abt Associates, 1998:App. 1, p. 2; Bureau of Justice Statistics, 1999:82). A breakdown of privately held inmate populations by state for 1999 is shown in Table 3. Of these inmates, 95% were minimum or medium security classification, with only 4% of privately held inmates having a maximum security designation (Abt Associates, 1998:25). As recently noted by the U.S. Federal Bureau of Prisons: "Compared to all prisoners held by state and federal prisons created by public employees, the private sector had a disproportionate number of minimum security prisoners and a few maximum security ones" (2000:109–110). At the end of 1997, only one private

TABLE 3   Number and Rated Capacity of Private Adult Correctional Facilities by Jurisdiction, Dec. 31, 1997, 1998, and 1999

Jurisdiction[a]	Number of Facilities			Rated Capacity		
	1997	1998	1999	1997	1998	1999
Arizona	5	6	6	4,748	6,860	6,860
Arkansas	2	2	2	1,200	1,200	1,885
California	19	24	24	10,292	11,294	11,462
Colorado	8	9	6	3,444	4,644	3,824
District of Columbia	1	1	1	866	866	866
Florida	10	10	9	6,223	6,255	5,465
Georgia	3	5	7	1,566	6,409	9,457
Idaho	1	1	1	1,250	1,250	1,250
Illinois	1	1	NA	220	220	NA
Indiana	1	1	1	670	670	670
Kansas	2	2	2	529	529	685
Kentucky	4	4	4	1,973	2,631	2,631
Louisiana	2	2	2	2,948	2,948	3,012
Michigan	1	1	1	480	480	480
Minnesota	1	1	1	1,338	1,338	1,338
Mississippi	5	6	6	3,176	4,650	4,700
Missouri	2	2	1	660	660	60
Montana	NA	1	1	NA	512	512
Nevada	1	1	1	500	500	500
New Jersey	1	1	1	300	300	300
New Mexico	6	7	7	3,836	4,864	5,322
New York	1	1	1	200	200	200
North Carolina	2	2	3	2,000	2,112	2,256
Ohio	2	2	4	2,256	2,256	4,140
Oklahoma	6	8	8	7,068	9,716	10,436
Pennsylvania	1	1	1	1,200	1,200	1,562
Puerto Rico	4	4	4	3,000	3,000	3,000
Rhode Island	1	1	1	302	302	302
Tennessee	5	6	6	5,628	7,326	7,326
Texas	41	43	42	27,139	29,690	29,820
Utah	1	1	2	400	400	900
Virginia	1	1	1	1,500	1,500	1,500
Washington	1	1	1	150	150	150

[a]The geographical location of facilities does not necessarily indicate contracting decisions made by agencies in those jurisdictions. Some states are contracting for the housing of their prisoners in other jurisdictions. Some states are providing sites for federal facilities. Data include facilities in operation and those under construction.

Source: Bureau of Justice Statistics, 1999.

prison facility in operation was designated exclusively for maximum security inmates, the South Bay Correctional Facility in Florida, operated by Wackenhut (Abt Associates, 1998:25).

THEMES IN THE DEBATE ABOUT PRISON PRIVATIZATION

The Cost Conundrum

Certainly, a most significant issue regarding private prisons to be resolved in the twenty-first century is the issue of whether or not private prisons can be operated more cheaply than state prisons while still achieving comparable performance. Although there are situations in which the evidence suggests that private prisons are more cost-effective than state-operated prisons, the data are not uniform across the sites and generalizations cannot be made across jurisdiction or region of the country (Shichor, 1995:136; see also Thomas, 1996). "Determining whether and how privatization saves the government money is difficult in many jurisdictions because no publicly managed prisons exist that are similar enough to warrant direct comparison with private facilities" (Abt Associates, 1998:34). *Thus, when privatized facilities are found to be more cost-effective, the salient question is: why and under what conditions?*

Because an essential argument in favor of prison privatization is that private vendors can provide "more for less," clearly some explanation is in order regarding exactly how private vendors might accomplish this goal (Shichor, 1995). Even though cost savings are not listed by most correctional administrations as being the most important rationale for utilizing private contractors, clearly cost-effectiveness remains one of the central arguments made on behalf of the private prisons industry. As privatization scholar Charles Logan notes: "[A]mong claims made for the superiority of propriety [private] prisons, the most frequent and most salient...is that they will be less expensive, or at least more efficient" (Logan, 1990:76). The financial stakes in this debate are enormous. In California, for example, corrections has become the fastest-growing state budget category since the mid-1980s—and by the mid-1990s outpaced spending on education—rendering enormous chunks of the state budget available to private prison vendors for the delivery of correctional services (Petersilia, 1994). Not surprisingly, then, stakeholders on both sides of the privatization debate cling to reports that each finds favorable.

Calculating costs for operating private prison systems across jurisdictions is a very complex matter, requiring a conflation of comparison costs between facilities often differing by jurisdiction, type of inmate, inmate programming and service assignments, salaries of line and administrative staff, overall number of staff, and health care commitments for inmates, for example. This often results in an "apples and oranges" kind of comparison that critics argue render comparisons between facilities neither valid nor reliable (Shichor, 1995; General Accounting Office, 1996). Prison facilities often also differ in "reputation," which, although a somewhat qualitative variable, may dramatically influence operational life inside a prison (Silberman, 1995). The two primary claims about the cost utility of private prisons, however, are clear (see Shichor, 1995):

1. Private contractors can operate prisons more cheaply and efficiently than can state-based providers, resulting in cost savings for taxpayers.

2. The quality of services provided by private vendors will be greater than or equal to those provided by state-based providers.

The first difficulty often articulated regarding making valid and reliable cost assessments of performance between public and private correctional facilities is that costs are a highly regional phenomenon. Thus, when comparing costs, it is vital that the comparisons be made between as nearly similar institutions as possible in as nearly similar regions as possible (General Accounting Office, 1996:5; Thomas, 1996:12, n20). It would be patently unfair, for example, to compare the costs of operating a prison in the rural south to the costs of operating a prison in Houston, Texas, or California, as this would greatly distort the averages. As Abt Associates' 1998 detailed analysis of privatization further notes:

> The task of selecting fully comparable prisons is difficult, if not impossible. Differences in the age, health, gender, and security risk of inmates would imply differences in the reported cost per inmate-day even among equally efficient prison facilities. The same may be said for differences in the size of the inmate population and regional differences in the cost of labor and materials. One could use regression analysis to "correct" for these differences if there were a large enough number of roughly comparable prisons in a given system. In the absence of such data, the only available alternative is to adjust on a case-by-case basis. Not surprisingly, this approach leaves room for considerable disagreement over the appropriate scale of the adjustment factors (Abt Associates, 1998:App. 1, fn 7).

Where savings from prison privatization have been demonstrated, they are consistently derived from a narrow set of sources: hiring fewer staff with lower benefits, choosing to serve mostly minimum and medium security inmates who are healthy, and operating in relatively newer facilities with more efficient designs and newer equipment. Arguably, the greatest level of savings, however, is achieved in staffing-related expenses. "Prisons are extremely labor-intensive, with approximately 65 to 70% of the costs of operating a prison related to staff salaries, fringe benefits, and overtime" (Austin and Irwin, 2001:73). As privatization proponent Charles Thomas notes, "it is generally acknowledged that private-sector fringe benefits—most particularly retirement benefits—are less generous than those made available to public employees" (1996:10).

The recent GAO report on prison privatization and cost is often cited as the most reliable study on the topic (Abt Associates, 1998:37). It closely examined five studies in California, Texas, Washington, Tennessee, and New Mexico. The study analyzed both operational cost and quality of service issues. This report is worth quoting at length:

> These studies offer little generalizable guidance for other jurisdictions about what to expect regarding comparative operational costs and quality of service if they were to move toward privatizing correctional facilities. First, several of the studies focused on specialized inmate populations, such as those in pre-release situations, that limited their generalizability to a wider inmate population. Second, methodological weaknesses in some of the comparisons—such as using hypothetical facilities or non-random survey

samples—make some findings questionable, even for the study setting. Third, a variety of differences in other states and regions could result in experiences far different from those of the states that were studied. For example, cost of living and a state's correctional philosophy could affect the comparative costs and quality of private and public facilities from state to state. Finally, the age or maturity of the private system could affect the relationship between private and public facilities in terms of costs and quality (1996:4).

Thus, assessing the true costs (and benefits) of private prisons is a very complex process.

Hidden Costs

One of the key difficulties involved in accurately calculating the true cost of a correctional operation has to do with so-called "hidden costs." The term "does not imply that [costs] are deliberately concealed, only that they are not easily discernible" (Logan and McGriff, 1989:2). Hidden costs include expenses that involve unforeseen events, such as expenses related to unexpected medical conditions, unexpected escapes, or unplanned damage to a facility. Because budgetary forecasting is generally done by singular institutional agencies, hidden costs generally first reveal themselves in cross-agency budget analyses when combined costs are more evident. As Logan and McGriff (1989) note: "[C]osts omitted from [single agency] correctional budgets can amount to one-third the value of those that are included." One of the key problems in forecasting costs in private, for-profit prisons is the continuous reality that unexpected things often happen in prisons. Whereas things such as per diem costs and services are relatively fixed, "unexpected" costs can be fairly substantial (Shichor, 1995). For example, in the aftermath of several high-profile escapes from CCA-operated prisons in Youngstown, Ohio, and Clifton, Tennessee, local jurisdictions paid for the expenses related to recapturing the escaped inmates. These costs, of course, then have to be added to the total cost of operating the private facility paid by the contracting jurisdiction. Moreover, "some of the apparent differences may not reflect actual savings but may instead be accounting artifacts…because public and private accounting systems are designed for different purposes; that is, public systems were not designed specifically for cost accounting (Abt Associates, 1998:iv).

Finally, an additional cost issue raised by evaluators of private prisons is that for-profit prison operations may be inclined to cut costs too far, resulting in a decreased level of service and safety for communities, inmates, and staff in and around correctional facilities that are privatized. Austin and Irwin's survey of private prisons revealed that "the number of staff assigned to private facilities per inmate population is approximately 15% lower than at public facilities," raising questions about cost versus safety (2001:83). Indeed, as recently noted by Hallett and Lee, a Tennessee legislative report from the state's Select Oversight Committee on Corrections, comparing public and private correctional facilities, stated:

> The number of injuries to staff and prisoners is a measure of the security and safety of the facility. During the fifteen-month evaluation period, South Central Correctional Center [the privately operated facility] reported significantly more injuries to prisoners

and staff than either Northeast Correctional Center or Northwest Correctional Center [both operated by the state], with 214 injuries reported as SCCC, 21 and 51 at Northeast Correctional Center and Northwest Correctional Center, respectively. The use of force is also reviewed when looking at the security and safety of a prison. The facilities have significantly different reported incidents of the use of force. South Central Correctional Center had 30 reported incidents, Northeast Correctional Center 4, and Northwest Correctional Center 6 (Tennessee Select Oversight Committee on Corrections, 1995:vii; as cited in Hallett and Lee, 2000:234; *bracketed text added for clarity*).

The survey conducted by James Austin and John Irwin also "revealed a greater number of inmate-on-inmate assaults per 1,000 at private prisons than at public facilities" (2001:81).

In sum, the few highly detailed studies on the cost-effectiveness of private prisons available have failed to reveal dramatic savings produced by private prisons. Part of the problem in demonstrating cost savings for private prisons is that the overall scale of prison privatization remains small. That is, as John Irwin and James Austin point out, currently the percentage of inmates held in private facilities is well under 10% in every state. Assuming that private prison facilities could achieve a 10% cost savings for 10% of a given state's inmates, the resulting savings would still be only a net savings of 1%: 10% of 10% is 1% (Austin and Irwin, 2001:73). Thus, large-scale cost savings are unlikely to be generated by privatization of prisons at its current scale of implementation. Moreover, in the relatively few evaluation studies designed to control for differences in public versus private accounting systems, inmate population differences, and staffing levels, the data remain inconclusive for the cost-effectiveness of private prisons. It must be said, however, that "only a very small percentage of those facilities operated by private firms have been evaluated" using appropriately designed studies (Abt Associates, 1998:46). The Abt Associates report concludes:

> Our conclusion regarding costs and savings is that the few existing studies and other available data do not provide strong evidence of any general pattern. Some states may be willing to pay high prices for private imprisonment if they need the beds to solve short-term deficiencies. In other states, expenditures for contracting may indeed be lower than for direct public provision. However, the bottom line with respect to savings is difficult to discern given the data and the assumptions made by analysts. Drawing conclusions about the inherent superiority of one or the other mode of provision, based on a few studies, is premature (1998:v).

Clearly, more work on this issue will be undertaken in the twenty-first century.

Construction of Prison Facilities

The available evidence on the cost-effectiveness of privatized construction of prison facilities strongly suggests that there are indeed significant cost savings produced when private companies contract with jurisdictional entities to build a prison facility (Shichor, 1995; Thomas, 1996). The reasons for this are numerous. First, private corporations are not bound by existing state contracts with suppliers and can "shop around" in their acquisition of building materials. Second, private companies are able to avoid the need to comply with governmental oversight in contract allocation and decision making, thus saving time. Third, private contractors are free from the sometimes lengthy approval process in procurement of materials, enabling private corporations to purchase and deliver necessary materials more efficiently to remote prison construction sites. In sum, it is clear from the literature that private contractors are indeed able to build prison facilities more cheaply and more quickly than are state contractors (Fitzgerald, 1991; Thomas, 1996).

Creaming, Skimming, and Cherry Picking

Since the vast majority of privatized correctional facilities in the United States serve either juvenile or minimum-medium security populations, researchers remain uncertain about performance issues in addition to the cost issues outlined above. "When privatization advocates talk about cutting expenses not through a cheaper work force but through the employment of fewer well-qualified workers, they may target more the soft-end operations, which usually have less custody and more human service components in their everyday operation" (Shichor, 1995:137). For example, corporate interest in running juvenile facilities is in large part due to the fact that many juveniles incarcerated therein are awaiting trial and have no required treatment programming attached to their custody (the same may be said for most inmates in adult jails) (Anon. 1996). As noted corrections researchers Todd Clear and George F. Cole argue: "Most privatization plans call for skimming off the best of the worst—the non-serious offenders who can be efficiently processed. Thus the government-run part of the correctional system faces the possibility of having to manage only the most costly, most intractable offenders on a reduced budget, and with the worsened fiscal and personnel situations that would result from such a development" (1994:513).

Creaming, skimming, or *cherry picking*, then, refers to the practice of private corporations contracting primarily for those inmates in the prisoner population that are the easiest to deal with and the cheapest to manage (Clear and Cole, 1994; Bureau of Justice Statistics, 1996). Prisoners who have violent tendencies or who have communicable diseases such as AIDS, for example, are traditionally shunned by private industry contractors. Put another way, creaming refers to the practice of the taking of the "best" offenders available in a population for the contract of private services—such as counseling and drug/alcohol treatment—in order to yield the highest profits. As noted above, fully 45% of all privatization contracts are for low- or minimum-security-risk inmates. Since many public facilities are required by law to deal with a broader spectrum of inmates, achieving accurate comparisons to the performance of privately run facilities becomes problematic.

Free Market Competition (Benefits) versus Service-Provider Captivity (Risks)

Many commentators on prison privatization have also issued warnings against the possibility of jurisdictions becoming "captive" to prison service vendors (Bowditch and Everett, 1991; Walzer, 1991; Shichor, 1995). That is, once a jurisdiction delegates its authority to manage and operate a correctional facility to a private corporation, the jurisdiction also runs the risk of becoming overly dependent on that corporation for services. Since only two corporations are frankly large and experienced enough to handle most large-scale prison privatization contracts (CCA and Wackenhut), and given the fact that the U.S. Department of Justice recommends using only experienced and capable private prison corporations for such contracts, a question emerges about how much "choice" a jurisdiction actually has—especially in the event that they wish to terminate a service contract with a private prison corporation.[2]

In an ideal free-market system, numerous providers exist to serve customers' needs—and customers enforce efficiency by virtue of their option to cease transacting with one provider in favor of another. In conditions where competition among vendors is limited, however, so are customers' options. So, for example, in a case where only a limited number of private prison vendors are large or experienced enough to handle a multilevel (minimum, medium, maximum security) inmate population, clearly the benefits of the free-market system become less powerful.

One of the key justifications for privatization put forward by its proponents is that private contractors operate more efficiently than their public-sector counterparts because they are subject to the forces of competition. Proponents argue that because state-based service providers are often locked into contracts with other state agencies and/or local service agencies, there is much less flexibility available to governmental jurisdictions in managing the facility (Logan, 1990; Fitzgerald, 1991). This lack of flexibility is put forward as a cause of governmental inefficiency and excessive costs to taxpayers, because governmental bureaucracies must follow governmental rules and have no incentive to downsize. Privatization proponents argue that private contractors have no such allegiances to state agencies and are not bound by similar procurement rules, thus being able to shop around for competitive prices and workers.

Two issues have emerged regarding the claimed benefits of competition in the context of for-profit prisons, however: (1) truly competitive bidding is often not realized (or required) in the bidding process (jurisdictions just go with the lowest bidder), and (2) the private prisons industry is itself dominated by two major providers, Corrections Corporation of America and Wackenhut Corrections Corporation, thus limiting the operational amount of true competition in the industry itself (Bureau of Justice Statistics, 1996). As prison privatization researcher David Shichor notes: "When private companies hold monopolies, they also lose their efficiency and flexibility, like in the cost of public utilities" (1995:17).

The "captivity" danger, then, is this: Because private vendors such as Wackenhut and CCA have become so large—and because one of the key criteria in the awarding of contracts is a "demonstrated ability to handle populations like those under consideration"—they have a competitive advantage in contract bidding of all kinds (National Institute of Justice, 1987:33). Evidence of the monopolistic power private prison corporations have acquired was recently demonstrated by the remarks of CCA spokeswoman Peggy Lawrence and CCA President Doctor Crants, after losing two separate service contracts, one with the state of South Carolina and the other with Washington, DC: "The government needs us to stay in that business," and "The fact of the matter is that D.C. needs us more than we need D.C." (Anon., 1997a). Although arguably, in state-based correctional operations there is a state-based monopoly, some are made uncomfortable by the prospect of governmental jurisdictions becoming overly dependent on private, for-profit corporations.

Finally, the possibility of bankruptcy must be considered and accounted for in any contract for private prison services (National Institute of Justice, 1987). Should a private contractor find itself out of business or unable to deliver the level of service required (the latter happened to CCA in a South Carolina facility), the state would be liable for resuming its stewardship of the state prisons. This is problematic because it would put governmental jurisdictions in the position of having to reallocate commitments, with any money saved by privatization directed back to its corrections functions. In addition, numerous commentators have noted that the probable transition costs of the state moving back in to take control of a privatized facility could be considerable (Robbins, 1998). Privatization researchers have now suggested that separate insurance policies be taken out by jurisdictions to guard against private-vendor bankruptcy and that these must be factored into the cost assessment of privatization contracts (Gilbert, 2000b).

Moral, Racial, and Ethical Issues

Clearly, the overriding moral or ethical issue surrounding the emergence of for-profit prisons is the fact that the industry's stock-in-trade is human beings: The more people locked up, the more profitable is the industry. Some fear that this new incentive for incarceration puts the traditional criminological goal of reducing crime in danger (Hallett and Lee, 2000). Moreover, some see privatized prisons as a repeal of the Emancipation Proclamation, particularly since a disproportionate number of prisoners throughout the U.S. correctional system are African American, while the large majority of private prison shareholders are white (Jackson, 2000).

Other questions concern the objectivity standards of political supporters of privatized prisons, who, often being recipients of campaign contributions from large corrections corporations, end up voting favorably on privatization initiatives. As documented recently in Tennessee, Corrections Corporation of America widely donated campaign monies to pro-privatization candidates (Hallett and Lee, 2000). Although no ethical breach is automatic, many argue that even the appearance of such a connection between policy and politics is inherently suspect (Ethridge and Marquart, 1993:38; Shichor, 1995).

One final ethical issue bears mentioning. Although in the United States it is clear that criminal justice policy has moved away from the ethic of rehabilitation in favor of an ethic of punishment, it is also clear that the experiences of prisoners while they are in prison are powerful determinants of their behavior after release (Pepinsky and Quinney, 1991; Silberman 1995). Given the concerns about the elevated level of violence in private facilities mentioned above, questions emerge about the potential long-lasting and negative impacts private prisons can have regardless of the short-term benefit of cost savings. The vast majority of offenders (98%) are eventually released into society. As Matthew Silberman notes: "Many prisons create an environment that encourages predators in the prison population to terrorize and exploit…inmates who might otherwise do their time without difficulty. Second, danger to the public results from the production of violent individuals learning to survive in a violent world. In other words, the American prison system both reflects and contributes to the high level of violence in contemporary society" (Silberman, 1995:1).

Contract and Monitoring Issues

Because the state is delegating its authority to govern the lives and freedom of the inmates it sends to a private corporation, and because life in prison takes place well outside public view, it is necessary for the state to monitor closely the level of service provided by contractors. "The function of monitoring is to ensure that the private operator is in compliance with the provisions of the contract" (Shichor, 1995:119). For a combination of reasons, independent evaluation of the performance of privatized facilities is vital for contract enforcement as well as a thorough accounting of the merits and deficits of prison privatization generally. It is important to note the difference between monitoring and evaluation. *Monitoring* refers to the processual and continuous examination of the level of service provided by vendors. *Evaluation* refers to a broader, more impact-based set of examination criteria, which may include issues of monitoring but extend beyond these to an examination of the efficacy of private prisons as a whole.

A central concern in the area of monitoring is the cost involved, especially because the nature of the monitoring required for a privatized prison goes well beyond the requirements of ensuring cost compliance. A special effort must be made on the part of the state to ensure that daily life inside the prison is under way within legal bounds. Thus, "monitoring is intended to ascertain that prisoners are securely incarcerated (thus protecting the public and penalizing those breaking the law), that the inmates themselves are being adequately treated (without violating their rights or providing unreasonable punishment), and that reasonable rehabilitation efforts are being provided" (National Institute of Justice, 1987:47). Needless to say, this can be quite an involved undertaking. The National Institute of Justice notes the following about the state of Pennsylvania's monitoring plan: "The State of Pennsylvania's Legislative Budget and Finance Committee in its October 1985 report stated that the law should designate a specific agency as responsible for monitoring private prisons; this process should include periodic [on site] inspections, evaluations, and specification of minimum standards" (1987:47).

Privatization researcher Charles Logan emphasizes the merits of outside monitoring: "Here, the point is that independent monitoring promotes objectivity and rigor in the overall supervision of a prison. It is easier to be consistent when imposing standards of outsiders than when enforcing them on ourselves or our colleagues" (1990:207). The Institute, however, notes that "[t]here are two disadvantages of on-site monitoring. First, it is expensive to maintain the monitor and provide the required resources such as secretarial support, telephone, equipment, and materials.…The second problem with the on-site monitoring is the possibility that the monitor would be co-opted by the contractor's staff" (1987:49). In sum, intensive monitoring is a costly— but necessary—part of any privatization undertaking.

High Turnover

A key and related issue for corrections is its continuous high turnover of staff. In fact, corrections, more than any other criminal justice profession, has the highest rate of turnover (Cole, 1994). High turnover leads to instability within the institution and the corresponding administrative need for continual recruitment and training. This results in a disproportionate number of inexperienced and untrained staff.

Reasons for the high turnover rate in corrections are numerous. First, corrections tends to be a fairly low-paying field, with comparatively modest benefits. Second, corrections is often very dangerous work, exacting a high level of work-related stress. Finally, another key reason for the high level of turnover among correctional workers is the relatively meager opportunity for advancement in the ranks (Cole, 1994). Taken together, these factors can lead to problems with staff morale, tardiness and absenteeism, and a general state of turmoil (Clear and Cole, 1994). In the context of privatized prisons, these problems have all been documented and may be worse than those in the public sector:

> [P]rivately financed institutions can cut costs by paying lower salaries and can reduce costs even further by providing no or minimum pension and fringe benefit packages. However, lower salaries could attract less qualified staff who would require extensive high quality training, and this would offset some of the cost savings. My personal observation has been that privately funded agencies offer lower salaries and have very high staff turnover rates. In fact, many of the best qualified private sector staff eventually apply for public sector probation positions that offer more job security and higher salaries. The high turnover rate must impact the quality of services that are provided, a factor that should be considered in any cost analysis formula [Alan M. Schuman, Director, Social Service Division, Superior Court of the District of Columbia] (in Shichor, 1995:194).

Legal Issues

The prevailing legal issue involved in privatization has revolved around the extent to which a state may constitutionally delegate its authority to punish. Specifically, legal questions surrounding the ability of a state to delegate its authority to make punishment decisions—and the liability associated with having made them—has been a center-stage legal debate in the area of prison privatization. As Shichor notes: "Many critics and even supporters agree that when a government deprives its citizens of their liberty, it exercises state power" (1995:52). Thus, the central legal issues involved in the area of privatizing prisons involve *delegation of the state's authority* to use force or make forceful decisions. In perhaps the most significant legal development on the privatization front in recent years, the U.S. Supreme Court recently ruled in

Richardson v. *McKnight*, 521 U.S. 300 (1997), that guards at a privately run prison facility in Clifton, Tennessee, are not entitled to the same level of immunity from liability that state guards are sometimes afforded. As Justice Stephen Breyer stated for the court: "Our examination of the history and purpose of the industry…reveals nothing special enough about the job or about its organizational structure that would warrant providing these prison guards with a governmental immunity" (Anon., 1997b). In his written opinion, Justice Antonin Scalia also noted that "this decision is sure to artificially raise the cost of privatizing prisons. Whether this will cause privatization to be prohibitively expensive, or instead simply divert state funds that could have been saved or spent on additional prison services, it is likely that tax-payers and prisoners will suffer as a consequence" (Anon., 1997d).

The legal questions surrounding prison privatization, however, involve more than just the issue of whether a privately paid guard can use force against an inmate as a delegate of the state, but also whether representatives of a private company may engage in behavior or decision making (e.g., writing disciplinary reports/revoking privileges) that has any detrimental effect upon an inmate whatsoever. A prevailing concern here is that privately paid guards—supervised directly by company, not state, representatives—owe primary allegiance to the company but act "under color of law" on behalf of the state under 42 U.S. Code Section 1983. Other questions regarding the accessibility that privately held inmates have to legal materials and due process issues surrounding the interstate transfer of inmates from one state to another are working their way through the courts at this writing.

ENDNOTES

1. According to the U.S. Department of Justice, the incarceration rate for persons in state and federal prisons or in local jails at the end of 1999 was 682 per 100,000 residents. The incarceration rate (per 100,000 resident population) for sentenced prisoners under jurisdiction of state and federal correctional authorities alone on December 31, 1999 was 486.

2. The National Institute of Justice asks "What evaluation criteria should be used?" in reference to RFP responses from private contractors. In top priority, NIJ lists: "Contractor qualifications: 'quality, relevance, or recency of projects of a similar nature conducted or completed by the contractor and ability to meet time constraints'" (1987:33).

REFERENCES

ABT ASSOCIATES INC. (1998). *Private Prisons in the United States: An Assessment of Current Practice*. Cambridge, MA: Abt.

ANON. (1996). *Nashville Banner*, May 20, p. B4.

ANON. (1997a). CCA deal breakdown; drops shares 22%. *Nashville Banner*, March 21, p. E1.

ANON. (1997b). Court rejects immunity for CCA prison guards: Ruling may slow push to privatization. *Nashville Banner*, June 23.

ANON. (1997c). Push for privatization boosts CCA. *Tennessean*, May 9, p. E1.

ANON. (1997d). CCA loses Supreme Court "test" case. *Tennessean*, June 24.

AUSTIN, J., and J. IRWIN (2001). *It's about Time: America's Imprisonment Binge*, 3rd ed. Belmont, CA: Wadsworth.

BOHM, R. M., and K. HALEY (1997). *Introduction to Criminal Justice*. New York: Glencoe/McGraw Hill.

BOWDITCH, C., and R. EVERETT (1991). Private prisons are not more efficient than public prisons. In *America's Prisons: Opposing Viewpoints*. San Diego, CA: Greenhaven Press.

BUREAU OF JUSTICE STATISTICS (1996). *Correctional Populations in the United States, 1994*. Washington, DC: U.S. Department of Justice.

BUREAU OF JUSTICE STATISTICS (1999). *Sourcebook of Criminal Justice Statistics*. Albany, NY: U.S. Department of Justice.

CLEAR, T., and G. F. COLE (1994). *American Corrections*. Belmont, CA: Wadsworth.

COLE, G. F. (1994). *The American System of Criminal Justice*, 6th ed. Belmont, CA: Wadsworth.

DONZIGER, S. (1996). *The Real War on Crime: The Report of the National Criminal Justice Commission*. New York: HarperCollins.

DUFFEE, D., and E. MCGARRELL (1990). *Community Corrections: A Community Field Approach*. Cincinnati, OH: Anderson Publishing.

ETHRIDGE, P., and J. MARQUART (1993). Private prisons in Texas: The new penology for profit. *Justice Quarterly*, 10(1):29–48.

FEDERAL BUREAU OF PRISONS (2000). Private prisons in the United States, 1999: An assessment of growth, performance, custody standards, and training requirements. Washington, DC: U.S. Federal Bureau of Prisons.

FITZGERALD, R. (1991). Private prisons: More effective than public prisons? In *America's Prisons: Opposing Viewpoints*. San Diego, CA: Greenhaven Press.

GENERAL ACCOUNTING OFFICE (1996). *Private and Public Prisons. Report to Subcommittee on Crime, Committee on Judiciary, House of Representatives*. Washington, DC: U.S. Government Printing Office.

GILBERT, M. J. (2000a). How much is too much privatization in criminal justice? In D. Shichor and M. Gilbert (eds.), *Privatization in Criminal Justice: Past, Present and Future*. Cincinnati, OH: Anderson Publishing, pp. 41–78.

GILBERT, M. J. (2000b). Not a true partner: Local politics and jail privatization in Frio County, In D. Shichor and M. Gilbert (eds.), *Privatization in Criminal Justice: Past, Present and Future*. Cincinnati, OH: Anderson Publishing, pp. 171–206.

HALLETT, M. A., and J. F. LEE (2000). Public money, private interests: The grass roots battle against CCA in Tennessee. In D. Shichor and M. Gilbert (eds.) *Privatization in Criminal Justice: Past, Present, and Future*. Cincinnati, OH: Anderson Publishing, pp. 227–244.

JACKSON, J. (2000). Hundreds arrested as protests turn disruptive. *Washington Post*, August 2, p. A22.

IRWIN, J., and J. AUSTIN (1997). *It's about Time: America's Imprisonment Binge*, 2nd ed. Belmont, CA: Wadsworth.

LOGAN, C. (1990). *Private Prisons: Cons and Pros*. New York: Oxford University Press.

LOGAN, C., and B. W. MCGRIFF (1989). *Comparing Costs of Public and Private Prisons*. Washington, DC: National Institute of Justice.

MCCARTHY, B. (1987). *Intermediate Punishments: Intensive Supervision, Home Confinement, and Electronic Surveillance*. Monsey, NY: Willow Tree Press.

NATIONAL INSTITUTE OF JUSTICE (1987). *Issues in Contracting for the Private Operation of Prisons and Jails*. Washington, DC: U.S. Department of Justice.

PEPINSKY, H. E., and R. QUINNEY, (eds.) (1991). *Criminology as Peacemaking*. Bloomington, IN: Indiana University Press.

PETERSILIA, J. (1994). Debating crime and imprisonment in California. *Evaluation and Program Planning*, 17(2):165–177.

QUINNEY, R. (1974). *Critique of Legal Order: Crime Control in Capitalist Society*. Boston: Little Brown, pp. 60–74.

RAND (1997). *Mandatory Minimum Drug Sentences: Throwing Away the Key or the Taxpayer's Money?* Los Angeles: Drug Policy Research Center.

ROBBINS, I. (1998). Statement before the joint Senate–House Judiciary Committee of the Oregon legislature. Delivered September 30.

SHICHOR, D. (1995). *Punishment for Profit: Private Prisons/Public Concerns*. London: Sage Publications.

SILBERMAN, M. (1995). *A World of Violence: Corrections in America*. Belmont, CA: Wadsworth.

TENNESSEE SELECT OVERSIGHT COMMITTEE ON CORRECTIONS (1995). *Comparative Evaluation of Privately-Managed Corrections Corporation of America Prison (South Central Correctional Center) and State-Managed Prototypical Prisons (Northeast Correctional Center, Northwest Correctional Center)*. Nashville, TN: SOCC, February.

SELECT OVERSIGHT COMMITTEE ON CORRECTIONS TENNESSEE (1997). Transcript from testimony at public hearings. Nashville, TN: SOCC.

THOMAS, C. (1995). *Correctional Privatization: The Issues and the Evidence*. Toronto, Ontario, Canada: Fraser Institute.

THOMAS, C. (1996). Testimony regarding correctional privatization. Subcommittee on Crime, House Committee on the Judiciary, Washington, DC.

TOUCHE ROSS & CO. (1987). *Privatization in America: An Opinion Survey of City Governments on Their Use of Privatization and Their Infrastructure Needs*. New York: Touche Ross.

WALZER, M. (1991). Private prisons are unjust. In *America's Prisons: Opposing Viewpoints*. San Diego, CA: Greenhaven Press.

chapter 21

Court-Ordered Reform of Jails

Past, Present, and Future

Wayne N. Welsh, Ph.D.

ABSTRACT

A major dilemma of criminal justice in a democratic society is how to process suspects and punish law violators in a humane and rational manner. The prevalence of court orders to reform unconstitutional conditions of confinement in U.S. jails and prisons, including unprecedented overcrowding, indicates a significant gap in our current ability to do so and an important opportunity for change. In this chapter the scope of jail and prison crowding and court-ordered reform is discussed and critical issues for the future are presented. A coordinated approach to problem analysis and policy design is emphasized.

INTRODUCTION

If the public, through its judicial and penal system, finds it necessary to incarcerate a person, basic concepts of decency, as well as reasonable respect for constitutional rights, require that he be provided a bed.[1]

Not the least of the Sheriff's problems is the abysmal design of the jail. Architecturally, the jail is a gross case of malpractice in design.[2]

Replacement [of the jail] must occur regardless of the source of funds....The Court's power in this regard is a negative one: it cannot order [the] respondent board of supervisors to appropriate funds. But it can, and will, order the facility closed, if necessary, to eliminate unlawful conditions.[3]

> This court will not tolerate the miserable overcrowding in the jail which was existent in March when these hearings began. The responsible executives in the Sheriff's Office, Board of Supervisors, and the County Executive have offered nothing whatever in response to this most pressing problem.[4]

Over the past 30 years, courts found conditions of confinement in U.S. jails to be in violation of constitutional guarantees such as the Eighth Amendment (banning cruel and unusual punishment) and the Fourteenth Amendment (guaranteeing due process rights). In 1992, 27% of the nation's large jails (i.e., 100 inmates or more) were under court order to reduce overcrowding or improve general conditions of confinement (U.S. Department of Justice, 1993). At midyear 1996, U.S. jails held or supervised a record 591,469 persons (U.S. Department of Justice, 1997a). Overcrowding, the problem most frequently cited in court orders, severely limits an institution's capacity to provide adequate safety, medical care, food service, recreation, and sanitation. Correctional and government officials have been ordered to make sweeping changes to comply with court directives: to reduce chronic overcrowding, to improve medical care and recreation services, to increase staffing levels and improve training, to make use of early release mechanisms, even to build new facilities—all under the watchful eye of the court (Welsh, 1995).

Change will be neither immediate nor wholesale. Current trends will not easily be reversed. Problems shaped by powerful forces over time are likely to persist into the twenty-first century:

- Overcrowding will persist despite the continued proliferation of intermediate sanctions and community corrections.
- Crime rates will continue to fluctuate, but punishments will remain driven more by political forces than by any documented "crime problem." Criminal justice as a policy priority will diminish, however, as economic conditions command greater attention.
- We will observe an increasingly rule-oriented correctional environment but fewer lawsuits challenging jail conditions. Basic inmate rights will be upheld, but courts will be increasingly hesitant to institute large-scale reforms.
- The major advocates of jail reform will be a select group of highly specialized experienced attorneys ("repeat players").

However, there is also reason to expect more effective and coordinated policy responses based on lessons from the past:

- Interagency problem solving and initiatives involving criminal justice, government, and community agencies will increase.
- As resources dwindle, public officials will be held more accountable for their policies: There is greater need to match resources to policy. We will continue to need cost-effective intermediate punishments.
- Standards for correctional confinement will continue to become increasingly specific and mandatory; there will be fewer "deviant jails."

The outcomes of countervailing trends cannot easily be predicted. Any prediction of future events, of course, must be based on observations from the past.

CHARACTERISTICS OF JAILS

Jails, in contrast to prisons, are operated at the municipal or county rather than the state or federal level; they house convicted offenders generally serving one year or less of time; and they also house pretrial detainees, typically about half of the jail's daily population (Advisory Commission on Intergovernmental Relations, 1984). Jails are also characterized by a high rate of turnover. There is a constant flow of inmates into and out of a jail, with the average inmate staying less than a week. The politics and demographics of jails, therefore, are different from those of state or federal prisons, and separate analyses of jail overcrowding and court intervention are required.

CAUSES OF OVERCROWDING

Overcrowding has consistently been identified as one of the most serious problems facing criminal justice systems (Gettinger, 1984; Grieser, 1988; U.S. Department of Justice, 1988). However, potential driving forces of problems such as overcrowding often remain undiagnosed. Judges who order change and government officials who formulate policies often make decisions on the basis of very limited causal theories. Like most social problems, jail overcrowding is multiply determined, and informed policy choices require a careful analysis of the causes and scope of the problem.

Crime Rates

To what degree, if any, do increases in crime explain jail overcrowding? Did crime rates explode without warning, leading to drastic shortfalls in correctional capacities? Although problems with official crime statistics are well known (e.g., Skogan, 1975), there is little support for the crime-causes-overcrowding hypothesis. In fact, the National Crime Surveys (NCS) show relatively stable crime victimization rates in the 1970s (U.S. Department of Justice, 1991), and declines in personal theft (–15%), household crimes (–18%), and violent crimes (–10%) between 1981 and 1988 (U.S. Department of Justice, 1991a). Stabilization or declines in most crime rates have continued, with declines in 1994–1995 the largest since the survey began in 1973 (U.S. Department of Justice, 1997b). The Uniform Crime Reports (UCRs), based on crimes reported to police, show increases in reported crime for most categories between 1964 and 1980. From 1980 to 1989, total UCR index crimes decreased by 3.5%, although violent crimes increased by 11.1% for this period (U.S. Department of Justice, 1992a). Although the two measures of crime yield somewhat different results, no dramatic increases in crime are substantiated by either.

Over the same time periods that crime rates stabilized or decreased, correctional populations soared. The number of prisoners under the jurisdiction of state or federal correctional authorities increased 150% between 1980 and 1991 (U.S. Department of Justice, 1992b). The number of jail inmates incarcerated by local authorities rose by 169% between 1978 and 1991 (U.S. Department of Justice, 1992a). Clearly, dramatic increases in incarceration rates were not driven by increases in crime.

Legal and Political Environments

Variations in local punishment practices influence overcrowding and the probability of judicial intervention. Incarceration rates reflect differences in the laws and legal cultures of different areas, including differences in the harshness of local policies regarding punishment (Kizziah, 1984; Klofas, 1987, 1990; Welsh et al., 1990). For example, to the degree that particular jurisdictions use incarceration as a preferred sanction, there are increased demands for correctional space and services. Where high incarceration rates are accompanied by low rates of prisoner expenditures, it becomes less likely that constitutionally acceptable standards of conditions (e.g., adequate medical care, food services, clothing, sanitation, inmate safety) will be met and prisoner lawsuits become more likely (Welsh, 1992a,b). Inadequate correctional spending may reflect a punitive political climate, a fiscally strapped county, or both, but the net effect is that jail conditions deteriorate and judicial intervention becomes more likely.

Demographic, Economic, and Social Conditions

To what degree do social conditions contribute to jail overcrowding? Conflict theorists suggest that incarceration rates are influenced by the fluctuating needs of dominant elites to maintain social control. High unemployment, for example, may lead to an unproductive and frustrated "surplus population." Dominant interests may feel threatened and increase their use of incarceration as a means of controlling the underclass (Rusche and Kirchheimer, 1939; Carroll and Doubet, 1983; McCarthy, 1990). Others have suggested that economic inequality fuels incarceration. Areas characterized by higher minority compositions and higher poverty also display more aggressive criminal justice responses and expenditures, including higher rates of imprisonment (Myers and Talarico, 1987).

Another approach examines how demographic shifts contributed to overcrowding (Blumstein, 1988). The mid-teens are the peak risk years for criminality, but the mid-twenties are the peak risk years for imprisonment, due to the greater seriousness of offenses committed by older offenders. According to Blumstein, crime rates began to rise in 1964 (when a large 1947 birth cohort reached age 17), but imprisonment rates didn't begin to rise until 1972 (when the 1947 cohort reached age 25). Crime rates began to increase again in 1980, when a large 1961 birth cohort ("echo" boomers) reached age 19. Because the 1961 cohort passed the peak age for imprisonment by the1990s, Blumstein predicted that prison populations would begin to decline once again. No such declines in jail or prison populations have been forthcoming, although rates of increase have slowed somewhat.

Resources and Expenditures

Criminal justice expenditures have traditionally been the primary responsibility of local (county and city) governments, but an increased burden on cities and counties has further constrained options to reduce jail overcrowding. From 1985 to 1988, justice spending increased more than government spending for any other activity, including education, health, and welfare (U.S. Department of Justice, 1990a). Increases in correctional expenditures were by far the most pronounced. These trends reflect the increased priorities of jail and justice issues on the policy agenda and increased strain on local government budgets.

According to government and correctional officials, resource shortages contributed to court orders by limiting new jail construction and by limiting the implementation of improvements (e.g., increased staff levels, improved medical care) needed to comply with court decrees (Welsh et al., 1990). However, policymakers must share responsibility for historically placing jail needs low on the list of policy priorities. Inadequate resources can never be an adequate justification for the state's depriving people of their constitutional rights (see *Gates* v. *Collier*, 1974; *Miller* v. *Carson*, 1975).

Public Attitudes and the "Get-Tough" Movement

To what degree has the public thirst for punishment contributed to jail overcrowding and court orders? Recent reforms have included restrictions or abolition of parole, mandatory minimum sentences, determinate sentencing, sentencing enhancements (e.g., for weapons, use of violence), and longer sentences. Cullen and colleagues (1985) trace much of this development to a growing crisis in authority which confronted the nation in the 1960s. Diminished confidence by voters in the nation's leaders created a threat to some politicians (electoral vulnerability) and an opportunity for others who could convince voters that they were capable of reestablishing the moral order.

While conservative values have dominated recent responses to crime, public opinion is less retributive and more complex than is commonly thought. For example, Cullen et al. (1985) found that a majority of Texas residents polled felt that the courts were too easy on criminals (77%) and felt that prison inmates should serve their full sentence (58%). However, many of these same respondents said that rehabilitation was an important function of prison (79%), and 72% favored some type of community-based corrections instead of simply "building as many prisons as needed." In surveys of two Ohio cities, Skovron et al. (1988) found that a majority of respondents (80% and 70% for the two cities) favored allowing prisoners to earn early release credits through good behavior and to participate in education or work programs while in prison. A large majority (90% and 87%) also favored the development of local programs to keep nonviolent and first-time offenders active and working in the community. There is little doubt that the "get-tough" movement has strongly influenced criminal justice policy, but the public has many voices, and many perceive a need for rational change in correctional planning and operations (Welsh et al., 1991).

COURT INTERVENTION

The Role of the Courts

Until the mid-1960s, the courts followed a "hands-off" policy regarding corrections. Courts refused to hear prisoner rights cases, essentially viewing the inmate as a "slave of the state" who had forfeited his or her rights as a consequence of his or her crime (Bronstein, 1980). This trend was reversed by the Supreme Court decision in *Cooper* v. *Pate* (1964). *Rhodes* v. *Chapman* (1981) represented the first time that the Eighth amendment was interpreted by the Supreme Court in the context of jail or prison overcrowding. The Court indicated that "conditions must not involve the wanton and unnecessary infliction of pain, nor may they be grossly disproportionate to the severity of the crime warranting punishment" (Call, 1986:245). Reviews of court decisions can be found elsewhere (e.g., Bronstein, 1980; Jacobs, 1980; Call, 1986; Cooper, 1988).

The Legal Process: Judges, Lawyers, and Defendants

Different judges adopt different roles in crafting remedies and monitoring compliance, and they do so at different stages of a case. Early in the remedy-crafting stage, judges often adopt a "facilitator" role, encouraging litigants to negotiate and develop plans to address jail problems (Welsh, 1995). Over time, though, judges often find it necessary to set limits as negotiations stall. Judges then shift toward a more active "ratifier–developer" role whereby they approve some plans presented by litigants but begin adding their own modifications and remedies. Judicial options are limited when resistance to change by county officials is pronounced, leading to a more autocratic and tough-minded judicial role.

The type of legal representation that prisoners obtain critically influences the outcome of lawsuits. Prisoner advocacy groups such as the ACLU have an ideological commitment toward jail reform and tend to seek extensive relief for plaintiffs. Repeat players (frequent litigants such as the ACLU) also enjoy competitive advantages (Galanter, 1975): greater ability to structure the transaction; expertise; lower startup costs; informal relations with court and government officials; ability to adopt optimal litigation strategies and issues; and bargaining credibility. Indeed, "ideologically committed" attorneys tend to target jail jurisdictions with histories of underfunding and overcrowding; they tend to file more allegations of constitutional violations; and they tend to receive greater relief than either private attorneys or public counsel who represent inmates in jail cases (Welsh, 1992a).

When the leaders of county government (e.g., county supervisors or commissioners) are named by inmate attorneys as defendants, lawsuits are often bitterly contested. Because these officials are responsible for allocating funds and personnel to jails, it seems a wise strategy to include them as defendants. However, they also command considerable resources, including a well-staffed legal department which handles the county's legal business. Not surprisingly, lawsuits involving county officials tend to last a long time and often involve bitter disputes not only with plaintiffs but with different county agencies, as government officials attempt to deflect blame for jail problems (Welsh et al., 1990; Welsh and Pontell, 1991; Welsh, 1995).

Court-Ordered Change and Compliance

Court orders against county jails put pressure on entire criminal justice systems to alter the processing of accused and convicted offenders. Police book suspects into the jail, the courts try them, jails house them, and probation provides programming for both pretrial and sentenced offenders. Pressures are also felt by city or county government officials, who are responsible for financial and personnel allocations to the jail.

Court-ordered remedies have shaped dramatic policy changes. For example, court-imposed jail population caps have resulted in the early release of sentenced inmates, citing the release of arrestees, expanded pretrial release programs, and the construction of new jails. Orders to protect inmate safety and provide adequate supervision often required substantial increases in staffing levels. Orders to provide inmates with adequate recreational time outside cells required both equipment and staff personnel. Orders to improve medical care required that doctors and nurses be hired, that medical equipment and supplies be purchased, and that medical records be kept. Where prison officials have been ordered to ensure inmates' access to lawyers and legal materials, visitation rights have been extended, and prison libraries have been created or expanded to provide access to law books.

Just because a court issues orders to improve jail conditions, however, does not necessarily mean that action by county officials is immediate or automatic. One study found that jail lawsuits lasted four to five years on average (Welsh, 1992a), with some extending 13 years or more. Special masters and contempt orders provide judges with two means of furthering compliance.

Special masters, usually corrections experts or lawyers familiar with correctional law, have frequently been used by judges to gather information on jail conditions and procedures, to monitor compliance with court directives, and in some cases, even to informally mediate disputes between litigants (Anon., 1979; Brakel, 1979; Nathan, 1979; Montgomery, 1980). The threat of a contempt order is used as a method of last resort when all other attempts to enforce compliance with the court's orders fail. A finding of civil contempt may lead to fines or even jail sentences for recalcitrant defendants. On March 16, 1987, Judge Spurgeon Avakian found Santa Clara, California, county supervisors in contempt of court for failing to build 96 new jail cells on time. He fined the supervisors $1000 each and sentenced them to serve five days in their own jail. In response, the county launched an aggressive media campaign criticizing the judge and successfully lobbied the state legislature to reduce the liability of government officials. The point became moot when the contempt order was annulled by the California Court of Appeals on September 17, 1987 (*Wilson* v. *Superior Court*, 1987), and Judge Avakian resigned from the case. Potential benefits of contempt orders must therefore be carefully weighed against the possibility of further retrenchment.

IMPACTS OF COURT-ORDERED REFORM

Changes in Institutional Conditions

While the impact of court orders is limited by legal and pragmatic constraints (e.g., limited judicial authority; defendants' willingness and ability to comply), significant changes have certainly occurred. Evidence from cases in Alabama (Yackle, 1989), Georgia (Chilton, 1991), Texas (Martin and Ekland-Olson, 1987; Crouch and Marquart, 1989), Louisiana (Harris and Spiller, 1977), and New York (Storey, 1990; Harland, 1991) suggests that court orders have contributed to improvements in staffing levels, disciplinary procedures, inmate safety, medical care, recreation, visitation, food services, sanitation, inmate classification procedures, and access to courts.

Certain issues, such as jail capacity, the physical condition of jail facilities, and staffing are generally perceived by the courts as necessary components of reform. In 34 of 43 California jail lawsuits examined by Welsh (1995), courts ordered jail officials to reduce overcrowding. In 13 cases, direct orders to improve staffing levels were issued. In 16 cases, judges handed down orders to build new jails or expand existing capacity.

Several examples illustrate the centrality of these issues and the ability of the courts to motivate change. In Alameda County (*Smith et al.* v. *Dyer et al.*, 1983), Judge Richard A. Bancroft proclaimed that "the time for footdragging is over" and "replacement must occur regardless of the source of funds." In Placer County (*Offield et al.* v. *Scott*, 1977), Superior Court Judge William A. Newsom stated: "The county jail is an antiquated facility designed to meet the needs of a different era" (May 12, 1977, p. 1). In Fresno (*In re Morgan, In re Ransbury*, and *Consolidated Cases*, 1983), Superior Court Judge Frank J. Creede stated: "Full compliance with recognized constitutional standards and with the 1980 California Minimum Jail Standards can be achieved only with the construction of a new detention facility" (Mar. 27. 1985, p. 12). In San Diego (*Hudler et al.* v. *Duffy et al.*, 1980), Superior Court Judge James L. Facht diagnosed the major jail problems as overcrowding and inadequate staffing, calling the jail an "architectural nightmare" that mitigated against proper supervision and observation of inmates.

Organizational Impacts

Jail administration has changed substantially as a result of court orders. Modern information systems and scientific classification procedures have replaced archaic methods in many jails. The courts have also helped define clearer professional standards and guidelines for institutional living conditions (Feeley and Hanson, 1986, 1990) and have created a need for better-educated modern correctional "managers" who can anticipate and prevent problems (Jacobs, 1980; DiIlulio, 1987, 1990). There is little doubt that court orders have increased the bureaucratization of the jail and required more accountability from public officials.

Unintended Impacts

There has been much speculation about the negative or unintended impact of court orders. Critics have attributed diverse effects to court orders: reduced inmate respect for staff; increased rule violation by inmates; reduced staff morale; increased uncertainty in decision making by guards; and increased assaults by inmates on guards and on each other (Anon., 1973; Glazer, 1975, 1978; Alpert et al., 1986; Martin and Ekland-Olson, 1987; Ekland-Olson and Martin, 1988; Crouch and Marquart, 1989). It is likely, however, that disruptions attributable to court orders are temporary aberrations brought about by rapid shifts in the power structures and regulatory mechanisms of institutions (Crouch and Marquart, 1989). Management and administration practices play a large role in shaping the new order that emerges in the postdecree phases of lawsuits.

Systemwide Impacts

Although the criminal justice system is often viewed as a "nonsystem" due to its decentralized and fragmented nature, dramatic changes in political environments, such as the imposition of court orders, create demands to tighten the "loose coupling" that normally characterizes criminal justice organizations (Hagan, 1989). Responses may include the formalization of exchange relations between different agencies (e.g., creation of jail task forces and committees) and the development of cooperative interagency innovations (e.g., new criminal justice programs). Less positive responses include struggles for resources and disagreements over appropriate agency responses to jail problems.

In jurisdictions from California (Welsh and Pontell, 1991) to New York (Storey, 1990; Harland, 1991), city and county jails implemented or increased the use of various pretrial release mechanisms to reduce jail populations to court-imposed limits. For example, "citation release" in California and "desk appearance tickets" in New York require that misdemeanor suspects sign a written promise to appear in court, and suspects are then released at the jail prior to arraignment. In several California cities, police officials reported adjustments in arrest policies in response to jail release procedures (Welsh, 1993). Police perceived that jail citations had hurt police credibility and morale, and some suggested that officers wouldn't "waste their time" booking misdemeanors any more. They also suggested that officers were less likely to enforce outstanding warrants as a result of liberal jail release policies. However, neither large-scale nor long-term changes were detected by statistical analyses. Police organizational culture (i.e., a "crime- fighting" orientation) and a motivation by public officials to avoid blame for unpopular policies may partially explain pronouncements by police officials that court orders to reduce jail overcrowding have impaired police capacity to protect public safety.

Numerous case processing and sentencing alternatives have been adopted by local criminal courts as a result of court orders against jails in Baltimore (Dunbaugh, 1990), California (Welsh, 1990; Welsh and Pontell, 1991), New Orleans (Baiamonte, 1990), New York (Storey, 1990; Harland, 1991), and Philadelphia (Babcock, 1990). For example, early screening programs have been implemented in attempts to remove weak cases that are likely to be discharged later and to speed processing of those that are being held awaiting decisions on bail or some other form of pretrial release. Pretrial release programs such as ROR (release on own recognizance), more liberal forms of bail (e.g., 10%), and supervised release are now widely used in many jurisdictions.

Postconviction sentencing alternatives such as work programs, community service, boot camps, and electronic surveillance have also proliferated as a result of court orders. The utility of these "intermediate sanctions" (Morris and Tonry, 1990) in reducing jail populations may be limited, however, as perceived liability by public officials often results in stringent eligibility criteria (e.g., no history of violence or drug abuse).

Without the specter of court orders, it is unlikely that we would have witnessed this bandwagon return to "alternatives to incarceration" (Austin and Krisberg, 1982). The popularity of "intermediate sanctions" today lies largely in their "band-aid" utility for reducing soaring incarceration costs and complying with court-imposed jail population caps rather than a liberal shift in correctional philosophy.

There is little doubt that correctional systems have been forced to increase their expenditures as a result of court orders, at least temporarily. Increases in institutional capacity, staffing, and service delivery surely require expenditures, and courts have occasionally been quite explicit in directing such expenditures (Welsh, 1995).

PRISONER LITIGATION: END OF THE ROAD?

Several legal and policy decisions over the past few years have limited but certainly not ended court-ordered reform of jails and prisons. In *Wilson* v. *Seiter* (1991), the Supreme Court ruled that conditions of confinement were not unconstitutional unless deliberate indifference to basic human needs could be demonstrated. It is not clear that this ruling had a chilling effect on prisoner litigation, but it certainly increased the burden of proof upon prisoners.

The *Violent Crime Control Act of 1994* represented an explicit attempt by Congress to legislate prisoner lawsuits (in the federal courts, at least) out of existence, but this has not proven to be the case. Section 20409 of the act attempted to reduce the role of federal courts in several ways (Call and Cole, 1996):

- The court may not find a violation of the Eighth Amendment in a jail or prison crowding case unless the plaintiff demonstrates that he or she has personally suffered from cruel and unusual punishment.

- When an inmate satisfied the personal harm requirement, the remedy shall extend no further than necessary to remove the unconstitutional conditions.

- No population caps may be imposed unless unconstitutional conditions of crowding have demonstrably inflicted cruel and unusual punishment on particular prisoners.

- All court orders imposed for Eighth Amendment violations must be reviewed at two-year intervals if requested by the defendants.

Call and Cole argued effectively that this politically inspired attempt to stamp out prisoner litigation is more "smoke than fire," it will not accomplish desired legislative ends, and it will not bring about a substantial change in federal court intervention. For example, in regard to personal harm, the Supreme Court ruled that an inmate alleging cruel and unusual punishment does not have to prove present harm as long as he or she can prove that the conditions subject him or her to an unreasonable risk of future harm (*Helling* v. *McKinney*, 1993). As for the "narrowest possible remedy" rule, judges generally believe that they follow this rule anyway. The third provision suggests that if crowding and specific harm to specific inmates are proven, the only requirement is that two or more inmates be affected. Such requirements are not onerous.

It is unlikely that the act will eliminate class action lawsuits in overcrowding cases, since it allows consolidation of individual lawsuits quite easily. Regardless of the act's intent, its overall effects on prisoner lawsuits are not likely to be great. Section 20409 was probably added to the Violent Crime Control Act at the last minute to gain needed conservative political support to pass the overall act (Call and Cole, 1996).

Last, but not least, the *Prison Litigation Reform Act* (PLRA) was signed into law in April 1996, hidden in an obscure appropriations bill called the Balanced Budget Down Payment Act. Its stated intent was to limit frivolous lawsuits filed by prisoners, but "the PLRA in fact impedes all litigation dealing with prisoners, including cases dealing with issues of health, safety, and serious constitutional violations" (National Prison Project, 1997). Provisions included the following:

- Section 802 imposes limitations on the ability of the federal courts to issue injunctions, by consent of the parties or after trial, for constitutional and statutory violations in prisons, jails, and juvenile detention facilities. The section also gives district attorneys and other state or local officials the right to intervene in certain types of cases.

- Section 803 requires prisoners to exhaust administrative remedies before bringing a lawsuit, expands courts' ability to dismiss lawsuits filed by prisoners, and imposes restrictions on attorney fees that can be awarded to prevailing counsel.

- Section 805 requires courts to prescreen lawsuits filed by prisoners and expands grounds for dismissal of such lawsuits.

Those who would deny or restrict the constitutional rights of prisoners have little cause for celebration at this time. Many of the provisions of the PLRA (especially Sections 802 and 803) are being challenged on constitutional grounds in lawsuits across the country, and several challenges to the act have already been successful (National Prison Project, 1996). While neither definitive nor comprehensive rulings by the Supreme Court have yet been issued, it is likely that legislative tampering with the intent of the Constitution, if perceived, will test the patience and resolve of even the most conservative Supreme Court justice.

IMPLICATIONS FOR CRIMINAL JUSTICE POLICY

Jail overcrowding is the result of a complex interaction of social and political forces. Competing problem definitions and causal explanations have been accompanied by uncertainty and a sense of urgency. Under such conditions, a "garbage-can" model of decision making prevails: policymakers seize upon readily available solutions rather than weighing options and formulating an optimal plan (Cohen et al., 1972). As a result, policies adopted may be ineffective, inefficient, or inconsistent. For example, early release policies may be implemented by local officials to reduce jail overcrowding at the same time as mandatory sentences adopted by the state send more people to jail. To counteract such tendencies, more attention needs to be paid to structuring and defining the jail overcrowding problem. If problem analysis is incomplete or inaccurate, policies may fail because they either find the wrong solution to the right problem or they are aimed at the wrong problem. A policy design approach focuses attention on the match between problem definition and proposed solutions. Seven aspects of policy design (adapted from Ingraham, 1987) are relevant to local jails.

1. *Degree of goal consensus versus level of conflict*. At present, jail policies are rarely tied to explicitly stated goals, purposes, or fiscal limitations. More consideration needs to be devoted to the unique purposes of jails, tempered by practical and fiscal constraints. If consensus is not possible, reasonable compromises must be realized.

2. *Placement on policy agenda*. Time and resources must be devoted to arriving at a solution. Conflict resolution and group-building techniques have proven effective in gaining consensus in a wide variety of policy settings (e.g., Susskind and Cruikshank, 1987). Kaufman (1985) describes team-building techniques used by the National Institute of Corrections to facilitate the formulation of solutions to prison overcrowding by state policymakers; Harland (1991) describes similar strategies with New York jail policymakers.

3. *Availability of alternative choices*. A complete list of policy alternatives and consequences should be articulated. For example, neither building nor using intermediate sanctions will be effective in all settings. Comprehensive needs assessments in each locality should be undertaken so as to define the need for future jail space, the feasibility of intermediate sanctions, and the costs (both financial and social) of pursuing different policy alternatives.

4. *Diversity of stakeholders*. The more heterogeneous are participants in the policy process, the more likely is conflict over policy options. Jail overcrowding is the policy arena for diverse actors: county supervisors, district

attorneys, sheriffs, probation departments, judges, and state legislators. Absent interagency cooperation or communication, many policies meet unexpected resistance and noncompliance. The diverse views of key actors must be identified and considered if effective responses are to develop.

5. *Level of required expertise to formulate policy.* Expertise includes technical and political competence, level of direct contact with the problem, and level of understanding of the problem. Policymakers must carefully locate and integrate expertise in a variety of areas: jail population forecasting; jail policy advocacy; design and administration of programs in jails, courts, probation, and other agencies; and planning. It must not be assumed that policymakers themselves possess the necessary range of required expertise.

6. *Resources demanded by the policy versus those available.* Assuming that agreement can be reached on problem definition and policy goals, it is essential to match resources to policy (Mullen, 1985). Either resources must rise to the level required by policy, or policy must be tailored to meet resource constraints. "Get-tough" sentencing policies, for example, should not be contemplated unless necessary jail and prison space can be ensured. Minnesota's sentencing guidelines were explicitly tied to resource considerations (Blumstein, 1987; Miethe and Moore, 1989).

7. *Implementation responsibility and determination of performance criteria.* Assuming that other policy requirements can be met (e.g., resources, agreement on problem and goals, commitment to achieving a solution), any new policy must contain a plan for monitoring its progress and evaluating its effectiveness over a specified period of time. A dearth of valid evaluations of new policies has seriously hindered progress in solving the jail crowding problem.

CONCLUSIONS

In this chapter we have attempted to advance our understanding of jail problems and reforms by integrating diverse perspectives on the causes, evolution, and impacts of court orders against jails. Substantial shortcomings in both policy design and research on jail problems have hindered solutions to overcrowding and other problems. We may not yet have learned how to punish in a humane and rational manner, but the courts have contributed enormously to an important window of opportunity to do so.

Over the past 30 years, court orders have forced social systems to become more selective about the use of incarceration. Court orders have raised awareness of jail problems and have created a more receptive climate for sentencing alternatives, public education, and other innovations. Building new jails has proven to be a simplistic, expensive, and ineffective response to overcrowding (Busher, 1983; Hall, 1985), while increased law enforcement and incarceration have proven to be simplistic responses to crime (Clear and Harris, 1987; Walker, 1990). Even in jurisdictions that have undergone extensive building programs, overcrowding persists and little change in crime has resulted. Fiscal crisis and court-imposed population caps have contributed to the widespread adoption of intermediate sanctions. It is not yet clear, however, that intermediate sanctions signal the emergence of a more rational system of sentencing and punishment (Morris and Tonry, 1990). Such policies may merely provide temporary "band-aid" solutions for overburdened correctional systems.

Long-neglected economic and social realities suggest a pressing need to reexamine our willingness and capability to punish. "Get-tough" anticrime policies have contributed to jail overcrowding, court orders, and resource crisis in local government. Such policies have also contributed to an increasingly criminalized urban underclass (Wilson, 1987). The United States now has the highest rate of incarceration in the world and incarcerates black males at a rate four times that of South Africa (Mauer, 1990).

Jail overcrowding and court orders result from a dynamic confluence of social, political, and legal forces, and solutions to complex problems are unlikely to be quick or easy. At the same time, the current state of affairs should be viewed as a considerable opportunity. Our need for efficient and just policy choices requires a more careful process of problem analysis, policy design, and policy evaluation than ever before. Well-planned research can open the door for coordinated policy innovation rather than a "piecemeal political patchwork of minor ameliorations" (Mattick, 1974:822). The major obstacle to a more rational system of punishment is the tendency to seize upon unrelated, simplistic solutions at the expense of more coordinated but complex plans informed by policy-relevant research. The dangers of faulty problem analysis, "knee-jerk" change, and poor evaluations of new criminal justice policies should be clear by now. While the future should be informed by the past, it need not be doomed by it.

ENDNOTES

1. Judge William P. Gray, *Stewart et al.* v. *Gates et al.*, 450 F. Supp. 583 (C.D. Cal. 1978), 450 F. Supp. at 588.
2. Judge James L. Facht, *Hudler et al.* v. *Duffy et al.*, No. 404148 (Cal. Super. Ct., County of San Diego, May 12, 1980), 21.
3. Judge Richard A. Bancroft, *Smith et al.* v. *Dyer et al.*, Nos. 74184, 63779, 76086, 750121 (Cal. Super. Ct., County of Alameda, Aug. 15, 1983).
4. Judge Bruce Allen, *Branson et al.* v. *Winter et al.*, No. 78807 (Cal. Super. Ct., County of Santa Clara, Order of Nov. 22, 1982), 4.

REFERENCES

ADVISORY COMMISSION ON INTERGOVERNMENTAL RELATIONS (1984). *Jails: Intergovernmental Dimensions of a Local Problem.* Washington, DC: The Commission.

ALPERT, G. P., B. CROUCH, and C. R. HUFF (1986). Prison reform by judicial decree: The unintended consequences of *Ruiz* v. *Estelle.* In K. C. Haas and G. P. Alpert (eds.), *The Dilemmas of Punishment.* Prospect Heights, IL: Waveland Press, pp. 258–271.

ANON. (1973). Judicial intervention in corrections: The California experience—An empirical study. Note. *UCLA Law Review,* 20:452–580.

ANON. (1979). "Mastering" intervention in prisons. Note. *Yale Law Journal,* 88:1062–1091.

AUSTIN, J., and B. KRISBERG (1982). The unmet promise of alternatives to incarceration. *Crime and Delinquency*, 28:374–409.

BABCOCK, W. G. (1990). Litigating prison conditions in Philadelphia: Part II. *Prison Journal*, 70(2):38–49.

BAIAMONTE, J. V. JR. (1990). *Holland v. Donelon* revisited: Jail litigation in Jefferson Parish, Louisiana, 1971–1991. *Prison Journal*, 70(2):38–49.

BLUMSTEIN, A. (1987). Sentencing and the prison crowding problem. In S. D. Gottfredson and S. McConville (eds.), *America's Correctional Crisis: Prison Populations and Public Policy*. Westport, CT: Greenwood Press.

BLUMSTEIN, A. (1988). Prison populations: A system out of control? In M. Tonry and N. Morris (eds.), *Crime and Justice: A Review of Research*, Vol. 10. Chicago: University of Chicago Press.

BRAKEL, S. J. (1979). Special masters in institutional litigation. *American Bar Foundation Research Journal*, 3:543–569.

BRONSTEIN, A. J. (1980). Offender rights litigation: historical and future developments. In I. P. Robbins (ed.), *Prisoners' Rights Sourcebook*, Vol. 2. New York: Clark Boardman, pp. 5–28.

BUSHER, W. (1983). *Jail Overcrowding: Identifying Causes and Planning for Solutions*. Washington, DC: U.S. Department of Justice, Office of Justice Assistance, Research and Statistics.

CALL, J. E. (1986). Recent case law on overcrowded conditions of confinement: An assessment of its impact on facility decisionmaking. In K. C. Haas and G. P. Alpert (eds.), *The Dilemmas of Punishment: Readings in Contemporary Corrections*. Prospect Heights, IL: Waveland Press.

CALL, J. E., and R. COLE (1996). Assessing the possible impact of the violent crime control act of 1994 on prison and jail overcrowding lawsuits. *Prison Journal*, 76: 92–106.

CARROLL, L., and M. B. DOUBET (1983). U.S. social structure and imprisonment: A comment. *Criminology*, 21:449–456.

CHILTON, B. S. (1991). *Prisons under the Gavel: The Federal Court Takeover of Georgia Prisons*. Columbus, OH: Ohio State University Press.

CLEAR, T. R., and P. M. HARRIS (1987). The costs of incarceration. In S. D. Gottfredson and S. McConville (eds.), *America's Correctional Crisis*. Westport, CT: Greenwood Press.

COHEN, M. D., J. G. MARCH, and J. P. OLSEN (1972). A garbage can model of organizational choice. *Administrative Science Quarterly*, 17:1.

COOPER, P. J. (1988). *Hard Judicial Choices*. New York: Oxford University Press.

CROUCH, B. M., and J. W. MARQUART (1989). *An Appeal to Justice*. Austin, TX: University of Texas Press.

CULLEN, F. T., G. A. CLARK, and J. F. WOZNIAK (1985). Explaining the get tough movement: Can the public be blamed? *Federal Probation*, 49:16–24.

DIIULIO, J. J., JR. (1987). *Governing Prisons: A Comparative Study of Correctional Management*. New York: Free Press.

DIIULIO, J. J., JR. (ed.) (1990). *Courts, Corrections, and the Constitution*. New York: Oxford University Press.

DUNBAUGH, F. M. (1990). Prospecting for prospective relief: The story of seeking compliance with a federal court decree mandating humane conditions of confinement in the Baltimore City Jail. *Prison Journal*, 70:57–73.

EKLAND-OLSON, S., and S. J. MARTIN (1988). Organizational compliance with court-ordered reform. *Law and Society Review*, 22:359–383.

FEELEY, M. M., and R. P. HANSON (1986). What we know, think we know and would like to know about the impact of court orders on prison conditions and jail crowding. Presented at the meeting of the Working Group on Jail and Prison Crowding, Committee on Research on Law Enforcement and the Administration of Justice, National Academy of Sciences, Chicago.

FEELEY, M. M., and R. P. HANSON (1990). The impact of judicial intervention on prisons and jails: A framework for analysis and a review of the literature. In J. J. DiIulio, Jr. (ed.), *Courts, Corrections, and the Constitution*. New York: Oxford University Press.

GALANTER, M. (1975). Afterword: Explaining litigation. *Law and Society Review*, 9:347–368.

GETTINGER, S. H. (1984). *Assessing Criminal Justice Needs*. Washington, DC: U.S. Department of Justice, National Institute of Justice.

GLAZER, N. (1975). Towards an imperial judiciary? *Public Interest*, 41:104.

GLAZER, N. (1978). Should judges administer social services? *Public Interest*, 50:64–80.

GRIESER, R. C. (1988). *Wardens and State Corrections Commissioners Offer Their Views in National Assessment*. Research in Action, NCJ-113584. Washington, DC: U.S. Department of Justice.

HAGAN, J. (1989). Why is there so little criminal justice theory? Neglected macro- and micro-level links between organization and power. *Journal of Research in Crime and Delinquency*, 26:116–135.

HALL, A. (1985). *Alleviating Jail Overcrowding: A Systems Perspective*. Washington, DC: U.S. Department of Justice, National Institute of Justice, Office of Development, Testing, and Dissemination.

HARLAND, A. T. (1991). Jail crowding and the process of criminal justice policymaking. *Prison Journal*, 71(1):77–92.

HARRIS, M. K., and D. P. SPILLER, JR. (1977). *After Decision: Implementation of Judicial Decrees in Correctional Settings*. National Institute of Law Enforcement and Criminal Justice, Law Enforcement Assistance Administration. Washington, DC: U.S. Government Printing Office.

INGRAHAM, P. (1987). Toward more systematic consideration of policy design. *Policy Studies Journal*, 15:611–628.

JACOBS, J. B. (1980). The prisoners' rights movement and its impacts, 1960–80. In N. Morris and M. Tonry (eds.), *Crime and Justice*, Vol. 2. Chicago: University of Chicago Press.

KAUFMAN, G. (1985). The national prison overcrowding project: Policy analysis and politics, a new approach. *Annals of the American Academy of Political and Social Sciences*, 478:161–172.

KIZZIAH, C. A. (1984). *The State of the Jails in California*. Report 1: *Overcrowding in the Jails*. Sacramento, CA: Board of Corrections, State of California.

KLOFAS, J. (1987). Patterns of jail use. *Journal of Criminal Justice*, 15:403–412.

KLOFAS, J. (1990). The jail and the community. *Justice Quarterly*, 7:69–102.

MARTIN, S. J., and S. EKLAND-OLSON (1987). *Texas Prisons: The Walls Came Tumbling Down*. Austin, TX: Texas Monthly Press.

MATTICK, H. W. (1974). The contemporary jails of the United States: An unknown and neglected area of justice. In D. Glaser (ed.), *Handbook of Criminology*. Skokie, IL: Rand McNally, pp. 777–848.

MAUER, M. (1990). *Americans behind Bars: A Comparison of International Rates of Incarceration*. Washington, DC: Sentencing Project.

McCARTHY, B. R. (1990). A micro-level analysis of social structure and social control: Intrastate use of jail and prison confinement. *Justice Quarterly*, 7:325–340.

MIETHE, T. D., and C. A. MOORE (1989). *Sentencing Guidelines: Their Effect in Minnesota.* Research in Brief, NCJ-111381. Washington, DC: U.S. Department of Justice, Office of Justice Programs, National Institute of Justice.

MONTGOMERY, E. (1980). Force and will: An exploration of the use of special masters to implement judicial decrees. *University of Toledo Law Review,* 52:105–123.

MORRIS, N., and M. TONRY (1990). *Between Prison and Probation: Intermediate Punishments in a Rational Sentencing System.* New York: Oxford University Press.

MULLEN, J. (1985). Prison crowding and the evolution of public policy. *Annals of the American Academy of Political and Social Science,* 478:31–46.

MYERS, M., and S. TALARICO (1987). *The Social Contexts of Criminal Sentencing.* New York: Springer-Verlag.

NATHAN, V. M. (1979). The use of masters in institutional reform litigation. *University of Toledo Law Review,* 10:419–464.

NATIONAL PRISON PROJECT (1996). Prison litigation reform act: The good, the bad and the ugly. *The National Prison Project Journal,* 11(2):1–2.

NATIONAL PRISON PROJECT (1997). *Overview of the Prison Litigation Reform Act* (PLRA). Washington, DC: American Civil Liberties Union Foundation. www.npp.org/plraover.htm.

RUSCHE, G., and O. KIRCHHEIMER (1939). *Punishment and Social Structure.* New York: Russell and Russell.

SKOGAN, W. G. (1975). Measurement problems in official and survey crime rates. *Journal of Criminal Justice,* 3:17–32.

SKOVRON, S. E., J. E. SCOTT, and F. T. CULLEN. (1988). Prison crowding: Public attitudes toward strategies of population control. *Journal of Research in Crime and Delinquency,* 25:150–169.

STOREY, T. S. (1990). When intervention works: Judge Morris E. Lasker and New York City jails. In J. J. DiIulio, Jr. (ed.), *Courts, Corrections, and the Constitution.* New York: Oxford University Press.

SUSSKIND, L., and J. CRUIKSHANK (1987). *Breaking the Impasse: Consensual Approaches to Resolving Public Disputes.* New York: Basic Books.

U.S. DEPARTMENT OF JUSTICE (1988). *Police Chiefs and Sheriffs Rank Their Criminal Justice Needs.* NCJ-113061. Washington, DC: U.S. Government Printing Office.

U.S. DEPARTMENT OF JUSTICE (1990a). *Justice Expenditures and Employment,* 1988. NCJ-124132. Washington, DC: U.S. Government Printing Office.

U.S. DEPARTMENT OF JUSTICE (1991a). *Criminal Victimization in the U.S.,1989.* NCJ-129391. Washington, DC: U.S. Government Printing Office.

U.S. DEPARTMENT OF JUSTICE (1992a). *National Update,* Vol. II, No. 1. NCJ-137059. Washington, DC: U.S. Government Printing Office.

U.S. DEPARTMENT OF JUSTICE (1992b). *Prisoners in 1991.* NCJ-134729. Washington, DC: U.S. Government Printing Office.

U.S. DEPARTMENT OF JUSTICE (1993). *Jail Inmates,* 1992. NCJ-143284. Washington, DC: U.S. Government Printing Office.

U.S. DEPARTMENT OF JUSTICE (1997a). *Prison and Jail Inmates at Midyear 1996.* NCJ-162843. Washington, DC: U.S. Government Printing Office.

U.S. DEPARTMENT OF JUSTICE (1997b). *Criminal Victimization, 1973–95.* NCJ-163069. Washington, DC: U.S. Government Printing Office.

WALKER, S. (1990). *Sense and Nonsense about Crime.* Pacific Grove, CA: Brooks/Cole.

WELSH, W. N. (1990). A comparative analysis of court orders against California county jails: Intervention and impact. Ph.D. dissertation, University of California, Irvine, CA.

WELSH, W. N. (1992a). The dynamics of jail reform litigation: A comparative analysis of litigation in California counties. *Law and Society Review*, 26(3):591–625.

WELSH, W. N. (1992b). Court orders and county correctional expenditures: Power of the purse? *Law and Policy*, 14:277–311.

WELSH, W. N. (1993). Changes in arrest policies as a result of court orders against county jails. *Justice Quarterly*, 10: 89–120.

WELSH, W. N. (1995). *Counties in Court: Jail Overcrowding and Court-Ordered Reform*. Philadelphia: Temple University Press.

WELSH, W. N., and H. N. PONTELL (1991). Counties in court: Interorganizational adaptations to jail litigation in California. *Law and Society Review*, 25:73–101.

WELSH, W. N., H. N. PONTELL, M. C. LEONE, and P. KINKADE (1990). Jail overcrowding: An analysis of policymaker perceptions. *Justice Quarterly*, 7:341–370.

WELSH, W. N., M. C. LEONE, P. T. KINKADE, and H. N. PONTELL (1991). The politics of jail overcrowding: Public attitudes and official policies. In J. A. Thompson and G. L. Mays (eds.), *American Jails: Public Policy Issues*. Chicago: Nelson-Hall, pp. 131–147.

WILSON, W. J. (1987). *The Truly Disadvantaged*. Chicago: University of Chicago Press.

YACKLE, L. W. (1989). *Reform and Regret*. New York: Oxford University Press.

CASES

Cooper v. *Pate*, 378 U.S. 546 (1964).

Gates v. *Collier*, 501 F.2d 1291 (5th Cir. 1974).

Helling v. *McKinney*, 113 S. Ct. 2475, 53 Cr. L. 2229 (1993).

Hudler et al. v. *Duffy et al.*, No. 404148 (Cal. Super. Ct., County of San Diego, May 12, 1980).

Miller v. *Carson*, 401 F. Supp. 835 (M.D. Fla. 1975).

In re Morgan, In re Ransbury, and *Consolidated Cases*, Nos. 281302-0, 281438-2, 284164-1, 308318-5, 316580-0, 286040-1, 285427-1, 289487-1, 289488-9, 287160-6 (Cal. Super. Ct., County of Fresno, Jan. 12, 1983).

Offield et al. v. *Scott*, No. 46871 (Cal. Super. Ct., County of Placer, May 12, 1977).

Rhodes v. *Chapman*, 452 U.S. 337 (1981).

Smith et al. v. *Dyer et al.*, Nos. 74184, 63779, 76086, 750121 (Cal. Super. Ct., County of Alameda, Aug. 15, 1983).

Wilson v. *Seiter*, 49 U.S.L.W. 2264 (1991).

Wilson v. *Superior Court* (Branson), 240 Cal. Rptr. 131 (Cal. App. 6 Dist. 1987).

chapter 22

Sentencing into the Twenty-First Century

Sentence Enhancement and Life without Parole

Etta F. Morgan, Ph.D. and Robert T. Sigler, Ph.D.

ABSTRACT

The disposition of offenders at the sentencing stage has cycled from extreme punishment to extreme treatment throughout history. Each peak is characterized by the creation of statutes that enable the increased use of the preferred disposition. We are presently at the peak of a punishment cycle. As the twenty-first century unfolds, it is likely that we will move toward a treatment orientation. We anticipate that in the next cycle, community corrections will be enhanced and expanded.

INTRODUCTION

As we move into the twenty-first century, the conservative trend that emerged in the 1970s has continued to dominate justice system policy. Prison populations continued to grow throughout the 1990s and are expected to continue to expand in the immediate future (Wees, 1996). Community corrections programs are being framed in terms of alternative sanctions but continue to be developed and expanded at a slow pace, with emphasis on control, punishment, and retribution potential rather than on treatment or rehabilitation potential.

CYCLES IN ORIENTATION TOWARD THE SENTENCING OF CRIMINAL OFFENDERS

Punishment and treatment represent two extremes on a continuum of approaches for the disposition of offenders who have been found or pled guilty to the offenses they have committed. Punishment stresses the protection of society through the use of incarceration and tends to have elements of retribution, incapacitation, and deterrence. Treatment stresses the protection of society by changing the offender so that he or she stops committing crimes, and it tends to have elements of rehabilitation and reintegration. It is rare in practice to have one extreme to the exclusion of the other, with most systems changing emphasis rather than eliminating programs when public sentiment changes. Orientation toward the punishment or treatment of convicted offenders has vacillated from treating the offender as if he or she had no rights or reason to expect help to treating the offender as a person who retains his or her rights and who should receive education, training, and psychological services (Smith and Berlin, 1988).

Bartollas (1980) identifies four waves of treatment reform. During the colonial period in the United States, punishment dominated as the philosophy for disposition of convicted offenders with severe penalties, such as the stocks, whipping post, and gallows seen as appropriate dispositions. Treatment-oriented reform emerged after the war for independence, producing the prison. A second wave of reform in the latter part of the nineteenth century produced the reformatory. A third wave of reform in the early twentieth century produced individual treatment, and the medical model emerged during the mid-1900s in a fourth wave of reform. He notes that punishment became dominant in the 1970s but suggests that support for rehabilitation will reemerge in the coming years.

Although shifts are not necessarily distinct or universal, clear shifts in orientation can be observed. When punishment dominates, laws are passed making incarceration easier to apply with provisions for longer sentences; the use of prison as a disposition increases, putting pressure on correctional systems. The response of correctional systems, combined with factors such as increasing costs, overcrowding, the incarceration of relatively mild offenders for long periods of time, and deterioration of the quality of life in prisons, produces a reaction against the use of prisons. Crime rates do not decline and punishment is projected in the media as an ineffective strategy. Public sentiment changes and treatment-oriented reformers press for a treatment-oriented response to the criminal offender to reduce crime. Laws, policies, and practices are adopted to change the orientation of the correctional system. At the extreme point in the swing to treatment, the system "treats" and releases all offenders. Offenders spend very little time incarcerated, and some of the released/nondetained offenders commit spectacular new crimes. Crime is not reduced. Treatment is projected as a failure in the public media. Public sentiment changes and treatment falls into disfavor. Punishment-oriented reformers press for a more restrictive system to provide protection from criminal offenders and to reduce crime.

The rehabilitation ideal is believed to have dominated corrections throughout the nineteenth and twentieth centuries (Allen, 1981). Although the treatment/punishment cycle is relatively pervasive, there appears to be a continuous shift toward more humane, if not more treatment-oriented, use of incarceration. That is, with each cycle some treatment-oriented programs tend to remain in place (education, vocational training, work release) and, with the exception of the death penalty, punishments have tended to become less severe than has historically been the case (corporal punishment, severity of the prison environment).

The alternating preference for punishment or treatment predates use of the prison as a sentence. Shifts in the cycle from treatment to punishment can be seen in the development of the workhouse or the development of the English Poor Laws. The development of the prison as a disposition in the late seventeenth century was the product of a reform movement that sought to reduce crime through the treatment of criminal offenders and was to replace less humane dispositions, such as corporal punishment and capital punishment. By the early eighteenth century, sentiment had changed, and while the prison was maintained, the colonial assembly reimposed the English criminal code, including capital punishment and whipping (McKelvey, 1977).

Clear peaks in the cycles are difficult to identify during the nineteenth century because of the different rates of development of prison systems in the various states. Although some states had well-established systems that progressed through stages of development and reform, other states did not build prisons until the latter part of the century (McKelvey, 1977). In states with well-developed systems, pressure for reform began to develop in the early nineteenth century, with much of the controversy emerging from the debate on the preference for either solitary confinement or congregate confinement. This pressure produced the use of indeterminate sentences, prison societies, probation and parole, and the reformatory movement, with firm discipline and education defined as part of the treatment process (McKelvey, 1977). Houses of refuge emerged for the treatment of children with an emphasis on training and inculcation of proper moral standards (Bernard, 1992). By the end of the nineteenth century, the cycle was shifting, as reflected in statues providing for longer sentences for minor offenders, the use of some mandatory sentences, habitual offender statutes, restrictions on the use of parole, and statutes criminalizing vagrancy. Overcrowding became common, and operations of reformatories came to resemble those of earlier prisons, with increased emphasis on control; the spread of the reformatory philosophy declined. The costs of maintaining prisons became an issue, existing institutions were expanded, and living conditions deteriorated. Contract labor, convict lease systems, and prison industries were developed as legitimate forms of punishment and as a way of reducing the costs of maintaining a prison system as a reaction to charges of the lack of a need for collegiate and hotel prisons (McKelvey, 1977). Houses of refuge fell into disrepute, and the focus of these institutions shifted to the control of children (Bernard, 1992).

At the turn of the century, reform was emerging in the form of the separation of children from adult offenders, the development of the juvenile court (Bernard, 1992), and the reemergence and expansion of the reformatory movement (McKelvey, 1977). Growing interest in mental health and its application to criminal offenders led to expanded indeterminate sentencing and defective delinquent statutes. In practice, treatment-oriented reformers sought to replace mark and ratings systems (an earlier treatment innovation) with clinical prognosis as a basis for determining release of imprisoned offenders. The medical model for treating offenders began to emerge. Much of the legislative reform during this period focused on the use of convict labor and was driven as much or more by economic factors as by treatment–punishment factors.

In the late 1920s, the focus shifted to the failure of the system to correct offenders, with studies indicating high failure rates on parole and among released offenders. The use of prison as a disposition increased, overcrowding became an issue, and most states undertook construction of expanded prison systems. During the mid-1900s, legislative action and practice produced classification systems that were based on offender risk. Educational and vocational training programs remained but were not supported adequately. Special programs were developed for incorrigible offenders, and prison violence increased. New programs such as movies and organized sports were implemented on the basis of potential for maintaining peace in the institution. Prison disturbances increased and the public became concerned.

In the 1930s and 1940s the medical model emerged and classification shifted, with an emphasis on classifying inmates for treatment and on an upgrading of the status of parole, beginning with the federal system and moving to the states (McKelvey, 1977). Studies of the impact of prisonization (Clemmer, 1958) appearing in the 1940s added to the shift toward treatment, as did rapidly emerging therapies such as psychodrama and guided group interaction. Legislation and practice emerged permitting the implementation and expansion of the medical model of treatment, including enabling statutes, modified death penalty statutes, and expanded good time provisions (McKelvey, 1977).

By the 1970s, sentiment had shifted away from treatment. Rehabilitation was perceived as a failure, with the severity of crime perceived as increasing and the safety of the public decreasing because of the emphasis on treatment in the correctional system (Fogel, 1978; Allen, 1981). The juvenile court became more legalistic (Bernard, 1992). Reformers who advocated punishment as the correct function of sentencing prevailed and incarceration became prominent. Legislative initiatives restored determinate sentences, abolished parole, reestablished or strengthened habitual offender provisions, increased the use of sentence enhancement, and developed sentencing guidelines. As a result, the incarceration rate more than doubled between 1973 and 1983 (Currie, 1985). This trend has continued, and presently, correctional systems are unable to house all of those sentenced to state incarceration, despite aggressive construction programs (Wees, 1996).

MEDIATING INFLUENCES

A number of factors work to mediate the impact and, to some extent, the visibility of treatment–punishment cycles. First, the shift is not complete. There is an identifiable group of treatment-oriented reformers which is relatively stable over time. When punishment is dominant, they continue to argue for treatment. There is a similar group of punishment-oriented reformers who continue to argue for punishment when treatment dominates orientation toward the disposition of criminal offenders. Although the size of these groups is undetermined, it appears probable that most people are relatively uninformed and uncommitted to punishment or to treatment; thus, the shift from one extreme to the other is likely to reflect a relatively small shift on the part of the uninvolved majority, permitting justice agencies to resist full implementation of reform measures.

Diffusion of concepts, particularly as reflected in legislation and policy development, is slow. Reform will begin in one state and spread to other states over many years. As a result, at any one time there are likely to be states in which punishment is still dominant, whereas a treatment orientation prevails in others. In addition, later adaptations may be less extreme than the original models, whether it be legislation or policy. System resistance to change also moderates the impact of extreme legislation. Judges may choose to avoid judicial notice of sentence enchantment conditions, particularly in plea-bargained cases when punishment is dominant, or give longer sentences from a range of sentences when treatment dominates. Correctional institutions may maintain treatment programs with decreased emphasis during punishment peaks and find ways to retain "dangerous" offenders during treatment peaks.

Correctional professionals change the terms and rationales for the programs that they want to maintain, expand, or develop. Practitioners speak in terms of risk control, effective correctional intervention, restorative or community justice, and structured sanctioning policy development (Harris, 1998) instead of treatment, rehabilitation, supervision, and equitable sentencing.

CONTEMPORARY PRACTICES

Punishment presently dominates policy, legislation, and practice regarding convicted offenders. Society is moving toward dependence upon punishment to deter criminals from criminal activity. The inclination to punish is an emotional reaction which becomes salient with the violation of social sentiments (Garland, 1990). The social sentiments that Garland addresses are referred to as the conscience collective by Durkheim (1965).

If punishment is merely an expressive institution that serves to release psychic energy, it has no objective or intended goal. If punishment simply occurs, without an objective to be achieved, it is not particularly useful other than in the context of retribution. If there is no action against the collective sentiment, there is no need for a reaction to protect the collective sentiment. If punishment functions to create a community that is harmonious and unified, the effects of punishment are positive. Punishment should be perceived as a part of the cultural matrix that supports a complex pattern of rules and sentiments (Garland, 1990). Punishment can be perceived as a symbolic issue in society that directly affects the psychological and overall development of people in a society. Politically, the extent of punishments in a society represents the definitive authority that is maintained by the political order of that society.

Because all the facets of a society are interrelated in the social order, like other social factors, punishments and all other dispositions available to the justice system are determined by means of inclusion or exclusion in the social group (Garland, 1990). It is the preferences of the conscience collective that are implemented by a select few who are elected to office. In most cases, legislators attempt to codify in law what they believe to be the wishes of the public, or at least that portion of the public who elected them to office. Other agencies, such as the police and the courts, are also sensitive to what are perceived to be the wishes of the public. It should be noted that these wishes generally are not empirically determined but reflect the beliefs of elected or appointed officials. It has been suggested that, to some extent, legislation and its implementation tend to reflect the sentiments of those persons with political and personal power (Headley, 1989).

Three types of legislative initiatives reflect a shift in orientation toward punishment: habitual offender statues, other sentence enhancement alternatives, and determinate sentencing (with reduction or elimination of the use of parole). These statutes are enacted to control dangerous or serious criminal offenders. An increase in public safety through the use of incarceration to control severe offenders is characteristic of periods in which punishment dominates disposition philosophy.

These initiatives developed in the federal system. Sentencing disparity, particularly insufficiently punishing sentences for some offenders, became an important issue for Congress during the 1970s. Congress charged the U.S. Parole Commission with the task of developing a plan to address the problems involved in sentencing offenders. The plan that was developed was short-lived because of lack of judicial acceptance. The second plan advanced involved rewriting the federal criminal code, but it, too, was not implemented successfully. The third plan focused on sentencing reform and proposed a comprehensive criminal law package, the Comprehensive Crime Control Act of 1984, and included the Sentencing Reform Act (Wilkins et al., 1993).

The purpose of the Sentencing Reform Act was to enhance the ability of the criminal justice system to combat crime through an effective, fair sentencing system. To achieve this goal, Congress identified three objectives: (1) the sentence imposed would be the actual sentence served, except for "good-time" credits, and the possibility of parole would not be a factor; (2) there would be uniformity in sentencing practices; and (3) the sentence would be proportional to the defendant and the offense (Wilkins et al., 1993). Several states have followed the federal model by enactment of similar sentencing procedures that provide for sentence enhancements for the career criminal. Common characteristics of sentence enhancement statues are: the imposition of a greater sentence for persons convicted under another statutory provision; the application of procedures for sentence hearings; and the use of titles that classify them as sentence enhancing statutes (Rafaloff, 1988:1090).

HABITUAL OFFENDER STATUTES

In an attempt to reduce recidivism, many states have enacted habitual offender acts. This is a direct response to evaluations that question the effectiveness of correctional programs in reducing criminality (Maltz, 1984). Maltz concluded that (1) nothing works or is an effective deterrent to reducing recidivism, and (2) getting tough works if the intervention is tough enough. States that have enacted habitual offender acts hold the belief that getting tough works.

Much of the research in this area has focused on the career patterns of dangerous and repeat offenders, who are the targets of habitual offender legislation. One group of studies focuses on the operation of special programs at the law enforcement and prosecution level and reports mixed results (Blumstein and Moitra, 1980; Phillips and

Cartwright, 1980; Weimer, 1980). A number of studies focus on the outcomes of special programs for the treatment of dangerous and career criminals and also tend to report mixed results (Van der Werff, 1981; Hoffman and Beck, 1982; Tennent and Way, 1984).

Habitual offender statues tend to reflect most clearly the preference for incarceration as a disposition. Forty-three states had adopted legislation providing mandatory sentencing for offenders who demonstrated repeated violations of felony statutes by 1983 (U.S. Department of Justice, 1983). This approach to controlling the crime problem was adopted without the benefit of supporting research and with, at best, limited consideration of the potential consequences. Reservations have been expressed by some correctional professionals and academic researchers, who suggest that habitual offender acts may prove to be costly and ineffective; others suggest that the use of imprisonment would be cost-effective.

Attempts to understand the "criminal," the person who earns his or her livelihood by committing criminal acts, have dominated criminology since its inception. Research indicates that as much as 80% (Shinnar and Shinnar, 1975) or 85% (Wolfgang et al., 1972) of serious crimes are committed by habitual offenders. Habitual offender acts attempt to control this population by assigning longer sentences to repeat felony offenders.

Concern about repeat offenders is not new. Proposed solutions are varied and have been present since the beginning of the use of prisons. Judges have taken prior criminal history into account when sentencing an offender, and they have used and do use longer sentences to control habitual or career criminals. The indiscriminate use of longer sentences for repeat offenders is not effective because plea bargaining, lack of information, and other factors can and do reduce the judge's freedom in assigning a sentence. The use of automatic sentencing has been present since as early as 1926 (Inciardi, 1986), when legislation very similar to current habitual offender legislation was introduced in the New York legislature, with a mandatory life sentence following a fourth felony conviction. Contemporary proposals for selective incapacitation (Blackmore and Welsh, 1983; Janus, 1985), which are the product of both a desire to control career offenders and pressure to contain the growth of prison populations, are an updated version of an old response to an enduring problem.

Attempts to develop an effective operational definition for habitual offenders have led to the reduction of this concept to a specific number of felonies, thus creating a condition in which offenders captured by the statute may not be the career criminals sought. Relatively nondangerous offenders could commit three mild felonies (a popular threshold for many legislatures), plead guilty to all three, and receive a harsh sentence for a fourth mild felony offense. The career criminal or the person with a criminal orientation would avoid the statute by bargaining for a plea to a reduced charge (a misdemeanor), by leaving the jurisdiction after posting bond and avoiding a conviction, or by moving from jurisdiction to jurisdiction during his or her criminal career.

Habitual offender acts have sentence enhancement provisions (add one or more years to the sentence when two or more prior convictions exist) that mandate the use of a life-without-parole sentence for some (usually on the fourth felony conviction), regardless of the dangerousness or level of commitment to criminal behavior. Other statutes provide for life without parole sentences because of the severity or offensiveness of an act. These statutes permit the assignment of a life-without-parole sentence when an offender's behavior is so dangerous that society has an interest in incarceration for public safety and/or for punishment. If the statutes are effective, there should be two life-without-parole populations. One is composed of offenders (who may not be career criminals) who have committed extremely offensive and dangerous acts, usually involving an element of physical assault; the other is a group of career criminals who frequently have no personal violence in their offense history. Habitual offenders tend to be the younger, more violent, and more assertive offenders (Irwin, 1981; Flanagan, 1982). If the habitual offender acts are ineffective, a third group of life-without-parole inmates is created. This group of offenders exhibits relatively mild levels of criminal activity and is not dangerous.

The growth in prison populations has been attributed to changes in the orientation of the justice system (MacKenzie et al., 1988). Prior to 1980, growth in Louisiana prisons was related to demographic changes in the general population, but the rapid growth of Louisiana's prison population in the early 1980s has been attributed to a number of changes in the law which increased the severity of sentences (MacKenzie et al., 1988). Similar statutes have been adopted in many states.

The cost of maintaining the life-without-parole population is high. If the use of these recent more severe statutes is heavy, a department of corrections might be required to build a new prison every two or three years just to accommodate new life-without-parole offenders. These prisons would be expensive, secure facilities requiring more and better qualified staff. Thus, in addition to adding the cost of staffing and maintaining new institutions to the operating budget of a department of corrections, the cost per inmate would increase as well.

SENTENCE ENHANCEMENT

Legislators in most states have passed sentence enhancement statutes. Legislators failed to realize the impact that sentence enhancements would have on prison populations and prison management. Sentence enhancements have contributed greatly to the problem of prison overcrowding in many states. For this reason, many prison officials have reconstructed their programs to accommodate the increase in population. The overall effects of punitive sentence reforms extend beyond the inmate population increase and prison management to include the management of human and material resources (Luttrell, 1991:54).

Many sentence enhancement acts focus on the use of firearms. The federal model is the Armed Career Criminal Act. Criminal justice administrators trying to comply with the requirements of the Armed Career Criminal Act found that its application as a sentence enhancement depended on judicial interpretation. The Armed Career Criminal Act's original objective was to punish habitual and/or repeat offenders, who are sometimes referred to as *career criminals*. The statute failed, however, to define the career criminal, thereby leaving the definition of such a person to the sentencing authority.

On the state level, firearm laws have been changed to shift discretionary powers in some states from the judges and parole boards to the prosecutors and police. In some states there tends to be an overuse of sentence enhancements with those identified as serious repeat offenders, while in others there is a tendency to avoid using these enhancements as the law mandates.

California's gun crime sentence enhancements include a one-year additional sentence if the offender or the accomplice is in possession of a gun during the commission or attempted commission of a felony. Actual use of a gun during a felony mandates an additional two-year sentence. An additional two years is added to the sentence if the perpetrator is armed during a sexual offense; in all cases using a firearm adds a third year to the sentence (Lizotte and Zatz, 1986).

In a study conducted by Lizotte and Zatz (1986) which covered a three-year period, data revealed that use of a firearm does not significantly affect the length of sentence to prison. The sentence enhancer is not used for first convictions of any type, and sentences were influenced more by the length of time required to process the case than by mandatory sentences. The use of firearms did begin to influence the sentence length, with the fourth or later arrest increasing the sentence length by 14 months. For the fifth and subsequent arrests, the sentence length increased by 29 months whether or not the prior arrests involved firearms (Lizotte and Zatz, 1986). The firearm sentence enhancer is not used until the fifth and later offenses for rape, although the California Penal Code mandates a three-year add-on sentence to the sentence for rape when a firearm is used. Courts in California, like those in many other states, use the sentence enhancer only for the most serious repeat offenders (Lizotte and Zatz, 1986).

Massachusetts statutes mandate a sentence of one year for persons carrying a firearm illegally. This enhancer does not establish an add-on sentence in relation to another felony; it is associated directly with possession of a firearm. With this enhancer in place, police officers have been granted unlimited discretion in terms of selective policing. As a means of "protecting" a particular group of citizens, the police decide who will be frisked and whether or not to report when a gun is found (Lizotte and Zatz, 1986).

In Michigan, if a person is convicted of possessing a firearm during the commission of a felony, the law mandates a two-year add-on sentence. Michigan officials have responded in two different ways to this law. In some instances they have chosen to "throw the book" at the defendant if the defendant is considered a serious repeat offender. Michigan officials have also found ways to avoid using or lessening the effect of the Felony Firearm Law, such as (1) adjusting the sentence for the mandatory two-year add-on sentence, (2) adjudicating the defendant as innocent of all charges, (3) adjudicating the defendant as guilty of all charges except the Felony Firearm Law, or (4) adjudicating the defendant guilty of a misdemeanor, at which point the Felony Firearm Law cannot be applied (Lizotte and Zatz, 1986).

In addition to firearm sentence enhancers, there are also drug enhancement sentences. In response to citizen outcry for more stringent drug laws, Congress passed the Anti-Drug Abuse Act of 1986. Under this act, mandatory provisions concerning the quantity of drugs involved were established. Mandatory sentences range from a minimum of 10 years without parole for 1 kilogram or more of heroin or 5 kilograms or more of cocaine to a minimum of five years for lesser amounts of either drug (Wilkins et al., 1993). If an offender has prior convictions, the mandatory sentence is doubled. In instances in which death or serious bodily injury occurred due to the use of a controlled substance, the mandatory minimum sentence is 20 years. The 1986 act also provided sentence enhancements for location of the distribution, age of purchaser, and pregnancy of purchaser (Wilkins et al., 1993).

Habitual offender acts are also sentence enhancement acts. In addition to the use of life without parole, habitual offender statutes use sentence enhancements for lower levels of repeat offenses. Thus, a second conviction might call for two to four additional years, and a third conviction might call for five to 10 additional years.

RESTRICTED HOUSING

Statutes were enacted that limited the ability of departments of corrections to house some offenders in specific types of housing. Some of these restrictions are explicit; others are implicit or related to classification restrictions. Explicit statutes identify classes of offenders who cannot be housed in specific types of facilities. For example, Alabama statutes prevent murderers, those who commit manslaughter while driving under the influence of alcohol, drug dealers, and offenders convicted of a sexual offense from receiving community status. Thus, they cannot be placed in facilities such as halfway houses or work release centers. As a result, these offenders are returned to the community from at least a minimum security correctional facility.

Habitual offender statutes, particularly those with life-without-parole provisions, produce a similar effect. Because a life-without-parole offender has no reason to avoid escape, he or she must be kept in at least medium security correctional facilities. Sentencing enhancing provisions have less impact but delay the time the offender will spend in secure facilities (most classification schemes consider length of sentence remaining to be served as well as severity in determining classification).

DETERMINATE SENTENCES AND PAROLE

In the middle 1970s, justice model–based determinate sentencing began to emerge as an alternative to rehabilitation-based indeterminate sentencing (Cullen and Gilbert, 1982). Determinate sentencing was used until the latter part of the nineteenth century. Indeterminate sentencing developed as a product of treatment-oriented reform and was well established by the beginning of the twentieth century. In the 1970s, punishment-oriented reformers pressed for sentences to be suited to the crime. The provisions for shorter sentences were acceptable to many rehabilitation-oriented reformers, who perceived the justice system as victimizing the offender, with set sentences reducing the degree of victimization. Programs to help offenders could remain in place but would not be related to release. By the beginning of the 1980s, 12 states and the federal system had adopted some form of determinate sentencing, but the justice model was not fully adopted in any jurisdiction. In many cases, the differences in legislation reflected the outcome of a debate between conservatives and liberals about the severity of the sentencing provisions and the range of offenses that should be addressed with incarceration. Other differences include the amount of discretion permitted, the abolishment or modification of parole, and the use of good time to reduce prison sentences (Cullen and Gilbert, 1982).

INTO THE TWENTY-FIRST CENTURY

Punishment as the appropriate disposition of convicted offenders is dominant at present. This preference for punishment developed in the 1970s and has influenced legislation, policy, and practice. Legislation enhancing habitual offender statutes, providing for determinate sentencing, restricting the ability of departments of corrections from housing some offenders in some types of housing, and providing longer sentences when specific conditions are present has increased the number of offenders sentenced to prison, provided for longer sentences, and made prisons more difficult to administer. The practical consequences of these actions have been to produce overcrowded prisons and to reduce the ability to use punishment to control offenders.

Punishment tends to become dominant when treatment is perceived as ineffective in curing offenders, crime is perceived as increasing, and the risk of the public to criminal victimization is seen as increasing. Punishment is perceived to have a deterrent effect, and long incarceration is perceived to have an incapacitation effect. It is anticipated that the combination of deterrence effect and incapacitation effect will reduce victimization by reducing crime. In particular, the identification of severe and persistent offenders and their subsequent incarceration is expected to greatly reduce crime by incarcerating a relatively small number of offenders. It was noted earlier that this strategy, as reflected in the application of habitual offender statutes, has not effectively removed serious offenders from society.

The ability to sentence severe offenders to prison and to maintain them for long periods of time is effectively prevented by overcrowding, which is caused by implementation of the various sentencing reform statutes. Prisons were overcrowded when the shift from treatment to punishment began. A series of judicial decisions in the 1960s established minimal standards for humane living conditions that continued to be reinforced into the 1970s. A central position in many of these decisions addressed population density, forcing many prison systems to reduce the number of inmates housed in existing facilities, thus defining many operating prisons as overcrowded. In many cases, court orders prevented, and in some cases still prevent, exceeding specific population limits for specific jails, correctional facilities, and correctional systems. While more recent decisions have modified the earlier rulings, upper population limits are in place for many correctional institutions. The mandatory provisions of many statutes forces the placement of specific offenders in prison for minimum periods of time. To accept these prisoners, other offenders must be released. When mandatory provisions apply to relatively mild offenders such as shoplifters, more serious offenders are released though a number of compensatory provisions enacted by legislatures at the request of system components. Although most correctional systems have responded with rapid expansion, new construction cannot keep up with the flow of new inmates into the system.

When overcrowding occurs and is capped at the state level, prisoners sentenced to the department of corrections remain in the county jail until a bed becomes available. In most states, the county jails are full. In many instances, they are under a court order capping jail population, and pressure is brought to bear on the court system to reduce the flow of offenders sentenced to incarceration. As a result, more serious offenders with fewer convictions (assault) are given probation, and less serious offenders with longer records (shoplifters) are incarcerated.

As the problems develop, secondary adaptations that avoid some of the statutory provisions emerge. For example, the court might not take judicial notice of the presence of three prior felony convictions when sentencing a specific offender, thus avoiding the mandatory prison sentence or the need to enhance the sentence appropriate for the offense. Pressure to use incarceration remains, producing an uneasy balance in the sentencing process, which causes some less severe offenders to be incarcerated while more severe offenders are released. When added to the process that causes some more severe offenders to be released rather than some less severe offenders, the degree of risk to which society is exposed increases rather than decreases.

Statutes with mandatory sentence enhancement and mandatory life without parole provisions are vulnerable to court challenge. The mandatory provision in many of these statutes has been included to answer criticism that such acts are discriminatory. If the imposition of a sentence is applied automatically to a set of circumstances related to the offense, it is not discriminatory. The decision to avoid taking judicial notice of conditions requiring the application of a mandatory sanction effectively removes the direct link between the conditions relative to the crime and the sentence. At some point, it is probable that the application of these statutes will be challenged as discriminatory.

As we enter the twenty-first century, it is probable that there will be a shift in philosophy from a preference for punishment in the disposition of offenders to a preference for treatment as a disposition for criminal offenders. It will be held that punishment is expensive and does not work. The construction costs of new prisons are high; however, the more substantial costs lie in operating budgets. As more prisons are brought on line, the operating budgets of correctional systems increase. This growth mandates either increased taxes or reduction in the budgets of other state government activities. News articles will begin to focus on the cost issue and ask the questions "What are we receiving for this investment?" and "Is what we receive worth higher taxes or poorer highways?" The belief that offenders who are incarcerated become worse and that all offenders cannot be locked up for life will be advanced along with examples of mild offenders who are serving life-without-parole sentences. The argument will emerge that it is not enough to lock people up—something must be done to reduce the likelihood that they will continue to commit crimes. As a result, a situation in which public sentiment for treatment will develop, producing a new wave of treatment-oriented reform.

Although the exact nature of these reforms cannot be determined, a number of reactions are probable. Community corrections is presently advanced as the next stage in the development of an effective treatment agenda for offenders. Community corrections continues to refer to a variety of programs that are located in the community with little attention given to conventional definitions of community corrections or to purpose and function. As a result, community corrections is a relatively vague entity encompassing such a variety of programs that most people can identify a community corrections program that they find acceptable. In essence, many programs defined as community corrections are not treatment-oriented in the pro-offender sense. Home detention, halfway houses, shock probation, and similar programs can be perceived as having punishment elements. Although statutory revision would not be required to implement community corrections as a disposition, it is probable that statues defining or expanding the scope of various community corrections sentencing alternatives will be enacted. It is also likely that additional enabling legislation and legislation supporting development and dissemination of community corrections will be enacted.

Contemporary concern with the perceived increase in the amount and severity of violence may moderate the response to pressure to modify sentencing provisions. If the focus on sentence enhancement and life without parole sentences focuses on the number of relatively mild offenders captured by these statutes, these statutes may be revised such that they apply only to those who commit the most serious assault/weapons-linked felonies. It is likely that mandatory sentence enhancements will be softened. Drug-related enhanced sentencing provisions may prevail unless the tendency to identify drug use as a cause of crime moderates. The expansion of the adoption of determinate sentencing will moderate; however, statutes in place are likely to remain in place. While determinate sentences reflect the positivist perspective and are keyed to the crime rather than to the characteristics and needs of the offenders, determinate sentences do not prevent the application of treatment programs, particularly if the next shift to a treatment perspective focuses on community corrections as treatment.

REFERENCES AND BIBLIOGRAPHY

ALLEN, F. A. (1981). *The Decline of the Rehabilitative Ideal: Penal Policy and Social Purpose.* New Haven, CT: Yale University Press.

BARTOLLAS, J. S. (1980). Practitioner's attitudes toward the career criminal program. *Journal of Criminal Law and Criminology*, 71:113–117.

BATES, R. L. (1981). Search and seizure: The effect of unrecorded misdemeanor corrections on enhancement statutes. *American Journal of Trial Advocacy*, 4:739–760.

BENNETT, R. (1983). A favorable decision for recidivists facing life sentences without parole. *St. Louis University Law Journal*, 27:883–894.

BERNARD, T. J. (1992). *The Cycle of Juvenile Justice.* New York: Oxford University Press.

BLACKMORE, J., and J. WELSH (1983). Selective incapacitation: Sentencing according to risk. *Crime and Delinquency*, 29(4):505–527.

BLUMSTEIN, A., and J. KADANE (1983). An approach to the allocation of scarce imprisonment resources. *Crime and Delinquency*, 29(4):546–559.

BLUMSTEIN, A., and S. MOITRA (1980). The identification of career criminals from chronic offenders in a cohort. *Law and Policy Quarterly*, 2:321–334.

BONTICY, M. K. (1983). Proportionality review of recidivist sentencing. *DePaul Law Review*, 33:149–182.

BRAUCHI, R. (1983). From the wool sack: Inconsistencies in Supreme Court decisions on recidivists. *Colorado Law*, 12:1658–1659.

CARNEY, L. (1980). *Corrections: Treatment and Philosophy*. Upper Saddle River, NJ: Prentice Hall.

CLEMMER, D. (1958). *The Prison Community*. New York: Holt, Rinehart and Winston.

CONNOUR, W. F. (1982). Habitual offender issues. *Res Gestae*, 26:86.

CULLEN, F. T., and K. E. GILBERT (1982). *Reaffirming Rehabilitation*. Cincinnati, OH: Anderson Publishing.

CURRIE, E. (1985). *Confronting Crime*. New York: Pantheon Books.

DAVIS, W. L. (1982). Recent developments in persistent felony offender cases. *Kentucky Bench and Bar*, 46:10.

DUNFORD, O., and D. S. ELLIOTT (1984). Identifying career offenders using self-reported data. *Journal of Research in Crime and Delinquency*, 21:57–86.

DURKHEIM, E. (1965). *The Rules of the Sociological Method*. New York: Free Press.

FELDMAN, S. W. (1984). The habitual offender laws of Tennessee. *Memphis State University Law Review*, 14:293–335.

FLANAGAN, T. (1982). Correctional policy and the long-term prisoner. *Crime and Delinquency*, 28(1):82–95.

FLANAGAN, T. (1985). Sentence planning for long-term inmates. *Federal Probation*, 49(3):23–28.

FOGEL, D. (1978). *We Are the Living Proof*, 2nd ed. Cincinnati, OH: Anderson Publishing.

FORST, B. (1984). Selective incapacitation. *Judicature*, 68:153–160.

GARLAND, D. (1990). Frameworks of inquiry in the sociology of punishment. *British Journal of Sociology*, 41:1–15.

GOTTFREDSON, M., and T. HIRSCHI (1986). The true value of lambda would appear to be zero: An essay on career criminals, criminal careers, selective incapacitation, cohort studies, and related topics. *Criminology*, 24(2):213–233.

GRANT, I. (1985). Dangerous offenders. *Dalhousie Law Journal*, 9:347–382.

GREENWOOD, W. (1980). Career criminals presentation: Potential objectives. *Journal of Criminal Law and Criminology*, 71:85–88.

GREENWOOD, P., J. CHAIKEN, J. PETERSILIA, and M. PETERSON (1978). *The RAND Habitual Offender Project: A Summary*. Santa Monica, CA: RAND Corporation.

HARRIS, M. K. (1998). Exploring the implications of four sanctioning orientations for community corrections. *Federal Probation*, LXII(2):81–94.

HEADLEY, B. (1989). Introduction: Crime, justice, and powerless racial groups. *Social Justice*, 16(4):1–9.

HOCHBERGER, R. (1980). Justice bar recidivist sentence. *New York Law School Journal*, 83:1.

HOFFMAN, P. B., and J. L. BECK (1984). Burmont: Age at release from prison and recidivism. *Journal of Criminal Justice*, 12:617–623.

INCIARDI, J. (1986). *Criminal Justice*. New York: Harcourt Brace Jovanovich.

IRWIN, D. (1981). Sociological studies of the impact of long-term confinement. In D. Ward and K. F. Schoen (eds.), *Confinement in Maximum Custody*. Lexington, MA: Lexington Books.

JACKSON, F. (1984). Second-degree burglary held a serious felony. *Los Angeles Daily Journal*, 97:2.

JANUS, M. (1985). Selective incapacitation: Have we tried it? Does it work? *Journal of Criminal Justice*, 3:117–129.

KINDELL, L. R. (1983). Ohio adopts a mandatory sentencing measure. *University of Dayton Law Review*, 8:425–441.

KRAMER, R. C. (1982). From habitual offenders to career offenders: The historical construction and development of criminal categories. *Law and Human Behavior*, 6:273–293.

LANGAN, P., and L. GREENFELD (1983). *Career Patterns in Crime*. Washington, DC: U.S. Department of Justice, Bureau of Statistics.

LIZOTTE, A., and M. ZATZ (1986). The use and abuse of sentence enhancement for firearms offenses in California. *Law and Contemporary Problems*, 49(1):199–221.

LUTTRELL, M. (1991). The impact of the sentencing reform act on prison management. *Federal Probation*, 55(4):54–57.

MACKENZIE, D. L., G. S. TRACY, and G. WILLIAMS (1988). Incarceration rates and demographic change hypothesis. *Journal of Criminal Justice*, 16(3):212–253.

MALTZ, M. (1984). *Recidivism*. San Diego, CA: Academic Press.

MARSHALL, L. (1980). The constitutional infirmities of Indiana's habitual offender statute. *Indiana Law Review*, 13:597–626.

MCKELVEY, B. (1977). *American Prisons: A History of Good Intentions*. Montclair, NJ: Patterson Smith.

MONAHAN, J. (1981). Identifying chronic criminals. In D. Ward and K. F. Schoen (eds.), *Confinement in Maximum Custody*. NCJ-77087. Lexington, MA: D.C. Heath.

MORAN, T. J. (1982). Separation of powers and the Illinois habitual offender act: Who sentences the habitual criminals? *Loyola University of Chicago Law Journal*, 13:1033–1053.

MORRIS, N. (1951). *The Habitual Criminal*. Cambridge, MA: Harvard University Press.

MORRIS, W. (1983). Colorado's habitual criminal act: An overview. *Colorado Lawyer*, 12:215.

MUELLER, N. R. (1982). Attacking prior convictions in habitual criminal cases: Avoiding the third strike. *Colorado Lawyer*, 11:1225–1230.

PECK, D., and R. JONES (1981). The high cost of Alabama's habitual felony offender act: A preliminary assessment. *International Journal of Offender Therapy and Comparative Criminology*, 29(3):251–264.

PETERSILIA, J., P. HONIG, and C. HUBOY (1980). *Prison Experience of Career Criminals*. Washington, DC: U.S. Department of Justice.

PHILLIPS, J., and C. CARTWRIGHT (1980). The California career criminal prosecution program one year later. *Journal of Criminal Law and Criminology*, 71:107–112.

PINDUR, W., and S. P. LIPEC (1981). Prosecution of the habitual offender: An evaluation of the Portsmouth commonwealth's attorney major offender program. UNIVERSITY OF DETROIT JOURNAL OF URBAN LAW, 58:433–457.

RADZINOWICZ, L., and R. HOOD (1980). Incapacitating the habitual criminal: The English experience. *Michigan Law Review*, 78(3):1305.

RAFALOFF, J. (1988). The armed career criminal act: Sentence enhancement or new offense? *Fordham Law Review*, 56:1085–1099.

SHILTON, M. K. (1995, February). Community corrections acts may be Rx system needs. *Corrections Today*, 32:34–36, 66.

SHINNAR, E., and K. SHINNAR (1975). The effects of the criminal justice system on the control of crime: A qualitative approach. *Law and Society Review*, 23(4):547.

SHORE, J. M. (1984). An evaluation of Canada's dangerous offender legislation. *Les Cahiers Droit*, 25:411–426.

SMITH, A. B., and L. BERLIN (1988) *Treating the Criminal Offender*. New York: Plenum Press.

SORENSON, C. W. (1980). The habitual criminal act. *Nebraska Law Review*, 59:507–537.

SUPREME COURT (1980). Cruel and unusual punishment: Life sentences for repeated nonviolent felonies. *Harvard Law Review*, 94:87–96.

TENNENT, G., and C. WAY (1984). The English special hospital: A 12–17 year followup study. *Medical Science and Law*, 24:81–91.

U.S. DEPARTMENT OF JUSTICE (1983). *Setting Prison Terms*. Washington, DC: Bureau of Justice Statistics.

VAN DER WERFF, C. (1981). Recidivism and special deterrence. *British Journal of Criminology*, 21:136–147.

WEES, G. (1996). Inmate population expected to increase 43% by 2002. *Corrections Compendium*, April, pp. 1–4.

WEIMER, D. L. (1980). Vertical prosecution and career criminal bureaus: How many and who? *Journal of Criminal Justice*, 8:369–378.

WEST, D. J., and R. S. WRIGHT (1981). A note on long-term criminal careers. *British Journal of Criminology*, 21:375–376.

WILHEIM, M. G. (1982). Recidivist statutes. *Washington Law Review*, 57:573–598.

WILKINS, L. T. (1980). Problems with existing prediction studies and future research needs. *Journal of Criminal Law and Criminology*, 71:98–101.

WILKINS, W. JR., P. NEWTON, and J. STEER (1993). Competing sentencing policies in a "war on drugs" era. *Wake Forest Law Review*, 28:305–327.

WILLIAMS, K. M. (1980). Selection criteria for career criminal programs. *Journal of Criminology Law and Criminology*, 71:89–93.

WOLFGANG, M., M. FIGLIO, and T. SELLIN (1972). *Delinquency in a Birth Cohort*. Chicago: University of Chicago Press.

YOUNG, J. (1980). Constitutional law: Texas habitual offender statute. *American Journal of Criminal Law*, 8:209–216.

PART VII

Gender and Race Issues in the Twenty-First Century

No work in criminal justice is complete without referring to issues of gender and race. The twenty-first century is here, and still we talk about equality issues. We see both women and minorities struggling for changes to occur. Changes are still being advocated and we wait for the day (hopefully, not another century) when all members of the human race are treated as persons deserving of the same opportunities.

Today, women are being arrested at higher rates than ever before. Women also continue to be victims of crimes. Witness the continuing cases of domestic violence and rape, and witness those women who find themselves being sexually harassed. During this new century, it is incumbent upon all who have power to develop a strategy that will combat violence against all women and minorities. Roslyn Muraskin and Martin O'Connor discuss the discrimination that is ever present and the continuing need to develop policies to protect women. Discrimination still exists in the twenty-first century; an agenda for change needs to be developed. The acts of rape and domestic violence have drawn parallels with that of sexual harassment. The law has seen and treated women the way that men have viewed and treated women. Men who harass are not pathological but rather, people who exhibit behaviors that have been characteristic of the masculine gender role. Each year, women experience sexual harassment, yet cultural mythologies consistently blame the victim for sexual abuse and act to keep women in their place. Hopefully, in the twenty-first century, women will finally secure the same rights and opportunities afforded to men.

There are other challenges facing females, one of the most serious being the problem of incarcerated women who have HIV. Women are the fastest-growing infected group. Lanier, Braithwaite, and Arriola point out strides that have been realized with providing incarcerating populations who are HIV positive with proper health care. Institutionalized people are one of society's most ostracized groups. Like the leper colonies of the eighteenth century, today's correctional facilities tend to segregate from the rest of society the disempowered, the poor, drug users, and those who are violent. Victims of HIV and AIDS face considerable stigma and social isolation even when not incarcerated. Women who belong to these high-risk groups (drug users, economically disadvantaged, and women of color) are concentrated in correctional institutions. Current mandatory sentencing requirements and increased sentence lengths for drug offenders mean that more at-risk women will remain incarcerated.

Effective policies are very much needed in the twenty-first century. Policies that include community corrections and good educational and treatment programs are an absolute necessity.

Gender and race have been identified as perhaps the most consistent extralegal factors that influence criminal justice personnel and juries concerning offensive behaviors. The creation of laws denoting acceptable boundaries of behavior also establishes and maintains both an economic and a social hierarchy within society. Economically, this means that only certain people or organizations are able to participate in the exchange relationship for the production and distribution of goods and services. In our country, most meaningful economic opportunities have been blocked for women and minorities. The fact that gender difference is embedded in our structure, and thus influences not only our language but also the meanings associated with that language, suggests that the law itself must be structured to eliminate gender difference in its meaning. Race is a topic that many people feel uncomfortable discussing, but it touches every segment of society in numerous ways. The racial injustices encountered by minority groups affect society as a whole indirectly. Rights that we take for granted are only rights until new legislation is introduced to remove them. In the past we were led to believe that the removal of discretionary powers for particular offenses would solve the problems associated with discriminatory practices, but it has not. In this century we must be willing to examine and correct the way that we have seen racism influence law.

How do we envision the role of women in twenty-first century policing? Hale and Lanier describe how policing will change in this millennium with the expansion of private security, higher education requirements for police applicants, and changes in employment practices due to affirmative action policies and antidiscrimination legislation. Nearly 40 years have passed since women first gained entry into police patrol in the United States by Title VII of the Civil Rights Act of 1964. Policewomen have been placed on patrol, which has advanced policing from the reactive to the proactive stance now advocated. Crime prevention duties historically performed by policewomen will be performed by both female and male police officers in the twenty-first century. Because of the public's concern with increasing juvenile delinquency and the increase in adolescent drug and alcohol abuse, police officers will continue to provide more services directly related to the prevention of adolescence drug use and to process cases of juveniles involved in drug trafficking. Research over the past decades demonstrates that women are extremely effective as police officers. Women police have transformed police work. Several recommendations are made by Hale and Lanier to ensure police women's continued success in the twenty-first century. They conclude, as we all should, that women who currently serve as police officers must recognize that they would not have these jobs without Title VII of the Civil Rights Act of 1964.

chapter 23

Women and the Law

An Agenda for Change in the Twenty-First Century

Roslyn Muraskin, Ph.D. and Martin L. O'Connor, J.D.

ABSTRACT

The twenty-first century is here. The past several hundred years have seen women struggling for equality—struggling to help make changes occur. Today, we still advocate change. Change in the criminal justice system is part of the change needed.

Women are being arrested at higher rates than ever before, although males are still the predominant groups in correctional facilities. Women are also more the victims of crimes than ever before. Witness the cases of domestic violence, the cases of rape, and women who find themselves being sexually harassed. The contention is that the continuum of violence against women includes sexual harassment as well as domestic violence. As women gain more equality, they become harassed by employers in a manner that is akin to criminal violence. During this new century a strategy must be developed to combat all violence against women. The argument is made that while the public has slowly recognized the dynamics of rape and domestic violence, cases of sexual harassment need to taken seriously and dealt with seriously.

INTRODUCTION

Historically, women have been discriminated against by law. Women have, in fact, sometimes been victimized by policies designed to protect them. During the last decades, women have been especially strong in arguing for equality. The history of women's struggles has taught us that litigation is simply a catalyst for change. A change in attitude is still needed, discrimination still exists, and women continue to struggle. When Abigail Adams wrote to her husband, John, who helped to write the Constitution of the United States, she told him to "remember the ladies." The ladies still wish to be remembered. Controversy still abounds.

Women's issues still infuse every aspect of social and political thought. As early as 1913, Rebecca West stated: "I myself have never been able to find out precisely what feminism is. I only know that people call me a feminist whenever I express sentiments that differentiate me from a doormat." Women's basic human rights are inextricably linked to our treatment by and with their participation in today's political world. Due to the fact that the lives of women are reflections of what they do, what they say, and how they treat each other, women as participating members of the human race are ultimately responsible for human affairs.

What, then, is the agenda for change in the criminal law in the twenty-first century? There is no way to guarantee both men and women equal protection of the laws unless we are committed to the elimination of all gender discrimination. The criminal justice system over the years has slowly come to grips with an understanding of women and justice. In the twenty-first century, more and more cases are being heard and will be heard in the courts, where legal procedures and precedents have been established to ensure that complainants will receive a fairer hearing than envisioned previously. Courts need to allow time for discovery of evidence as well as the opportunity to hear expert testimony in cases of sexual violence.

The data continue to show that women are involved in the criminal justice system in numbers greater than before. Crimes such as rape, domestic violence, and sexual harassment are all part of the continuum of violence against women. Rape is not a crime of sex; it is a crime of power. It is "an act of violence, an assault like any other, not an expression of socially organized sexuality" (MacKinnon, 1979:218). The fact that rape is acted out in sex does not mean that it is an act of male sexuality. Rape is simply an act of violence. Think of the social construction of battering. "Take a moment and think about the image that comes to mind when you hear words like *domestic violence, spouse abuse, wife battering*, and *women battering*. Close your eyes and think about an assault between two adults who are in an intimate relationship. Visualize the events leading up to the assault and the event itself. Who is the perpetrator? Who is the victim? What is the context surrounding the assault?" (Eigenberg, 2001:15).

The acts of rape and domestic violence have drawn parallels with that of sexual harassment. If sex or sexual advances are unwanted, if they are imposed on a woman who is in no position to refuse, why is this act any different from rape or domestic violence? Some consider sexual harassment a lesser crime, and that itself is questionable, but it is, nevertheless, an act of violence against women. Both women and men spend the better part of their day at work. Sexual harassment is sexual discrimination and attention must be paid to these acts. In recent years there has been a current of public discussion about the cases of women accused and sometimes convicted of assaulting and killing partners who abuse them. The actual volume of these cases is relatively small, but the attention given the cases illuminates the larger problem for which they have come to stand: the common disparity of power between men and women in familial relationships. And now what about working relationships?

If a sexual crime is a crime of power, all these acts constitute the subordination of women to men. This continues the powerlessness in the criminal law of women as a gender. "If sexuality is set apart from gender, it will be a law unto itself" (MacKinnon, 1979:221).

HISTORY

The fact is that when this country was founded, it was founded on the two principles that (1) "all men are created equal" and that (2) "governments derive their powers from the consent of the governed." Women were not included in either concept. The Constitution of the United States did not include women as citizens or as person with legal rights. Women were not considered persons under the Fourteenth Amendment to the Constitution, which guaranteed that no state shall deny to "any person within its jurisdiction the equal protection of the laws." Remember the words of Justice Miller in the case of *Bradwell* v. *Illinois*: "The paramount destiny of women is to fulfill the noble and benign offices of wife and mother. This is the law of the Creator. And the rules of civil society must be adopted to the general constitution of things, and cannot be based upon exceptional cases" (Muraskin, 2000:9). Therefore, in the face of the law, women had no rights—women did not exist on a legal footing with men.

The women's movement was the most integrated and populist force in this country. More than 80 years later, after women won the right to vote, a right granted to women *after* the slaves were freed, women still wait for the promise of the Declaration of Independence, that of equality before and under the law.

There existed under the English common law the "rule of thumb," which allowed a husband to beat his wife with a whip or stick no wider than his thumb. The husband's prerogative was incorporated into the law of the United States. The sad fact is that several states had laws on the books that essentially allowed a man to beat his wife with no interference from the courts. Blackstone referred to this action as the "power of correction." For too many decades women have been victims of sexual assault. Each act of "sexual assault is recognized as one of the most traumatic and debilitating crimes for adults…" (Roberts, 1993:362). The victimization of women has been most prevalent and problematic for the criminal justice system. As pointed out by Susan Faludi (1991): Women's advances and retreats are generally described in military terms: battles won, battles lost, points and territory gained and surrendered. In times when feminism is at a low ebb, women assume the reactive role—privately and most often covertly struggling to assert themselves against the dominant cultural tide. But when feminism becomes the tide, the opposition doesn't simply go along with the reversal, it digs in its heels, brandishes its fists, builds wall and dams.

"Under the federal constitution and most state constitutions, women have not yet been raised to the status of constitutional protections enjoyed by males" (Thomas, 1991:95). Gender-neutral language does not solve the problem either. All such language does is to allow employers to hide the discrimination that is prevalent.

SEXUAL HARASSMENT

Women represent half of the national population. They are deserving of the same rights and opportunities as are afforded men. There exists the rhetoric of gender equality, but it has still to match the reality of women's experiences. The case of Anita Hill and Supreme Court Justice Clarence Thomas defined sexual harassment as occurring when unwelcome sexual advances, requests for sexual favors, and other verbal or physical conduct of a sexual nature are made a condition of employment, are used in employment decisions, affect an employee's work performance, or create an intimidating, hostile, or offensive working environment. The Supreme Court upheld these guidelines in 1986 in the case of *Meritor Savings Bank* v. *Vinson*, where it ruled that sexual harassment is sexual discrimination and illegal under Title VII of the Civil Rights Act of 1964.

As the law has been interpreted, prohibition against sexual harassment in the workplace includes any remark or behavior that is sufficiently severe or pervasive. In a typical "hostile environment" case, a victim suffers a number of sex-related inquiries, jokes, slurs, propositions, touching, or other forms of abuse. There exists no litmus paper test that can tell us whether a work environment is hostile or abusive. Courts look at the frequency and severity of the conduct, whether it is physically threatening or humiliating, and whether it interferes with an employee's work performance. Courts require that the victim show some proof of harm, but the victim of the harassment does not have to demonstrate psychological injury or show that he or she had a nervous breakdown in order to state a claim of sexual harassment (*Harris* v. *Forklift Systems, Inc.*, 1993).

An important issue regarding sexual harassment is whether the harassment should be measured from the viewpoint of the *reasonable woman* or *reasonable person* perspective. What some men may view as "horseplay," women may view as harassment. A 1991 ruling by the Court of Appeals for the Ninth Circuit held that the "appropriate perspective for judging a hostile environment claim is that of the 'reasonable woman.'" However, the United States Supreme Court in several cases has adopted and reiterated that harassment should be measured from the viewpoint of the "reasonable person" (*Harris* v *Forklife Systems, Inc.*, 1993; *Oncale* v. *Sundowner Offshore Services, Inc.*, 1998).

In 1997, the United States Supreme Court was faced with an interesting question regarding a sexual harassment lawsuit. Is it appropriate to sue for sexual harassment a sitting President of the United States? Lower federal courts decided that it would be inappropriate to sue the President for sexual harassment while still in office. The United States Supreme Court unanimously reversed and held that the lower courts abused their discretion in delaying the sexual harassment case. The Court said that the Federal District Court "...has jurisdiction to decide this...[sexual harassment]...case...[and]...like every other citizen who properly invokes that jurisdiction...[this plaintiff]...has a right to an orderly disposition of her claim..." (*Clinton* v. *Jones*, 1997). The Court, in effect, said that no matter what one's rank or station in life, if an appropriate claim of sexual harassment exists, an alleged victim of sexual harassment shall not have her or his day in court delayed simply because the alleged harasser is the President of the United States.

In regard to sexual harassment, a question that frequently arises is employer liability. It has not been uncommon for employers to adopt a "see no evil" defense. In short, some employers do little to prevent sexual harassment and then contend that they have a policy that forbids such harassment, so they are not liable for any harassment that may take place in the workplace. In *Faragher* v. *City of Boca Raton* (1998) and *Burlington Industries* v. *Ellerth* (1998), the Supreme Court made a very important ruling in regard to employer liability. In *Faragher*, Beth Ann Faragher worked as a part-time lifeguard and was severely and repeatedly harassed (lewd remarks, touching, etc.) by her lifeguard supervisors. She complained to a nonharassing supervisor, who told her "...the City doesn't care...." Although lower courts found the supervisors liable for harassment, the courts also found that the city was not liable since it had an antiharassment policy and did not know of the harassment. A main issue in the case that the lower courts seemed to ignore was that the city of Boca Raton did not disseminate its sexual harassment policy to the lifeguards or train its employees with respect to sexual harassment. One of the questions that arose was whether an employer can create an antiharassment policy, put it in a file, keep no track of the harassment activities of its employees, and then escape liability for sexual harassment by producing the policy when sued.

The Supreme Court in *Faragher* and *Ellerth* swiftly put a stop to this "see no evil" defense. The Court found that employers are liable whenever a supervisor's harassment culminates in an employment action such as a discharge, demotion, or undesirable assignment. In addition, the Court said that when no tangible employment action is taken, the employer is also liable for the harassment unless the employer can show that (1) the employer exercised reasonable care to prevent and correct promptly any sexually harassing behavior, and (2) the employee unreasonably failed to take advantage of preventive or corrective opportunities provided by the employer. In *Faragher*, since the city did not disseminate an appropriate sexual harassment policy to the beach employees and keep track of their conduct, the city failed to exercise reasonable care in preventing the supervisor's misconduct. In an extraordinary exercise of its power, the United States in *Faragher* not only reversed the lower court decisions, but also sent the case back to the district court with a directive that a judgment be entered in Faragher's favor. *Fargher* and *Ellerth* provide that employers cannot easily escape liability by saying "I did not know of the harassment." These cases make it clear that for an employer to avoid liability for sexual harassment, the employer must not only have in place a comprehensive sexual harassment policy, but must also communicate that policy to the workforce and train all its employees with respect to that policy. In addition, an employer must carefully monitor the work environment, adopt a zero-tolerance policy regarding sexual harassment, and take swift action to enforce the harassment policy where appropriate.

When Title VII was created, did Congress have only traditional notions of gender discrimination in mind (i.e., discrimination by men against women, and vice versa)? This issue has troubled the courts for some time because when Title VII was contemplated by Congress, the word *sex* was added to the bill on the floor of the House of Representatives at the last minute by opponents of the measure in an attempt to prevent its passage (110 Cong. Rec. 2577-84, 1964). Hence there is little legislative history to guide the courts in its interpretation of the word *sex*. Nevertheless, in *Oncale* v. *Sundowner Offshore Services, Inc.* (1998), the United States Supreme Court clearly answered this question. Joseph Oncale was sexually harassed by other men (sexually humiliated, assaulted in a sexual manner, and threatened with rape). The lower courts held that Title VII does not cover same-sex sexual harassment so it dismissed Oncale's sexual harassment claim. The Supreme Court in a unanimous opinion reversed that decision and said that nothing in Title VII precludes a same-sex sexual harassment claim.

Sexual harassment law is largely judge-made law, and some have expressed concern that the words and phrases used by the courts—"that the conduct must be severe or pervasive...that a reasonable person would find hostile or abusive..." are so vague that "...as a practical matter...[these decisions]...let unguided juries decide whether sex-related conduct engaged in by an employer is egregious enough to warrant damages..." This concern was raised by Justice Scalia in *Harris* v. *Forklift Systems, Inc.*, (1993) but he noted: "Be that as it may, I know of no alternative...." However, the real problem is not the words or phrases of the law of sexual harassment. Commonsense evaluations by judges and juries can distinguish between appropriate activity in a workplace and sexual harassment. Nevertheless, if sexual harassment is to be significantly reduced or eliminated, gender power balances in our society must be changed, and the values underlying the law of sexual harassment (equal treatment, nondiscrimination, and fair play) must be internalized by all who function in our workplaces.

THE NEED FOR A NATIONAL COMMITMENT TO END VIOLENCE AGAINST WOMEN

Addressing violence against women requires a national commitment and a national remedy. Toward this end, in the early 1990s, Congress began assembling a mountain of data about gender violence. A summary of this data was included in the dissenting opinion of Supreme Court Justice David Souter in *United States* v. *Morrisson*, (2000:1761–1763):

- Three out of four American women will be victims of violent crimes sometime during their lives.
- Violence is the leading cause of injuries to women ages 15 to 44.
- As many as 50% of homeless women and children are fleeing domestic violence.
- Since 1974, the assault rate against women has outstripped the rate for men by at least twice for some age groups and far more for others.
- Battering is the largest cause of injury to women in the United States.
- An estimated 4 million women in the United States seek medical assistance each year for injuries sustained from their husbands or other partners.
- Between 2000 and 4000 women die every year from domestic abuse.
- Arrest rates may be as low as 1 for every 100 domestic assaults.
- Partial estimates show that violent crime against women costs this country at least $3 billion a year.
- Estimates suggest that we spend $5 to $10 billion per year on health care, criminal justice, and other social costs of domestic violence.
- The incidence of rape rose four times as fast as the total national crime rate over the past 10 years.
- According to one study, close to one-half million females now in high school will be raped before they graduate.
- One hundred twenty-five thousand college women can expect to be raped during this or any year.
- Three-fourths of women never go to the movies alone after dark because of the fear of rape, and nearly 50% do not use public transit alone after dark for the same reasons.
- Forty-one percent of judges surveyed in a Colorado study believed that juries give sexual assault victims less credibility than other victims of crime.
- Less than 1% of rape victims have collected damages.
- An individual who commits rape has only 4 chances in a 100 of being arrested, prosecuted and found guilty of any offense.
- Almost one-fourth of convicted rapists never go to prison and another one-fourth received sentences in local jails, where the average sentence is 11 months.
- Almost 50% of rape victims lose their jobs or are forced to quit because of the crime's severity.
- The attorneys general from 38 states urged Congress to enact a civil rights remedy, permitting rape victims to sue their attackers because "the current system of dealing with violence is inadequate."

Based on this extensive data, which were collected over four years, Congress has found that crimes of violence motivated by gender have a substantial adverse effect on interstate commerce, by deterring potential victims from traveling interstate, from engaging in employment in interstate business...[and being]...involved in...[other]... interstate commerce..." (H.R. Conf. Rep., No. 103–711, 1994:385).

Because of its findings, Congress deemed it necessary to supplement the inadequate State remedies in combating gender violence by creating and passing the Violence Against Women Act (VAWA) in 1994. This Act attacked violence against women in several ways. First, it provided substantial sums of money to States for education, rape crisis hotlines, training criminal justice personnel, victim services, and special units in police and prosecutors' offices to deal with crimes against women. The Act specifically provided incentives for the enforcement of statutory rape laws, the payment of the cost of testing for sexually transmitted diseases for victims of crime, and studies of campus sexual assaults, and the battered women's syndrome. As a condition of receiving federal monies states would have to demonstrate greater efforts toward arresting and prosecuting domestic violence offenders. Several states changed and strengthened their domestic violence laws and moved from policies of arrest avoidance in domestic cases to mandatory arrest policies.

Second, criminal provisions of the VAWA provide that it is a federal offense to cross state lines with the intent of contacting a domestic partner when the contact leads to an act of violence. In addition, the Act also makes orders of protection enforceable from one state to another.

Third, the civil rights component of the Act permitted a victim of gender violence to sue his or her attacker and seek compensatory and punitive damages for a crime of violence motivated in part by gender animus. Victims of gender violence were thus empowered to bring lawsuits against their attackers even if the prosecutors were unwilling or unable to pursue a criminal action.

Finally, the Act was an important vehicle to raise the consciousness level of the nation to the problem of violence against women. The VAWA was not the millennium, but an important first step by our national government in its commitment to combat gender violence.

Shortly after the VAWA became law, it encountered a significant constitutional challenge. In the Fall of 1994, a young woman named Christy Brzonkala enrolled in college at Virginia Polytechnic Institute. Early in her freshman year, Christy alleged that she was gang raped by two other students named Crawford and Morrison who were also varsity football players. Subsequently, Christy reported the attack and became severely emotionally disturbed and depressed. She sought assistance from a University psychiatrist, was prescribed anti-depressant medication, stopped attending classes and eventually withdrew from the University. Neither man was ever charged with a crime.

The victim filed a complaint against Morrison and Crawford pursuant to University procedures. Virginia Tech held a hearing and Crawford produced an alibi witness who said that he left the room before any sexual activity occurred. Morrison admitted having sexual contact with Christy even though she had told him twice, "no." After a hearing, Morrison was suspended for two semesters. There was insufficient evidence to punish Crawford.

Subsequently, a University official set aside Morrison's punishment as being "excessive when compared to other cases…" The victim then became the first to file a lawsuit against her attacker and Virginia Tech under the newly created VAWA. Although the case began as a victim suing her alleged rapists, by the time the case reached the United States Supreme Court, some called the case a clash between feminism and federalism (*American Spectator*, Dec. 1999/Jan. 2000, v. 32, No. 12 pp. 60–61).

Unfortunately, under the concept of federalism (sharing of power between the state and federal government) the United States Supreme Court, by a narrow margin (5 to 4), ruled that Congress did not have the constitutional authority to create this federal civil remedy. Chief Justice Rehnquist writing for the majority said: "[I]f the allegations—[of rape by the football players]…are true, no civilized system of justice could fail to provide her a remedy for the conduct of respondent Morrison. But under our federal system that remedy must be provided by the Commonwealth of Virginia, and not by the United States…." Four justices disagreed. They contended that "…Congress has the power to legislate with regard to activity that in the aggregate has a substantial effect on interstate commerce…" The impact of the *Morrison* decision is that civil remedies designed to assist women who have been victims of violence will be balkanized. Women will have to seek legislative approval in communities throughout the United States so that they are authorized to bring lawsuits against their attackers for gender violence. In response to the *Morrison* decision, the city of New York became one of the first U.S. communities to create such a remedy for victims of gender violence.

The VAWA has been an important national vehicle in addressing the issue of violence against women. It is unfortunate that this important federal civil remedy relied on by the victim in *Morrison* has been ruled unconstitutional. Nevertheless, the other provisions of the act are still intact and billions of federal dollars will still flow to states over the next few years to support various provisions of the act. Violence against women still requires an urgent national response.

SUMMARY

The law has seen and treated women the way that men have viewed and treated women. Like the crime of rape, sexual harassment is not an issue of lust; it is an issue of power. Similarly, the crime of domestic violence is also one of power. In voluntary sexual relationships everyone should exercise freedom of choice in deciding whether to establish a close, intimate relationship. Such freedom of choice is absent in cases of sexual harassment. Similar to rape, incest, and battering, sexual harassment may be understood as an extreme acting out of qualities that are regarded as supermasculine: aggression, power, dominance, and force. Men who harass are not pathological but rather, people who exhibit behaviors that have been characteristic of the masculine gender role. Most sexual harassment starts at the subtle end of the continuum and escalates over time. Each year, women experience sexual harassment, yet cultural mythologies consistently blame the victim for sexual abuse and act to keep women in their place.

Women who speak about victims of sexual harassment use words such as *humiliating, intimidating, frightening, financially damaging, embarrassing, nerve-wracking, awful* and *frustrating*. These are not words that are used to describe a situation that one enjoys.

Historically, the rape of a woman was considered to be an infringement of the property rights of man. Sexual harassment is viewed in the same light. The message for this, the twenty-first century, is the recognition that changes are needed. We can no longer blame the messenger. We need to understand the message. There is no questions that what is referred to as "women's hidden occupational hazard," sexual harassment, is sexual victimization. The fact that sexual harassment exists demonstrates that it must be understood as part of the continuum of violence against women. In a typical sexual harassment case, the female accuser becomes the accused and the victim is twice victimized. This holds true in cases of rape, domestic violence, and cases of harassment. Underlying the dynamics of the situation is the profound distrust of the woman's word and a serious power differential between the accused and the accuser.

What actions are being taken? As noted in this chapter, more and more cases are coming to light. There is the understanding that conduct that many men consider unobjectionable may very well offend women.

AGENDA FOR CHANGE

Litigation is occurring. Although we do not have a federal equal rights amendment, there are states that recognize its potential worth. As an example, the use of male terms to indicate both sexes is slowly being examined. There are those who choose to use gender-neutral terms. Note the use of *reasonable person*. Words are meant to have definitive meaning. "Words are workhorses of law" (Thomas, 1991:116). Sexual harassment is a major barrier to women's professional and personal development and a traumatic force that disrupts and damages their personal lives. For ethnic-minority women who have been sexually harassed, economic vulnerability is paramount. Women feel powerless, not in control, afraid, not flattered by sexual harassment. As stated previously, women's basic human rights are inextricably linked to their treatment by and with their participation in today's political world.

As they did in the *Paula Jones* case, the courts need to continue to look at the totality of circumstances. One action where no evidence of extreme emotional distress exists cannot be construed to be an act of harassment regardless of the political atmosphere. Calling an act harassment simply because a person makes an accusation will not create the change that is needed.

What, then, is the agenda for change in this century? More needs to be done by elected officials, public policymakers, religious institutions, educational institutions, the criminal justice system, the media, and business and labor organizations. For justice to be gained, everyone must be concerned with the long arduous fight for freedom and equality for everyone. It was Gloria Steinem who noted that cultural myths die hard, especially if they are used to empower one part of the population. We must do whatever is necessary to fight oppression and alleviate repressive conditions wherever they exist. The struggle of women continues under the law. There is no way to allow both sexes automatically to enjoy equal protection of the laws unless we are committed to the elimination of all sexual discrimination. The criminal justice system over the years has slowly come to grips with the needed understanding of both women and justice. Recent Supreme Court cases have noted that sexual harassment as such creates a hostile environment that defies "a mathematically precise test," calling for an examination of all the circumstances of a case. In this new century more cases will be heard, and legal procedures and precedents will be established to ensure that complainants will receive a fairer hearing than before. For justice to be gained, everyone must be concerned with the long arduous fight for freedom and equality for everyone. Women's agenda is that by representing half the population, we must be willing to meet the challenge.

Women deserve the same rights and opportunities afforded men. There has existed/ does exist/will exist the rhetoric of gender equality (yesterday, today, and tomorrow), but it has yet to match the reality of women's experiences. The question remains: Are men ready? The twenty-first century is here; are we all ready to meet the challenges necessary for much needed change? In the words of Abigail Adams, "remember the ladies."

REFERENCES

EIGENBERG, H. M. (2001). *Woman Battering in the United States: Till Death Do Us Part.* Prospect Heights, IL: Waveland Press.

FALUDI, S. (1991). *Backlash: The Undeclared War against Women.* New York: Crown Publishers.

MACKINNON. C. A. (1979). *Sexual Harassment of Working Women.* New Haven, CT: Yale University Press.

MURASKIN, R. (2000). *It's a Crime: Women and Justice,* 2nd ed. Upper Saddle River, NJ: Prentice Hall.

ROBERTS. A. R. (1993). Women: Victims of sexual assault and violence. In R. Muraskin and T. R. Alleman (eds), *It's a Crime: Women and Justice.* Upper Saddle River, NJ: Prentice Hall.

THOMAS, C. S. (1991). *Sex Discrimination.* St. Paul, MN: West Publishing

CASES

Bradwell v. *Illinois,* 83 U.S. 130 (1872).

Burlington Industries v. *Ellerth,* 524 U.S. 742 (1998).

Clinton v. *Jones,* 520 U.S. 681 (1997).

Faragher v. *City of Boca Raton*, 542 U.S. 775 (1998).

Harris v. *Forklift Systems, Inc.*, 510 U.S. 17 (1993).

Meritor v. *Savings Bank, FSB* v. *Vinson*, 4777 U.S. 57, 106 S. Ct. 2399, 91 L.Ed.2d. 49 (1986), 239.

Oncale v. *Sundowner Offshore Services, Inc.*, 523 U.S. 75 (1998).

United States v. *Morrison*, 120 S. Ct. 1740 (2000).

chapter 24

New Directions for Incarcerated Women with HIV in the Twenty-First Century

The Corrections Demonstration Project

Mark M. Lanier, Ph.D., Ronald L. Braithwaite, Ph.D.,
and Kimberly R. Jacob Arriola, Ph.D.

ABSTRACT

In this chapter we review the challenges facing female HIV-positive offenders and outline the latest research and policy programs. Although most research attention has been directed toward male inmates, incarcerated women, like women not under custodial care, are the fastest-growing infected group. We therefore outline factors driving the increased threat to women. Demographic, epidemiological, and social determinants are discussed. Futhermore, unique problems faced by women are presented. A theoretical discussion provides suggestions for effective interventions. Over the past few years tremendous strides have been realized in providing incarcerated populations who are HIV positive with health care. However, a glaring deficiency has been postrelease treatment. A new initiative funded by the Centers for Disease Control (CDC) and the Health Resources and Services Administration (HRSA) is addressing that problem. That initiative, the Corrections Demonstration Project (CDP), a longitudinal, multistate, multijurisdiction program that seeks to rectify that omission, is described in the conclusion.

INTRODUCTION

Institutionalized persons are one of society's most ostracized groups. Much like leper colonies of the eighteenth century, today's "correctional" facilities segregate from the rest of society the disempowered, the poor, drug users, and the violent. Also like leper colonies, inhabitants of these institutions face serious medical threats. Contemporary threats include acquired immunodeficiency virus (AIDS), hepatitis, human immuno-deficiency virus (HIV), and tuberculosis. Unlike leper colonies, however, most of the inhabitants of modern penal colonies will one day reenter society—some infected with serious, contagious diseases, and many unarmed with knowledge about the disease and prevention.

Like lepers, in addition to physical separation, the stigma associated with insti-tutionalization further isolates the incarcerated from "mainstream" society. Victims of HIV and AIDS also face considerable stigma and social isolation even when not incarcerated. In addition, in our society women and people of color have a history of being marginalized and of being disempowered by sexism and racism. When any person is a member of each of these groups simultaneously, the psychological and physical pressures are immense. Women who belong to these high-risk groups (drug users, economically disadvantaged, and women of color) are concentrated in correctional institutions.

Medical researchers have the formidable task of identifying a vaccine that prevents the spread of HIV and treatments that improve the longevity and quality of life for those already infected. Social scientists have the task of developing theory, which can be used to guide policy initiatives that slow the spread of HIV. Recently, medical breakthroughs have started to increase the length of life for AIDS patients, but a cure or vaccine remains an enigma. Social scientists have also had mixed results: AIDS cases are decreasing among certain high-risk groups but are rapidly increasing among heterosexual women and people of color (indicating that gender- and ethnic-specific theoretical guides are needed). AIDS and HIV continue to spread through all societal groups. If current trends continue, the number of incarcerated Americans will increase, victims of HIV/AIDS will multiply, and the burdens faced by correctional systems will intensify [Centers for Disease Control (CDC), 1991a]. In short, the cost in physical, emotional, and fiscal terms will escalate as we enter the twenty-first century unless effective theoretically driven and culturally appropriate policies are implemented now.

The following discussion concentrates on incarcerated populations with a special focus on women. This population was selected for several reasons. First, high-risk groups are concentrated in correctional facilities, affording correctional administrators an ideal opportunity to positively influence the at-risk behaviors of this captive group (Lanier and McCarthy, 1989). Second, heterosexual females comprise the largest-growing group to be HIV infected. Third, women who are under correctional supervision have been seriously neglected by researchers and in the AIDS literature (Altice et al., 1998). We agree with Young and McHale's statement that "the problem of the HIV positive woman prisoner is something that it is to be hoped will soon be the subject of more detailed research" (1992:89).

In this chapter we describe the current problems facing these women and provide a theoretical model which if used to shape correctional policy could reduce the occurrence of HIV and decrease the stigma suffered by those already infected. The policy suggestions would make humane treatment more normative for those incarcerated and for those returning to mainstream society. Finally, a recent study designed to provide a link between correctional systems and community health care is described as an illustrative example of theory and research in practice. Despite the focus on incarcerated women, the treatment information, theoretical model, and policy suggestions (e.g., the Corrections Demonstration Project) presented are applicable with any at-risk incarcerated group.

WOMEN WITH HIV AND AIDS

AIDS is the third-leading cause of death among all U.S. women between the ages of 25 and 44. AIDS is the leading cause of death among African-American women, and it is the fifth-leading cause of death for white women between 25 and 44 years of age (Legg, 1996; MMWR, 1996). Despite these alarming numbers, relatively few women are currently infected compared to men. As of December 31, 1999, the Centers for Disease Control (CDC) reported that 124,045 of the 733,374 Americans with AIDS were female (CDC, 1999).

The largest identified risk factors for women are intravenous drug use and sexual activity with male drug injectors. Thirty-four percent ($N = 15,464$ in 1999) of the known HIV-positive women contracted the disease as the result of injecting drugs (CDC, 1999). This is alarming when considering that many women in our society inject drugs. It has been estimated that as many as 500,000 women use intravenous drugs in the United States (Wofsky, 1987). Forty percent ($N = 4281$ in 1999 and 47,946 cumulative) of the women with HIV were infected through heterosexual contact. Only 1% ($N = 119$) in 1999 and 3% ($N = 3668$) cumulative have been infected through blood transfusions, and 32% in 1999 had unknown, or unreported, causes of infection (CDC, 1999).

AIDS IN CORRECTIONAL FACILITIES

AIDS has already been identified as the leading cause of death in some correctional facilities (New York State Commission of Corrections, 1986; CDC, 1989). In fact, "the number of AIDS-related deaths in prison has increased 84% since 1991, making AIDS the fastest rising cause of State inmate deaths" (U.S. Department of Justice, 1996: 5). As the number of cases of HIV and AIDS continues to rise across the country, more correctional systems can expect AIDS to be become a major source of inmate demise. It is also suggested as being an increasing reason for litigation (Anderson et al., 1998). The exact number of incarcerated persons who are HIV positive is unknown (Hammett, 1988). However, some estimations that can be made based on the research suggest that between 1 and 19% are HIV positive.

In one study from 430 correctional facilities that reported the results of HIV antibody testing in 1991 (42 states, the District of Columbia, and Puerto Rico) 65,724 inmates were HIV positive (Anon., 1992). At year end in 1994, 2.3% of the 999,693 state and federal prison inmates were infected with the HIV virus (U.S. Department of Justice, 1996). In state prisons, 21,749 inmates were HIV positive (2.5% of the total) and in federal prisons, 964 or 1.1 percent (U.S. Department of Justice, 1996:1). Of all inmates in U.S. prisons, 4489 (0.5%) had confirmed AIDS and 17,480 were HIV positive. More recent data show that this has increased since 1994 to 28,249 inmates with HIV (Bureau of Justice Statistics [BJS], 1995:552, 600).

In Massachusetts it has been reported that around 5% of the 735 females who elected to have an AIDS antibody test in 1993 were HIV positive, compared to just 2% of the male inmates (Hammett et.al., 1995:16). In 1994, the HIV seroprevalence rate for state inmates ranged from 0.2 to 20.1% for women (U.S. Department of Justice, 1996:6). The rate for women surpassed that of male inmates, who had rates from 0.1 to 12.0% (U.S. Department of Justice, 1996:6). Overall, the rate for female inmates was 3.9% while it was 2.4% for male inmates. Interestingly, unlike men (who had higher rates among inmates over 25 years old) age was not a predictive factor with female inmates (Vlahov et al., 1991:1130). It is apparent that many incarcerated women have AIDS, a significant number are HIV positive, and many more are at risk.

Incarcerated Women

Nationwide, there are approximately 864,900 females who are under correctional supervision and who are held in secured facilities (BJS, 1996). Most of these women are held in state and federal correctional institutions. There has been an explosion in the number of women sentenced to these facilities since 1984 (BJS, 1996:554). From 1984 to 1994, the number of females sentenced increased from 19,205 per year to 60,069 (BJS, 1996:556). There has been a correspondingly large increase in the number of women detained in jails. In 1988 there were 28,187 women incarcerated in jails, while by 1993 the number had increased to 44,600 (BJS, 1996:549). The tremendous increases have been caused by new drug policies (Brewer et al., 1998). If these trends continue, a significantly higher number of women will be under correctional supervision in this century.

Most of the men and women who are incarcerated in correctional facilities are parents and many have used "serious" drugs (Center on Addiction and Substance Abuse, 1998). More than three-fourths of all women in prisons in 1991 had children, and two-thirds had children under the age of 18 (BJS, 1994). Also, in 1991, 36.5% used cocaine or crack and 14.8% had used heroin (BJS, 1994b:622). Thus, many incarcerated mothers are at risk for HIV infection. Reasons for the disproportionate number of infected female inmates are presented next.

UNIQUE PROBLEMS

Incarcerated women and prison officials face many problems related to HIV. For infected women (and men) the sophistication and availability of medical care is suspect in some systems. For administrators, the medical expenses associated with caring for HIV inmates are high. For example, New Jersey prison authorities report that the average cost associated with caring for an infected inmate (from diagnosis to death) was $67,000 and that the average length of hospitalization was 102 days. However, this amount is considerably lower than the $140,000 and 160 days of hospitalization that was estimated for the first 100,000 nonincarcerated AIDS patients (Anon., 1986). One source found that correctional budgets have been overwhelmed by the cost of new treatments, which have sent the annual expense of treating an HIV-infected patient from about $2000 to as much as $13,000 (Purdy, 1997). The state of Florida spends over $6.7 million a year for the care of inmates with HIV (Anon., 1994).

Medical Problems

Biological factors give women a disproportionately high probability of contracting HIV, and consequently, AIDS, compared to men with similar risk behaviors. Women who are most likely to become infected come from socially and economically deprived groups. Therefore, they may also receive inferior medical treatment. Thus, greater risk coupled with insufficient medical care places women at increased risk of premature death due to AIDS.

According to the findings of several studies, gender-specific diseases also have implications that are more serious for women who are HIV positive. One study found that among women suffering from cervical cancer, those who were HIV positive had a median of 10 months until death, compared to a median of 23 months for women who were HIV negative (Maiman et al., 1990). It has also been shown that gynecological infections develop much more rapidly in women who are HIV positive (Minkoff and DeHovitz, 1991). For example, pelvic inflammatory disease (PID) progresses more rapidly in women who are HIV positive. HIV-positive women also appear to have a large number of infections with vaginal candidiasis (Rhoads et al., 1987). The Centers for Disease Control (CDC) reported that for HIV-infected women, "the prevalence of cervical dysplasia on Papanicolaou (Pap) smear for HIV positive women was eight to eleven times greater than the prevalence of dysplasia for women residing in the respective communities" (CDC, 1991b:23). Finally, it has also been suggested that, "seropositive women with herpes infection might shed virus more frequently than women not infected with HIV and thereby pose an increased risk of HIV transmission to sexual partners" (Minkoff and DeHovitz, 1991:2254).

Compounding Medical Problems

There are also factors that increase both the threat and severity of HIV infection in correctional facilities. Related diseases are also increasing in correctional health systems.

Tuberculosis

Of the diseases closely related to HIV infection that are increasing in correctional facilities, the most prevalent is tuberculosis (TB). According to the editors of the *Journal of the American Medical Association*, "[t]he recent emergence of multi-drug-resistant

TB (tuberculosis) as an important opportunistic infection of HIV infected people underscores the need for secondary HIV-prevention services in correctional facilities. Persons in correctional institutions are at increased risk for TB because of high prevalence of HIV infection and latent TB, overcrowding, poor ventilation, and the frequent transfer of inmates within and between institutions" (1993:23).

After being controlled for over 40 years, TB is once again posing a major health threat. According to Dixie Snider of the CDC, "[a]t no time in recent history has tuberculosis been as much concern as it is now, and legitimately so, because tuberculosis is out of control in this country" (Altman, 1992). A particularly dangerous strain, resistant to standard antituberculosis drugs (isoniazid, rifampin, and streptomycin), has been identified in 16 states. The recent outbreaks of TB primarily involve HIV-positive persons. However, since TB is spread through airborne droplets, others are also at risk. Close, prolonged contact (such as is found in correctional facilities) increases risk of infection. In one case, it was reported that more than 50 health care workers were infected from a single patient, although none have yet developed TB (Altman, 1992). However, like HIV, TB can remain dormant for years. Healthy persons can harbor the TB bacillus for years without being ill. For these reasons, and due to the concentrations of high-risk individuals found in correctional facilities, some medical experts are arguing for centering detection and treatment efforts among the incarcerated (DiFerdinando, in Altman, 1992).

There are also indications that as a group, incarcerated women have more health problems than male prisoners (Waring and Smith, 1990:5). Concerns with gynecological care are also unique to female populations.

Contraceptive Devices

Among all the reported cases of AIDS among women, 80% occurred in women in the childbearing years (ages 15 to 44). Of these, 20% are between the ages of 20 and 29, and many were probably infected while teenagers (CDC, 1999). Thus, safe contraceptive devices are a relevant concern for women.

Women who are HIV positive cannot take it for granted that the use of common contraceptive methods is safe for either the woman or her sexual partners. First, Minkoff and DeHovitz stated that, "[t] here are several reasons to be cautious about the use of intrauterine devices….they may render the woman more infectious….The woman herself might be rendered more susceptible to ascending infections and hence PID" (1991:2255). Second, oral contraceptives have also generated theoretical debate as to whether or not they alter the natural course of HIV disease among women (Grossman, 1984; Minkoff and DeHovitz, 1991). Finally, research is lacking on the effect of microbiocides.

Psychological Stress

Compared to other infected groups, women who are infected with HIV or AIDS face increased psychological pressures. For example, many economically disadvantaged women are also the primary, and often sole, caretakers for their dependent children.

Others are thus financially and emotionally dependent on them. When these women have HIV/AIDS, they also have the concern of caring for others while often ill themselves. Incarceration forces a separation and additional stress for the woman, who must now rely on others or the state to care for her dependents.

Social Stigmata

Groups that are most highly represented among those HIV infected already belong to highly stigmatized groups—women of color and intravenous drug users (Richardson, 1988). While women of color comprise 23% of all the women in the United States (Bureau of the Census, 1995) more than three-fourths (77%) of female AIDS cases are among African Americans and Hispanics, and rates for African Americans and Hispanic women are 16 and 7 times higher, respectively, than those for white women (CDC, 1995b). According to Wiener, "[h]istorically, these women have been tangled in a web of poverty, illness, and oppression; by the dictates of racism and poverty, they are disempowered, disenfranchised, and alienated from traditional sources of help and support" (1991). Young and McHale added that "HIV infection makes visible and explicit the hidden and implicit links between conceptions of disease and criminality. Both are seen as (symbolically or literally) life-threatening. The HIV positive prisoner is a deadly icon of a psychosocial malaise" (1992:90). Others have also articulated how societal sexism, racism, and classism have affected public perceptions of HIV and women (Anastos and Marte, 1989; Marte and Anastos, 1990). McKenzie (1989) argued that HIV-positive women's legal rights have also been neglected.

Self-efficacy

Most theoretical models addressing risk reduction practices have included self-efficacy as a central component. Several factors (drug and alcohol use, poverty, cultural norms, gender roles, and sexuality issues) have been identified as decreasing women's self-efficacy (Wermuth et al., 1991:132). Also according to Wermuth et al., "[w]hen individuals believe they can exercise control over actions and situations that might pose a risk for HIV infection, they are more likely to exercise that control (Bandura, 1989). However, the extent to which this holds true for individuals with less actual control over their material and relational world's remains to be learned. For example, Mondanaro (1987) points out that women at greatest risk for AIDS are those with the least amount of control over their lives" (1991:133–134). Of all women in our society, those who are incarcerated probably have the least control over their lives. Thus, the thesis that lack of control results in decreased self-efficacy would be more consequential for incarcerated women.

Finally, women who are HIV positive may also not enjoy the widespread and organized support that gay men have. When current or past incarceration is also present, stigma may intensify, and with current practices, support may decrease.

In summary, gender influences social, biological, and treatment consequences of AIDS (Minkoff and DeHovitz, 1991). So far, an overview of the demographics, behaviors, and problems facing incarcerated women has been presented. In the next section, treatment options are reviewed. Theoretical guides that may prove useful for slowing the spread of HIV among women, policy recommendations, and an illustrative program conclude the chapter.

HIV/AIDS MEDICAL TREATMENT

On a positive note, medical advances have greatly increased the longevity of AIDS patients. This trend should continue. A complete cure or preventive vaccine remains elusive, however. The latest treatment regimes are presented in this section.

Most of the HIV treatment regimens include two components. The first involves the use of prophylactic drugs to prevent and treat opportunistic infections. The second component is the use of antiviral drugs to reduce replication of the virus (Linsk, 1997). Most recent increases in life span have been due to advances in prophylactic drugs (Linsk, 1997:70). For example, substantial progress has been made in developing and testing drugs to prevent the many otherwise fatal opportunistic infections caused by bacteria, fungi, protozoa, or other viruses in people with HIV-weakened immune systems (Cooper, 1996:160). The most vivid examples are a variety of treatments that prevent *Pneumocystis carinii* pneumonia (PCP). These treatments range from a simple dose of a sulfa drug to complex management using aerosolized pentamidine (Linsk, 1997:70).

The most successful treatment innovation to combat HIV and AIDS is the "cocktail" approach (Anon., 1997). Previously people with AIDS had only one drug option: zidovudine (AZT). There are at least nine separate drug combinations that can work in more than 100 different combinations (Leland, 1996:64). The first clinical trials of these combination drugs (reverse transcriptase inhibitors) were shown to have benefits, including prolonged survival and fewer "AIDS-defining events," when given to asymptomatic individuals with relatively early-stage disease, compared to AZT alone (Fauci, 1996). AZT in combination with other reverse transcriptase drugs, such as didanosine (ddI) and zalcitabine (ddC), has been found to be greatly superior to AZT treatment alone (Cooper, 1996:160).

Following these medical breakthroughs came improvements in the capability of protease inhibitors to block virus replication (Fauci, 1996:276). Use of this new class of drugs in combination with first-generation reverse transcriptase inhibitors holds great promise for improved control of HIV and AIDS (Fauci, 1996:276). The greatest gains have been made by using different combinations of drugs that attack HIV at different stages of its replication process (Markowitz, 1996). Reverse transcriptase inhibitors disrupt the HIV enzyme soon after HIV infects a cell—much earlier than when protease inhibitors are involved (Markowitz, 1996:2). Consequently, survival and delay of AIDS progression are significantly improved among those patients receiving combination therapy [U.S. Department of Health and Human Services (U.S. DHHS), 1997]. Combination therapy with ritonavir (a protease inhibitor) plus two reverse transcriptase inhibitors (such as AZT and ddC) is significantly more effective than reverse transcriptase inhibitors alone (Voelker, 1996:436; U.S. DHHS, 1997:1). With these types of treatments, AIDS-related illnesses (including opportunistic infections and cancers) and deaths have decreased (U.S. DHHS, 1997:2).

Advances in combination therapy and the introduction of protease inhibitors have permitted sustained suppression of plasma viral load to undetectable levels in patients in various clinical trials (St. Louis et al., 1997). These findings make plausible the possibility of substantially improving the survival and quality of life of HIV-infected persons through chemotherapy (St. Louis et al., 1997:10). Consequently, medical personnel are starting to consider HIV to be a chronic, manageable disease rather than a death sentence (Leland, 1996:64). This means not only fewer deaths but also more people living with HIV and AIDS.

Because of these advances, many people with HIV are living longer and have more productive lives than 10 years ago; however, the vast majority still eventually succumb to the disease (Cooper, 1996:160). Consequently, rather than quickly succumbing to illnesses such as *Pneumocystis carinii* pneumonia (PCP), patients suffer from what is commonly referred to as *wasting syndrome* (severe weight loss, chronic diarrhea, and fever) or from the more difficult-to-treat opportunistic infections, such as *Mycobacterium avium* complex (MAC) or cytomegalovirus (CMV) (Cooper, 1996:160).

To date, these antiviral drugs have been tested largely on white males. Thus, little information is available regarding possible gender or ethnic differences in the efficacy, or toxicity, of antiviral medication (Leland, 1996; Kloser, 1997). Differences between the response of women and men to some treatments may be attributed to differences in size, body fat, and hormonal environments (Kelly, 1995). Additionally, women of childbearing age must be monitored carefully for pregnancy so that appropriate management can take place early in a pregnancy (Kloser, 1997:180).

If racial and ethnicity differences in the efficacy of AIDS-related drugs are found, questions can be anticipated that ask if the differences truly derive from race or ethnicity, or if they derive from differences in standard of living and access to health care experienced by different racial/ethnic groups (Kelly, 1995:52). For example, African-American and Latino patients generally have more advanced HIV disease when they begin taking medication (Kelly, 1995). In this situation, the use of antiviral medication has often been less effective.

It has been estimated that 90% of the world's population of HIV patients cannot access the more effective, and expensive, treatments (Voelker, 1996:435). Thus for many, the new drugs and treatment modalities remain illusive (Leland, 1996). What does this mean for HIV-positive inmates and correctional administrators?

HIV/AIDS Treatment in Prison

Prison environments are not the ideal location for AIDS patients (Leland, 1996:67) although correctional settings provide an improvement over the health environment in which some HIV-positive offenders would otherwise reside (Braithwaite et al., 1996). Prisoners with AIDS become sick at twice the speed of those on the outside (Hope and Hayes, 1995:12). In addition, among prison populations there is a greater likelihood that a person's HIV status is unknown, and it is this group of patients (the unknowing) who are most likely to come in too late for effective treatment (Anon., 1997). Moreover, efforts to treat HIV and AIDS within prisons have been severely hampered by uneven medical care and a short supply of the promising new treatments described here (Purdy, 1997). For example, while the drugs AZT (zidovudine) and bactrim (for *Pneumocystis carinii* pneumonia prophylaxis) have been available in most correctional systems, other treatments widely used among nonprisoners with HIV, such as pentamidine, ddI, and ddC, and combinations therapies are much less available (Stein and Headley 1996:4). Some prison systems are following old treatment protocols that do not take advantage of the new drugs, especially protease inhibitors (Purdy, 1997:1). More important, resistance to AZT is almost certain to develop when given the monotherapy (one drug at a time) commonly used in prison settings (Markowitz, 1996:4). Despite these obstacles, correctional settings provide much needed data and give many inmates access to medication and counseling that they otherwise would not receive (Braithwaite et al., 1996).

The quality of treatment also varies from prison to prison and state to state, often depending on whether court actions have forced improved medical care (Purdy, 1997:28). Courts have mandated that prisons must meet community standards (Braithwaite et al., 1996). Some prison systems (currently, very few) continue to put HIV-positive prisoners in isolation or special units, depriving them of limited programs and recreational opportunities available to other inmates (Berkman, 1995:1618). Other correctional systems do not permit prisoners to participate in clinical studies, denying them the potential benefits of promising new treatment approaches (Stein and Headley, 1996:3). In addition, now that treating HIV and AIDS is becoming as complex as treating cancer, with drugs and dosages carefully calibrated to each patient's medical condition, specialists are required. Unfortunately, many infected inmates are being treated by primary-care doctors and see a specialist only occasionally, if at all (Purdy, 1997:1). AIDS care should be delivered by the best medical care providers possible, not those lacking specialization (Voelker, 1996:438). Dr. Altice of Yale Medical School, who treats inmates in Connecticut's prisons, stated that "[p]rison doctors around the country are not trained specialists. We used to say that AIDS treatment is primary care. This is no longer true. We would no more have the average primary care provider deliver chemotherapy to cancer patients, than we would have the same people provide complex HIV treatment" (cited in Purdy, 1997:28).

An additional concern is the fact that the recent combination therapies require incredibly demanding regimens (Leland, 1996:69). Some drugs have to be taken with food, others on an empty stomach (Leland, 1996:69). Most correctional systems are crowded and must operate on a strict timeline, making this type of specialized care difficult and often impossible.

Finally, the organization of health care systems within prisons operates according to a "sick-call model." In other words, they respond to discrete and immediate health problems (e.g., injuries, specific illnesses) (Smith and Dailard, 1994). Systems designed in such a way lack the flexibility that HIV-positive inmates require.

Just to provide one illustration, consider the fact that since inmates are not trusted with the responsibility of controlling their own medication, prisoners who require medication on a regular basis must follow a rigorous procedure. AIDS patients who are incarcerated will require this medical attention several times a day. Concerns have also been raised because inmates going to the medical dispensary numerous times daily to receive medication pose a security risk (Purdy, 1997:28). Consequently, correctional medical staff may have difficulty accepting or understanding the need for the large number of pills required or the frequency with which they must be administered (Kelly, 1995:67). As a result, prisoners often miss doses of medication (Smith and Dailard, 1994:82), thus interfering with adherence to the treatment regime.

When patients divert from the required medical regimen, they risk cultivating a strain of the virus that is resistant to one or more of the drugs (Leland, 1996:69). These drug-resistant viruses threaten the general and prison public health as well as that of the HIV-infected patient. This growing concern is illustrated by the increasing spread of multidrug-resistant tuberculosis (Linsk, 1997:70). Therefore, adherence to drug regimens is critically important (Purdy, 1997:28) despite the difficulty imposed on correctional administrators.

Making sure that inmates get uniform care is a problem not only when they are released, but also when they move from one prison to another. A prisoner's medical records may fail to follow her as she moves through the prison system, and prison health care providers rarely coordinate treatments with community-based physicians once a prisoner is released (Smith and Dailard, 1994:82). Continuity of care is critically important to prisoners with HIV, but the concerns and realities presented here make it difficult to provide consistent treatment (Smith and Dailard, 1994:82).

As we enter the next century, treatment of HIV and AIDS patients will improve. The lives of those infected will increase in length and quality. At the same time, the complexity of treatment and the expenses associated with these treatments will severely test even the best-funded correctional systems (Solomon et al., 1989). Systems experiencing financial burdens will be hard pressed to provide effective treatment. To date, the medical community is still uncertain about the ethnic and gender effects of the newest treatment protocols. This situation will soon be remedied; however, should differences be found, the complexities facing correctional administrators will increase geometrically. In addition to considering medical care, prevention should be of paramount concern since HIV-positive people living longer could lead to increased infections. In the next section we review promising theoretical models that may meet prevention needs.

THEORETICAL MODELS

Lacking a cure or preventive vaccine, slowing further spread of HIV among women in correctional facilities is urgent. However, the most commonly used theoretical models have difficulty encompassing the needs and experiences of women of color, those most likely to be found in correctional facilities. Commonly used theories (Feldman and Johnson, 1986) to develop AIDS interventions are the AIDS Risk Reduction Model (ARRM) (Catania et al., 1990), Social Cognitive Theory (Bandura, 1994), and models founded on the Health Belief Model (Becker, 1974; Maiman and Becker, 1974; Rosenstock, 1974; Rosenstock et al., 1988). Unfortunately, several problems are evident with these models (Lanier and Gates, 1996; Wingood and DiClemente, 1997) which result in their unsuitability for use with those most likely to be incarcerated. These models fail to consider the contextual issues of rationality, psychosocial issues, class, gender, or ethnicity (Cochran and Mays, 1993).

Each of the theoretical models is based on the concept of rationality. Concerning the ARRM, Lanier and Gates noted: "[T]he ARRM is based on assumptions concerning the rationality of human behavior....Concerning possibly hedonistic adolescents, such a cost/benefit analysis may have little relevance. This may be especially true when faced with the prospect of immediate sexual and/or drug-induced gratification, opposed to the remote possibility of contracting a disease that may not manifest symptoms for several years" (1996:540).

These theories also focus on decision making as being individualistic. Gasch et al. (1991) noted that African-American women are more likely to focus on family and community norms when making decisions. Another psychosexual variable focuses on the concept of power and control. Findings show that women in heterosexual relationships are more psychologically, economically, and socially dependent on the male (Kelley and Thibaut, 1978; Wingood and DiClemente, 1997). Thus, the male yields power over the female and this presumably affects sexual negotiations (e.g., using condoms) (Wingood et al., 1993). Indeed, research has found males to refuse using condoms against his female partners' wishes (Wingood and DiClemente, 1997).

The models also fail to consider the effect of socioeconomic factors. Income differentially affects women of color because they are less likely to finish high school and more likely to have extremely low household incomes (Diaz et al., 1994). In fact, when the rates of HIV/AIDS are adjusted for socioeconomic factors, analyses reveal that the incidence is higher in areas having lower income as compared to those areas with higher incomes (Morse et al., 1991; Fife and Mode, 1992). Among women who acquired AIDS through heterosexual contact, over 80% of the African-American women have incomes under $10,000 compared to under half (49%) of the white women (Wingood and DiClemente, 1997). Wingood and DiClemente added that taking precautions against HIV/AIDS might be complicated by the immediate concern of caring for their families (1997).

Finally, each of the theoretical models also fails to consider the influence of gender and ethnicity. Models that fail to account for these variables are problematic. For one thing, "gender-blind models" assume "static" sex roles and may neglect social processes that could influence risk reduction strategies (Wingood and DiClemente, 1995). What is needed are gender and culturally sensitive theoretical models.

One promising theoretical guide is the "theory of gender and power" (Connell, 1987). According to Gold (1984), most epidemiological research defines *gender* based on biological sex rather than gender differences, which are not just biological but also result from "prevailing socially defined societal norms that dictate appropriate sexual conduct" (Wingood and DiClemente, 1997). The theory of gender and power moves beyond this rudimentary classification by addressing social norms that influence sexual behavior; further, it considers power differentials in relationships, although only in a male/female classification. Incarcerated women are also in a subordinate position due to their incarceration.

The theory of gender and power considers the division of labor, the structure of power, and the structure of cathexis. This theory is particularly useful for explaining why economically disadvantaged minority women (those found most often in prison) are more likely to have HIV (Wingood and DiClemente, 1997). First, the sexual division of labor—the preponderance of unpaid work associated with housework and childcare, coupled with inequalities in education and wages—explain why socioeconomic factors influence African-American women's greater vulnerability to HIV. The women, and her children, are economically dependent on the better paid male partner. Second, power differentials between the genders contribute to greater exposure since the "stronger" partner holds authority and coercive power. Wingood and DiClemente (1997) illustrated this by describing sexual politics which limit (and more commonly deny) accessibility of condoms in schools, lack of efforts devoted to development of a device to protect women from HIV, and norms supporting male control over condom use. Finally, the structure of cathexis characterizes the erotic and affective influences in sexual relationships. It provides an explanation for why many women are passive in demanding safe sex, since they are more focused on securing basic living accessories for themselves and family from the more economically secure male, who may not desire to practice safe sex. This also explains how the sex ratio in the African-American community favors the male, since there fewer males are available (due to premature death, incarceration, etc.), which further weakens the woman's "bargaining" position.

The theory of power and gender is useful for explaining why economically disadvantaged racial- and ethnic-minority women face greater risk; it is less useful for providing methods of behavior change. It can provide a basis for HIV prevention policies directed at incarcerated women (discussed next) which also include models for behavior change.

POLICY RECOMMENDATIONS

Incarcerated women face a myriad of social, economic, psychological, and medical problems. Infection and the threat of infection with HIV and AIDS create additional stress. Obviously, sane, humane, and realistic care of women infected with HIV is necessary. However, it is also critical that effective preventive programs implemented and evaluated (Gaiter and Doll, 1998; Hammett et al., 1998). Due to the vast diversity found among incarcerated women, no single strategy can be considered effective. A combination of case management, individual counseling, group sessions, role playing, and constant reinforcement while incarcerated needs to be supplemented with post-release treatment. This constellation of strategies may prove effective with women under correctional supervision. The eclectic approach suggested here should be based on a theoretical model that incorporates power and gender (such as the theory of gender and power).

Case Management

A comprehensive strategy would take a case management approach toward prevention and treatment. Each woman would be assigned to a treatment or educational program based on her unique past experiences and practices. For example, commercial sex working females could be grouped with similar women for individual counseling and group sessions. Experts who are sensitive to each woman's history and (perceived) degree of rationality should devise the specific program. Social Justice for Women has suggested than an interdisciplinary group comprised of clinicians, psychologists, department of corrections employees, parole workers, and others be used to collaborate on "medical management, psychosocial services, family counseling, discharge planning,...[and] early consideration for parole" (Waring and Smith, 1990). Such a team-centered approach would be more likely to address the sometimes-overlapping problems facing these women comprehensively and congruently.

Counseling

Both group and individual sessions should be used for educational purposes. Groups sessions have shown some value (Valdiserri et al., 1987) and peer-led sessions have great potential. Incarcerated women who are seen as positive role models by other inmates should be recruited and enticed to lead the group sessions. Peer-led sessions may be more effective with inmates since they may resist the educational efforts of correctional officials. Groups should be formed based on the experiences of each inmate. For example, bakers or bikers should be grouped together so that they can relate and share common past risky experiences and jointly develop resistance devices unique to their culture. In part, this grouping based on prior experiences will help identify and perhaps improve existing social networks.

Role-playing should be a major component (e.g., teaching female commercial sex workers how to demand that customers and sexual partners use condoms). The group leaders and those who develop the program should base it on proven theoretical models. It must be stressed that such programs should be rigorously evaluated by neutral outside observers.

Health Services

Health services for incarcerated women show great potential. For example, some women who are incarcerated may not have been able to take advantage of comprehensive health services (dental, gynecological, etc.) prior to incarceration. (One goal of health educators within the correctional setting should be to make inmates aware of community services that are available upon their release.) Correctional institutions should conduct mandatory HIV screening at intake (commonly done in many correctional systems) and at six-month intervals for the first 18 months of incarceration (a less frequent practice).

All women's facilities should also have HIV treatment facilities where the latest drug therapy is provided on a timely basis. It is not improbable that many incarcerated women would also volunteer to participate with testing new HIV and AIDS drugs prior to FDA approval (see Young and McHale, 1992, for further discussion of this).

Postrelease Services

Virtually all incarcerated women are eventually released back into the community. Being cognizant of their rights after parole, they should be strongly encouraged to continue participation in counseling sessions, drug therapy, and whatever AIDS/HIV prevention and/or treatment program that was devised for them while under correctional supervision. Many incarcerated persons could also be monitored with alternative means of control such as community corrections.

Alternative Sanctions (Community Corrections)

Since most women are not incarcerated for violent offenses, and since women's sentences are typically much shorter than men's (BJS, 1990), perhaps it would be more humane and cost-effective for women who develop symptomatic AIDS to be supervised in community corrections. Community corrections offer several benefits. For one thing, community health care services are available. Young and McHale noted that "...A considerable difference does exist in both choice and standard of care in relation to prisoners with HIV....A HIV positive patient has a far wider choice of care outside prison...he [sic] may seek psychotherapeutic care and counseling to bring him to terms with the fact that he has AIDS or is HIV positive. If he has the means, he may also obtain care from 'alternative' medical practitioners..." (1992:97). Courts have also recognized this fact. At least one prisoner with AIDS was ordered released from a federal prison because he could not receive adequate medical care (Young and McHale, 1992). More support groups also exist in the community. Despite the potential negative influences, family and friends would be available to assist women physically, financially, and emotionally.

McCarthy (personal correspondence August 12, 1997) cited four additional factors that should be considered. First, community corrections should be used increasingly for humanitarian reasons. For one thing, the mortality rate is higher among incarcerated persons. Second, from a managerial perspective, community corrections solve many potential problems. One issue facing correctional administrators is whether or not to segregate HIV-infected individuals; only a few systems still do so (Braithwaite et al., 1996). Inmate violence against those infected is a related problem. In addition, detention personnel have been found to be uncomfortable supervising HIV-positive offenders (Lurigio, 1989). Community corrections eliminates each of these administrative concerns for inmates who do not pose a threat of violence to community members, and again, most women are incarcerated for nonviolent offenses.

Third, monetary concerns should be considered. Prisons are designed to be punitive institutions. They are not hospitals. Thus, care for critically ill inmates' demands replicating services that are already available through the health care sector. Many institutions cannot afford expensive drugs needed to fight AIDS (such as azdothymidine [AZT] and cocktail combinations). The National Institute of Justice (NIJ) has found that many inmates who are eligible for AZT and who need it are not receiving it while incarcerated (Young and McHale, 1992).

Finally, community corrections are preferable for infectious reasons. TB and other infectious diseases are becoming an increasing problem in close-custody correctional institutions. "The circumstances and conditions in custody, including overcrowding and lack of privacy, may foster high risk behaviors such as unprotected anal sex, drug injecting, tattooing; and self-injury with consequent blood-spillage" (Dolan et al., 1990). It is also much more likely for inmates who would otherwise be heterosexual to engage in homosexual activity (often called "prison homosexuality") while incarcerated. Since condoms are often not provided to inmates, this behavior is even more risky. Incarcerated HIV and AIDS patients thus pose additional problems for other inmates and staff (see McCarthy and McCarthy, 1997, for additional information on community corrections).

Many of the difficulties described above are being addressed in one federally funded program. This iniative is described next.

RESEARCH INITIATIVES

One promising new initiative is the federally funded HIV in Corrections Demonstration Project (CDP). The Centers for Disease Control (CDC) and Prevention and the Health Resources and Services Administration (HRSA) have selected six state public health departments—California, Florida, Georgia, Massachusetts, New Jersey, and New York, and the Chicago Department of Health—to collaborate with state and local departments of corrections and community-based organizations to implement programs promoting continuity of care for HIV-positive and at-risk inmates and recent releasees from correctional facilities. Racial, ethnic, and linguistic minorities and women are the primary focus of the CDP, as these groups are overrepresented in corrections and/or heavily affected by the HIV epidemic. The goals of this initiative are to (1) increase access to HIV/AIDS primary health care and prevention services, (2) improve HIV transitional services between correctional facilities and the community, and (3) develop organizational supports and networks of comprehensive HIV health and social services. To determine the extent to which these goals are met, a comprehensive research evaluation effort has also been funded that is conducted simultaneously with the projects.

The Health Services and Resources Administration funded the Rollins School of Public Health (RSPH) of Emory University as an Evaluation and Program Support Center (EPSC) to conduct a multisite evaluation of the grantees' activities. Abt Associates serves as a subcontractor to RSPH on this project but functions as an equal partner in the implementation of the EPSC. Each of the seven grantees has allocated resources to state-level evaluators who oversee data collection and serve as liaisons between the project staff and the EPSC. For example, in Florida, the program is funded through the Department of Health and is titled Linking Inmates Needing Care (LINC). The evaluation team consists of one or two people representing each state grantee, the EPSC, and members from two organizations that have been funded to provide technical assistance. The state-level evaluators may be housed in universities, public health departments, and research organizations devoted exclusively to research and /or policy issues. This eclectic group of researchers, who have very diverse educational and practical backgrounds, has worked continuously with the EPSC to develop a research strategy that will evaluate the effectiveness of their programs. The entire research team has met via conference call, site visits, and grantee meetings for the past year.

The CDP is being implemented in county jails, state prisons, juvenile detention facilities, and Offices of Community Corrections (a system that is unique to Massachusetts) within the seven states. All states have programs in at least two of these settings, and some states will offer services in all four. There are four core program types, at least two of which are offered in each state. These are (1) facility-based HIV treatment and discharge planning with follow-up case management or prevention case management in the community for HIV-infected or high-risk clients; (2) facility-based infectious disease screening (HIV, STD, TB, and hepatitis), (3) facility-based HIV prevention and peer education programs; and (4) staff training for corrections and community providers. The following sections describe the multisite evaluation approach that the EPSC is taking with the seven projects.

The EPSC has opted to take a matrix evaluation approach. This involves varying levels of participation in the selected evaluation components. Not all grantees are responsible for contributing client-level data to all aspects of the cross-site evaluation. Instead, all grantees contribute to aspects of the cross-site evaluation, depending on what service components (HIV/AIDS treatment/case management/discharge planning constellation, HIV/AIDS prevention, disease screening, staff training) they devoted the most resources to and in which setting (prisons, jails, juvenile facilities) these components are being implemented. Grantees are collecting aggregate data for all services that they are providing. However, for service components on which grantees are placing a greater emphasis, client-level data are being requested instead. The EPSC will then generate program-level data based on this information. The grantees have provided full endorsement of this approach to the cross-site evaluation and are now in the process of collecting the data that they will contribute to the cross-site evaluation.

Aggregate data are being requested from the grantees on a quarterly basis; the client-level data forms are being requested bimonthly. Considerable time has been spent refining the five client-level data forms so that they are not only user friendly but also capture information that is valid and reliable. Thus, these forms have undergone extensive revision, particularly the baseline and follow-up interviews. The purpose of the five client-level data forms is to determine to what extent clients are engaged successfully in case management, which seeks to help them to get into key services, such as HIV and other medical care, mental health and substance abuse treatment, housing, benefits, and employment. Although the program goals extend beyond meeting these needs, they make up the primary focus of the evaluation. Case managers also want to help clients integrate into society, connect with their families, and reduce their risk of transmitting HIV. Each of the forms that were developed to capture the service components that were presented previously is described briefly.

The baseline interview (Form 1) is conducted by the case manager inside the correctional facility during one of the first three sessions and gathers information about the client on which key services he or she was connected to before incarceration. The questions about drug and alcohol use serve as an indication of the client's ability to engage in care and make appointments. The questions about corrections will allow evaluators to look at the success of the program in the context of the client's offense, as well as to assess the effectiveness of the program for clients who have been incarcerated for more or less time. The interview is not a needs assessment, nor is it meant to substitute for a psychosocial assessment.

The form that captures significant client contacts in the facility (Form 2) is completed by the corrections case manager and is completed each time the client sees the case manager or another relevant staff person. The case manager completes this after each client contact. The form documents the level of effort required on the part of the case manager to develop the discharge plan in the correctional environment.

Form 3, the status at release form, gathers basic data about the client at release. This is completed by the case manager after the client is released. In addition to the discharge plan itself, which outlines specific appointments, general referrals, and areas where no linkages were made or necessary, this covers information on the release data, whether the client was released with medications, and if the client is expected to receive postrelease services. Some of the areas covered may not be a component of every grantee's program, which is fine. Grantees will not be judged on services that they do not intend to provide.

The postrelease services/status form, Form 4, is intended to take a "snapshot" of the client every 30 days after release, for as long as he or she is receiving services. This form is completed by the case manager every 30 days after the client has been released from the facility. The case manager reports the client's status on the key services and also completes a form tabulating the date and duration of each contact and indicates the general nature of the session. For the first 30-day period, there is a special set of questions to be answered regarding the extent to which the client followed up on the discharge plan completed at release.

A staff person who is not the client's primary case manager conducts the follow-up interview (Form 5) in the community after release. This can be another staff person at the agency/CBO or an independent interviewer. The interview takes place either three months after the last formal client contact with the program or six months after release, whichever comes first. If the client does not receive services in the community after release, the interview should be conducted three months after release. The content and purpose of this interview mirrors that of the baseline interview.

The discharge planning/case management aggregate data form (Form 6) is completed only if client-level data are not being collected on clients from the given facility. There is no need for project staff to complete this form if client-level data are being collected. The purpose of this form is to report the number of clients receiving services through the program inside facilities and in the community. In addition, the form tabulates the number of clients receiving basic discharge planning services.

The HIV prevention/education programs form (Form 7) captures, in aggregate form, all grant-funded single and multiple-session HIV prevention programs conducted in jails, prisons, juvenile facilities, and Office of Community Corrections programs. This form is not intended for use with informal HIV prevention activities; every prevention message conveyed by a grant-funded staff person is not being captured by this form. Instead, the purpose of this form is to measure the dose of HIV prevention services the grantees are offering, the utilization of peer educators, the language appropriateness of the sessions that are offered, and the demographic characteristics of the participants.

Form 8, the peer educator training process data report, captures information concerning who is being trained under the peer education programs. It gathers specific demographic information (i.e., gender, ethnicity, race, and primary language), the number of peers recruited, and the number who actually complete training. The purpose of this form is to examine the extent to which the people being trained accurately reflect the population demographic characteristics of those being served.

Form 9, the disease screening aggregate data form, is intended to capture the extent to which facilities are engaging in enhanced disease screening as a result of this funding. This form captures the proportion of people who test positive for a range of infectious diseases, including HIV, TB infection, syphilis, and chlamydia. This form also captures the type of follow-up care that clients received after being tested, such as posttest counseling, partner notification services, and treatment. Importantly, this form captures the demographic characteristics of the people who are undergoing screening, to verify that those who are screened represent the target populations.

Finally, form 10 captures information about the type and intensity of staff training that is offered and utilized. This form also allows grantees to report the types of staff members who are undergoing training and the titles of the sessions that are conducted. The purpose of this form is to document the staff training that is funded by this grant and conducted for medical, correctional, and community-based staff.

Although obviously not an experimental design, this program and evaluation are a major step toward improving the health care of HIV-positive individuals. Equally important, the educational component of the same program will help retard the spread of HIV.

SUMMARY AND CONCLUSIONS

Administrators of correctional facilities are going to face increasing problems related to HIV and AIDS. More women than men will develop AIDS since women are more likely to be infected than to infect men (European Study on Heterosexual Transmission of HIV, 1992; Padian et al., 1991). Between 1980 and 1994, the number of incarcerated women increased 386% (Edna McConnell Foundation, 1995). If current incarceration trends continue, women are also going to be incarcerated at greater rates in this century. As more incarcerated women with HIV develop symptomatic AIDS, correctional health care costs will rise dramatically. The current climate of tax reduction is likely to persist, forcing consideration of community-based corrections for economic reasons. The expense and complexity with the recent treatment modalities also favor a community-based approach for HIV positive inmates. Elimination of duplicated government services (specifically, public health care and correctional health care) will further add to the impetus for increasing the use of community sanctions. Current mandatory sentencing requirements and increased sentence lengths for drug offenders mean that more at-risk women will remain under correctional supervision for longer periods of time (Lanier and Miller, 1995). From a medical viewpoint, these resultant overcrowded conditions are not conducive to effective treatment or prevention for those uninfected, further supporting community-based options for HIV positive women. The burdens on correctional officers, inmates, medical staff and society will geometrically increase during the twenty-first century unless effective policies are implemented. Correctional administrators must therefore seriously and rigorously engage in HIV educational and treatment programs. Community corrections should be one increasingly used option. LINC and the state initiatives funded through CDP provide unique comprehensive efforts that seek to link incarcerated HIV positive inmates with community care providers in an effort to improve health and decrease the spread of HIV. On another positive note, correctional administrators are in an excellent position, through programs like CDP and LINC, to reach one high-risk group and thus help slow the spread of HIV among the general population.

ACKNOWLEDGMENTS

The Florida Department of Health, Bureau of HIV/AIDS (contract C0AW4), and the Duval County Health Department (contract DV127) not only supported this research with funding but also provided encouragement and expertise.

REFERENCES

ALTICE, F. L., F. MOSTASHIRI, P. A. SELWYN, P. J. CHECKO, R. SIGHN, S. TANGUAY, and E. A. BLANCHETTE (1998). Predictors of HIV infection among newly sentenced male prisoners. *Journal of Acquired Immune Deficiency Syndrome Human Retroviral*, 18:444–453.

ALTMAN, L. K. (1992). Deadly strain of tuberculosis is spreading fast, U.S. finds. *Themes of the Times: Sociology*. New York Times. Upper Saddle River, NJ: Prentice Hall.

ANASTOS, K., and C. MARTE (1989). Women: The missing persons in the AIDS epidemic. *Health/PAC Bulletin*, 19(4)6–13.

ANDERSON, J. F., J. BURNS, and L. DYSON (1998). Could an increase in AIDS cases among incarcerated populations mean more legal liabilities for correctional administrators? *Journal of Crime and Justice*, 21(1)41–52.

ANON. (1986). Prisons confront dilemma of inmates with AIDS. *Journal of the American Medical Association*, 255(8):2399–2404.

ANON. (1992). HIV prevention in U.S. correctional system, 1991. *Journal of the American Medical Association*, 268(1):23.

ANON. (1994). Program developed for AIDS infected inmates. *States Legislatures*, 20(1):7–8.

ANON. (1997). Policy prescription for HIV. *American Medical News*, April 28.

BANDURA, A. (1994). Social cognitive theory and exercise of control over HIV infection. In DiClemente and Peterson (eds.), *Preventing AIDS: Theories and Methods of Behavioral Intentions*. New York: Plenum Press, pp. 25–54.

BECKER, M. (1974). The Health Belief Model and personal health behavior. *Health Education Monographs*, 2:220–243.

BERKMAN, A. (1995). Prison health: The breaking point. *American Journal of Public Health*, 85(12)1616–1618.

BRAITHWAITE, R., T. HAMMETT, and R. MAYBERRY (1996). *Prisons and AIDS: A Public Health Challenge*. San Francisco: Jossey-Bass.

BREWER, V. E., J. W. MARQUART, and J. L. MULLINS (1998). Female drug offenders: HIV-related risk behavior, self-perceptions and public health interpretations. *Criminal Justice and Policy Review*, 9(2):185–208.

BUREAU OF JUSTICE STATISTICS (1994a). *Women in Prison*. March. Annapolis Junction, MD: Bureau of Justice Statistics Clearinghouse, March.

BUREAU OF JUSTICE STATISTICS (1994b). *Sourcebook of Criminal Justice Statistics, 1991*. Washington, DC: U.S. Department of Justice.

BUREAU OF JUSTICE STATISTICS (1995). *Sourcebook of Criminal Justice Statistics, 1994*. Washington, DC: U.S. Department of Justice.

BUREAU OF JUSTICE STATISTICS (1996). *Sourcebook of Criminal Justice Statistics, 1995*. Washington, DC: U.S. Department of Justice.

BUREAU OF THE CENSUS (1995). *Women in the United States*. Washington, DC: Bureau of the Census, August.

CATANIA, J., S. KEGELES, and T. COATES (1990). Toward an understanding of risk behavior: An AIDS risk-reduction model. *Health Education Quarterly*, 17:53–92.

CENTER ON ADDICTION AND SUBSTANCE ABUSE (1998). *Behind Bars: Substance Abuse and America's Prison Population*. New York: CASA.

CENTERS FOR DISEASE CONTROL (1989). Florida: AIDS primary cause of death in prison. *CDC Weekly*, 2:7.

CENTERS FOR DISEASE CONTROL (1991a). AIDS in women: United States. *Morbidity and Mortality Weekly Report (MMWR)*, 265(1)23–24.

CENTERS FOR DISEASE CONTROL (1991b). Risk for cervical disease in HIV-infected women, New York City. *Morbidity and Mortality Weekly Report*, 265(1):23–24.

CENTERS FOR DISEASE CONTROL (1995a). AIDS associated with injecting-drug use, United States, 1995. *Morbidity and Mortality Weekly Report (MMWR)*, 45(19):392–398.

CENTERS FOR DISEASE CONTROL (1995b). Update: AIDS among women, United States 1994. *Morbidity and Mortality Weekly Report*, 44(5):81–84.

CENTERS FOR DISEASE CONTROL (1996a). *Morbidity and Mortality Weekly Report*, Vol. 8, No. 2.

CENTERS FOR DISEASE CONTROL (1996b). *HIV/AIDS Surveillance: Year-End Edition*. Atlanta, GA: Centers for Disease Control.

CENTERS FOR DISEASE CONTROL (1999). *HIV/AIDS Surveillance Report*, 11:2, December.

CLEARY, P., T. ROGERS, E. SINGER, J. AVORN, N. VAN DEVANTER, S. PERRY, and J. PINDYCK (1986). Health education about AIDS among seropositive blood donors. *Health Education Quarterly*, 13:317–329.

COCHRAN, S. D., and V. M. MAYS (1993). Applying social psychological models to predicting HIV-related sexual risk behaviors among African Americans. *Journal of Black Psychology*, 19:142–154.

CONNELL, R. W. (1987). *Gender and Power: Society, the Person and Sexual Politics*. Stanford, CA: Stanford University Press.

COOPER, E. C. (1996). Treatment of HIV disease: Problems, progress, and potential. In J. M. Mann and D. J. M. Tarantola, (eds.), AIDS *in the World II*. New York: Oxford, University Press, pp. 159–164.

DIAZ, T., S. Y. CHU, J. W. BUEHLER, et al. (1994). Sociodemographic differences among people with AIDS: Results from a multistate surveillance project. *American Journal of Preventive Medicine*, 10:217–222.

DOLAN, K., M. DONOGHOE, and G. STIMSON (1990). Drug injecting and syringe sharing in custody and in the community: An exploratory survey of HIV risk behavior. *Howard Journal*, 29(3):177–186.

EDNA MCCONNELL FOUNDATION (1995). *Seeking Justice: Crime and Punishment in America*. New York: The Foundation.

FAUCI, A. (1996). Much accomplished, much to do. *Journal of the American Medical Association*, 276:155–156.

FELDMAN, D. A., and T. M. JOHNSON (1986). *The Social Dimensions of AIDS: Method and Theory*. Westport, CT: Praeger.

FIFE, D., and C. MODE (1992). AIDS incidence and income. *Journal of Acquired Immunodeficiency Syndrome*, 5:1105–1110.

GAITER, J., and L. DOLL (1998). Improving HIV/AIDS prevention in prisons is good public health policy (editorial). *American Journal of Public Health*, 86: 1201–1203.

GASCH (1991).

GROSSMAN, C. (1984). Possible underlying mechanisms of sexual dimorphism in the immune response: Act and hypothesis. *Journal of Steroid Biochemistry*, 34:241–251.

HAMMETT, T. (1988). *AIDS in Correctional Facilities: Issues and Options*. Bureau of Justice Statistics Report. Washington, DC: National Institute of Justice.

HAMMETT, T. R. WIDOM, J. EPSTEIN, M. GROSS, S. SITRE, and T. ENOS (1995). *1994 Update: HIV/AIDS and STDs in Correctional Facilities*. Washington, DC: U.S. Department of Justice.

HAMMETT, T., J. GAITER, and C. CRAWFORD (1998). Reaching seriously at-risk populations: Health interventions in criminal correctional facilities. *Health Education and Behavior*, 25:99–120.

HOPE, T., and P. HAYES (1995). A clear pattern of neglect: Prisons and the HIV crisis. *Gay Community News*, 20(4)12–15.

KELLEY, H. H., and J. W. TRIBAUT (1978). *Interpersonal Relations: A Theory of Interdependence*. New York: Wiley.

KELLY, E. (1995). Expanding prisoners' access to AIDS-related clinical trials: An ethical and clinical imperative. *Prison Journal*, 75(1)48–69.

KLOSER, P. (1997). Primary care of women with HIV disease. Pp. 177–191. In D. Cotton and D. H. Watts (eds.), *The Medical Management of AIDS in Women*. New York: Wiley.

LANIER, M., and S. GATES (1996). An empirical assessment of the AIDS Risk Reduction Model (ARRM) employing ordered probit analyses. *Journal of Criminal Justice*, 24(6):537–547.

LANIER, M., and B. R. MCCARTHY (1989). AIDS awareness and the impact of AIDS education in juvenile corrections. *Criminal Justice and Behavior*, 16(4):395–411.

LANIER, M., and C. MILLER (1995). Attitudes and practices of federal probation officers toward pre-plea/trial investigative report policy. *Crime and Delinquency*, 41(3):364–377.

LEGG, J. L. (1996). HIV testing in women: A growing worry. *Patient Care*, 30(9)147–158.

LELAND, J. (1996). The end of AIDS? The plague continues, especially for the uninsured, but new drugs offer hope for living. *Newsweek*, 128(23)64–71.

LINSK, N. L. (1997). Of magic bullets and social justice: emerging challenges of recent advances in AIDS treatment. *Health and Social Work*, 22(1):70–75.

LURIGIO, A. (1989). Practitioner's views on AIDS in probation and detention. *Federal Probation*, 53(4):16–24.

MAIMAN, L., and M. BECKER (1974). The Health Belief Model: Origins and correlates in psychological theory. *Health Education Monographs*, 2(4):337–353.

MARKOWITZ, M. (1996). Booklet. Protease inhibitors. AEGIS: International Association of Physicians in AIDS care.

MARTE, C., and K. ANASTOS (1990). Women: The missing persons in the AIDS epidemic: Part II. *Health/PAC Bulletin*, 20(1):11–18.

MCCARTHY, B. R., and B. J. MCCARTHY (1997). *Community-Based Corrections*, 3rd ed. Pacific Grove, CA: Brooks/Cole.

MCKENZIE, N. (1989). The changing face of the AIDS epidemic. *Health/PAC Bulletin*, 19(4):3–5.

MINKOFF, H., and DEHOVITZ (1991). Care of women infected with the human immunodeficiency virus. *Journal of the American Medical Association*, 226:2253–2258.

MORSE, D. L., L. LESSNER, M. G. MEDVESKY, D. M. GLEBATIS, and L. F. NOVICK (1991). Geographic distribution of newborn HIV seroprevalence in relation to four sociodemographic variables. *American Journal of Public Health*, 81:25–29.

NEW YORK STATE COMMISSION OF CORRECTIONS (1986). *Acquired Immunodeficiency Syndrome: A Demographic profile of New York State Mortalities 1982–1985*. Albany, NY: The Commission.

PADIAN, N. S., C. SHIBOSKI, N., and P. JEWELL (1991). Female-to-male transmission of human immunodeficiency virus. *Journal of the American Medical Association*, 266:1664–1667.

PURDY, M. (1997). As AIDS increases behind bars, costs dim promise of new drugs. *New York Times*, 146, p. A 1.

RHOADS, J. L., C. WRIGHTS, R. R. REDFIELD, and D. S. BURKE (1987). Chronic vaginal candidiasis in women with human immunodeficiency virus infection. *Journal of the American Medical Association*, 257:3105–3107.

RICHARDSON, D. (1988). *Women and AIDS*. New York: Methuen.

ROSENSTOCK, I. (1974). The Health Belief Model and preventive health behavior. *Health Education Monographs*, 2(4):355–386.

ROSENSTOCK, I., V. STRECHER, and M. BECKER (1988). Social learning theory and the Health Belief Model. *Health Education Quarterly*, 15(2):175–183.

SMITH, B., and C. DAILARD (1994). Female prisoners and AIDS: On the margins of public health and social justice. *AIDS and Public Policy Journal*, 9(2):78–85.

SOLOMON, D., A. HOGAN, R. BOUKNIGHT, and C. SOLOMON (1989). Analysis of Michigan Medicaid costs to treat HIV infection. *Public Health Reports*, 105(5):416–424.

ST. LOUIS, M. E., J. N. WASSERHEIT, and H. D. GAYLE (1997). January. Editorial: Janus considers the HIV pandemic—Harnessing recent advances to enhance AIDS prevention. *American Journal of Public Health*, 87(1):10–13.

STEIN, G. L., and L. D. HEADLEY (1996). Forum on prisoners' access to clinical trials: Summary of recommendations. *AIDS and Public Policy Journal*, 11(1):3–20.

U.S. DEPARTMENT OF HEALTH AND HUMAN SERVICES (1997). Study confirms that combination treatment using a protease inhibitor can delay HIV disease progression and death. *NIAID News*. Washington, DC: U.S. DHHS.

U.S. DEPARTMENT OF JUSTICE (1996). *HIV in Prison, 1994.* (1996). Washington, DC: U.S. Department of Justice, March.

VALDISERRI, R., D. LYTER, L. KINGSLEY, L. LEVITON, J. SCHOFIELD, J. HUGGINS, M. HO, and C. RINALDO (1987). The effect of group education on improving attitudes about AIDS risk reduction. *New York State Journal of Medicine*, 87(5):272–278.

VLAHOV, D., F. BREWER, K. CASTRO, J. NARKUNAS, J. SALIVE, J. ULRICH, and A. MUNOZ (1991). Prevalence of antibody to HIV–1 among entrants to U.S. correctional facilities. *Journal of the American Medical Association*, 265:1129–1132.

VOELKER, R. (1996). Can researchers use new drugs to push HIV envelope to extinction? *Journal of the American Medical Association*, 276(6):435–438.

WARING, N., and B. SMITH (1990). *The AIDS Epidemic: Impact on Women Prisoners in Massachusetts.* Boston: Social Justice for Women.

WIENER, L. S. (1991). Women and human immunodeficiency virus: A historical and personal psychosocial perspective. *Social Work*, 36(5):375–378.

WINGOOD, G., D. HUNTER, and R. DICLEMENTE (1993). A pilot study of sexual communication and negotiation among young African-American women: Implications for HIV prevention. *Journal of Black Psychology.* 19:190–203.

WINGOOD, G., and R. DICLEMENTE (1995). Understanding the role of gender relations in HIV prevention research. *Journal of Public Health*, 85:4.

WINGOOD, G., and R. DICLEMENTE (1997). Prevention of human immunodeficiency virus infection among African-American women: Sex, gender and power and women's risk for HIV. In D. C. Umeh (ed.), *Cross-Cultural Perspectives on HIV/AIDS Education.* Trenton, NJ: African World Press.

WOFSKY, C. B. (1987). Intravenous drug abuse and women's medical issues. *Report of the Surgeon General's Workshop on Children with HIV Infection and Their Families.* Washington, DC: U.S. Department of Health and Human Services.

YOUNG, A., and J. MCHALE (1992). The dilemmas of the HIV positive prisoner. *Howard Journal*, 31(2):89–104.

chapter 25

The Administration of Justice Based on Gender and Race

Etta F. Morgan, Ph.D.

ABSTRACT

Empirical research persistently finds evidence that the administration of justice is discriminatory by race and gender. Efforts to reduce discrimination by reducing discretion at the sentencing stage have not been effective. It appears that more fundamental changes in the justice system and in the values expressed by members of society will be needed if we are to establish a fair and efficient system of justice from arrest to incarceration.

The administration of laws by our criminal justice system has come under scrutiny for various reasons. It has been suggested that the influence of extralegal factors is more important in determining the outcome of a case than the law itself. Gender and race have been identified as perhaps the most consistent extralegal factors that influence criminal justice personnel and juries concerning offensive behaviors. In this chapter we review the literature that examines the influence of race and gender on decisions within the criminal justice system from initial contact with law enforcement to sentencing.

A THEORETICAL BEGINNING

Laws of U.S. society, whether civil or criminal, represent the acceptable boundaries of behaviors established by various social contracts inherent in our society. In the past, U.S. society was represented by stability and long-term relationships, unlike the temporary, unstable relationships of today (Rubin, 1996). As a result of this shift in relationships and social changes, there is some disorder. According to Rubin (1996), "the images of disorder…reflect two very different things…the disorder that grows out of a society in transition…[or] a society that has institutionalized continual change. (Institutionalization refers to the process of making something permanent, either by law or because people take it for granted)" (p. 4).

The creation of laws denoting acceptable boundaries of behavior also establishes and maintains both an economic and a social hierarchy within society. Economically, this means that only certain individuals or organizations are able to participate in the exchange relationship for the production and distribution of goods and services (Rubin, 1996). In a country like the United States, which perpetuates a patriarchal Anglo-Saxon society, most meaningful economic opportunities have been blocked for women and minorities. According to strain theorists (Merton, 1957; Durkheim, 1965; and Messner and Rosenfeld, 1997), blocked opportunities, both socially and financially, cause crime and deviant behaviors, thereby placing society in an anomic state. When society is in an anomic state, its social controls are not functional. Therefore, the exchange relationship in society is no longer a legitimate enterprise of goods and services but becomes one with an illegal component because the population's desires and goals are uncontrollable. As a means of regaining control, the criminal justice system uses extralegal factors to control those members of society who have deviated from their respective places in the social and economic hierarchy.

Merton (1957) suggests that a society which places enormous emphasis on material success, although its institutionalized means of achieving this success is not equally obtainable for all members of the population, creates strain within society. As a result, people respond to this strain in various ways. Merton (1957) identifies five modes of adaptation in response to the strain in society. Some of these modes—innovation, retreatism, and rebellion—have been labeled as deviant behaviors. One could assume that these modes of adaptation have been labeled as deviant behaviors because the person rejects the institutionalized means of achieving cultural goals. However, we should note that the retreatist and rebellionist modes of adaptation also reject the cultural goals. The goals and means conflict in society directly affects society's ability to maintain social control over its members.

Messner and Rosenfeld (1997) state that individuals are in pursuit of the American Dream, which they define as "a broad cultural ethos that entails a commitment to the goals of material success to be pursued by everyone in society, under conditions of open competition" (p. 6). Therefore, "the American Dream itself exerts pressures toward crime by encouraging an anomic cultural environment…the anomic pressures inherent in the American Dream are nourished and sustained by a distinctive *institutional balance of power* [emphasis in the original] dominated by the economy" (p. 68). Members of society are constantly encouraged to pursue the American Dream, but the avenues available to achieve this dream are not the same for all members of society. Some members of society have been hindered from achieving the American Dream because of their race or gender. Specifically, the American Dream is based on a class system, and as a result, it helps to maintain the class hierarchy by denying members of certain racial and gender groups the opportunity to participate fully in the accumulation of wealth by socially acceptable means. The class hierarchy in the United States devalues blacks and women. However, the structure of the class hierarchy does have an inherent value system that determines the degree of devaluation of certain members of society. The devaluation of persons based on the class system can be characterized as follows: (1) white men are valued more than all other persons, (2) white women are valued more than black women and men, and (3) black women are valued more than black men. This devaluation continues throughout the socialization process of our children and into the workplace.

Previously, girls and boys were socialized differently in preparation for various occupational roles. In terms of educational training, boys were most often encouraged to take math and science courses, while girls were directed toward courses more closely related to their prescribed gender roles. As a result, women were most often hired in occupations that earned much less than men (Doyle and Paludi, 1991). As society continues to change economically, so does the path that leads to the American Dream change from "education, hard work, luck, and motivation" (Rubin, 1996:8) to anything goes. Ironically, Merton (1968) suggested that the American Dream creates and destroys American society.

THE PATHWAY TO CIVIL RIGHTS AND AFFIRMATIVE ACTION

U.S. society has always functioned according to the ideology of a preferential system. Privilege and opportunity for success in the United States has been determined by one's race, class, and gender. Although the passage of the Thirteenth Amendment and the Civil Rights Act of 1866 gave blacks the same rights as whites, it has never really come to fruition. Instead, southern states responded with state legislation which became known as Black Codes, in an attempt to "keep blacks in their places." Congress then responded by enacting the Fourteenth (providing the foundation for civil rights and affirmative action legislation) and Fifteenth (prohibited discrimination based on race, not other factors) amendments, in hopes of curtailing the differential treatment of blacks and to ensure that blacks (males) had the right to vote.

Women did not receive voting rights along with the black man; instead, they (black and white women together) continued to fight for the right to vote for many years. According to Aptheker (1982), the relationship that developed among Elizabeth Cady Stanton, Frederick Douglas, and Susan B. Anthony during the struggle to abolish slavery "was an alliance unable to survive the post Civil War crucible of racism, male supremacy, and class collaboration" (p. 42). When members of the Equal Rights Association supported passage of the Fifteenth Amendment, Stanton and Anthony resigned from the organization and focused on the National Woman Suffrage Association "with little or no further interest in the cause of Afro-American freedom" (Aptheker, 1982:49). Under the leadership of Susan B. Anthony, the National American Woman Suffrage Association embraced a racist and classist position on the importance of gaining the right to vote for white women (Davis, 1981). Anthony suggested that the white woman's ability to vote represented a power to be contended with which could have a profound impact politically (Davis, 1981). Therefore, she actively campaigned for the right of white women to vote. It was not until the passage of the Nineteenth Amendment that black women were given the right to vote. Still, those persons opposed to black women having the right to vote instituted various measures to keep them from exercising that right (Aptheker, 1982). It was not until the Voting Rights Act of 1965 that blacks (men and women) begin to register and vote in record numbers. Voting was not the only area in which blacks and minorities experienced differential treatment. The lack of an equal and quality education for black children was the basis for legal challenges to the previous educational system.

In 1787 and 1847, black parents filed a petition requesting the desegregation of Boston's public schools. The petition filed in 1787 failed, but the 1847 petition was argued before the Massachusetts Supreme Court in 1849. By 1855, Boston's public schools were desegregated (Aptheker, 1982). It should be noted that the Massachusetts decision was the precedent used for the decision in *Brown* v. *Board of Education* (1954). The U.S. Supreme Court ruled in *Brown* that the segregation of public schools was unconstitutional and in violation of the Fourteenth Amendment; however, many states believed that the *Brown* ruling was another example for federal interference and chose instead to ignore the decision, and as a result, many school districts came under federal court orders to desegregate or face the penalties. A few years later (1957), the Civil Rights Commission was established as "an independent, bipartisan, fact-finding commission" (Jordan, 1985:21) which would investigate any allegations of civil rights violations. Another area in which blacks encountered discrimination was in employment.

According to Fair (1997), "there were white jobs and black jobs....In those days, merit was not the basis for employment....No matter how well educated or accomplished a black worker was, he or she could not obtain a job explicitly reserved for whites, mostly men" (p. 116). In the past, jobs were first filled with white males, and if any positions were left in which a black was permitted to work, he or she was given the job. Although President Roosevelt issued an executive order requiring the elimination of discrimination based on race, creed, color, or national origin for purposes of employment, future administrations ignored it. It was not until the Kennedy administration that overt discrimination was outlawed in 1964 by Titles II, VI, and VII of the Civil Rights Act. It was also during this administration that women were afforded protection against discrimination and the Equal Employment Opportunity Commission was established.

Another accomplishment of the 1960s was the passage of the Voting Rights Act of 1965, which was enacted to ensure that all persons would have the right to vote. Also, under the Johnson administration, federal affirmative action law became compulsory. With all the good faith doctrines in place which specifically prohibited acts of discrimination based on race, gender, creed, color, or national origin, in both the public and private sectors in education, employment, housing, and so on, some gains were made in an attempt to replace the inequalities of the past with positive changes in all spheres of society. For example, women and blacks were employed in occupations that were previously closed to them. They were able to earn higher wages than ever before and be in positions of authority, including high-level management positions (Fair, 1997). Educational opportunities that had been unavailable for various reasons were obtainable as a result of affirmative action programs. Also, persons were able to purchase or lease homes in *any* area of a city as a result of affirmative action programs. But programs created to provide equal access and opportunity, such as affirmative action, were challenged in the courts.

In *Regents of the University of California* v. *Bakke* (1978), the plaintiff claimed that he had been denied admission to Davis Medical School because of their special admissions program which reserved 16 of 100 seats for various minorities and therefore had created a case of reverse discrimination. The Supreme Court ruled that Bakke should be admitted to Davis and that any programs that specifically establish quotas are unconstitutional. The Court's ruling suggested that race could be considered along with other factors in determining admission, but it should not carry more weight than any other factor. This case opened the door for several other cases involving "reverse discrimination."

Another important case involving affirmative action was *United Steelworkers of America* v. *Weber* (1979). In this case the company and the employees' union worked together to formulate an acceptable affirmative action plan. An employee who was not selected for the training program, which had been instituted as a part of the affirmative action plan, felt that he had been discriminated against. However, the Supreme Court ruled that companies and employees' unions were permitted to devise an affirmative action plan because "its purposes mirrored those of Title VII...[and] the plan was only a temporary measure" (Fair, 1997:130). These are not the only cases that have challenged affirmative action programs, but they do represent some of the issues raised as a result of affirmative action programs.

Affirmative action is an integral part of the progress of blacks and minorities in this country. Without its programs, some opportunities would never have been available to blacks and minorities. According to Fair (1997), "affirmative action was not established as a subsistence program for the poor...affirmative action was an antidiscrimination policy" (p. 158). The attack on affirmative action began with institution of the Philadelphia Plan (Fair, 1997) and has continued. Affirmative action has not eliminated racial or gender discrimination, nor have all of its effects been positive, but the overall impact of affirmative action cannot be dismissed as insignificant. The ideology of inclusiveness, equality, and opportunity encompassed in affirmative action creates a better society for all people, and discrimination, regardless of where it occurs—in court, on the job, or at school, and so on—indirectly affects all persons in society in a negative way.

THE ADMINISTRATION OF LAW

In a collection of essays on law, crime, and sexuality, Smart (1995) explores two very powerful arguments: (1) that law is gendered, and (2) that the law itself is used as a gendering strategy. A further examination of these arguments will perhaps assist us in understanding the treatment of women in the criminal justice system. The idea that the law is gendered is based upon three specific phases: "(a) law is sexist; (2) law is male; and (3) law is gendered" (Smart, 1995:187). What do we really mean when we say that the law is sexist? First, there have always been dual standards for men and women in our society. These standards and laws established by our society have placed men in a more advantageous position while causing women to be disadvantaged in the areas such as material resources and opportunities (Smart, 1995). Additionally, lawmakers for the most part have chosen to ignore the harm caused to women as a direct result of laws that have been advantageous for men (Smart, 1995). For example, most prostitution laws focus on female prostitutes, not males, "but courts have been almost as reluctant to find an equal protection violation in statutes that criminalize only female prostitution as they have been in male-only statutory rape laws" (Bartlett, 1993:716). In most instances, the person that profits from prostitution is male, yet seldom is he prosecuted for pimping (Bartlett, 1993).

Instead, women are considered the problem regardless of the circumstances because they are continually being viewed as irrational and incompetent, but the problem is not with women. According to Smart (1995), "[the] law suffers from a problem of perception which can be put right such that all legal subjects are treated equally" (p. 188). It is therefore necessary to change the perception of women from that of mother, sister, and homemaker to whatever roles they so desire, especially since role expectations are so much a part of our thought processes, actions, and reactions. If these roles are no longer gender specific, perhaps we can start eradicating differential treatment of men and women.

The fact that sexual difference is embedded in our structure and as such influences not only our language but also the meanings associated with that language suggests that the law itself must be structured to eliminate sexual difference in its meaning. Language is power, if it is the accepted language. For example, this country has fought to remain monolingual instead of embracing a bilingual society. Nowhere is it more evident than in our schools that we do not want a truly bilingual society. Persons who do not identify English as their first language are viewed differently in this society. Soto (1997) notes: "The voices of the bilingual parents, community leaders, and bilingual educators…rang out loudly but were disregarded and silenced by 'more powerful elements'…it was evident that current educational structures…have encouraged the disenfranchisement of the less valued and less powerful" (p.1). We must remember that the same educational structure determines our perceptions and beliefs about the members of our society. That same structure also determines the meaning we associate with our language. It is through language usage that social control is dictated.

Because law is directly related to politics and most of our politicians are males, our laws reflect the beliefs of the male majority when laws are written; therefore, women are judged based on male criteria. In the present state, the laws of this country must be changed to reflect ideals that represent universal values that gender neutral and truly objective, based-on-people standards, not on male standards. In the past, laws referred to the idea of the "reasonable man," suggesting that only men could be reasonable and thereby excluding women as logical beings. To deconstruct law as gendered, Smart (1995) suggests that "…we begin to analyse law as a process of producing fixed gender identities rather than simply as the application of law to previously gendered subjects" (p. 191). Finally, the argument of law as a gendering strategy suggests that over time, laws have excluded and included women from various positions in society. Smart (1995) notes "that nineteenth-century law brought a more tightly defined range of gendered subject positions into place. We can also see how law and discipline 'encouraged' women to assume these identities or subjectivities" (p.195).

Laws, in any society, define behaviors that are deemed unacceptable based on the morals and values of the community at large. They also determine who will be punished (Price and Sokoloff, 1995). In societies that are not very complex, informal rather than formal methods are used as means of social control. Both society and individuals are presumably protected by laws. These laws may prescribe punishments, direct or restrain certain actions, and access financial penalties (Reid, 1995). Price and Sokoloff (1995) state that "the law protects what those in power value most" (p. 14). Laws are created and passed by legislative bodies composed mainly of rich white men and persons who share their interests (Price and Sokoloff, 1995). Laws are the mechanism by which the dominant class ensures that its interests will be protected (Quinney, 1975). However, challenges to specific laws are not uncommon (Price and Sokoloff, 1995).

Historically, women have been considered the property of their fathers or husbands without full acknowledgment of them as individuals with rights granted by the Constitution (Price and Sokoloff, 1995). Several cases have come before the Supreme Court concerning the rights of women. In the landmark case of *Reed* v. *Reed* (1971), the Supreme Court ruled that women were indeed persons and should be treated as such under the U.S. Constitution. The Court stated that the Fourteenth Amendment clause "does not deny to States the power to treat different classes of persons in different ways...[it] does, however, deny to States power to legislate that different treatment be accorded to persons placed by a statute into different classes on the basis of criteria wholly unrelated to the objective of that statute. A classification "must be reasonable, not arbitrary, and must rest upon ground of difference having a fair and substantial relation to the object of the legislation..." (*Reed* v. *Reed*, 1971).

According to the justices, preference based on gender which is used merely to reduce the number of court hearings that could arise because two or more persons are equally entitled is directly in violation of the Fourteenth Amendment clause forbidding arbitrariness, nor can gender be used as a preventive measure against intrafamily controversies (*Reed* v. *Reed*, 1971). Based on this ruling, the Court recognized women as individuals with the right to individualized treatment, but it did not identify gender in relation to the suspect-classification argument under the Fourteenth Amendment.

It was not until *Frontiero* v. *Richardson* (1973) that the Court attempted to rule that gender was a suspect classification which "must be subjected to strict judicial scrutiny" (p. 677). This case involved differential treatment of men and women in the military in regards to their respective spouses being classified as dependents. The ruling by the Court also stated that the current statute was in violation of the due process clause of the Fifth Amendment. Justice Powell suggested that the Court should not rule on gender as a suspect classification because the Equal Rights Amendment (ERA) had been approved by Congress and it would eliminate the need for such a classification (*Frontiero* v. *Richardson*, 1973). Unfortunately, the states did not ratify the ERA.

Women were still seeking equal rights during the Ford and Carter administrations, although the Court ruled in *Craig* that "classification by gender must serve important governmental objectives and must be substantially related to achievement of those objectives" (*Craig* v. *Boren*, 1976). Yet this case did not a have true impact on constitutional law; instead, it most notably suggested that there were changes in alliances among the justices. These cases represent only small legal gains by women.

According to Hoff (1991), "some of the most disturbing gender-biased decisions the Supreme Court has reached in the last seventeen years have involved pregnancy cases...[O]ther recent decisions are either discouraging or disquieting for the cause of complete female equality, especially where redistributive economic issues are at stake" (p. 251). Knowing that many households are now headed by women has not moved Congress or the Supreme Court to properly address the comparable worth issue. Instead, they avoid the comparable worth issue as though it were a plague. Women must decide "whether they prefer equal treatment as unequal individuals (when judged by male standards) or special treatment as a protected (and thus implicitly) inferior group" (Hoff, 1991:274). The legal system has not always treated women and girls fairly, and this could be due in part to the perceptions that men (who are the majority in the legal system) have of females (Price and Sokoloff, 1995). A prime example is the difficulty associated with passage of the Anti-Violence/Domestic Violence Act, presented to Congress during the 2000 session. The bill almost did not pass because of several insignificant items that were attached to the bill that had nothing to do with stopping violence against women. It is unfortunate that in the twenty-first century, women are still being treated as less than equal. This unequal treatment extends from civil law to criminal law, too. Roberts (1994) states that "the criminal law most directly mandates socially acceptable behavior. Criminal law also helps to shape the way we perceive women's proper role" (p. 1). Women who do not adhere to prescribed gender roles and commit criminal offenses are viewed differently by our criminal justice system. This issue is discussed more fully in the following section.

FEMALE CRIMINALITY

Female crime is not as prevalent as that of males and previously had not been considered a social problem (Belknap, 1996). Women are also more likely than males to commit fewer and less serious violent crimes (Mann, 1984a; Pollock-Byrne, 1990; Simon and Landis, 1991; Belknap, 1996). Yet we have been led to believe that female crime has reached outlandish proportions and far exceeds male crime. The basis for this information has been the Uniform Crime Reports (UCR), complied by the FBI from data supplied by law enforcement agencies.

According to Steffensmeier (1995), these data (UCR) are problematic in assessing female crime patterns. Steffensmeier (1995) suggests the following: (1) the changes in arrest rates may be related more to "public attitudes and police practices...than actual behaviors; (2) because of the broadness of categories they include "dissimilar events and...a range of seriousness"; and (3) the definition of serious crime as used by the UCR tends to lead one to believe that serious female crime has risen dramatically, when in fact, women have been arrested more for the crime of larceny, "especially for shoplifting" (p. 92) than any other type I offense. Previous research (Steffensmeier, 1980; Mann, 1984a; Naffine, 1987; Simon and Landis, 1991) has revealed that overall, female crime rates have remained fairly stable in most areas. The notable changes are in the areas of "less serious property offenses and possibly drugs" (Belknap, 1996:58).

To better assess the rate of female crime, Steffensmeier (1995) completed a 30-year study of arrest statistics. Although the study examined trends in individual offenses, of particular importance here are the trends by type of crime based on male/female arrests. The type of crimes chosen to develop trends for male/female arrests were "violent, masculine, Index ('serious'), and minor property" (Steffensmeier, 1995:94). He found that female participation in masculine crimes increased slightly, which led to more arrests, but this was not the case for violent crimes. Steffensmeier (1995) again attributes the increase in arrests for index crimes as a result of an increase in the number of women committing larcenies. Women have also had an increase in arrest rates for minor property crimes (Steffensmeier, 1995; Belknap, 1996). Simpson (1991) suggests that violent behavior varies among women and it is difficult to separate the individual influence of race, class, and gender because they are so intermingled.

EXTRALEGAL FACTORS

Gender

Having examined briefly female criminality, we now turn our attention to the processing of female criminal cases by the criminal justice system. It has been suggested (Steffensmeier, 1980; Chesney-Lind, 1982; Frazier et al., 1983; Harvey et al., 1992; Farnworth and Teske, 1995; Spohn and Spears, 1997) that women receive differential treatment during the processing of criminal cases. The differential treatment may be negative or positive. For example, Steffensmeier (1980) suggested that the likelihood of future offending and the perceived danger to the community influenced the preferential treatment of women in the criminal justice process and as a result increased their chances of receiving probation instead of prison. Yet Chesney-Lind (1982) discovered that female juveniles have always received negative differential treatment. She noted that the females were processed into the juvenile justice system as a result of status offenses and received institutionalization more often than male juveniles.

Frazier et al. (1983) examined the effect of probation officers in determining gender differences in sentencing severity. In their study, they collected data from presentence investigation reports with various information concerning the offender as well as recommendations from the probation officers regarding sentences. According to Frazier et al. (1983) "there is a strong relationship between gender of offender and final criminal court disposition...[P]robation officers' recommendations have major effects and...being female greatly increases the likelihood of receiving a nonincarceration sentence recommendation" (pp. 315–316). In an international comparison of gender differences in criminal justice, Harvey et al. (1992) found that women were processed out of the criminal justice system more often than men. Their study also revealed that men who were processed through the criminal justice system were convicted and imprisoned at a higher rate than women worldwide. Harvey et al. (1992) note "that criminal justice worldwide operates differentially by gender (but not necessarily in a discriminatory way)" (p. 217).

In another study, Farnworth and Teske (1995) found some evidence of gender disparity in relation to charge reductions if there was no prior criminal history. The absence of prior offending was noted to increase the possibility of probation for females. Based on the selective chivalry thesis, Farnworth and Teske (1995) discovered that "white females were twice as likely as minority females to have assault charges changed to nonassault at sentencing" (p. 40). There was also supportive evidence which suggested that the use of discretionary powers influenced informal rather than formal decisions (Farnworth and Teske, 1995).

More recently, Spohn and Spears' (1997) study of the dispositions of violent felonies for both men and women revealed that more men (71.4%) than women (65.0%) were prosecuted, but their conviction rates were very similar, and major differences appeared in sentencing. For example, men were incarcerated 77.4% of the time versus 48.2% for women. Overall, women normally served "428 fewer days in prison" (p. 42) than men. This study also found that charge reduction or total dismissal of charges was more likely for women than for men. Spohn and Spears (1997) state: "Females were more likely than males to have injured their victims....Female defendants were much less likely than male defendants to have a prior felony conviction. Females were charged with and convicted of less serious crimes and were less likely...to be charged with or convicted of more than one offense...less likely than males to have used a gun to commit the crime or to have victimized a stranger....[F]emales were more likely to have private attorneys and to be released prior to trial" (p. 42). Based on their findings, Spohn and Spears (1997) suggest that violent women offenders are looked upon differently by judges for various reasons, such as: (1) women may be perceived as less dangerous to the community; (2) women may have acted as an accomplice instead of being the primary perpetrator; (3) the risk of recidivism is less for women; and (4) there is a better chance of rehabilitating women offenders. Spohn and Spears (1997) also found an interaction between race and gender that is discussed in the following section.

Race

In many instances we are led to believe that any race other than minorities is pure, but Headley (1995) noted that centuries of interbreeding have eliminated most "pure" races. He further stated that "human genes occur in every imaginable combination...[and] many people fit into more than one racial category or none at all....Our highly race-conscious society attributes greater meaning and significance to skin color than the objective realities could possibly justify" (Headley, 1995:23–24). Race is a topic that many people feel uncomfortable discussing, but it touches every segment of society in numerous ways. Perhaps we tend not to discuss race because then we are forced to acknowledge that U.S. society is flawed, and these flaws include "historic inequalities and longstanding cultural stereotypes" (West, 1994:6). The racial injustices encountered by minority groups indirectly affect society as a whole.

Higginbotham (1992) noted that the U.S. system of injustice has been constructed and reconstructed since the founding of the United States. Perhaps one of the most important facts about minorities still has not been fully realized, and that is that minorities have human rights. According to Higginbotham (1992), several factors have contributed to the injustices experienced by blacks. For example, during slavery "many legal decisions" (p. 253) were influenced by "the economics of slavery" (p. 253). Slave masters were to have total control over the slaves, and "total submission" was expected of blacks. Another factor in the development of the U.S. legal process was "whether or not blacks were inherently inferior to whites" (Higginbotham, 1992:255). These and other factors have resulted in adverse legislation, adjudication, and racial deprivation of minorities in this country (Higginbotham, 1992). "The legal process has never been devoid of values, preferences, or policy positions....The legal process has always acted as an expression of social control" (Higginbotham, 1992:257).

The main objective of legislation and criminal court processing is controlling blacks and minorities. The race card becomes very evident in the processing of criminal cases. Some researchers (Mann, 1989, 1995; Spohn and Spears, 1997) have found a relationship between race and gender. Mann (1989, 1995) studied the treatment of minorities from arrest to incarceration and found that arrest rates for black women exceed those of other ethnic groups, which could be due in part to law enforcement biases based on racial stereotyping. In other instances, black women received higher bails, were not adequately represented in court, received longer sentences, and served more time in prison. According to Mann (1989), "minority women offenders [are] doubly discriminated against because of their gender and race/ethnicity status" (p. 95). Spohn and Spears (1997) also noted that incarceration rates were influenced by the gender of the defendant. Specifically, they found that "[e]ven after taking other legal predictors of sentence severity into account, the incarceration rate for black males is 17.9 percentage points higher than the rate for white females, 14 percentage points higher than the rate for black females, and 5.6 percentage points higher than the rate for white males" (Spohn and Spears, 1997:50–51). The differences in sentencing is also evident as it relates to the death penalty.

Foley (1987) discovered that in capital cases "there was a highly significant relationship between the race of the offender and the race of the victim...with persons adjudicated guilty of an offense against a white victim more likely to be convicted of a serious offense than persons adjudicated guilty of murder of a black victim" (pp. 460–461). Foley's findings of capital sentencing in the post-*Gregg* decision are the same as Bowers and Pierce (1980), Paternoster (1983), and Radalet (1981). Based on their research, Aguirre and Baker (1991) concluded that "blacks have been subjected to systematic racial discrimination throughout most of the United States and throughout the entire history of the imposition of capital punishment in this country" (p. 40).

The imposition of the death penalty is not just racially biased, but it is also gender biased. Currently (as of the summer of 2001), there are 3650 males and 53 females (a total of 3703 inmates) serving time under the sentence of death (NAACP Legal Defense and Educational Fund, Inc., 1997). Since capital punishment was reinstated in 1976, there have been 403 executions. Of these executions, only one (Velma Barfield) was a woman. For some, this may come as a surprise, but historically, it is not. There have been 398 confirmed executions of women since 1632 and according to Streib (1988) "for the 346 for whom race is known, 229 (66%) were black and 108 (31%) were white" (p. 2). Recent data suggest that women (as a gender) receive only 1 to 2% of the total death sentences imposed, and of that 1 to 2%, black women receive 25% of the death sentences imposed (Streib, 1990). However, being sentenced to death does not always mean an execution is forthcoming. The reversal rate of women sentenced to death is approximately 98% (Streib, 1990). We (society) are willing to sentence women to death, but we (society) are not willing to execute them.

THE FUTURE

We are currently in a regressive phase of affirmative action. The gains in educational and employment opportunities experienced by blacks and minorities will soon be overshadowed by a consistent reduction in growth in these areas. Attitudes and behaviors that were controlled because of affirmative action will no longer be suppressed because there will no longer be consequences for exhibiting those attitudes and behaviors. Pipes and Lynch (1996) asserted that there may be a "lowering [of] legal standards against sex-based discrimination" (p. 30). Although this issue was raised in response to California Civil Rights Initiative's Bona Fide Qualifications clause, it should be a national concern because states tend to pass the same or similar legislation. Based on the attitudes of the current political forces in control of our Congress, the recent elimination of affirmative action, and the overall racial climate in this country, the discriminatory practices in the administration of justice will only increase.

One might wonder how the elimination of affirmative action will impact the administration of justice for women. The elimination of affirmative action will send a strong message to women indicating that their place is in the home, not in the workplace. The paternalistic forces of our society have started a reduction in opportunities for women in the workplace since there are no longer any safeguards to ensure that equally qualified women be given the same consideration as men. In the future, fewer women will be entering the workplace in professions previously considered male professions. Instead, those men in positions of power will revert back to the traditional standards of networking with only the "old boys," who have some type of direct connection to the company: a relative or a friend. Women who have achieved some power will find their authority being undermined or challenged by the male associates in the company who are in positions of power or are being groomed for advancement, while they will remain stagnant until they either retire or are forced to leave because of unbearable conditions. The camaraderie between men will continue to increase since important "information, resources and support" (Shukla and Tripathi,

1994:1280) are gained from these interactions while women are excluded. Lyness and Thompson (1997) suggest that women have not risen above the glass ceiling but have instead discovered a second and higher ceiling, which would imply that with the elimination of affirmative action, the workplace atmosphere will become one of intolerance and discrimination.

The elimination of affirmative action will eventually affect sexual harassment legislation. In time, the paternalistic forces will suggest that women who desire to work in a male-dominated profession expect to be treated "like one of the boys," which means that there is no need to watch one's language or gestures. In other words, all behaviors are acceptable to the "boys." Most of the paternalistic males will consider women who remain in occupations more closely related to their prescribed gender roles as conforming to the norm and as women who are trying to help their mates rather than being too independent. In these occupations there will not be the lack of respect for women, again because these women are conforming. The woman who is viewed as independent, intelligent, and aggressive will continue to be considered a threat to some males, especially those who believe in stereotypical gender roles.

The impact of affirmative action will also be noted in race relations in this country. We have already experienced a regression in terms of race relations. Instead of becoming closer as one nation, we have again become a nation divided by color. Since blacks have never really been assimilated into U.S. society, it was not difficult to dissimilate from mainstream society. Blacks have been the only group of people to come to this country and not be truly accepted as members of this country, but instead, be treated as a people here on a temporary journey. We have not yet brought closure to the racial incidents of the 1960s, and already the problems of the 1990s are on the rise. Incidents of the 1990s, such as police brutality, the hanging of a black youth in Virginia, the burning of black churches, the destructive painting and burning of homes owned by blacks in predominately white neighborhoods, racial slurs directed at interracial couples and their children, and so on, are all indicators that we have not progressed to the point that we are able to live in harmony as a diverse population. Instead, many persons of various ethnic backgrounds live in a constant state of fear. The land of opportunity is sometimes the land of a daily nightmare. Yet we say that we do not need affirmative action. Affirmative action was, in some instances, the only mechanism by which to introduce persons of different ethnic backgrounds to each other. As a result, persons were able to move beyond the stereotypes they once held about a particular group of people. Interaction assists in our understanding of each other. The criminal justice system will not be immune from the impact of race relations in this country.

Race again will become more prevalent in the administration of justice. The current regressive state of the criminal justice system represents a shift from the rehabilitative model of treating offenders to one of increased incarceration due in part to society's low level of tolerance for any type of offender. Those persons most affected during increased periods of protecting society from the criminal elements are blacks, the poor, and legally underrepresented. These persons are usually more visible to law enforcement and are therefore more likely to be arrested and processed into the criminal justice system.

Although there are mandatory sentences and supposedly, safeguards to ensure that the laws are applied in a nondiscriminatory fashion, we will see an increase in the arrest, conviction, and incarceration rate of blacks and other minorities because prosecutors will revert to scare tactics to encourage cooperation and admission of guilt. The uneducated and underrepresented black or minority offender will once again be railroaded to prison. The administration of justice will also affect women. Women who come before the criminal justice system will be treated more harshly because they will be considered disreputable women with no morals and values. They will be viewed as women who have ventured away from their prescribed gender roles and are therefore in need of guidance. Of course, this guidance can only be achieved by incarceration, and as a result we will have an increase in the incarceration rate of women, regardless of the offense.

Prison overcrowding will reach enormous proportions because of this new attitude toward blacks and minorities, along with the lack of tolerance on the part of those in power to devise alternative methods to deal with minor offender problems. The overall mentality will be to eliminate those who they deem to be offensive. For a period of time, those in power will try to break the spirits of the oppressed groups in an attempt to regain total control of all persons in society.

We must remember that affirmative action was only a temporary "fix" for a problem that has existed since the beginning of this country (Citrin, 1996). Unfortunately, some members of the citizenry were misinformed and led to believe that affirmative action was a permanent solution to this age-old problem. Affirmative action was only the beginning of the termination of rights and equality in this country. We will find that during each session of Congress, some rights previously granted will be legislated away unless we as a society begin to voice our concerns. Rights that we take for granted are rights only until new legislation is introduced to remove them. Although it may take several years for us to realize the full true impact of this legislation, we are already beginning to see the ripple effects. The educational system, the brain center of any society, has already been affected. For example, new guidelines for admission in some universities and colleges will eliminate specific groups from educational opportunities beyond high school. Other are asking for unitary status so that they may resegregate their school districts and not be required by the courts to provide an equal, high-quality education to all members of a metropolis. Without education, we create a population of illiterates who will become society's problem, supported by taxpayers in some form of social service or in the criminal justice system. Those in power who desire to control the members of society are better able to do so with an illiterate populace. We are slowly moving toward becoming a mechanical society, as identified by Durkheim in his book *The Division of Labor in Society* (1964).

CONCLUSIONS

Study after study continues to find evidence that our criminal justice system is plagued by discriminatory practices. In the past we were led to believe that the removal of discretionary powers for particular offenses would solve the problems associated with discriminatory practices, but it has not. To solve any specific problem, we must first make changes in the total program. The problems of the criminal justice system are merely extensions of society's problems. As a society, we must be willing to examine and correct "the way racism has influenced the law" (Washington, 1994:22) as well as gender if we are to establish a fair and efficient system of justice from arrest to incarceration. In the words of Cornell West (1994): "In these downbeat times, we need as much hope and courage as we do vision and analysis; we must accent the best of each other even as we point out the vicious effects of our racial divide and the pernicious consequences of our maldistribution of wealth and power" (p. 159).

REFERENCES AND BIBLIOGRAPHY

AGUIRRE, JR., A., and D. BAKER (1991). *Race, Racism, and the Death Penalty in the United States*. Berren Springs, MI: Vande Vere.

APTHEKER, B. (1982). *Woman's Legacy: Essays on Race, Sex, and Class in American History*. Amherst, MA: The University of Massachusetts Press.

BARTLETT, K. (1993). *Gender and Law: Theory, Doctrine, Commentary*. Boston: Little, Brown.

BELKNAP, J. (1996). *The Invisible Woman: Gender, Crime and Justice*. Belmont, CA: Wadsworth.

BLOMBERG, T., and S. COHEN, (1995). *Punishment and Social Control: Essays in Honor of Sheldon L. Messinger*. Hawthorne, NY: Aldine DeGruyter.

BOWERS, W., and G. PIERCE (1980). The pervasiveness of arbitrariness and discrimination under post-Furman capital statutes. *Crime and Delinquency*, 26(4):563–635.

CHEMERINSKY, E. (1997). What would be the impact of eliminating affirmative action? *Golden Gate University Law Review*, 27(3):313–344.

CHESNEY-LIND, M. (1982). Guilty by reason of sex: Young women and the juvenile justice system. In B. Price and N. Sokoloff (eds.), *The Criminal Justice System and Women*. New York: Clark Boardman, pp. 77–105.

CITRIN, J. (1996). Affirmative action in the people's court. *The Public Interest*, 22:39–48.

CULLIVER, C. (1993). *Female Criminality: The State of the Art*. New York: Garland Publishing.

DALY, K. (1994). *Gender, Crime and Punishment*. New Haven, CT: Yale University Press.

DAVIS, A. (1981). *Women, Race and Class*. New York: Random House.

DOYLE, J., and M. PALUDI (1991). *Sex and Gender: The Human Experience*. Dubuque, IA: Wm. C. Brown.

DURKHEIM, E. (1964). *The Division of Labor in Society*. New York: Free Press.

DURKHEIM, E. (1965). *The Rules of the Sociological Method*. New York: Free Press.

FAIR, B. (1997). *Notes of a Racial Caste Baby: Color Blindness and the End of Affirmative Action*. New York: New York University Press.

FARNWORTH, M., and R. TESKE, JR. (1995). Gender differences in felony court processing: Three hypotheses of disparity. *Women and Criminal Justice*, 6(2):23–44.

FLOWERS, R. (1995). *Female Crime, Criminals and Cellmates: An Exploration of Female Criminality and Delinquency*. Jefferson, NC: McFarland & Co.

FOLEY, L. (1987). Florida after the Furman decision: The effect of extralegal factors on the processing of capital offense cases. *Behavioral Sciences and the Law*, 5(4):457–465.

FRAZIER, C., E. BOCK, and J. HENRETTA (1983). The role of probation officers in determining gender differences in sentencing severity. *The Sociological Quarterly*, 24:305–318.

HARVEY, L., R. BURNHAM, K. KENDALL, and K. PEASE (1992). Gender differences in criminal justice: An international comparison. *British Journal of Criminology*, 32(2):208–217.

HEADLEY, J. (1995). *Race, Ethnicity, Gender and Class: The Sociology of Group Conflict and Change.* Thousand Oaks, CA: Pine Forge Press.

HEIDENSOHN, F. (1995). *Women and Crime.* New York: New York University Press.

HIGGINBOTHAM, A., JR., (1992). Race and the American legal process. In P. Rothenberg (ed.), *Race, Class and Gender: An Integrated Study.* New York: St. Martin's Press, pp. 250–258.

HILL, G., and E. CRAWFORD (1990). Women, race, and crime. *Criminology,* 28(4):601–625.

HOFF, J. (1991). *Law, Gender and Injustice: A Legal History of U.S. Women.* New York: New York University Press.

JORDAN, B. (1985). Still two nations: One black, one white? *Human Rights,* 13(1):21.

LYNESS, K., and D. THOMPSON (1997). Above the glass ceiling? A comparison of matched samples of female and male executives. *Journal of Applied Psychology,* 82(3):359–375.

MANN, C. (1984a). *Female Crime and Delinquency.* Tuscaloosa, AL: University of Alabama Press.

MANN, C. (1984b). Race and sentencing of female felons: A field study. *International Journal of Women's Studies,* 7(2):160–172.

MANN, C. (1989). Minority and female: A criminal justice double bind. *Social Justice,* 16(4):95–114.

MANN, C. (1993). *Unequal Justice: A Question of Color.* Bloomington, IN: Indiana University Press.

MANN, C. (1995). Women of color and the criminal justice system. In B. Price and N. Sokoloff (eds.), *The Criminal Justice System and Women: Offenders, Victims, and Workers,* 2nd ed. New York: Clark Boardman, pp. 118–135.

MERLO, A., and J. POLLOCK-BYRNE (1995). *Women, Law, and Social Control.* Boston: Allyn & Bacon.

MERTON, R. (1957). *Social Theory and Social Structure.* New York: Free Press.

MERTON, R. (1968). *Social Theory and Social Structure,* 2nd ed. New York: Free Press.

MESSNER, S., and R. ROSENFELD (1997). *Crime and the American Dream,* 2nd ed. Belmont, CA: Wadsworth Publishing.

MORGAN, E. (1995). Men, morals, and murder. In N. Jackson (ed.), *Contemporary Issues in Criminal Justice: Shaping Tomorrow's System.* New York: McGraw-Hill, pp. 83–92.

NAACP LEGAL DEFENSE AND EDUCATIONAL FUND (1997). *Death Row, U.S.A.* New York: NAACP.

NAFFINE, N. (1987). *Female Crime: The Construction of Women in Criminology.* Sydney, New South Wales, Australia: Allen & Unwin.

NORTHWESTERN UNIVERSITY SCHOOL OF LAW (1994). Symposium: Gender issues and the criminal law [special issue]. *Journal of Criminal Law and Criminology,* 85(1).

PATERNOSTER, R. (1983). Race of victim and location of crime: The decision to seek the death penalty in South Carolina. *Journal of Criminal Law and Criminology,* 74(3):754–785.

PIPES, S., and M. LYNCH (1996). Smart women, foolish quotas. *Policy Review,* 78:30–32.

POLLOCK-BYRNE, J. (1990). *Women, Prison and Crime.* Belmont, CA: Brooks/Cole.

PRICE, B., and N. SOKOLOFF (1995). The criminal law and women. In B. Price and N. Sokoloff (eds.), *The Criminal Justice System and Women: Offenders, Victims, and Workers.* New York: McGraw-Hill, pp. 11–29.

QUINNEY, R. (1975). *Class, State and Crime: On the Theory and Practice of Criminal Justice.* New York: Longman.

RADALET, M. (1981). Racial characteristics and the imposition of the death penalty. *American Sociological Review,* 46(6):918–927.

REID, S. (1995). *Criminal Law,* 4th ed. Upper Saddle River, NJ: Prentice Hall.

ROBERTS, D. (1994). The meaning of gender equality in criminal law. *Journal of Criminal Law and Criminology,* 85(1):1–14.

RUBIN, B. (1996). *Shifts in the Social Contract: Understanding Change in American Society*. Thousand Oaks, CA: Pine Forge Press.

SHUKLA, A., and A. TRIPATHI (1994). Influence of gender and hierarchical position on interpersonal relations at work. *Psychological Reports*, 74(3):1280–1282.

SIMON, R. (1993). *Rabbis, Lawyers, Immigrants, Thieves: Exploring Women's Roles*. Westport, CT: Praeger.

SIMON, R., and J. LANDIS (1991). *The Crimes Women Commit, the Punishments They Receive*. Lexington, MA: Lexington Books.

SIMPSON, S. (1991). Caste, class, and violent crime: Exploring differences in female offending. *Criminology*, 29(1):115–135.

SMART, C. (1995). *Law, Crime and Sexuality:Essays in Feminism*. London: Sage.

SOTO, L. (1997). *Language, Culture, and Power: Bilingual Families and the Struggle for Quality Education*. Albany, NY: State University of New York.

SPOHN, C., and J. SPEARS (1997). Gender and case processing decisions: A comparison of case outcomes for male and female defendants charged with violent felonies. *Women and Criminal Justice*, 8(3):29–59.

STEFFENSMEIER, D. (1980). Assessing the impact of the women's movement on sex-based differences in the handling of adult criminal defendants. *Crime and Delinquency*, 26:344–357.

STEFFENSMEIER, D. (1995). Trends in female crime: It's still a man's world. In B. Price and N. Sokoloff (eds.), *The Criminal Justice System and Women: Offenders, Victims, and Workers*. New York: McGraw-Hill, pp. 89–104.

STREIB, V. (1988). *American Executions of Female Offenders: A Preliminary Inventory of Names, Dates, and Other Information*, 3rd ed. Cleveland, OH: Author.

STREIB, V. (1990). Death penalty for female offenders. *University of Cincinnati Law Review*, 58(3):845–880.

VOLOKH, E. (1997). The California civil rights initiative: An interpretive guide. *UCLA Law Review*, 44(5):1335–1404.

WASHINGTON, L. (1994). *Black Judges on Justice: Perspectives from the Bench*. New York: New Press.

WEST, C. (1994). *Race Matters*. New York: Vintage Books.

CASES

Brown v. *Board of Education*, 347 U.S. 483 (1954).

Craig v. *Boren*, 429 U.S. 190, 197 (1976).

Frontiero v. *Richardson*, 411 U.S. 677 (1973).

Gregg v. *Georgia*, 428 U.S. 153, 96 S. Ct. 2909, 49 L.Ed.2d. 859 (1976).

Reed v. *Reed*, 404 U.S. 71, 92 S. Ct. 251, 30 L.Ed.2d, 255 (1971).

Regents of the University of California v. *Allan Bakke*, 438 U.S. 265 (1978).

United Steelworkers of America v. *Weber*, 443 U.S. 193 (1979).

chapter 26

The New Millennium

Women in Policing in the Twenty-First Century

Donna C. Hale, Ph.D. and Mark M. Lanier, Ph.D.

ABSTRACT

In this chapter we envision the role of women in twenty-first century policing, in part, by examining the perceptions of undergraduate and graduate criminal justice students. Students identified problems and issues that patrol women as pioneers, settlers, and opportunists (Lanier, 1996) encountered in the male-dominated police occupation during the past 40 years. We describe how policing will change in the beginning of this millennium with the expansion of private security, higher education requirements for police applicants, and changes in employment practices due to affirmative action polices and antidiscrimination legislation. We conclude with several policy recommendations critical to the continued success of women in policing.

INTRODUCTION

In this chapter we examine the role of women in policing in the twenty-first century. Nearly 40 years have passed since women first gained entry into police patrol in the United States by Title VII of the Civil Rights Act of 1964. Beginning in the mid-1960s and continuing through the 1990s, researchers examined the nature and function of police work itself (see Wilson, 1968, 1978; Bittner, 1970; Westley, 1970; Reiss, 1971; Klockars, 1985; Skolnick and Bayley, 1986; Greene and Mastrofski, 1988; Skogan and Hartnett, 1997). As this chapter demonstrates, placing policewomen on patrol contributed to advancing policing from the reactive, crime-fighter mentality of the first three quarters of the twentieth century to the proactive, more service-oriented police advocated now (Miller, 1999).

Women have only had a role in policing since early in the twentieth century (Hale, 1992). Until the passage of the Equal Employment Opportunity Act (1972), policewomen occupied clerical positions, conducted activities concerning children (e.g., the juvenile bureau), and/or served as decoys in undercover investigations (House, 1993). When women went on patrol in 1972, they came under scrutiny regarding whether or not they could successfully complete the activities associated with patrol work (Milton, 1975).

The entry of policewomen coincided with research on the function of police which concluded that police work is actually more service-oriented than law enforcement. In *Varieties of Police Behavior*, James Q. Wilson (1968) coined the terms for styles of police work as *law enforcing* (primarily arrest duties), *order maintenance* (keeping the peace functions), and *community service activities*. In the revised version of *Varieties of Police Behavior*, Wilson (1978:ix–x) discussed the consequences of research on policing since the mid-1960s:

> [I]deas have consequences. Ten years ago, the police were popularly portrayed as "crime fighters" who "solved crimes" by investigation and "prevented crimes" by patrol. Police officers may privately have then known that this view was simplistic, if not false, but few pointed that out. Today, there are few big-city chiefs who use the old phrases. They speak instead of "order maintenance," "community service," "family crisis intervention," and "police–citizen cooperation" and they ask hard questions about the role of detectives, the best uses of patrol time, and the need for investigative priorities.

The publication of Wilson's second edition of *Varieties* (1978) occurred about the same time as proactive police officers were returning to foot patrol after years isolated from the community in patrol cars (i.e., the Newark and Flint foot patrol projects). In the late 1970s and early 1980s, patrol officers were often resistant to the return of foot patrol because they viewed it as an ineffective use of their time. These officers had become accustomed to the sanctuary of the patrol car, where they spent the majority of their shift time isolated from the public they were assigned to patrol. Ironically, putting police officers in patrol cars was a consequence of the professionalization of policing of the early 1900s. The patrol car was used to increase the response time of the police.

An examination of Wilson's research (1968, 1978) that scrutinized the functions of policing, combined with Trojanowicz and Bucqueroux's (1990) description of community policing, and finally, Goldstein's analysis of problem-oriented policing (1990) all depict police activities that police women historically conducted in U.S. police departments of the early twentieth century. That is, much of the work of the early policewomen was preventive by nature. These policewomen—many trained in social work—patrolled the streets looking for young girls and children in amusement parks, taverns, movie theaters, and at railway/bus stations and dance halls, where all types of vice crimes were prevalent (Appier, 1992; Odem and Schlossman, 1991).

In our synopsis of the future of women in policing, we find that the crime prevention duties historically performed by policewomen will continue to be the ones that both female and male police officers will provide in the twenty-first century. Because of the public's concern with increasing juvenile delinquency and the increase in adolescent drug and alcohol abuse, police officers will continue to provide more services directly related to the prevention of adolescence drug use and to process cases of juveniles involved in drug trafficking. Initially, police officers were trained as D.A.R.E. officers (drug prevention specialists), to work with children at both the elementary and secondary school levels.

The major operational difference between the nineteenth- and early twentieth-century police women was that the pre-1972 policewomen were relegated to preventive duties concerning women and children (duties that men did not want to do). The post-1972 policewomen performed the same patrol duties as policemen. However, in the twenty-first century, more women will enter police work due to the crime prevention and service aspects of community policing. Women will also be attracted to police work because of the opportunity to work with victims of crime. The research of the past 40 years supports the fact that women as police are extremely effective (Miller, 1999) in communicating with victims of crime (Kennedy and Homant, 1983; Homant and Kennedy, 1984). Women are also effective at defusing volatile situations, and making arrests (Grennan, 1987).

To begin our exploration of the future of women in policing, we examine how the role of women in police work is perceived by law enforcement undergraduate and graduate students, who will comprise the police force of the twenty-first century. This is followed with a discussion of how students perceive past and present policing. Finally, we discuss strategies to increase the role of women in policing in the next millennium.

METHODOLOGY: STUDENTS' PERCEPTIONS OF WOMEN IN AMERICAN POLICING

The first author of this chapter instructed undergraduate students in two sections of "Police Operations and Management" to list problems, or issues, that women encountered when they entered patrol work in 1972. The majority of these students were seniors and had completed both "Introduction to Criminal Justice" and "Policing a Democracy" (a traditional police and society course) classes.

Next, students were asked to think about the entry of women in patrol work in the context of people who settled the American West. The term *pioneers* was used to refer to those Americans who went west and "blazed a trail" for those who followed. The pioneers' followers were *settlers* who benefited from the pioneers' hard work. The last group of people moving west were labeled *opportunists* because they benefited both from the labors of the pioneers and the continued efforts of the settlers to make expansion of the West easier for all those in later periods.

The next assignment required students to take the results of the first exercise described above one step further. They were to address how leaders/managers facilitated the entry of women into patrol during the last 40 years. The students were asked to address the problems and issues identified for the three periods of women in law enforcement (pioneers, settlers, and opportunists) to Fyfe et al.'s (1997) discipline continuum, which includes recruitment and selection; training and socialization, supervision and policy formation, reward and incentive system, and punishment.[1]

The second author utilized a graduate law enforcement course to solicit information on the future role of women in policing. The class of 24 students contained approximately 15 career law enforcement officers, including several women. The students were older and many are approaching the end of their current careers. The specific assignment was to read an article on female police typologies (Lanier, 1996). The students were to critically evaluate the two linked typologies presented (settlers, pioneers, and opportunists and a second clique group typology). Next, the students were asked to develop a future typology projecting the role of female police into the new century. The results (presented under the findings section) were instructive, based on the age, maturity, and experiences of the career officers.

Unlike the Western analogy given the undergraduate class, the graduate class was required to read and critically evaluate an article that presented typologies of female police officers (Lanier, 1996). In this article, *pioneers* were described as the first females to participate in regular patrol duties, who had 13 or more years of experience, generally had a high school education at the time of initial employment, and whose career ambition was to survive. The *settlers* were officers with 8 to 12 years of police experience, a high school and two-year college education, and desired primarily just to "do the job." The final group, *opportunists*, had less than 7 years' experience, were educated with at least an Associate degree, and desired to progress in policing. These temporal typologies were supplemented with a classification dividing officers by group differences (e.g., clique group membership). After critically evaluating the initial classifications, the students made projections about female police into the next century.

FINDINGS

Table 1 presents a summary of the undergraduate students' responses to this exercise. This table identifies the major problems for women police pioneers as stereotypes of police work, such as "men's work" or "lack of physical strength/endurance required to do men's work." Women did not have either community support or male officer support to do the job, resulting in the pioneers' alienation and isolation within the police department, the community, and their own families. Much of what these undergraduate students identified was stereotypical and sexist in nature. Students pointed out that the women patrol officers were pioneers and did not have mentors to help them assimilate into the organizational culture of police patrol.

For the settlers, students' responses were similar to what they had identified as problems or issues for the pioneers. Women on patrol from 1981 to 1988 still experienced lack of support from family and friends, faced resentment and sexual harassment from male officers, and their physical abilities to use force and firearms were questioned. Although settlers' confidence levels may have benefitted from the pioneers' mentoring, the settlers still had to work twice as hard to prove themselves. Students' statements

TABLE 1   Problems or Issues for Women on Patrol: Three Typologies, 1972–1997

Pioneers, 1972–1980	Settlers, 1981–1988	Opportunists, 1989–1997
Traditionally, police work "men's work" because of size and males as authority figures.	Benefit from mentoring of pioneer women	More acceptance by males because older ones that pioneers and settlers encountered have retired
Question of women's physical ability to do "men's work"; women believed not to have biological physical strength/endurance to do patrol work.	Still resentment from peers	
	Lack of support—family and friends	Continued research that women are effective on patrol
Police as "men's work" paid more money and did not require college education.	Still expected to prove themselves able to do patrol	Change in police work from crook catching to community-oriented policing
Fear that women not authoritarian enough to do patrol, especially arrest, using a weapon, or physically tackling or chasing suspects; also, concern that criminals would not respond to policewoman's request.	Sexual harassment	As policing becomes more professional in requirements for college-educated cops, less resentment expected toward women on patrol
	Agility testing changed	
	Lack of promotions—glass ceiling	
	Lack of physical facilities for women	
Consequently, policewomen encountered resentment and lack of support from male officers; policewomen experienced alienation and isolation within police department	Face that hired because of political correctness	Still problems of harassment and discrimination
Policewomen lacked community support.	Not trusted with firearms	Few women have been promoted to first and middle management positions
Policewomen had no mentors to advise them regarding patrol	Entry of more college grads	
	Research shows women effective with communication with victims and in mediations	Women still have problems with family care issues
Policewomen's psychological stress of not being accepted or trusted in patrol contributed to own lack of self-esteem.		Still lack of confidence by peers
	Psychologically alone	Policewomen need to mentor and develop networks if they are to succeed
Stereotypes of women—patrol not their sphere; wives of police officers opposed because of safety and potential for romantic involvement.	Policewomen working twice as hard to prove selves	
	Wearing same male uniform	Women don't support each other; become "one of boys" to be accepted
Stress of lack of family support, lack of child care when doing shift work.		
Sexism: "What's a nice girl like you…?"		Advancement of women on patrol taken for granted by young women today who think all obstacles are gone
Policewomen as "outsiders," not part of "boys' club."		
1960s violent in United States; policemen did not handle violent episodes appropriately.		Still wearing male uniform
Patrol work viewed as "crook catching," not problem-oriented or community policing.		
President's Commission stated that women should be in patrol.		
The entry of women in patrol guaranteed by the passage of the Equal Employment Opportunity Act and the Equal Employment Opportunity Commission to oversee its enactment is the gateway for women as patrol officers.		
Required in beginning to wear skirts; then changed to male uniform; uniform not adjusted for female anatomy.		

that the policewomen were striving continually to prove themselves is reminiscent of the mythical Sisyphus, who was condemned eternally to repeat the cycle of rolling a heavy rock up a hill in Hades only to have it roll down again as it nears the top. Students do indicate that research has shown that policewomen are effective in dealing with victims and in situations were mediation is necessary (e.g., domestic conflict). Students' comments about women who remained in police work was that these women were determined to survive and not to become discouraged by their experiences.

During the third period, 1989–1997, students indicated that the opportunists still experienced harassment, discrimination, and lack of male officers' confidence that policewomen could do the job. The students' concerns are substantiated by Brown's (1994) findings that only one-third of policemen in her study accepted women as colleagues.

For the third period, students indicated that since more of the current police officers were both younger and college graduates, they might have less resentment toward women police. However, students acknowledged that policewomen still experience discrimination and harassment, and few women are promoted to management positions. Consequently, students recommended that the more senior policewomen, who had advanced through the glass ceiling, should mentor the junior policewomen for promotion. Students realized the contributions of research supporting the effectiveness of women on patrol. Unfortunately, the students pointed out that the "opportunist" policewomen not only still encounter obstacles from their male peers, but currently experience the ingenuous beliefs by novice policewomen that all the barriers against women in policing have been removed. Finally, students emphasized that women on patrol are still wearing the male uniform (i.e., one designed for the male physique with no accommodation for the female anatomy). The students' comments find support in Connie Fletcher's (1995) interviews with policewomen who describe the problems they encounter with the male-designed police uniform.

Table 2 provides more specific information on how students felt that managers and supervisors addressed the problems and issues identified for women in policing in each of the three time periods. An examination of the students' responses reveals their increased awareness over the three periods for managers and supervisors to recognize the stereotypes that women police encountered when they were assigned to patrol, traditionally a male duty. One suggestion that students emphasized was the development and implementation of training for both male and female officers regarding the obstacles that women in policing have encountered because of these stereotypes.

Students recommend that research findings reporting policewomen as effective in both mediating conflicts and community policing strategies must be incorporated into the training academy curriculum along with weapons and physical agility training for policewomen. The use of sensitivity training for men to women's issues and educating officers about sexual harassment policy needs to be included as well. Students also note that incentives need to be in place for promotions but that benefit packages are also necessary for both women and men for maternity/paternity[2] leaves as well as more "family-friendly programs" such as flex-time and shift standardization for officers with families. As a last resort, students point out that punishments should be in

TABLE 2 Women on Patrol: Leadership and Discipline, 1972–1997

Type of Police Women	Identification of Problems/Issues	Recruitment and Selection	Training and Socialization	Supervisors and Policy Formation	Reward and Incentive System	Punishment
Pioneers, 1972–1980	No one to answer questions Women suffered resentment from other officers Suffered through harassment No public respect Not taken seriously Abuse Discrimination No training	Advertise/knowledge Factory worker High school/college athletes Physical standards Women without families of own Advertise in areas frequented by women Applications made more available to women	Treat equally Physically fit (running, pushups, situps) Gun training Ride-alongs with male officers Specialized training Sensitize to opposite sex	Partner with an experienced officer Advance women to supervisory positions	Equal promotion As women prove themselves, they should move up the ranks Promote one female (the best) to a higher position for women to look up to	Suspend pay Demotions
Settlers, 1981–1988	Still dealing with resentment Maternity leave Nontraditional Denied power positions Harassment Good-old-boy system	Use successful women officers to go out and recruit	Academy Sensitize to opposite sex Specialized training	Partners with experience (male or female) Sexual harassment policy Advance women to supervisory positions	Equal promotions Equal pay Maternity leave Family friendly work environment	Extra training No promotion Demotions Desk work
Opportunist, 1989–1997	Resentment Still nontraditional (women should be at home) Old stereotypes Under microscope Equal pay and responsibilities	Colleges Athletes Colleges Pass entrance exams Pass physical agility tests Use successful women to recruit	Academy Helping others Specialized training Sensitize to opposite sex	Family friendly Accountability (leadership) Partners with experience (male or female) Workshops	Equal promotions Equal pay Maternity leave Women police chiefs Family friendly work environment	Desk duty Graveyard shift Demotions Patrol work Same punishment for women and men

place for officers who harass other officers or who are hostile to the presence of women in policing. An article in *USA Today* describes training programs that police departments have developed focusing on sexual harassment (Heckeroth and Barker, 1997).

The comments of the undergraduate students were supported by the former president of the International Association of Chiefs of Police (IACP), Darrell L. Sanders. He stated that "the number of female police officers has continued to grow slowly over the past decade" (1997:6). He identified several issues that the IACP will help police women to address in the twenty-first century. These concerns include the development and continuation of "aggressive and balanced recruiting policies, the steady promotion of female officers to higher ranks and the eventual breaking of the 'glass ceiling' to ensure a strong presence by women at leadership levels" (Sanders, 1997:6).

Graduate Students' Examination of Women in American Policing

The graduate students devoted considerable effort to this assignment. Many interviewed women in policing, many reflected on their own experiences, and all provided projections as to what the future holds for women in policing. With few exceptions, the graduate students accepted and agreed with the typologies developed by Lanier (1996). However, what are of interest for our purpose are the projections they made. This exercise employed a modified form of the Delphi technique that relies on "experts" to make projections about the future. The primary finding was that policewomen in the twenty-first century would continue to do what they do well: mediate disputes and provide a reassuring presence. The number of females in policing was projected to increase due primarily to economic necessities. Further women in management and supervisory roles would increase, having an increasingly positive effect on women in particular and policing in general.

DISCUSSION

Neither the numbers of women entering policing, nor the numbers of women being promoted to management and supervisory roles, has increased significantly. The reasons for this are difficult to explain to students, public officials, and, perhaps even police personnel. Why is it that over the past half century so few women have entered police work? Why have police departments not reached Peter Horne's (1979) prediction that 50% of sworn police officers would be women by the year 2000? Why is it impossible to implement the Independent Commission on the Los Angeles Police Department report's (1991) recommendation that the Los Angeles Police Department should have 50% of its sworn officers as women by the year 2000? Why is it that we have the revealing statistics from the 1998 Uniform Crime Reports that just over 10% (10.5) of total police agencies (U.S. Department of Justice, 1998:296) are sworn police women? The U.S. Bureau of Labor Statistics (1998) reports that women as "police and detectives" has risen from 5.7% in 1983 to 10.4% in 1995 and to 11.8% in 1997. Why is it that very few women become police chiefs? The following comments attempt to provide answers to these fundamental questions.

First, more women should be interested in police work for several reasons. It is an occupation that does not require specific educational requirements, although more police departments require a college degree. As many other jobs that are blue-collar, male-dominated occupations (e.g., construction, electricians, and welders) police work offers more pay, fringe benefits, authority, and autonomy than do jobs in female-dominated fields (Dubeck and Borman, 1996). Also, higher pay and greater status are associated with men's jobs (Williams, 1989:132; Jacobs, 1993:49). Police work is a blue-collar occupation where "affirmative action policies and anti-discrimination legislation permits women's entry" (Williams, 1989:142) to the workplace.

Also, it is important to indicate that the television and movie industries have played a role in shaping the public's perception of a policewoman's role in the traditionally male domain of patrol and investigation. The police officer's job is glamorized and often depicts policewomen right alongside policemen fighting crime on a day-to-day basis.

However, very little of the actual experiences of policewomen are depicted in television, movies, and videos (Hale, 1998). The discrimination, sexual harassment, and restrictive policies that women experience in police work do not make box office sales and pay for production costs and advertisements. In reality, women may not actually think of policing as a career option because of the shift work, may think of it as "dangerous work," or have been socialized to accept the more traditional occupations for women without a college education (e.g., secretarial or service). Police recruiters must address these issues in their recruitment strategies to attract women to police work (see Hale and Wyland, 1993). In addition, successful police women should be used as recruiters to attract more women to the field. Mentoring programs designed to facilitate the promotion of women to supervisory and managerial positions must be implemented to facilitate the advancement of women once they enter the police department (Sanders, 1997).

Furthermore, police departments should take advantage of how their jobs are presented in the media. Undoubtedly, our students, who are the twenty-first-century police officers, have been exposed to the image of women in policing by their tele-vision viewing. In fact, the *Journal of the American Medical Association* (1992) reported that the typical American child spends 27 hours a week watching television (see Stossel, 1997). Consequently, our present college students are (and their successors will be) exposed to an image of police women in such television programs as *NYPD Blue, Crime Scene Investigation (CSI), Third Watch, Homicide, Law and Order*, and the *X-Files*. Many of our freshman criminal justice students announce their career ambition as either "profiler" or FBI agent. Where do they see profilers and FBI agents? On weekly series such as *Profiler* and the *X-Files*. Sam and Scully are successful in their weekly investigations of serial killers and unusual "paranormal" crimes. Also, the steady information stream of crime investigations broadcast on local and national news and the weekly news programs keeps the viewing audience up to date on all the latest crime investigation techniques (DNA testing, hair and fiber analysis). The television audience is introduced to expert "criminal profilers" associated with the Federal Bureau of Investigation's (FBI) Behavioral Sciences Unit (e.g., John Douglas, Robert Ressler, and Ann Burgess).

The writers and producers of these television "cop shows" can work with actual police departments to send a positive message to the viewing audience by depicting women as successful and effective police officers. For example, actual policewomen advised the producers of the now classic *Cagney and Lacey* television series regarding the roles of Christine Cagney and Mary Beth Lacey as New York City police detectives.

Although television may portray women police officers as accepted by their peers and successful on the job, audiences should be cautioned that this is television and not reality[3] (Hale, 1998). Hollywood glorifies Kanter's (1977) concept of a "tokenism" show—casting a woman in a highly visible nontraditional profession or occupation. For example, script writers may include scenes where the policewoman encounters some initial resentment/harassment from male officers; but eventually she overcomes their hostility and is accepted by the peer group. Furthermore, it is rare for a script to depict male officers acknowledging that a policewoman earned her promotion rather than receiving it because of affirmative action policies.

However, Hollywood does not show on its weekly episodes the recurrent discrimination and harassment that policewomen or other professional women encounter from their peers when they enter nontraditional jobs of policing (*Law and Order* and *Homicide*), law (*L.A. Law* and *The Practice*), and medicine (*ER* and *Chicago Hope*). After all, the purpose of the series is to solve the crime, win the case, save the patient, not to address personnel matters. Rarely does the television audience hear the complaints from the women's peers that they got these jobs because of affirmative action and quotas; these people are often referred to as "tokens" in a negative manner. The audience does not hear the stories that Connie Fletcher's (1995) policewomen disclosed about their experiences in the police academy, in the police locker room, or on the streets when they needed backup and it was not there. After all, our weekly episodes are for entertainment; Connie Fletcher's book is read by college students and policewomen.

Consequently, a caveat (i.e., "let the viewer beware") to television aficionados and movie buffs that "real life" policewomen's experiences are not always similar to those of the policewomen "captured in the camera lens." In the everyday work world, the policewoman is a token, a representative of women in nontraditional police work. Therefore, as a token, if the policewoman succeeds, she is applauded; but unlike the policeman, the policewoman must continue to prove herself incident after incident after incident. As a token, if she fails, her failure symbolizes the failure of her gender, not her individual failure or the particular situation itself. If a man fails, he fails; his failure is not symbolic of all men; it is his failure, his situation.

For example, Shannon Faulkner was highly visible as the lone female cadet at the Citadel and was viewed as a failure when she withdrew. Her failure was seen by many as a reflection on her gender, not the obstacles she encountered in a historically male-dominated organization. Her physical unpreparedness was used to explain her failure. There was no acknowledgment of her status as the only woman in the traditionally male organization, or recognition of the resentment and ostracism she experienced. The same scenario is true for women in policing or for women in any traditionally male profession or occupation.

IMPLICATIONS

From this discussion based on undergraduate and graduate classes, there are several ways that we can utilize to increase the numbers of women entering police work.

In the Classroom

Instructors in secondary and college classrooms should present information about the roles of women in the nontraditional field of policing, as well as in law and corrections. It is important to illustrate to students that it is just not women in the field of criminal justice that encounter these situations, but that women in other traditionally male professions (business, engineering, law, and medicine) and occupations (carpenters, construction, electricians, and welders) experience the same actions. It is also paramount to discuss that ethnic- and-racial-minority males also experience many of the same obstacles as women police do. This illustrates to students that it is *both* a gender and a racial issue, not necessarily male versus female.

From this chapter itself, it is clear that college students assimilate information from class to class over their four years in higher education. Classroom instructors and authors of textbooks should include information about women (and minorities) in the criminal justice workplace. It does not take much time in any class (e.g., introductory criminal justice or policing classes) to discuss the entry of women (and minorities) into police work. These concepts can easily be incorporated with course material on the establishment of police departments in England and United States and why men were on patrol and women did not have a role in policing until the late nineteenth century. Certainly, discussion related to the President's Commission on Law Enforcement and the Administration of Justice's (1967) emphasis on the recruiting of more qualified people to work in the criminal justice system is another opportunity to include information on the role of women in policing. As students progress through their college years, more information on women in policing can be included in their courses. Once again, information from Tables 1 and 2 was based on senior law enforcement students in a police operations and management course.

In graduate courses similar pedagogical strategies can be utilized. However, it is important to recognize that graduate students are generally older, in-service professionals who may be more optimistic about the future of policewomen because they have witnessed firsthand the implementation of strategies by management to facilitate both the entry and advancement of women as sworn officers. Conversely, many graduate students realize that women have entered police work as a direct result of affirmative action policies, and their male colleagues do not automatically accept them as equals. The older students understand that women are attracted to police work due to the nature of the work as well as the opportunity that policing provides for a higher salary than the traditional occupations for women (i.e., secretarial and service positions) do.

Use of the Media in the Classroom

Today, we rely on the media not only for entertainment but to keep us informed and apprised of what is happening in our world. This is unmistakable from the ever-increasing number of movies and videos, television talk shows, news tabloids, and weekly news series. In the very near future, computers will become conventional both in the workplace and at home. The *Wall Street Journal* reported that for the first time, households in the United States with personal computers exceeded 40% (Anon., 1997c). This statistic supports the notion that as we become more familiar with computers and the Internet, we will begin to rely on its technology to provide us with access to unlimited information.

Consequently, it is important to use the media in the classroom to increase students' awareness of just how the opinions and attitudes of an audience are influenced by what they read and observe. Therefore, in the next section of this chapter we describe how one futuristic television series, *Star Trek* (airing in the mid-1960s), depicted the changing roles of women in a nontraditional workforce. When the instructor uses illustrations like this, it provides an opportunity to discuss with students how captivating television can be and how it may reinforce stereotypes of women in nontraditional occupations and professions. Also, it provides an occasion to dialogue with students about tokenism and acceptance of women in the workplace.

Star Trek: A Depiction of Women's Work and Women's Place in Space Travel

When we examine the future of women in policing, it is interesting to compare the expansion of the roles of women in policing over the years with the development of the women characters and their roles in the television series *Star Trek*. In 1966, *Star Trek* first aired with Lieutenant Uhura (actress Nichelle Nichols) and Nurse Christine Chapel, later Dr. Christine Chapel (actress Majel Barrett). Nichelle Nichols was cast as Lieutenant Uhura, the first black woman in space *and* on television in a nonstereo-typical role as communications specialist. It should not be surprising that she was given the job but not the autonomy that a man would unquestionably have had. This is acknowledged by Nichelle Nichols, who complained that her character, Lieutenant Uhura, never got off the bridge and her dialogue was limited to variations of "all hailing frequencies open, sir" (Gibberman, 1991:143). Lieutenant Uhura remained a communications officer for 20 years.

An interesting aside was that Nichelle Nichols became actively involved in the real space program as a recruiter for NASA (Gibberman, 1991:55) where she "...worked for NASA's education and recruitment program and became known as the 'First Lady of Space'" (Gibberman, 1991:143). This illustration can serve as an example to recruitment of women in police (e.g., perhaps contracting with Gillian Anderson, who plays the highly successful FBI agent Dana Scully, to serve as a recruiter for women in law enforcement).

In the *Star Trek: Next Generation* (1987–1994) series, the audience was introduced to several women in nontraditional roles. For example, Dr. Beverly Crusher was a follow-up to Dr. Leonard "Bones" McCoy from the original series. Counselor Deanna Troi (actress Marina Sirtis) was the empathic ship's counselor. In later episodes she was portrayed as more of a psychiatrist. The actress Diana Muldaur cast as Dr. Kate Pulaski, the chief medical doctor, portrayed another doctor. Denise Crosby's character, Tasha Yar, was security chief and was killed during the first season.

The third televised series, *Star Trek: Deep Space 9*, introduced Major Kira Nerys as second in command (Bajoran Liaison) of Deep Space Nine. Lieutenant Jadzia Dax was operations officer, and science officer of Deep Space Nine.

The fourth series, *Star Trek: Voyager*, presented Captain Kathryn Janeway, Kes as the medical technician on the *USS Voyager*, and Lieutenant B'Elanna Torres as chief engineer. The latest addition to the cast of *Voyager* was a Borg "Seven of Nine." The evolution of the Star Trek series parallels the progress that women have made in policing from crime prevention specialists trained in social work and nursing to a small number of police chiefs in metropolitan areas. However, as we show in our conclusion, much remains to be accomplished.

CONCLUSIONS

The four *Star Trek* series depict the evolution of women's roles in future space expeditions. Similarly, the functions of police women have evolved, expanded, and improved over the past nine decades since Alice Stebbins Wells became the first sworn policewoman with the power to arrest and carry a gun. This trend will continue as increasing numbers of women enter police work and reach management positions where they can develop and implement policy. We also anticipate increasing numbers of females entering the profession and having a lasting impact. With the acceptance of policewomen by their peers and supervisors, their token status will diminish and they will no longer be considered an anomaly in policing. However, the majority of police departments will not reach the often cited goal of 50%, if any. The impact of gender socialization, work norms, family obligations, and childrearing desires will continue to limit some women.

Interestingly, rather than the role played by female police changing, the role of male officers is projected to change more. Community policing and proactive strategies dictate greater interaction with citizens, thus forcing *successful* male officers to learn interactional techniques from their female counterparts.

As a final thought, we would like to share the observation that one constant characteristic of policing is that it is constantly changing. Policing changes, as it should, to reflect changing social conditions and to rectify its own faults (corruption, deviance, excess, etc.). The continuous change will persist. We would like to suggest trends that will influence how and when the police change.

In this century, policing will change in some fundamental ways. First, private security will greatly increase the number of people working in law enforcement and order maintenance. Many major U.S. cities already have security officers in fast-food restaurants, malls, convenience stores, and other locations. Presumably, this trend will continue and escalate. Some private security officers now make more money than municipal police officers do. If trends against increasing taxation continue, government budgets will not allow municipal salaries to compete with private industry. Will the best-and-brightest police applicants consequently be drawn to private security? How will this affect policing? Female police?

Trends in criminal justice education will also affect the police force of the twenty-first century in the United States. Although there are no specific educational requirements for the police officer position (Career Information Center, 1996:57), many local and state police departments are beginning to require at least 60 credits of college, or a four-year degree in criminal justice. This requirement is due primarily to the large number of applicants that police departments receive whenever they advertise positions. Even in situations where only a high school degree is required, college graduates who flock to take the police examinations should score higher and perform at higher levels than their high school graduate counterparts at the oral interview stage of the police selection process. Optimistically, the entry of more college-educated police officers should be favorable for women entering patrol. These college graduates in criminal justice should have more favorable attitudes toward women in police because of their exposure to the research on the effectiveness of women as police officers.

Competition for police officer positions "will be keen," since the availability of positions depends on funding available to police departments (Career Information Center, 1996:57). Unlike correctional officer positions, which will increase steadily in the twenty-first century (Brindley et. al., 1997:105), the total number of police officers positions available will "rise slowly…[with] openings to replace officers who retire or leave their jobs for other reasons" (Career Information Center, 1996:57).

Second, the United States will continue to be a pluralistic society. The proportions of what we currently consider "minorities" will escalate. Currently, Caucasians are the minority in some California universities. This demographic shift will also affect policing. Other cultures have different views of the police. To provide two dichotomies, for often good reasons, the English generally hold police in high respect, whereas Mexicans generally fear the local police. How will this affect policing? All this diversity will require a tolerant, interactive, and highly qualified police officer.

Third, medical advances, lifestyle changes, and improved nutrition will result in Americans living longer. As our society continues to "gray" into the next century, will the older members of society desire meaningful employment (such as policing?). Will an Equal Rights Amendment include letting the elderly become police officers, just as it did women? For example, the Aurora, Colorado police department hired two recruits in their fifties who were starting a second career after retiring from their first. Again, the ramifications may fundamentally change policing, perhaps for the better.

A setback for police women occurred on November 3, 1997, when the U.S. Supreme Court "let stand California's groundbreaking Proposition 209, a ban on race and gender preference in hiring and school admission. Affirmative action foes predicted that other states now will follow California's lead" (Anon., 1997a). Christine Williams (1989:142) specifies that "affirmative action policies and anti-discrimination legislation are necessary for women to enter blue-collar occupations where they encounter "often explicit and organized resistance." Furthermore, she believes that "affirmative action policies and anti-discrimination legislation… allow [women] the possibility to transform these male-dominated organizations."

As we have described in this chapter, women police have transformed—made a difference—in police work. And without affirmative action policies beginning with Title VII in 1972 and subsequent antidiscrimination legislation, women would have been denied entry to police patrol duties. What can we do to prevent all the advances that women have made in policing from eroding? We have several recommendations to offer to ensure police women's continued success in the twenty-first century.

First, organizations concerned with the advancement of women in policing must meld with similar organizations to form stronger coalitions to lobby for the continuation of affirmative action and antidiscrimination programs. These organizations include the National Association of Women Law Enforcement Executives (NAWLEE), the International Association of Women Police (IAWP), the National Center for Women and Policing, the National Organization for Black Law Enforcement Officers (NOBLE), and the International Association of Chiefs of Police (IACP). This solidarity will present a strong lobby advocating for the continuation of all current law enforcement recruitment, training, and advancement programs. The coalition must convince law enforcement agencies that the research on women in policing, and changes in the nature of police work itself, support the need for women to remain and to continue advancement in police departments.

It is vital for educational institutions (high schools, community colleges, colleges, and universities) to implement programs that prepare young women for success in nontraditional occupations such as policing. Programs should include sports programs that teach young women interpersonal skills necessary to be competitive in the workplace (Marcus, 1997:88). Junior police academies is another way that law enforcement agencies can work with secondary schools to educate and prepare students for future careers in law enforcement (National Association of Veteran Police Officers, 1997).

Criminal justice programs in community colleges, colleges, and universities need to emphasize to students that *diversity* is essential if police departments are to be successful in performing their duties. The community the police serve is not only *diverse* in its needs, but the community's population is *diverse*–it is not composed only of white males. Research supports that victims of crime benefit from the presence of women police officers.

An additional goal of higher education is to provide future police officers with the knowledge and skills to do their jobs well. Not only do students need courses in law, communication, and psychology; they must also be able to analyze situations and write thorough reports. College classroom instruction must prepare students to perform well at both the written and oral interview stages of the police personnel selection process. When women students score higher on the tests, they cannot be told that they only got the job because of affirmative action or a quota system.

Our last recommendation is for individuals to become knowledgeable about political platforms and vote for those candidates who support strong affirmative action and anti-discrimination legislation. Women who are currently police officers must recognize that they would not have these jobs without Title VII of the Civil Rights Act of 1964.

Finally, we must all work together to keep the momentum going for the advancement of women in policing. We do not want our achievements compared to the labors of Sisyphus.

ENDNOTES

1. These categories were taken from Fyfe et al.'s Chapter 12 on "Discipline." The authors point out that "discipline is a responsibility that permeates a police department, that is shared by everyone in it, and that results from several nonpunitive processes that often are not included in lists of disciplinary activities....Punishment fits at the end of this list and should come into play when none of these more positive disciplinary functions has produced the desired results" (p. 409).
2. Women state troopers in Massachusetts expressed dissatisfaction with a new policy that permitted the state police physician (not the woman's doctor) to determine when a pregnant officer should be put on modified duty. Modified duty specifies that officers "can't walk the beat, make traffic stops or even drive police vehicles" (Anon., 1997b:A8).
3. A content analysis of over 100 movies/videos produced since 1972 to the present concluded that by the end of the presentation, the police woman (either patrol, detective, or chief) is "kept in her place." The movie/video concludes with her as either injured, dead, or leaving police work to marry usually another police officer. The success of a woman police chief in *Fargo* (1996) is downplayed at the end with a bedroom scene where she is seen assuring her husband that his winning second place for his stamp design is valuable. At no time does he compliment her on her success with solving the crime and apprehending the criminals.

ACKNOWLEDGMENTS

The authors acknowledge and thank the students for their participation in the class exercises. We also thank Margaret Burkholder at Shippensburg University for preparing Tables 1 and 2.

REFERENCES

ANON. (1997a). Court ruling could end affirmative action. *Sentinel*, Carlisle, PA, November 4, p. A6.

ANON. (1997b). State troopers unhappy with pregnancy policy. *Sentinel*, Carlisle, PA, October 16, p. A8.

ANON. (1997c). U.S. households with PCS exceed 40% for the first time. *Wall Street Journal*, June 10, p. B9.

APPIER, J. (1992). Preventive justice: The campaign for women police, 1910–1940. *Women and Criminal Justice*, 4(1):3–36.

BITTNER, E. (1970). *The Functions of the Police in Modern Society: A Review of Background Factors, Current Practices, and Possible Role Models*. Chevy Chase, MD: National Institute of Mental Health.

BRINDLEY, D., R. M. BENNEFIELD, N. Q. DANYLIW, K. HETTER, and M. LOFTUS (compilers) (1997). 20 hot job tracks. *U.S. News & World Report*, 123(16):95–106.

BROWN, M. C. (1994). The plight of female police: A survey of NW patrolmen. *The Police Chief*, 61(9):50–53.

Bureau of the Census (1998). *Statistical Abstract of the United States*. Washington, DC: U.S. Government Printing Office.

Career Information Center (1996). *Public and Community Services*. 6th ed., Vol. 11. New York: Macmillan.

Dubeck, P. J., and K. Borman (eds.) (1996). *Women and Work: A Handbook*. New York: Garland Publishing.

Federal Bureau of Investigation (1998). *Crime in the United States*. Uniform Crime Reports. Washington, DC: U.S. Department of Justice.

Fletcher, C. (1995). *Breaking and Entering: Women Cops Break the Code of Silence to Tell Their Stories from the Inside*. New York: Pocket Books.

Fyfe, J. J., J. R. Greene, W. F. Walsh, O. W. Wilson, and R. C. McLaren (1997). *Police Administration*, 5th ed. New York: McGraw-Hill.

Gibberman, S. R. (1991). *Star Trek: An Annotated Guide to Resources on the Development, the Phenomenon, the People, the Television Series, the Films, and Novels and the Recordings*. Jefferson, NC: McFarland & Company.

Goldstein, H. (1990). *Problem-Oriented Policing*. New York: McGraw-Hill.

Greene, J. R., and S. D. Mastrofski (eds.). (1988). *Community Policing: Rhetoric or Reality?* New York: Praeger.

Grennan, S. A. (1987). Findings on the role of officer gender in violent encounters with citizens. *Journal of Police Science and Administration*, 15(1):78–85.

Hale, D. C. (1992). Women in policing. In G. W. Cordner and D. C. Hale (eds.), *What Works in Policing: Operations and Administration Examined*. Cincinnati, OH: Anderson Publishing, pp. 125–142.

Hale, D. C. (1998). Keeping women in their place: An analysis of policewomen in videos, 1972–1996. In F. Y. Bailey and D. C. Hale (eds.), *Popular Culture, Crime, and Justice*. Belmont, CA: West/Wadsworth, pp. 159–179.

Hale, D. C., and S. M. Wyland (1993). Dragons and dinosaurs: The plight of patrol women. *Police Forum*, 3(2):1–6. Highland Heights, KY: Academy of Criminal Justice Sciences.

Heckeroth, S. E., and A. M. Barker (1997). Police department efforts to deter sexual harassment. *USA Today*, 125(2626):64–67.

Homant, R. J., and D. B. Kennedy (1984). A content analysis of statements about policewomen's handling of domestic violence. *American Journal of Police*, 3(2):265–283.

Horne, P. (1979). Policewomen: 2000 A.D. *Police Journal*, 52(1):344–357.

House, C. H. (1993). The changing role of women in law enforcement. *The Police Chief*, 60(10):139–144.

Independent Commission on the Los Angeles Police Department (1991). *Report of the Independent Commission on the Los Angeles Police Department*. Los Angeles, CA: The Commission.

Jacobs, J. A. (1993). Men in female-dominated fields: Trends and turnover. In C. L. Williams (ed.) *Doing "Women's Work": Men in Nontraditional Occupations*. Thousand Oaks, CA: Sage Publications, pp. 49–63.

Kanter, R. M. (1977). *Men and Women of the Corporation*. New York: Basic Books.

Kennedy, D. B., and R. J. Homant (1983). Attitudes of abused women toward male and female police officers. *Criminal Justice and Behavior*, 10(4):391–405.

Klockars, C. B. (1985). *The Idea of Police*. Thousand Oaks, CA: Sage Publications.

Lanier, M. M. (1996). An evolutionary typology of women police officers. *Women and Criminal Justice*, 8(2):35–57.

MARCUS, M. B. (1997). If you let me play…a basketball or a hockey puck may shatter the glass ceiling. *U.S. News & World Report*, 123(16):88, 89.

MILLER, S. L. (1999). *Gender and Community Policing: Walking the Talk*. Boston: Northeastern University Press.

MILTON, C. H. (1975). Women in policing. In J. T. Curan and R. H. Ward (eds.), *Police and Law Enforcement 1973–1974*, Vol. II. New York: AMS Press, pp. 230–245.

NATIONAL ASSOCIATION OF VETERAN POLICE OFFICERS in association with New Century Productions and Sol Productions (1997). *Future Cop*. Washington, DC: NAVPO.

ODEM, M. E., and S. SCHLOSSMAN. (1991). Guardians of virtue: The juvenile court and female delinquency in early 20th-Century Los Angeles. *Crime and Delinquency*. April, 37(2); pp. 186–203.

PRESIDENT'S COMMISSION ON LAW ENFORCEMENT AND THE ADMINISTRATION OF JUSTICE (1967). *The Challenge of Crime in a Free Society*. Washington, DC: U.S. Government Printing Office.

REISS, A. J., JR. (1971). *The Police and the Public*. New Haven, CT: Yale University Press.

SANDERS, D. L. (1997). 21st-century issues for women in policing. *Police Chief*, 64(1):6.

SKOGAN, W. G., and S. M. HARTNETT (1997). *Community Policing, Chicago Style*. New York: Oxford University Press.

SKOLNICK, J. H., and D. H. BAYLEY (1986). *The New Blue Line: Police Innovation in Six American Cities*. New York: The Free Press.

STOSSEL, S. (1997). The man who counts the killings. *Atlantic Monthly*, 279(5):86–105.

TROJANOWICZ, R., and B. BUCQUEROUX (1990). *Community Policing: A Contemporary Perspective*. Cincinnati, OH: Anderson Publishing.

WESTLEY, W. A. (1970). *Violence and the Police: A Sociological Study of Law, Custom, and Morality*. Cambridge, MA: MIT Press.

WILLIAMS, C. L. (1989). *Gender Differences at Work: Women and Men in Nontraditional Occupations*. Berkeley, CA: University of California Press.

WILSON, J. Q. (1968, 1978). *Varieties of Police Behavior: The Management of Law and Order in Eight Communities*. Cambridge, MA: Harvard University Press.

PART VIII

Conclusions

chapter 27

The Future Is Now

Summing Up

Roslyn Muraskin

Crime is a problem that did not disappear in the preceding centuries nor will it disappear in the twenty-first century. Can we predict the future with any precision? Probably not. What is predicted is that crime will remain with us forever. Perhaps, there will be different kinds of crime, as noted in this work, but crime remains a factor of life. Even if the crime index is down, individual events create the impression that certain kinds of crime are out of control; take the example of drug abuse. We can present no easy solutions or answers.

We know that in place already is sophisticated technology that will aid in the solving of crimes. We know that we face a growing, aging correctional population, presenting new problems in terms of special care in the health of inmates. The media continue to focus on the negatives of the criminal justice system, and therefore the politicians tell us that we need to build newer and bigger and better correctional facilities. This is not how to solve the crime problem.

We know that by the year 2006, the baby boomers of today will be old enough to commit criminal acts. Based on demographics, we will have an ever-larger number of people as defendants in the criminal justice system than envisioned previously. Prediction is a risky business, but we need to review the trends. What we need is the use of advanced technology that can put information in the hands of law enforcement officers quickly. "Three strikes and you're out" was not the answer for the twentieth century, and it certainly will not be the answer for this new century. If we were to multiply the number of felons in each state, we would have correctional facilities with larger populations than those of some states.

It is possible that the year 2001 could be the one in which the United States calls a halt to its long love affair with capital punishment as predicted by the magazine *The Nation*. We believe that executions will increase throughout this first decade and not lessen until later in the century. The moratorium on the death penalty in Illinois, the growing number of death row exonerations, the advances of DNA technology, the Columbia University study (2000) of a broken capital punishment system, the slight decrease in the national total of executions in the year 2000, the demise of the electric chair in Florida, and growing pressure from abroad will *not* make a difference for at least a decade. To many of us this is depressing.

There exists little doubt that drug users will continue to provide much of the fodder for our rapidly expanding correctional system unless people take notice that there are alternatives to incarceration for drug users. The funds that we currently spend on drug interdiction, law enforcement, the courts, and incarceration should allow us to make substantial progress in improving treatment available to those who need it. Time will tell.

Gangs will continue to grow, and not simply from the lower economic classes, but from the middle classes as well. If the family continues to deteriorate together with other social control institutions, we can expect much more gang activity than has existed previously. Gangs are not going to dissipate soon, if ever. There is hope, however, if the advice of the experts is heeded and communities take the necessary initiatives to develop policies that will provide the necessary resources to stem the tide of gang activities.

If the availability of sexually explicit materials delivered by radio, television, books, films, computer services, and dial-a-porn is identified as a social problem, it will become essential that a better understanding emerge as to why those interested in seeing and hearing such material is so resistant to change. Why is it that consumers of most pornographic materials are males? Is it not that we need better sex education than we have currently in an effort to reduce the interest in pornography? These kinds of questions underlie the current debate about the effects of pornography on attitudes toward sex and toward women.

Community policing will be revisited in this new century and will become acceptable in today's world. As noted in this book, the community policing concept will become embedded in the strategies of policing. Citizen police academies will become common, with citizens being involved directly in crime prevention and control strategies. Included in this concept will be private security organizations, which will function alongside the community police.

The function of the Bill of Rights in the twenty-first century will be simply to protect the rights of minorities, whomever they might be. It does not seem, at this writing, that there will be a sweeping denial of basic human rights in the United States. But increased crime and violence would result in a strain on the social fabric, and such strains will determine the shape of the criminal justice system in the new century.

Will we see a new kind of juvenile justice system in this country? As critics and supporters look back to the first 100 years of the juvenile court, both can agree that the founding principles and original intent of a separate court for youth have faced serious challenges. Critics may argue that flawed assumptions and failed performance should justify dismantling of the system. It may be, however, that transformations and emerging paradigms will be evidence of a system capable of adapting to social and political change while meeting the challenges of the twenty-first century.

If incarceration rates continue to rise, we may see privatization of correctional institutions. The prevailing legal issue will revolve around the extent to which a state may constitutionally delegate its authority to punish. The legal questions surrounding prison privatization, however, involve more than just the issue of whether a privately paid guard can use force against an inmate as a delegate of the state. Also involved is the question of whether representatives of a private company may engage in behavior or decision making that has any detrimental effect whatsoever on an inmate. In examining victims' rights, the stark contrast between the sheltered lives of the privileged classes in gated communities and the misery endured by the inhabitants of out-of-control "free-fire zones" and "no-man's lands" will serve as an indictment of the gross inequities imposed by the problem of differential access to justice.

The issues of gender and race will continue to plague us until such time as we understand that equality or parity is the answer. More needs to be done by elected officials, public policymakers, educational institutions, the criminal justice system, the media, and business as well as by labor organizations. It was Gloria Steinem who noted that cultural myths die hard, especially if they are used to empower one part of the population. There is no way to allow both genders and all minorities to enjoy the equal protection of the laws, unless and until we are committed to the elimination of all gender discrimination. In this new century, more cases will be heard, and legal procedures and precedents will be established to ensure that complainants will receive fairer hearings than before. There has existed for centuries the rhetoric of both gender and racial equality, but it has yet to match everyday life experience.

The twenty-first century is here. Plans are needed to quell the fear of crime; plans are needed to hold the crime rates down, not simply for a few years, but forever. Action is needed. The rhetoric continues. Every time a crime of great magnitude occurs, the populace and the politicians are enraged. But rage does nothing without some plan of action to back it up. Concrete plans and policies are required. By linking yesterday to today and then to tomorrow, we may see some improvement. Crime in this century (as in preceding centuries) will not simply go away, unless we are smart enough to plan this moment. We must have a "vision for change."

Epilogue

chapter 28

Criminal Justice
in the New Millennium

The Crises of System and Science[1]

David V. Baker, Ph.D. and Richard P. Davin, Ph.D.

ABSTRACT

The criminal justice issues facing U.S. society in the coming decades of the new millennium will continue to challenge the institutional effectiveness of our nation's system of justice administration as long as the manner in which criminal justice as an academic discipline responds to these issues remains wholly inadequate. Criminal justice scholars must take notice of the inextricable link between the current condition of justice administration in the United States and the lack of scientific veracity in the discipline of criminal justice. Our central thesis in this epilogue is that the present state of affairs for both the U.S. system of justice administration and the discipline of criminal justice are in institutional states of *crisis*. Unquestionably, the system under which justice professionals dispense criminal justice in U.S. society is far removed from the constitutionally prescribed canons of equity, fairness, and impartiality. What's more, we place accountability for this crisis at the doorstep of the criminal justice discipline for its inattention to exploring meaningful reforms required to alleviate the systemic misfortunes of justice administration in U.S. society. Here, we provide a straightforward and candid look at the *tragedy* of American criminal justice. Moreover, we advance a rational course of action that, if adopted by the criminal justice discipline, would go far in ameliorating the tragedy.

INTRODUCTION

Visions for Change: Crime and Justice in the Twenty-First Century explores some of the more notable issues confronting justice administration in the second millennium. But what is most important, the selections brought together in this book clearly identify issues that, in the coming decades, will seriously challenge both the institutional effectiveness of justice administration and the academic integrity of criminal justice. Any consideration of the future prospects of the U.S. system of justice administration or the veracity of criminal justice as an academic discipline must at once take notice of their inextricable connectedness and their current condition. Regarding the present state of affairs, we believe that both the U.S. system of justice administration and the discipline of criminal justice are in states of institutional *crisis*. The processes and procedures under which justice professionals dispense justice in U.S. society are far removed from the constitutional canons of equity, fairness, and impartiality. Moreover, the manner in which the discipline of criminal justice has responded to the blatant inequities of justice administration remains wholly inadequate. As a result, we place at the doorstep of the criminal justice discipline much of the accountability for the lack of attention paid to the institutional reforms required to alleviate the systemic *misfortune* of justice administration in United States society. Thus, our purpose in this epilogue is to provide a straightforward and candid explication of the *tragedy* of American criminal justice and to advance what we believe to be a reasonable course of action toward amelioration of the *tragedy*.

THE CRISIS IN JUSTICE ADMINISTRATION

According to Trebach, "[i]f rights are to have real meaning for the great mass of people, we must not only inscribe them in constitutions and statutes—we must support these freedoms by powerful institutions as well."[2] But Marable may have put it best when he said, "like the rest of United States society, white society has designed the American legal system essentially for whites."[3] The ideological premises of *racism, sexism,* and *classism* are fully institutionalized and systemic in the U.S. criminal justice system. In one of the most comprehensive studies on the adverse impact of crime and criminal justice on American minority groups, the National Minority Advisory Council on Criminal Justice acknowledged that the "laws and public policies in the United States reflect the contradiction of a society attempting to act within an egalitarian ideological posture while treating minorities with direct, blunt and flagrant inequality."[4] Indeed, patterns of institutional discrimination are so pervasive in the U.S. system of justice administration that it is one of society's most oppressive institutions.[5] Structured inequality remains deeply embedded in American criminal justice because the discriminatory conduct of justice professionals is built into the system's structure and legitimated by U.S. cultural beliefs and legal codes.[6] Justice professionals can no longer deny the consequences of structural inequality as aberrant, obscure, tangential, and unimportant in the administration of justice. Structural inequality is not fragmented and isolated in our system of justice; rather, it is endemic, integral, and central to its processes and procedures. It is indisputable that race, ethnic, gender, and class inequality are clearly associated with racial profiling and selective law enforcement, the vicious brutality waged against nonwhite minorities by state and federal police agents, the violent sexual exploitation of female inmates by male prison guards, the torture and murder of custodial populations by prison guardians, the politicalization of crime as a nonwhite problem, the warehousing of blacks and Latinos in our nation's jails and prisons, the prosecutorial impotence in gaining convictions for hate crime, the violence-related morbidity and mortality in Latino communities, the capriciousness with which our society imposes death as punishment, and the continued pacification of critical race theory and feminist thought concerning U.S. criminal justice.[7] In this regard, the criminal justice discipline can no longer summarily reject as inconsequential the constitutional mandate that even nonwhite minority Americans are to be afforded the fundamental rights of due process of law and equal protection of the law. Such is the *crisis* of justice administration in U.S. society.

Police Lawlessness

The use of violence and brutality has a long history in American policing, and unfortunately, its use remains just as pervasive and widespread in contemporary law enforcement.[8] The historically based literature also explains that white police officers have aimed their violent and brutal methods mostly at race and ethnic minorities.[9] Race is integral to police brutality because police consider minority persons more dangerous and arousing of more suspicion than white persons. A recent report by Human Rights Watch on police brutality in U.S. cities noted that "[r]ace continues to play a central role in police brutality in the United States...Police have subjected minorities to apparently discriminatory treatment and have physically abused minorities while using racial epithets. Each new incident involving police mistreatment of an African American, Hispanic American or other minority—and particularly those that receive media attention—reinforces a belief that some residents are subjected to particularly harsh treatment and racial bias."[10]

High-profile cases such as the police brutality and violence surrounding Rodney King, Abner Louima, Amadou Diallo, Tyisha Miller, and the atrocities associated with the antigang unit based in the Los Angeles Police Department's Rampart Division limit our societal notion of police lawlessness to out-of-control rogue city cops. Yet police violence is often collaborative among different agencies. For example, a recent review of several hundred complaints of Mexican migrants found that agents patrolling the United States–Mexico border incessantly violate their civil rights, including illegal searches of persons and private property, verbal, psychological, and physical abuse, child abuse, deprivation of food, water, and medical attention, torture, theft, excessive force, assault and battery, and murder. The victims of this violence lodged complaints against the United States Border Patrol, the Immigration and Naturalization Service, United States Customs, the United States Port Authority, the Sheriff's Departments of San Diego, Vista, San Marcos, Fallbrook, and Riverside, the San Diego Police Department, the California Highway Patrol, and the California National Guard.[11]

Although thousands of allegations of police abuse are filed every year with law enforcement agencies, the extent of police brutality is actually unknown. Nevertheless, Human Rights Watch reported that roughly 12,000 civil rights complaints alleging police abuse were filed with the United States Department of Justice in 1999.[12] Despite these numbers, there is very little accountability of police for brutality.[13] Of the complaints reported by Human Rights Watch, only 31 officers were convicted of crimes under civil rights statutes. One reason for the lack of police accountability for abusive tactics is a reluctance of local and federal prosecutors to take on police brutality cases.[14]

Aggressive and arbitrary police practices also target black and Latino motorists along many of the nation's interstate highways as part of the federal government's "war on drugs" campaign. In Maryland, for example, blacks account for only 17% of motorists but 73% of drivers stopped and searched by police on Interstate 95 for possible drug trafficking. Yet 76% of all drivers on that interstate are white. In Illinois, while Latinos are 8% of the state's population, they account for 30% of the drivers stopped by police. The racial profiling and targeting of black and Latino motorists has become so pervasive that minorities now refer to the practice as D.W.B—"driving while black (brown)." Law enforcement agencies across the country also systematically target minority travelers, including pedestrians, motorists, and airline passengers.[15] United States Customs inspectors regularly strip-search minorities under the notion that they may be smuggling drugs into the United States. The U.S. Supreme Court sanctioned these practices in *Whren* v. *United States*.[16] The Court essentially gave tacit approval to police to conduct searches during traffic stops of minority motorists by severely undermining motorists' Fourth Amendment protections against unreasonable searches and seizures by allowing police to use state traffic codes to usurp probable cause or reasonable suspicion.[17] The Court ruled that police are not required to inform motorists that they can deny consent to police to search their car and that police are not required to inform a motorist that after the initial reasons for a traffic stop are resolved, the motorist is free to leave.

One could suggest that bias-motivated crimes may be proliferated by law enforcement's insensitivity to criminal activity directed at minority groups. Many victims of bias-motivated crimes fail to report incidents of hate crime to police agencies because the victims often fear reprisal from those very institutions designed to protect against hate crimes. Because the U.S. criminal justice system has not fully institutionalized an antihate movement within its ranks, antihate efforts have been ineffective in bringing justice for the victims of hate crimes.[18] For example, undocumented immigrants are unlikely to report hate crimes out of fear that an investigation of the incident would reveal that they are in the country illegally and, as a result, would be turned over to the INS for deportation. Another problem with reporting hate crime is that many police officers do not understand what constitutes a hate crime, particularly line officers who tend to be the most cynical about bias-motivated conduct. In this regard, when a young black gay man reported to Los Angeles police officers that three white skinheads had beaten and stabbed him, the officers ridiculed him by calling him names, pulled on his earrings, and told him the attack was his fault.[19] Moreover, prosecutors are extremely selective in choosing which cases involving hate crimes to prosecute in that racial stereotypes often influence the perceptions of jurors.[20] For example, the U.S. Justice Department prosecuted only 22 of the more than 8000 reported hate crimes committed in 1997.[21] Gay men and lesbians also have been subjected to unprovoked violence by police officers and other forms of police harassment. Because of their reluctance to report crimes and their distrust of the criminal justice system, gay men and lesbians are more attractive victims for perpetrators of bias crime.[22]

Courts and Partiality

Most Americans presume that notions of fundamental fairness characterize our nation's courts. While the adversarial nature of criminal proceedings ostensibly offers a semblance of fairness, it nevertheless reproduces the inequalities endemic throughout the system. Arguably, state and federal prosecutors possess unbridled discretion to file criminal charges against persons suspected of crime.[23] They alone determine the number of criminal counts to be filed against a criminal suspect and the seriousness of the charges to be filed against a suspect. Characteristics of the crime, the criminal, and those of the victim commonly influence prosecutorial discretion. Basing prosecutorial discretion upon unjustifiable (extralegal) standards is unconstitutional. But that such factors as race and ethnicity enter into prosecutorial decision making remains a critical issue in the administration of justice. Indeed, such U.S. Supreme Court cases as *Ah Sin* v. *Wittman*,[24] where only Chinese people were prosecuted for illicit gambling, *Butler* v. *Cooper*,[25] where trial delays imposed on black defendants were used to force them into accepting plea bargains, and *U.S.* v. *Clary*,[26] where only black defendants were prosecuted as crack cocaine dealers in federal courts attest to the sociohistorical significance of prosecutors' abuse of discretion on racial grounds. Race continues to be a critical factor influencing prosecutorial decision making.[27] One study on prosecutorial decisions to reject or dismiss charges against felony defendants in Los Angeles reveals that prosecutors dismiss charges at the initial hearing stage in 60% of all cases involving white male defendants, but they similarly dismiss charges in only 46% of all cases involving black and Hispanic male defendants. In contrast, prosecutors fully prosecute 26% of all criminal cases involving white male defendants, but they fully prosecute 39% of all cases regarding black male defendants and 42% of all cases concerning Hispanic male defendants.[28]

Prosecutorial misconduct proves particularly heinous in murder cases. Over the last several decades, some 67 defendants have received death sentences as a direct result of prosecutorial misconduct even though roughly half of the defendants in these cases were subsequently released. Scholars contend that prosecutorial misconduct is on the rise because efforts to deter prosecutorial misconduct have proven largely unsuccessful. For example, the U.S. Supreme Court held in *Brady* v. *Maryland*[29] that prosecutors are under a constitutional duty to disclose evidence favorable to the accused. Despite *Brady*, scholars have documented several hundred murder cases that have been reversed because of prosecutorial and police misconduct.[30] Moreover, prosecutors rarely face criminal charges for misconduct, as attested to by the fact that of those documented cases of prosecutorial misconduct, not one prosecutor was ever convicted of criminal conduct or even disbarred. Adding to the problem of prosecutorial accountability for misconduct is that they enjoy absolute immunity from civil liability. In fact, prosecutors found to have engaged in misconduct are often elevated to the bar as judges.[31]

In one of the more appalling cases of prosecutorial misconduct in the United States, a federal District Court in Pennsylvania threw out the first-degree murder conviction of Lisa Lambert for brutally murdering Laurie Show on the morning of December 20, 1991. Laurie Show was a 16-year-old high school student killed with a knife to her neck. Lambert had received a life sentence and, consequently, was raped by a custodial guard while in prison. The federal district court found the prosecutor's conduct in the Lambert case so egregious that the court forbid the prosecution from retrying Lambert and referred the prosecutor's conduct to the state's disciplinary board and to the U.S. Attorney's office. In April 1997, the court ordered Lambert's immediate release because the court found 25 separate instances of prosecutorial misconduct and expressed its view that the police committed perjury and fabricated and destroyed crucial evidence, that witnesses were intimidated, and that the prosecutor knowingly used perjured testimony in this case in which the death penalty was sought.[32]

Racism also pervades the U.S. jury system. With historical roots to the Norman conquest of England in 1066, the jury system reinforces the idea of fairness in Anglo-American jurisprudence. The United States adopted the jury system in the Sixth Amendment, by which "in all criminal prosecutions, the accused shall enjoy the right to a speedy and public trial by an impartial jury." Yet considerable evidence suggests that throughout the history of U.S. criminal justice, minorities have been methodically disenfranchised from full and equal participation in the jury system. All-white juries have been used selectively to ensure the guilt of nonwhite defendants accused of crimes against whites. The pervasiveness of institutionalized racism continues in the American jury system today. One study examined four specific determinants of disproportionate racial representation on juries: racial discrimination in jury selection procedures, socioeconomic barriers preventing full-community participation by blacks and other racial minorities, judicial discrimination that allows racially distinguished jury representation, and institutional racism and bureaucratic discrimination all perpetuate judicial race and ethnic inequality in the United States.[33] To these scholars, the jury system as a whole and jury selection in particular are grounded on Anglo-controlled institutions and structural ideas of supremacy.

Jury nullification has also played a significant role in ensuring the judicial impunity with which white people can victimize blacks and other nonwhite minorities in the United States.[34] Historically, all white racist juries often disallowed convictions of whites accused of murdering blacks throughout the history of the South. The practice continues today. To some scholars, minority defendants must begin to draw upon unconventional methods to accommodate the inherent imbalance in the scales of justice. In his review of the doctrine of jury nullification as an effective means by which blacks may rectify the injustices they often receive at the hands of the U.S. criminal justice system, former U.S. attorney Paul Butler contends that black jurors must recognize the inherent racism in U.S. criminal justice and respond by neutralizing and mitigating racism's effect upon their communities. To Butler, black jurors are legally and morally bound to nullify their fact-finding charge in favor of racially driven decision making because black defendants are better judged by other blacks, who are far more likely than whites to understand the social, political, economic, historical, and cultural contexts of black criminality.[35]

Sentencing Disparity

Criminology literature is filled with empirically based evidence that whites are dealt with far more leniently than nonwhite minorities in the criminal justice system. One illustration of the oppressive relationship between America's minority populations and justice administration is the representativeness of race and ethnic minorities in the criminal justice system. Moreover, the overrepresentation of a population in the criminal justice system permits researchers to examine the operation of extralegal factors, such as biased attitudes and perceptions, in the processing of the population by the criminal justice system. Several studies have examined the extent to which Latinos suffer ethnic discrimination in criminal court processes.[36] Latinos tend to receive harsher prison sentences from courts and serve more time in prison than do whites convicted of similar crimes. Latinos are also less able to make bail than whites and more likely to have court-appointed counsel. A study of two southwestern cities found that Latinos who were tried for a crime and found guilty rather than simply entering a guilty plea as part of a plea-bargaining agreement received far harsher sentences.[37] Another study of Latinos convicted of felonies in California found that a Latino's prior criminal record was a significant predictor of sentence length, but that prior criminal record accounted for little or no variation in sentence length among other race and ethnic groups.[38] In California, then, Latinos with prior records are processed in a systematically different way than persons without prior records, and the use of sentence enhancements is essentially restricted to Latinos. A similar study found that Latinos have higher conviction rates and more likely to be sentenced to prison than Anglos.[39] Even in states that do not have significant Latino populations tend to subject their Latino populations to inequitable treatment of the criminal justice system. A study of Latinos in Nebraska found that they are arrested and charged with misdemeanor offenses at a considerably higher rate than Anglos. Latinos were usually charged with more counts, received higher fines, and were sentenced to more probation time than Anglos. In effect, a higher rate of conviction for misdemeanor offenses ensures that Latinos will have a higher rate of prior offenses, which is considered a valid predictor of future convictions, thereby setting the stage for future disparate encounters with the criminal justice system. Moreover, fines and probation are feasible methods of controlling the Latino population economically and socially without jeopardizing their labor power.[40]

To the National Minority Advisory Council on Criminal Justice, the displacement of American Indian sovereignty by the encroaching Anglo-European system of laws and values has had pernicious, debilitating effects on the American Indian community. The Council noted that "the discriminatory law enforcement experienced by American Indians is perpetuated in the U.S. judicial system, where it assumes the more subtle form of institutionalized discrimination and racism."[41] The most recent compilation and analysis of new data on American Indians by the United States Department of Justice supports this contention by revealing an extremely disturbing portrait of American Indians as offenders of violent crime in the United States.[42] The incarceration rate of American Indians is about 38% higher than the national rate, with some 4% of the American Indian population in custody or otherwise under the control of the American criminal justice system. Although American Indians constitute less than 1% of the U.S. population, nearly 2% of all federal cases filed in U.S. district courts in 1997 were against American Indians, with roughly half of these cases for such violent crimes as murder and rape. American Indians are subjected to more abuse by the correctional system than any other minority group, particularly when they attempt to identify with their native cultures, such as "wearing head-bands, using native languages, maintaining long, braided hair, enjoying native music, or securing culture-related leisure and educational materials."[43] American Indian prisoners serve more of their sentences than do non–American Indian prisoners. It is not surprising that American Indian prisoners' ethnic distinction exerts such a strong and independent effect upon the proportion of time an American Indian prisoner will be incarcerated before release.[44] Much of the criminality attributed to American Indians can be attributed to social disorganization and economic deprivation in reservation communities.[45] Concern for these issues appears to be beyond the concern of our national leaders, as well as preserving American Indian rights. In fact, the first study of the voting behavior of U.S. trial judges on American Indian rights and law finds that conservative federal judges are significantly less likely to support Indian litigants are than are more liberal federal judges.[46]

The federal prison population has increased by over 640% over the last 30 years. Moreover, whites are significantly underrepresented in federal prison populations compared to their overall representation in the United States population. In contrast, nonwhite minorities are significantly overrepresented in the federal prison population. While 58% of all federal prisoners are white, 39% are black, 31% are Latino, and Asian Americans and American Indian prisoners constitute about 1.7% of the federal prison population, respectively. Most federal prisoners have been sentenced to between five and 10 years, and over 60% of them are imprisoned for nonviolent drug offenses. A recent analysis of federal correctional facilities inmate survey data reveals that blacks and Latinos are being discriminated against in the judicial system and that this differential treatment results in a larger percentage of blacks and Hispanics being incarcerated in comparison to whites. Socioeconomics, language barriers, child-rearing practices, and family structure account for higher black and Latino incarceration rates in federal prisons.

In response to concerns over increasing crack cocaine use in inner cities, in 1986 Congress enacted disproportionately harsher penalties for possessing crack cocaine than for possessing powder cocaine under the auspices that crack cocaine is far more potent and socially disruptive than powder cocaine. The minimum sentence for possession of 5 grams of *crack* cocaine is five years in prison for first-time offenders, and a 10-year-to-life minimum prison sentence for persons arrested with more than 10 grams. But the same minimum five-year sentence is not given to defendants in possession of powder cocaine unless they are arrested with at least 500 grams. Federal sentencing guidelines, then, require 100 times more powder cocaine for the minimum five-year sentence than what is needed to invoke the minimum sentence for crack cocaine. Consequently, the average sentence for possession in federal convictions is 3.2 months for powder cocaine and 30.6 months for crack cocaine. Yet in a special report to the Congress, the U.S. Sentencing Commission denied that these statistical variations are indicative of racial bias in the use of this federal sentencing law:

> One of the issues of greatest concern surrounding federal cocaine sentencing policy is the perception of disparate and unfair treatment for defendants convicted of either possession or distribution of crack cocaine. Critics argue that the 100-to-1 quantity ratio is not consistent with the policy, goal, and mission of federal sentencing—that is to be effective, uniform, and just. While there is no evidence of racial bias behind the promulgation of this federal sentencing law, nearly 90 percent of the offenders convicted in federal court for crack cocaine distribution are African-American while the majority of crack cocaine users is white. Thus, sentences appear to be harsher and more severe for racial minorities than others because of this law. The current penalty structure results in a perception of unfairness and inconsistency.[47]

Minority defendants disproportionately receive harsher sentences for crack cocaine violations than white defendants because crack cocaine cases involving nonwhite defendants are prosecuted more often in federal courts, where penalties for drug possession are far more severe than in state courts. As a result, blacks and Latinos account for 97% of all defendants prosecuted in federal courts for crack cocaine violations, whereas whites are only 3% of crack cocaine defendants prosecuted in federal courts. In fact, no whites were federally prosecuted for crack cocaine offenses from 1988 through 1994 in 17 states. California convicted one white defendant for crack cocaine violations, Texas convicted two, New York convicted three, and Pennsylvania convicted two. Federal arrests for powder cocaine violations are also made disproportionately by race and ethnicity. White persons account for 32% of all federal arrests for powder cocaine violations; blacks account for 27% and Latinos account for 39%.[48] To Michael Tonry, the racially disparate impact of the nation's "war on drugs" as evidenced by these statistics was highly foreseeable by the architects of the campaign against drug trafficking and drug use. For one, urban police departments have found it far easier to focus the drug war on disadvantaged minority neighborhoods than on suburban white neighborhoods.

> For a variety of reasons it is easier to make arrests in socially disorganized neighborhoods, as contrasted with urban blue-collar and urban or suburban white-collar neighborhoods. First, more of the routine activities of life, including retail drug dealing, occur on the streets and alley in poor neighborhoods. In working-class and middle class neighborhoods, many activities, including drug dealing, are likelier to occur indoors. This makes it much easier to find dealers from whom to make an undercover buy in a disadvantaged urban neighborhood than elsewhere.
>
>   Second, it is easier for undercover narcotics officers to penetrate networks of friends and acquaintances in poor urban minority neighborhoods than in more stable and closely knit working-class and middle-class neighborhoods. The stranger buys drugs on the

urban street corner or in an alley or overcoming local suspicions by hanging around for a few days and then buying drugs, is commonplace. The substantial increases in the numbers of black and Hispanic police officers in recent decades make undercover narcotics work in such neighborhoods easier....

Both these differences between socially disorganized urban neighborhoods and other neighborhoods make extensive drug-law enforcement operations in the inner city more likely and, by police standards, more successful. Because urban drug dealing is often visible, individual citizens, the media, and elected officials more often pressure police to take action against drugs in poor urban neighborhoods than in other kinds of neighborhoods.[49]

Eugenics

A concern among social ethicists is the extent to which medical experimentation takes place in the United States. Indeed, many Americans have suffered the atrocities of human subject medical experimentation by agencies of the federal government. Historically, poor black women have suffered from brutal experimentation, particularly in gynecological surgeries. A 925-page report released in 1995 by the Advisory Committee on Human Radiation Experiments reviewed 4000 experiments in which mostly race and ethnic minorities, indigent patients, poor pregnant women, and mentally retarded schoolchildren were the subjects of radiation experiments conducted by the federal government. One estimate is that up to 400,000 children have undergone nasal irradiation therapy, including infant children with Down's syndrome. In another case, the federal government purposely exposed about 6 million people to radiation when it deliberately destroyed a nuclear-powered rocket over Los Angeles. And from the 1930s and to the early 1970s, researchers with the United States Public Health Services intentionally left untreated 600 indigent and illiterate black men living in Alabama infected with syphilis, to observe the natural progression of the disease on human beings.[50] Human subject medical experimentation continues today. In 1989, African-American and Latino parents were not notified that one of two measles vaccines given to their infant children in Los Angeles was experimental and which the Centers for Disease Control in Atlanta warned had been used throughout developing countries with an increased death rate among female infants.[51]

Human subject medical experimentation is no less prevalent in the U.S. criminal justice system. A University of Washington experiment exposed prisoners' testicles to radiation.[52] The *Los Angeles Times* most recently reported that in 1997, Stanford University and the California Youth Authority tested a powerful psychiatric drug (Depakote) on 61 teenage inmates at a state correctional center in Stockton to determine whether the drug would make young offenders less aggressive. The director of the California Youth Authority acknowledged that the experiment did not comply with a law prohibiting medical research on prisoners. As a result, California's governor has ordered the state's attorney general and inspector general to investigate the "propriety and legality" of the experiment. To some scholars, correctional medical personnel have essentially abdicated their professional and ethical obligations and contributed to the ill-treatment and outright torture of prisoners in the U.S. penal system.[53]

Gender and Criminal Justice

The etiology of female criminality, criminal justice outcomes and female offenders, and whether police, judges, correctional officers, and other criminal justice professionals victimize female prisoners remain ambiguous to social scientists because criminologists, legal scholars, and social scientists have simply ignored female criminality.[54] While the representation of females in the U.S. criminal justice system as both offenders and victims has increased significantly over the last several decades, the criminological literature addressing inequalities in the administration of criminal justice has remained focused primarily on the male offender. The conventional sociological and criminological perspectives are inadequate in explaining the peculiarity and uniqueness of female criminality. Schulhofer has analyzed the male-dominated nature of the criminal law and the administration of criminal justice and addresses the inherent complexities of applying existing criminal justice theory and practice to female victimization and offending. He advances the proposition that a feminist theory must be constructed to make clear the particularistic nature of female criminality and victimization. To effectively combat gender inequality in the criminal justice system, the theory must guide its practice away from the male-dominated ideologies of inequality toward a gender-specific, or gender-sensitive, structure of policies and practice.

Yet many nonwhite female scholars hold further that feminist constructions of crime theory have left out their particular concerns.[55] Minority women are overburdened with the social conditions of unemployment, poverty, and racism. Evidence suggests that the vast majority of minority female offenders are poor, uneducated, and unskilled.[56] Minority women, poor women, and economically dependent women experience discrimination in the criminal justice system. The average female offender is a minority woman between the ages of 25 and 29 who had either never been married or who before incarceration was a single parent living alone with one to three children.[57] Yet Mann points out that "the most cogent conclusion one can draw from an examination of the minority woman offender in the United States criminal justice system is that despite awakening interest in female criminality, little attention is devoted to the Black, Hispanic, or Native American female offender."[58] All the same, as racial minorities and female, nonwhite women are *doubly* discriminated against at every level of the criminal justice system—from arrest to incarceration. Of women in their twenties, the criminal justice system controls one in 100 whites, one in 56 Latinos, and one in 37 blacks. Minority women, especially black women, are disproportionately represented in our nation's prisons and jails compared with white women. Minority women are more likely to be incarcerated than white women because race and ethnic bias against minority women by criminal justice professionals increases their likelihood of arrest and conviction. For example, research suggests that conviction rates are lower for women released on bail than women who remain in jail pending trial. Since minority women are often poorer than white women and cannot easily raise the bail necessary for release, courts are more likely to convict minority women than white women. Women released on bail are less likely to be incarcerated even if they are convicted, but judicial officers are less likely to release minority women on bail or on their own recognizance.

In 1998, nearly 500,000 females under the age of 18 were arrested and charged with a criminal offense. Most of these young girls were arrested for theft crimes, simple assault, drug and liquor law violations, curfew violations, and runaways. Nevertheless, police agencies arrested nearly 18,000 juvenile females for violent crimes, including murder and nonnegligent manslaughter, forcible rape, robbery, and aggravated assaults. Moreover, nearly 3% of juvenile females arrested end up in public or private detention, correctional, and shelter facilities. Despite an increase in the number of studies focusing on female criminality, there remains a dearth of gender-specific explanatory research on why females, especially juvenile females, engage in crime. As many scholars studying female crime have noted, much of the research on female criminality has relied on male criminality models to explain female criminality. Yet there are peculiarities as to why females commit crime. For example, it has been estimated that nearly one-third of all female children in the United States suffer sexual abuse before their eighteenth birthday. Sexual abuse of female children often leads to early traumatic experiences associated with depression and mania. Most female crack addicts have a history of sexual abuse. Childhood sexual abuse is a predictor for HIV sexual risk behaviors among incarcerated women. A history of child sexual abuse also increases the vulnerability of women to adult sexual and physical victimization. Belknap and her associates point out that girls' increased risk of sexual and nonsexual physical abuse, especially incest, are significant factors in explaining gender differences in offending. Their data suggest that despite varying problems and experiences of delinquent girls, the prevailing notions among these girls are their feelings of being disrespected, their abusive and sexist backgrounds, and their belief that the juvenile justice system is sexist.[59]

The female imprisonment rate is at its highest percentage in U.S. history. The number of female prisoners in the United States has increased by over 400% since the early 1980s. The number of women incarcerated in state and federal prisons rose to nearly 85,000 inmates in 1998—constituting 6.5% of the U.S. prison population.[60] With an increase in the female prison population has come an increase in the risk of sexual assault of female inmates by male correction officers. The pervasiveness of sexual assaults of female inmates results from the U.S. criminal justice system having left female prisoners virtually unprotected from abuse by male prison guards, staff, and wardens. This is especially true in California, Texas, and in federal prisons, where more than a third of nation's female inmates are housed. Although the abuse of women prisoners occurs nationwide, the extent and frequency of the abuse of female prisoners cannot be accurately determined since prisons fail to keep records of assaults. Female inmates are subjected to rape, sexual assault, and unlawful invasions of privacy, including prurient viewing during showering and dressing. The sexual abuse of female inmates includes such atrocities as "forced abortions, women prisoners left stripped and bound for weeks, and inmates taken off the grounds to work as prostitutes." *Lucas* v. *White*, for example, meted out to the public that female inmates have been sold as sex slaves to male inmates. Apparently, male inmates paid prison guards to allow them into female inmate cells while temporarily held in male detention centers. The Women's

Rights Project recently issued a comprehensive report detailing the sexual abuse of women in prisons in California, Washington, DC, Michigan, Georgia, and New York. The report found that male correctional employees have vaginally, anally, and orally raped female prisoners. Another study described prison life for female inmates as tantamount to "a climate of sexual terror that women are subjected to on a daily basis."

One reason why sexual assaults of female inmates by males guards remains pervasive in the U.S. penal system is that it is extremely difficult for female inmates to realize their constitutional protections against male correctional officers' sexual misconduct since the testimony of sexually abused female inmates is often discounted or ignored, a disturbing lack of prosecutions for custodial sexual misconduct, a failure of lawsuits by women prisoners attempting to hold male corrections officers criminally liable for sexual misconduct, and the prevalence of misconduct by male guards remains relatively unknown outside the prison system. To correct for the inadequacies of prison officials to sufficiently control the violent behavior of prison employees against female inmates and to take complaints of female prisoners seriously, one legal scholar suggests that the class action lawsuit may prove a feasible option for women inmates since class action lawsuits attract "significant publicity" and allow courts to characterize the abuses as occurring in a "sexualized environment" within the prison system.[61]

Official criminal justice statistics claim that women suffer some 100,000 rapes and attempted rapes every year in the United States. But the National Crime Victimization Survey estimates that nearly 200,000 rapes and attempted rapes take place each year. The disparity between these two figures means that roughly half of all rapes and sexual assaults go unreported to law enforcement. Other victimization surveys confirm that the actual incidence of rape is far more prevalent than is actually accounted for by law enforcement agencies and official victimization reports. In this regard, about 20% of all adult women and 15% of college-aged women are raped or sexually assaulted during their lifetimes. More than half of all rapes and sexual assaults reported to police involve girls under 18 years of age, and 16% of these rapes are adolescent girls younger than 12 years old, with 96% of them being assaulted by someone they know. As for the race of rape victims, American Indian women and women of mixed races are far more likely to suffer rape than white, black, or Asian American women. American Indian women comprise more than 34% of women raped each year, women of mixed race are about 24%, African-American women are about 19%, white women are about 18%, and Asian-American women constitute 7% of women raped in the United States each year.[62] Rape is an intraracial crime, with female rape victims most often assaulted by someone of the same race. Yet black men who victimize white women are far more likely to be sentenced to prison and to receive longer sentences than other assailants. Moreover, the death penalty, in both its legal and extralegal (lynchings) forms, has been disproportionately imposed on blacks males accused of raping white women. Although *Coker* v. *Georgia* prohibits the use of capital punishment for the rape of an adult woman where no death results, the rate of black executions for rape in the United States is nine times the rate of white executions for rape—black men constitute nearly 90% of all prisoners executed for rape.[63]

But white men have sexually attacked black women with legal impunity. One of the most troubling statistics on black rape in the United States is that no white man has ever been executed for the rape of a black woman in the history of American criminal justice.[64]

The Death Penalty

Despite a net decrease in the number of criminal homicides in the United States over the past 30 years, the number of persons sentenced to death has increased by more than 1100% over the same period. Condemned inmate populations have increased from 134 inmates in 1973 to 3703 inmates by October 1, 2000.[65] Death penalty jurisdictions have sentenced more than 6881 capital offenders to death since the early 1970s. Most condemned prisoners are nonwhite minorities. State penitentiaries in California, Texas, and Florida confine almost half of all death row inmates in the United States. Then again, it is also significant that state prisons in Arizona, California, Florida, and Texas hold more than 75% of all Latino prisoners sentenced to death. Blacks, Latinos, American Indians, and Asian Americans comprise nearly 54% of all death row inmates, but taken together, these groups represent one-fifth of the overall U.S. population. Considering their representation in the overall U.S. population, blacks continue to be disproportionately represented as death row inmates. Indeed, about 43% of all death row inmates are black and account for more than three times their proportionate representation in the U.S. population. Native Americans are also disproportionately represented as death row inmates; their representation on death row is twice that of their representation in the U.S. population. Yet Asian-American and Pacific Islanders and Latinos are proportionately represented in death row populations. Latinos are 9% of the nation's death row population and Asian Americans are 1%.

The pace of executions in the United States has also increased since the U.S. Supreme Court reinstated capital punishment in 1976. Capital punishment jurisdictions executed eleven capital offenders between 1976 and 1983, but as of February 2001, authorities had executed 692 condemned prisoners with Texas, Virginia, and Florida accounting for about half of all executions.[66] With 98 executions conducted in 1999, death penalty jurisdictions performed more executions in that year than in any other year since 1951, when 105 prisoners were put to death. Jurisdictions executed 85 prisoners in the year 2000, and another eighteen executions are scheduled to take place over the next several months.

Investigators view the imposition of death in the United States as a systematic pattern of differential treatment of nonwhite minorities.[67] Nearly half of all prisoners executed in the United States since 1976 have been nonwhite minorities, and in 83% of these cases the race of the victim has been white.[68] One of the most troubling statistics concerning the imposition of capital punishment in the United States is that a black man is 20 times more likely to be executed for killing a white man than is a white man for killing a black man. A Latino is about twice as likely to be executed for killing a white man than is a white man for killing a Latino. Jurists, legal scholars, and social scientists have looked to the U.S. Supreme Court to redress the effects of racism in the application of the death penalty. Yet the major capital punishment cases handed down by the Court concerning the application of the death penalty in the United States indicate that the Court has moved from a position of formally recognizing that imposition of the death penalty is imbued with racial prejudice, as noted in *Furman* v. *Georgia*,[69] to imposing what many scholars and jurists believe are meaningless procedural safeguards established in *Gregg* v. *Georgia*,[70] to an acceptance of the risk of racial prejudice in imposing the death penalty in *McCleskey* v. *Kemp*.[71] The U.S. Supreme Court held in *McCleskey* that empirically based statistical evidence showing that blacks who kill whites are more likely to be executed than white defendants who kill blacks does not "prove that race enters into any capital sentencing decisions or that race was a factor in petitioners' cases." Nonetheless, post-*McCleskey* research has found that black defendants with white victims are more likely to be charged with aggravated murder and tried as capital offenders than other defendant–victim racial combinations.[72] As such, prosecutorial discretion amounts to intentional discrimination against black defendants with white victims.

To some scholars, an escalating rate of executions in the United States increases the possibility that innocent defendants will be executed.[73] The possibility of executing an innocent defendant has increased so significantly that the American Bar Association has called upon capital punishment jurisdictions not to carry out the death penalty until jurisdictions can ensure that they have significantly reduced the risk of executing innocent persons. This plea is not without merit. Capital punishment researchers have identified some 350 cases where defendants have been wrongfully convicted of murder in the United States since 1900. Of these cases, states sentenced 159 defendants to death, 23 prisoners were actually executed, and another 22 condemned prisoners came within 72 hours of being executed before their innocence had been established and they won release. The Death Penalty Information Center reports that 93 condemned prisoners have been released from death rows across the country through evidence of their innocence since 1973. The majority of innocent defendants released from death row have been nonwhite minorities, and over one-third of these defendants had been wrongfully convicted in Florida and Illinois. Innocent defendants spent an average of 7.5 years on death row before being released, and in eight of the cases identified by researchers with the Death Penalty Information Center; DNA evidence was a significant contributing factor in establishing defendants' innocence. Social critic Alan Berlow has identified several facets of the process under which the U.S. criminal justice system imposes the death penalty that have increased the prospect that wrongfully convicted prisoners will be executed. Death-qualified juries, a "take-no-prisoners" mentality of jurists and politicians, the lack of resources required to fund public-defender organizations, an ever-increasing public condemnation of heinous criminality, an indifference of jurists to the possibility of wrongful convictions, the incompetence of defense counsel, the lawlessness of police officers and prosecutors in suppressing exculpating evidence, and the increasing complexity of the appeals process have all added to the equation that the U.S. criminal justice system's mechanism of imposing death as punishment is faulty, impractical, and ineffectual.[74] Our only hope of remedying the problem of executing innocent persons is to declare a moratorium on the death penalty.

In summary, nonwhite minority populations are at risk regarding the criminal justice system. By *at risk* we refer to the fact that the population's representation in the criminal justice system is greater than its representation in the general population. In this sense, the representation of nonwhite populations in U.S. society suggests that nonwhites have a higher degree of contact with the criminal justice system. We expect this since the social conditions of racial and ethnic populations in U.S. society increase their chances of coming into contact with a social institution that legitimatize their oppressed status. As a result, the high degree of representativeness for nonwhites in the criminal justice system portrays their oppressed position in the United States. In this regard, the disproportionate representation of nonwhite populations in the U.S. criminal justice system amounts to a mechanism of disparate social control: That is, racial and ethnic oppression and subjugation result in higher rates of crime and criminal sanctions for minority persons. The disproportionate representation of nonwhites in the U.S. criminal justice system illustrates the selectivity used by legal institutions. As the principal vehicle for defining deviance in society, the criminal justice system uses selectivity to process persons for deviant labels. A central dynamic in any societal system of intergroup domination and subordination is social control through institutional apparatuses such as the criminal justice system. To legitimate its presence in society, the criminal justice system uses a process of selectivity to reinforce the differential position of racial and ethnic populations in the structure of opportunity in U.S. society. Accordingly, the official task of law enforcement officers, prosecutors, judges, juries, and correctional officers is to protect dominant group interests. That is, the U.S. criminal justice system maintains the social arrangement between dominant and subordinate groups by defining any social behavior engaged in by members of subordinate groups that the dominant group perceives as a threat to their interests as criminal.[75] Moreover, this process of selectivity is inversely associated with a racial or ethnic population's position in the structure of opportunity. Consequently, the restricted access of nonwhites to the U.S. opportunity structure increases their selective treatment by the criminal justice system. This is the crisis of justice administration in the United States.

THE CRISIS IN THE DISCIPLINE OF CRIMINAL JUSTICE

The current state of justice administration poses fundamental challenges to criminal justice as an academic discipline that defies its veracity. Regrettably, disciplines other than criminal justice have proffered much of our scientific understanding of the difficulties facing justice administration in the United States. For example, critical race theory, critical race feminism, and critical white studies have put forward some of the most perceptive and discerning work on the structure and dynamics of U.S. criminal justice.[76] Criminal justice will remain ill equipped to critically evaluate and challenge the crises of justice administration until the discipline begins to do more than simply provide descriptive profiles of the system. In effect, justice studies do nothing more than reinvent, and in many regards, outright advocate the system's status quo.

Criminal justice investigators must employ advanced theoretical frameworks and research methodologies to examine the sociological effects of inequitable justice policies. Critical theory has developed an explanatory framework that examines the structure and dynamics of the U.S. criminal justice system. The research conducted subsequent to this explanatory framework has produced information unmistakably verifying inequality as an inherent quality of U.S. criminal justice. We are not suggesting that critical theory has produced the final word or uncovered with ultimate certainty the workings of the U.S. system of justice administration. But we are suggesting that to attain academic and scholarly integrity, criminal justice must develop theoretical and explanatory frameworks that move beyond simple description and expand its research efforts toward empirically based explanation and projection. Criminal justice must ground its future academic endeavors in sound explanatory frameworks because to continue a pattern of description, devoid of theory and empiricism, will subject the discipline to continued criticism that will eventually challenge the discipline's academic prowess directly. Already, the discipline occupies a dubious status within the greater academic and scientific community.

We suggest that criminal justice will face a number of problems should it continue on its present course. First, without a sound theoretical and empirical foundation, the discipline's attempt at structural explanations of crime, criminality, and criminal justice behavior are imprudent. Second, without the requisite academic foundations, any policy implications toward crime amelioration are irresponsible. Third, given its current posture, criminal justice remains hopelessly useless to challenge the pervasiveness of social inequality that is so deeply embedded in the U.S. system of justice administration. Fourth, since criminal justice professionals and agents view themselves as somehow apart from the greater social system (i.e., the proverbial "we" versus "them" mentality), the relationship between the justice administration system and the American people will remain adversarial.

In looking forward to the new millennium, we offer a direction for criminal justice that promises to elevate the discipline to a higher level of academic and scientific integrity, and one that promises to truly assist in the amelioration of the problems so inherent in the current system. We recommend that criminal justice enjoin from its role as advocate for the status quo of justice administration and pursue a more critical perspective. Criminal justice as an academic discipline must adopt the role of "objective" observer and prepare for its role as a system antagonist. Criminal justice must vigorously call for substantive change, it must espouse equality and eschew criminal justice system practices that violate principles of equity. In general, criminal justice must move from its posture as static reporter to a dynamic agent for social change.

One must recognize that the criminal justice system is located and operates within the greater society and not apart from it. The discipline is not an outside observer, overseer, or enforcer. The criminal justice system is located within a capitalist culture where social inequality of race, gender, and class is imperative to its survival. Subsequently, one must keep in mind that the criminal justice system is a progeny of, and an advocate for, the privileged classes. It is a system of the privileged, by the privileged, and for the privileged. One must also recognize that the criminal justice system bears responsibility for the crime problem in at least equal proportion to the greater community. From the enactment of target-specific law to its selective enforcement, prosecution, adjudication and final disposition, the criminal justice system fosters and facilitates the very crime it purports to control or eradicate. Aided by big government, big business, and big media, the criminal justice system overwhelmingly focuses its attention on the crimes and criminality of the lower echelons of society, to the poor, to the homeless, to the indigent, and to the racial, ethnic, and gender minorities. Moreover, criminal justice places blame for crime and criminality squarely on the shoulders of powerless persons. Criminal justice agents pay only token and infrequent attention to the miscreance of government, business, and the criminal justice system itself. In fact, a good deal of the behavior of the powerful classes escapes definitions of criminality altogether. When it does meet criminal criteria, more often than not a completely different set of jurisprudential principles surface.

In conclusion, we agree whole heartedly that there will always be a demand for a criminal justice system. There are those among us who would rape, rob, and pillage, or otherwise threaten our safety, security, and well-being. But those who do such things are among all of us, not relegated only to the lower echelons or powerless segments of our society. Nevertheless, any response to such things must always be tempered with equity, it must be humane, and it must keep an eye toward improving the human condition and the social structure in which it exists. We also agree that there will always be the need for an academic discipline of criminal justice, a proactive force that serves in the best interest of both the system and the citizen—all the citizens. By design or by consequence, academia has always exacted its influence on culture, social structure, and social policy. It is naive to continue with the principle that the academy must remain neutral and purely objective in the study of human affairs. Alternatively, we think the charge of the academy is to employ objective and sound means to seek truth wherever it lies, and then to deliver that truth. We strongly hold that it is the responsibility of academia to occupy a position of advocacy for the betterment of social life; for academia to claim any other position, particularly one of neutrality, is simply derelict. The discipline of criminal justice will never realize a respectable niche in the scientific community, nor will it substantively influence or improve its counterpart system of justice, until it is properly aligned with the search for truth and until it develops and employs the proper tools with which to conduct that search.

ENDNOTES

1. We dedicate this epilogue to the memory of Detective Charles Douglas "Doug" Jacobs III. Detective Jacobs, a member of the Riverside Police Department in Riverside, California, was killed in the line of duty during the writing of this essay. Detective Jacobs was one of our most distinguished graduate students at Chapman University's Coachella Valley Campus where the authors of this epilogue teach as adjunct faculty in the Criminal Justice Department. Detective Jacobs had just completed all of the requirements for the Master of Arts degree in criminal justice. We'll miss our friend.

2. A. Trebach. 1964. *The Rationing of Justice*. Piscataway, NJ: Rutgers University Press, p. 205.

3. Manning Marable. 1983. *How Capitalism Underdeveloped Black America: Problems in Race, Political Economy and Society.* Boston: South End Press, p. 113.

4. National Minority Advisory Council on Criminal Justice. January 1982. *The Inequality of Justice: A Report on Crime and the Administration of Justice in the Minority Community.* Washington, DC: National Institute of Law Enforcement and Criminal Justice.

5. Adalberto Aguirre, Jr., and David V. Baker. 1991. *Race, Racism and the Death Penalty in the United States.* Berrien Springs, MI: Vande Vere Publishing. Adalberto Aguirre, Jr., and David V. Baker. 1994. *Perspective on Race and Ethnicity in American Criminal Justice.* New York: West Publishing. Adalberto Aguirre, Jr., and David V. Baker. 2000. *Structured Inequality in American Society: Critical Discussions on the Continuing Significance of Race, Ethnicity, Gender, and Class.* Upper Saddle River, NJ: Prentice Hall.

6. Jonathan H. Turner, Robert Singleton, Jr., and David Musick. 1984. *Oppression: A Socio-History of Black–White Relations in America.* Chicago: Nelson-Hall.

7. For comprehensive reviews of racial discrimination in the U.S. criminal justice system, see generally Randall Kennedy. 1997. *Race, Crime, and the Law.* NY: Pantheon Books. Coramae Richey Mann. 1993. *Unequal Justice: A Question of Color.* Bloomington, IN: Indiana University Press. Jerome G. Miller. 1996. *Search and Destroy: African-American Males in the Criminal Justice System.* New York: Cambridge University Press. Kathryn K. Russell. 1998. *The Color of Crime: Racial Hoaxes, White Fear, Black Protectionism, Police Harassment, and Other Macroaggressions.* NY: New York University Press. Samuel Walker, Cassia Spohn and Miriam DeLone. 1996. *The Color of Justice: Race, Ethnicity, and Crime in America.* Belmont, CA: Wadsworth. Robert D. Crutchfield, George S. Bridges, and Susan R. Pitchford. 1994. "Analytical and Aggregation Biases in Analyses of Imprisonment: Reconciling Discrepancies in Studies of Racial Disparity." *Journal of Research in Crime and Delinquency,* 31, 2, pp. 166–183. Angela J. Davis. 1996. "Benign Neglect of Racism in the Criminal Justice System." 94 *Michigan Law Review* 1660. Michael Tonry. 1995. *Malign Neglect: Race, Crime, and Punishment in America.* New York: Oxford University Press. Alfred Blumstein. 1993. "Racial Disproportionality of U.S. Prison Populations Revisited." 64 *University of Colorado Law Review* 743.

8. Myriam E. Gilles. 2000. "Breaking the Code of Silence: Rediscovering 'Custom' in Section 1983 Municipal Liability." 80 *Boston University Law Review* 17. Jennifer E. Koepke. 2000. "The Failure to Breach the Blue Wall of Silence: The Circling of the Wagons to Protect Police Perjury." 39 *Washburn Law Journal* 211. Mary M. Cheh. 1996. "Are Lawsuits an Answer to Police Brutality?" In William A. Geller and Hans Toch (editors), *Understanding and Controlling Police Abuse of Force.* New Haven, CT: Yale University Press. Kenneth Adams. 1996. "Measuring the Prevalence of Police Abuse of Force." In William A. Geller and Hans Toch (editors), *Police Violence: Understanding and Controlling Police Abuse of Force.* New Haven, CT: Yale University Press. Susan Bandes. 1999. "Patterns of Injustice: Police Brutality in the Courts." 47 *Buffalo Law Review* 1275. Carl B. Klockars. 1996. "A Theory of Excessive Force." In William A. Geller and Hans Toch (editors), *Police Violence: Understanding and Controlling Police Abuse of Force.* New Haven, CT: Yale University Press. David S. Cohen. 1996. "Official Oppression: A Historical Analysis of Low-Level Police Abuse and a Modern Attempt at Reform." 28 *Columbia Human Rights Law Review* 165. David Dante Troutt. 1999. "Screws, Koon, and Routine Aberrations: The Use of Fictional Narratives in Federal Police Brutality Prosecutions." 74 *New York University Law Review* 18. Alexa P. Freeman. 1996. "Unscheduled Departures: The Circumvention of Just Sentencing for Police Brutality." 47 *Hastings Law Journal* 677. National Minority Advisory Council on Criminal Justice. January 1982. *The Inequality of Justice: A Report on Crime and the Administration of Justice in the Minority Community.* Washington, DC: National Institute of Law Enforcement and Criminal Justice, p. xxxiii.

9. Gregory H. Williams. 1993. "Controlling the Use of Nondeadly Force: Policy and Practice." 10 *Harvard BlackLetter Journal* 79. Robert E. Worden. 1996. "The Causes of Police Brutality: Theory and Evidence on Police Use of Force." In William A. Geller and Hans Toch (editors), *Police Violence: Understanding and Controlling Police Abuse of Force*. New Haven, CT: Yale University Press. Christopher A. Love. 1998. "The Myth of Message-Sending: The Continuing Search for a True Deterrent to Police Misconduct." 12 *Journal of the Suffolk Academy of Law*, 45. Marshall Miller. 1998. "Police Brutality." 17 *Yale Law and Policy Review* 149. Alison L. Patton. 1993. "The Endless Cycle of Abuse: Why 42 U.S.C. 1983 Is Ineffective in Deterring Police Brutality." 44 *Hastings Law Journal* 753. Tara L. Senkel. 1999. "Civilians Often Need Protection from the Police: Let's Handcuff Police Brutality." 15 *New York Law School Journal of Human Rights* 385. "Police Brutality Must End." *Progressive*, 64, 4, April 2000, p. 8. Jonathan Sorensen, James Marquart, and Deon Brock. 1993. "Factors Related to Killings of Felons by Police Officers: A Test of the Community Violence and Conflict Hypotheses." *Justice Quarterly*, 10, pp. 417–440. Donna Coker. 2000. "Piercing Webs of Powers: Identity, Resistance, and Hipe in LatCrit Theory and Praxis: Shifting Power for Battered Women: Law, Material Resources, and Poor Women of Color." 33 *University of California, Davis Law Review* 1009.

10. Human Rights Watch. April 1998. *Shielded from Justice: Police Brutality and Accountability in the United States*. New York: Human Rights Watch. Gregory H. Williams. 1993. "Controlling the Use of Non-deadly Force: Policy and Practice." 10 *Harvard BlackLetter Journal* 79. *Report of the Independent Commission on the Los Angeles Police Department*. July 1991. For example, Waegel reported that during investigations of criminal activity involving nonwhite persons, he overheard police officers say: "Maybe Hitler was right, he just had the wrong group," "You've got to understand, these people are animals, and we're here to keep the peace among animals"; and "What's another dead nigger anyway?" See Walter Waegel. 1984. "How the Police Justify the Use of Deadly Force." *Social Problems*, 32, p. 148. Similarly, transcripts of squad-car communications following the Rodney King incident revealed that officers of the Los Angeles Police Department (LAPD) referred to African Americans as "gorillas in the midst"; "sounds like monkey slapping time"; "I would love to drive down Slauson with a flame thrower…we would have a barbecue"; and regarding Mexican Americans, "I almost got me a Mexican last night but he dropped the damn gun too quick." LAPD Detective Mark Fuhrman admitted in taped interviews introduced as evidence in the O. J. Simpson murder trial that he had assaulted and used racial slurs against blacks and Latinos: "I used to go to work and practice (martial arts)." "Niggers, they're easy to practice my kicks." "How do you intellectualize when you punch the hell out of a nigger? He either deserves it or he doesn't." Even Fuhrman's boss, LAPD Chief Daryl Gates (now retired), called on the public for an insurgency to constitutionally prescribed judicial safeguards for criminal suspects. Chief Gates advocated the view that some people should be "taken out and shot on the spot," and that black persons are different from "normal" people and are, therefore, deserving of different types of police tactics—namely, life-threatening strangle holds. In the immediate aftermath of the Tyisha Miller, persons overheard Riverside Police Department officers referring to the traumatized family members as a Kwanzaa gathering.

11. Michael Huspek, Roberto Martinez, and Leticia Jimenez. 1998. "Violations of Human and Civil Rights on the U.S.–Mexico Border, 1995 to 1997: A Report." *Social Justice*, 25, 2, pp. 110–129. See Human Rights Watch. December 1998. *United States Detained and Deprived of Rights: Children in the Custody of the U.S. Immigration and Naturalization Service*. New York: Human Rights Watch. April 1995. *United States Crossing the Line: Human Rights Abuses along the U.S. Border with Mexico Persist amid Climate of Impunity*. New York: Human Rights Watch. June 1992. *Brutality Unchecked: Human Rights Abuses along the U.S. Border with Mexico*. New York: Human Rights Watch. Amnesty International. 1998. *Human Rights Concerns in the Border Region with Mexico*. London: Amnesty International. The American Friends Service Committee. February 1992. *Sealing Our Borders: The Human Toll*. Third Report of the

Immigration Law Enforcement Monitoring Project, A Project of the Mexico–U.S. Border Program. *Los Angeles Times.* "When Agents Cross over the Borderline: Law Enforcement: Charges of Wrongdoing in Border Patrol Have Forced Even Loyalists to Call for Reforms." April 22, 23, 24, 1993. Human Rights Watch. May 1992. *Brutality Unchecked: Human Rights Abuses along the U.S. Border with Mexico.* Human Rights Watch. May 1993. *Frontier Injustice: Human Rights Abuses along the U.S. Border with Mexico Persist amid Climate of Impunity.* Human Rights Watch. April 1995. *Crossing the Line: Human Rights Abuses along the U.S. Border with Mexico.* Human Rights Watch. January 1997. *Human Rights Violations by INS Inspectors and Border Patrol Agents Continue; Attorney General Reno Urged to Address Abuse Problem.*

Children are no less the victims of police violence. Human Rights Watch charged the U.S. Immigration and Naturalization Service (INS) with violating the rights of children in custody. Roughly one-third of the more than 5000 unaccompanied children detained by the INS are held in punitive, jail-like detention centers even though these children have committed no crimes. Most of them are detained for administrative reasons. Many of these children are locked up in prison-like conditions with other juveniles accused of murder, rape and drug trafficking. The children are forbidden to speak their native languages, instructed not to laugh, and even forced to ask permission to merely scratch their noses. Some of the children are strip-searched and restrained by handcuffs during transport. In other words, basic human rights to protection and care are being denied these children. See Human Rights Watch. April 1997. *Slipping through the Cracks: Unaccompanied Children Detained by the U.S. Immigration and Naturalization Service.* Human Rights Watch Children's Rights Project. New York: Human Rights Watch.

12. Human Rights Watch. April 1998. *Shielded from Justice: Police Brutality and Accountability in the United States.* New York: Human Rights Watch. Human Rights Watch World Report 2001. U.S. Human Rights Development. Police Abuse. New York: Human Rights Watch.

13. Susan T. Peterson. 1999. "Torts—Official Immunity Survives Police Misconduct: But Should It? *Kelly* v. *City of Minneapolis*, 598 N.W.2d 657." 27 *William Mitchell Law Review* 1433. Brandon Garrett. 2000. "Standing While Black: Distinguishing *Lyons* in Racial Profiling Cases." 100 *Columbia Law Review* 1815. The Mollen Commission Report. 1994. *Commission Report of the City of New York Commission to Investigate Allegations of Police Corruption and the Anti-corruption Procedures of the Police Department.* St. Clair Commission Report. 1992. *Report of the Boston Police Department Management Review Commission.* Christopher Commission Report. 1991. *Report of the Independent Commission on the Los Angeles Police Department.* Alexa P. Freeman. 1996. "Note, Unscheduled Departures: The Circumvention of Just Sentencing for Police Brutality." 47 *Hastings Law Journal* 677. Amnesty International. September 1999. *United States of America: Race, Rights and Police Brutality.* Report AMR 51/147/99. Amnesty International. September 1999. California: Update on Police Brutality. Report AMR 51/150/99.

14. Jennifer E. Koepke. 2000. "The Failure to Breach the Blue Wall of Silence: The Circling of the Wagons to Protect Police Perjury," 39 *Washburn Law Journal* 211. John V. Jacobi. 2000. "Prosecuting Police Misconduct," 2000 *Wisconsin Law Review 789.* Jerome H. Skolnick and James J. Fyfe. 1993. *Above the Law: Police and the Excessive Use of Force.* New York: Macmillan International. Leadership Conference on Civil Rights. *Justice on Trial: Racial Disparities in the American Criminal Justice System.* Leadership Conference Education Fund. Alexa P. Freeman. 1996. "Unscheduled Departures: The Circumvention of Just Sentencing for Police Brutality." 47 *Hastings Law Journal* 677.

15. *Los Angles Times.* "Corrosive Racial Profiling Must End, Clinton Insists." June 10, 1999. *Time.* "It's Not Just in New Jersey." June 14, 1999. *Los Angeles Times.* "Can a Traffic Offense be D.W.B. (Driving While Black)?" March 9, 1997. American Civil Liberties Union. June 1999. Special Report. *Driving While Black: Racial Profiling on Our Nation's Highways.* New York: ACLU.

16. 517 U.S. 806 (1996).

17. David A. Harris. 1997. "'Driving While Black' and All Other Traffic Offenses: The Supreme Court and Pretextual Traffic Stops," *Journal of Criminal Law and Criminology*, 87, 2, pp. 544–582.

18. Terry A. Maroney. 1998. "The Struggle against Hate Crime: Movement at a Crossroads," 73 *New York University Law Review* 564.

19. *Los Angeles Times*. "It's Time to Handcuff the Police." April 26, 1995.

20. Cynthia Kwei Yung Lee. 1996. "Race and Self-Defense: Toward a Normative Conception of Reasonableness." 81 *Minnesota Law Review* 367. Angela J. Davis. 1998. "Prosecution and Race: The Power and Privilege of Discretion." 67 *Fordham Law Review* 13. Sheri Lynn Johnson. 1993. "Racial Imagery in Criminal Cases." 67 *Tulane Law Review* 1739. Anthony V. Alfieri. 1995. "Defending Racial Violence." 95 *Columbia Law Review* 1301. Anthony V. Alfieri. 1998. "Race Trial." 76 *Texas Law Review* 1293.

21. Michael Lieberman. 2000. "Statement of the Anti-Defamation League on Bias-Motivated Crime and the Hate Crimes Prevention Act." 21 *Chicano-Latino Law Review* 53. Tanya K. Hernandez. 1990. "Bias Crimes: Unconscious Racism in the Prosecution of 'Racially Motivated Violence.'" 99 *Yale Law Journal* 845.

22. Note. 1989. "Developments in the Law: Sexual Orientation and the Law." 102 *Harvard Law Review* 1508.

23. Charles P. Bubany and Frank F. Skillern. 1976. "Taming the Dragon: An Administrative Law for Prosecutorial Decision Making." 13 *American Criminal Law Review* 473. Bennett L. Gershman. 1992. "The New Prosecutors." *University of Pittsburgh Law Review* 393. Robert L. Misner. 1996. "Recasting Prosecutorial Discretion." 86 *Journal of Criminal Law and Criminology* 717.

24. 198 U.S. 500 (1905).

25. 554 F.2d 645 (4th Cir. 1977).

26. 846 F. Supp. 768 (E.D.Mo. 1994). See also Charles R. Lawrence. 1987. "The Id, the Ego, and Equal Protection: Reckoning with Unconscious Racism." 39 *Stanford Law Review* 317. Knoll D. Lowney. 1994. "Smoked Not Snorted: Is Racism Inherent in Our Crack Cocaine Laws?" 45 *Washington University Journal of Urban and Contemporary Law* 121.

27. Angela J. Davis. 1998. "Prosecution and Race: The Power and Privilege of Discretion." 67 *Fordham Law Review* 13.

28. Cassia Spohn, John Gruhl and Susan Welch. 1987. "The Impact of the Ethnicity and Gender of Defendants on the Decision to Reject or Dismiss Felony Charges." *Criminology*, 25, pp. 175–191.

29. 373 U.S. 83 (1963).

30. Kenneth Williams. 2000. "The Deregulation of the Death Penalty." 40 *Santa Clara Law Review* 677. Barry Scheck, Peter Neufeld, and Jim Dwyer. 2000. *Actual Innocence: Five Days to Execution and Other Dispatches from the Wrongfully Convicted*. New York: Doubleday.

31. Darryl K. Brown. 2000. "Criminal Procedure Entitlements, Professionalism, and Lawyering Norms." 61 *Ohio State Law Journal* 801.

32. *Lambert* v. *Blackwell*, No. 96-6244, Dist. Ct., E.D.Pa. 1997.

33. Hiroschi Fukurai, Edgar Butler, and Robert Krooth. 1991. "Where Did Black Jurors Go? A Theoretical Synthesis of Racial Disenfranchisement in the Jury System and Jury Selection." *Journal of Black Studies*, 22, pp. 196–215. See also B. Applegate, J. Wright, R. Dunaway, F. Cullen, and J. Wooldredge. 1993. "Victim-Offender Race and Support for Capital Punishment: A Factorial Design Approach." *American Journal of Criminal Justice*, 18, pp. 95–115.

34. Adalberto Aguirre, Jr., and David V. Baker. 1991. *Race, Racism and the Death Penalty in the United States*. Berrien Springs, MI: Vande Vere Publishing. Adalberto Aguirre, Jr., and David V. Baker. 1994. *Perspective on Race and Ethnicity in American Criminal Justice*. New York: West Publishing.

35. Paul Butler. 1995. "Racially Based Jury Nullification: Black Power in the Criminal Justice System." 105 *Yale Law Review* 677. Paul Butler. 1997. "Race-Based Jury Nullification:

Case-in-Chief." 30 *John Marshall Law Review* 911. Compare Andrew D. Leipold. 1997. "Race-Based Jury Nullification: Rebuttal (Part A)." 30 *John Marshall Law Review* 923. Randall Kennedy. 1997. *Race, Crime, and the Law*. New York: Pantheon Books. Alan W. Scheflin. 1972. "Jury Nullification: The Right to Say No." 45 *Southern California Law Review* 168. Phillip B. Scott. 1989. "Jury Nullification: A Historical Perspective on a Modern Debate." 91 *West Virginia Law Review* 389. Roscoe C. Howard, Jr. 2000. "Changing the System from Within: An Essay Calling on More African Americans to Consider Being Prosecutors." 6 *Widener Law Symposium Journal* 139.

36. Jorge L. Carro. 1981. "Impact of the Criminal Justice System on Hispanics." In *National Hispanic Conference on Law Enforcement and Criminal Justice*. Washington, DC: U.S. Department of Justice, pp. 361–382. U.S. Commission on Civil Rights. 1970. *Mexican Americans and the Administration of Justice in the Southwest*. Washington, DC: U.S. Commission on Civil Rights. Juanita Diaz-Cotto. 1996. *Gender, Ethnicity, and the State: Latina and Latino Prison Politics*. Albany, NY: SUNY Press. Malcolm D. Holmes and Howard C. Daudistel. 1984. "Ethnicity and Justice in the Southwest: The Sentencing of Anglo, Black, and Mexican American Defendants," *Social Science Quarterly* 65, pp. 265–277. T. Miethe and C. Moore. 1986. "Racial Differences in Criminal Processing: The Consequences of Model Selection on Conclusions about Differential Treatment." *Sociological Quarterly* 27, pp. 217–237. Roger Peterson and John Hagan. 1984. "Changing Conceptions of Race: Toward an Account of Anomalous Findings of Sentencing Research." *American Sociological Review*, 49, pp. 56–70. Charles Pruitt and James Wilson. 1983. "A Longitudinal Study of the Effect of Race on Sentencing." *Law and Society Review* 17, pp. 613–635. Cassia Sophn, John Gruhl, and Susan Welch. 1981. "The Effect of Race on Sentencing: A Reexamination of an Unsettled Question." *Law and Society Review*, 16, pp. 71–88. James Unnever, Charles Frazier and John Henretta. 1980. "Racial Differences in Criminal Sentencing." *Sociological Quarterly*, 30, pp. 197–205.

37. Gary LaFree. 1985. "Official Reactions to Latino Defendants in the Southwest." *Journal of Research in Crime and Delinquency*, 22, pp. 213–237.

38. Marjorie Zatz. 1981. "Differential Treatment in the Criminal Justice System by Race/Ethnicity." Paper presented at the annual meeting of the American Sociological Association (August) in Toronto, Ontario, Canada.

39. Susan Welch, John Gruhl, and Cassia Spohn. 1984. "Dismissal, Conviction, and Incarceration of Latino Defendants: A Comparison with Anglos and Blacks." *Social Science Quarterly*, 65, pp. 257–264.

40. Ed A. Muñoz, David A. Lopez and Eric Stewart. 1998. "Misdemeanor Sentencing Decisions: The Cumulative Disadvantage Effect of 'Gringo Justice.'" *Hispanic Journal of Behavioral Sciences*, 20, 3, pp. 298–320.

41. National Minority Advisory Council on Criminal Justice. January 1982. *The Inequality of Justice: A Report on Crime and the Administration of Justice in the Minority Community*. Washington, DC: National Institute of Law Enforcement and Criminal Justice.

42. U.S. Department of Justice. Office of Justice Programs. Bureau of Justice Statistics. February 1999. *American Indians and Crime*. Washington, DC, NCJ 173386. For a review of the criminological literature on American Indians, see Donald E. Green. 1993. "The Contextual Nature of American Indian Criminality." *American Indian Culture and Research Journal*, 17, 2, pp. 99–119.

43. Coramae Richey Mann. 1993. *Unequal Justice: A Question of Color*. Bloomington, IN: Indian University Press, p. 235.

44. S. Feimer, F. Pommerstein, and S. Wise. 1990. "Marking Time: Does Race Make a Difference? A Study of Disparate Sentencing in South Dakota." *Journal of Crime and Justice*, 13, 1, pp. 86–102.

45. Ronet Bachman. 1991. "An Analysis of American Indian Homicide: A Test of Social Disorganization and Economic Deprivation at the Reservation County Level." *Journal of Research in Crime and Delinquency*, 28, 4, pp. 456–472. Ronet Bachman. 1991. "The Social

Causes of American Indian Homicide as Revealed by the Life Experiences of Thirty Offenders." *American Indian Quarterly*, 15, 4, pp. 469–493.

46. Ronald Stidham and Robert A. Carp. 1995. "Indian Rights and Law before the Federal District Courts." *Social Science Journal*, 32, 1, pp. 87–97.

47. U.S. Sentencing Commission. April 1997. Special Report to the Congress. *Cocaine and Federal Sentencing Policy*. U.S. Sentencing Commission. February 1995. Special Report to the Congress. *Cocaine and Federal Sentencing Policy*.

48. *Los Angeles Times*. "War on Crack Targets Minorities over Whites." May 21, 1995. *Riverside Press-Enterprise*. "Cocaine Sentencing High on List of Racial Issues." November 2, 1995.

49. Michael Tonry. 1995. *Malign Neglect: Race, Crime, and Punishment in America*. NY: Oxford University Press, pp. 105–106.

50. James H. Jones. 1993. *Bad Blood: The Tuskegee Syphilis Experiment*. New York: *Free Press*. San Bernardino Sun. "U.S. to Apologize for Syphilis Study." April 9, 1997. *Los Angeles Times*. "Facing the Same of Tuskegee." May 18, 1997.

51. *Los Angeles Times*. "CDC Says it Erred in Measles Study." June 17, 1996.

52. *Chronicle of Higher Education*. "Making Amends to Radiation Victims." October 13, 1995. *Chronicle of Higher Education*. "Radiation Probe Taps Records Spanning 30 Years." October 13, 1995.

53. Michael S. Vaughn and Linda G. Smith. 1999. "Practicing Penal Harm Medicine in the United States: Prisoners' Voices from Jail." *Justice Quarterly*, 16, 1, pp. 176–231.

54. H. Allen and C. Simonsen. 1992. *Corrections in America*. New York: Macmillian Publishing, p. 350. I. Moyer. 1985. "Academic Criminology: A Need for Change." *American Journal of Criminal Justice*, 9, pp. 197–212.

55. Angela P. Harris. 2000. "Race and Essentialism in Feminist Legal Theory." In Richard Delgado and Jean Stefancic (editors). *Critical Race Theory: The Cutting Edge*, 2nd ed. Philadelphia: Temple University Press, pp. 261–274.

56. D. Stanley Eitzen and Maxine Baca-Zinn. 1992. *Social Problems*. New York: Simon & Schuster, p. 488.

57. American Correctional Association. 1990. *The Female Offender: What Does the Future Hold?* VA: Kirby Lithographic Company.

58. Coramae Richey Mann. 1989. "Minority and Female: A Criminal Justice Double Bind." *Social Justice*, 16, 4, pp. 95–114.

59. Joanne Belknap, Kristi Holsinger, and Melissa Dunn. 1997. "Understanding Incarcerated Girls: The Results of a Focus Group Study," *Prison Journal*, 77, 4, pp. 381–405.

60. U.S. Department of Justice. Bureau of Justice Statistics. *Sourcebook of Criminal Justice Statistics, 1999*. "Female Prisoners under Jurisdiction of State and Federal Correctional Authorities." Washington, DC: U.S. Department of Justice, p. 514, Table 6.40.

61. Amy E. Laderberg. 1998. "The 'Dirty Little Secret': Why Class Actions Have Emerged as the Only Viable Option for Women Inmates Attempting to Satisfy the Subjective Prong of the Eighth Amendment in Suits for Custodial Sexual Abuse." 40 *William and Mary Law Review* 323. See also Martin A. Geer. 2000. "Human Rights and Wrongs in Our Own Backyard: Incorporating International Human Rights Protections under Domestic Civil Rights Law—A Case Study of Women in United States Prisons." 13 *Harvard Human Rights Journal* 71.

62. U.S. Department of Justice. Office of Justice Programs. Bureau of Justice Statistics. February 1999. *American Indians and Crime*. Washington, DC, NCJ 173386.

63. Adalberto Aguirre, Jr., and David V. Baker. 1991. *Race, Racism and the Death Penalty in the United States*. Berrien Springs, MI: Vande Vere Publishing. Adalberto Aguirre, Jr., and David V. Baker. 1994. *Perspective on Race and Ethnicity in American Criminal Justice*. New York: West Publishing

64. Ronald B. Flowers. 1990. *Minorities and Criminality*. New York: Praeger.

65. This figure includes prisoners confined by the U.S. military and the U.S. government. NAACP Legal Defense and Education Fund. *Death Row*, USA. October 1, 2000.
66. Amnesty International. 1998. *Statistics on the Death Penalty in 1998*.
67. For a review of this literature, see Adalberto Aguirre, Jr., and David V. Baker. 1991. *Race, Racism and the Death Penalty in the United States*. Berrien Springs, MI: Vande Vere Publishing. Adalberto Aguirre, Jr., and David V. Baker. 1994. *Perspective on Race and Ethnicity in American Criminal Justice*. New York: West Publishing.
68. NAACP Legal Defense and Educational Fund. Death Row, U.S.A. October 1, 2000.
69. 408 U.S. 238 (1972).
70. 428 U.S. 153 (1976).
71. 481 U.S. 279 (1987).
72. Jon Sorensen and Donald H. Wallace. 1999. "Prosecutorial Discretion in Seeking Death: An Analysis of Racial Disparity in the Pretrial Stages of Case Processing in a Midwestern County." *Justice Quarterly*, 16, 3, pp. 559–578. Robin H. Gise. 1999. "Rethinking *McCleskey* v. *Kemp:* How U.S. Ratification of the International Convention on the Elimination of All Forms of Racial Discrimination Provides a Remedy for Claims of Racial Disparity in Death Penalty Cases." 22 *Fordham International Law Journal* 2270.
73. Richard C. Dieter. July 1997. *Innocence and the Death Penalty: The Increasing Danger of Executing the Innocent*. New York: Death Penalty Information Center. Staff Report by the Subcommittee on Civil and Constitutional Rights Committee on the Judiciary One Hundred Third Congress, First Session. October 1993. *Innocence and the Death Penalty: Assessing the Danger of Mistaken Executions*. New York: Death Penalty Information Center.
74. Alan Berlow. 1999. "The Wrong Man." *Atlantic Monthly*, pp. 66–91.
75. Richard Quinney. 1970. *The Social Reality of Crime*. Boston: Little Brown. Richard Quinney. 1977. *Class, State, and Crime: On the Theory and Practice of Criminal Justice*. New York: Longman. Austin Turk. 1969. *Criminality and Legal Order*. Skokie, IL: Rand McNally. William Chambliss and Robert Seidman. 1971. *Law, Order and Power*. Reading, MA: Addison-Wesley.
76 For comprehensive compilations of these works, see Richard Delgado and Jean Stefancic. 2001. *Critical Race Theory: The Cutting Edge*, 2nd ed. Philadelphia: Temple University Press. Adrien Katherine Wing. 1997. *Critical Race Feminism: A Reader*. New York: New York University Press. Richard Delgado and Jean Stefancic. 1997. *Critical White Studies: Looking behind the Mirror*. Philadelphia: Temple University Press. Juan F. Perea, Richard Delgado, Angela P. Harris, Stephanie M. Wildman and Jean Stefancic. 2000. *Race and Races: Cases and Resources for a Diverse America*. Eagan, MN: West Group. Derrick Bell. 2000. *Race, Racism and American Law*, 4th. ed. New York: Aspen Publishers.

Index